QUMRAN
and the
HISTORY
of the
BIBLICAL TEXT

QUMRAN
and the
HISTORY
of the
BIBLICAL TEXT

EDITED BY

Frank Moore Cross and Shemaryahu Talmon

Harvard University Press

Cambridge, Massachusetts

and London, England

Library of Congress Cataloging in Publication Data
Main entry under title:
Qumran and the history of the Biblical text.

   1. Dead Sea scrolls—Addresses, essays, lectures.
2. Bible. O. T.—Criticism and interpretation—
Addresses, essays, lectures. I. Cross, Frank Moore.
II. Talmon, Shemaryahu.
BM487.Q58   221.4'4
ISBN 0–674–74360–1
ISBN 0–674–74362–8 (Pbk.)

PREFACE

The discovery of manuscripts in the Wilderness of Judah has stimulated a period of unparalleled activity and progress in the study of the biblical text. What had appeared for a long while to be secure limits to the field of textual criticism have disappeared, and new positions and new theories, especially of the early history of the biblical text, have emerged from first interpretations of a mountain of textual data extracted from ancient scrolls. So radical has been the change in our understanding and outlook that the field is in flux if not in chaos; the older handbooks surveying the field of biblical textual criticism are hopelessly obsolete. In view of this state of the discipline, we have designed a collection of essays to introduce the serious student to this new or rather transformed field of textual research. Some of the papers chosen are general surveys of the field; some are programmatic essays propounding new theories; several are first publications of new manuscript data of revolutionary importance. The final studies, hitherto unpublished, state the present outlook of the editors, and suggest new approaches to the fundamental task of textual criticism. Appended is a list of published manuscripts or manuscript fragments from the Judaean desert, and bibliography.

Frank Moore Cross
Shemaryahu Talmon

CONTENTS

QUMRAN
and the
HISTORY
of the
BIBLICAL TEXT

SHEMARYAHU TALMON

THE OLD TESTAMENT TEXT

I

We shall examine here the first stages in the history of the transmission of the Old Testament text over a period of approximately 500 years, starting with *c*. 300 B.C. For the preceding phases in the history of the text woefully little historical evidence is available, and none of it is contemporary. Any account of the development of the text prior to *c*. 300 B.C., i.e. in the Persian period, not to mention the periods of the Babylonian Exile or of the First Temple, must perforce rely upon conjecture and, at best, upon deductions and analogies derived from later literature and later manuscripts.

The beginning of what may properly be called the history of the Old Testament text roughly coincides with the final phases of the canonisation of the Old Testament books, a subject which has been discussed in the preceding section. During the period under review, the Jewish scribes and sages decided on, and carried out, the minute fixation of the consonantal text of the scriptures in the original Hebrew tongue.

Concurrently, the Old Testament books were translated into other Semitic languages—Aramaic and Syriac—and also into non-Semitic languages—Greek, and subsequently Latin. This intense activity of editing and revising resulted, at the end of this period (first half of the third century A.D.), in the first comprehensive scholarly enterprise, Origen's *Hexapla*.[1] In its six columns Origen presented a synoptic view of the then current Hebrew text of the Old Testament and its Greek translations: (1) The Hebrew Old Testament in Hebrew letters; (2) this same text transcribed in Greek letters; (3–6) the Greek versions of Aquila, Symmachus, the Septuagint and Theodotion.[2]

The work of the Jewish scribes affected, as we have said, only the Hebrew consonantal text. To the best of our present knowledge, no fully fledged system of recording vowels in Hebrew had yet been invented, with the exception of the use of some consonants as *matres lectionis*, i.e. as indicators of a few basic long vowel values. The pronunciation of Hebrew words, as it was current in that period, can, however, in some cases be ascertained by means of retroversion from their rendering in translations, and in some instances from their transcription into the vocalised Greek or Latin alphabets.

The absence of vowels meant that many a Hebrew consonant group could be differently pronounced, and from this resulted the fact that a variety of meanings could be attached to one and the same word in the original. When ultimately vowels were introduced into the Hebrew text of the Bible, these pronunciation variants sometimes became the bases of *variae lectiones*.

The lack of any system of interpunctuation in written Hebrew at that time was another factor which gave rise to different interpretations of many passages. These diverging interpretations may also in the end turn up as variants in versions which are based on fully interpunctuated manuscripts.

The full establishing of these features of the text which are complementary to the basic Hebrew consonantal text, namely the vowel system(s), interpunctuation, and the subdivision of the text into paragraphs (*sᵉdārim* and *pārāšōṭ*), was carried out by the various schools of Massoretes, vocalisers and interpunctuators who flourished in the last

[1] Cf. v, 14.
[2] For a short presentation of the salient characteristics of these versions, cf. B. J. Roberts in *Cambridge History of the Bible*, Vol. 2, ed. G. W. H. Lampe, pp. 13–26.

quarter of the first millennium A.D. These late aspects of the textual transmission of the Bible do not come within the orbit of our present exposition.[1]

II

There is probably no other extant text, ancient or modern, which is witnessed to by so many diverse types of sources, and the history of which is so difficult to elucidate as that of the text of the Old Testament. The task of the scholar who endeavours to trace the antecedents of the text as we know it today is further complicated by the fact that he is concerned with sacred literature, every word of which is considered to be divinely inspired and therefore infallible. However, having been handed down by human agents for more than two millennia, the text of the scriptures suffered from the shortcomings of man. It became faulty to a greater or less degree and even at times distorted. It must therefore be subjected to scholarly critical analysis like any other ancient literary document.

The Old Testament books were handed down, as has been said, not only in their original Hebrew or, in some passages, Aramaic tongue, but also in a variety of translations into Semitic and non-Semitic languages. All these textual traditions, as we know them today, differ from one another. What is more, even the witnesses to one tradition, in the original language or in a translation, often diverge from one another. As a result, the scholar who takes a synoptic view of all the sources at his disposal is confronted with a bewildering plethora of *variae lectiones* in the extant versions of the Old Testament books. This fact obviously does not become apparent in the common editions of the Old Testament, in Hebrew or in translation, which are in everyday use. However, it should be borne in mind that the printed editions represent the end of a long chain of textual development and of editorial activities which were aimed at unifying the sacred texts. These late editions can in no way be taken to exhibit faithfully the autographs of the biblical authors. In fact not one single verse of this ancient literature has come to us in an original manuscript, written by a biblical author or by a contemporary of his, or even by a scribe who lived immediately after the time of the author. Even the very earliest manuscripts at our disposal, in Hebrew or in any translation language,

[1] On this subject cf. B. J. Roberts, *op. cit.* pp. 1–26.

are removed by hundreds of years from the date of origin of the literature recorded in them.

Even a cursory perusal of the sources available immediately reveals
that not one tradition and not one manuscript is without fault. Each
and every one patently exhibits errors which crept into it during the
long period of its transmission, in the oral stage, when written by hand,
and even, though to a lesser degree, when handed down in the form
of printed books.

It should, however, be stressed that these errors and textual divergences between the versions materially affect the intrinsic message
only in relatively few instances. Nevertheless this may occur. Some
examples of variants significant from a theological or ideo-historical
angle may in fact be found. In most instances the differences are of a
linguistic or a grammatical nature, which resulted either from the
unpremeditated impact of the linguistic peculiarities of successive
generations of copyists, or from their intentional attempts to adjust
the wording of scripture to changing concepts of linguistic and stylistic
norms.

The above remarks do not, however, absolve us from accounting
for the fact that the further back the textual tradition of the Old Testament is followed, i.e. the older the biblical manuscripts perused, and
the more ancient the records which come to the knowledge of scholars,
the wider is the over-all range of textual divergence between them. The
existing variants, therefore, cannot be simply explained as having
arisen solely from the cumulative effect of imperfect copying and
recopying of the text over many centuries. The very earliest biblical
manuscripts known—and in this respect the biblical scrolls from
Qumrân[1] are of decisive importance—exhibit practically all types of
variants found in later witnesses. This fact indicates that variation as
such in the textual transmission cannot be laid exclusively at the door
of careless scribes, or of sometimes unscrupulous, and sometimes well-
meaning, emendators and revisers. One has to consider the possibility,
as scholars have indeed done, that individual variants, and also groups
or even types of variants, which have been preserved in the ancient
versions, both in Hebrew and in translations, may derive from divergent
pristine textual traditions. That these divergent traditions are today
represented in the extant witnesses only in what amount to haphazard

[1] See below, pp. 182–7.

remains, can be explained as resulting from the endeavour of later generations to establish for each version one officially acclaimed standard text. After the establishment of such an official standard, new copies would have been based from the very start on the *textus receptus*. In the course of time, earlier non-standard manuscripts would also have been emended to conform to it. In the ensuing process of unification, which was inspired both by religious-dogmatic and scholarly motives, divergent texts almost automatically went out of circulation, or were more or less systematically suppressed. After a given period in the history of the text, a period which differs from version to version, all manuscripts of a version can be reduced to a very restricted number of prototypes. In some instances, as is the case with the Massoretic and the Samaritan Hebrew texts, all manuscripts conform to one basic text form. In other words, the later the witnesses which are reviewed, the more pronounced their conformity, and the fewer their divergences, both in number and type.

The scholar whose interest lies in tracing the history of the text cannot rely upon the end products, but must turn for information to the earliest sources available. In doing so he is faced with an *embarras de richesse* of variant and often conflicting readings even in the most ancient witnesses to the text. It now becomes his task not only to sketch the lines of these developments, but also to attempt the reconstitution of the original wording, or wordings, of the text. He will sift the available evidence, and discard from the outset obvious faults and errors. He will try to establish manuscript families, as far as this is possible. All manuscripts which can be affiliated with each other will then be considered as one composite witness to a reading found in them. Any decision with regard to the importance of a reading cannot be based merely on counting manuscripts. They have to be assessed and their intrinsic value taken into account. At the apex of this long and complicated process of collation and critical analysis, the investigator may carefully conclude that with the available evidence no 'first' text form can be established. Or else, more optimistically, he may attempt to reconstitute the presumed pristine texts of each of the major versions individually. It then still remains to be debated whether these proto-texts of the extant versions can be reduced to one common stem, or whether, at least in part, they must be considered to represent intrinsically independent textual traditions. Even if by retracing the steps of textual development we may be able to arrive at the *Ur-text* of this version or that, the question still remains open whether we shall ever be able to recover the *ipsissima verba* of a biblical author.

III

In pursuing the chain of development of the Old Testament text, we may discern four distinct main stages in its transmission between its initial inception at a time varying from book to book, and its form in the days of Origen.

The initial stage, that of the not provable but highly probable oral phase of the biblical literature, lies outside the scope of our present investigation, since by its very nature it precedes written documentation. It should, however, be pointed out that originally oral variations may ultimately turn up as textual variants between duplicate texts within the Old Testament. Such instances are found in two versions of one and the same psalm embedded in a book of the Former Prophets and Psalms (e.g. 2 Sam. 22 = Ps. 18), in Chronicles and Psalms (e.g. 1 Chron. 16: 8–36 = Ps. 105: 1–15; 96: 1–13; 106: 1, 47–8), or in the Book of Psalms itself (e.g. Ps. 31: 2–4*b* = 71: 1–3; 60: 7–14 = 108: 8–14).[1] Again, we meet with two or even three presentations of a piece of biblical literature in parallel passages in the Former and Latter Prophets (2 Kings 18: 13—20: 19 = Isa. 36: 1—38: 22 = 2 Chron. 32: 1–20; 2 Kings 25: 1–22 = Jer. 39: 1–10 = 52: 4–27; 2 Kings 25: 27–30 = Jer. 52: 31–4). To some extent also quotations from an earlier book in a later one may exhibit textual variants. However, in these cases literary licence and a possible tendency towards intentional variation or rephrasing on the part of the writer who is borrowing may lie at the root of the present divergences.

It goes without saying that in using the term oral tradition we do not exclude the transmission of some biblical books or parts of them in manuscript form even at this stage. The question rather is one of the relative preponderance of the two vehicles of transmission of literary material, the oral and the written. For this reason it is completely unwarranted even to attempt, with the means currently available, to delineate what cannot be known—namely the process of transition from the stage of mainly oral tradition to that of preponderantly

---

[1] On this theme cf. also pp. 185 ff.

written transmission. In all likelihood the process was gradual, with the weight progressively shifting from the former to the latter. Without aiming at precision, in view of the foregoing remarks, it may be said that the period of the Babylonian Exile after the destruction of the First Temple, i.e. the middle of the sixth century B.C., could be taken as a rough dividing line. The definite shift of emphasis from oral to written transmission of the biblical books would thus have become clearly apparent during the period of the Return, i.e. at the end of the sixth and in the fifth century B.C., in what, from a wider historical viewpoint, may be termed the Persian period. These considerations indicate, as will be further shown, that in attempting an elucidation of the history of the text we cannot concern ourselves exclusively with literary issues, but have to look out also for social and political phenomena whose impacts made themselves felt in its development.

The preponderance of written transmission of Old Testament books after the return from the Exile still does not make this second phase of development a ready subject for textual study in the strict sense of the term, since it is not yet represented by manuscript evidence. Any conclusions with regard to the history of text at that time lack a documentary basis. They are grounded solely on inference from subsequent phases of development and on theoretical considerations rooted in other fields of biblical research and transferred from them to the study of the text. Textual study proper commences in the next stage with the appearance of accessible manuscripts of Old Testament books.

The third phase begins, according to the present state of our knowledge, in the early third century B.C. For several reasons this phase must be considered the pivot around which any investigation into the history of the Bible text turns. At this stage, the written transmission of biblical literature finally and, to all intents and purposes, completely replaced oral tradition. With this transition went the gradual formal sanctification of the books which were accepted as scripture, culminating at the end of this phase, i.e. by the turn of the eras, in the establishment of the complete and closed Old Testament Canon. The very fact that an attempt was made to compile a definite codex of the sacred lore of the community shows that those who undertook it sensed that a period in the history of Israel and of its literature had come to a close, and that a new era of basically different literary standards and norms had begun. In instigating the canonisation of those books, they

intended to ensure the faithful preservation of the spiritual heritage
of preceding generations. At the same time they purported to draw a
definite line between this acknowledged body of written sacred literature and contemporary non-sacred books on the one hand, and on the
other hand between it and the emerging new type of rabbinic literature
which was to be only orally transmitted. Again, as has been shown in
the section on the Canon, we are concerned with a gradual process, of
which many aspects still cannot be adequately examined for lack of
reliable evidence. Yet it would appear that the progressive demarcation
of the books accepted as scripture over against all other writings extant
at that period was a prerequisite for the ensuing preoccupation with
the exact wording which aimed at guaranteeing an unimpaired textual
transmission. No such tendency is apparent in the preceding phase.
It seems that only with the emerging concept of a clearly circumscribed
canon of inspired literature could there develop this concern for the
exact preservation of its wording. We have no reason to suppose that
much heed was paid to the text of non-sanctified writings, nor does the
traceable textual history of writings of this kind, such as Ecclesiasticus,
substantiate such an assumption. Since they had no claim to have been
conceived under divine inspiration, variants in their transmitted wordings were regarded as of no consequence.

IV

The internal Jewish trends outlined above were intensified by another
set of factors. In the period under review, Israel was drawn into the
orbit of hellenistic culture, which heavily influenced contemporary
Jewish culture. The resulting contact with the Greek world of letters
had a decisive impact on the transmission of the Old Testament. Jewish
scribes emulated Greek scribal techniques and terminology, and adopted
their insistence on exactitude in handing down written records and
literary works.[1]

This development occurred at an opportune moment in the history
of the Old Testament text, when its translation into other languages
was first undertaken. The demand for a translation of the Hebrew
scriptures into Aramaic probably arose during the Babylonian Exile
or immediately after the return of the exiles to Palestine, i.e. in the

---

[1] Cf. S. Lieberman, *Hellenism in Jewish Palestine* (New York, 1950), pp. 3–46.

Persian period. Aramaic being the *lingua franca* of the time, it was adopted by many Jews in their intercourse with the non-Jewish world. Being a Semitic language, closely related to Hebrew, it eventually achieved the status of a sister tongue to Hebrew even in the internal life of the Jewish people, especially in the Babylonian Diaspora, but also in Palestine. At first, the translation of the scriptures into Aramaic was most probably sporadic and undirected. It was left to the individual communities to tend to the needs of their members by providing a vehicle which would make the message of the sacred writings understandable also to those whose command of the mother tongue had become insufficient for this purpose. Lacking authorised supervision, the resulting translation often assumed the form of a somewhat free paraphrase of the original, rather than of an accurate rendering into the translator's language. But even when a word-by-word translation was attempted, divergence from the Hebrew *Vorlage* was inevitable. Translation from one language into another always produces inaccuracies since there is no exact correspondence between the vocabulary and the syntax of the two, even if they belong to the same language family. Moreover, the probably divergent first renderings of the Hebrew scriptures into Aramaic were based on originals which may well have differed among themselves to a smaller or larger degree, for reasons set out above.

The same considerations apply with additional force to the translation of the Old Testament books into Greek, a non-Semitic language. This translation was required, for reasons similar to those mentioned above, by Jews living within the sphere of hellenistic culture, whether in Ptolemaic Egypt, where the Jewish community of Alexandria was the focal point, or in Palestine. Tradition maintains that in this case official non-Jewish agents also showed interest in rendering the Old Testament into Greek, and instigated a properly supervised scholarly translation. This tradition will be further discussed subsequently. The pseudepigraphic *Letter of Aristeas* credits King Ptolemy II Philadelphus (285–246 B.C.) with having inaugurated the translation of the Pentateuch into Greek by seventy sages. As a result of their concerted effort, the Septuagint, commonly designated LXX, was in the Pentateuch less open to the uncontrolled impact of translators' idiosyncrasies. It contains indeed fewer deviations from the Hebrew text here than in the renderings of the other books. But it is still open to discussion whether this reputedly official undertaking is to be considered the first attempt at translating the Old Testament or parts of it into Greek and to have provided the impetus to further ventures of the same kind, or whether it should rather be viewed as an event which crowned a long series of previous diffuse attempts with a standardised version.

The first wave of translation of the Hebrew Old Testament into other languages, Semitic and non-Semitic, perforce resulted in the creation of variants and types of variants in the then extant witnesses to the text. The ensuing embarrassing textual diversity of the versions of the sacred books soon called for the application of the methods of textual analysis and textual criticism to remedy this deficiency. As stated above, the ground for this new approach had been laid by the conjunction of scholarly norms borrowed from the Greeks with the care for the accurate transmission of the inspired literature which had developed within Judaism. This attitude towards the text characterises the fourth period of its history.

V

We have already indicated that the fourth phase in the textual history of the Old Testament may be reckoned to extend from the end of the last century B.C. to the beginning of the third century A.D. It is marked by a vigorous process of textual standardisation which affected practically all versions. In order to include within this time-span the activities of Jewish and Samaritan scribes who applied themselves to the stabilisation of the Hebrew text, and of Christian, and to some extent also of Jewish, scribes and scholars who dealt with the Greek Bible, the upper and lower limits have been chosen with some latitude. The dates could be lowered by half a century or so at both ends as far as the Hebrew text is concerned. Also in this phase we have to take into account the impact of socio-political events on the history of the text, especially the emergence of Christianity and the destruction of the Second Temple in A.D. 70. The finalisation of the rift between the Synagogue and the Church which was incomparably more important and decisive than any preceding clash of the main stream of Judaism with deviating movements, and the insistence of both Jews and Christians on basing the cardinal tenets of their conflicting beliefs on the sacred scriptures, necessitated the clear definition of the text on which these claims were grounded. Further, the destruction of the

Second Temple seriously impaired the social cohesion of Jewry which had previously ensured some unity of the text, or at least had prevented its dissolution into innumerable streamlets of textual tradition. The renewed dispersion of Jews over a large geographical area, the disruption of existing socio-religious centres and the creation of new pivotal agencies with the possible resulting diversification of the biblical textual traditions, required counteraction. The propagation of one, universally recognised text form was considered indispensable for ensuring the continuity of the national unity. Rabbinic literature, Hebrew fragments of the Old Testament from after A.D. 70 such as those from Wadi Murabba'at and Massada,[1] and some subsidiary evidence from the ancient versions, witness to the emergence of a Hebrew *textus receptus*, the prototype of the Massoretic text which was finally established almost a millennium later.

Correspondence between the developments of the Hebrew and non-Hebrew versions terminates somewhere at the end of the first century A.D. By then the division between them is in fact no longer a division along linguistic lines, but reflects the schism between the Synagogue and the Church and their different attitudes to the text. The process of textual unification referred to above affected not only the rabbinic Hebrew Bible and the Samaritan Hebrew Pentateuch but also seems to be observable in the Jewish Aramaic translations of the Old Testament books, especially in the Targum Onkelos to the Pentateuch. As against this, if we may judge by Origen's enterprise, and by some preceding Greek evidence from Qumrân, Christian scholars were indeed also bent on editing, and probably on stabilising, the various extant Greek translations, but apparently did not attempt to weld them into one solely acceptable textual tradition. This interpretation of the available evidence is borne out by the subsequent fate of the Greek Bible which after Origen's time was also subjected to recurrent revisions which in practice sometimes amount to new translations. This state of affairs brought about the renewed efforts of Jerome some two centuries later to provide the Church with a new Latin version, the Vulgate, based on the then extant form of the *hebraica veritas*.[2] The Vulgate was intended to supersede the Old Latin version then in use, itself derived from the Greek and therefore presenting in many cases readings which deviated considerably from the current Hebrew text. True, there is

---

[1] See below, pp. 182–6.   [2] See v, 16 in the present volume.

no comparable evidence on hand for the Jewish-Hebrew text in the period under review. At the beginning of the second century manuscript Hebrew evidence comes abruptly to an end, and the text remains unattested for some seven centuries until the appearance of the earliest medieval Hebrew manuscripts. However, the basic similarity between the Hebrew textual traditions at the two extreme points of this timespan, which is not impaired by the persistence of individual variants or even the emergence of new ones, bears out the above statement that after the first century A.D. one single Hebrew text type gained the upper hand and that deviant types practically went out of circulation.

VI

At this point of our investigation we have to turn our attention to the history of biblical textual research as it has developed since the rediscovery of the Samaritan Hebrew Pentateuch by Pietro della Valle in 1616. The Samaritan text was made available to scholars shortly afterwards when Morinus first printed it in 1632 alongside the other versions in the Paris Polyglot. Its many deviations from the Massoretic text, later estimated at about six thousand, were soon observed. It was further established that approximately one third of these *variae lectiones* could be traced also in the Septuagint. This concurrence enhanced the doubts which had been raised concerning the veracity of the Massoretic text. It was maintained that, having been revised by the rabbis after the destruction of the Temple, in the first half of the second century A.D., it did not represent the *ipsissima verba* of the divinely inspired message, but a faulty text, resulting from *incuria librariorum* or from wilful malicious tampering with it on the part of the Jews. As against this it was claimed that the Septuagint had never been subjected to such interference, and therefore represented the biblical text in its prerevision stage. If it was not altogether a true image of the pristine form of the divine word, it certainly came closer to it than any other version. The alignment of the Hebrew Samaritan version with the Greek in so many instances seemed to strengthen the position of the defenders of its accuracy. True, the history of the Samaritan community remained to a large extent shrouded in mystery, but its seclusion throughout more than a millennium appeared to imply that its version of the Pentateuch had been safeguarded from the impact of the biased Jewish revision. It was therefore accepted as a true reflection of the Hebrew Pentateuch as that had been extant before the rabbis exerted their influence on it.

It hardly needs stressing that the discussion at that time, and into the eighteenth century, arose almost exclusively from theological considerations and not from detached scholarly observation. Textual criticism was employed in order to prove the claim that the Greek Bible adopted by the Church was the only true manifestation of the divine message. Accordingly, the Hebrew text of the Synagogue was relegated to an inferior status. The Reformation had, however, instigated a counter movement. Its reliance on the Hebrew text accorded the latter a new place of honour in biblical studies. It was indeed agreed that the Massoretic text exhibited a text form which had been fixed and codified by numerous successive generations of Jewish scribes and sages, and that it bore the imprint of their redactional activities. But, it was argued, this very preoccupation of those early scholars with the accurate preservation of the text, and the uninterrupted supervision of its transmission, had saved it from the corroding impact of insufficiently controlled copying which had been the lot of the other versions. Collations of the available Hebrew manuscripts which were prepared at the end of the eighteenth century by Kennicott and de Rossi, and which superseded all previous endeavours, proved their basic identity.[1] The rich crop of individual variants which were recorded in the apparatus of these works at first sight appeared to disprove the compactness and stability of the Hebrew text. However, closer scrutiny more and more strengthened the conviction that almost all of them can and should be classified as intentional or unintentional secondary scribal alterations. In any case, they could not offset the clear impression that the consonantal text of practically all Massoretic manuscripts showed no deviation of any consequence. All exhibited a tradition which was identical to the smallest *minutiae*, even in recording anomalous phenomena such as the *puncta extraordinaria*, and the unconventional spelling or pronunciation of certain words. The lesson to be drawn from Kennicott's, de Rossi's and other such collations was summarised at the end of the eighteenth century by E. F. C. Rosen-

---

[1] M. H. Goshen-Gottstein has recently provided us with new insights into the phase of research into the history of the Massoretic text which is briefly discussed here. See his 'Hebrew Biblical Manuscripts', *Biblica*, XLVIII (1967), 249–77.

mueller as follows: 'This whole range of variants...leads moreover
to the simple recognition that all surviving codices are relatively late
in relation to the *originals*...they all represent *one recension*, all stem
from one *source*...'[1] It is imperative to underline Rosenmueller's
reference to *originals* (in the plural), and his conclusion that all medieval
Hebrew manuscripts derive from one single recension, i.e. a revised text
source. They are therefore to be regarded as one composite witness.
Moreover, they can in no way be viewed, without further analysis,
as a faithful reflection of the original Hebrew text. Their collation can
only help us to reconstitute or recapture the prototype of the Massoretic
recension, not the pristine Hebrew Bible.

    This line of argument by which the extant *variae lectiones* in Masso-
retic manuscripts were shown to be of secondary origin was further
elaborated in the early nineteenth century to include also the Samaritan
Pentateuch text. In his dissertation *De Pentateuchi Samaritani Origine*
(1815), W. Gesenius subjected this version for the first time to a proper
textual analysis, leaving aside theological considerations. After collect-
ing and categorising the variant readings in the Samaritan, comparing
them whenever possible with parallel readings in other non-Massoretic
sources, he concluded that in the overwhelming majority of cases these
variants resulted from a Samaritan revision of the same basic text
exhibited by the Massoretic text, and therefore cannot be considered
to present evidence for an original independent text tradition. Even
the concurrence of the Samaritan in so many instances with the
Septuagint could not affect this conclusion. Gesenius' successors did not
materially add to his findings, but only put in sharper relief the dependence of the Samaritan Version on the Massoretic text, and thus further
diminished the former's text-critical value. Z. Frankel defined the
Samaritan as a faulty recension full of mistakes and scribal redactions,
based on the Massoretic text,[2] a view subscribed to by S. Kohn in
numerous publications, and summed up by him as follows:

The Samaritan and the Massoretic text are not two divergent copies of one
book, but the Samaritan is related to the Massoretic text in the way that a
new edition, carefully revised, is related to an older one; it not only improves

---

[1] E. F. C. Rosenmueller, *Handbuch der biblischen Kritik und Exegese*, I (Göttingen,
1797), p. 244; quoted by E. Preuschen, *ZAW*, IX (1889), 303. (Translation by the editors.)
[2] Z. Frankel, *Ueber den Einfluss der palaestinischen Exegese auf die alexandrinische
Hermeneutik* (Leipzig, 1851), p. 242.

on it in content—though in this instance it is mainly the opposite of improvement—but it is also modernised in regard to language and orthography.[1]

Rosenmueller's well-balanced 'one-recension' theory which, it is to be noted, he had applied to the Massoretic text only, was pushed into the background by the more sweeping 'archetype theory' propounded by P. de Lagarde about a century ago. In Lagarde's formulation all Hebrew manuscripts derived from one single exemplar, not one recension. This hypothetical manuscript admittedly did not faithfully mirror the original text, but patently contained numerous deviations from it which had been faithfully transmitted and preserved in all extant manuscripts: 'The result is that our Hebrew manuscripts of the Old Testament all go back to one single exemplar, and have even faithfully reproduced as corrections the correcting of its scribal errors and taken over its fortuitous imperfections.'[2] It was tacitly assumed or even expressly conceded, e.g. by J. G. Sommer, that that unique proto-Massoretic manuscript either derived directly from the Temple or else was based upon a copy of the complete Canon which had been kept there before the fall of Jerusalem in A.D. 70, although it achieved its final form only somewhat later.[3]

Lagarde widened the scope of his investigation by applying a similar method to the Greek tradition. He argued that all the available Greek manuscripts could be reduced to the three basic local recensions of Origen, Hesiod and Lucian, from which scholars could trace their way back to the original Septuagint. Taken as a whole the Greek tradition represented a textual family which differed from the Massoretic text. Although it must be viewed as an unsatisfactory translation of the original, this tradition can be employed, by way of comparison, to go behind the archetype which underlies the Hebrew manuscripts: 'We could only penetrate behind this archetype of the Massoretic text by conjecture, were it not for the fact that the Greek version of the Old Testament opens up the possibility of making use of at least a poor translation of a manuscript belonging to a different family.'[4]

---

[1] S. Kohn, 'Samaritikon und Septuaginta', *MGWJ*, xxxviii (1895), 60. (Translation by the editors.)

[2] P. de Lagarde, *Anmerkungen zur griechischen Uebersetzung der Proverbien* (Leipzig, 1863), p. 2. (Translation by the editors.)

[3] J. G. Sommer, *Biblische Abhandlungen* (Bonn, 1846), p. 79; further: J. Olshausen, *Die Psalmen* (Braunschweig, 1853), pp. 15–17.

[4] P. de Lagarde, *ibid.* n. 18. (Translation by the editors.)

The various manifestations of the Old Testament text could, according to this theory, be likened to the branches of a tree, all of which had grown from one stem in diverse stages of bifurcation. There remained little doubt that an analysis and comparison of the main versions, chiefly of the Massoretic text and the reconstituted Septuagint buttressed by the Hebrew Samaritan Pentateuch version, would lead scholars to the very *Ur-text* common to all. The Greek tradition was deemed especially valuable for the purpose of purging the Old Testament of anti-Christian falsifications which allegedly had been introduced into the Massoretic text by the rabbis. This consideration, more theological than textual, fixed the *terminus non ante quem* of the reputed Jewish *Ur-exemplar*. It could not precede the emergence of Christianity, indeed not the first centuries A.D., since one had to allow some time for the Jewish–Christian controversy to develop.[1] The final fixation of the proto-Massoretic text was soon connected with the members of the Sanhedrin of Jamnia that flourished in the days of the Emperor Hadrian (first half of the second century A.D.), and especially with Rabbi Aqiba, probably the most prominent rabbi of the early Christian era. In some such formulation Lagarde's *Ur-text* theory, which was incorrectly considered an elaboration of Rosenmueller's 'one recension' theory, carried the day. Scholars differed in their opinions as to how the basic Massoretic text had been established—whether a deliberate choice had been made by some official Jewish body (Olshausen), or whether, rather haphazardly, a readily available manuscript had been made the basis of the standard text (Noeldeke).[2] But they concurred on the basic issue—the presupposed existence of an archetype. The situation was succinctly summarised at the end of the nineteenth century by F. Buhl:

Of the style and manner in which this authorized text was constructed we unfortunately know nothing definitely. This much only is plain, that the very conception of such an authorized form of text implies the existence of a definite standard manuscript, which was pronounced the only allowable one. In so far, the relatively recent but already widespread theory, that all extant manuscripts point back to one single archetype, is decidedly correct.[3]

[1] For a summary of Lagarde's views see A. Rahlfs, *P. de Lagardes wissenschaftliches Lebenswerk* (Göttingen, 1928), pp. 75–82.

[2] Th. Noeldeke, *Alttestamentliche Literatur*, I (Leipzig, 1868), pp. 22–5.

[3] F. Buhl, *Canon and Text of the Old Testament*. Translated by J. Macpherson (Edinburgh, 1892), p. 256.

Buhl subscribed to the idea that this standard text was officially pro-
claimed, and soon pushed its way

in a remarkably short time wherever the Pharisaic influence extended. On the
other hand, the equally widespread theory that this primitive codex obtained
this position by mere arbitrary choice, or by the manuscripts of the several
books that by chance were at hand being bound together into one standard
Bible, is by no means certain.[1]

But he was less sure than Lagarde that we can reach back behind this
archetype by comparing the Hebrew version with the extant Greek.
It is important, he says,

to determine the exact relation between the Massoretic text and the Archetypal texts of Aquila, Symmachus, and Jerome. In a remarkable way the
Hebrew manuscripts, which were certainly derived from the most diverse
regions, seem to form a unity over against those translators, because the
variations present in these are only extremely seldom repeated in any one
manuscript. Evidently the rigid stability of form which resulted from the
labours of the Massoretes called into being new standard texts, on which the
manuscripts are directly dependent, which, however, were themselves
collateral with the manuscripts used by those translators.[1]

VII

The validity of some of Lagarde's arguments was questioned already
in his lifetime. Within thirty years after the inception of the *Ur-text*
theory the onslaught on it from various quarters forced its adherents
to modify their rigid position, and ultimately resulted in the conception
of new rival hypotheses. P. E. Kahle drew attention to Hebrew manuscripts from the Cairo Geniza stemming from the end of the first and
the beginning of the second millennium A.D. which exhibited variants
in the secondary phenomena of the Hebrew text (vocalisation, punctua-
tion, etc.). These derived from different Massoretic systems, and seemed
to indicate that the Hebrew tradition was less solidified than Lagarde
had assumed.[2] But since these manuscripts were much too late, and
their variants did not really affect the consonantal text, their evidence
could not be adduced to disqualify the *Ur-text* hypothesis.

[1] Buhl, *ibid.*

[2] P. Kahle's work of a lifetime is summarised in his *The Cairo Geniza*. The Schweich
Lectures of the British Academy 1941 (London, 1947; 2nd ed. Oxford, 1959).

More decisive were the strictures raised by V. Aptowitzer. His collection of biblical quotations in rabbinic literature, a field which had
not been explored at all by earlier scholars, brought to light a wealth
of variant Hebrew readings, which were sometimes reflected also in
one or another of the versions.[1] In spite of attempts to diminish the
value of this evidence, by explaining the variations as arising from
quotation by heart, or from intentional alteration of the original on
the part of the quoting authors, it stands to reason that it severely
undermines the theory of a single Jewish *Ur-text*. It would be hard
to explain the persistence of variants in rabbinic literature, even when
these occur merely in quotations, if indeed the text of that one manuscript had ousted all others since the days of Rabbi Aqiba.

The very existence of variant quotations in rabbinic writings and
in their exegetical comments, particularly in Midrash literature, which
mirror a text that deviates from the Massoretic text, dealt a severe blow
not only to the *Ur-text* hypothesis, but also to the less rigorous 'one
recension' theory. Rival theories were now put forward. All of these
set out to account for the co-existence of divergent text traditions of
the Old Testament in the pre-Christian rabbinic and the early Christian
period, in Hebrew as well as in Aramaic, in Greek and possibly also
in Latin translations, as are exemplified in: (*a*) divergent textual
traditions exhibited in quotations in rabbinical literature; (*b*) parallel
Aramaic translations of the Pentateuch, which indeed stem from a
period later than the one under discussion here, but most probably
derive from pre-Origenic prototypes, namely Targum Onkelos which
possibly originated in Babylonia, and certainly was redacted there,
Pseudo-Jonathan, of Palestinian origin, and a third Aramaic version
which until recently had been known only from excerpts, and therefore
had been named the Fragment Targum, but now has been proved to
represent in fact a fully fledged Jerusalem Aramaic translation;[2] and

---

[1] V. Aptowitzer, *Das Schriftwort in der rabbinischen Literatur: Prolegomena. Sitzungsberichte der Kaiserlichen Akademie der Wissenschaften, philosophisch-historische Klasse*,
Band 153, Abhandlung VI (Vienna, 1906). The 'Prolegomenon' was followed by a
detailed investigation into quotations from the Former Prophets in rabbinic literature,
published in four separate instalments. Cf. further I. Abrahams, 'Rabbinical Aids to
Exegesis' in *Essays on Some Biblical Questions of the Day. By Members of the University
of Cambridge* (London, 1909), pp. 172 ff.

[2] See A. Diez Macho, 'The recently discovered Palestinian targum: its antiquity
and relationship with the other targums', *Supplements to Vetus Testamentum*, VII,
Congress Volume Oxford 1959 (Leiden, 1960), 222–45.

(c) the propagation of diverse Greek translations exhibited in an almost codified form in the parallel columns of the *Hexapla*, and sometimes preserved in the form of variant-quotations from the Old Testament in the Apocrypha, the New Testament and the writings of the early Church Fathers, and also in Jewish hellenistic literature, especially in the works of Flavius Josephus.

The most extreme of the new theories was that of the 'vulgar texts' proposed by Paul Kahle which may be considered the very opposite of Lagarde's *Ur-text* hypothesis, and with some qualifications also of the 'one recension' theory. As stated, both these hypotheses take for granted that all extant versions of the Old Testament books, and also most of the intra-versional textual variants, can in the last analysis be reduced, at least in theory if not always in practice, to one common text base which was the only acclaimed, or possibly even the only extant, text form of the Old Testament at the beginning of the Christian era. Though differing as to the characterisation of the 'archetype' as a 'recension' or as a single manuscript, neither of these two hypotheses seems to have taken into consideration the antecedents of the pre-supposed archetype. It would, in fact, appear that in both the respective archetype was believed to have represented the very first text form of the Old Testament books, not preceded by any divergent predecessors. In other words, all present divergences in the extant versions must be considered to have arisen after the archetype had been established and had been officially accepted. The archetype is viewed, as it were, as a riverhead running off into numerous rivulets, all of which, however, can be retraced to the original source.

Now, it may be said that Kahle would be prepared to subscribe to such a description of the issue as far as the latter part of the simile is concerned, namely the diversification of the Old Testament text tradition in the post-Jamnia period. He would also agree that many variants in the diverse versions are of a secondary nature, resulting from intentional or accidental scribal alterations. But on the other hand he would maintain that on the whole the more important witnesses to the Old Testament text, such as the primary Hebrew Massoretic and Samaritan versions, and the basic Greek and Aramaic translations, represent in essence text forms which preceded Lagarde's model-codex or Rosenmueller's arch-recension. The 'vulgar texts' school does not consider the archetype to be the riverhead, but rather the confluence of preceding varying text traditions. These pristine traditions were unified to a considerable degree by the endeavour of generations of tradents within the Jewish, Samaritan and Christian communities who established the (proto)-Massoretic *textus receptus*, the Samaritan consolidated version of the Pentateuch and the Septuagint respectively. But they never fully succeeded in completely suppressing older and purer, i.e. non-revised, 'vulgar' texts within their own official tradition, which was determined by linguistic peculiarities and religious dogma, nor could they ever establish one common archetype of the Old Testament books.[1]

It is the great merit of Kahle that he attempted to push the inquiry into the history of the text in all its ramifications beyond the *terminus non ante quem* which his predecessors had tacitly or explicitly considered as the starting point for their investigations, namely the end of the Second Commonwealth or the beginning of the period after the destruction in A.D. 70. In his understanding of the matter, the then already extant *textus receptus* of each single version marked the apex of a long chain of development in the course of which divergent text-traditions had been progressively abolished. The creation of the Septuagint as portrayed in the pseudepigraphical *Letter of Aristeas*, the compact Aramaic Targums, the Massoretic text and the Samaritan Version are the crowning events in a process of textual unification which had been set on foot by the needs of socio-religious-organisations: the Synagogue, the Samaritan community and the Church.

Without, to the best of my knowledge, stating so explicitly, Kahle in fact applied to the research into the history of the Old Testament text ideas and principles which concurrently emerged in the study of biblical stylistics and literature. Quite correctly, he considered textual history as a phenomenon of a socio-religious kind and endeavoured to map out its place in actual communal life, i.e. to establish, in Gunkel's terminology, its 'Sitz im Leben'.

It follows that in many instances an ancient variant, or a Bible quotation which differs from the authoritative texts, exhibits a *wirkliche Variante*, i.e. a true variant which is a remnant of a pristine text-tradition that had escaped the levelling influence of the official redactions. Inter-version variants may have resulted from the fact that the

---

[1] Similar ideas had been already presented *in statu nascendi* by A. Geiger. See e.g. his remarks on the Samaritan text in: *Nachgelassene Schriften*, IV (Berlin, 1876), 67.

individual versions finally crystallised at different stages of the textual transmission of the Old Testament. Variant quotations survived predominantly in texts which did not come under the scrutiny of the official revisers. They should be considered sediments of 'vulgar', i.e. popular traditions that had been in use before the introduction of each respective *textus receptus*.

VIII

It hardly needs stating that by virtue of its being the very antithesis to the *Ur-text* and the *Ur-recension* theses, Kahle's theory of 'vulgar texts and *textus receptus*' was from the outset rejected by the followers of Lagarde and Rosenmueller. But scholars who were inclined to embrace the new idea also called for the correction of some of its constituent elements. They fully recognised a diversity of the textual traditions of the Old Testament as already existing in the very first stages of its manuscriptal transmission—the point on which Kahle had based his arguments—and they accepted his attempt to account for this diversity by trying to retrace the steps of the textual development before the emergence of a standard text. It was nevertheless considered imperative to smooth out some features of his theory which had justifiably evoked criticism. Kahle had brought into clear focus the natural, uncontrolled transmission of the 'vulgar' traditions, thus freeing them from the rigidity of a conception which supposes the *Ur-text* or the *Ur-recension* to be scholarly creations. Yet he postulated that very same 'academic' setting for the Massoretic *textus receptus*. His presentation of the process by which this model text came about suffers from all the misconceptions which led the *Ur-text* thesis to postulate an abstract scholastic procedure—a procedure for which there is little evidence that it corresponded with socio-historical realities. His assumption that the *textus receptus* should be viewed as resulting from the concerted efforts of a rabbinic academy, especially that of Jamnia, and that its exclusive status was achieved by what amounts to a wholesale *auto-da-fé* of all diverging manuscripts, is neither substantiated by any historical evidence nor plausible. The emergence of the *textus receptus* should be conceived of as a protracted process which culminated in its *post factum* acclamation in the first or at the latest in the second century A.D., as has been stated previously.

Some of the opposition to the *Vulgärtexte* theory, when not attributable to dogmatic rather than rational, scholarly motives, probably has its roots in the reluctance of scholars to accept the bewildering 'disorderliness' implied by that thesis in place of the much more systematic theory of an *Ur-text*. But its impact on the issue under review was soon felt. As normally in scholarly discussion and evaluation, some novel intermediate theories were produced which, by way of synthesis, combined salient features of the opposing schools. It may be said that basically, the attempt was made to bring some method into the madness of the uncontrolled vulgar texts, and at the same time little was needed to square Kahle's *textus receptus* with Lagarde's Hebrew *Ur-text* or Rosenmueller's *Ur-recension*, all of which in fact were considered to be mirrored with some deviations in the present Massoretic text.

We shall consider here two propositions which purport to take into account the diversity of the actual textual traditions from the very moment at which they become known to us in manuscript form or in quotations in early post-biblical Jewish and Christian literature, and to avoid at the same time the disturbing diffuseness of the vulgar texts if seen as pristine independent traditions.

Setting out from Kahle's premises, and probing into the antecedents of the various text forms in which the Old Testament is extant, in Hebrew as well as in translations, and especially in Greek, A. Sperber attempted to reduce all versions in their variations to two basic textual traditions: one is supposedly derived from Judah and is represented most clearly by the Massoretic text; the other stems from Ephraim, and is best recognised in the Samaritan Hebrew Pentateuch. Both have their offshoots in the major Greek textual families, in manuscripts A and B.[1] The admitted initial dichotomy of the biblical text-tradition, carried back by Sperber's hypothesis into pre-exilic times, is fundamentally opposed to the 'one *Ur-recension*' and the 'one *Ur-text*' theories. The difference between one textual tradition and two is qualitative, and not merely quantitative. On the other hand Sperber invalidated to a high degree the originality of the 'vulgar texts', which Kahle had assumed, by presenting them as derivations from a preceding

[1] Sperber's criticism of the archetype theory may be found in his *Septuagintaprobleme* (Stuttgart, 1929). For a presentation of his own views see 'New Testament and Septuagint', *JBL*, LIX (1940), 193–293.

pristine textual tradition which diverged from the prototype of the present Massoretic text. Sperber further introduced into the discussion the idea of 'local traditions' which figures prominently in the most recent theory, yet to be described, perceiving in the Samaritan not merely the product of a late dissident Jewish group, but rather the best-preserved representative of a North-Israelite (namely Ephraimite) text type, and in the Massoretic text its South-Israelite (Judaean) counterpart.

In the same manner as Kahle had applied, as was suggested, Gunkel's exclusively literary concept of the 'Sitz im Leben' to the sphere of biblical textual history, so Sperber appears to have transferred to the study of the text the notion of a geographical dichotomy of the pentateuchal literature inherent in the sigla J and E which, according to some views, are taken to represent the Judaean–Jahwistic and the Ephraimite–Elohistic traditions respectively. At the same time he abandoned the evaluation of the diverse text types which is concomitant with Kahle's very terminology, 'vulgar texts' versus *textus receptus*, and repaired to a purely descriptive division of the extant representatives of the text.

S. Liebermann,[1] on the other hand, took up the qualitative differentiation between the witnesses to the text, applying it, however, not to 'textual traditions', but to types of manuscripts which were extant in the crucial period of the last one or two centuries B.C. and the first one or two centuries A.D. His division between manuscripts as 'base' (φαυλότερα), 'popular' (*vulgate* or κοινότερα) and 'excellent' (ἠκριβω-μένα) also has some 'local' affiliations, since the first were supposedly unworthy copies found mainly in the hands of uneducated villagers, the second class was widely used in cities for study purposes, even in schools and rabbinic academies, whereas only the third type had binding force and was meticulously transmitted by the learned sages of Jerusalem. It goes without saying that only the latter group can be taken to represent faithfully the pristine text of scripture, whereas the others must be judged inferior, their variants being in the nature of secondary deviations. Here Lieberman, without stating so expressly, obviously presupposes the existence of some basic text of exclusive validity which is best mirrored in the manuscripts.

It is important, again in reference to later theories pertaining to the

[1] Cf. *Hellenism in Jewish Palestine.*

history of the text which are yet to be discussed, to put in relief Liebermann's threefold division of biblical manuscripts at the end of the
Second Temple period, and the assumption that the three types were
anchored and transmitted in different localities. One may also detect
in his system a sociological dimension in so far as the above types are
affiliated with different strata of Jewish society: illiterate or semi-
illiterate country people on the one hand, and 'academicians' on the
other hand, with an intermediate, less precisely delineated group
including city dwellers of all kinds.

IX

At this stage of our investigation we turn to the presentation of some
issues which have caused novel developments in the theories about the
history of the text.

It was said above that the third phase in the early history of the
text, which coincides approximately with the hellenistic and the early
Roman period, i.e. the last three centuries B.C., must be considered
crucial for our investigation. The final and complete transition from oral
tradition to written transmission, the gradual canonisation of the books
which were deemed holy, the emerging processes of translation of the
Hebrew Bible into other languages, and the impact of hellenistic literary
norms and techniques, make this stage the very centre of our inquiry.

To the above considerations must be added one other factor which
looms very large in contemporary research into the issue under review.
It necessitates, in fact, a reopening of the discussion on the history of
the text, and a re-evaluation of theories which had been formed at the
end of the nineteenth and in the first half of the twentieth century. We
refer to the collection of manuscripts and fragments from the Judaean
Desert, also known by the misnomer 'The Dead Sea Scrolls', which
include numerous scrolls and thousands of fragments of biblical books.
Since 1947 when the new finds were first reported, an incessant stream
of discoveries, so far only published in part, illuminates that phase in
the history of the text.

The above documents are of two groups, quite disparate from the
standpoint both of chronology and of their sociological provenance.
One group hails from Qumrân which is situated some five miles south
of Jericho and two miles west of the shores of the Dead Sea. It precedes

the destruction of the Second Temple (A.D. 70)—so important an event for the textual history of the Old Testament—and derives from the dissident Jewish sect of the 'New Covenant'.[1] The other consists of scattered manuscript finds from the region to the south of Qumrân, Wadi Murabbaʻat (halfway between Jericho and ʻEin Gedi), Naḥal Zeʼelim and Massada, and exhibits the textual tradition of what has been styled by G. F. Moore 'normative' Judaism.

The latter fragments, which date from the Bar-Kochba revolt (middle of the second century A.D.), do not shed much light on our problem because they provide evidence for only some sections of a few Old Testament books, and because they present a text which had already been almost wholly adjusted to the prevailing *textus receptus*.[2] These documents therefore do not bear on the phase of textual development at present under review. The biblical manuscripts from Qumrân, on the other hand, some of which are dated by scholars in the third and many in the second and first centuries B.C., have added a new dimension to the criticism of the biblical text and to the study of its history, both in the original Hebrew and in the earliest ancient versions, especially in Greek.[3] Some of these manuscripts are quite extensive. Thus in the case of the First Isaiah Scroll (1QIsᵃ), we have a virtually complete copy of the biblical book. This, like many other manuscripts from Qumrân, precedes the oldest extant manuscripts of any part of the Old Testament in the Hebrew Massoretic tradition by more than a millennium, and those in Greek or any other translation by several centuries. They are thus of unsurpassed importance for an investigation into the third phase of the history of the text, and into the processes of its transmission.

The new material often helps in elucidating the genesis and the history of individual variants in which one or more of the ancient versions differ from the Massoretic text. They also open up new possibilities for the recovery, or the reconstruction, of the factors which underlie textual variation. The sifting of these cases, their

[1] The reader will find a valuable summary of the literature and the ideology of this group in F. M. Cross, jun., *The Ancient Library of Qumrân* (revised edition, New York, 1961).

[2] See Y. Yadin, *The Finds from the Bar Kokhbah Period in the Cave of Letters* (Jerusalem, 1963).

[3] See D. Barthélemy, O.P., 'Les Devanciers d'Aquila', *Supplements to Vetus Testamentum*, x (Leiden, 1963).

classification, and a statistical assessment of the frequency of their appearance, may make possible the systematic presentation of the processes which can be proved empirically to have been conducive to the emergence of *variae lectiones*. The pertinent information gained from these first-hand sources, because of their scope and their primacy, should enable scholars to improve on previous attempts along these lines.

Prior to the discovery of the Qumrân Scrolls, observations on the skill and the peculiarities of the ancient copyists of the text could be inferred only from the analysis of variants which are found in medieval Hebrew manuscripts, or had to be abstracted from deviating translations in the ancient versions. With the pre-Christian Hebrew Scrolls from Qumrân at our disposal, we are now in a position to verify principles established by inference, and to put them to a practical test. The Scrolls afford us a completely new insight into ancient scribal craft and give us an unparalleled visual impression of the physical appearance of the manuscripts in which the biblical *variae lectiones* arose. We can now observe at close range, so to say *in situ*, scribal techniques of the Second Temple period which left their impression on the text in subsequent stages of its history. We can perceive the conditions which were the breeding ground of the variants that crop up in the extant witnesses to the text of the Old Testament.

There is nothing specifically sectarian in the external appearance of the Qumrân Scrolls, in the scribal customs to which their copyists adhered, or in the majority of the deviant readings found in them. The impression of dissent that goes with the biblical Scrolls from Qumrân derives from the secession of their scribes from normative Judaism, and has no roots in the manuscripts as such. That is to say, it must be attributed to the socio-historical processes which engulfed these Scrolls, but in no way to their textual or manuscript character. Genetically the biblical texts from Qumrân are 'Jewish'. They became 'sectarian' in their subsequent history.

What makes the evidence of the Scrolls especially valuable is the fact that they present not just a horizontal cross-section of one stabilised version, such as is the Massoretic *textus receptus*. Because of their diversity, the kaleidoscope of the textual traditions exhibited in them, their concurrence here with one, here with another of the known versions, or again in other cases their exclusive textual individuality, the biblical manuscripts found at Qumrân, in their totality, present in a nutshell, as it were, the intricate and variegated problems of the Hebrew text and versions. The concentration of processes which obtain in the history of the text in a comparatively small corpus of manuscripts, small in comparison with the bulk of Hebrew (Massoretic and Samaritan), Aramaic, Syriac, Greek, Latin, etc., manuscripts which have to be sifted, collated and compared in the course of the critical work on the text—a corpus which moreover is relatively homogeneous with respect to time and provenance—make the Qumrân Scrolls an ideal subject for a study of these processes. Although the results gained from an analysis of the Qumrân material cannot be applied without qualification to the wider field of comparative research into the Massoretic text and the versions, we may derive from them certain working hypotheses which have then to be verified by application to the wider problem.

Thus the situation at Qumrân reflects on a basic issue in Old Testament textual research, namely the debated problem of the very establishment of a Hebrew *textus receptus*. The coexistence of diverse text-types in the numerically, geographically and temporally restricted Covenanters' community, the fact that some or most of the conflicting manuscripts had very probably been copied in the Qumrân scriptorium and that no obvious attempts at the suppression of divergent manuscripts or of individual variants can be discovered in that voluminous literature, proves beyond doubt that the very notion of an exclusive *textus receptus* had not yet taken root at Qumrân.

We have no reason to doubt that this 'liberal' attitude towards divergent textual traditions of the Old Testament prevailed also in 'normative' Jewish circles of the second and first centuries B.C. According to rabbinic testimony, even the model codices that were kept in the Temple precincts—the *ʿazārāh*—not only exhibited divergent readings, but represented conflicting text-types.[1] Phenomenologically speaking, the situation that prevailed in the *ʿazārāh* of the Temple may be compared, though with qualifications, with the one that obtained in the scriptorium at Qumrân. The difference consists in the fact that in the end the Temple codices were collated, probably in the first century A.D. and, what is more important, that rabbinic Judaism ultimately

[1] See S. Talmon, 'The Three Scrolls of the Law that were Found in the Temple Court', *Textus (Annual of the Hebrew University Bible Project)*, II (1962), 14–27.

established a model text and strove to banish deviant manuscripts from circulation. But at this stage the comparability of Jewish 'normative' with Qumrân practice breaks down. The active life-span of the Covenanters' community ends some time in the first century B.C., although sporadic attempts at restoration have repercussions in the first and possibly into the second century A.D. However, even the latest manuscripts from Qumrân which provide evidence of the local history of the text in the crucial period, the last decades before the destruction of the Temple, do not give the slightest indication that even an incipient *textus receptus* emerged there, or that the very notion of a model recension was ever conceived by the Covenanters.

The coexistence of varying text forms of the Old Testament, and the absence of any noticeable attempt at establishing one universally recognised recension of binding force, must have confronted the Qumrân scribes with the problem of what attitude to take towards these conflicting textual traditions, which had not yet been assessed and evaluated. The individual scribe could solve this problem by adhering faithfully to the manuscript which he had chosen, or had been assigned, as the *Vorlage* for his own copy. In a reasonable number of instances he could perpetuate parallel readings which he found in other manuscripts that were at his disposal, by noting them in the margins or between the lines of his own copy, or sometimes by integrating them in his text-base, in which case he would create a double reading.[1] Now these devices, which were a common stock-in-trade of the ancient Bible scribes regardless of their socio-religious affiliations, are mere practical expedients that may work fairly well, up to a certain point, for the individual copyist, but cannot satisfactorily solve the problem of the community's disposition towards divergent, but equally well-documented, readings. In manuscripts which are intended for public use, critical annotations must be kept to a practical minimum. In fact, even these relatively few marginal entries will tend to disappear at subsequent copyings by sheer routine omission, unless they are absorbed into the text proper. Even where authoritative guidance is absent we may find a spontaneous tendency towards the simplification and the stabilisation of the textual traditions of scripture and other hallowed books. This process cannot be expected to culminate in

[1] See S. Talmon, 'Double Readings in the Massoretic Text', *Textus*, I (1960), 144–84.

complete unification but it will effectively circumscribe the scope, and reduce the number, of textual types which are allowed a continued existence until, if ever, conscious official redactional activities set in.

The impending gradual disappearance of variant readings, which on objective grounds could not be declared to be intrinsically inferior to those which happened to have taken root in the predominant textual traditions, may well have been viewed with misgivings by those concerned with the preservation of scripture. The practical advantage of acquiring a fairly standardised text-type for communal-cultic purposes was offset by an understandable apprehension for the—to all intents and purposes—irrecoverable loss of valid and venerated textual traditions of the biblical books, which perforce would result from the process outlined above. Contradictory as it may sound, such *pro* and *ante* deliberations seem to have produced diverse manuscript and non-manuscript techniques of variant preservation which helped to balance the scale which was tipped in favour of the text-tradition(s) that became increasingly predominant, to the exclusion and practically complete suppression of less favoured *variae lectiones*.

Here again, a comparison with attitudes and techniques that were current in other communities is in order. In rabbinic circles, the prevalence of such trends of thought may have been responsible for the perceptible latitude in the employment of the text in scholarly discussion which conspicuously contrasts with the unceasing efforts to establish an exclusive *textus receptus* for public worship and for official text-transmission. Whereas deviant readings were banned from the books which were earmarked for these latter categories, they were readily accepted and used as bases for midrashic exposition.[1] At times it appears that such an officially discarded variant was not employed merely as a convenient peg upon which to hang a midrash that was to hand, but rather that the midrash in question was constructed on a variant that had been barred from the *textus receptus*, in order to give it a non-manuscript lease of life. This supposition especially applies to the specific type of the *'al tiqrē'* midrash in which an established reading is suspended as it were, and another reading becomes the point of departure for an ensuing midrashic comment, by means of the introductory formula: 'do not read...but rather read...'. A famous case

[1] See S. Talmon, 'Aspects of the Textual Transmission of the Bible in the Light of Qumrân Manuscripts', *Textus*, IV (1964), 125–35.

in point is the *'al tiqrē'* midrash (Bab. Tal. Berakot 64a) which hinges on reading in Isa. 54: 13 *bōnayik* = 'thy builders', instead of *bānayik* = 'thy sons' (cf. τέκνα; Targum *bānāk*), a variant which now has turned up in 1QIsᵃ as an emended reading *bᵒnaykī*. Similarly the midrash 'do not read (the flesh of) his arm but (the flesh of) his offspring' (Bab. Tal. Shab. 33a) can be anchored in the different text traditions of Isa. 9: 19. Here the Massoretic text (= 1QIsᵃ) reading: 'they shall eat every man the flesh of his own arm' = *zᵉr(ō)'ō* is abandoned for the variant reading *zarʿō* = 'his offspring' which underlies the Aramaic paraphrastic rendering: 'they shall plunder everyone the goods of his neighbour', and Symmachus' τοῦ πλησίον αὐτοῦ. Both readings were apparently conflated in the main stream of the Septuagint tradition: τοῦ βραχίονος τοῦ ἀδελφοῦ αὐτοῦ.

We do not mean that every extant *'al tiqrē'* midrash can be shown to have arisen from an already identifiable textual variant. This certainly is not the case. *Variae lectiones* which supposedly triggered off the emergence of many midrashim of this type have been lost for us together with the (suppressed) manuscripts which exhibited them. Moreover, this specific type of midrash progressively degenerated. The *'al tiqrē'* formula was then often employed even when the midrash in question could not be related to an actually extant reading, though this had originally been by definition a *sine qua non* requirement. Ultimately it became a mere exegetical *Spielelement*.[1] Conversely, the introductory formula of a genuine *'al tiqrē'* midrash was often dropped, so that now the same exposition is sometimes preserved both with and without that formula.

In a majority of cases the textual variations involved are of the simplest and most common types: interchange of graphically similar letters or of auricularly close consonants; haplography or dittography; continuous writing of separate words or division of one word into two; *plene* or defective spelling (as in the cases adduced above); metathesis; differences of vocalisation, sometimes entailing a change of verb conjugations. Some cases of more complicated textual phenomena do not materially affect the over-all impression.

The ambivalence of the request for a generally recognised standard

[1] See I. L. Seeligmann, 'Voraussetzungen der Midraschexegese', *Supplements to Vetus Testamentum*, i. Congress Volume Copenhagen, 1953 (Leiden, 1953), 150–81, and iii, 8 in the present volume.

text of scripture, and the concomitant apprehension over the resulting loss of possibly valuable readings, may have produced yet another technique of variant preservation in the early Church. The recording of different text-traditions in the parallel columns of Origen's *Hexapla* was a way out of this dilemma. On the one hand it ensured the continued preservation of probably widely accepted text forms. On the other hand, with the help of a system of critical symbols by which omissions or additions in the Greek in comparison with the Hebrew text could be indicated, the basis for the establishment of an officially acknowledged and critically guaranteed text was created. In this case, as also in the case of the rabbinic *'al tiqrē'* formula, the critical symbols were subsequently not properly recorded in copies made of or from Origen's work. This may have resulted simply from scribal carelessness. However, in view of our foregoing remarks it is reasonable to surmise that this apparently merely technical deficiency was helped along, so to say, by the postulated disinterestedness of the Church in the centuries after Origen in establishing one exclusive, binding text-tradition of scripture.

We seem to be able to discern three main types of technique intended to counterbalance the impact of standardisation which affected the textual transmission of the Old Testament in all its ramifications in various degrees of intensity and at various stages of its development:

(1) Internal manuscript notation of variant readings, either in the text-base, leading to the emergence of double-readings, or else in the margins, as exhibited, e.g., in the Qumrân Scrolls and probably also in some *qerē* readings in the Massoretic text.[1]

(2) The preservation of variant readings in parallel text-traditions. In its earliest form this technique may be observed in the retention of *variae lectiones* in parallel passages in the Former Prophets and Chronicles, etc., and from it may have been derived the basic idea which underlies Origen's *Hexapla*.

(3) Extra-manuscript preservation of variants in midrashic-homiletic exegesis.

x

The situation which obtains at Qumrân holds out one more possibility of comparison in respect of another aspect of the history of the text.

---

[1] See the chapter by B. J. Roberts (vol. 2, pp. 1–10).

In conformity with a basic characteristic of Second Commonwealth Judaism, the Covenanters' religious concepts were Bible-centred. Their original literary creations, such as the War-Scroll, the *Hōdayōt*, the Sectarian Manual, and the Zadokite Documents, swarm with verbatim Bible quotations, paraphrases and allusions. Their most fundamental beliefs and practices reflect the attempt to recapture, and typologically to re-live, biblical Judaism. This scriptural piety produced the *pēšer* technique,[1] so indicative of the Covenanters' system of Bible hermeneutics, by the aid of which biblical history was actualised, and made existentially meaningful. In this unceasing process of quotation, interpretation and adaptation, the text at Qumrân was exposed to a fate which is comparable to that which the *hebraica veritas* experienced on a wider scale in rabbinic Judaism and in the orbit of Jewish and Christian communities that had recourse to translations of the Hebrew original. The deliberate insertion of textual alterations into scripture for various reasons of style and dogma, the uncontrolled infiltration of haphazard changes due to linguistic peculiarities of copyists or to their characteristic concepts and ideas, which may be observed in the wider transmission of the text, have their counterparts in the 'Qumrân Bible'. The study of these phenomena at Qumrân is again facilitated by the comparative compactness of the material and by the decidedly more pronounced manner in which they are manifest. We thus encounter in the Qumrân writings developments of biblical text-transmission which may be considered prototypes of phenomena that emerge concurrently and subsequently in the text-history of the Old Testament in Jewish and Christian tradition, albeit in less concentrated form, and at different grades of variation.

That the sum total of the biblical documents from Qumrân may be seen to present the issue of the 'Massoretic text and the versions' in miniature, derives further support from one more characteristic of that material. The Qumrân manuscripts exhibit, as already stated, a basic homogeneity with regard to time and provenance. There are no grounds to doubt that these manuscripts were written in Palestine, and that a great majority, if not all, were copied at Qumrân. It may also be considered as established that, with the exception of some odd items, the bulk of the manuscripts in the Qumrân library was copied within a span of not much more than three hundred years, approxi-

---

[1] On the *pēšer*, cf. also pp. 225 ff.

mately from the beginning of the third century B.C. to the middle of the
first century A.D. In view of these circumstances, the marked diversity
of textual traditions which can be observed in these scrolls presumably
derives from the temporal and/or geographical heterogeneity of the
Vorlagen from which the Qumrân manuscripts, or some of them, were
copied. Thus, in addition to the horizontal cross-section view of the
text at Qumrân during the last phases of the Second Commonwealth
period, this material also affords a vertical cross-section view of the
transmission of the text, which reflects different chronological layers,
geographical areas and social strata. These circumstances further
enhance the similarity of the problems relating to the text at Qumrân
with those appertaining to the wider issue of the relations of the
Massoretic text and the versions and, therefore, give rise to new
definitions of their historical development.

XI

Before presenting in detail the impact of the Judaean Desert Scrolls on
existing theories of the text-history of the Old Testament and their
importance for the formation of new theories, it may be useful to
summarise the main conclusions which can be drawn from the material
published up to the present.

(1) Different books of the Old Testament differ in their textual
history and furnish different sets of problems. Restraint should therefore be exercised in subjecting textual processes observed in one book
to an analysis which is based on the analogy of issues which obtain in
another book. In the last resort, the textual development of almost each
individual book must be viewed separately. Thus we can observe in
the Hebrew tradition of the Pentateuch at Qumrân the same relative
textual compactness, and the same relative sparseness of variant readings, which have already been pointed out in the Septuagint Pentateuch.
On the other hand the extant copies of the book of Isaiah, and above all
the complete First Isaiah Scroll (1QIs^a), present us with a veritable
crop of *variae lectiones*. It has moreover become quite clear that, e.g.,
the book of Samuel and the book of Jeremiah were current at the time
in clearly discernible deviant Hebrew text-traditions. All this goes to
show that the text of these and similar books was still in a state of flux.
Only a careful synopsis of the results achieved by a detailed analysis

of the individual books may ultimately lead to more general conclusions with regard to the over-all history of the Old Testament text.

(2) The Hebrew scrolls from Qumrân prove beyond doubt the actual existence of variant readings in the biblical books of the hellenistic and Roman periods which until their discovery had been beyond the scope of textual research proper. They have added a kaleidoscopic wealth of individual readings for practically all books of the Old Testament, represented in the Qumrân library whether by substantial manuscript finds or sometimes even by only small fragments. Some of these *variae lectiones* are to be found also in:

(*a*) the textual traditions of the main versions, in Hebrew or in translation;

(*b*) quotations in post-biblical writings (Apocrypha, early Christian, hellenistic-Jewish and rabbinic literature); and even

(*c*) medieval Hebrew manuscripts.

In view of the arguments presented earlier, we may assume a genetic relationship between Qumrân variants and identical or similar readings found in the first two sets of the above witnesses which precede the final stabilisation of the Hebrew text. As against this it is probable that the comparatively rare congruence of *variae lectiones* in the third group, i.e. in medieval Hebrew manuscripts or in medieval Jewish commentaries with Qumrân readings, is merely accidental. In most instances the similarity seems to have been caused by the equal but independent impact of the same scribal habits on widely separated sets of manuscripts.

(3) All the extant major versions of the Old Testament, as we know them today, are already represented in Qumrân manuscripts, not only in individual readings, but also in the form of prototypes of their textual traditions. This observation applies principally to the Hebrew Massoretic and the Samaritan (Pentateuch) versions, and to the Septuagint. But manifold affinities with the Aramaic Targums, the Syriac Peshiṭta, and in rare cases even with Jerome's comparatively late Vulgate (end of fourth century A.D.) can also be observed. It is self-evident that this circumstance will weigh heavily in the appreciation of the individual development of these sources and of their common history.

XII

In view of the foregoing presentation of the manuscript finds from Qumrân, it can hardly cause surprise that these discoveries required a reopening of the inquiry into the history of the Old Testament. The resulting scholarly discussion of this issue, and not a mere comparative textual research into the diverse versions, brought about a renewed confrontation of the rival theories of Rosenmueller in Lagarde's version of it, and of Kahle. On the one hand it was claimed with full justification that the presence of the prototype of the Massoretic text among the Qumrân manuscript finds, e.g. in fragments of the Pentateuch or the Second Isaiah Scroll (1QIs[b]) and others, proved the existence of an early precursor of the *textus receptus* at a time which considerably preceded the date presupposed by the followers of the *Ur-recension* and the *Ur-text* schools. On the other hand it was argued that the 'vulgar texts' theory is fully vindicated by the host of textual variants and also of clearly discernible different textual traditions in the bulk of the Qumrân material. The stalemate that resulted from the *pro* and *contra* arguments which could now be buttressed by tangible evidence, unlike the situation which obtained in the stage of the discussion referred to above, again became the point of departure for the conception of a novel theory.

The foundations for a new interpretation of the available material were laid by W. F. Albright.[1] His ideas were soon embraced by a group of predominantly American scholars, and were further developed and succinctly summarised by F. M. Cross:

Any reconstruction of the biblical text before the establishment of the traditional text in the first century A.D. must comprehend this evidence: the plurality of text-types, the limited number of distinct textual families, and the homogeneity of each of these textual families over several centuries of time. We are required by these data...to recognize the existence of *local texts* which developed in the main centers of Jewish life in the Persian and hellenistic age.[2]

[1] W. F. Albright, 'New Light on Early Recensions of the Hebrew Bible', *BASOR*, 140 (1955), 27–33.

[2] F. M. Cross, jun., 'The Contribution of the Qumrân Discoveries to the Study of the Biblical Text', *IEJ*, XVI (1966), 85. The author's preceding studies of this problem are listed in the notes to that article.

After at first accepting Albright's terminology, Cross is to be com-
mended for subsequently introducing a significant change of terms into
the system advocated by Albright who had referred to 'local recensions'. Says Cross:

Against Albright, we should argue, however, that the local textual families
in question are not properly called 'recensions'. They are the product of
natural growth or development in the process of scribal transmission, not
of conscious or controlled textual recension.[1]

These considerations are in line with the arguments presented above,
and disclose a welcome recognition of the fallacy of the concept of a
'scholastic-academy recension', a concept which haunted practically all
preceding theories about the history of the text. However, notwithstanding this difference, the 'local recensions' theory in its 'local texts'
variation absorbed some prominent features of its predecessors which
it built into its own system, as will be shown. The following quotation
summarises the basic concepts of the new school:

Three textual families appear to have developed slowly between the fifth
and first centuries B.C., in Palestine, in Egypt, and in a third locality, presumably Babylon. The Palestinian family is characterized by conflation,
glosses, synoptic additions and other evidence of intense scribal activity, and
can be defined as 'expansionistic'. The Egyptian text-type is often but not
always a full text. In the Pentateuch, for example, it has not suffered the
extensive synoptic additions which mark the late Palestinian text, but is not
so short or pristine as the third or Babylonian family. The Egyptian and
Palestinian families are closely related. Early exemplars of the Palestinian
text in the Former Prophets, and pentateuchal texts which reflect an early
stage of the Palestinian tradition, so nearly merge with the Egyptian, that
we are warranted in describing the Egyptian text-type as a branch of the Old
Palestinian family. The Babylonian text-type when extant is a short text.
Thus far it is only known in the Pentateuch and Former Prophets. In the
Pentateuch it is a conservative, often pristine text, which shows relatively
little expansion, and a few traces of revision and modernising. In the books
of Samuel, on the contrary, it is a poor text, marked by extensive haplography
and corruption.[2]

An analysis of the above quotation discloses the dependence of the
'local texts' theory on its predecessors. It may be described as a new
synthesis, arrived at by sifting the major contentions of earlier views,

[1] *Ibid.* note 21.   [2] *Ibid.* p. 86.

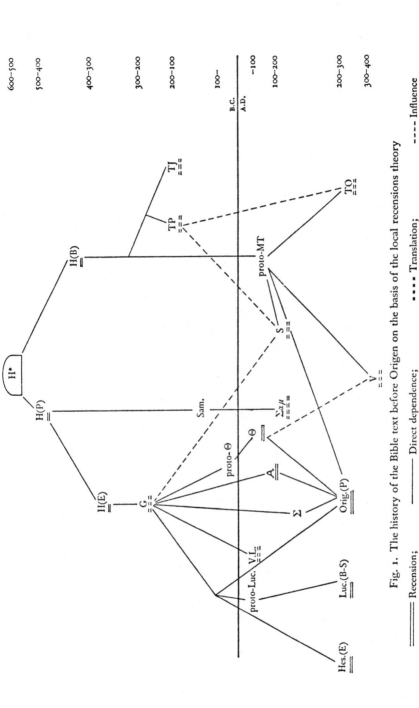

Fig. 1. The history of the Bible text before Origen on the basis of the local recensions theory

═══ Recension; ─── Direct dependence; ∙∙∙ Translation; ----- Influence

H*	The postulated proto-Hebrew text of the Bible	MT	The Massoretic text
H(P)	The Palestinian Hebrew recension	Σαμ	The Samaritan Greek translation—Samaritikon
H(E)	The Egyptian Hebrew recension	TP	The Palestinian Aramaic Targum
H(B)	The Babylonian Hebrew recension	TJ	Targum Jonathan to the Prophets
Sam.	The Samaritan Hebrew (Pentateuch) text	G	The Basic Greek translation—Septuagint

S	The Syriac Targum—Peshitta	Orig.	Origen—Hexapla
TO	Targum Onkelos	Hes.	Hesychius
Θ	Theodotion	Luc.	Lucian
A	Aquila	V.L.	Vetus Latina
Σ	Symmachus	V	Vulgata

600–500
500–400
400–300
300–200
200–100
100—
B.C.
A.D.
100–200
200–300
300–400

discarding some items and maintaining others, and subsequently welding them into a novel structure. It is interesting to remark that although initially the conceivers of the 'local recensions/texts' theory seemed to view themselves as being in line with the basic ideas of the Lagarde–Rosenmueller school, in later presentations of it no reference is made to the *Ur-text/Ur-recension* theory. The very concept of solidified textual traditions, however, whatever term may be applied to characterise them, is apparently tacitly accepted. Further, the assumption of *three* 'local recensions' or 'traditions' is not intrinsically opposed to the 'one recension/manuscript' theory. Of the presupposed three textual recensions or families, in fact only one, namely the Palestinian, has some claim to having been presented by the proponents of the 'three local texts' school as an independent, fairly clearly circumscribed entity, recognisable by specific textual peculiarities. The so-called 'Egyptian' text-type is regarded as derived from the Palestinian, and is presumed to have broken off from it at some time in the early fourth century to begin its independent development. The definition of the third family is not too clear either and its locale can be defined only as being 'presumably Babylon'. This text also obviously originated in Palestine, but had come into final form in Babylon in the sixth century. It is assumed that it had developed there during the interval between the fifth and the second centuries B.C., was reintroduced into Palestine some time after the Maccabean period, and by the end of the first century A.D. had established itself as the dominant or standard Jewish text.[1] Without stating it explicitly, the 'local texts' theory appears to presuppose the existence of an *Ur-text* in Palestine at some time before the Babylonian Exile from which the two major types, the Babylonian and the Palestinian, and the latter's derivative, the Egyptian, emerged at later stages in the post-exilic period. It appears that as a result of the now available material, which is several hundred years older than the material on which scholars of the 'pre-Qumrân' generations could base their arguments, the date of the implied *Ur-text* is also pushed back by some centuries.

In a way, the new theory in its major aspects also resembles Sperber's parallel-transmission system. Both assume different locales for the emergence of the different traditions: here post-exilic Palestine and Babylon; there pre-exilic North and South Palestine. Again we are

---

[1] *Ibid.* p. 91.

transported into the realm of purely hypothetical statements, arrived at by deductions and reconstructions which lack any material, i.e. manuscript, basis.

The very idea of 'local' texts underlies not only Sperber's 'two traditions' theory, but also the system of 'three manuscript types' elaborated by Lieberman, who had not only already posited a tripartition of the biblical textual tradition, but had also affiliated the diverse manuscript types with different types of localities, though in Palestine. One further point is to be noted, namely that the differentiation in value between a standard/received and a vulgar text, introduced into the discussion by Kahle, had been taken up with significant variations in Lieberman's distinction between 'inferior local school texts', 'Jerusalem vulgar manuscripts', and the 'most exact copies of the temple'. Such a value judgement is now applied again by Cross to characterise his three local families: the Palestinian text is conflate and expansionistic, the Egyptian is presented as a predominantly full text, and the Babylonian, in the main, as a short pristine tradition. The shortcomings of this characterisation become apparent when it is applied in detail to the textual tradition of different biblical books in the families thus distinguished. It then transpires that, as if refusing to submit to the scholar's natural quest for order, in the books of Samuel, for example, the Babylonian, somewhat unexpectedly, 'is a poor text, marked by extensive haplography and corruptions'.

One cannot help suspecting that the proposed tripartition of the Old Testament text tradition into a Palestinian, a Babylonian and an Egyptian family in some way echoes the widely accepted three-pronged transmission of the New Testament text in Palestinian, Antiochian (Syrian) and Egyptian versions. Though in itself such a transfer of theories is certainly permissible and could be constructive, it remains doubtful whether in the present case it can be justified in view of the differing attitudes which the Synagogue and the Church took towards the text transmission of their holy scriptures. It has been pointed out above that whereas the former strove gradually to abolish deviant readings and text-types, the latter, possibly because of its heterogeneous composition, attempted to accommodate the diverse traditions that had emerged in the main daughter churches. An unqualified application of a theory which arises from an investigation into the history of the New Testament text to the history of the Old Testament text perforce results in a distortion of the issue and in yet-to-be-proved, or unprovable, hypotheses.

Summing up, we may say that in spite of its appeal the 'three local texts' theory cannot really explain satisfactorily the 'plurality of text-types' at the end of the pre-Christian era. It could indeed account for the 'limited number of distinct textual families' extant at that time. But one is inclined to attribute this feature of the text transmission to two factors: (*a*) historical vicissitudes which caused other textual families to disappear; (*b*) the necessary socio-religious conditions for the preservation of a text-tradition, namely its acceptance by a sociologically integrated and definable body. It is this latter aspect of the problem which safeguarded the preservation of the (proto-)Massoretic text which ultimately became the standard text of the Synagogue, the Samaritan Hebrew Pentateuch version which gained authoritative status in the Samaritan community, the Greek Bible that was hallowed by the Church, and the diverse textual traditions saved for us by the Judaean Desert Covenanters in a form from before standardisation. This tradition complex should be viewed as representing the remains of a yet more variegated transmission of the Old Testament books. Contradictory as it may sound, one is almost inclined to say that the question to be answered with regard to the history of the Old Testament text does not arise from the extant 'plurality of text-types' but rather from the disappearance of other and more numerous textual traditions.

These considerations do not necessarily call for an unqualified acceptance of Kahle's theory of a '*textus receptus* and vulgar texts' which, as already stated, suffers from the over-emphasis put on pre-supposed but unsubstantiated conscious, official redaction processes. All we can say is that from the very first stage of manuscript transmission of the Old Testament text the material which is available to us witnesses to a wide variety of textual traditions which seemingly mirror fairly exactly the state of affairs which obtained in the pre-manuscript state of transmission. In other words, the extant evidence imposes on us the conclusion that from the very first stage of its manuscript transmission, the Old Testament text was known in a variety of traditions which differed from each other to a greater or less degree. As a result of undirected, and possibly in part also of controlled, processes of elimination, the majority of these variations went out of use. The remaining traditions achieved by and by the status of a *textus receptus* within the socio-religious communities which perpetuated them. These standardised texts were preserved for us in the major versions of the Hebrew Bible and its translations.

Hebrew Biblical Manuscripts

Their History and Their Place in the HUBP Edition (¹)

M. H. GOSHEN-GOTTSTEIN – Jerusalem

To Chaim Rabin
Friend and Colleague
On his Fiftieth Birthday

1. The renewed activity in textual studies of the Bible has led of necessity to a revival of interest in Hebrew biblical manuscripts. It stands to reason that in the present state of a general re-evaluation

---

(¹) This study bears the imprint of the oral presentations on which it is based. This may explain the unwieldy subtitle which hints at the subjects treated together — the history of the Hebrew Bible text, the *Problemgeschichte* and the practice in the new edition of the Hebrew University Bible Project (HUBP). Keeping to the form of the original papers serves also, as usual, as an excuse for the large number of footnotes. Some of the points made here are touched upon in the Introduction to my recent 'Sample Edition' of Isaiah, especially §§ 16-18, 73-77, and should be read in conjunction with it. Slight changes of stress and formulation are intentional. This study is to a large extent a provisional summary of my work on the text of medieval Hebrew MSS, started soon after the first discovery of Qumran Scrolls, but is not meant to submit the detailed evidence on which my view is based; that would mean writing a special volume. Apart from the common abbreviations, the following *sigla* for my recent publications should be noted: *TL = Text and Language in Bible and Qumran* (1960); *BMU* = "Biblical Manuscripts in the United States", *Textus* 2 (1962); *RTBT* = "The Rise of the Tiberian Bible Text", *Biblical and Other Studies*, ed. A. Altmann (1963); *TPTC* = "Theory and Practice of Textual Criticism", *Textus* 3 (1963); *ISE = The Book of Isaiah: Sample Edition with Introduction* (1965); *PSCT* = "The Psalms Scroll — A Problem of Canon and Text", *Textus* 5 (1966). In my work on the text of Hebrew MSS I have been ably assisted by Dr. A. Hurwitz and by Mr. M. Bar-Asher of the HUBP, to whom I should like to express my thanks. The responsibility for the views put forward is solely mine.

we cannot yet fully appreciate the change in our overall picture of the development of the Hebrew Bible text. On the one hand, we have already grown accustomed to the idea that no other type of evidence for the Bible text is known to us for such a length of time as that of Hebrew MSS, and this seems almost too natural to need further comment. On the other hand, attitudes to, and evaluations of, Hebrew MSS which have developed during a period of about two centuries still linger on, and perforce influence our judgment. It is, therefore, a matter of course that we do not, as yet, possess any theory which tries to integrate all the known facts into one historical framework. The present study will deal mainly with the problem of Hebrew 'medieval' (1) MSS as part of an attempt at such a theory. The remarks about earlier periods are thus intended, not as an investigation in its own right, but as a sketch of the background against which medieval manuscripts should be seen and as an outline of the pre-medieval history.

2. Our evidence at present (2) suggests a division of the history of Hebrew biblical MSS (3) into three major periods, with an evident cleavage between the second period and the third (4). Our witnesses from the first two periods are of great importance both for our knowledge of the development of the Bible text and for our understanding of the text itself. In other words: their readings can materially change our understanding of the text (5). Although these witnesses have only recently become available to scholarship — and are still partly

---

(1) For the term cf. below, § 7.

(2) But for the basic problem discussed in *PSCT*, one might feel more confident that our results with regard to the details of the second period are there to stay. We are too much in the middle of new discoveries to claim finality for the picture we attempt to paint. The borders between the periods may therefore stand in need of future revision, apart from the inevitable borderline cases.

(3) This discussion deals only with the periods of MS evidence, not with the earlier transmission of the text.

(4) Cf. below, § 6.

(5) According to the position set forth in *ISE* § 3 f., I am not talking in terms of preferability for the reconstruction of the *Urtext*. Those scholars whose primary aim is such a reconstruction would adopt the formulation that those witnesses can sometimes get us nearer the *Urtext*.

unpublished — nobody would contest their place (¹) in a 'critical'
edition of the Bible text (²).

3. The first period starts around 300 B.C.E.; to what degree the
picture emerging for that period holds true for the preceding 'Persian'
period in the history of the Second Jewish Commonwealth is anybody's
guess (³). This period is characterized by a diversity of textual traditions undreamt of two decades ago. It may already be said today
that at the stage of *examinatio* the 'Massoretic Text' (⁴), in comparison
with these traditions, often yields one out of two or more hyparchety-
pal variants which for the time being seem irreducible (⁵). Whether
we shall be able to subdivide these traditions into more or less fixed
'recensions' and whether it is useful to add at this juncture identifying
labels according to the habitats of Jewish communities, is a matter

(¹) Whether they will occupy pride of place (cf. *ISE* § 8) obviously
depends on future finds.
(²) One is almost afraid to use this term. I just refer to an edition
of the text with an apparatus adducing the readings from various types
of witnesses.
(³) Cf. *ISE* § 6. It is most tempting to push the limits upwards,
beyond the earliest fragments from Qumran. But the outcome of past
speculation beyond the limits of the evidence should teach us a lesson.
(⁴) Especially SPERBER has repeatedly suggested dropping the definite article from '*the* Massoretic Text'. Cf., e.g., A. SPERBER, *A Grammar
of Massoretic Hebrew*, 1958, § 36. Cf. below, n. 3, p. 270. It seems inevitable that the different senses in which the term was used have become
confused. In the light of our results in this study (cf. especially below, § 24)
we might as well keep the article, at least for the purpose of text-critical
discussions (as opposed to the problems of the Tiberian *textus receptus*.
Cf. below, n. 6, p. 272, *ISE* § 74 and *RTBT*, Ch. VIII. Just now the
re-issue of C. D. GINSBURG, *Introduction to the Massoretico-Critical Edition of the Bible* (New York 1966) has come into my hands. In the 'Prolegomenon' to this edition H. M. ORLINSKY wages war, amongst other
things, against all the editors of Bible editions and translations who dar-
ed use the term 'massoretic' on their title-page. (The last editor who has
committed this 'sin' is, I think, ORLINSKY himself, although his note
34 does not clarify his responsibility). I am not convinced that his
pronouncements against '*the* massoretic text' (p. IX ff.) have lessened
the general confusion. I hope that the present paper will clarify the facts;
but I may have to return to an evaluation of ORLINSKY's statements on
another occasion.
(⁵) Cf. *TL* p. 161. The present discussion deals with traditions in
Hebrew only.

which needs further discussion (¹). This diversity in Hebrew manuscript tradition is paralleled by extra-Hebrew witnesses, and the
combined evidence must be taken into consideration. It is this period
that offers the greatest challenge to the student of the Bible text (²),
who, quite naturally, is mainly interested not in textual dynamics
per se but in 'material' insights. In contradistinction to what will be
said later (§ 22), it should be stressed that the types of readings and
the textual development which previously could only be illustrated
from extra-Hebrew sources, can now be more or less paralleled
from Hebrew MSS (³). But it should be stressed no less that such a
statement is to be understood typologically. We are in need of many
more material finds before the theoretical importance of the insights
gained during the past years will be equalled by factual gains in the
sphere of variant readings (⁴).

4. The second period may be said to centre in the first century
C.E. (⁵) and seems to have come to a close in the first half of the second

(¹) Cf. *ISE*, Ch. I, n. 15.

(²) If evidence were needed, the first two apparatuses of *ISE* may
be taken as an illustration.

(³) Differently put, these MSS contain both ever-fresh variations
such as caused by the 'law of scribes' (cf. *TL*, p. 159) and 'real variants'
(*ibidem*, p. XIII). All this is stressed in contradistinction § 22 to below.

(⁴) Cf. n. 5, p. 244, above and § 30, below.

(⁵) I am not sure that our paleographical knowledge is precise enough
to fix very narrow limits (cf. *PSCT*, n. 15). A date in the first century
B.C.E. for the beginning of this period seems acceptable, even without
pressing too much the argument from halachic activity in the generation
of Hillel and the statement of JOSEPHUS, *Contra Apionem* I, 42: τοσού-
του γὰρ αἰῶνος ἤδη παρῳχηκότος οὔτε προσθεῖναί τις οὐδὲν οὔτε ἀφελεῖν αὐτῶν
οὔτε μεταθεῖναι τετόλμηκεν. Even though it is based on Deut 4,2 and meant
to impress foreigners, we have no right to discard this explicit testimony.
The turn of the era must be presupposed also because of the activity of
'book correctors'. For this problem, which will not be discussed here,
cf., e.g. S. LIEBERMANN, *Hellenism in Jewish Palestine*, 1950, p. 20 f.
See also S. TALMON, *Textus* 2, p. 14 f. and now M. BEER, *Bar Ilan Annual*
II, 1964, p. 136 f., and the references mentioned there.

Most recently F. M. CROSS has put forward strong arguments for an
extremely low dating of the final rift between Jews and Samaritans
(cf. *Harvard Theological Review* 59 [1966] 201 f.). I should like to suggest
that it may be no coincidence if his date for the final branching off of the
Samaritan Pentateuch turns out to be the first century B.C.E. (*ib*. p. 211).
While it would not be unusual that in such a situation of religious tension

century (^{1}). Since our material evidence comes to an abrupt end at
that point, it stands to reason that our picture would emerge somewhat less schematic if later evidence were available. But in the light
of the Rabbinic activity around 100 C.E., this picture — which in a
slightly different shape is of long standing (^{2}) — is probably more
or less correct. The first century C.E. (^{3}) is emerging more and more
as the decisive phase in the stabilization and growing predominance
of what I have termed elsewhere the 'Massoretic type' (^{4}). By the
end of the second period that type had become absolutely dominant —
deviating details notwithstanding. Again, whereas previous descriptions of the history of the Bible text had to be pieced together without
the benefit of Hebrew evidence, the picture which now emerges fits
the combined evidence of Hebrew MSS, Versions and Rabbinic literature (^{5}). To put it differently, the ratio between 'real variants' (^{6})
and text diminishes during that period, but the readings can still be

textual differences tend to become part of a general interplay of cause and
effect, the final breach may have been one of the factors which resulted
in further unification of the 'Jewish' text-tradition. Hence the gradual
emergence of that century as the turning point in the history of the Hebrew
text and as the beginning of the second period.

(^{1}) For a discussion it may be useful to agree on convenient, if somewhat arbitrary, terms. Chronologically 'pre- and post-Christian' may not
be too far off the mark, but the term would be badly chosen. Since we
have to reckon with Tannaitic activity as a major influence in the process
of standardization (see below, § 31) 'pre-Tannaitic' may, perhaps, be suggested for the first period and 'Tannaitic' for the second.

(^{2}) Cf. the sources mentioned below: n. 2, p. 258; n. 4, p. 263;
n. 1, p. 270; and see § 31.

(^{3}) It remains to be seen to what extent a more exact limitation is
borne out by the facts. In *ISE* § 13 the 'period of the Destruction of
the Temple' — the last third of the first century and the first third of
the second century — has been suggested. But cf. the problems mentioned
above, n. 2 (p. 244), and n. 5 (p. 246).

(^{4}) Cf. *ISE* § 14.

(^{5}) The results of the study of the Peshitta and the Aramaic Versions
will have to be integrated, and it is to be hoped that recent activity in
these fields will lead to a study of the aspects affecting our problem.
The results of my own unpublished attempts in this field corroborate the
picture. Cf. *ISE*, Ch. I, n. 25; cf. *ibidem*, Ch. IV as regards Rabbinic
Literature. See also "Prolegomena to a Critical Edition of the Peshitta",
TL, p. 175 f.

(^{6}) As opposed to variations caused by the 'law of scribes'; cf. above,
n. 3, p. 246.

of importance for our understanding of the Bible text ([1]). To be sure, we must be careful not to press our present evidence for the trend towards a more or less stabilized text or to make *ex silentio* arguments bear too much weight. But attention should be paid to the fact that from the 'destruction period' ([2]) no Bible texts of the 'non-Massoretic type ' have so far come to light ([3]).

5. The end of the first two periods marks the decisive turning point in the history of the Hebrew Bible text. To put it, perhaps, somewhat boldly: the two periods we have tried to describe lead up to the very point which was the reconstructed starting-point of theories about the history of Hebrew biblical manuscripts current until two decades ago. Working back from medieval Hebrew MSS, and connecting the result with what could be inferred from the history of the Bible Versions and Rabbinic Literature, our predecessors were able to reconstruct a point of departure more or less identical with the end of the second period ([4]). This identity is neither coincidental nor self-evident, and this question will need some further discussion.

6. The turning-point reached is remarkable for an additional reason. For the first two periods Hebrew and non-Hebrew evidence runs on roughly parallel lines and all the evidence can be fitted into one picture. As from the end of the second period this 'parallelism' is disturbed: the third period of non-Hebrew evidence, down to the days of Jerome ([5]), as yet lacks any comparable Hebrew evidence; the third period of Hebrew MSS starts centuries later ([6]). It is here

([1]) Cf. *ISE* § 13 f. and above, n. 5, p. 245.

([2]) The problem of the Nash Papyrus need not be gone into on this occasion. If 11QPs[a] should turn out to be datable to this period, this statement may stand in need of revision. Cf. above, n. 2, p. 244.

([3]) The much quoted Torah-scrolls with variant readings (from the כנשתא דסיירום etc.) are not of the 'non-Massoretic' type. Cf. *ISE*, Ch. I, n. 26. For the facts cf., e.g., M. H. SEGAL, *Məvo ha-Miqra IV*, 1950, p. 880 f.

([4]) For details see below, n. 1, p. 270.

([5]) For our discussion it is immaterial whether any independent use of the Hebrew text by a Christian source later than Jerome can be detected. The anonymous Greek version of Habakkuk III is probably earlier; cf., e.g. GOOD, ''The Barberini Greek Version of Habakkuk III'', *Vetus Testamentum* 4 (1954) 29.

([6]) The facts can be described by counting the periods differently, e.g., by leaving a blank in the 'Hebrew' column for the period 3rd–9th

that we are most likely to misinterpret what seems to be our evidence. We have just begun to understand that the history of about four decisive centuries — about 300 B.C.E. to 100 C.E. — was telescoped until this generation for lack of evidence. It seems improbable that new evidence of similar impressiveness will ever come forward (¹), from the span of about six to seven centuries, until the emergence of the earliest MSS of the 'Massoretic period' (²); but the gap is too large to be made light of. On the other hand, it must be admitted that the state of the text reached at the end of the second period does not require any further intermediary stage for the 'Massoretic' MSS to have developed from (³).

7. We have thus reached the third period (⁴). The term 'Massoretic' may be used in this connection to indicate that none of the Hebrew biblical MSS known today which were written after ca 150 C.E. antedates the activity of the Massoretes (⁵); for the moment ' medieval' (⁶) is an equally acceptable term for that period. In quantity these by far outnumber all other Hebrew MSS, and until our generation this was the only Hebrew evidence. To be sure, these witnesses provide

---

century, and assigning the medieval Hebrew MSS to period IV. The variants found in the Arabic Version of R. Saadia Gaon hardly go typologically beyond what is found in early medieval Hebrew biblical MSS.

(¹) I am on record (*Ha'arez* 15.1.1965) as having said that I would be more than surprised should we ever come across a find of Hebrew MSS where a whole lot (as opposed to one or two MSS) written after the beginning of the second century would turn out to be of a non-Massoretic type. In other words, it is more than improbable that there will ever be a discovery of a hoard of non-Massoretic type MSS, similar to that of Qumran Cave IV, written in that period.

(²) For the difference of terms cf. *ISE* § 74.

(³) It should be noted that this is an attempt to differentiate between main stages. For the possible developments after the second period, cf. below, §§ 20, 31.

(⁴) It may not be without interest to compare the 'periodization' suggested from quite a different point of view by B. KENNICOTT *Dissertatio Generalis* § 14 f. (Unless otherwise stated, I quote from the augmented reissue by BRUNS, 1783).

(⁵) I am not aware of any witness certainly datable before the ninth century. Earlier datings are still in need of proof.

(⁶) In order to avoid terminological difficulties (cf. *TL* p. 160, *ISE* § 74), witnesses from the first and second periods are termed here 'premedieval'.

an excellent illustration of textual dynamics, and they deepen our knowledge of the development of the Bible text in the technical sense. But ever since these were first studied in larger numbers, about two centuries ago, it was obvious that their contribution to the understanding of the text itself is extremely doubtful (¹). We must therefore ask ourselves whether the retention of this type of evidence in the apparatus is due to more than mere habit and inertia. Perhaps in the light of the type of evidence available today, the time has come to disregard the readings of medieval MSS completely and to free the apparatus from meaningless ballast? If it is true that these MSS contribute practically nothing to an attempt to reach back to an earlier textual stage, perhaps the consequences must be drawn? Those who wish to study textual dynamics in their own right or to investigate the changes introduced by medieval scribes will turn to the original collections; other scholars may safely ignore that material. This problem cannot be brushed aside, because it has both theoretical and practical implications. We must, therefore, turn to the history of this question as it took shape in recent generations (²).

8. All views on the text of medieval Hebrew biblical MSS held by scholars in the past and at present are based primarily on the collations published in the end of the eighteenth century by Kennicott and de Rossi (³). In spite of assertions to the contrary (⁴), and of some material additions in the form of further readings, mainly due to the

---

(¹) For the contrast cf. below § 22. The criteria for judging MSS in the time of Kennicott and in this generation are different, but the judgments are not as unconnected as appears at first sight. If we bear in mind that scholars in those days tended to accept the very identity of readings as proof of relationship, the widespread disappointment even in those days is telling. Cf. below, § 10.

(²) The following paragraphs had to be written in some detail because I have been unable to find a description of the *Problemgeschichte* which I can regard as absolutely correct and to which the reader could be referred. Much of the material for a full-length study is referred to in the notes to these paragraphs and it is hoped that our discussion will be sufficient within the present framework.

(³) B. KENNICOTT, *Vetus Testamentum Hebraicum cum Variis Lectionibus*, 1776-80; J. B. DE ROSSI, *Variae Lectiones Veteris Testamenti*, 1784-88; J. B. DE ROSSI, *Scholia Critica*, 1798.

(⁴) Cf. especially below, § 20.

diligence of Ginsburg (^{1}) nothing typologically new was discovered after their time (^{2}). It is therefore not really surprising that after a relatively short period of violent discussion in the nineteenth century most scholars in our time hold a view substantially identical with what had been stated back in the seventeen-nineties.

9. Kennicott's collations (^{3}) were not undertaken as a purely philological work. They were one of several enterprises (^{4}) resulting from the onslaught of the 'Critica Sacra', and were intended to be of theological significance. Both text-critical and theological positions were at stake ever since the implications of the *Sola Scriptura* and *Theopneustia* ideologies had developed to their logical end. The Reformers had placed the Hebrew text on a pedestal and it was this text on which severe doubts had been cast. Whether it was *Iudaeorum malitia* or *incuria librariorum* (^{5}) was for many a question of secondary importance. Only the extensive study of Hebrew MSS could give an answer to the issue itself.

10. Against this theological background, the judgments and views expressed by scholars at that time (^{6}) and their strong accusations and

---

(^{1}) The material adduced by STRACK is hardly worth mentioning in this context. Cf. below, n. 3, p. 266.

(^{2}) Of course, anything printed before the work of KENNICOTT must be regarded as superseded, although not all the variants published in the edition of the Bible by J. H. MICHAELIS (1720) were included by KENNICOTT. Practically all modern studies which use Hebrew variants are based on the collations of KENNICOTT and DE ROSSI.

(^{3}) Unless specification is necessary, KENNICOTT's name alone will be mentioned, because most of the discussion turned on his work and because its arrangement made it more influential, although from the scholarly point of view DE ROSSI's work was more exact. Cf. below: n. 1, p. 252; and n. 2, p. 255. As *sigla* K–R will be used.

(^{4}) Cf. the editions and collations from MILL until BENGEL and until WETTSTEIN and, in other fields, those of SABATIER and HOLMES-PARSONS. The study of Hebrew MSS had its special aim, but it was part of a larger movement. The term 'Critica Sacra' is used here in its general sense, not as the title of a collection.

(^{5}) See L. DIESTEL, *Geschichte des Alten Testamentes*, 1869, p. 326 f., 345 f.

(^{6}) The theological overtones remind us that but for the theological implications the work would never have been carried out. Perhaps even our generation is less free from theological predilection than we like to admit. Cf. for the field of N.T. studies the latest Presidential Address to

counter-accusations (¹) must be understood. From the point of view of the theory of one fixed immutable Hebrew text the sheer mass of readings was overwhelming (²) and some scholars even felt the need to explain it away (³). Many readings previously known from the Greek seemed all of a sudden paralleled by Hebrew variants (⁴). These

---

the SBL of K. W. CLARK, "The Theological Relevance of Textual Varia- tions in Current Criticism of the Greek New Testament", *Journal of Biblical Literature* 85 (1966) 1 f. and his statement (p. 5): "The only objective and justification of textual criticism is that it's emended text should give access to a clearer insight and a deeper faith." Cf. *TPTC* p. 137. We should also remember the remark of H. S. NYBERG, *Zeit- schrift für die alttestamentliche Wissenschaft* 52 (1934) 244 repeated *Studien zum Hoseabuche*, 1935, p. 14 "Diese Geringschaetzung ist nur als Antithese gegen das alte kirchliche Dogma von der Verbalinspiration zu verstehen. Die ganze Psychose kann nur durch nüchterne philologische Betrachtung überwunden werden".

(¹) From a perusal of the literature of the second half of the 18th century it seems that various scholars occupied different positions on a 'scale' of attitudes towards the received Hebrew text, and consequently had to defend their position on both sides. Even KENNICOTT — who certainly was interested in overstating the importance of the readings (cf. also below, n. 4) — started out by turning against denigrations of the Hebrew text; cf. B. KENNICOTT, *The State of the Printed Hebrew Text of the Old Testament Considered*, 1753, p. 556 f. J. H. MICHAELIS turned against KENNICOTT's claims, but he himself was considered by others to exaggerate the importance of the Hebrew variants (cf. ref. below, n. 4, p. 253). At the other end of the scale we find the extreme position of O. G. TYCHSEN (cf. n. 3). The rather sloppy work of some of KENNI- COTT's assistants helped to make things easier for his opponents.

(²) Cf. e.g., the evaluation of J. C. DOEDERLEIN, *Auserlesene Theolo- gische Bibliothek* II, 7, 1782. p. 483 f.

(³) The most radical attempt was made by O. G. TYCHSEN, *Tentamen de Variis Codicum*, 1772; *Befreyetes Tentamen*, 1774. Whereas this work is better known for the 'Transkriptionstheorie', taken up in our time by F. X. WUTZ, its major aim was to defend the received Hebrew text and to explain the deviations as coming from 'inferior' sources (written by Christians, women, etc.). Cf. also below n. 2, p. 270, and n. 3, p. 275. In any case, his extreme position did some good in making scholars more critical towards the 'Varientenrummel'.

(⁴) To be sure, many scholars were dimly aware that most of these 'readings' were secondary harmonization, simplificationss, etc. But we must not forget that at least one variation of the יָךְ / ךָ type (cf. below n. 3, p. 281) was discussed on many occasions. I am referring, of course, to the famous חסידך problem in Ps 16,10, which was judged to be of the utmost theological importance. KENNICOTT himself was very out-

variants seemed thus of the greatest importance and their use in any
exegetical-critical work was imperative. Textual critics were at liberty
to plough through the collations and to dig up what they thought
useful for their purpose (¹). They have done so ever since (²).

11. On the other hand some scholars were not slow to recognize
that very little could be actually gained and that the huge mass of
readings consisted mostly of secondary scribal changes, parallelisms,
normalizations, harmonizations or free associations (³). In fact, for
them the old theory of the one 'Massoretic Text' seemed vindicated
de facto, only the picture (⁴) which had emerged was somewhat more

---

spoken in his claim and his influence is felt in all the subsequent discussion. Cf. his *Dissertatio Generalis*, § 49: "Quanquam vero manuscriptorum
vetustissimi non superant aetatem annorum 800 vel 900, tamen desumti
fuerunt hi ex manuscriptis qui ipsis antiquiores erant, idque fortasse per
quaedam secula: auctoritas vero eorum, dum saepius confirmant versiones
antiquas, assurgit ad aliquot secula A.C." Cf. also the more sophisticated
discussion of DOEDERLEIN, *loc. cit.*, (n. 2, p. 252), p. 523.

(¹) The summary of DOEDERLEIN, *loc. cit.*, II, 9, 1783, p. 675 is
quite typical. According to his summary we should be content " dass
hie und da eine Lesart verborgen steckt, die der Ausleger sucht und als
Rest der alten Recension betrachten kann, dass Untersuchung, Prüfung und Wahl der Materialien, welche hier ausgelegt sind, dazu dienen
kann, dass wir in der biblischen Kritik doch einige Schritte vorwärts
kommen".

(²) It seems superfluous to voice again objections to the procedure
of R. KITTEL's *BH*. Cf. below n. 5, p. 264. It is somewhat surprising,
however, to find out that in our generation a scholar should come forward
with an appeal for readings from Hebrew MSS to be used more frequently
in everyday exegetical work — an appeal which does not betray much
knowledge of the problems involved and illustrated by rather unsuitable
examples. See F. S. NORTH *Jewish Quarterly Review* 47 (1956) 77 f. Cf.
below, n. 3, p. 284.

(³) Cf. *TL* 45 f., 57 f. DOEDERLEIN, *loc. cit.*, 653 f. gives a striking
example of how, on closer inspection, practically none of the readings
from the apparently deviating MS K 1 stands up to scrutiny. See also
below, § 25 f.

(⁴) In spite of certain differences in stressing details, leading scholars
of that time, like DOEDERLEIN, EICHHORN and MICHAELIS came to similar
results. Thus, J. G. EICHHORN, *Einleitung* II, 1781, p. 239 summed up
immediately after the first volume of KENNICOTT appeared: " Schreibfehler in Menge und brauchbare Lesarten äusserst wenige " (and this
according to the criteria of that generation). This statement remained in
EICHHORN's standard work throughout the editions. Cf. 4th ed. II,

complicated than before. It was thus quite natural that a scholar at that time could sum up his impressions in the form of a 'one-recension theory' which was destined to get mixed up hopelessly, almost a century later, with Lagarde's ' archetype theory '. Rosenmueller, one of the half-forgotten foremost critics of that time was the first to formulate the results of his study of the huge collections in philological terms (¹): "Dieser ganze mit so viel Aufwand von Zeit und Kosten zusammengefuehrte Variantenwust giebt übrigens das einfache Resultat dass alle noch vorhandenen Codices im Verhaeltnis zu den Originalen sehr jung sind... dass sie saemmtlich zusammen *eine* Rezension (²) darstellen, aus einer Quelle geflossen sind, und dass folglich aus ihnen für die etwa verdorbenen Stellen des hebräischen Textes wenig oder

---

p. 700, and *ib.* p. 707: "die Geschichte des Hebr. Textes lehrt, dass seine Hauptfehler älter sind als alle unsere noch vorhandenen kritischen Hülfsmittel..." Cf. MICHAELIS, *Oriental. und Exeget. Bibliothek* 11 (1876), p. 72 f. esp. p. 95 f., as well as the appendix containing the dispute between him and KENNICOTT.

(¹) J. G. ROSENMUELLER, *Handbuch der bibl. Kritik und Exegese* I, 1797, p. 244. This publications is not available to me and I cannot verify the exact title and the quotation. I quote after E. PREUSCHEN *ZAW* 9 (1889) 303. Since PREUSCHEN had pointed to the formulation of 1797, it is not clear why scholars went on quoting ROSENMUELLER as if his view was formulated in 1834 only. Cf. below n. 3, p. 261, and n. 1, p. 264). (I have not searched for other possible statements of ROSENMUELLER on the subject. He does not mention it in his preface to the reprint of J. SIMONIS' edition of the Bible [1828]). By the way, there was no real need to rediscover ROSENMUELLER's view, since it was quoted in DIESTEL's standard work in 1869 (*loc. cit.* [n. 5, p. 251], p. 594, quoted as *Handbuch d.... Literatur*). DIESTEL took the 'one-recension' formulation as representative of the view taken by scholars who summed up KENNICOTT's work. He does not yet as much as mention LAGARDE! Cf. below, n. 4, p. 263.

(²) The term 'Rezension' in ROSENMUELLER's writings has to be understood in the sense in which it was current since it was introduced by J. S. SEMLER (1765) into New Testament studies. For the history of our problem it may not be uninteresting to point out that SEMLER's term *recensiones* superseded J. A. BENGEL's term *nationes*. The two terms thus foreshadowed the later 'local recension' from K. LACHMANN's time down to our own (cf. below, n. 2, p. 257 and *ISE*, Ch. I, n. 15). Cf. now for N.T. studies B. M. METZGER, *The Text of the New Testament*, 1964, pp. 112 f., 119 f. The term 'Rezension' in those days was not yet understood as implying almost complete 'official' regulation. Hence it is accepted throughout this study and the term "one-recension' theory is used. But cf. below, § 31.

gar keine Hülfe zu erwarten ist" (¹).   The 'one-recension' theory was
the result of a level-headed analysis of the collations of Kennicott (²);
it was never seriously challenged or disproved (³), and its substance
remains true to this day (⁴).

(¹) This remains the most important criterion; cf. above n. 1, p. 250;
n. 1 and n. 4, p. 253. In the words of EICHHORN, *loc. cit.*, II, 706:
"Die suesse Hoffnung muss man aufgeben, dass er [the Hebrew text]
selbst bei einem moeglichst vollstaendigen kritischen Apparat zu seiner
voelligen urspruenglichen Reinigkeit wieder gelangen werde".

(²) The attitude to the text was shaped by the analysis of KEN-
NICOTT's collection and in spite of its special features DE ROSSI's work
was never allowed the same influence. Cf. above, n. 3, p. 251. It should
be remembered that KENNICOTT did not note variants in vocalization;
hence the impression of a unified text was even greater. Cf. below, n. 1,
p. 282. Of course, KENNICOTT advanced good reasons for leaving out
the vocalization — the amount of work involved, the different types of
MSS, etc. — but the omission should also be viewed in the light of the
'vowel-war', which had not yet abated at that time. Cf. DOEDERLEIN
loc. cit., p. 508, and see the telling remark of MICHAELIS, *Orient. etc. Bibliothek*, 23, p. 104: "bey allem meinem Unglauben an das Alter der
Puncte waeren mir diese doch sehr wichtig gewesen". Cf. TYCHSEN,
Tentamen, p. 182 f., and *Befreyetes Tentamen*, p. 144: "Ein grosser Fehler
ist es, dass Hr. D. K. sich nicht um die Vergleichung der Punkten (*sic*)
bekümmert hat. Denn da er durch seine Varianten-Samlung den maso-
rettischen Text zu verbessern zur Absicht hatte, die Punkte aber ein
wesentliches Stück desselben ausmachen, so hätte er sie auch vergleichen
lassen sollen... Sagt man, dass die Punkte oder die Aussprache eine
neuere Erfindung der Juden sind und ein jeder Ausleger das Recht
habe sie nach Belieben zu ändern, und dass daher die Consonanten blos
authentisch sind, so sezt man unausgemachte Sachen als ausgemacht
voraus, etc. etc.".

(³) Statements in the literature to the contrary rest on the misunderstanding discussed below, § 15 f.

(⁴) I am not concerned here with the felicitousness of this formulation
or with the term itself. Cf. below, § 31. Some statements in the literature are worded to convey the impression that the 'one-recension'
theory was already suggested by SPINOZA. It should be made clear,
therefore, that not only is there the difference in the textual theory, indicated by the term 'Rezension', but SPINOZA's statement is simply a paraphrase of the well-known story about 'the three Scrolls of the Law that
were found in the Temple Court'. This can be seen if one cares to check
the discussion in *Tractatus Theologico-Politicus*, end of Ch. 9. The statement itself reads: "... *credo scribas pauca admodum exemplaria reperisse,
forte non plura quam duo vel tria*". For the story of those scrolls cf.
most recently S. TALMON, *Textus* 2 (1962), p. 14 f.

12. In spite of certain formulations in the beginning of the second half of the nineteenth century (¹), matters might have rested there, but for Lagarde. Students of the history of a problem have got used to the fact that posterity tends to connect a certain theory with a certain man, regardless of his predecessors. Whatever our feelings about Lagarde as a person, his stature as a master of textual criticism was unrivalled. In spite of his waverings between theology and philology, he did more than anyone else to lay the foundations of textual criticism of the Bible as a philological discipline (²). Together with this went his penchant — his strength or weakness, as one prefers to see it — to formulate very outspoken and extreme theses which tended to acquire an axiomatic character. It was his clear-cut and attractive formulation which became the basis for subsequent discussion of our subject, and earlier formulations were soon erroneously equated with his view. A spurious dilemma began to bedevil all later statements, and a perusal of many studies and handbooks reveals that hardly anyone has managed to state the exact positions ever since (³).

13. The quotation of the famous 'archetype theory', first formulated just over a century ago, is in order (⁴): "es ergiebt sich also, dass unsere hebräischen handschriften des alten testaments auf ein einziges exemplar zurückgehn, dem sie sogar die korrektur seiner schreibfehler als korrektur treu nachgeahmt und dessen zufällige unvollkommenheiten sie herübergenommen haben. Über diesen archetypus des masoretischen textes würden wir nur durch conjectur hin-

(¹) Cf. below, esp. n. 3, p. 261.

(²) The present writer is probably not the only one who often wonders wistfully whether the place of P. DE LAGARDE as a combination of all-round textual critic and Semitist has ever been filled. Precisely because the man and his views were often objectionable (see also below, n. 4, p. 258), his merits should not be belittled. LAGARDE did not reach his goal, and the specialization in the generations since then has carried us further and further away from it. Cf. *TL*, p. XIV, and my *Hebrew and Semitic Languages*, 1965, p. 26.

(³) I can only hope that I have got the facts right and that no further misunderstandings will occur; but, unfortunately, misunderstandings copied from book to book are almost ineradicable. Cf. also below n. 6, p. 272.

(⁴) LAGARDE, *Anmerkungen zur griechischen Übersetzung der Proverbien*, 1863, p. 2. I have tried, in general, to reproduce LAGARDE's orthography.

ausgelangen können, wenn uns nicht die griechische version des
alten testaments die möglichkeit verschaffte, wenigstens eine schlechte
übersetzung eines einer andren familie angehörenden manuscripts zu
benutzen''. According to this picture, the Hebrew and the Greek
texts were likened to two witnesses representing two textual families.
The conclusion to be drawn from all the existing Hebrew MSS was
thus that they all went back to one archetype, one single manuscript(¹).

14. No sooner had this theory been formulated than the misunderstandings began. Lagarde had not bothered to base his view on
any analysis of readings in Kennicott and de Rossi. He rested his
case at this stage exclusively on what could be regarded as a 'stemmatic
proof' based on common characteristics — a type of proof acceptable
according to the rules of textual transmission in cases in which texts
were developing without outward influence or regulation (²). The

(¹) It has not always been emphasized that LAGARDE assumed a
parallelism in the development of the Hebrew and the Greek texts, that
is, he maintained that in both cases we may attempt to reach back to the
respective archetypes. There remained, however, an important difference.
The aim for the Greek was the reconstruction of 'hyparchetypes' — the
famous 'local recensions' — which would then enable scholars to work
their way back to the original Septuagint. For the Hebrew there was no
more than that one assumed 'archetype'. For the temptation to put forward similar theories to account for the facts in related fields of textual
inquiry, cf. below, n. 1, p. 272, and n. 3, p. 281. For the somewhat belated
introduction of such a theory into the study of the Vulgate, especially
by H. QUENTIN, and the present state of the issue in that field cf. now
R. A. KRAFT, *Gnomon* 37 (1965) 777 f.

(²) For a long time I have been wondering how the misunderstanding about LAGARDE's 'proof' (see below) could arise, and how most of his
contemporaries were apparently unable to take his argument at its face
value. The following seems to be a possible explanation: The scholars
in the sixties of the last century to whom LAGARDE's formulation was ad-
dressed were Semitists and theologians, however thorough their training in
classical philology. LAGARDE's way of argument, as well as the very term
'archetype', were taken over from K. LACHMANN. But in 1863 only
thirteen years had passed since LACHMANN had finalized his textual theory
in the introduction to his edition of Lucretius (1850). The theory and
the way of argument were quite novel, and LAGARDE's fellow-Semitists
and theologians could not really be expected to appreciate that LAGARDE
rested his case exclusively on the slender evidence of 'common mistakes'
etc., completely ignoring the whole issue of variant readings which in
previous generations had stood in the centre of the argument. One might

common exterior signs, *puncta extraordinaria* and *literae suspensae,*
which appeared at the same places in the Hebrew MSS were deemed
sufficient proof (¹) for the assumption of one common ancestor text.
Nothing more was needed to prove the case. This completely theoretical construction was soon to be buttressed by two further pillars (²).
First came a late Arabic story about a Scroll of the Law saved from
Bittir from which other scrolls were said to have been copied — a
story which was taken as historical proof (³), fixing the time of the
archetype in the reign of Hadrian. Second — an unbelievable argument which was later on deliberately glossed over by others because of
its unpleasant affinities to a certain type of literature — was the
'theological' proof, i.e. a certain chronological difference between MT
and LXX was alleged to prove the wilful tampering of the Rabbis
with the text from anti-Christian motives. Such tampering could
only have succeeded, in Lagarde's contention, because all later manuscripts derived from the selfsame copy. (⁴). In other words: the arche-

---

object that theologians should have been familiar with LACHMANN's
method from his work on the N.T., but before 1850 he had not yet developed his system. We have the word of U. v. WILAMOWITZ-MOELLENDORFF,
Geschichte der Philologie, 1921, p. 59 that the edition of Lucretius was
the decisive step. Cf. also G. PASQUALI, *Storia della Tradizione e Critica
del Testo,* 1952, p. 3. The influence of LACHMANN on LAGARDE is, of
course, obvious in his treatment of the 'local recensions' of the LXX.
Cf. above, n. 2, p. 254, and below, n. 1, p. 264.

(¹) LAGARDE stressed that he considered his statement in 1863 as
proof; see, e.g., LAGARDE, *Symmicta* I, 1877, p. 50; II, 1880, p. 120.

(²) LAGARDE, *Materialien zur Geschichte und Kritik des Pentateuchs*
I, 1867, p. XII and the references there.

(³) *Loc. cit.*: "... eine mir damals unbekannte notiz, die als ein histo-
risches zeugniss für jenen damals nur durch combination gefundenen
satz gelten darf".

(⁴) "... um die mit huelfe der LXX angestellten berechnungen der
christen zu widerlegen, nach denen der Messias im jahre 5500 der welt
erschienen war. Solche fälschungen (welche die kirchenväter so oft den
juden vorwarfen) sind nur denkbar, wenn sie an Einem exemplare vor-
genommen werden konnten, aus dem alle übrigen abschriften des textes
zu entnehmen waren. Aquila ... hat seine übersetzung offenbar nur an-
gefertigt, damit das im Interesse des grimmigsten christenhasses gedok-
terte hebräische alte testament ja den auständigen ' Gebildeten' nicht
unbekannt bliebe...." Can one really do more than add exclamation marks
with A. GEIGER, *Jüdische Zeitschrift* 7 (1869) 312? This incredible argumentation was quickly disposed of in a masterly study of A. KUENEN,
De Stamboom van den Masoretischen Tekst des O.T., 1873 (I have used

type theory had been formulated in 1863 on purely theoretical grounds, and it was bolstered up and given a chronological setting in 1867. It should be emphasized that these and only these points were Lagarde's 'proofs', and the problem of variants was never mentioned. These points were repeated over and over again (¹), but no attempt was made by him to answer any of the queries raised (²). If Lagarde was forced to come back to the issue it was only in order to guard his priority rights (³).

---

mainly the German translation in BUDDE's edition of KUENEN, *Gesammelte Abhandlungen*, 1894, p. 82 f.). Cf. below, n. 4, p. 263. In the light of the history of this problem it is rather unfortunate that the author of a recent well-known handbook on the Bible text found it necessary to say in this context — I am sure, in ignorance of LAGARDE's argument — that in the "movement for fixing an authoritative text of the Hebrew Bible... the name most prominently associated with it is that of Rabbi Aqiba, probably the most renowned Rabbi of the early Christian era, and a notorious anti-Christian". See B. J. ROBERTS, *The Old Testament Text and Versions*, 1951, p. 25.

(¹) Cf. *Materialien, Symmicta* I, *loc. cit.*, and especially his discussion of his priority rights, *Symmicta* II, 1880, p. 120 f. and *Mittheilungen* I, 1884, p. 22 f.

(²) *Mittheilungen, loc. cit.*, does not disprove anything. The arguments against LAGARDE are summarized below, § 17 f. Cf. also n. 4, p. 263.

(³) Cf. above, n. 1. An elaborate description of the theory in its historical context was given in 1870, reprinted *Symmicta* I *loc. cit.*: " Im jahre 1863 habe ich in den anmerkungen zur griechischen übersetzung der proverbien bewiesen (ich betone dies zeitwort), dass alle bisher bekannten handschriften des jüdischen kanons aus Einem archetypus stammen. am nächsten läge es, diesen archetypus für das exemplar der sammler jenes kanons zu halten, das natürlich officiell war. auffallen würde dann die stellenweise ausserordentlich grosse fehlerhaftigkeit des überlieferten textes. man könnte zu deren entschuldigung freilich sagen, dass der unter Esdras amtierende ausschuss die widersprüche des deuteronomikers etwa gegen den elohisten übersehen hat, also auch wohl fehler in den worten nicht bemerkt haben kann... indessen abgesehen von anderen erwägungen, haben wir ein, allerdings durch die mündliche überlieferung eines für geschichtsschreibung und geschichtsauffassung absolut unbegabten volkes hindurchgegangenes, also mit mehr oder weniger unzuverlässigem stoffe vermengtes ausdrückliches zeugnis dafür, dass jenes urexemplar unseres textes der zeit Hadrians angehoert... glaublich erscheint jene nachricht insoferne, als eine in den schweren zeiten unter Hadrian sich sammelnde gemeinde frommer juden leicht in der lage sein konnte, sich mit einem einzigen exemplare ihrer heiligen schriften begnügen zu müssen, und als das ansehen der männer, welche sich eines solchen exemplares bedient hatten, unschwer diesem buche eine grössere bedeu-

15. It is not easy to understand today how a theory built on so
insecure a foundation was so warmly welcomed (¹). I would go so
far as to suggest that the main reason was that very misunderstanding
against which Lagarde tried unsuccessfully to guard himself (²). His
contemporaries took it for granted that his theory was only a refinement of the view expressed on the basis of the K–R collations, with
slight variations, ever since the days of Rosenmueller — especially
in Lagarde's own time by Olshausen. They talked of the theory of
Olshausen and Lagarde (³) — and Lagarde's formulation appealed to

---

tung verschaffte, als sein innerer wert philologischer kritik gegenüber ihm
verliehen haben würde... was aber jene überlieferung als in der grundan-
schauung richtig erweist, ist der umstand, dass unser text des jüdischen
kanons mindestens an Einem punkte gegen das christentum gerichtete
correcturen enthält, mithin sein archetypus aus der christlichen zeit
stammen muss...".

(¹) The first scholar of note who accepted the theory was none other
than Th. NOELDEKE, *Die alttestamentliche Literatur*, 1868, p. 241. But
according to the popular character of that book he did not state expressly
that this was LAGARDE's view. In scholarly discussion he reiterated his
acceptance of the view five and ten years later (see HILGENFELD's *Zeitschrift für wissenschaftliche Theologie*, 1873, p. 445; *Zeitschrift der Deut-
schen Morgenländischen Gesellschaft* 32 [1878] 591). There is therefore
no justification for LAGARDE's complaint (*Mittheilungen*, loc. cit., pp. 22;
210) that his theory met with the 'Hohn der Zunft'. Since later literature states that the theory was accepted by J. WELLHAUSEN in the fourth
edition (1878, p. 620 f.) of F. BLEEK, *Einleitung in das A.T.*, it should be
noted that A. H. KAMPHAUSEN had already done that in the third edition
(1870, p. 733). This is apparently the first textbook which mentions the
theory in the name of J. OLSHAUSEN next to LAGARDE. KAMPHAUSEN's
formulation shows that he did not appreciate the difference between
LAGARDE's formulation and the older view: "... besitzen wir denselben
wesentlich nur in Einer Recension, d.h. alle unsere Hebr. Handschriften
gehen auf ein einziges Exemplar zurueck, dass man... zur Musterhand-
schrift erklaerte, und dann mit ganz sklavischer Treue abschrieb". Cf.
ib., p. 802. But it was probably WELLAUSEN's acceptance that was
decisive. Cf. n. 3, p. 269.

(²) There is no evidence that scholars tended to welcome the theory
because of the allegedly similar state of textual transmission, claimed at
that time for the Vedas by M. MUELLER. But the parallel was suggested
by A. GEIGER, *Jüdische Zeitschrift* 3 (1864) 78 f. and was taken up in
BLEEK–WELLHAUSEN, loc. cit.,

(³) WELLHAUSEN, loc. cit., described the theory as that of OLSHAUSEN
and added (p. 621): "Um die weitere Verbreitung dieser sehr plausibeln
Hypothese OLSHAUSENS's hat sich LAGARDE verdient gemacht" and ex-

them because he had added further 'proofs' (¹). Soon the 'one recension' theory and the 'archetype' theory had become fused into one.
Rosenmüller was quoted as having said more or less the same thing
as Lagarde (²) — and it would seem that some scholars who were
annoyed by Lagarde's unsavoury habit of repeatedly starting some
'priority quarrel' enjoyed pointing out that in this case it was Lagarde
who had forgotten his predecessors (³). It was a somewhat tragico-

---

pressly stressed that "LAGARDE überschaetzt hier... seine Originalität".
In the same vein, although not so outspoken, were the remarks of NOEL-
DEKE, *Hilgenfeld's Ztschr.* and *ZDMG, loc. cit.* (n. 1, p. 260). Such re-
marks forced LAGARDE to stress his priority rights; cf. below, n. 1 f., p. 263.

(¹) The widespread acceptance in the eighties of the last century
can be seen from various statements in the literature. W. ROBERTSON
SMITH, *The O.T. in the Jewish Church*, 1881, p. 70 f., 398 — through
whose influence the theory was accepted in England — stated "I know
of no attempt to refute the argument". Slightly different was B. STADE,
ZAW 4 (1884) 302: "Es ist bekanntlich eine noch nicht alte Erkenntniss,
dass der massoretische Texte des A.T. auf eine einzige Handschrift zurueck-
geht. Und wiewohl die Variantensammlung zu jedem beliebigen Capitel
des A.T. diese Annahme für jeden philologisch Geschulten als nothwendig
erweisen müsste, vernimmt man zuweilen dagegen noch Widerspruch".
Note that STADE connects the theory with the result of collations of variants. F. BUHL, *Kanon und Text des A.T.*, 1891, p. 259 summed up:
"Insofern ist die verhaeltnissmaessig neue, aber schon sehr verbreitete
Annahme, dass alle vorhandenen Handschriften auf einen Archetypus
zurückweisen, entschieden richtig".

(²) Since handbooks are mainly responsible for perpetuating the
formulations of summaries, I single out the wording of BUHL, *loc. cit.*,
p. 261: "Die Abstammung aller Handschriften von einem Archetypus ist
behauptet worden von ROSENMUELLER... OLSHAUSEN... LAGARDE...
NOELDEKE." And he adds: "Eine ganz eigentuemliche Formulierung
hat LAGARDE dieser Hypothese gegeben". This is a fair example of the
way the two theories had become fused and BUHL's formulation was copied
up to our own generation. Cf. R. GORDIS, *The Biblical Text in the Making*,
1937, p. 45. I. L. SEELIGMANN, *Tarbiz* 25 (1956) 118 also fell victim to the
statements of his predecessors, in spite of some attempt to differentiate
between views. See also below, n. 4, p. 263.

(³) OLSHAUSEN was named as the originator of the theory as soon
as discussion started; cf. above, n. 1, p. 260 STADE, *loc. cit.* (above, n. 1),
pointed to ROSENMUELLER's statement in the preface to the Bible edition of
1834, and PREUSCHEN, *ZAW* 9 (1889) 303 rediscovered the statement from
1797 (cf. above, n. 1, p. 254). Finally C. H. CORNILL, *ZAW* 12 (1892) 309
rediscovered the position of J. G. SOMMER, *Biblische Abhandlungen*, 1846,
p. 79. ROSENMUELLER had talked about a 'recension' but SOMMER was the

mic situation that had developed: scholars had enthusiastically embraced Lagarde's formulation, but named his alleged predecessors into the bargain. Lagarde fought tooth and nail to make it clear that

---

first to suggest an exact description — of course without using the term 'archetype': "... da alle Handschriften und Ausgaben des hebr. Textes nicht nur im Allgemeinen Einer Recension angehören, sondern ursprünglich sammt und sonders aus Einem Exemplar der bereits vollendeten Schriftsammlung — vielleicht war es ein zu besonderem Ansehen gelangter Tempelcodex — herstammen...". It should be emphasized that SOMMER was not only the first to formulate the 'archetype' theory but also the first to differentiate it clearly from the 'one recension'. Cf. below, n. 2, p. 270. OLSHAUSEN, *Die Psalmen*, 1853, p. 18 wrote in a very similar vein, without any mention of SOMMER. According to him, an official 'recension' — very similar to the later 'massoretic' one — already existed in early Christian times. Since this 'recension' contains obvious mistakes which were not corrected, we must assume that it was based on one single MS for each part of the Bible, which was often damaged but was followed "mit sklavischer Treue". The recension itself had probably been arranged at the end of the first century B.C.E.

Even LAGARDE's 'proof' had practically been mentioned already by OLSHAUSEN, two years before the *Anmerkungen* appeared. In his *Lehrbuch der hebräischen Sprache*, 1861 § 31a OLSHAUSEN stated: "Wenn in einigen Stellen des Alten Testamentes die Finalform eines Buchstaben in der Mitte des Worts oder umgekehrt die gewöhnliche Form am Ende gefunden wird, so ist der Grund davon darin zu suchen, dass in dem Exemplare der heiligen Schriften, welches die diplomatische Grundlage der heutigen Textesrecension bildete, der Schreiber entweder mit Absicht oder durch Versehen eine andre Wortabteilung statuirte..." There can be little doubt that in fact LAGARDE only added some refinement in his formulation of the 'proof' as well as the very term 'archetype' to this theory. WELLHAUSEN's judgment of the actual contribution of LAGARDE (cf. above, n. 3, p. 260) therefore seems justified.

It remains an unsolved problem whether LAGARDE — who was quick to censure others for ignorance of the literature — was really completely unaware of his predecessors. As shown above, (n. 1, p. 260), KAMPHAUSEN knew about OLSHAUSEN in 1870, but NOELDEKE adduced OLSHAUSEN's view in 1873 (see n. 3, p. 260) as mentioned to him in a private talk, and LAGARDE maintains (*Mitth.*, I, p. 23) that OLSHAUSEN himself "von mir seiner zeit ausdrücklich befragt, erinnerte sich nicht, sich über den hier behandelten gegenstand einmal öffentlich geäussert zu haben". There remains the possibility that LAGARDE propounded his view independently, and once the facts were pointed out to him tried to defend his priority rights by stressing the slight differences. OLSHAUSEN himself appears to have remained completely quiet and did not claim his rights, perhaps because of his official position or else because he himself had omitted to credit SOMMER.

his theory was different from any other (¹), that he did not accept Olshausen's position, that nobody had ever put forward any of his, Lagarde's, proofs, and that his proofs were different *toto caelo* (²). Hence it was his theory only — a theory different from their's (³). But he did not succeed (⁴), and scholars went on talking about 'archetype' and 'recension' as if they were synonyms and quoting Rosenmüller etc. as the first to have put forward Lagarde's theory (⁵).

(¹) For details cf. *Symmicta* II, 1880, 120 f. and *Mitth.*, *loc. cit.*

(²) Almost the whole discussion centered around OLSHAUSEN's priority. Only in the '*Nachtraege*', *Mitth.* I, p. 381, did LAGARDE hear of the note about ROSENMUELLER, to be published that year (1884) in the *ZAW*, and he identified ROSENMUELLER's view with that of OLSHAUSEN, as opposed to his own. As far as I can see in the literature available to me, LAGARDE returned to the issue finally in 1886, in his review of CORNILL (*Mitth.* II, p. 49 f.) On that occasion he mentions for the first time that the question of variant readings may also be of importance for proving the existence of the archetype. Here he seems less confident about the dating of the archtype in the time of Hadrian, and even finds it worth mentioning that the archetype "erheblich über 750 hinaufreicht" (the date is based on a wrong premise in that context and need not concern us here). Cf. below, n. 2, p. 265, and n. 1, p. 270.

(³) *Mitth* I., p. 24: "Da ich Wert darauf lege, das oben wiederabgedruckte zuerst erkannt zu haben...".

(⁴) Right at the beginning of the discussion the particular position of LAGARDE had been stressed by GEIGER, *Jüdische Zeitschrift* 7 (1869) 312 f. in his review of LAGARDE's *Materialien* (1867). For GEIGER the commonly accepted position of his day was that there was practically one text as from the second century C.E. In other words, he bears witness that the 'one recension' theory was the reigning one. (cf. above n. 1, p. 254): "Im Gegensatze zu diesem wohlbezeugten Resultate stellt Herr LAGARDE in dem Vorworte zu den "Materialien" eine Ansicht auf, die wir als eine Probe seltsam launenhafter Kritik nicht vorenthalten wollen..." Thus, LAGARDE's first opponent stressed the difference. LAGARDE took notice of the review only by some personal sneers (*Mitth.* I, p. 22). Nor did he ever trouble to refute KUENEN, *Stamboom* (cf. above, n. 4, p. 258), who was the only one at the time who had attempted to undermine LAGARDE's structure by reasoned argument and who had formulated afresh a 'one-recension' formula ("In één woord: al onze codices vormen te zamen ééne familie"). The most correct assessment of the differences of position given right after LAGARDE's death is the summary by E. KOENIG, *Einleitung in das Alte Testament*, 1893, p. 88, but he, too, missed a number of points. As for BUHL, cf. above n. 2, p. 261.

(⁵) Thus, e.g., B. STADE, *Lehrbuch der Hebräischen Grammatik*, 1879 p. 20, mentions LAGARDE as having put forward a view about one recen-

16. It seems a reasonable assumption that the lack of differentiation between the two formulations (¹) had a share in preventing scholars from drawing the necessary consequences for their theoretical positions — and here we return for a moment to the text-critical practice. As long as the Hebrew manuscripts were viewed as belonging to one recension (²), there was at least a theoretical justification for their use in the critical apparatus and for connecting their readings with those of the ancient versions. A 'recension' is not watertight (³). But an 'archetype' is, by definition, only one manuscript. *Ex hypothesi* the belief in an archetype should have meant that all medieval readings were secondary changes in the transmission and hence could only be used for the reconstruction of that archetype. They could never be simply used side by side with readings from the versions (⁴), and such statements as 'read with G 4 MSS' or the like should have been disallowed on theoretical grounds. One might even have envisaged a difference of procedure between 'exegetical practitioners' according to their adherence to one theory or the other, with the adherents of the 'archetype theory' abstaining from the use of Hebrew MSS.

17. Nothing of the kind happened (⁵). Scholars were quick to accept the 'archetype theory' (or what they thought it to be), although they differed in their opinions as to how that archetype had come into

---

sion ("eine einzige Recension"). In *ZAW* 4 (1884) 302 he mentions correctly, "eine einzige Handschrift" — without realizing the difference — and then goes on to equate this with ROSENMUELLER's view.

(¹) In the eighteen eighties 'Archetypus' was already a well-established term. But it may be that the term 'Rezension' was not longer free any more from ambiguity. Cf. above, n. 2, p. 254; n. 2, p. 257.

(²) That is, until the seventies of the last century, because only by then had LAGARDE succeeded in making an issue of the question.

(³) Cf. below, § 21 f.

(⁴) I am not concerned at present with the actual correctness of retroversions (cf. *TPTC*), but with the practice of adducing readings in the apparatus, which ran counter to what theory should have taught. The consequences which should have been drawn from the 'archetype' theory seem to me self-evident. Looking for a discussion of such a problem in general literature I found this application of the theory affirmed by H. KANTOROWICZ, *Einfuehrung in die Textkritik*, 1921, p. 24. For my suggestion on handling the evidence, cf. also *ISE*, § 23.

(⁵) Quite typically, R. KITTEL, *Über die Notwendigkeit und Möglichkeit einer neuen Ausgabe der Hebräischen Bibel*, 1902, p. 5, having mentioned the differences of opinion about the 'archetype' theory, adds: "Für unsern

being (¹). In practice nothing changed and Hebrew readings were quoted as before (²). But perhaps the time was too short for the exegetical and text-critical practice to be influenced by the new theory.

Zweck verschlägt der Streit wenig". It is largely thanks to his *Biblia Hebraica* that two generations of Bible scholars were reared on this way of looking at the evidence. Cf. also, n. 2, p. 253, and below, n. 2.

(¹) OLSHAUSEN, *Psalmen*, p. 18 had assumed a "pharisäische Redaction" whereas Lagarde tried to pin down the historic situation in which there was literally just one MS left (cf. above, n. 3, p. 259). (KUENEN, *Ges. Abhandl.*, p. 118 turned also against this detail). NOELDEKE, *Die alttest. Literatur*, p. 241 thought that one MS had been chosen more or less by chance, "... dass man ziemlich planlos nach einer Handschrift griff, weit mehr besorgt darum, einen einzigen als einen guten Text zu bekommen". Cf. also BLEEK–KAMPHAUSEN, *Einleitung*, p. 802. A few years later the idea of 'deliberate suppression' of other MSS was added to the description (NOELDEKE, *Zeitschrift f. Wiss. Theol.* 1873, p. 444 f. Cf. below, n. 4, p. 288. It was probably because of NOELDEKE's preoccupation with the history of the Qoran that he saw the acceptance of the Hebrew archetype in the light of the action of OTHMAN, in utter disregard of the different historical situations. (This is not intended to deny that the comparison of the histories of Qoran and Bible texts may yield instructive illustrations, if cautiously applied; cf. also GORDIS, *Tarbiz* 27 [1958] 454 f.).

This picture of the Rabbis ruthlessly ordering all other texts to be suppressed (or destroyed) was only too readily accepted as explaining the later actions of the Massoretes, too. Cf. KAHLE, *Cairo Geniza*², 1959, p. 141 f., and my criticism, *RTBT*, Ch. IV. That picture mainly grew out of the misunderstanding of the institution of '*Geniza*', which was mentioned in connection with the dearth of MSS again and again, at least since the days of WALTON (*Prolegomena* IV, 8): "Ratio etiam probabilis reddi potest cur non habemus codices Hebraeos... quia scil. post Masoretharum criticam et punctationem ab omnibus receptam Judaeorum magistri omnes codices his non conformes ut profanos et illegitimos damnarunt..."; cf. also H. L. STRACK, *Prolegomena Critica*, 1873, § 6.

For a summary of opinions by the end of the last century as to the choice of the archetype, cf. BUHL, *Kanon*, p. 259 f. More or less the same opinions were expressed as regards the origin of the recension, a number of scholars claiming that the MSS chosen were actually the best; cp. e.g. the position of KAHLE, *Masoreten des Ostens*, 1913, p. XVIII, against GRESSMANN. For a summary of the Rabbinic sources with regard to the question of the possible 'archetype' and the different types of MSS cf. LIEBERMANN, *Hellenism in Jewish Palestine*, 1950, p. 20 f.

(²) The first scholar of that generation who seriously attempted to carry out the demand that the exegesis of a book should start off with the use of the ancient witnesses and should be preceded by a systematic

For no sooner had the 'archetype theory' become accepted than the gradual rejection of Lagarde's extreme position started (¹). Just as scholars had not really bothered to examine Lagarde's reasoning and his position was accepted under a partly false impression, so they did not bother to disprove Lagarde's proof formally by unmasking the fallacy of his stemmatic argumentation and by rejecting his theory on those grounds. Thirty years after 1863 it began to be realized somehow that the particular history of massoretic MSS made them defy the usual stemmatic procedures — and hence Lagarde's proof was no proof at all (²). But this was not the decisive argument. To be sure, the weight of the work done by those of his younger contemporaries who had worked on Hebrew MSS, especially that of Strack (³), was thrown against Lagarde, although their actual

---

evaluation of those witnesses was C. H. CORNILL, *Ezechiel*, 1886 (cf. also the review of LAGARDE, *Mitth.* II, p. 49 f.) CORNILL accepted LAGARDE's thesis enthusiastically and even tried to strengthen it by reintroducing the problem of variants (cf. n. 2, p. 263, and n. 2, p. 272). But he then went on to quote Hebrew readings without so much as realizing the dilemma. Nor did LAGARDE comment on it in his review.

(¹) The reasons given in the literature for the rejection of the 'archetype' theory are many and varied, showing a correlation with the subject each scholar happened to be dealing with; cf. also n. 1, p. 269, and n. 1, p. 274. An interesting example is F. ZIMMERMAN, *Jewish Quarterly Review* 34 (1944) 459, dealing with the problem of double readings, who claims as first reason for LAGARDE's fall: "In the first place, scholars have noticed that in quite a number of instances the massoretic context contains obvious variants placed side by side." Cf. below, n. 1, p. 285.

(²) During LAGARDE's lifetime KUENEN (cf. above, n. 4, p. 258, and n. 4, p. 263) remained the only one to have written a proper refutation, but also he was not aware of the basic fallacy of LAGARDE's argument based on the *puncta extraordinaria*, etc. Immediately after LAGARDE's death E. KOENIG, *Einleitung* etc., 1893, p. 88 f., and H. L. STRACK *Einleitung*, etc., ⁴1895, p. 172 questioned the validity of that argument, followed by V. APTOWITZER, *Das Schriftwort in der Rabbinischen Literatur*: *Prolegomena*, Sitzungsberichte Akad. Wien, Phil.-Hist. Kl. Bd. 153, 1906, p. 5. A remark on the subject from D. H. MUELLER's classroom, quoted by APTOWITZER, clearly exposes the weakness of LAGARDE's argument. The main issue, however, was the return to the evaluation of variants, and LAGARDE's real argumentation was pushed aside. Cf. esp. below n. 5, p. 275; n. 2, p. 278.

(³) STRACK was the only one in the decade before APTOWITZER who repeatedly rejected LAGARDE's formulation even though he did not add further evidence. Cf. preceding note and his paper in *Semitic Studies*

findings did not really change the overall picture as known from the collections of Kennicott and de Rossi. But nothing of what they said actually countered Lagarde's basic argument about the *puncta extraordinaria*, etc. Trying to reconstruct the history of our problem, one is tempted to conclude that since Lagarde's theory had never really been accepted just on its own merits, but rather as a continuation and logical conclusion from the positions of his predecessors, which were based on the study of variants, it sufficed to point out forcefully that the overall evidence of variants now available precluded the assumption of an archetype. It was first and foremost a return to the evaluation of variant readings which dethroned the Lagardian formulation (¹).

18. Once the Lagardian structure had begun to collapse, further attacks were readily interpreted as having dealt it the final blow. Scholars were now only too eager to accept the contention of Aptowitzer (²) that the variants in Rabbinic literature suffice to nullify Lagarde's formulation(³). Since the type of material on which Aptowitzer based his argument was relatively unknown to most theologians and had hardly been used seriously in the previous discussion of the

---

in Memory of A. Kohut, 1897, p. 571 — basing his opposition especially on the large number of marginal notes to codices — and *Dictionary of the Bible*, IV, 1902, p. 28.

(¹) Cf. E. KOENIG, *loc. cit.*, C. STEUERNAGEL, *Lehrbuch der Einleitung in das A.T.*, 1912, p. 20 f. See the list of B. J. ROBERTS, *O.T. Text and Versions*, 1951, p. 27. But cf. below, n. 3, p. 283. It must, of course, be remembered that not all the scholars whose views are mentioned in such lists were in a position to express a view based on first-hand study.

(²) *loc. cit.*, p. 3 f.

(³) "Dieses Argument fällt mit dem Nachweis solcher Varianten einfach weg". It is characteristic of the atmosphere in those days that nobody paused to ask whether the argument based on variations in *Rabbinic* sources had any necessary bearing on the theory of an archetype assumed for *Bible* MSS. In any case, I have not seen that anyone suggested this rather obvious counter-argument. All later discussions revolved around the question to what degree one should assume 'quotation by heart'. (For a similar problem in the study of the Peshitta cf. *TL*, p. 196 f.) An interesting argument recently put forward from 'orthodox' quarters is that because of the strict regulations as to the conditions of writing down Scripture, the Rabbis intentionally refrained from exact quotations. Cf. R. MARGULIES, *Bible and Massora* (in Hebrew), 1964, p. 47 f. It is not clear how this explanation accounts for the great majority of quotations which agree with MT.

subject (¹), its impact was considerable and made many scholars decide finally against the archetype formulation (²).   It thus began to become customary for scholars to propagate the view that Lagarde's theory was still basically true, but had to be slightly modified.   His position was almost right — with the stress on 'almost'; his formulation was too extreme and should be tuned down; one must allow for more flexibility, etc. (³).   It is not without reason that we attempted previously to analyze the development through which the 'one-recension' theory got mixed up with the Lagardian position.   Since most scholars around the turn of the century were convinced that Lagarde's predecessors had intended to put forward his theory and that there was only one theory accepted by most leading scholars during the latter half of the nineteenth century, none of Lagarde's opponents was able to state in so many words that the seemingly new, 'almost Lagardian' position was in fact nothing else but a return to the

(¹) Even so, it had come up sporadically, especially since the days of KENNICOTT, and STRACK had stressed it in his dissertation.   A list of his predecessors is given by APTOWITZER, p. 8.

(²) The statements of KAHLE in his young days show clearly that his anti-Lagardian position was influenced by APTOWITZER.   This is foreshadowed in a long footnote, *Masoreten des Ostens*, 1913, p. XVIII f. and developed in his "Untersuchungen zur Geschichte des Pentateuchtextes", 1915 = *Opera Minora*, 1956, p. 31.   APTOWITZER's work is not even mentioned in *Cairo Geniza*!

(³) A typical formulation, e.g., STEUERNAGEL, *loc. cit.*, p. 22: "... dass jene These in abgemilderter Form doch ein gewisses Recht hat".   Similarly, KAHLE, *Opera Minora*, p. 33: "Seit ungefähr 100 n. Chr. ist in den offiziellen jüdischen Kreisen unser masoretischer Konsonantentext als *textus receptus* betrachtet worden — so könnte man vielleicht LAGARDE's Hypothese modifizieren".   The formulation, some decades later, of O. EISSFELDT is not much different, but he allows for more flexibility; cf. *Einleitung*², 1956, p. 838: "die... These... ist in dieser Form nicht mehr haltbar..."; cf. 3rd ed., p. 929f. See below, n. 2, p. 270, and n. 3, p. 283.   It should be noted that EISSFELDT also writes as if his view is directly opposed to LAGARDE's thesis, and the reader is not really made aware that LAGARDE's formulation had been rejected by practically all scholars since the beginning of this century.   One may compare the slightly varying formulations of J. REIDER, *Prolegomena... to Aquila*, 1916, p. 81 f.; A. BENTZEN, *Introduction to the O.T.*, I, 1948, p. 51 f.; D. Winton THOMAS in H. H. ROWLEY (ed.), *The Old Testament and Modern Study*, 1951, p. 244 f. B. J. ROBERTS, *loc. cit.*, p. 25; M. NOTH, *Die Welt des A.T.*, 1953, p. 245, etc. My own formulation in *TL*, p. XI, reflects the common state of misinformation; the formulation in *ISE* § 75 is correct, as far as it goes.

view formulated by the father of the 'one recension' theory, back
in 1797 (¹).

19. At no stage, however, did the pendulum swing back towards
an even more 'positive' evaluation of Hebrew readings, such as was
suggested by some scholars in Kennicott's times. If there was not
sufficient proof for assuming an archetype, there was not more than
what could be encompassed within one recension (²). To be sure,
back in the eighteen-eighties matters had looked different for a short
moment, when Hebrew MSS with completely different readings were
said to exist. But the forgeries were soon detected (³), and the result
of the disappointment may, in a way, have indirectly even strengthened the general opinion that no readings of 'importance' could ever be
found in genuine MSS.

20. Thus, by the first quarter of this century, practically all
specialists were agreed on what amounted in fact to a 'one recension'
theory (⁴). The main difference as compared with the position of

(¹) It may be added that since scholars have not been aware of the
differences of position, the outline of the *Problemgeschichte* suggested
here should be judged only in the light of the primary sources concerned.

(²) This may explain why the issue of studying variants from biblical MSS was practically reopened only in the thirties of this century.
Cf. P. VOLZ, *ZAW* 54 (1936) 104: "Mir scheint dass die Annahme eines
Archetypus daran gehindert hat in der Untersuchung der hebr. Handschriften auf Wert usw. vorwärts zu kommen". But (p. 106): "Der Ertrag
der Variantensammlung ist, wie ich aus eigner eingehender Beobachtung
weiss, ganz abgesehen von der Frage des Archetypus, sehr gering".

(³) As for FIRKOWICH, cf. my recent remarks in *Tarbiẓ* 33 (1964) 149f.
It is most unfortunate that J. M. ALLEGRO has attempted to warm up
the SHAPIRA affair in a popular book, connecting it afresh with the Qumran
discoveries and insinuating gross errors committed by the leading Bible
scholars and archeologists in those days. (*The Shapira Affair*, 1965).
ALLEGRO has not adduced a shred of new evidence or so much as attempted to refute the arguments brought forward in recent discussions. Any
attempt to clear the Shapira forgeries will first have to get rid of the evidence I submitted in *Journal of Jewish Studies* 7 (1956) 187 f. See the
London *Jewish Chronicle*, Nov. 12, 1965 and cf. also O. RABINOWICZ,
"The Shapira Scroll: A Nineteenth-Century Forgery", *JQR* 56 (1965) 1 f.

(⁴) Sometimes a formulation was copied which reminds one of J. G.
SOMMER's statement (cf. above n. 3, p. 261), but seems to have been
some kind of 'compromise'. As far as I can see, it occurs first in S. R.
DRIVER, *Notes... on... Samuel*, 1890, p. xxxvii: "All MSS belong to
the same recension, and are descended from the same imperfect archetype."
This was taken over, e.g., by J. REIDER, *loc. cit.* (cf. above, n. 3, p. 268).

Rosenmüller was that it became now usual to quote a date for the recension, mostly by simply relying on the date suggested by Lagarde for the 'archetype', but sometimes by pushing it slightly up or down ([1]). Apart from minor fluctuations ([2]), the problem could be regarded as settled, and remained so up to the time of the recent discoveries. In this context one cannot but point out that the work of Kahle and his followers on the vocalization systems dealt, in a way, only an additional blow to the Lagardian theory ([3]). Statements in the literature

---

The only one in our generation who built his own thesis on the 'archetype' theory is R. GORDIS, *The Biblical Text in the Making*, 1937, p. 45 f. He believes in one single MS on the margins of which variant readings had been noted. His picture is somewhat like that of NOELDEKE in *ZDMG* 32, p. 591. In private talk he stressed that he did not think of the archetype in the Lagardian sense, that no other MS was in existence at the time, but rather as *the* MS, out of a larger number, which became the basis for all the later ones. Cf. now his slightly modified exposition in *Tarbiz* 27 (1958) 444 f., where he stresses that the large number of variants in Hebrew MSS need not influence the verdict on the issue of the archetype.

([1]) In a way, the suggestion to recognize a 'second period' (cf. above, §4) is little more than an attempt to get into one framework the various dates suggested for the 'archetype' on the basis of ancient Rabbinical and historical literature, since the days of SOMMER and OLSHAUSEN (cf. above, n. 3, p. 261). For the problem of evaluation of Rabbinical sources cf. also the references above, n. 5, p. 246 and in GORDIS's discussion (cf. preceding note and his reply to ALBRIGHT in *JBL* 37 [1938] 330). The connection with the early Christian period has been claimed at least since R. Simon; cf. BUHL, *Kanon*, p. 261. More scholars accepted the suggested date in the first century C.E. than is usually realized; cf. especially Th. NOELDEKE, *Zeitschr. f. wiss. Theol.*, 1873, p. 446 and LAGARDE's slight withdrawal (above n. 2, p. 263).

([2]) The formulation of O. EISSFELDT, *Einleitung*[2], p. 833 is typical of a position which assumes a rather considerable degree of fluctuation (cf. above, n. 3, p. 268), probably influenced by KAHLE (see below). But nobody went as far as to suggest a typological differentiation among Hebrew MSS. In the light of § 23 f. below, it should be added that the last one to maintain that against the uniformity of the rest of the recension there are a few MSS which are seriously deviating was SOMMER (cf. above n. 3, p. 261). But from his discussion it would seem that his remark was rather in the nature of claiming Christian etc. origin for deviating MSS, after the fashion of TYCHSEN (cf. above, n. 3, p. 252): "Allerdings giebt es nebenher auch etliche hebräische Codices die einer andern Reihe von Abschreibern, zum Theil sicher Judenchristen, angehören...; aber auch diese Gattung gehört mit den aecht jüdischen Codices derselben Recension an".

([3]) Cf. e.g., the introduction to R. KITTEL, *Biblia Hebraica*[3], p. XIII. KAHLE's remarks on problems of textual variants remained incidental

which may create the impression that it was mainly Kahle's work that overthrew the 'archetype' theory are not borne out by the facts (¹). Kahle published the first major summary of his views (²) when the anti-Lagardian movement had won the day and he never added new evidence against the 'archetype theory'(³). His main contribution

---

and he never attempted to study the Geniza material in this respect systematically; cf. *BMU*, Ch. II. The provocative statement of A. SPERBER (cf. above n. 4, p. 245): "There never existed The Massoretic Text and consequently never will be" has little to do with the subject under discussion here. But such statements easily lend themselves to misinterpretation.

(¹) Thus, e.g., it is difficult not to understand A. BENTZEN, *Introduction*, I, p. 56, as if it is because of KAHLE that "we have to abandon the theory of the archetype". Similarly E. WÜRTHWEIN, *Der Text des A.T.²*, 1963, p. 26. More correctly R. H. PFEIFFER, *Introduction to the O.T.*, 1948, p. 79. Cf. below, n. 3. Precisely because of H. M. ORLINSKY's many just strictures against KAHLE one would have wished that his description of the position in *Journal of the American Oriental Society* 61 (1941) p. 84 f. had been more exact, the more so since younger scholars have copied the details on his authority. As far as I can make out, according to ORLINSKY, too, it was KAHLE who attempted to refute LAGARDE. But LAGARDE, according to him believed in the 'one-recension' (not the 'archetype'!), whereas KAHLE rejects the theory of a one-text tradition. Since the idea of 'one-recension' is right, ORLINSKY upholds LAGARDE. ("In the second third of the nineteenth century, ROSENMUELLER, OLSHAUSEN and LAGARDE, especially the last-named, advanced the view, which is held by practically all competent scholars today, that all preserved MSS of the Hebrew text of the O.T. go back to the one recension which came to domination in the first-second century A.D. at the latest. In this I concur".) I can only add that I wonder whether ORLINSKY would have identified his position with that of LAGARDE, had he been aware of the exact facts. As his words stand, they are part of a total position for LAGARDE against KAHLE, as regards both the Hebrew and the Greek textual traditions. Furthermore, in spite of the strong words of ORLINSKY against GORDIS (cf. *JAOS* 60 [1940] 30 f.), both these pupils of M. L. MARGOLIS happen to be the only ones who maintained, around 1940, that LAGARDE was right. Since I tend to assume at least a partial misunderstanding, I agree with ROBERTS, *JJS* 1 (1949) 147 that the apparently considerable differences between the positions of KAHLE and ORLINSKY are exaggerated.

(²) Published in 1915; cf. above n. 2, p. 268.

(³) The few variants from MSS with Palestinian vocalization published in *Masoreten des Westens* II, 1930, p. 22* f. did not change the picture at all. Cf. below, n. 3, p. 272. I should think it fair to state that KAHLE's main point was that in the light of the different systems of traditions of vocalization, "es scheint dass erst die exakte Arbeit die die

was an argument *ex analogia* ([1]) from his own theory about the work
of the Massoretes ([2]). It was thus no specific evidence ([3]), but rather
the overall weight of Kahle's position, which made some scholars
adopt a view in favour of a certain textual fluctuation even after the
second century C.E. ([4]) It would, therefore, be correct to sum up
that Kahle's ([5]) writings made it finally clear that Lagarde's formulation was erroneous and that Kahle went further than his predecessors
in assuming fluctuations within the 'one recension' ([6]). On the theo-

---

Punktation des Konsonantentextes erforderte, einen wirklich einheitlichen
Konsonantentext — in Palästina wie in Babylonien — durchsetzte"
(*Opera Minora*, p. 32). Perhaps one may say that whereas KAHLE's predecessors had rejected LAGARDE's formula, but had thought of the 'one-
recension' as being almost of an archetypal nature, KAHLE saw larger
divergences within the recension which became unified through later
gradual convergence. Cf. below, n. 2, p. 273. This may explain why
some authors of handbooks credited KAHLE with overthrowing LAGARDE's
thesis (cf. above, n. 1, p. 271). It should be stressed that what KAHLE
put forward was a somewhat refined view, but not based on any new and
relevant evidence. In a way, he refined the picture drawn by his anti-
Lagardian predecessors, just as LAGARDE had done with the statements
of OLSHAUSEN, etc.

([1]) Cf. especially *Opera Minora*, p. 26. It cannot be shown here in
detail how the argument *ex analogia* played a large part in KAHLE's
theories in general. Cf. also *RTBT*, n. 42, and *TL*, p. 176.

([2]) This did not prevent him mixing up facts about the text and
about vocalization, and claiming that CORNILL in his comparisons of the
Petrograd Codex of 916 with the printed text "in all the details of punc-
tuation of such a long and difficult text he was able to find only about a
dozen slight variations" (cf. *Cairo Geniza*[2], p. 63). Because of the interest of CORNILL's position for the history of our subject (cf. above, n. 2,
p. 263; n. 2, p. 265) I cannot but note that KAHLE got the facts wrong.

([3]) ROBERTS, *JJS* 1 (1949) 152 sums up, rightly, that the variants
collected by KAHLE have little bearing on textual questions. Cf. above,
n. 3, p. 271.

([4]) Even some of those who favoured KAHLE's modification of the
theory felt he pressed his point too much, Cf. ROBERTS, *loc. cit.*

([5]) For KAHLE's lack of interest in Tiberian Geniza material cf. *BMU*
p. 35 f. See above, n. 3, p. 270.

([6]) KAHLE's opening sentences on the two senses in which 'textus
receptus' is used (*Opera Minora*, p. 26) can be wholeheartedly endorsed.
His summary (*ib.*, p. 33) is in line with what had been said by his predecessors. ROBERTS, *O.T. Text*, went even beyond KAHLE when he stated
that "the theory collapses when it is argued that the archetype belongs
to the second century A.D., or some such early date. The MSS on which

retical side, the victory of the 'one recension' theory — regardless of
the terms or words used — was thus well established by the end of the
first third of this century, and it has remained victorious throughout
the second third.   What seemed to Kahle and his opponents a major
clash between their positions was no more than a minor difference of
views which did not really affect the basic common theory (¹).   It
was a difference as regards the degree of internal unity that scholars
were ready to allow the recension at *ca* 150 C.E., with Kahle opting
for the picture of a broader basis and a partial later ironing-out of
variations (²).

21. In the context of our present study it should be stressed that
at no point of the discussion did the theoretical position have any
repercussion on the everyday practice of the use of Hebrew variants
by 'practitioners' of textual criticism.   Hebrew variants were continued to be quoted as before, and their use was not felt to constitute
any problem (³).   On the other hand, the end of the first third (⁴) of

---

it is based belong in the main to the twelfth century A.D. and later"
(p. 24) and "... until final emergence of the standard archetype text of
the ben Asher Massoretes, which received official status by the decree of
Maimonides in the twelfth century A.D." (p. 29).   Bearing in mind the
history of the term 'archetype', this is either an unfortunate use of the
term or a mistaken presentation.   My objections to ROBERTS' formulation on another occasion (cf. *RTBT*, n. 126; see also above, n. 4, p. **258**)
have been attacked by him in *Journal of Theological Studies* 15 (1964)
253 f. (but see *ib.*, p. 331).   I shall try to reduce differences of opinions
between us to a minimum in a future paper.

(¹) Cf. also above, n. 1, p. **271**. Possibly some writers tended to
overstress the differences between positions precisely because there are
too few facts.

(²) In a way, the differences and possible combinations between the
'family-tree theory' and the 'wave theory' in linguistic theory may be
compared.

(³) Cf. above, § 16. Of course, had anyone been asked about the
theoretical basis, he might have answered that since the ' archetype '
formulation had been rejected, there was no bar to using Hebrew variants.
It should be noted that the scholars who took part in the theoretical discussion or wrote the handbooks were usually not those who carried out
the actual text-critical work. Cf. below, n. 7, p. **274**.

(⁴) Cf. below, § 23. HEMPEL was the first scholar who approached
the problem methodically, and was aware of the necessary connection
between the Lagardian theory and text-critical practice. His study in

this century marks a renewed interest in the old problem of the 'value' of those variants and their sources ([1]). This problem was to appear in a new perpective about the middle of the century ([2]). It has been mentioned above ([3]) that the K–R readings have remained the basis for any view expressed on the subject of Hebrew variants and that none of the additional material published since has altered the overall picture ([4]). Therefore, any judgment expressed in our generation is, by necessity, hardly more than a restatement of the opinions put forward in the second half of the eighteenth century, whether pro or con ([5]). Our main advantage over our predecessors lies, therefore, in our ability to view medieval Hebrew MSS against the background of pre-medieval ones ([6]), and to attempt to create some interaction between theoretical insights and text-critical–exegetical practice ([7]).

22. The results of our investigations force upon us the conclusion that pre-medieval Hebrew biblical MSS are *typologically* different from medieval ones. Only now that different types of readings can be adduced from pre-medieval MSS can it be fully appreciated that what sets medieval MSS apart is the fact that they contain practically exclusively variations of the types which can arise again and again

---

ZAW 48 (1930) 187 f. is a step forward. Had I been aware of that article a dozen years ago, when I first turned to this subject (*Biblica* 35 [1954] 429 f.), I could have saved myself some remarks.

([1]) Whereas by the end of the 19th century the disappointment with K–R's collections is given as the reason for the discontinued interest in Hebrew MSS (cf., e.g., STRACK, *Semitic Studies... Kohut*, 1897, p. 562), other reasons were also put forward now; cf. n. 1, p. 266, and n. 2, p. 269.

([2]) Cf. *Biblica, loc. cit.* = *TL*, p. 51 f.

([3]) Cf. above, § 8.

([4]) If anything, the basic textual uniformity has only been underlined by the publication of medieval MSS which belong to other traditions than the 'Tiberian receptus' one.

([5]) It seems not impossible that the very fact that scholars of our generation were not always educated to work for themselves from the primary collections but rather got acquainted with Hebrew readings through sporadic and selective quotations, has created among many a wrong evaluation of the material and fostered unjustified expectations. Cf. above, n. 5, p. 264.

([6]) Cf. above, § 7 and n. 6, p. 249.

([7]) For attempts to combine the two aspects cf. the introductions to *TPTC* and *ISE*. Cf. above, n. 3, p. 273.

through scribal activity ([1]), Among tens of thousands of readings from medieval witnesses which were checked in this connection it was hard to find even a handful which were not immediately explicable as having arisen through harmonization, simplification, etc. To be sure, all these occur in Hebrew MSS from the first two periods and can be amply adduced from the Versions. But there they exist side by side with 'real variants' ([2]). It is precisely the existence of 'real variants' that has made the pre-medieval MSS a new challenge to textual criticism ([3]); it is their absence that marks medieval MSS ([4]). This is the reason why scholars have been disappointed ever since Kennicott's collections became known and why the study of medieval Hebrew MSS was previously said to be little more than an illustration of textual dynamics ([5]). On the other hand, it is the considerable number of variants, formally common to medieval Hebrew MSS and pre-medieval sources, which we tend to attribute to the ever active and repeated force of the 'law of scribes' that creates the illusion ([6]) of a genetic connection between medieval MSS on the one hand and pre-medieval ones and the Versions on the other. It is that apparent formal identity which has caused scholars ever since Kennicott's time to state that, in spite of the generally disappointing results, there are some readings of 'value' in medieval MSS, which

([1]) For the various types cf., e.g., *TL*, p. 45 f., 57 f. The problem of ' simple ' scribal mistakes and omissions is not dealt with here. Cf. below, n. 4, p. 279, and n. 6, p. 285. Cf. also the discussion in B. M. METZGER, *The Text of the New Testament*, 1964, p. 186 f.

([2]) For the term cf. *TL*, p. XIII. The existence of borderline cases, here as elsewhere, does not invalidate the differentiation.

([3]) Cf. now also TALMON, *Textus* 4 (1964) 95 f.

([4]) This may, perhaps, be put differently: were we to put medieval and pre-medieval MSS together indiscriminately and have them sorted out according to types of variations, the new typological arrangement would turn out to be identical with the chronological one. Cf. *ISE*, § 17.

([5]) As a corollary; because of this, any attempt at ordering all medieval witnesses into families according to stemmatic principles is doomed to failure, just like LAGARDE's attempt to assume a Hebrew archetype according to LACHMANN's principles. It may be truly said that the Massoretic activity made the usual criteria inapplicable. Cf. § 17 and n. 2, p. 278. — Cf. also *ISE*, §§ 17, 76. This is not to deny, of course, that individual MSS can be shown to be connected. Cf. already the discussion of DOEDERLEIN, *Auserlesene... Bibliothek* II, 9, 1783, p. 650 f.

([6]) Cf. below, § 25 f. The connection would cease to be an illusion only after a specific relationship is proved.

'confirm' (or are confirmed by) the readings of the versions, and those readings have taken their place in the apparatuses next to the re-troversions.

23. Having restated the argument against the assumption of genetic relationship between medieval and pre-medieval witnesses as seen from our newly-gained vantage ground (¹), we may turn back and look at the attempts during the past fifty years at studying me-dieval MSS (²). It may be useful to distinguish between two main lines of inquiry: the attempt to detect MSS which deviate in their whole textual structure from the standard text (³) to such a degree that their deviations may be said to point towards extra-massoretic connec-tions, so that these specially selected MSS may serve as the basis for the apparatus of medieval MSS (⁴), and the attempt to select from all

(¹) Cf. above, n. 2, p. **274**. In the past years I have repeatedly come back to the investigation of the problem, hoping that more pos-itive results could be gained. The following paragraphs have been written after a fresh analysis of the material adduced in the various studies.

(²) The published studies known to me are (in chronological order: P. VOLZ, *Studien zum Text des Jeremia*, 1920, p. IX f.; J. HEMPEL, *ZAW* 48 (1930) 187 f.; S. H. BLANK, *HUCA* 8 (1932) 229 f.; J. HEMPEL, *ZAW* 52 (1934) 254 f., J. W. WEVERS, *ZAW* 61 (1948) 43 f.; H. GESE, *ZAW* 69 (1957) 55 f.; W. H. BROWNLEE, *The Text of Habakkuk in the Ancient Commentary from Qumran*, 1959, p. 124 f. Available to me are also the following unpublished Princeton dissertations: W. A. BELING, *The Hebrew Variants in the First Book of Samuel compared with the Old Greek Recensions*, 1947; J. F. ARMSTRONG, *A Study of the Alternative Readings in the Hebrew Text of the Book of Isaiah and their Relation to the Old Greek Recensions*, 1958.

(³) For this purpose it makes practically no difference whether we take as 'standard' the text of VAN DER HOOGHT used by KENNICOTT, the Venice *Biblia Rabbinica*, or the Aleppo Codex or use some statistical mean. Cf. n. 3, p. **278**.

(⁴) This, again, is a restatement of observations such as DOEDERLEIN, *Auserlesene... Bibliothek* II, 9, 1783, p. 641 f.: "Kennikot [!] hingegen sammlet, ohne den Versuch... seine gefundenen Lesarten zu vergleichen oder das Gewicht seiner Handschriften abzuwägen". Cf. below, n. **1**, p. **278**. The first to restate this clearly is HEMPEL (*ZAW* 48 [1930] 195): "es ist unzulässig, ohne Prüfung des Characters der betreffenden Hand-schrift eine innermasoretische Abweichung kritisch zu verwerten oder auch nur mitzuverwerten" Cf. below, n. **1**, p. **279**. This is echoed more weakly by VOLZ, *ZAW* 54 (1936) 100 f. Since "Die Jesaiah-Rolle und das

the medieval readings taken together those that formally agree with readings in pre-medieval sources so that genetic relations are allegedly proved ([1]).

24. The analysis of all the studies which pursue the first line of inquiry ([2]) has yielded an unequivocal result: among all the MSS and fragments known so far there is not even one the deviations of which can be significantly connected with any non-Massoretic tradition ([3]). We possess no medieval manuscript ([4]) which, on the strength of its readings, may be termed 'valuable' or be worthy of our attention more than any other. Having attempted to come to an 'evaluation' of MSS ([5]) in order to fulfil the demand that MSS should not be counted

---

Problem der hebräischen Bibelhandschriften" (1954) I have tried to argue that the problems of the textual character of the apparently deviating MSS as a whole and of the typology of changes must be investigated before any further step in this field can be made.

([1]) The second line of approach is basically the one usual in KEN-NICOTT's times, whereas the first one is methodologically novel — in spite of the fact that the most deviating MSS were, of course, noticed by KEN-NICOTT, BRUNS, etc. I need not add that I use the term 'structure' in this context as against 'atomistic' comparisons of readings; cf. *TL*, index. Since I am not well enough acquainted with the procedures in N.T. studies, I can only register that also in N.T. textual criticism the evaluation of readings as part of a textual structure is mentioned as a novel approach; cf. K. W. CLARK, *JBL* 85 (1966) 16.

([2]) This includes the published studies by HEMPEL, GESE and myself as well as the work carried out at the HUBP. VOLZ did not really pursue this line, and BLANK only touched upon the problem by the way. Nevertheless, his study serves to point out — much against his own intentions — that the MSS wrongly attributed by KAHLE to BEN-NAFTALI (cf. *RTBT*, Ch. VI) do not stand apart from the textual side. For the problem of publishing all the details on which this summary is based; cf. above, n. 1, p. 243.

([3]) My attempts to ' salvage' even one single MS onto which others could be pegged have proved abortive. Cf. *ISE*, § 77.

([4]) Caution bids us say that none has survived, but I doubt very much whether there was ever any such MS. A chapter explaining the rarity of medieval Hebrew codices has been included in many studies since the days of WALTON; cf., e.g., STRACK, *Prolegomena Critica*, 1873, § 6. See also DE ROSSI, *Scholia Critica*, 1798, § 15 ("unde antiquissimorum codicum hebr. summa raritas").

([5]) Our tabulations are based both on quantity and on typology.

but weighed (¹), we are finally driven to admit that the history of the transmission of Hebrew medieval MSS is such that this famous rule is inapplicable (²). There exists no MS which deserves special attention in the sense that it 'weighs' more; there are only MSS with smaller or larger numbers of readings (³). But as one starts to investigate them, they melt into nothing (⁴), and the huge mass of variations does not finally yield a single variant which is significantly, decisively and undoubtedly connected with a pre-medieval tradition.

(¹) The weakness of ' counting' readings was stressed two centuries ago, especially by those scholars who strongly opposed KENNICOTT's work; cf. O. G. TYCHSEN, *Tentamen*, 1772, p. 134 f. *Befreyetes Tentamen*, 1774, p. 150 f. See also H. L. STRACK, *Sem. Stud*... *Kohut*, p. 561 and above n. 4, p. 276.

(²) This is, in fact, also the result of H. GESE, *ZAW* 69, p. 66. Having written against the undiscriminating use of medieval MSS (cf. *TL*, p. xf.; *ISE*, § 18), I am forced to admit that I now doubt even more whether after the 'discrimination' there remains anything to use. This is, again, the outcome of the history of medieval MSS under the influence of Massoretic activity, and again these MSS defy the application of the text-critical rules of the game. Cf. above, § 17, and n. 5, p. 275.

(³) For the standard, cf. above, n. 3, p. 276. It is with grave misgivings that I approach the conclusion that statements made in KENNICOTT's times to the effect that we possess only MSS with more or less scribal mistakes and that finally the *textus receptus* is our only yardstick, are not really so far off the mark, although they seem to carry us back to 'Buxtorfian fundamentalism'. Cf. above nn. 3 f., p. 253. Now, that we can check the ninth and tenth century model codices, such a statement does not look as preposterous as it did when the attack on the *textus receptus* was in full swing. Again, I suspect that in the deprecation of the *textus receptus* there was also a good deal of carry over from N.T. studies. Cf. the somewhat similar remark in *RTBT*, § 44, and my cautionary note below, n. 3, p. 289. Were I not afraid of overstating my case, I would consider a very provocative formulation, i.e., that in our case the *textus receptus* functions practically like the 'archetype' and that we might disregard the MSS by way of *eliminatio codicum descriptorum*. This sounds, of course, like a *reductio ad absurdum* of the Lachmannian method Cf. below, n. 3, p. 283.

(⁴) Cf. now the result of GESE (above, n. 2) which should be seen in the light of HEMPEL, *ZAW* 1930, p. 193; 1934, p. 273, i.e., that those MSS which seem to stand out at first sight turn out to have the greatest number of obvious mistakes. HEMPEL's result with regard to K 69 in Deuteronomy, which only at first sight seems to have affinities with the Samaritan text, is borne out by our investigations of Genesis and Exodus.

25. In order to enable others to judge for themselves, a full new collation ([1]) of the MSS ([2]) which seemed most 'promising' is being published in the HUBP edition — considerably fuller than the collation published by Kennicott, not least because the vocalization and the differences of hands have been noted. From the thousands of readings checked from K 30 93 96 150 ([3]), it is difficult to 'salvage' a handful which might be possibly more than the result of harmonization etc. etc. — certainly a far cry from the claim of special value. Thus we get as the yield from Isaiah ([4]):

7,8	– MT	ובעוד ששים וחמש שנה
	K96	עשרים
11,6	– MT	וענל וכפיר ומריא
	K30 ([5])	+ ואריה
13,3	– MT	גם קראתי גבורי לאפי
	K96	ביכורי (?)

([1]) Cf. for this issue, H. S. NYBERG, *ZAW* 52 (1934) 244 and see above, n. 4, p. 276.

([2]) As against the more extreme suggestion *TL*, p. XI, four MSS were finally included. As long as we find it necessary to adopt this system, the details of the MSS to be chosen may vary from book to book. Cf. below, § 30 and n. 4, p. 283.

([3]) The general character of these MSS had been noticed by KEN-NICOTT, BRUNS, DOEDERLEIN, etc. It is interesting to remember that K93 was once said to be a MS written by a Gentile and that on the strength of the judgment of H. OPITZ, K150 was thought to represent the 'true' MT until KENNICOTT, *Diss. General.*, 1780, p. 83. After prolonged examinations of K96 and 150 I now doubt — against *TL*, p. XI — whether K150 is really the more noteworthy of the two. But the initial impression (*TL*, p. 56), that K96 150 should be studied in the first place, has been confirmed.

([4]) The present list includes those places where an explanation of the reading from context, parallel, etc. does not obviously suggest itself, without limiting the examples to cases where similar extra-Hebrew readings exist. It thus specifically excludes cases such as were mentioned as illustrative of the 'law of scribes' (cf. above, n. 1, p. 275), but may include what is actually a scribal mistake. On rechecking the collation of K–R others may, of course, find, an instance to add or to omit.

([5]) Details as to second hands, lack of vocalization, etc., are not taken into consideration on this occasion.

36,17 – MT	ארץ לחם וכרמים
K30	(¹) + ומים
44,14 – MT	לכרת לו ארזים
K96	(²) אלהים
51,6 – MT	וצדקתי לא תחת
K150	(³) תאחר

From the whole book of Isaiah one can quote only one variant which
makes one really prick up one's ears:

18,4 – MT	כחם צח עלי אור כעב טל בחם קציר
K30	ביום

This reading occurs in about a dozen other MSS as well as LXX,
Pesh, Vulg.; and while the graphic similarities are such that the variant
could have arisen again independantly in medieval MSS, the case
remains remarkable (⁴).

26. It may be of some interest to mention in this connection some
provisional results of our study of Geniza fragments (⁵). First and
foremost: leaving aside the mass of 'pseudo-readings' which are connected with different methods of vocalization (⁶), the overall picture
of the text in Geniza fragments is completely identical with that of
the codices collated for K–R etc. The Geniza has not turned out
to have been in any way a repository for aberrant texts which were,

(¹) This case should probably be omitted, both because of the idiomatic character and because of the letters of כרמים.

(²) LXX: ὃ ἔκοψε ξύλον ἐκ τοῦ δρυμοῦ, ὃ ἐφύτευσε κύριος... is no more
than an interesting parallel to the same train of thought.

(³) Cf. *ISE* app. ad. loc. This is the only case which may remain
from K150. But this one too should probably be weeded out; cf. Is 46,13.

(⁴) This is the only instance in the entire book which fulfils the conditions which would make it a candidate for the 'extramassoretic trickle'
(cf. below, § 29). The question of its 'value' *per se* is outside the scope of
this discussion.

(⁵) The hopes expressed in *TL*, p. XI had already been damped in
BMU, Ch. II.

(⁶) It is hoped that we shall be able, before long, to publish a study
exemplifying the various types of vocalized texts using Tiberian vowel
graphemes.

allegedly, condemned to oblivion. Since earlier studies of Geniza material were not concerned with the problem of variant readings and no systematic inquiry had been carried out, there was some hope that Geniza fragments might help in clarifying our ideas about the 'Massoretic recension'. This hope must be given up, although we may always run into a fragment which at first sight seems to contain a large number of readings ([1]). Though not all the Geniza fragments are known to us as yet ([2]), the following readings from Isaiah, culled from a few hundred fragments of this book checked so far, may illustrate our point. Leaving aside variants of Divine names and of the types ‏כְּ / ‏יך‎ , ‏אל‎ / ‏על‎ / ‏ממצרים‎ / ‏מן מצרים‎ ([3]) as well as omissions, homoioteleuta, etc., we are faced with variants which can arise again and again. Thus ([4]):

22,12 – MT		‏ולקרחה ולחגר שק‎
F ([5])		‏ולחגרת‎
37,26 – MT	‏הלא שמעת למרחוק אותה עשיתי מימי קדם‎	
F	‏למימי‎	
42,3 – MT		‏לאמת יוציא משפט‎
F		‏משפט יוציא‎
47,5 – MT		‏שבי דומם ובאי בחשך‎
F		*om.*
52,10 – MT		‏וחפץ ה׳ בידו יצלח‎
F		‏יצליח‎

([1]) The large number of Geniza fragments has helped to enlarge the sum total of MSS, partly or fully preserved, and has thus given us an even broader basis for statements on medieval MSS. Quite often a reading quoted as unique by K–R can now be adduced from a Geniza fragment too. The fragments from 'Listeners' Codices' (*BMU*, p. 39 f.) have not turned out to change the picture. Inversions of textual portions in a very few fragments need further investigation.

([2]) This summary is based, of course, on the study of fragments from the entire Bible. Altogether several thousand fragments have been studied.

([3]) Cf. above, n. 4, p. 252.

([4]) The following are examples of some of the types.

([5]) F = Fragments. A system has yet to be devised for quoting the fragments. In the present context the exact shelfmark is given only where the fragment as a whole is of interest.

These instances can be multiplied manifold; they are paralleled by
thousands of 'readings' in K–R and amount to nothing. The same is
true for variations in vocalization which indicate a different sense (¹).
Thus, e.g.

18,6 – MT		יֵעָזְבוּ יַחְדּו
F		יַעַזְבוּ
19,22 – MT		וְנָגֹף ... נָגֹף וְרָפוֹא
F		נָגֹף וְרַפָּא
52,6 – MT		לָכֵן יֵדַע עַמִּי
F		יָדַע

Only one fragment is interesting in this respect, i.e., T-S A 10,5, because
it has a considerable number of changes, among them in

52,12 – MT		וְלַפֹּשְׁעִים יַפְגִּיעַ
F	(²)	וְלִפְשָׁעִים

Among the simplifications an outstanding instance, hitherto unattested, is

19,4 – MT		וְסִכַּרְתִּי אֶת מִצְרַיִם
F	(³)	וּמָסַרְתִּי

We are thus left with the one and only instance of a remarkable variant in the Geniza fragments, and it need hardly be added that this
is again בְּיוֹם instead of בָּהֶם in 18,4.

27. For those books of the Bible which have already been checked (⁴) the results gained for Isaiah are paralleled, and there is no reason to assume that further investigations of MSS and fragments from

---

(¹) These cannot be paralleled, of course, from K and only rarely
from R. Cf. above, n. 2, p. 255.

(²) LXX: καὶ διὰ τὰς ἁμαρτίας αὐτῶν παρεδόθη In KENNICOTT's generation such a reading would have been hailed as being of significance.

(³) I cannot help remarking that this reading would have fitted
perfectly into 1QIsᵃ.

(⁴) At the time of writing, complete or exploratory studies have been
carried out on the Law and the Prophets. First results of an investigation
of books from the Hagiographa indicate that the picture may be different

other books are going to enable us to uphold the notion of a 'valuable' medieval MS (¹). Thus the provisional result for Jeremiah is
that only two variants from the above named MSS are possibly worthy
of note:

27,22 –	MT	בבלה יובאו
	K96	יובלו
48,2 –	MT	חשבו עליה רעה
	K150	מחלמה + (²)

There can be no doubt that our evidence fully upholds the 'one recension' (³) theory. But the existence of MSS like K 30, 93 96 150 (⁴)

---

to a very slight degree only. Today it seems that the expression 'weak
link' used *ISE*, § 18 is an exaggeration, born out of caution. What remains in medieval MSS to make us suspect a reading as genetically connected with pre-medieval sources is next to nil. I am afraid that with
the disappearance of the 'weak link' our view is fully validated and practical consequences will have to be drawn before long.

(¹) While studying the so-called 'Psalms Scroll' (11QPsª) it seemed
at first sight as if readings from medieval MSS are uniquely paralleled by
the scroll. What finally remained was

Ps 119,2 – MT	בכל לב ידרשוהו
11QPsª = K245	עת

For the problem of readings in that scroll cf. *PSCT*.

(²) Some other MSS read מלחמה instead of רעה. No reading in Jeremiah
approaches the 'quality' of ביום quoted above pp. 280, 282 from Isa 18,4.

(³) According to the criteria applied here, the study of the variants
— far from overthrowing the Lagardian thesis — comes almost near
upholding it. Cf. above, § 17; n. 3, p. 268; n. 3, p. 278. It is rather for
theoretical considerations that one is bound to limit LAGARDE's formulation to being only 'almost right'. I would go so far as to suggest that
those studies during the past thirty-five years which have attempted to
approach the problem by applying what amounts to structural criteria
lead *de facto* to this 'almost right' formulation — of course not in
the way LAGARDE had pictured the process nor on the strength of his
arguments. From a different point of view cf. the summary of HEMPEL
ZAW 1930, p. 95: "Mit ungeheurer Zähigkeit hat die Judenschaft der
Zeit nach den staatlichen Katastrophen *einen* Text durchgesetzt, so
dass nur geringe Spuren der einstigen Differenziertheit dem Schicksal
der Ausmerzung entgangen sind. Das ist das Richtige an der These
LAGARDE's".

(⁴) The numbers may change, of course, from book to book. Cf.
above, n. 2, p. 279 and below, n. 3, p. 287.

still remains a problem which forces us to tread cautiously. At least as long as we remain in the dark as to the state of MSS between the second and the ninth centuries, more than one explanation may be suggested ([1]). But no explanation which assumes the existence of what is in substance a greater diversity than can be encompassed within 'one recension' is acceptable.

28. The second line of inquiry ([2]) — the study and selection of readings as such, regardless of their source — could be hardly expected to yield results different from those suggested by Kennicott and his contemporaries. If every formal agreement between a reading in a Hebrew medieval MS and a pre-medieval source can be valued as indicative of a genetic connection ([3]), the result can be impressive, indeed. If that procedure is accepted, not only can the ' archetype'

([1]) The possible influence of the type of codex — vulgar, private official, etc. — on the text has been suggested repeatedly. Cf., e.g., TYCH-SEN, *Befreyetes Tentamen*, p. 159; STRACK, *Prolegomena*, 33; *BMU*, Ch. II. As regards the textual basis — as opposed to vocalization, etc. — no such differentiation emerges from the evidence at our disposal, although 'Listeners' Codices' were usually written with less care. It should be remembered that the four MSS quoted by us do not differ outwardly in any way from hundreds of other 'Massora'- or 'Study'-codices (according to the classification in *BMU, loc. cit.*). No evidence could be found for the existence of a vulgar sub-recension suggested by HEMPEL, *ZAW*, 1934, p. 254. In any case, during the last decade we have learned to be very hesitant in talking of 'vulgar' MSS. Cf. already *TL*, p. 67.

([2]) It may be more than coincidence that this line of approach was developed in dissertations written under the guidance of H. S. GEHMAN. From the written material it does not seem that the approach taught by GEHMAN is a conscious theoretical renunciation of method, influenced by attitudes like the 'Critique Rationelle' in N.T. research. The remarks of W. H. BROWNLEE (cf. above, n. 2, p. 276) can be hardly termed a contribution to our discussion.

([3]) WEVERS, *loc. cit.*, p. 75, maintains expressly "that the Hebrew variants have perpetuated pre-Massoretic traditions which were the basis for certain readings in G and the later Greek recensions". For BELING the comparison with the versions is sufficient proof "that these Hebrew variants from the Massoretic text in I Samuel are actually pre-Massoretic". NORTH (cf. above, n. 2, p. 253) goes so far as to accept any Hebrew variant for his exegetical needs, without any corroboration from the versions, provided it meets the following conditions: it is contextually not less difficult than the received text, it seems not to be attributable to scribal error and it is explicable.

theory be disproved ([1]), but even the 'one recension' theory can be made to look questionable. We have as yet only one objective way to declare out of court the evidence gained by such indiscriminate hunting for readings ([2]): Our newly gained insight into the typological limitation of readings in medieval MSS as opposed to pre-medieval witnesses ([3]). But even if we admit this yardstick and accept the conclusion that all medieval MSS must be dealt with as one family, representing one recension or even 'almost' one archetype, there remain those very few instances ([4]) which make one wonder whether the 'one-recension' central current did not allow the occasional drop to trickle in from the side. It must, however, be stressed that while this remains a possibility, we have not yet encountered even *one* instance where the assumption of a genetic relationship between a MS from the Massoretic period ([5]) and a pre-medieval source differing significantly from the received text is an absolute necessity ([6]).

29. This position may be formulated in a slightly different fashion in order to ensure fairness to possible opponents. Almost all our evidence from medieval MSS would be explicable as a secondary

---

([1]) WEVER's dissertation was the first attempt to use the apparent identity of readings in Hebrew MSS with the Greek for disproving the 'archetype' theory. ARMSTRONG in his dissertation sets out to investigate also the truth in the thesis of O. H. BOSTRÖM, *Alternative Readings in the Hebrew Book of Samuel*, 1918. The main point of BOSTRÖM's thesis had also been taken up by ZIMMERMANN (cf. above, n. **1**, p. **266**) and by WEVERS, *JBL* 65 (1946) 307 f. The whole issue has lately been studied extensively by S. TALMON.

([2]) For me, personally, the issue is settled. The problem remains how to prove the case ' objectively'.

([3]) Cf. above, § 22.

([4]) If we adopt the system of indiscriminate use of all MSS, the number of readings which are apparently connected in a significant way with pre-medieval witnesses is somewhat larger than in our example above, § 25, but incomparably smaller than suggested in the dissertation of WEVERS, etc. The material in *ISE*, Apparatus III may be used for illustrating the question.

([5]) For the definition, see *ISE*, § 74e.

([6]) It may be useful to remember that, of course, not all the apparently identical readings in a version, on the one hand, and Hebrew MSS from the first or second period, on the other hand, should be rated as genetically connected, the more so since the 'law of scribes' never ceased to be operative. Cf. above, § 22, and already *TL*, p. 67 f.

development from a common archetype (¹) and practically all of it as belonging to one 'recension'. Were it not for the disturbing 'almost', the whole chapter on medieval MSS could be regarded as closed and our apparatus be freed from them once and for all. But since scholars, especially during the first half of this century, were justly forced to the conclusion that our witnesses cannot be reduced to one archetype, we cannot be absolutely sure that a few extra-Massoretic variants did not trickle into the central current even after the recensional decisions or standardizations were carried out in the first and/or second centuries C.E. Once this possibility is not absolutely ruled out in theory — though of no consequence in practice — the door is thrown open for those who wish to maintain that we possess no sure yardstick to decide, whether in a given case we can unreservedly deny that formal identity between readings may be interpreted as genetic relationship. It lies in the nature of the subject that the case against genetic relationship is based on the analysis of the evidence as a whole and that those who wish to ignore the typological proof mentioned above may use that apparent excuse in order to go on declaring as 'valuable' any reading from Kennicott, etc. they fancy. I can do no more than hope that this attempt at pointing out that a tiny remnant of doubt cannot be overcome will not be misused, and that scholars will accept the position advocated here: that the possibility of infiltration of extra-Massoretical variants into the Massoretical 'central current' is so negligible that for all practical purposes it may be disregarded, and that medieval Hebrew MSS are therefore without practical value for any attempt to reach back into the early history of the Bible text (²).

30. Yet another point must be mentioned to which insufficient attention has been paid. Since no one in this century has independently worked through the evidence from medieval MSS for the whole

(¹) For the present argument 'archetype' may be understood in the sense of a master model codex, the tradition of which served as a basis for correcting other MSS.

(²) Anyone who wishes to base a reconstruction of the Bible text on Hebrew medieval variants must offer specific proof for his procedure. But since it is inevitable that a considerable time will elapse before the view outlined here is more widely accepted, fellow students would justifiably find fault with an edition that completely ignores the Hebrew evidence and thus does not serve scholars of different persuasions and demands. Cf. above, § 7 and below, n. 1, p. 290.

Bible, it is inevitable that scholars tend to take the results gained in
the analysis of one book as indicative of the state in the entire Bible (¹).
In other fields of inquiry into the Bible text it has become customary
in recent years to sound a note of caution and to stress the demand
that each book, or group of books, of the Bible ought to be investigated in its own right and that the results gained for one book are not
necessarily valid for all the books of the Bible as a whole (²).   In our
views of the growth of the Hebrew 'Massoretic Text', as gained from the
analysis of both medieval and pre-medieval MSS, there is nothing that
induces us to assume that the fate of all the books was absolutely
identical (³). On the other hand, we have as yet no reason to assume
slightly different histories for different books, apart from the obvious
slight differences of 'spread' of readings connected with the liturgic
position of the books (⁴).   However, the analysis of readings such as in
the Book of Kings may at least justify the mentioning of the possibility that different results may be obtained for different books (or
parts) (⁵) of the Bible and that, accordingly, we may have to reckon
with different 'breadths' of the 'central current' and different strengths
of the 'trickle' from the side.   But whatever the possible slight differences in detail — the main conclusion remains.

31. Our inquiry has thus brought us back to the point of departure
at the end of what we have termed the second period in the history
of Hebrew MSS, i.e., around 100 C.E. While future evidence may show

---

(¹) For the MS basis for our statements, cf. above n. 2, p. 281, and
n. 4, p. 282.

(²) Cf. *ISE*, § 10.

(³) For the difference of MSS as regards various books cf. above
n. 2, p. 279; n. 4, p. 283. Thus, e.g., for Kings K70 seems to stand out
and for 1 Sam also K 89 174 187 have to be considered. Among these
is K 89, the alleged age of which has given rise to discussions. But this
MS does not stand out at all in Isaiah.

(⁴) There exists as yet no comprehensive study of the relationship
between the 'spread' of variants and the liturgical use of the individual
book of the Bible. The relatively stronger standardization of the text
of the Peshitta in the Pentateuch is a case in point. Cf. also *TL*, p. 175.
In any case, the state in medieval Hebrew MSS is only one aspect of a
larger question. On the other hand, Samuel and Kings offer specific problems because of the parallel texts.

(⁵) WEVERS is cautions enough to add that his results may hold true
only as regards the Book of Kings.

that the 'recension' was rather broader than we tend to assume now, and that the end of the second period must be pushed beyond the second century C.E. ([1]), the analysis of Hebrew medieval MSS allows us at present to identify *grosso modo* the textual tradition of these MSS with that of the 'central current' tradition of *ca* 100 C.E. ([2]). However, as regards the choice of terms, the term 'recension' has acquired a sense slightly different from that understood in the generation of Rosenmüller. It is thus open to discussion because of the connotation of official interference ([3]). Since in the past whatever meagre evidence for 'official' approval and disapproval has been blown up into a picture of imposing the 'official' text of the Rabbis by force and consigning all rival texts to extermination ([4]), it may be more cautions to talk about the 'central current' tradition ([5]). On the other hand, the type of halachic discussion pursued by the Rabbis in the first century C.E. presupposes one more or less binding text. I prefer, therefore, the picture of a 'main current' tradition, constantly narrowing down ([6]) until its predominance ('central current') in the first century C.E. was a matter of course. The text used by the Tannaites for halachic discussions was, so to speak, the 'ideal' core of this tradition, with other texts, acceptable just as well to a broader public, differing from it only slightly. The 'official' text was thus part and parcel of a somewhat broader current of textual tradition and served at the same time as a

([1]) This possibility is mentioned here in order to stress that the view outlined here allows for marginal changes of facts which may be caused by future surprises. Cf. above, § 6.

([2]) No futher intermediary state is theoretically necessary (cf. above, § 6), but a certain breadth of the tradition with some further standardizing remains a possibility, though not on the exaggerated lines suggested by KAHLE.

([3]) Cf. *ISE*, Ch. I, nn. 12, 15. The idea of official pressure appears in various descriptions under various guises. Cf., on the one hand, the statements mentioned above, n. 1, p. 265 and, on the other hand, e.g. VOLZ, *Studien zum Text des Jeremia*, 1920, p. XIV, who talks about the 'amtliche Arbeitsplan der Synagogue'. See also *ZAW* 54 (1936) 104 f. My resistance to previous exaggerations should not be interpreted as denying any 'officiality' altogether. Cf. *RTBT*, § 26.

([4]) Cf. above, n. 1, p. 265, and *RTBT*, § 23 f.

([5]) I am ready to accept any better term, if it helps to express the issue more clearly.

([6]) Possibly with differences as regards different books; Cf. above, § 30.

centre for further standardization and unification. For binding
halachic or liturgic (^{1}) purposes there was thus, in fact, one model text;
that text became the 'ideal' centre of the tradition out of which it had
grown, together with which it continued to exist (^{2}), and which it
re-influenced to the point of creating the illusion of there having
been 'almost' an archetype (^{3}).

32. I trust that the preceding discussion has shown how the investigation of the problem connected with the arrangement of the apparatus of the HUBP edition has led us to suggest a theory which accounts for the facts known so far, and how the theory has become inter-

(^{1}) See above, n. 5 f., p. 246. For the view of R. GORDIS, which
takes into consideration the textual problem with regard to Rabbinic
discussion, cf. above, n. 4, p. 269. Cf. also the views of S. TALMON,
Textus 2 (1962) 14 f.; 4 (1964) 126 f. The Rabbinic discussion is such
as presupposes *one* text, and the textual questions mentioned in it concern mostly *plene* and defective spellings. On the other hand, the
analysis of readings in medieval MSS according to types shows quite clearly that the fluctuation was strongest in matters of copulative *waw*, prepositions, etc., as opposed to 'meaning-words', and with regard to the former
full unification within the recension was probably never achieved. Hence
the difficulty of dealing with these elements in the apparatus; cf. *TL*,
p. 59 (which today I would formulate somewhat differently).
  (^{2}) To put it differently. Precisely because the differences had already
become minimal, the texts could co-exist, until the few 'extra-central
current' variants were finally swallowed up in the MSS or practically
drowned in the mass of new secondary variants.
  (^{3}) Talking about LAGARDE and KAHLE above, n. 1, p. 257, and n. 1,
p. 272) I have remarked on the tendency of scholars to advance the same
type of explanation repeatedly for different sets of problems. KAHLE's
way of solving the problems in various fields of biblical textual studies by
a 'pluralistic' theory is an outstanding example; cf. *TL*, p. 66 f. The main
doubt in the correctness of my views remains that I, likewise, try to understand the development of the consonantal *textus receptus* on lines similar to those of my view on the development of a *textus receptus* of vocalization and accentuation, as outlined in *RTBT*. But if no mistakes as to
the facts can be pointed out against my theory, I am ready to take the
blame that I repeat myself in rejecting the imputation of highhanded
arbitrariness of which, in turn, both the Tannaites and the Massoretes
have been accused, unless specific and unequivocal proof is offered. If
we have to allow for LAGARDE's and KAHLE's personal equations to have
influenced their theories, I might as well let myself be influenced by my
own. Cf. *TPTC*, n. 18, For a kindred discussion in N.T. textual criticism
cf. now K. W. CLARK, *JBL* 85 (1966) 5.

connected with the practice of constructing the apparatus of medieval MSS. The time is not yet ripe and the last remaining queries not yet fully disposed of. Hence an edition of this type cannot altogether dispense with the quotation of readings from medieval MSS (¹). The practical solution — a separate apparatus exhibiting both full collations from MSS which appear to be of special interest and all the readings which may conceivably be judged by some scholars to be of value (²) — remains a compromise which, in practice, may not justify all the efforts bestowed on it. (³). I hope this discussion may turn out to be a modest contribution towards the clarification of our views on the history of the Bible text as a whole, and especially on Hebrew MSS — both on the level of suggesting a theory of textual development, and on the practical level of allotting a place to Hebrew MSS within the framework of the new edition of the Bible.

(¹) In writing a text-critical study or commentary, unconnected with the HUBP edition, I would not hesitate leaving out those witnesses altogether. Cf. above, n. 2, p. 286.

(²) The separation of the medieval evidence in an apparatus of its own is for me a matter of principle. As for the size, it may be noted that Apparatus III in *ISE* gives the fullest selection to be published since the selection of J. C. DOEDERLEIN and J. H. MEISNER, edited right after the publication of DE ROSSI's collations. Cf. *ISE*, §§ 16, 77.

(³) It has been our endeavour not to evade the problems posed on the theoretical level, even if the practical gain for the understanding of the Bible text is next to nil.

DIE VORLAGE DER ISAIAS-SEPTUAGINTA (LXX) UND DIE ERSTE ISAIAS-ROLLE VON QUMRAN (1QIsᵃ)

JOSEPH ZIEGLER

UNIVERSITÄT WÜRZBURG

I

FÜR DEN biblischen Textkritiker ist die vollständige Isaias-Rolle (1QIsᵃ; in diesem Beitrag einfach mit "Qu" bezeichnet) der wertvollste Fund von Qumran; denn sie enthält eine Textform, die von dem masoretischen Text ("M") in zahlreichen Varianten abweicht (im Gegensatz zur unvollständigen zweiten Isaias-Rolle, die M ganz nahe steht). In vielen Abhandlungen ist der Textcharakter von Qu untersucht worden; es seien hier die folgenden genannt (die Zahl in eckigen Klammern bezeichnet die Nummer, unter der die Aufsätze in der von Chr. Burchard zusammengestellten *Bibliographie zu den Handschriften vom Toten Meer*, Berlin 1957, stehen).

A. ALLGEIER, "Der Isaiastext der Funde am Toten Meer," *Jahresber. d. Görres-Gesellschaft* 1950 (Köln, 1951), 50–52 [1401].

D. BARTHÉLEMY, "Le grand rouleau d'Isaïe trouvé près de la Mer Morte," *RB*, LVII (1950), 530–49 [86].

W. BAUMGARTNER, "Der palästinische Handschriftenfund," *ThRsch*, 17 (1948/49), 338–343 [109].

M. BURROWS, "Variant Readings in the Isaiah Manuscript," *BASOR*, 111 (1948), 16–24; 113 (1949), 24–32 [234].
"Orthography, Morphology, and Syntax of the St. Mark's Isaiah Manuscript," *JBL* 68 (1949), 195–211 [235].

O. EISSFELDT, "Varianten der Jesaja-Rolle," *ThLZ*, 74 (1949), 221–226 [397].

M. D. GOLDMAN, "The Isaiah Mss.," *Austr. Bibl. Review*, 1 (1951), 1–22 [461].

M. H. GOTTSTEIN, "Die Jesaia-Rolle im Lichte von Peschitta und Targum," *Bibl.*, 35 (1954), 51–71 [477].
"Die Jesaiah-Rolle und das Problem der hebräischen Bibelhandschriften," *Bibl.*, 35 (1954), 429–442 [478].

J. Hempel, "Vorläufige Mitteilungen über die am Nordwestende des Toten Meeres gefundenen hebräischen Handschriften," *Nachr. d. Akad. d. Wiss. in Göttingen. I. Philolog.-hist. Kl.*, 1949, 411–438 [523].
"Chronik," *ZAW* 62 (1949/50), 253 f. [524].
"Beobachtungen an der 'syrischen' Jesajarolle vom Toten Meer," *ZDMG*, 101 (1951), 138–173 [525].

P. Kahle, "Die textkritische Bedeutung der Jesaja-Rolle," *ThLZ*, 74 (1949), 93 [577].

O. Löfgren, "Zur Charakteristik des 'vormasoretischen' Jesajatextes," in *Donum Natal. H. S. Nyberg oblatum*, Uppsala, 1954, 171–184 [675].

J. T. Milik, "Note sui manoscritti di 'Ain Fešḫa," *Bibl.*, 31 (1950), 73–94, 204–225 [733].

F. Nötscher, "Entbehrliche Hapaxlegomena in Jesaia," *VT*, 1 (1951), 299–302 [777].

H. M. Orlinsky, "Studies in the St. Mark's Isaiah Scroll," *JBL*, 69 (1950), 149–166 (S. 152–155 zu חושב 32 6); *JJSt*, 2 (1950/51), 151–154 (zu חמת 42 25); *JNESt* , 11 (1952), 153–156 [795].

I. L. Seeligmann, "The Epoch-making Discovery of Hebrew Scrolls in the Judean Desert," *BO*, 6 (1949), 1–8 [961].

A. Vaccari, Besprechung der Ausgabe von Burrows, *Bibl.*, 34 (1953), 396–403 [231].

P. Wernberg-Møller, "Studies in the Defective Spellings in the Isaiah-Scroll of St. Mark's Monastery," *JSST* 3 (1958), 244–264.

J. Ziegler, "Der Handschriftenfund in der Nähe des Toten Meeres," *MüThZ*, 1 (1950), 23–39 [1241].[1]

Gelegentlich sind meine Arbeiten zur Is.- und Ier.-LXX zitiert:

J. Ziegler, *Untersuchungen zur Septuaginta des Buches Isaias* (= Alttest. Abhandlungen, XII, 3), Münster, 1934.
Beiträge zur Ieremias-Septuaginta (= Mitteilungen des Sept.-Unternehmens, VI), Göttingen, 1958.

Bei diesen textkritischen Untersuchungen von Qu mussten die Forscher auf Varianten stossen, die sich mit LXX-Lesarten berührten, und sie beurteilen. Dies ist auch bisweilen geschehen, aber gewöhnlich nur in kurzen Hinweisen und einfacher Aufführung der in Frage kommenden Stellen. Gottstein hat in seinem Beitrag über die Beziehung von Qu zu Pesch. Targ. auch jedesmal die LXX genannt, wenn sie mit Qu Pesch. Targ. gegen M zusammenging (es sind aber verschiedene fehlerhafte Angaben über die LXX gemacht).

[1] Der Beitrag von S. Segert, "Septuaginta rukopisy z Ain Fašcha," *Listy filol.*, 77 (1954), 293 f., [976], war mir nicht zugänglich.

Am ausführlichsten hat sich Orlinsky mit unserer Frage befasst und an zwei Einzelbeispielen ausführlich nachzuweisen versucht, dass die LXX-Lesarten nicht dazu berechtigen, die in Qu vorliegende Lesart auch in der Vorlage der LXX anzunehmen (siehe unter VIII zu 32 6 und 42 25). Orlinsky ist bekanntlich ein fanatischer Liebhaber von M und ebenso ein entschiedener Gegner von Qu: "MT has been transmitted unusually carefully, SM (=Qu), on the other hand, is an extraordinarily carelessly written text" *JNESt*, 11 (1952), 155. Es ist Orlinsky zuzustimmen, wenn er davor warnt, bei Varianten, die in Qu und LXX übereinstimmen, auf die gleiche hebr. Vorlage zu schliessen, aber es ist doch etwas zu spitz formuliert, wenn er schreibt: "a more patient and sober study of DSI (=Qu) and G would have shown how reckless and baseless the idea of associating DSI with G's Hebrew *Vorlage* really was" *JJSt*, 2 (1950/51), 152. Im Verlauf dieser Untersuchungen wird gezeigt werden, dass LXX zwar in ihrer Vorlage oftmals wie M gelesen hat, dass sie aber auch die Lesart von Qu gekannt und benutzt hat.

Für die vorliegende Studie wurde die Textausgabe von Millar Burrows, *The Dead Sea Scrolls of St. Mark's Monastery*, vol. I (New Haven, 1950), zugrunde gelegt. Eine wertvolle Hilfe bieten die Variae Lectiones von O. Eissfeldt, die 1951 als Sonderheft der *Biblia Hebraica* (=BH) erschienen und auch in der Neuausgabe des Isaias in der BH aufgenommen sind, weil hier die Sonderlesarten von Qu gegenüber M verzeichnet sind. Leider ist ihr Dienst nicht immer bereit, weil etliche Lücken und Mängel vorliegen, siehe Hempel, *ZAW*, 64 (1952), 64 f. Deshalb sind die beiden Nachträge von M. H. Gottstein, "Bemerkungen zu Eissfeldt's Variae Lectiones der Jesaiah-Rolle," *Bibl.*, 34 (1953), 212–221, und S. Loewinger, "New Corrections to the Variae Lectiones of O. Eissfeldt," *VT*, 4 (1954), 80–87, sehr dienlich.[2]

---

[2] Ein Wort an die "Variantensammler," das zugleich eine "correctio fraterna" sein soll. Hempel, *ZAW*, 64 (1952), 64, hält es bei der Besprechung von E.'s Variae Lectiones für "selbstverständlich, dass ein subjektives Moment bei der Auswahl der Varianten gar nicht zu umgehen ist; es sind diejenigen ausgelassen, die E. für rein grafisch oder grammatikalisch hält." Gottstein, *Bibl.*, 34 (1953), 213, nimmt Hempel's Äusserungen beifällig auf, meint aber, dass E. doch "gar zu subjektiv zu Werk gegangen" sei. Man kann von einem "subjektiven Moment" in dem Sinn reden, dass es eine Rolle spielt, wenn man nur gewisse Arten von Varianten aufnimmt, andere aber (z. B. die orthographischen) ausscheidet, und besonders dann, wenn man von einer gewissen Art von Varianten (z. B. von den grammatikalischen) nur eine Auswahl trifft. Diese Auswahl ist aber sehr leicht zu subjektiv, weil andere Textkritiker gerade die fehlenden Varianten für ihr Thema wichtig halten, und deshalb in den meisten Fällen ohne grossen Wert. Jedoch darf das "subjektive Moment" keine Rolle spielen in der Weise, dass man völlig inkonsequent verfährt; dies tadelt Gottstein mit Recht, siehe *Bibl.*, 34 (1953), 215[2], [7], 216[6].

Nur e i n "subjektives Moment" kann man nicht umgehen, weil es in der "fallibilitas humana" seine Wurzel hat. Ein jeder, der Varianten notiert, weiss, wie gross hier das Versagen ist; so sagt Gottstein, *Bibl.*, 34 (1953), 212: "Man glaube aber nicht,

Eine besondere Schwierigkeit für unsere Studie liegt darin, dass (1) an manchen Stellen die LXX ganz anders liest als M (und Qu), so dass eine andere Vorlage angenommen werden muss, und dass (2) sehr oft frei wiedergegeben wird, so dass bei zwei verschiedenen Vokabeln in M und Qu nicht gesagt werden kann, welche LXX in ihrer Vorlage las. Einige Beispiele sollen genannt werden. Zu (1) sei 21 10a und 37 27c genannt. Infolge der völlig abweichenden Wiedergabe in LXX kann nicht gesagt werden, dass LXX die in Qu überlieferte Variante 21 10a גדרי oder 37 27c הנשדף לפני קדים gelesen hat. Es wird so sein, dass LXX weder Qu noch M vor sich hatte, sondern einen anderen Text. Zu (2) mögen folgende Stellen zitiert werden:

13 10   (τὸ φῶς οὐ) δώσουσι] יהלו M; יאירו Qu.
13 16   (καὶ τὰς γυναῖκας αὐτῶν) ἕξουσιν] תשגלנה M; תשכבנה Qere Qu.
26 12   (εἰρήνην) δὸς (ἡμῖν)] תשפת M; תשפוט Qu.
48 21   (ὕδωρ . . .) ἐξάξει] הזיל M; הזיב Qu.

An allen Stellen lässt die freie Wiedergabe der LXX keinen Schluss auf die Vorlage zu. LXX kann sowohl M als auch Qu gelesen haben.

Deshalb bietet auch 47 13 die LXX-Wiedergabe οἱ ἀστρολόγοι keine Handhabe, um das Hapaxlegomenon des M הברו als "entbehrlich" zu bezeichnen. Auch οἱ ἀστρολόγοι ist Hapaxlegomenon der LXX und

dass hiermit das Rohmaterial erschöpft sei, und es wird noch so mancher 'Zusätze' bedürfen, bis alle Varianten definitiv verzeichnet sind." Dies ist jedoch wieder zu pessimistisch. Wenn die Sammlung der Varianten richtig gehandhabt worden wäre, dann hätte dies auf den ersten Hieb hin "definitiv" geschehen können. Deshalb seien hier drei Regeln genannt: (1) Man darf sich nicht mit e i n e r Kollation begnügen, sondern muss eine zweite, ja sogar eine dritte machen, (2) man muss die Kollation immer zu zweien machen, weil man viel leichter die Varianten übersieht als überhört, (3) man muss die Kollationen langsam, ohne jede Hast, machen.

Die Sammlung der Varianten soll geordnet (konkordanzmässig) vorgelegt werden. Gewiss ist es notwendig, die Varianten nach Kapitel und Vers geordnet vorzulegen, wenn sie im Apparat der BH aufgenommen werden sollen. Wenn sie jedoch in einem Sonderheft erscheinen, dann ist eine geordnete Zusammenstellung (wie es bei den "Orthographika" der Göttinger Sept.-Ausgabe in der Einleitung geschieht) erforderlich. So bleibt es dem Benützer erspart, noch einmal die Arbeit zu leisten, die der Sammler bereits gemacht hat. Bei dieser Darbietung der Varianten werden auch Versehen leichter ausgeschaltet. Zwei Beispiele seien genannt: (1) רומליה Qu, so (mit ו, bedeutsam für die LXX, siehe unter VII), fehlt bei Eissfeldt, nachgetragen von Hempel, ZAW, 64 (1953), 64 und ZDMG, 101 (1951), 140, und Gottstein, Bibl., 34 (1953), 215: 7 1 (von Hempel übersehen); 7 5; 7 9, aber 7 4 fehlt das ו, und 8 6 ist eine Lücke im Ms. (2) רונה so mit ו, nicht mit י, wie fehlerhaft die Ausgabe von Burrows hat: 14 7 (von Gottstein übersehen) und sonst überall, ausser 43 14; vielleicht mag diese Lesart (=M) andeuten, dass an dieser schwierigen Stelle nicht das Wort "Jubel" vorliegt. Somit wäre zu notieren: (1) רומליה 7 1, 5, 9; רמליה 7 4; 8 6 lacuna. (2) רונה 14 7; 44 23; 48 20; 49 13; 54 1; 55 12; ברונה 35 10; 51 11; 43 14 רנתמה (cf. M).

im Anschluss an das folgende οἱ ὁρῶντες τοὺς ἀστέρας = M Qu gewählt.
Der Übersetzer hat höchst wahrscheinlich bereits die Lesart von M vor
sich gehabt, die nicht anzutasten ist; dagegen ist Qu sekundär (gegen
Nötscher, *VT*, 1 [1951], 299).

II

Das P l u s, das LXX Qu gegenüber M bezeugen, ist unbedeutend. Es
betrifft zunächst (1) die Einfügung von Partikeln, die verhältnismässig
häufig ist, und dann (2) die Einfügung einzelner Wörter und Wendungen,
die selten ist.[3]

(1) Sehr oft ist die Konjunktion von LXX (καί) und von Qu
(ו copulativum) bezeugt, die in M fehlt.

καί LXX = ו Qu] om. M.

1 3; 1 8; 2 4; 3 7; 3 9; 3 19; 3 20; 3 21; 3 22; 5 6; 7 4; 13 8; 16 10; 16 41;
17 8; 17 14; (ו auch "20 MSS"); 30 19; 30 23; 31 5; 32 13; 34 2; 34 10; 34 16
36 15; 38 5; 39 6; 40 17; 41 2; 41 3 (2mal); 42 7; 42 21; 43 17; 44 11; 44 16
(ו auch "42 MSS"); 44 19; 45 14; 45 16; 45 23; 46 3; 46 6; 47 11 (2mal);
48 13; 48 16; 48 18; 48 20; 49 9; 52 5; 52 9; 52 13; 52 15; 53 4; 53 5; 53 11;
55 13; 56 6; 57 4; 57 13; 58 8; 58 9; 60 7; 60 13; 60 18; 61 8; 62 4; 65 20; 66 8
(ו auch "Var Ka"): 68 Fälle.

οὐδέ LXX = ולא Qu] לא M.

5 27; 13 18; 26 14; 35 9; 38 13 (2°); 40 28; 57 11; 64 4 (3): 8 Fälle.

δέ LXX = ו Qu] om. M.

26 11; 55 13 (ו auch "mlt HSS Q"); 64 8 (7): 3 Fälle.

---

[3] Es werden die gleichen Sigel und Abkürzungen wie in der Göttinger LXX-Ausgabe
verwendet: S, A–Q, *O* (=B–V; hexaplarische Rezension), *L* (lukianische Rezension),
C (Catenen-Gruppe), o*I* o*II*, *lI lII*, *cI cII* (hexaplarische, lukianische, Catenen-Unter-
gruppen). Bei starker Verteilung sind nur die Hauptzeugen genannt; wenn wenige
Zeugen eine Lesart überliefern, dann sind alle Hss. aufgeführt.
    Es ist auffallend, dass manche Textkritiker immer noch zu den kleinen Handaus-
gaben (Swete, Rahlfs) greifen, wenn sie eine LXX-Lesart zitieren. Gewiss mögen in
manchen Fällen die Handausgaben genügen, aber für textkritische Untersuchungen sind
sie unzureichend, zumal auch die hexaplarischen Lesarten in ihnen nicht verzeichnet
sind. Wenn man die Göttinger LXX-Ausgabe ignoriert, kann es passieren, dass man
völlig ungenügende und nichtssagende Angaben macht, z. B. zu 51 9 "Catena in XVI
prophetas, apud BH³, πλάτος," so Burrows, *BASOR*, 113 (1949), 26, und direkt von
Burrows übernommen, bei Milik, *Bibl.*, 31 (1950), 82⁸, ferner zu 40 10 "Also here DSI
follows some Greek translations" bei Goldman, *Austr. Bibl. Review*, 1(1951), 15, und zu
49 24". . . is also found in two Greek translations," *ebd.*, S. 16, — sehr zum Schaden der
Untersuchungen.

γάρ LXX = ו Qu] om. M.

2 11; 9 21 init. (19 fin. M); 41 29: 3 Fälle.

ἀλλά LXX = ו Qu] om. M.

7 17: 1 Fall.

Im ganzen sind es also 83 Fälle, wo LXX Qu die Konjunktion *et* bezeugen, während sie in M fehlt. Damit ist aber nicht gesagt, dass die LXX-Vorlage an allen Stellen auch ו gehabt hat; manchmal mag der griech. Übersetzer sie aus eigenem beigegeben haben.

Hierher gehören auch 43 19 ἅ *νῦν*: cf. ועתה Qu] om. ἅ M und 46 2 οἵ οὐ (δυνήσονται): cf. ולוא Qu] om. οἵ Bo Cypr. = M.

An den genannten Stellen ist καί einhellig bezeugt. Es lassen sich auch Stellen anführen, wo die Bezeugung von καί geteilt ist, wo also nur einige Rezensionen, Textgruppen, Unzialen, Minuskeln und Väterzitate καί überliefern, das als ו auch in Qu steht.

1 16   καθαροὶ γένεσθε = M] pr. και 93 130 ClemRom. Or. lat = Qu.
9 12 (11)   ἐπὶ τούτοις] pr. και 538 Syp = Qu.
10 4   ἐπὶ τούτοις] pr. και C 403–613 Syp = Qu.
15 2   πάντες] pr. και lI 449–770 Cyr. = Qu.
40 26   οὐδέν] pr. και Syh = Qu.
41 2   ἐκάλεσεν αὐτήν] pr. και 309 = Qu.
41 25   κληθήσονται] pr. και L = Qu.
42 1   κρίσιν] pr. και Bo = Qu et Matth 12 18.
42 11   ἐπαύλεις] pr. και αι Iust. = Qu.
43 3   ἐποίησα] pr. και Syp = Qu; pr. ιδου 46 538 Sa.
45 21   οὐκ ἔστι 2°] pr. και 233 534 = Qu.
46 2   οὐκ] pr. και 88 L = Qu.
46 13   τῷ Ισραηλ] pr. και Eus. Hi. = Qu.
52 2   κάθισον] pr. και L c II = Qu.
57 2   ἔσται] pr. και 106 88 147–233 Cypr. = Qu.
59 13   ἐλαλήσαμεν] pr. και 88 = Qu.
60 11   οὐ] pr. και L = Qu.
61 6   λειτουργοί] pr. και A–86–106 449–770 538 Bo = Qu.
63 10   αὐτός] pr. και S* A C = Qu "50 MSS."

An keiner einzigen Stelle kann mit Sicherheit gesagt werden, dass die genannten Zeugen in der hebr. Vorlage ו gelesen haben, weil sie nicht nach ihr ausgerichtet sind, ausgenommen 42 11 (Iust.). Es könnte der Fall sein bei *L*; aber auch für Lukian ist der Stil, nicht der hebr. Text entscheidend. Nur an der zuletzt genannten Stelle (63 10) ist sehr wahrscheinlich καί ursprünglich.

In den beiden Zusätzen 34 10 und 43 23 ist καί nicht einheitlich bezeugt:

34 10 ※ κ α ι (hab. Sᶜ *o II L* = Qu; om. V = M) ουκ εστιν ...

43 23 ο υ δ ε (Sᶜ A *cI II* = Qu; ουκ V *oI II L C* = M) εδουλευ-
σας ...

Oft steht der A r t i k e l in LXX Qu, während er in M fehlt.

8 9; 23 8; 44 23; 52 10 τ ῆ s γῆs = Qu] om. τ ῆ s M.

8 22; 45 9 τ ὴ ν γῆν.

9 19 (18); 24 20 ἡ γῆ.

14 12; 63 15 ἐκ τ ο ῦ οὐρανοῦ.

14 16 ὁ παροξύνων.

19 6 ο ἱ ποταμοί.

23 7 ἡ ὕβρις.

32 11 τ ὰ s ὀσφύας.

34 3 τ ὰ ὄρη.

41 18 τ ὴ ν ἔρημον.

45 10 ὁ λέγων.

52 14 ἀπὸ τ ῶ ν ἀνθρώπων.

Während an den genannten Stellen der Artikel einhellig überliefert ist, findet er sich an den folgenden Stellen nur in einigen Zeugen.

1 2 γῆ = M] pr η 147–36 410 534 538 613 = Qu.

14 16 σείων = M] pr. ο 88 *L C* = Qu.

66 2 τρέμοντα] pr. τον *lI* 544 = Qu.

Noch unsicherer als bei der Konjunktion ١ lässt die Setzung des Artikels in der LXX einen Schluss zu, dass er bereits in der hebr. Vorlage gestanden habe und dass somit die LXX-Vorlage und Qu in der Setzung des Artikels übereingestimmt hätten. Man kann deutlich beobachten, dass oft der Artikel sekundär ohne Rücksicht auf die Vorlage aus stilistischen Gründen eingefügt worden ist.[4] Auch die Einfügung von ה in Qu ist sekundär; deutlich zeigt dies 33 9 ἡ γῆ = Quᶜ] om. ἡ M Qu*. Auch parallele oder benachbarte Stellen erweisen, dass die Setzung bzw. Unterlassung des Artikels in LXX keinen Schluss auf die Vorlage ziehen lässt:

23 8 ἄρχοντες τ ῆ s γῆs = Qu] om. τ ῆ s M; vgl. 23 9 πᾶν ἔνδοξον ἐπὶ τ ῆ s (> M Qu) γῆs.

63 15 ἐκ τ ο ῦ οὐρανοῦ = Qu] om. τοῦ M parallel ἐκ τ ο ῦ (> M Qu) οἴκου.

_____

[4] Siehe meine *Beiträge zur Ier.-Sept.*, S. 114–169. Vierter Beitrag: Der Artikel in der Ier.-LXX.

Dies gilt besonders für den Is.-Übersetzer, der bekanntlich seine Vorlage frei wiedergibt.

P r o n o m i n a sind selten von LXX Qu gegenüber M bezeugt.

Pronomen separatum.

65 3   α ὐ τ ο ί = Qu] > M.

36 11   καὶ εἶπε π ρ ὸ s α ὐ τ ό ν = Qu] om. πρὸς αὐτόν M.

48 17   ἐ ν ᾗ πορεύσῃ ἐ ν α ὐ τ ῇ = Qu] om. ἐ ν ᾗ et ἐ ν α ὐ τ ῇ M.

66 21   λήμψομαι ἐ μ ο ί S A (εμαυτω)-Q C = Qu] om. ἐ μ ο ί O L = M.

Suffixum nominale.

1 31   ἡ ἰσχὺς α ὐ τ ῶ ν et αἱ ἐργασίαι α ὐ τ ῶ ν = Qu] om. α ὐ τ ῶ ν (bis) M.

26 18   σωτηρίας σ ο υ = Qu] om. σ ο υ M (im Text habe ich οὐκ für σου geschrieben).

53 12   διὰ τὰς ἀμαρτίας α ὐ τ ῶ ν = Qu] om. α ὐ τ ῶ ν M.

40 26   ἰσχύος = M] + αὐτοῦ 87* Sa = Qu.

Suffixum verbale.

44 13   ἔστησεν αὐτό = Qu] om. αὐτό M.

49 7   ὁ ῥυσάμενός σε = Qu] om. σε M.

65 1   τοῖς ἐμὲ μὴ ζητοῦσιν = Qu] om. ἐμέ M.

Präpositionen.

כ   34 12   ε ἰ s ἀπώλειαν: cf. Qu באפס] om. ε ἰ s M.

55 9   ὠ s ἀπέχει = Qu] om. ὠ s M.

62 5   ὠ s συνοικῶν = Qu] om. ὠ s M.

64 10 (9) ὠ s ἔρημος = Qu] om. ὠ s M.

66 3   ὠ s ὁ ἀποκτέννων = Qu] om. ὠs M.

ב   9 14 (13) ἐ ν μιᾷ ἡμέρᾳ = Qu] om. ἐν M.

37 38   ἐ ν τῷ οἴκῳ = Qu] om. ἐν M.

43 23   ἐ ν ταῖς θυσίαις σου = Qu] om. ἐν M.

6 10   καὶ τῇ καρδίᾳ: cf. בלבבו Qu] ולבבו M.

57 15   ἐν ἁγίοις 2°: cf. ובקדוש Qu] קדוש M.

ל   31 1   ε ἰ s Αἴγυπτον = Qu] om. εἰs M.

45 18   ε ἰ s κενόν = Qu] om. εἰs M.

49 4   καὶ ε ἰ s οὐθέν = Qu] om. εἰs M.

מן 18 7 ἐκ λαοῦ = Qu (parallel ἀπὸ λαοῦ = Qu M)] om. ἐκ M, vgl.
Hempel, *ZDMG*, 101 (1951), 167: "das hochgewachsene
Volk wird nicht als Gabe dargebracht, sondern stiftet selbst
Gaben."

29 9 ἀπὸ οἴνου = Qu] om. ἀπό M; es geht voraus ἀπὸ (> Qu M)
σικερα.

Sonstige Partikeln.

כי 7 4 ὅταν γάρ = Qu] om. γάρ M.

48 8 ὅτι ἀθετῶν = Qu] om. ὅτι M.

לא 58 13 τοῦ μὴ ποιεῖν = Qu] om. μή M.

ולא 38 18 οὐδὲ οἱ ἀποθανόντες = Qu] om. οὐδέ M.

עוד 54 9 ἐπὶ σοὶ ἔτι = Qu] om. ἔτι M.

אם 62 9 ἀλλ᾽ ἤ Sᶜ A–Q C = כיא אם Qu] om. ἤ S* O L = M.

Die genannten Qu LXX gemeinsamen Varianten sind zahlreich, aber
ohne Gewicht. Ebenso kann nicht gesagt werden, dass die Vorlage der
LXX immer mit Qu übereingestimmt hat. Häufig sind die LXX-Lesarten
durch den Stil des Übersetzers bedingt, der bekanntlich frei seiner Vorlage
gegenüber stand. Namentlich geht die Hinzufügung und Auslassung des
kopulativen ו und καί oftmals auf den Schreiber zurück, vgl. dazu
Gottstein, *Bibl.*, 35 (1954), 437–439.

(2) Bedeutsam sind die folgenden Wörter und Wendungen, die in
LXX Qu stehen, dagegen in M fehlen.

37 9 καὶ ἀκούσας ἀπέστρεψε = Qu] om. ἀπέστρεψε
M; vgl. unter X "Dubletten."

39 6 εἰς Βαβυλῶνα ἥξει = Qu] om. ἥξει M.

49 9 καὶ ἐν πάσαις ταῖς ὁδοῖς = Qu] om. πάσαις M.

51 23 τῶν ἀδικησάντων σε καὶ τῶν ταπεινωσάντων
σε = Qu] om. καὶ τῶν ταπ. σε M.

53 11 δεῖξαι αὐτῷ φῶς = Qu] om. φῶς M.

56 7 ἔσονται δεκταί = Qu יעלו] om. ἔσονται M.

60 19 φωτιεῖ σοι τὴν νύκτα = Qu] om. τὴν νύκτα M.

64 2 (1) καὶ κατακαύσει πῦρ τοὺς ὑπεναντίους (+σου
L Qu) = Qu] om. τοὺς ὑπεναντίους (σου) = M.

36 11 τῶν ἀνθρώπων τῶν] +καθημενων A cI II = Qu; +εστη-
κοτων V–Qᵐᵍ–οI II L C.

36 14 ὁ βασιλεύς] +ασσυριων 26 407 538 Sa = Qu.

An den Stellen 49 9; 51 23; 53 11; 60 19 haben LXX Qu das Ursprüngliche erhalten; deshalb ist ihre Lesart als Text anzunehmen und zu
übersetzen, siehe meinen Isaias-Kommentar der "Echter-Bibel" III
(Würzburg, 1958) zu den einzelnen Stellen. Die übrigen Stellen sind in
exegetischer Hinsicht nicht so wichtig; hier scheinen sekundäre Erwei-
terungen vorzuliegen, die M nicht kennt. Zu 56 7 ist zu bemerken, dass
ἔσονται nicht "innergriechisch" (so Gottstein, *Bibl.*, 35 [1954], 63) ist,
sondern LXX in ihrer Vorlage עלי (wie Qu) gelesen hat (BH retrovertiert
יהיו, setzt aber mit Recht ein Fragezeichen hinzu); auch sonst hat εἶναι
andere hebr. Äquivalente.[5] An den beiden letzten Stellen, wo die Bezeugung der mit Qu übereinstimmenden griech. Lesart geteilt ist, braucht
nicht die hebr. Lesart in der LXX-Vorlage angenommen zu werden.

III

Die Stellen, an denen LXX Qu ein M i n u s gegenüber M haben, sind
nicht so zahlreich wie die, welche ein Plus bezeugen. Auch hier kann
man unterscheiden: Auslassung (1) von Partikeln und (2) von einzelnen
Wörtern.

(1) om. καί LXX Qu] hab. M. 1 24; 6 1; 8 11; 13 22; 14 13; 17 8 (2mal);
30 23; 33 9; 37 26; 44 7; 45 11; 46 4; 46 13; 48 5; 48 7; 50 2; 51 16; 51 22;
56 3; 58 2; 64 4 (3); 64 6 (5); 65 7.

Dies sind 24 Fälle (beim Plus 83). Dies zeigt, dass LXX Qu gegenüber M sekundär sind; denn die asyndetische Verbindung ist ursprünglich.

An einigen Stellen lassen nur einige Zeugen καί bzw. δέ aus:

43 8   καὶ ὀφθαλμοί = M] om. καί 22–93 = Qu.
43 10   καὶ ὁ παῖς = M] om. καί 393 = Qu.
61 2   καὶ ἡμέραν = M] om. καί V Spec. = Qu.

49 21   τούτους δέ = M ואלה] om. δέ 534 Tert. = Qu.
54 16   ἐγὼ δέ = M ואנכי] om. δέ 88–*oII lII* 49* Bo = Qu.

Das Fehlen von καί besagt nicht, dass die genannten Zeugen nach
einer hebr. Vorlage ausgerichtet worden wären, die wie Qu ו nicht hatte.

An nur 3 Stellen fehlt der A r t i k e l in LXX Qu, während er in
M steht: 11 5; 64 8 (7); 66 22.

---

[5] Siehe *Beiträge zur Ier.-Sept.*, S. 35. Vgl. auch 57 2 ἔ σ τ α ι ἐν εἰρήνῃ יבוא שלום.

Auch hier hat der Übersetzer nur frei wiedergegeben, wenn er den Artikel nicht setzt.

Pronomina (Suffixa) fehlen selten.

11 15   πνεύματι = Qu]+*eius* M.
13 9   καὶ τοὺς ἀμαρτωλούς = Qu]+*eius* M.
21 14   ἄρτοις = Qu]+*eius* M.
26 8   ἠλπίσαμεν = Qu]+*te* M.
42 3   οὐ σβέσει = Qu]+*eam* M.
45 11   ὁ ποιήσας = Qu]+*eum* M.
46 6   ἐποίησαν = Qu]+*eum* M.
48 15   ἐκάλεσα = Qu]+*eum*M.
63 11   ὁ ἀναβιβάσας = Qu "pc MSS"]+*eos* = M.
 5 27   κοπιάσουσιν = Qu]+*in eo* M.

Sonstige Partikeln

44 20   Ψεῦδος = Qu] pr. הלוא M (ὅτι 1° 2° von LXX eingefügt).
52 6   τὸ ὄνομά μου = Qu]+ ※ δια τουτο V C = M et οι γ'.
60 20   δύσεται = Qu]+ ※ ετι = M et οι λ'.

(2) Einzelne Wörter fehlen manchmal in LXX Qu, während sie in M stehen. Das "Füllwort" *esse* fehlt 2mal, *omnis* 4mal.

 3 24   κονιορτός = Qu]+*erit* M.
 7 23   ἐκείνῃ = Qu] + ※ εσται L C = M et π'

11 9   τὸ ὄρος = Qu] pr. *omne* M = σ' εν παντι τω ορει.
14 18   ἐκοιμήθησαν = Qu] pr. *omnes illi* M.
21 16   ἡ δόξα = Qu] pr. *omnis* M.

56 6   om. πάντας Sa = Qu] hab. πάντας rel. = M.

Die Zufügung in M ist wohl sekundär.

An folgenden Stellen fehlen die genannten (manchmal in *O L C* vorhandenen) Wörter in LXX Qu.

26 3   fin. = Qu]+ελπιδι *O L* = M.
26 5   καταβαλεῖς = Qu]+*humiliabit eam* M.
26 6   πατήσουσιν αὐτάς = Qu]+*pes* M.
36 11   Ιωαχ = Qu] + ※ προς τον ραψακην V L C = M.
62 10   πορεύεσθε = Qu] + ※ πορευεσθε Q^{mg}–oI 403 Eus. = M.

Überall wird M den Vorzug gegenüber LXX Qu haben.

An einigen Stellen fehlen die genannten Wörter nur in einigen Zeugen der LXX und in Qu.

48 19 καὶ τὰ ἔκγονα τῆς κοιλίας σου = M] om. τῆς κοιλίας L = Qu.
59 21 εἶπε γὰρ κύριος (2°) = M] om. οI = Qu.

Auch hier verdient M den Vorzug gegenüber LXX Qu.

Die Auslassungen, die Qu LXX gegenüber M haben, sind der Zahl und dem Umfang nach unbedeutend, besonders dann, wenn man sich vor Augen hält, wie oftmals LXX ein Minus gegenüber M Qu hat, das dann Origenes gewöhnlich sub asterisco aufgefüllt hat. Nur zwei Stellen können genannt werden, wo LXX Qu im Minus gegenüber M überein-stimmen, und von ihnen kommt eigentlich nur die erste in Frage, nämlich 40 7–8, die bereits Kahle, *ThLZ*, 74 (1949), 93, besprochen hat: "Wir sehen, dass der Text der Rolle genau der hebräischen Vorlage der LXX entspricht." An der zweiten Stelle 55 1 fehlen in Qu infolge Homoioteleuton die drei Verba ואכלו ולכו שברו, dagegen in LXX nur die beiden letzten, die von V L^P C ※ καὶ πορευεσθε και αγορασατε aus ϑ' ergänzt worden sind. Hier wird LXX den ursprünglichen Text bezeugen, vgl. BH.

IV

In der Wortfolge stimmen LXX Qu gegenüber M an nur wenigen Stellen überein.

23 9 πᾶσαν τὴν ὕβριν = Qu] tr. M; om. πᾶσαν A 198.
60 7 δεκτὰ ἐπί = Qu "4 MSS"] tr. M.
61 7 ἐκ δευτέρας κληρονομήσουσι τὴν γῆν: cf. Qu *duplicia in terra sua possidebunt*] *in terra sua duplicia possidebunt* M.
62 8 Εἰ ἔτι δώσω τὸν σῖτόν σου: cf. *si dedero ultra triticum tuum* Qu] *si dedero triticum tuum ultra* M.

37 1 τὸν βασιλέα / Εζεκίαν = M] tr. Qu, cf. εζεκιας ο βασιλευς l I-36*–456.

Somit ist die Wortfolge nur selten geändert. Dies ist umso auffal-lender, als LXX sehr oft gegen M umstellt und ebenso Qu (siehe die Stellen bei Eissfeldt "invers"). Wenn hier LXX mit Qu zusammengeht, so ist damit nicht gesagt, dass bereits in der Vorlage der LXX die Um-stellung vorhanden gewesen sein muss. Nur 60 7 haben LXX Qu die ursprüngliche Wortfolge bewahrt, siehe BH und die Kommentare.

V

Sehr zahlreich sind die g r a m m a t i k a l i s c h - s y n t a k t i -
s c h e n Varianten, die LXX Qu gegen M bezeugen.

(1) N u m e r u s.

1 18 ὡς φοινικοῦν = Qu "4 MSS"] plur. M (parallel ὡς κόκκινον =
Qu M).

14 11 τὸ κατακάλυμμά σου = Qu "66 MSS"] plur. M.

15 2 ἐπὶ πάσης κεφαλῆς = Qu] plur. M.

43 23 τῆς ὁλοκαρπώσεώς σου = Qu] plur. M.

59 9 ἐν ἀωρίᾳ = Qu] plur. M (parallel σκότος = Qu M).

63 15 ἡ ἰσχύς σου = Qu] plur. M.

6 7 τὰς ἁμαρτίας σου = Qu] sing. M (parallel τὰς ἀνομίας σου:
sing. Qu M).

26 6 πραέων = Qu] sing. M (neben ταπεινῶν = Qu M).

32 7 ταπεινῶν = Qu] sing. M (parallel ταπεινούς = Qu M).

53 9 τοὺς πλουσίους = Qu*] sing. Quᶜ M (parallel τοὺς πονηρούς
= Qu M).

53 12 ἁμαρτίας 1° = Qu] sing. M (parallel τὰς ἀνομίας bzw. ἁμαρτίας,
siehe unter VI).

20 2 τὰ σανδάλιά σου = Qu] sing. M, ebenso 28 25 ἐν τοῖς ὁρίοις
σου.

37 19 und 60 21 ἔργα (χειρῶν).

41 2 κατὰ πόδας αὐτοῦ.

47 7 τὰ ἔσχατα.

57 10 ταῖς πολυοδίαις σου.

58 3 τὰς ψυχὰς ἡμῶν.

59 5 ἀσπίδων.

64 6 (5) διὰ τὰς ἀνομίας ἡμῶν.

64 8 (7) τῶν χειρῶν σου.

43 6 ἀπ' ἄκρων: cf. Qu] απ ακρου S oI C Tyc. = M.

66 19 σημεῖα Sᶜ A–Qᵗˣᵗ = Qu] σημειον S* O–Qᵐᵍ L C = M.

37 17 ※ τους οφθαλμους σου (im hexaplar. Zusatz) = Qu] sing. M.

36 12 πρὸς ὑμᾶς = Qu] sing. M (ad te).

56 5 αὐτοῖς 2° = Qu et α'σ'ϑ'] sing. M (ei).

9 21 (20) φάγεται = Qu] plur. M; "le ms. fait commencer le verset
20 par ויאכל comme la Sept." Barthélemy, RB, 57 (1950),
541.

10 29 καὶ παρελεύσεται 2°: cf. Qu] plur. M (es geht voraus καὶ
    παρελεύσεται 1° = Qu M, und es folgt καὶ ἥξει: Qu M
    aliter).

12 4 καὶ ἐρεῖς = Qu (wie 12 1 καὶ ἐρεῖς = Qu M)] plur. M (et
    dicetis).

16 4 ἀπώλετο = Qu] plur. M (Subjekt ὁ ἄρχων ὁ καταπατῶν = Qu
    M; BH "רמסים l").

33 23 ἀρεῖ = Qu] plur. M.

35 10 ἀπέδρα = Qu] plur. M (parallel καταλήμψεται αὐτούς: Qu M
    aliter).

42 11 εὐφράνθητι = Qu] plur. Syh = M.

62 2 καὶ καλέσει σε = M] et vocabunt Tyc. = Qu.

1 23 ἀγαπῶντες ... διώκοντες = Qu] sing. M (Subjekt ist οἱ
    ἄρχοντες; LXX om. כל).

2 18 κατακρύψουσιν: cf. Qu] sing. M (LXX zieht v. 18 zu v. 19, wo
    der Plur. steht).

3 25 καὶ οἱ ἰσχύοντες ὑμῶν = Qu] sing. M (LXX übersetzt frei).

5 3 οἱ ἐνοικοῦντες = Qu] sing. M (LXX übersetzt das kollektive
    יושב mit dem Plural, wie auch sonst, vgl. nur 12 6a LXX
    plur. gegen Qu M sing.).

6 10 ἀκούσωσι = Qu] sing. M (alle Verba stehen in der LXX im
    Plur.; Subjekt ist λαός im kollektiven Sinn. Das ו der
    Pluralform ישמעו gehört vor בלבבו; somit liegt in Qu falsche
    Worttrennung vor).

7 1 ἠδυνήθησαν = Qu et M LXX IV Reg 16 5] sing. M (vielleicht
    ist der Plur. ursprünglich, vgl. BH).

13 14 καὶ ἔσονται = Qu] sing. M (LXX setzt gegen M als Subjekt
    οἱ καταλελειμμένοι ein).

14 32 ἀποκριθήσονται = Qu] sing. M (LXX hat als Subjekt βασι-
    λεῖς = Qu; M scheint verderbt zu sein, vgl. BH).

16 10 εὐφρανθήσονται = Qu] sing. M (neben πατήσουσιν gegen
    Qu M sing.; LXX übersetzt frei, da sie die Vorlage nicht
    versteht).

21 9 συνετρίβησαν = Qu] sing. M (LXX ändert die Satzkonstruk-
    tion und nimmt ἀγάλματα, χειροποίητα als Subjekt).

23 2 διαπερῶντες = Qu] sing. M (Subjekt οἱ ἐνοικοῦντες = Qu M,
    und μεταβόλοι ✕⁶ Qu M sing.).

30 20 ἐγγίσωσί σοι = Qu] sing. M (Subjekt οἱ πλανῶντές σε = Qu
    M).

32 5 εἴπωσι 1° = Qu] sing. M Niphal (parallel εἴπωσι 2°: gegen M
    Niphal und יאמר Qu).

---

⁶ Das Zeichen ✕ besagt, dass in den genannten Zeugen entgegengesetzte Lesarten
stehen, steht also dem Gleichheitszeichen = gegenüber.

36 7 λέγετε=Qu et M IV Reg 18 22] sing. M et LXX IV Reg (die
      Rede folgt im Plural: πεποίθαμεν=Qu M).
36 8 μείχθητε=Qu et LXX IV Reg 18 23] sing. M Is. et M IV
      Reg (siehe zu 36 7).
39 6 καὶ λήμψονται=Qu] sing. M Is. Niphal et M LXX (λημφθή-
      σεται) IV Reg 20 18 (aktive Form in der LXX und deshalb
      Plural).
41 25 ἐρχέσθωσαν=Qu] sing. M (Subjekt ἄρχοντες=Qu M).
42 20 ἠνοιγμένα=Qu] sing. M (in LXX überall Plural).
50 10b οἱ πορευόμενοι=Qu] sing. M (in LXX überall Plural: gegen
      Qu M sing.).
51 3 εὑρήσουσιν=Qu] sing. M Niphal (in LXX aktive Form).
56 6 τοὺς φυλασσομένους=Qu] sing. M (LXX hat überall Plural-
      formen in diesem Vers=Qu M).
57 20 κλυδωνισθήσονται=Qu (Subjekt οἱ δὲ ἄδικοι).
58 5 καλέσετε=Qu] *vocabis* Cypr. Spec.=M.

6 3   ἐκέκραγον S A–Q L C (87ᶜ)=Qu] εκεκραγεν B 87*=M.
45 24 ἥξουσι Sᶜ A–Q=Qu "21 MSS Seb"] ἥξει S* O L C=M.

(2) T e m p u s.

2 11 καὶ ταπεινωθήσεται=Qu] perf. M (parallel καὶ ὑψωθήσεται ×
      Qu M).
5 5   ἀφελῶ=Qu] infin. abs. M (parallel καθελῶ × Qu M).
5 12 ἐμβλέπουσι=Qu] fut. M (parallel κατανοοῦσι=Qu M).
8 2   μάρτυρας . . . ποίησον=Qu (vgl. die Imperative 8 1 Λάβε und
      γράψον=Qu M).
10 26 καὶ ἐπεγερεῖ=Qu] part. M (in der LXX überall v. 24–34
      Future=Qu M).
14 24 ἔσται=Qu] perf. M (parallel μενεῖ=Qu M).
17 13 καὶ ἀποσκορακιεῖ=Qu] perf. M (es folgt διώξεται × Qu M).
26 19 ἐγερθήσονται . . . καὶ εὐφρανθήσονται=Qu et οι λ'; α' ϑ']
      imperat. M (es geht voraus ἀναστήσονται=Qu M; nach
      BH sind die Futurformen zu lesen).
27 6 καὶ ἐξανθήσει=Qu] perf. M (neben βλαστήσει=Qu M)
28 16 ('Ιδοὺ ἐγὼ) ἐμβαλῶ (besser ἐμβάλλω)=מיסד Qu] perf. M
      (nach הנה steht gewöhnlich das Partizip; deshalb fordert BH
      יᵒסֵד).
29 11, 12 (2°) καὶ ἐρεῖ=Qu] perf. M (das Futur ist in LXX sti-
      listisch geiordert, vgl. καὶ ἐρεῖ 1° v. 12 × לֵאמֹר Qu M).
33 10 λέγει=Qu] יֹאמַר M (LXX λέγει im Anschluss an die häufige
      Formel λέγει κύριος).
41 7 ἐρεῖ=Qu] part. M (ἐρεῖ stilistisch notwendig, vgl. καὶ ἐρεῖ
      41 6 fin.).

43 28 καὶ ἔδωκα = Qu] imperf. M וָאֲחַלֵּל (es geht voraus καὶ ἐμίαναν; BH fordert mit Qu die Punktierung 'וָאֶ).

45 16 καὶ πορεύσονται = Qu] perf. M (parallel αἰσχυνθήσονται καὶ ἐντραπήσονται × Qu M).

48 14 καὶ (>Qu) συναχθήσονται . . . καὶ ἀκούσονται = Qu] imperat. M

48 14 ἀγαπῶν σε: cf. אֹהֲבִי Qu] perf. M.

52 5 καὶ ὀλολύζετε: cf. Qu] imperf. M (siehe unter VIII).

53 7 ἀνοίγει 2° = Qu] imperf. M (bei ἀνοίγει 1° auch Qu wie M imperf.).

54 2 πῆξον: cf. יטי Qu] imperf. plur. M יטו (πῆξον = הטי BH; in v. 2 nur Imperative).

56 4 καὶ ἐκλέξωνται = Qu] perf. M (parallel φυλάξωνται = Qu M).

57 17 καὶ ἀπέστρεψα = Qu] infin. abs. M (neben καὶ ἐπάταξα αὐτόν: cf. Qu M).

59 4 πεποίθασιν . . . τίκτουσιν = Qu] infin. abs. M (auch die beiden anderen absoluten Infinitive sind mit λαλοῦσι und κύουσι übersetzt).

62 9 καὶ αἰνέσουσι = Qu] perf. M (neben φάγονται und πίονται = Qu M).

63 16 οὐκ ἐπέγνω = Qu] imperf. M (parallel οὐκ ἔγνω = Qu M).

66 2 καὶ ἔστιν = Qu] imperf. M (vgl. BH).

(3) Wechsel der Person.

7 14 καλέσεις = M] –σει S 311–46 = Qu.

33 17 ὄψεσθε = Qu] videbunt (oculi tui) M.

48 8 ἤνοιξα] –ξας 564 239 410 534 Sa = Qu; apertum est M (siehe unter VIII).

53 8 τοῦ λαοῦ μου = M] του λαου αυτου Syp = Qu.

60 21 χειρῶν αὐτοῦ = Qu] χ. μου lI lII–233 Tht. = M.

49 5 ὁ πλάσας με = M] ο πλ. σε 534 Sa = Qu.

51 18 (ὁ παρακαλῶν) σε = Qu] לָהּ M.

58 14 ἀναβιβάσει σε . . . ψωμιεῖσε = Qu] et sustollam te . . . et cibabo te M.

Vgl. auch 46 13 ἤγγισα τὴν δικ. μου] ηγγισεν η δικαιοσυνη μου 538 Syl Tert. (plur.): cf. קרובה Qu. Auch Pesch. und Targ. haben "Gerechtigkeit" als Subjekt, vgl. Gottstein, Bibl., 35 (1954), 61.

(4) Genus.

14 32 καὶ δι' αὐτοῦ = Qu] וּבָהּ M.

15 3 ἐν ταῖς πλατείαις αὐτῆς = Qu] εν ταις πλ. αυτου M.

Zahlenmässig sind es somit viele Stellen, wo LXX und Qu gegen M übereinstimmen. Aber bei diesen grammatikalisch-syntaktischen Varianten muss man sehr vorsichtig sein, wenn man auch sagen will, dass LXX überall so wie Qu in ihrer Vorlage gelesen hat. An den meisten Stellen forderte der griechische Stil, nicht die hebräische Vorlage, die mit Q übereinstimmende Wiedergabe.

VI

In der Vokalisierung (Punktation) treffen LXX und Qu manchmal zusammen.

5 28   ὡς στερεὰ πέτρα = כצור Qu] כַּצַּר M.

14 32   βασιλεῖς = מלכי Qu] מַלְאֲכֵי M.

15 3   περιζώσασθε = חגורו Qu] חָגְרוּ M.

21 7   ἀναβάτην 1° 2° und 21 9 ἀναβάτης = רוכב Qu] רֶכֶב M.

27 1   φεύγοντα = בורח Qu] בָּרִיחַ M.

34 13   αὐλή = חצר Qu] חָצִיר M.

40 10   μετὰ ἰσχύος = בחוזק Qu, vgl. Hempel, ZAW, 61 (1945/48), 282] בְּחָזָק M.

40 26   καὶ ἐν κράτει (ähnlich σ' ϑ' και κρατους) = ואמץ Qu] וְאַמִּיץ M.

41 26   ἀληϑῆ = צדק Qu] צַדִּיק M.

49 17   οἰκοδομηϑήσῃ (ähnlich α'ϑ' οικοδομουντες σε) = בוניך   Qu] בָּנָיִךְ M = σ' οι υιοι σου.

53 3   καὶ εἰδώς = ויודע Qu] וִידוּעַ M.

53 12   καὶ διὰ τὰς ἁμαρτίας (besser ἀνομίας) αὐτῶν = ולפשעיהמה Qu] וְלַפֹּשְׁעִים M.

54 11   καὶ τὰ ϑεμέλιά σου = ויסודותיך Qu] וִיסַדְתִּיךְ M.

55 10   εἰς βρῶσιν = לאכול Qu] לָאֹכֵל M.

57 15   ἐν ἁγίοις 2° = ובקודש Qu] וְקָדוֹשׁ M.

66 2   καὶ (+τον ΙΙ 544 = Qu, siehe unter ΙΙ) τρέμοντα = והחורד Qu] וְחָרֵד M.

66 12   τὰ παιδία αὐτῶν = ותיהמה[ויונק] Qu] וִינַקְתֶּם M.

Bei den genannten Stellen hat der Übersetzer die Lesarten von Qu entweder bereits in seiner Vorlage gelesen oder als Randnoten bzw. Korrekturen irgendwie gekannt und sie als "matres versionis" benützt.

Von den Lesarten können als ursprünglich betrachtet werden: 49 17 (BH: "l"); 53 12 (ἀνομίας ist anstelle von ἁμαρτίας 2° in den Text aufzunehmen; es ist nicht anzunehmen, dass zweimal hintereinander פשעים ursprünglich ist); 54 11 (BH: "prps"; besser ist: "l"); 66 12 (vgl. BH).

Bei den übrigen Stellen kann man geteilter Meinung sein, ob die Punktation des M oder die Lesart der LXX Qu den Vorzug verdient.

VII

Auch die Transkription der Eigennamen verrät, dass LXX in verschiedenen Fällen Qu näher als M steht. Dies ist schon gelegentlich festgestellt worden, siehe Hempel, *ZDMG*, 101 (1951), 140, und Milik, *Bibl.*, 31 (1950), 217. Die in Frage kommenden Eigennamen seien hier zusammengestellt.

1 9   Σόδομα: cf. Qu סודם,] סְדֹם M, ebenso an allen Stellen.
1 9   Γόμορα: cf. Qu עומרה] עֲמֹרָה M, ebenso an allen Stellen.
7 1   (υἱὸς) Ρομελίου: cf. Qu רומליה] רְמַלְיָהוּ M, ebenso 7 5; 7 9; 8 6; aber 7 4 (LXX aliter) steht in Qu רמליה, also ohne ו, siehe Anm. 2.
15 5   Σηγωρ: cf. Qu צעור] צֹעַר M.
21 13 Δεδαν V 544 Bo Hi. (δαιδαν S A–Q O C): cf. M דְּדָנִים] α′ σ′ δωδανιμ = L Qu דודנים.
36 3   Σομνας: cf. Qu שובנא] שֶׁבְנָא M, ebenso 36 11, 22; 37 2.

Die Transkriptionen 1 9; 7 1; 15 5 sind allgemein in der übrigen LXX gebräuchlich. Wiederum kann nicht sicher gesagt werden, dass der Is.-Übersetzer den o-Laut, der in Qu besonders gern eingefügt wird (man kann bei Qu direkt von einer kennzeichnenden o-Vokalisierung im Gegensatz zur a-Vokalisierung bei M sprechen), in seiner hebr. Vorlage gelesen hat. Jedoch hat er sicher die Lesarten mit dem Vokal o gekannt und sie als "matres transcriptionis" benützt. Wenn 21 13 Aquila und Symmachus (und von ihnen abhängig Lukian) mit ω transkribieren, so ist dies ein Beleg, dass sie eine alte Tradition wieder aufgreifen.

In M haben viele Eigennamen die langen altertümlichen Endungen יהו–, während in Qu die kurzen Endungen יה– stehen. Auch in der LXX sind durchweg die Eigennamen in der Art von Qu geschrieben, vgl. Ησαιας, Εζεκιας, Οζιας usw. Auch hier kann LXX wie M in ihrer Vorlage gelesen haben; aber ebenso war ihr die Form in Qu bekannt.

Auf die Endung von "Jerusalem" לם–, לַיִם– hat bereits Hempel, *ZDMG*, 101 (1951), 142, hingewiesen. Wenn LXX durchgehend Ιερουσαλημ wiedergibt, so mag dies ein Hinweis darauf sein, dass sie die Endung לם– als "mater transcriptionis" gekannt hat.

Doppeltes י liest Qu 23 1 כתיים, das auch LXX voraussetzt Κιτιέων (κιτιαιων S A B C; χετιειμ 239–306mg), und 23 12 Κιτιεῖς, wo auch M Ketib כתיים hat (M Qere aber כתים). Auch 23 1 ist nach LXX Qu כתיים zu lesen.

Die zuletzt genannten Stellen zeigen, dass keine Konsequenz vorhanden ist. Dies ist auch allgemein in Bezug auf die Transkription der Eigennamen zu beobachten. In Qu stehen noch viele andere Eigennamen mit dem o-Laut, der aber in LXX keine Aufnahme gefunden hat, z. B. 20 1 Ταναθαν (θαρθαν Qmg-οΙ = M)] תורתן Qu.

VIII

Buchstaben-Vertauschung

ו | י   18 6   καὶ καταλείψει: cf. ועזבו Qu] יֽעֲזְבוּ M; vgl. Loewinger, VT, 4 (1954), 81.

י | ו   21 2   οἱ πρέσβεις = צירי Qu] צוּרִי M.

         22 24   ἔνδοξος = כביד Qu (vid.)] כבוד M.

         33 13   γνώσονται = ידעו Qu] וּדְעוּ M.

         37 13   Σεπφαρ(ε)ιμ A L cI = ספריים Qu] σεπφαρουαιμ O–Qmg: cf. ספרוים M.

         52 5   καὶ ὀλολύζετε: cf. והללו Qu] יהילִלוּ M.

ז | ו   16 9   τὰ δένδρα σου: cf. ? ארזיך Qu] אֲרֻזֶּיך M; BH: "1 אַרְזֶּיך"

ב | מ   9 19 (18)   διὰ θυμόν = מעברת Qu] בְּעֶ M.

         46 6   ἐκ μαρσιππίου = מכיס M] ἐν μαρσιππω 534 Bo = בכֹ' Qu.

מ | ב   15 9   Ρεμμων] δηβων V Eus.; διβων 87–91; δεεβων 309–490 = דיבון Qu; δειμων B et οἱ γ' διμων = דימון M.

         65 14   ἐν εὐφροσύνῃ = בטוב Qu] מֽט' M.

מ | כ   40 17   εἰς (ως 88 93 87* 566 Cyr.lem) οὐθέν: cf. כאפס Qu] מֽא' M.

כ | ב   44 4   ὡς (ωσει) ἀνὰ μέσον = כבין Qu "10 MSS"] בבין M.

ב | כ   28 21   ἐν τῇ φάραγγι = בעמק Qu] כֽע' M.

ד | ר   23 10   ἐργάζου = עבדי Qu] עברי M.

         29 3   ὡς Δαυιδ = כדוד Qu] כַּדּוּר M, vgl. Loewinger, VT, 4 (1954), 82.

ר | ד   14 4   ὁ ἐπισπουδαστής: cf. מרהבה Qu] מֽד' M.

ה | ח   51 9   πλατος (im hexaplar. Zusatz) = רחוב Qu] רהב M.

         56 10   ἐνυπνιαζόμενοι = חוזים Qu; "pl MSS"] הֹזים M.

ה | ת   42 25   ὀργὴν (θυμοῦ αὐτοῦ) = חמת Qu] חֵמָה M.

         48 8   ἤνοιξας 564 239 410 534 Sa = פתחת Qu] ηνοιξα rel.; פִּתֵּחָה M; siehe oben unter V (3).

מ | ה   63 11   ὁ ἀναβιβάσας = המעלה Qu "pc MSS"] לֽם- M.

ן | מ   9 4 (3); 60 6 Μαδιαμ = מדים Qu] מדין M.

ת | י   35 9   εὑρεθῇ = ימצא Qu] תמצא M.

ד | ת   64 9 (8)   ἐν καιρῷ = לעת Qu] לעד M.

ע | א   28 22   καὶ ὑμεῖς = ואתם, vgl. Loewinger, VT, 4 (1954), 82¹: cf. ועתה Qu] ואתה M.

לא | לו   31 8   οὐκ = לוא Qu, לא "KOr"] לו M "Occ QOr."

לא | לו   49 5   πρὸς αὐτόν = לו Qu "9 MSS Q"] לא M.

על | אל   2 2   (καὶ ἥξουσιν) ἐπ' [αὐτό עלוהי Qu et עליו Mich 4 1] אליו M et LXX Mich 4 2 (πρὸς αὐτό).

         17 8   (πεποιθότες ὦσιν) ἐπί = על Qu] אל M.

         22 5   (πλανῶνται) ἐπὶ (τὰ ὄρη) = על Qu] אל M.

         36 7   Ἐπὶ (κύριον ... πεποίθαμεν) = על Qu] אל M.

אל | על   22 15   (Πορεύου ...) πρὸς (Σομναν) אל Qu] על M.

         29 12   (καὶ δοθήσεται ...) εἰς χεῖρας (ἀνθρώπου) אל Qu] על M.

65 6, 7 (v. 6 ἕως ἂν ἀποδῶ, v. 7 ἀποδώσω . . .) εἰς (τὸν κόλπον αὐτῶν) אל Qu] על M.

66 20 (ἄξουσι . . .) εἰς (τὴν ἁγίαν πόλιν) אל Qu] על M.

BH empfiehlt die Lesart von Qu LXX an folgenden Stellen: 40 17; 44 4; 23 10; 14 4; 42 25; 63 11; 49 5; von den genannten Stellen schwächt sie ihre Empfehlung durch "frt" oder "prb" ab: 23 10; 42 25; 63 11. Wenn hier LXX Qu zusammengehen, so ist nicht immer damit erwiesen, dass der Übersetzer auch so in seiner Vorlage gelesen hat. Dies gilt besonders für die Präpositionen על und אל; sie sind teilweise durch das Verbum bedingt, so ἐπί 17 8 36 7 durch πεποιθέναι, ebenso εἰς 29 12 durch διδόναι (im vorausgehenden Vers 11 ist die gleiche Wendung frei mit dem Dativ δῶσιν αὐτὸ ἀνθρώπῳ wiedergegeben; deshalb ist die Notiz in BH "1 c G אל" hinfällig) und vor allem 65 6, 7 durch die Wendung ἀποδιδόναι εἰς τὸν κόλπον, die auch Ps 78 (79) 12 und Ier 39 (32) 18 vorkommt.

48 8 ist vielleicht ἤνοιξας ursprünglich: ς ist infolge Dittographie ausgefallen, es folgt σου.

Lehrreich ist beim Eigennamen Madian 9 4 (3) und 60 6 der Wechsel מ | נ, der somit bereits auf hebr. Ebene erfolgt ist, siehe meine *Beiträge zur Ier.-LXX*, S. 66 f. Orlinsky, *JJSt*, 2 (1950/51), 151–154, tritt energisch dafür ein, dass 42 25 חמה des M ursprünglich sei und die Wiedergabe in LXX (ebenso in Targ. Pesch. Vulg. siehe BH) keinesfalls חמת voraussetze; aber LXX hat vielleicht חמת als "mater versionis" gekannt.

IX

Am bedeutsamsten sind solche l e x i k a l i s c h e Varianten, die ein anderes Wort bezeugen, weil sie für die Exegese entscheidend sind.

10 32 τὴν θυγατέρα = Qu Qere בת] בית M.

16 9 τὰ δένδρα σου, siehe bereits unter VIII.

23 10 ἐργάζου, siehe bereits unter VIII.

32 6 νοήσει: cf. Qu חושב] עשה M = *faciet* Vulg.

36 11 τῶν ἀνθρώπων = Qu האנשים] העם M = *populi* Vulg.

37 26 ἐν ὀχυροῖς: cf. Qu נצורים] נצים M: cf. *compugnantium* Vulg.

39 1 καὶ ἀνέστη = Qu ויהיה] ויחזק M = *et convaluisset* Vulg.

41 5 ἅμα = Qu יחדו] יחרדו M = *obstupuerunt* Vulg.

41 20 καὶ ἐννοηθῶσι = Quᶜ ויבינו: cf. *et recogitent* Vulg.] וישימו Qu* M.

44 20 δύναται ἐξελέσθαι: cf. Qu יוכיל] יציל M.

45 2 καὶ ὄρη = Qu והרדים] והדורים M: cf. *gloriosos terrae* Vulg.

45 8 εὐφρανθήτω: cf. Qu הריעו] הרעיפו M = *rorate* Vulg.

49 24 ἀδίκως: cf. Qu עריץ: cf. *a robusto* Vulg.] צדיק M.

50 2 ξηρανθήσονται = Qu תיבש] תבאש M = *computrescent* Vulg.

50 6 ἀπέστρεψα = Qu הסירותי = *averti* Vulg.] הסתרתי M.

44 16 (vorhexaplar. Zusatz) ἐν τοῖς ἄνθραξιν B; ἐπὶ τῶν ἀνθράκων
αυτου 449-770; ἐπὶ τοῖς ἄνθραξιν αυτου Q^mg (om. αυτου)
239-306 Syh^mg = Qu וֹעל גחליו] om. hic M, sed hab. v. 19.

51 9 (hexaplar. Zusatz) ἡ κατακόψασα L = Qu המחצת = percussisti
Vulg.] ἡ λατομήσασα V–oII C (ex α' σ' ϑ') = המחצבת M.

Ursprünglich sind LXX Qu 10 32 (BH: "l"); 23 10 (BH: "l frt";
streiche "frt"); 32 6; 45 2 (BH: "l?"; streiche das Fragezeichen); 49 24
(BH: "l"); 44 16 (BH: "l"); 51 9 (BH: "l").

Sedundär sind LXX Qu 16 9; 36 11 (stammt aus v. 12); 37 26 (erleichternde Lesart); 41 5; 45 8 (Qu bestätigt meine Vermutung, dass LXX
bereits הריעו vor sich gehabt hat, siehe *Untersuchungen zur Is.-Sept.*,
S. 157); 50 2 (erleichternde Lesart).

Verschiedene Stellen sind eigens zu besprechen. An den beiden
Stellen 41 20 und 50 6 hat LXX wohl die Lesart des M vor sich gehabt
und frei übersetzt; es ist aber möglich, dass die Lesart von Qu in der
Vorlage stand entweder als Textlesart oder als Randnote. 41 20 ist zum
Verbum שׂים das Nomen לב zu ergänzen, vgl.

41 22 ἐπιστήσομεν τὸν νοῦν.
47 7 ἐνόησας ... ἐν τῇ καρδίᾳ σου.
57 1 ἐκδέχεται τῇ καρδίᾳ.
57 11 οὐδὲ ἔλαβές με εἰς τὴν διάνοιαν αὐδὲ εἰς τὴν καρδίαν σου
(οὐδὲ εἰς τὴν καρδίαν σου ist Dublette, siehe *Untersuchungen zur Is.-Sept.*,
S. 77). Es ist deshalb mit ἐννοηθῶσι richtig wiedergegeben, wie die
benachbarten Wörter verlangen. Es ist sehr wahrscheinlich, dass die
Lesart von Qu als "mater versionis" bereits der LXX vorlag.

50 6 liegt in M die häufige Wendung vor "das Angesicht verbergen,"
von den Menschen als Subjekt nur 4mal (Exod 3 6; Isa 50 6; 53 3; 59 2),
von Gott jedoch 27mal (namentlich in den Psalmen) ausgesagt. Überall
übersetzt die LXX mit ἀ π ο σ τ ρ έ φ ε ι ν τὸ πρόσωπον Exod 3 6;
Deut (3mal); Pss (14mal); Ier 40 (33) 5; Ezek (3mal); auch Isa 8 17; 53 3;
54 8; 57 17; 59 2; 64 7 (6), also 6mal. Nur Iob 13 24 ist "warum verbirgst
Du Dein Angesicht" frei mit διὰ τί ἀπ' ἐμοῦ κρύπτῃ wiedergegeben.
Auch die Peschitta übersetzt diese Wendung wie die LXX, siehe Gottstein, *Bibl.*, 35 (1954), 62. Die jüngeren Übersetzer haben wörtlich
übersetzt: ἀ π ο κ ρ ύ π τ ε ι ν (α' Exod 3 6; Deut 31 18; Isa 8 17 u. ö.;
ϑ' Isa 59 2), κ ρ ύ π τ ε ι ν (σ' Isa 8 17; 54 8 u. ö.) τὸ πρόσωπον.

Es ist auffallend, dass nur 50 6 in Qu הסירותי steht, das wie eine
Retroversion des griech. ἀπέστρεψα aussieht, aber sicher keine ist. Es
ist auch nicht anzunehmen, dass in der Vorlage der LXX die Lesart von
Qu gestanden habe. Aber es ist deutlich zu sehen, dass die LXX-

Übersetzer eine gemeinsame Tradition kennen, die ihre Heimat nicht in Alexandrien, sondern in Palästina hat. Es mag so gewesen sein, dass für die Übersetzer gewisse "Richtlinien" ausgearbeitet worden sind, die Angaben über die Bedeutung und Wiedergabe verschiedener Wörter und Wendungen enthielten. Sie mögen zunächst an den Rand der Handschriften geschrieben sein (unsere Handschrift von Qumran enthält keine Randnoten, wohl aber die hebr. Sirach-Handschriften); vielleicht waren sie auch in getrennten "Wörterverzeichnissen" vorhanden. Man kann diese Lesarten als "lectiones auxiliares" oder besser (im Anschluss an die "matres lectionis") als "matres versionis" bezeichnen (siehe oben die "matres transcriptionis"). Sie sind dann gelegentlich vom Rand oder von der separaten Liste in den Text geraten (wie an unserer Stelle).

Ein weiterer Beleg für diese Annahmen ist die Stelle 32 6, die Orlinsky ausführlich besprochen hat, siehe *JBL*, 69 (1950), 152–155, und wiederholt *JJSt*, 2 (1950/51), 152; *JNEST*, 11 (1952/53), 153. Man kann wohl Orlinsky zustimmen, wenn er sagt, dass das Zusammengehen von LXX (und Targ.) mit Qu nicht beweist, dass beide Zeugen die Lesart von Qu auch in ihrer Vorlage gehabt haben. Aber es besteht doch die Möglichkeit (und dies soll hier gleich betont werden), dass die Lesart von Qu bereits dort stand. Bei Orlinsky steht Qu nicht hoch im Kurs; die von M abweichenden Varianten verdanken ihren Ursprung dem fehlerhaften mündlich tradierten Text: "The St. Mark's Isaiah Scroll derives from a text which was written (probably from dictation) from memory," *JBL*, 69 (1950), 165. Man darf jedoch nicht zu sehr den Ton auf die "mündliche" oder "gedächtnismässige" Tradition legen. Es ist auch nicht anzunehmen, dass so umfangreiche Texte "from memory" oder "from dictation" geschrieben worden seien, zumal auch, so viel ich sehe, Hörfehler nicht festgestellt worden sind. Deshalb ist es nicht richtig, in חושב "an unreliable oral variation" (*ebd.*, S. 165), zu sehen. Vielmehr ist die Lesart von Qu eine "mater versionis," die bereits in der Vorlage der LXX gestanden haben kann.

39 1 ist ebenfalls nicht sicher zu sagen, dass LXX wie Qu in der Vorlage gelesen hat. Aber wiederum ist dem Is.-Übersetzer die Qu-Lesart bekannt gewesen; dies zeigt die Parallelstelle 38 9 καὶ ἀνέστη = ויחי M Qu (von hier kam ויחי nach 39 1), ferner 26 19, wo ebenfalls חיה mit ἀνίστασθαι wiedergegeben ist: ἀ ν α σ τ ή σ ο ν τ α ι οἱ νεκροί.

Auch bei 44 20 kann nicht entschieden werden, ob LXX wie Qu in der Vorlage gehabt hat. Es ist eher wahrscheinlich, dass sie wie M gelesen hat und dass ihr die Lesart יוכל als "mater versionis" (aus 16 12, siehe unten) ebenfalls zur Verfügung stand. Bei der Verwendung des Verbums δύνασθαι bestehen d r e i Möglichkeiten:

1. Die Vorlage hat zwei Verba (dies ist der gewöhnliche Fall), z. B.

7 1 καὶ οὐκ ἠδυνήθησαν πολιορκῆσαι αὐτήν = M Qu.

36 14 οἳ οὐ δυνήσονται ῥύσασθαι ὑμᾶς = M Qu.

2. Die Vorlage hat nur das Hauptverbum; der Übersetzer übernimmt als Hilfsverbum δύνασθαι, z. B.

11 9 οὐδὲ μὴ δ ύ ν ω ν τ α ι (>M Qu) ἀπολέσαι.

20 6 οἳ οὐκ ἠ δ ύ ν α ν τ ο (>M Qu) σωθῆναι.

36 9 καὶ πῶς δ ύ ν α σ ϑ ε (>M Qu) ἀποστρέψαι.

36 19 μὴ ἐ δ ύ ν α ν τ ο (>M Qu) ῥύσασθαι.

3. Die Vorlage hat nur יכל im absoluten Sinn "vermögen," "imstande sein"; diesen absoluten Charakter hat der Übersetzer verkannt und musste so ein sinnentsprechendes Verbum beifügen, z. B.

16 12 καὶ οὐ μὴ δύνηται ἐξελέσϑαι αὐτόν (ἐξελέσϑαι αὐτόν sub ÷; om. M).

29 11 οὐ δύναμαι ἀναγνῶναι (ἀναγνῶναι sub ÷; om. M).

Weitere Beispiele in den *Untersuchungen zur Is.-Sept.*, S. 65, und in den *Beiträgen zur Ier.-Sept.*, S. 92 zu 20 9.

                              X

Die bis jetzt genannten Stellen zeigen, dass Qu von M abweichende, gewöhnlich sekundäre Lesarten kennt, die auch LXX als "matres versionis" benützte. Da kann es leicht vorkommen, dass D u b l e t t e n eindringen; es ist aber auffallend, dass nur wenige Stellen genannt werden können, wo "Dubletten" in Qu bew. LXX vorliegen.

37 9 καὶ ἀκούσας ἀπέστρεψε = Qu וישמע וישוב] וישמע M; וישב IV Reg. 19 9.

Als ursprüngliche Lesart ist mit IV Reg 19 9 וישב anzunehmen, siehe meinen Is.-Kommentar in der "Echter-Bibel" (BH "sed ? origin" ist zu Unrecht unschlüssig; bereits am Anfang von v. 9 steht richtig וישמע, das sicher nicht zweimal im gleichen Vers geschrieben wurde). Die Erklärungen, dass hier eine einfache "addizione," so Milik, *Bibl.*, 31 (1950), 86, oder "verschiedener Ausfall durch doppeltes Homoioarkton," so Hempel, *ZAW*, 62 (1949/50), 289, vorliege, treffen nicht das Richtige.

40 19 ἐποίησε: cf. Qu ויעשה מסך] נסך M.

Der in Qu vorliegende Text ist unklar. Hempel, *ZAW*, 61 (1945/48), 284, meint, dass "מסך für נסך 19, wohl unter dem Einfluss des neben פסל

häufigen מסכה" stehe. Jedoch ist in מסך ein Nomen als Objekt von ויעשה zu sehen. Sowohl Qu als LXX kannten die Lesart עשה. Der griech. Übersetzer benützte sie als "mater lectionis" und gab deshalb נסך mit ἐποίησε wieder. Der Schreiber von Qu wollte die alte ursprüngliche Lesart nicht unter den Tisch fallen lassen und schrieb "und er machte ein Gussbild." Jedoch passt die Satzkonstruktion nicht gut; man erwartet ויעשה מסך ופסל.

41 11 πάντες 2°: cf. Qu אנשי כול] אנשי M.

Man könnte כול als einfache Hinzufügung betrachten, die der Schreiber aus eigenem beigab; aber πάντες 2° der LXX zeigt, dass כול bereits vorlag (beeinflusst von πάντες 1° v. 11a). כול ist sekundär, siehe G. Fohrer, *VT*, 5 (1955), 249.

65 2 ἀπειθοῦντα καὶ ἀντιλέγοντα] מורה (so ist nach dem Photo zu lesen, nicht סורה, wie Burrows abdruckt) Qu; סורר M.

Wahrscheinlich hat LXX in ihrer Vorlage bereits die beiden Lesarten von M und Qu סורר ומורה gelesen. Dann hätten wir in der LXX eine Dublette, die allerdings ihr Doppelgesicht verloren hat, da die Wendung "widerspenstig und abtrünnig" an vielen Stellen vorkommt und ursprünglich ist, siehe meine *Untersuchungen zur Is.-Sept.*, S. 78. An unserer Stelle ist nur e i n Verbum und zwar das des M echt.

XI

Wenn neu entdeckte Handschriften uns geschenkt werden, dann erregt die Schreibung und Wiedergabe der G o t t e s n a m e n besonderes Interesse. So auch bei unserer Isaias-Rolle. Über die Gottesnamen hat P. Boccaccio in *Bibl.*, 32 (1951), 90–96, einen Beitrag "I manoscritti del Mar Morto e i nomi di Dio יהוה אל" geschrieben, jedoch keine Notiz von der Wiedergabe in der LXX genommen. Auch in anderen Aufsätzen ist über die Gottesnamen gesprochen worden, aber nur gelegentlich auf die LXX Bezug genommen, vgl. Burrows, "The Treatment of the Tetragrammaton," *BASOR*, 113 (1949), 31 f., und Hempel, *ZAW*, 62 (1949/50), 253. Um eine Übersicht zu gewinnen, seien die Stellen, an denen Qu in der Behandlung des Gottesnamens von M abweicht, zusammengestellt.

6 11 κύριε יהוה Qu, אדני M.

7 14 κύριος יהוה Qu, אדני M, ebenso 9 8 (7); 21 16.

28 2 κυρίου ליהוה Qu "mlt MSS Edd," לאדני M.

3 18 κύριος יהוה Qu* "mlt MSS" אדוני Qu^c; אדני M, ebenso 8 7.

3 17 ὁ ϑεός] κυριος C 46 403–613 =יהוה Quᶜ, "mlt MSS"; 'אד Q* M.

37 20 ὁ ϑεός 2°] יהוה M; κυριος ο ϑεος 86 = יהוה אל' Qu IV Reg 19 19.

49 7 κύριος =יהוה M] יהוה 'אד Qu;

38 11 τοῦ ϑεοῦ] יה Qu; יה יה M = α'ϑ' ια ια; σ' (τον) κυριον.

49 14 καὶ ὁ κύριος] και ο ϑεος A 88–oII L =ואל' Quᶜ; 'ואד Qu* M.

42 6 κύριος ὁ ϑεός] יהוה M; om. יהוה Qu: cf. Hempel, ZAW, 62
(1949/50), 253.

25 9 ὁ ϑεὸς ἡμῶν =אלהינו M] pr. κυριος S 393 538 Co Syp Ir.ˡᵃᵗ =
יהוה אל' Qu.

28 16 κύριος S A–Qᵗˣᵗ C =יהוה Qu*] κυριος κυριος O–Qᵐᵍ et κυριος
ο ϑεος L =יהוה 'אד Quᶜ M.

28 22 (παρὰ) κυρίου = יהוה Qu "4 MSS"] a domino deo Hi.; οι γ' +※
κυρίου =יהוה 'אד M.

30 15 κύριος S A 87* =יהוה Qu*] κυριος κυριος Q O C (87ᶜ) et
κυριος ο ϑεος L =יהוה 'אד Quᶜ M.

42 5 κύριος ὁ ϑεός =האל האל' Qu; יהוה האל M: cf. Hempel, ZAW,
62 (1949/50), 253] ο ϑεος 51; κυριος οII 407 410 Ir. Cyr.

49 22 κύριος B* A–Qᵗˣᵗ S L =יהוה Qu] κυριος κυριος O (Bᶜ)–Qᵐᵍ
C =יהוה 'אד M; dominus deus Hi.

50 5 κυρίου S* A–Qᵗˣᵗ L C] κυριου κυριου Sᶜ B–Qᵐᵍ–oI 36 ='אד
יהוה M; אל' 'אד Qu.

52 4 κύριος S A–Qᵗˣᵗ L =יהוה Qu] κυριος κυριος O– Qᵐᵍ =יהוה 'אד
M; κυριος ο ϑεος C.

54 6 ὁ ϑεός σου S A–Q O L C =אלהיך M] κυριος ο ϑεος σου 88
239–306 Bo (ημων pro σου) =אל' יהוה Qu.

61 1 κυρίου =יהוה Qu] +※ κυριου Qᵐᵍ =יהוה 'אד M.

61 11 κύριος S A–Qᵗˣᵗ L C] κυριος κυριος O–Qᵐᵍ =יהוה 'אד M;
dominus deus Hi. =אל' יהוה Qu.

65 13 κύριος =יהוה Qu*] +※ κυριος 407 613 Or. =יהוה 'אד Quᶜ M.

Ein Überblick über die genannten Stellen lässt keine klare Linie
sehen. Der griech. Übersetzer hatte ja bereits die Schwierigkeit, אדני mit
einem entsprechenden Wort wiederzugeben, nachdem κύριος für יהוה
festgelegt war. So ist 49 14 zweimal κύριος für אדני und יהוה verwendet.
Das bekannteste Beispiel ist Ps 109 (110) 1 (Εἶπεν) ὁ κύριος τῷ κυρίῳ
μου יהוה לאדני. Deshalb kann auch nicht gesagt werden, ob LXX wie
Qu יהוה in ihrer Vorlage 6 11; 7 14; 9 8 (7); 21 6; 28 2; 3 18 gelesen hat.
Dagegen hat sicher LXX wie Qu nur e i n e n Gottesnamen (M zwei)
an folgenden Stellen: 28 16; 28 22; 30 15; 49 22; 50 5; 52 4; 61 1; 65 13, ferner
38 11. Wahrscheinlich hat hier LXX mit Qu das Ursprüngliche bewahrt.
Dagegen stehen aber wieder Stellen, wo LXX mit M nur e i n e n Got-

tesnamen hat, während in Qu zwei stehen, so 37 20; 49 7; 25 9; 54 6.
Schliesslich hat LXX nur e i n e n Gottesnamen, während in Qu M zwei
stehen, so 50 5; 61 11.

E r g e b n i s . Eine stattliche Anzahl von Varianten konnte notiert
werden, die in LXX Qu gegen M übereinstimmen. Diese Übereinstim-
mung besagt aber nicht, dass überall die Vorlage der LXX die gleiche
hebr. Lesart wie Qu hatte. Es ist deutlich zu erkennen, dass Qu gerade
in vielen Fällen, wo sie mit LXX übereinstimmt, sekundäre, erleichternde
Lesarten gegenüber M bezeugt.

Jedoch ist erwiesen, dass bereits der LXX-Übersetzer die von M abweichenden Varianten in Qu kannte, entweder als Lesarten, die am Rand
seiner Vorlage standen (Randnoten), oder im Text angebracht waren
(Textkorrekturen), oder völlig die ursprüngliche Lesart, die in M steht,
verdrängt haben (sekundäre Lesarten). Es besteht auch die Möglichkeit,
dass solche Varianten, besonders die lexikalischen, die den Sinn anders
deuteten, von einer Gelehrtenschule mündlich tradiert und auch schrift-
lich in separaten Verzeichnissen fixiert wurden. Diese Lesarten kannte
sicher der Übersetzer und hat sie als "matres versionis" bzw. "transcriptionis" benutzt. Es besteht auch die Möglichkeit (und sie liegt sehr
nahe), dass ein Grossteil der aufgeführten Varianten von Qu bereits in
der LXX-Vorlage stand; denn wenn sie in Qu Aufnahme gefunden haben,
warum hätten sie nicht auch in der LXX-Vorlage stehen können? Somit
verraten LXX und Qu eine gemeinsame Textform, in der sich "gewisse
«schriftgelehrte» Tendenzen geltend machen, die dazu zu zwingen
scheinen, in ihr den Niederschlag einer bewussten Rezension zu sehen,"
wie richtig Hempel, *ZAW*, 62 (1949/50), 254, bereits "als vorläufiges
Ergebnis" feststellt. Nur ist der Is.-Übersetzer bzw. der Bearbeiter der
LXX-Vorlage konsequenter als der Rezensent von Qu, wie die durch-
gängige Schreibweise der Eigennamen Ρομελιας und Σομνας mit ο
(siehe unter VII) und die ständige Wiedergabe ἀ π ο σ τ ρ έ φ ε ι ν τὸ
πρόσωπον (siehe unter IX) zeigen, während Qu den ז Laut nicht überall
hat und nur einmal (50 6) das Verbum סור Hiphil bezeugt. Aber ganz
folgerichtig waren weder der Is-Übersetzer bzw. die Bearbeiter der LXX-
Vorlage noch der Rezensor von Qu, und dies ist auch nicht zu erwarten,
denn der Is.-Übersetzer war kein Aquila und der Bearbeiter von Qu bzw.
der LXX-Vorlage waren keine Schüler des Rabbi Aqiba. Diese Erkennt-
nisse sind das wichtigste Ergebnis der vorliegenden Untersuchung, mag
auch die Summe der LXX Qu gemeinsamen Lesarten (besonders wenn
man die Gegenprobe machen würde und die sehr zahlreichen Stellen
sammelte, wo LXX M gegen Qu oder LXX gegen M Qu geht) ὀλιγοστὸς
καὶ οὐκ ἔντιμος sein, um mit den Worten der Is.-LXX 16 14 zu schliessen.

DSIa AS A WITNESS TO ANCIENT EXEGESIS
OF THE BOOK OF ISAIAH *)

S. TALMON

In the very first attempt to clarify systematically the readings
deviating from the MT which were discovered in DSIa, Millar
Burrows defined the textual relationship between the scroll and MT
as follows: "Differing notably in orthography and somewhat in
morphology it agrees with the Masoretic text to a remarkable degree
in wording. Herein lies its chief importance, supporting the fidelity
of the Masoretic tradition. There are minor omissions, but nothing
comparable with those found in the Septuagint of some of the books
of the Old Testament. Words repeated in the MT are sometimes not
repeated in our manuscript: e.g. vi 2 שש כנפים; vi 3 קדוש (repeated
once); viii 9 התאזרו וחתו; xxxviii 11 יה; lvii 19 שלום; lxii 10 עברו.
Such omissions may have been made deliberately by a scribe who
did not have the modern scholar's concern for meter" [1].

This definition expresses rather a high estimate of DSIa as a witness
to the text of the Book of Isaiah. It was followed by similar statements
voiced by other scholars who set out to prove the antiquity and the
authenticity of the MT by drawing attention to the basic resemblance
between its textual tradition and that of DSIa.

This basic identity between MT, which is preserved to us only
in comparatively late manuscripts none of them from before the
ninth century A.D., and DSIa which beyond any doubt stems from
the pre-Christian era, surely implies that the scribe of DSIa must be
considered a fairly reliable workman who took great care to transmit
somewhat mechanically, but faithfully the intricacies of a textual
tradition held holy in his community. Just as did the scribes who
handed down the MT he sometimes copied passages in his manuscript
which were faulty and no doubt, without sense even to him.

As against this remarkable basic concurrence of DSIa with MT

---

*) A paper read at the Swedish Theological Institute in Jerusalem in May 1961.
The original text is printed here with slight alterations and with some notes
appended.

the former differs from the latter textually in a good number of instances, as is well known. Now, these deviations from MT are often quoted by the same scholars to prove the scribe's laxity and the unreliability of the text of DSIa.

It appears to us that this two-edged reasoning comes dangerously near to juggling of evidence. There can be no two measures by which to judge and evaluate this ancient manuscript. It is methodically unsound to give credit to DSIa where its tradition coincides with that of MT, while condemning it as unworthy of trust whenever it goes its own way, unless its direct dependence on MT or on its proto-type has been conclusively proved. It is in this respect that, wittingly or unwittingly, scholars have failed by taking recourse to an unproven conjecture as if it were an established fact: MT is applied as a yardstick to measure the textual tradition of DSIa, with the tacit assumption that Isaiah's prophecies were handed down in one single formulation which moreover was preserved most faithfully in the Massoretic Text. But actually this question, whether all versions of the Bible were derived from one ancestor or whether we have to assume a manifold textual tradition in the latter half of the Second Temple Period, or even in the very first stage of literary biblical composition, has constituted the bone of contention between two schools of textual scholars since the beginning of the twentieth century. Instead of judging DSIa by the axioms of an Urtext theory, we should use the new finds from the Judaean Desert as a test for this theory. By stating matters in this manner we are widening the scope of a mere investigation into the impact of DSIa on the study of the Book of Isaiah. This will call for further comments at a later stage.

Before proceeding we have to consider some additional factors. In spite of the alleged general textual integrity of DSIa it cannot be denied that in many instances the scroll is demonstrably faulty. By processes which sometimes can be reconstructed to a reasonable degree of certainty errors of various types were incorporated in the text of the scroll. Again, in some cases we can observe in the scroll attempts at improving imaginary or real misreadings which the scribe or the copyist found in his *Vorlage* and which often remained unchanged in the MT. These errors were assembled and roughly categorised already by Burrows in the article mentioned previously. They drew the special attention of Y. KUTSCHER [2]) and H. M. OR-LINSKY [3]) who, more than others, became convinced of the inferiority of DSIa as against the MT.

It must be conceded that erroneous readings due to failings of the copyists are more numerous in the scroll than in the MT. The same holds true for the number of attempts at correcting obviously faulty readings. But it should be stressed, on the other hand, that this process of textual revision is far from being complete. Many cases of a crux interpretum in the Hebrew Isaiah were left to stand unchanged in DSIa as they are in MT Statistically speaking we may say that only a minority of difficult passages in the book were smoothed over in DSIa while the great majority were transmitted in their unsatisfactory wording. This state of matters does not allow a clear-cut decision, whether in those instances in which the scroll presents a better reading than MT this is due to a secondary attempt at improvement or whether the scroll preserved here sometimes an original straightforward text. The maxim that the lectio difficilior should usually be given preference over a parallel smooth reading is a valid safeguard against hasty textual emendation. But it should not be considered an invariable rule by which to decide the relative value of variants.

From the foregoing discussion arises a rather multicoloured picture of DSIa as a witness to the text of the book of Isaiah. Even should the scroll ultimately be judged to be inferior to the MT this does not rule out the possibility that in many individual instances it has preserved readings superior in sense to those of MT, and textually more original than their parallels in MT. In order to form a balanced opinion of DSIa and the characteristics of its scribe the discussion should take its departure from an evaluation of the scroll by itself without setting MT as a standard for comparison. A reading of the scroll should first of all be judged by itself in order that we may decide whether it has any intrinsic value. At the second stage of such an investigation DSIa should be compared with other extra-Massoretic versions, with the Septuagint, the Peshitta, and to a lesser degree with the Targum, which probably perpetuate other independent textual traditions. Only after that a comparison with the MT is called for.

This comparison will often result in a deadlock, both versions presenting equally acceptable readings. Again in other instances we may arrive at the conclusion that both parallel readings cannot be considered original, but were derived from a common ancestor which sometimes can still be restored conjecturally.

Finally we should submit all the variant readings of a given passage to a synoptic analysis. This synopsis will often reveal a striking resemblance, even an identity, of DSIa with one or more of the extra-Massoretic versions. These textual concurrences are of great value, since they point to an ancient Jewish tradition current in Israel in the latter half of the Second Temple period.

II

The diversity of textual tradition which can yet be observed in our sources makes it sufficiently clear that at some stage or other in the history of the book of Isaiah different avenues were leading to its interpretation.

Our modern concept of the prophet's words is decisively influenced by the system of vowels and syntactical symbols, the *ta'amim*, with which the Massoretes endowed the biblical text during the ninth and tenth century A.D. This system embodies exegetical reflections which undoubtedly are deeply rooted in Jewish tradition. Still, they convey only one possible approach to the Bible. DSIa presents to us a text devoid of the Massoretic aids to its explanation. But it is free, on the other hand, from those explanatory symbols which transmit a historically dated interpretation of the Holy Writ, an interpretation that consituted the tradition of only one, however important, sector of the Jewish people.

Here the exegetical importance of DSIa becomes apparent. It is witness to a phase in Jewish interpretation of the book of Isaiah independent from that embodied in the Massoretic text. Furthermore, it often provides us with an excellent tool for a novel approach to the interpretation of Isaiah's prophecies. If we succeed to read the text of the scroll without unconsciously providing it with the vowel signs and text-divisions to which we became accustomed we sometimes will arrive at a new interpretation of a given passage which assumedly was in the mind of its scribe even where its consonantal text does not differ from that preserved in MT.

We shall now adduce some examples by which to put these theoretical considerations to the test of practical application. Starting from instances in which only a difference in pointing of a single word is assumed to constitute the variant, we shall then deal with cases of identical consonantal texts which were divided syntactically in different ways.

1. Different vocalization of single words.

We shall first adduce an example in which the scroll has a most

probably faulty pointing of a crucial word. However it is important
to show that this same pointing is mirrored partly in the translations
of the Sept., the Pesh. and the Targ.

a) Is. xix 10. MT: והיו שתתיה מדכאים, כל עשי שכר אגמי נפש

G: καὶ ἔσονται οἱ διαζόμενοι αὐτὰ ἐν ὀδύνῃ καὶ
πάντες οἱ ποιοῦντες τὸν ζῦθον λυπηθήσονται καὶ
τὰς ψυχὰς πονέσουσιν [4])

DSIa: והיו שותתיה מדכאים כל עושי שכר אגמי נפש

T: ויהון אתר בית שתי מהא כבישין אתר דהוו
עבדין סיכרא וכנשין מיא גבר לנפשיה

The RV translates the verse under review thus: "And her pillars
shall be broken in pieces, all they that work for hire shall be grieved
in soul". Here as in G's rendering אגמי נפש is tacitly equated with
עגם, probably on the basis of Job xxx 25: עגמה נפשי לאביון — "was
not my soul grieved for the needy". The root עגם is a *hap. leg.* This
may have been conducive to the substitution of א for ע, both in
MT and DSIa. T however seems to have thought of אגם — pond.

But we are mainly concerned with two other words in the verse.
In translating "her pillars" the RV obviously connected שתתיה with
שתת, from which also שת — "base, foundation" is derived. שֶׁכֶר was
taken as just a variant pronunciation of שָׂכָר — "wages".

The ancient versions, however ascribed these words a quite
different meaning. G's οἱ διαζόμενοι, which is preserved only
in some mss. but is nevertheless considered original, takes שתתיה as a
technical term which rather fits the context. The same verb translates
in Judg. xvi 14 the Hebrew root ארג.

It has been suggested that the Hebrew שתת is of Egyptian origin
and that it carries the meaning of "weaver, ropemaker" [5]).

The main Greek tradition renders שתתיה rather loosely ἐργαζόμενοι.

T's בית שתי מהא definitely connects שתתיה with שתה, to drink.
Now it appears that DSI's reading שותתיה points to the same concept.
שתת alongside שתה is employed by both MT and DSIa in Is. xxii 13:
אכל בשר ושתות יין ··· כי מחר נמות. Hence DSIa concurs with T in the
interpretation of the first half of the verse under review.

This leads to the assumption that DSIa's reading differed from
that of MT also in the second half of the verse, though their consonantal texts are identical. Here G's translation contains the clue.
שכר was rendered by G — ζῦθον, i.e., beer, the Hebrew word ob-

viously being read — שֵׁכָר. We suggest that this was also the reading of the scroll and that accordingly its text is to be translated: "And her drunkards (lit. drinkers) shall be downcast (depressed), all makers of beer (shall be) grieved in soul".

The argument advanced here goes to show that in the verse under discussion DSIa presents an ancient attempt of Jewish exegesis, one part of which is also reflected in the Targum while another part underlies the Greek translation. As already stated we think that in this case DSIa represents a misinterpretation of scripture. In the following example however we feel strongly that DSIa contributes to a better understanding of the biblical text.

b) Is. xxvi 9. MT: כי כַאֲשֶׁר משפטיך לארץ צדק למדו ישבי תבל

T: כמא דדינך מתקנין לארעא ...

G: διότι φῶς τὰ προστάγματά σου ἐπὶ τῆς γῆς

This is a case of an assumed variant which ordinarily would not attract the attention of a reader of the scroll since its consonantal text is identical with that of MT (excepting the *plene* writing of ישבי which is written defective in MT). The difference seems to lie in the second word which in MT is obviously taken as a particle and is pointed כַּאֲשֶׁר. The RV consequently translates the passage in a rather forced manner: "...for when thy judgements are in the earth, the inhabitants of the world learn righteousness".

The ancient translators had before them essentially the same text as is preserved in MT. But they could not make head or tail of it. T inserted a verb — מתקנין, which completes nicely the relative clause introduced by כמא, but is patently secondary [6]). G turned the particle into a noun — φῶς, reading, intentionally or unintentionally, כְּאֵשׁ for

כאשר. It appears that this is a step in the right direction. A noun seems to be required after the comparative "כ". Retaining the consonants of MT — כאשר, we propose to point the word כָּאֹשֶׁר or כָּאֵשֶׁר, and to translate the phrase—"for as happiness (sweetness) are your statutes to the (dwellers of the) earth, the inhabitants of the world learned justice". Thus is restored the parallelism of the verse which is now in full accord with the other sentences in the passage Is. xxvi 6-10.

The idea, that God's precepts (משפטים) produce happiness or sweetness (אֹשֶׁר) for their observers, recurs in Is. xxx 18: "...for the

Lord is a God of righteousness (משפט), happy (אשרי) are all they
that wait for him". And again in Is. lvi 2: "Happy (אשרי) the man
that doeth this... that keepeth the Sabbath from profaning it, and
keepeth his hand from doing any evil". We may further compare
Ps. cvi 3: אשרי שמרי משפט עשה צדקה בכל עת — "Happy are they that
observe the laws (and) he that doeth righteousness at all times".
Here we have the same combination of (אשר(י) – משפט – צדק(ה) that
supposedly is to be found also in the verse under review—Is. xxvi 9.

Our argument may be strengthened by a further consideration.
We assumed that the restored noun אֶשֶׁר–אֲשֶׁר carries the sense of
"happiness" or "sweetness" and that this sensation is bound up with the
notion of justice and righteousness. Now is it mere coincidence that
as against this injustice is compared to bitterness? We venture to
propose that Is. xxvi 9 is the very antithesis of the verse Am. v 7:
ההפכים ללענה משפט וצדקה לארץ הניחו, "Ye who turn justice to
bitterwood and cast down righteousness to the earth", are bound
to come to grief. The incompatibility of God's intentions and man's
acts is forcefully brought out in these mutually opposed scriptures
by the employment in both of them of the salient words (משפט–צדק(ה
לארץ–, modified by the antithetic concepts of אשר and לענה.

We wish to emphasize that the reading of Is. xxvi 9 that was
proposed here adheres to the consonantal text as transmitted both
in MT and DSIa. However, availing ourselves of the flexibility
inherent in the unpointed text of DSIa we achieved two results:
a) We were able to restore the hitherto only presupposed noun
אֶשֶׁר–אֲשֶׁר from which may have been derived also the word באשרי
in Gen. xxx 13. We may expect to find some further instances in the
MT in which this noun was erroneously taken as the relative pronoun
and was pointed אֲשֶׁר [7]). b) We could interpret satisfactorily the
verse under review and to place it into proper relationship with
other scriptures which express similar ideas.

2. Erroneous pointing coupled with the additional interchange
of two very similar letters, *yod* and *waw*, seems to have resulted in the
following variant:

a) Is. xix 9. MT: ובשו עבדי פשתים שריקות וארגים חורי

   DSIa: יבושו עובדי פשתים שריקות ואורגים חורו

The substitution of *yod* for *waw* in יבושו–וב(ו)שו is just another case of the alternate employment of the perfect and the imperfect and does not affect the sense of the verse. However, the interchange of חורי and חורו is of a different nature. Let it be stated that the reading of MT is supported by T's translation מצדן = nets, which points to a derivation of חורי from חור — hole. Also G render חורי as a noun βύσσον, deriving it probably from חור (Esth. i 6; viii 15). The weavers of that material (ארגים חורי) would be put to shame (αἰσχύνη λήμψεται) like the flax workers mentioned in the first part of the verse. This is roughly the rendering of the RV too: "moreover they that work in combed flax, and they that weave white cloth, shall be ashamed". לחדותא of the Pesh. is inconclusive since its meaning cannot be ascertained.

As against these DSI's reading חורו must obviously be explained as a perfect form (3. pers. pl.) of the verb חור and should probably be pronounced חָוְרוּ (or חָוֵרוּ — if pausal forms were employed in DSIa). This reading was already proposed tentatively by some commentators (cp. BH), prior to the discovery of DSIa. The second member of the verse thus contains a verb parallel to יבושו in the first member: "Ashamed shall be they that work in combed flax and weavers (of flax) shall wax pale".

b) The same parallelism of בוש–חור recurs in Is. xxix 22: לא ··· עתה יבוש יעקב ולא עתה פניו יחורו "Jacob shall not now be ashamed, neither shall his face now wax pale".

It could be argued that the scroll's reading in this verse should be viewed as an attempt of explaining away the *hap. leg.* חורי of MT. By employing the rule of *lectio difficilior* the MT should then be given priority over DSIa. But we shall immediately see that this rule cuts both ways. If it were to be applied categorically it would for example prove the superiority of DSIa over the MT in the following instance:

c) Is. xi 6. MT: ועגל וכפיר ומריא יחדו ונער קטן נהג בם

   DSIa: ועגל וכפיר ימרו יחדו ונער קטן נהג במה

Instead of the noun מריא, fatling, in the MT, DSIa has a verb in the perf. form — ימרו, which like מריא is derived from the same stem מרא with elision of the *aleph*. Again this reading had already been restored conjecturally before the discovery of the scroll. Now, the noun מריא is found several times in the O.T. (II Sam. vi 13; I Kings i 9, 19, 25; Is. i 11; xi 6 etc.), but there is not one single instance of the verb מרא being used. Therefore it is DSIa that in this case has preserved the more difficult reading.

The same division of MT and DSIa can be observed also in the translations. T's ופטים mirrors MT's מריא. On the other hand the rendering of Pesh. — נרעון "they will graze", concurs with DSIa's — ימרו. G surprisingly has conflated both interpretations, translating: καὶ μοσχάριον καὶ ταῦρος καὶ λεῶν ἅμα βοσκηθήσονται.

The reading of DSIa is stylistically better suited than that of MT. The verse thus contains four syntactically complete parts (a-b; a-c) each with its own predicate.

This stylistic superiority of DSIa over MT deserves serious consideration. But of even more importance is the exegetical and textual concord of DSIa, Pesh. and of one Greek tradition. There are no adequate reasons to explain this as due to the same trend of emendation independently conceived in a Hebrew, a Greek and the Syriac tradition. Similarly no direct interdependence between these three witnesses to the text of the Bible can be established. It therefore appears that their combined evidence points to an ancient source from which all three were derived. This, admittedly hypothetic source represented an exegetical tradition, based on a text varying from that of MT, which must have been firmly established in Jewish circles in the period of the Second Temple.

3. Different pointing coupled with an interchange of non-similar letters.

Is. xiv 11. MT: הורד שאול גאונך הֶמְיַת נבליך

DSIa: [הו]רד שאול גאונך המית נבלתך

The translation of MT: "Thy pomp is brought down to hell (and) the noise of thy viols" shows that we are confronted here with a parallelism in which the words הורד שאול are tacitly applied also to the second apocopated member. הֶמְיַת נבליך can be taken with some imagination as a parallel to גאונך. But DSIa's reading נבלתך — thy corpse, can by no means be combined with הֶמְיַת. The scribe obviously read the word as הֵמִית, conceiving it as a parallel to הורד שאול. Though "he killed your corpse" sounds somewhat unusual, this exegetical tradition is witnessed for also by the rendering of Sym.: ἐθανατώθη τὸ πτῶμά" σου. A reference to death is contained also in Theodotion's translation who apparently reads the noun הָמְות instead of the verb

הֵמִית: ὁ θάνατος κατέρρηξέν σε. T: תושבחת זמרך and G: ἡ πολλή σου
εὐφροσύνη mirror MT; while Pesh. presents elements of both interpretations: ומית כנרך — "and thy viol will die".

4. In some cases slight differences in the consonantal text of DSIa
suggest a syntactical arrangement that differs from the one indicated
by the massoretic accents.

Is. xxvi 16. MT: ה׳ בצר פקדוך צקון לחש מוּסָרך למו

          DSIa: ה׳ בצר פקדיך צקון לחשו מוסריך למו

          T: ה׳ בעקא הוו דכירין לדחלתך בעקתההון הוו
                          מלפין אולפן אוריתך ב(ו)חשי

The *atnach* under פקדוך indicates that in MT the second stichos
opens with the word צקון. The second half of this verse is admittedly
difficult. The apparent noun צקון is usually derived from צוק — distress, but is registered in the most recent dictionary of the Bible
(KOEHLER) as "unexplained". The RV took it as a verb from the
stem — יצק, and translated accordingly: "Lord, in trouble have they
visited thee, they poured out a prayer when thy chastening was upon
them". The first half of this translation corresponds roughly to the
ancient versions. But instead of interpreting מוסרך in the second half
as "chastening—affliction", G and T take it as a reference to God's
commandments — G: ἡ παιδεία σου. T: אוריתך. This is the sense
which the word מוסר usually carries in the Bible (e.g. Jer. xvii 23;
xxxii 33; Zeph. iii 27; Pr. viii 33; xii 1 etc.), and this is obviously
also the meaning of the plural מוסריך of DSIa.

Against MT and the versions which take לחש as a noun (G: μικρᾷ,
read: πικρᾷ; T: בחשי), DSIa has here a verb: לחשו. It seems that this
is paralleled by צקון, which in DSIa is probably a contraction of
צעקון. That צקון was understood as a verb by the writer of the scroll
may be deduced also from his reading פקדיך — thy precepts, a noun
parallel to מוסריך in the second stichos, instead of the verb פקדוך
in MT. The noun פקדים is frequently used in the Psalms and is, so
to speak, the catchword of Ps. cxix, where it is paralleled by תורה, חוק,
etc.

All this results in a different verse division in DSIa, and in a perfect
parallelism of members: ה׳ בצר פקדיך צ(ע)קון, לחשו מוסריך למו. We
suggest the following translation: "Lord, in distress they call out
your precepts, they whisper your commandments unto themselves".

We are fully aware that the few examples which were analysed here can only indicate the line of approach to the scroll of Isaiah which was advocated. A full investigation will result in proper appraisal of the scroll as a witness to ancient Jewish exegesis and of its writer as an exegete of no mean achievements. In conclusion we wish to state that the exegetical tradition underlying the scroll is reflected not only in ancient translations, as we set out to prove in this paper, but also in Talmudic and Midrashic literature. But this problem should be dealt with separately.

-----

[1]) M. Burrows, Variant Readings in the Isaiah Manuscript. *BASOR*, 111, 1948, pp. 16-17.

[2]) E. Y. Kutscher, *The Language and Linguistic Background of the Isaiah Scroll* (Hebrew). 1959.

[3]) S. his *Studies in the St. Mark's Scroll*. I-IV, JQR 43, 1952/53, pp. 329-340; V, IEJ 4, 1954, pp. 5-8; VI, HUCA 25, 1954.

[4]) The last passage in G is apparently a *Doppelübersetzung* influenced by Is. liii 10: ἀπὸ τοῦ πόνου τῆς ψυχῆς. Cf. J. Ziegler, *Untersuchungen zur Septuaginta des Buches Isaias*, 1934, p. 65.

[5]) S. L. Koehler — W. Baumgartner, *Lexicon in Veteris Testamenti libros*, 1953, s.v. שתת (p. 1015).

[6]) We tend to assume that this translation is moulded upon the pattern of the similar expression in Is. xlii 4: עד ישים בארץ משפט, where T translates: עד דיתקין בארעא דינא.

[7]) Prof. G. R. Driver has kindly drawn our attention to some of his notes in which he dealt with the root אשר and its occurrences in the O.T. S. *JThSt* 38, pp. 37, 43; *BiOr* 1, pp. 234-35; AJSL 52, p. 160. To the instances of the noun אשר mispointed אֲשֶׁר suggested by him we would add provisionally Is. xlii 4.

REDÉCOUVERTE D'UN CHAÎNON MANQUANT DE L'HISTOIRE DE LA SEPTANTE

DOMINIQUE BARTHÉLEMY

Pendant la répression du mouvement insurrectionnel de Ben Kosebah — si nous en croyons la mise en scène du « Dialogue » — Justin se plaignait auprès du juif Tryphon de l'attitude du rabbinat contemporain à l'égard de la vénérable version des Septante. Non seulement ils avaient l'audace de soutenir que l'interprétation donnée par leurs soixante-dix anciens réunis chez le roi d'Égypte Ptolémée n'était pas exacte en tous points (1), mais ils allaient jusqu'à prétendre donner eux-mêmes leur propre interprétation de l'Écriture (2), osant ainsi dénaturer ce vénérable héritage (3) et remplacer l'exégèse messianique traditionnelle des prophéties par des interprétations misérables, « qui se traînent à ras de terre » (4). Justin affirme sans ambages que c'est pour ôter une arme essentielle à la propagande chrétienne que les rabbins ont falsifié ainsi les prophéties en en retranchant maints passages qui laissaient entrevoir trop nettement la figure de Jésus-Christ (5).

Ne se bornant pas à ces accusations globales, Justin prétend nous donner en plusieurs cas, face à face, des exemples de l'interprétation traditionnelle des LXX et de celle du rabbinat contemporain (6). Il accepte même à contre-cœur la situation faite ainsi à la controverse chrétienne antijudaïque et s'efforce de n'argumenter qu'à partir de textes acceptés par ses adversaires (7). En plusieurs cas, il nous prévient incidemment qu'il les cite sous la forme où les lisaient ceux-ci (8).

Si l'on pouvait faire toute confiance à Justin, nous aurions donc en lui un témoin précieux d'une phase très importante de l'histoire du

---

(1) LXVIII, 7; LXXI, 1; LXXXIV, 3 (divisions et texte selon l'éd. d'ARCHAMBAULT, *Textes et Documents*, Picard, Paris, 1909).

(2) LXXI, 1.

(3) LXXXIV, 3.

(4) CXII, 4.

(5) LXVIII, 8; LXXI, 2; LXXII, 3; CXX, 5.

(6) CXX, 4; CXXIV, 2 et 3; CXXXVII, 3.

(7) LXXI, 2.

(8) CXXIV, 4; CXXXVII, 3.

texte grec de l'Ancien Testament. Ses innombrables citations souvent très longues, tirées de livres bibliques fort divers, nous auraient conservé le texte grec courant dans les milieux juifs orthodoxes du début du Second siècle. Mais certaines considérations ont empêché la critique contemporaine de se laisser entraîner par cet espoir. Même ceux qui ne nient pas, à la suite de Preuschen et de Schäder, l'authenticité du « Dialogue » sont forcés d'y reconnaître une bonne part de fiction et de repousser sa composition dans la seconde moitié du siècle. Aussi envisage-t-on volontiers le texte biblique très original attesté par Justin comme une recension personnelle de la LXX à partir des premières grandes traductions juives du Second siècle et spécialement de celle d'Aquila. Il importe enfin de faire remarquer que nous ne connaissons l'œuvre de Justin que par un unique ms. du xive siècle, et que la forme de ses citations bibliques a pu être sérieusement affectée par son passage à travers cette longue et étroite filière. Il semblait donc, jusqu'à une date toute récente, que le plus prudent fût de souscrire à ces lignes déçues et décevantes par lesquelles Rahlfs concluait une étude du texte biblique de Justin : « Für den LXX-Forscher ist unser Resultat insofern lehrreich als es wieder einmal zeigt wie vorsichtig man bei der Verwertung von Kirchenväter-Zitaten sein muss. » (1).

Mais au cours de la seconde quinzaine d'août 1952, les infatigables bédouins Ta'amré ont découvert dans une nouvelle grotte du désert de Juda d'importants fragments d'un rouleau de parchemin qui y avait été déposé lors de la révolte de Ben Kosebah (2). Ces fragments ont été acquis par le Musée Archéologique Palestinien, avec l'assentiment de Mr. Harding, Directeur des Antiquités de Jordanie, et nous sommes autorisés à en faire une première présentation aux lecteurs de la *Revue Biblique*. Il s'agit d'un texte grec des Petits Prophètes dont les parties conservées appartiennent à Michée, Jonas, Nahum, Habacuc, Sophonie et Zacharie. Comme on pourra s'en rendre compte par la planche ci-jointe (pl. I), la très belle onciale de notre ms. se situe au mieux vers la fin du 1er siècle après J.-C. (3), ce qui concorde avec le fait que

_____

(1) *ZNW.*, 1921, p. 198.

(2) C'est ce qu'indique de façon suffisamment certaine l'écriture des petits fragments de papyri hébréo-araméens trouvés dans la même grotte ainsi que les monnaies et documents datés trouvés en deux autres grottes toutes proches.

(3) Des *apices* inférieurs vigoureusement lancés vers la droite constituent la caractéristique la plus frappante de cette onciale au caractère très ferme. Ni l'*alpha* ni le *mu* ne présentent les signes de fléchissement qui apparaissent au début du second siècle. Le centre de gravité de l'écriture n'est ni surélevé ni surbaissé. Les apices obliques supérieurs qui apparaissent parfois dans le *delta*, l'*alpha* et le *lambda* ne manifestent aucune tendance à s'incurver.

le ms. était déjà très usagé lorsqu'il fut abandonné. L'abondance de textes découverts cette année ne nous permet pas d'aborder tout de suite la publication intégrale de ces nouveaux fragments bibliques, aussi me bornerai-je pour cette fois à situer cette nouvelle recension du texte grec dans son contexte littéraire et historique.

Voici tout d'abord un passage qui recouvre partiellement une importante citation faite par Justin au ch. cix du « Dialogue » : il s'agit de *Michée* iv, 3-7.

```
                                        ]πολλω[
                                        ]κρανκαισυνκοψου
                                        ]νεισαροτρακαιτασ
              ]μαχα[                     ]ανακαιουμηανθα
    σιβυ[      ]υτων[                    ]καιουμημα
    ρηεθν[     ]φεθνοσ[
 4  θωσινετιπολεμει[                     ]ονταιανηρ
    υποκατωαμπελουαυ[                    ]υκησ
    α[         ]ιουκεστινο[              ]οτ . τοστομα
 5  (tetr.)[   ]νδ[                      ]οτιπαν
    τεσοιλα . . πορε[                    ]ουαυτων
    ημεισδεπορε[                         ](tetr.) θεου
    ημω . ειστον[                        ]
 6                                       ]συνα
                                         ]ξωσ
 7                          ]ηνεκα[      ]θησω
                            ]νεισυ[      ]μμα
                            ]νηνεισεθνοσισχυρον
             ](tetragr.) επαυτωνεντωορεισει
                            ]ωστουαιωνοσ
```

Il suffit de comparer ce texte à celui de la citation de Justin pour constater qu'il lui est substantiellement identique. Voici les seules variantes qui les distinguent : v. 3. : ανθαρη/αρη Just.; v. 4 : καθι] σονται/καθισεται Just.; ibid. : εστιν/εσται (1) Just.; ibid. : το στομα/ στομα Just.; v. 5ᵃ : θε]ου/θεων Just. Aucune de ces variantes, on le voit, n'excède ce que l'on est en droit d'attendre des abâtardissements d'une tradition manuscrite aussi longue et étroite que l'est celle du texte de Justin.

La dimension des lettres est régulière, bien calibrée. Toutes ces caractéristiques s'accordent au mieux avec la Seconde moitié du Premier siècle; date qu'aucune particularité de détail ne vient contredire, bien qu'il soit difficile de trouver des parallèles parfaitement typiques.
(1) En cx, 4, Justin reprenant ce passage lit εστιν comme notre ms.

Les points où notre texte concorde avec celui de Justin contre les LXX sont beaucoup plus nombreux et typiques (1) : v. 3 : συνκοψουσι/ κατακοψουσι LXX; ibid. : μαχαιρας/ρομφαιας LXX; ibid. : τας ζιβυνας/ τα δορατα LXX; ibid : ου μη/ουκετι μη (1er) LXX; ibid. ου μη...ετι/ ουκετι μη (2e) LXX; v. 4 : ανηρ/εκαστος LXX; ibid. : των δυναμεων/ παντοκρατωρος LXX; v. 6 : ην εκακωσα/ους απωσαμην LXX; v. 7 : θησω/θησομαι LXX; ibid. : επ'αυτων εν τω ορει/επ'αυτους εν ορει LXX; ibid. : εως του αιωνος/εως εις τον αιωνα LXX.

Notons de plus que les lacunes du ms. sont beaucoup plus aisément remplies avec le texte de Justin qu'avec celui des LXX. Mais les concordances formelles qui viennent d'être relevées paraissent suffisamment démonstratives : en argumentant contre Tryphon, Justin citait Michée selon notre texte.

Je n'ai relevé dans le « Dialogue » qu'un autre passage très bref où ses citations des Petits Prophètes recoupent encore une fois nos fragments : il s'agit de *Zac.* ii, 12 où tous deux sont d'accord pour lire ἐκλέξεται contre αἱρετιεῖ de la LXX. Remarquons enfin, pour éviter une méprise, que le texte que donnent nos fragments pour *Mic.* v, 2 est très différent de celui que cite Justin. Cela tient seulement à ce que ce dernier ne cite pas directement Michée, mais en réalité reproduit la citation libre qu'en fait l'évangile de S. Matthieu.

Que nous ayons ainsi retrouvé dans une grotte de la Seconde Révolte le texte des Petits Prophètes cité par Justin, cela nous amène déjà à une première conclusion : c'est que Justin cite un texte juif réel, en vogue au moment où il situe son dialogue avec Tryphon. Nous n'avons donc pas affaire, comme on pouvait le craindre, à une mixture tardive et arbitraire : il n'invente rien. Seuls ses copistes peuvent être rendus responsables de quelques modifications facilitantes ou assimilantes. De là nous pouvons inférer que les autres citations de Justin, et elles sont aussi amples que variées, représentent très vraisemblablement, dans ce qu'elles ont d'original, une recension rabbinique de la Septante qui avait cours entre 70 et 135.

Il est en effet assez aisé de prouver, sur la base des fragments qui nous en sont parvenus, premièrement que notre texte n'est qu'une *recension de la Septante*, et deuxièmement que cette recension est l'œuvre de *lettrés juifs*.

Que notre texte ne soit pas une version originale mais une recension, un simple exemple suffira à le prouver en permettant de saisir sur le

---

(1) Pour l'établissement du texte de la LXX, je me base sur l'édition de J. Ziegler (Göttingen, Vandenhoeck & Ruprecht, 1943).

vif les procédés du recenseur. Voici deux versets d'Habacuc. On pour-
rait trouver nombre d'autres passages typiques dans nos fragments.
Le seul privilège de ces deux versets est de ne pas avoir été rendus
trop lacunaires par la dent des rats :

Hb. ii, 7 : **οὐχὶ** ἐξαί[φνη]ς ἀναστήσονται δάκνοντες **σε** καὶ ἐγνή[ψουσ]ιν
οἱ **ἀλεύοντες** σε καὶ ἔσῃ εἰς διαρπαγὰς αὐτ[οῖς].

Hb. ii, 18 : τί ὠφέλη**σεν** γλυπτόν ὅτι [ἔγλυψε]ν αὐτό **ὁ πλάσας**
αὐτὸ χώνευμα [**καὶ** φα]ντασίαν ψευδῆ ὅτι πέποιθεν ὁ πλάσας ἐπὶ τὸ
πλάσμα αὐτοῦ **ἐπ᾽αὐτό** [π]οιῆσαι εἴδωλα κωφά.

Il suffit de comparer ces deux versets au texte de la LXX et à
l'hébreu pour se rendre compte que toutes les modifications (en carac-
tères gras) du texte grec traditionnel s'expliquent par un souci de le
modeler plus exactement sur l'hébreu.

Il convient cependant d'ajouter qu'à côté de centaines de variantes
de ce type, on en trouve aussi un certain nombre où notre texte semble
s'éloigner à la fois de la LXX et du T.M. Cela peut vouloir dire alors
que le texte hébreu sur lequel le recenseur s'est basé différait du nôtre.
Ainsi en Hab. i, 17 où εκκεν]ωσει μαχαιραν αυτου (qui remplace αμφι-
βαλει το αμφιβλησтρον αυτου de la LXX) suppose qu'il lisait avec le
Pesher d'Habacuc de Qumrân חרבו au lieu de חרמו du T. M. Peut-être
faut-il faire entrer dans la même catégorie la substitution de αρτος à
μερις en *Hab.* i, 16. Notre recenseur aurait lu dans son texte hébreu
probablement abâtardi להם au lieu de חלק, modification que paraît
supposer aussi le targum de Jonathan.

Lorsqu'il quitte la base de la LXX pour essayer de rendre par ses
propres moyens le texte hébreu, il se montre souvent fort inconséquent.
Il lui arrive de faire preuve d'un littéralisme extrême qui violente la
syntaxe grecque : ainsi lorsqu'il ajoute επ᾽ αυτο en *Hab.* ii, 18 (cf. *supra*)
ou bien lorsqu'il laisse au nominatif sans aucun lien syntactique des
substantifs dont il a supprimé, par fidélité à l'hébreu, la préposition
introductive : ainsi en *Hab.* ii, 6 : οὐχὶ ταῦτα πάντα παραβολὴν κατ'
αὐτοῦ λήμψεται (1) καὶ πρόβλημα **διήγησις** αὐτοῦ. Ailleurs au
contraire il traduit de façon assez large. C'est ainsi que ערות est
traduit εξε]κενωσας en *Hab.* iii, 13, ou חבש : περιεσχ[ε]ν en *Jon.* ii, 6,
ou encore בריאה : στερεον en *Hab.* i, 16.

Je ne puis, dans les limites de cette simple présentation, m'attarder
à étudier une à une chaque option de notre réviseur anonyme. Notons
plutôt une conclusion intéressante qui semble se dégager du fait qu'il

---

(1) Le texte hébreu de notre recenseur supprime le *waw* final par haplographie.

ait pris pour base la LXX au lieu de se lancer dans une traduction
entièrement personnelle. Il est difficile de ne pas voir là un hommage
tacite rendu à la très grande diffusion dont jouissait alors, jusqu'en
Palestine, citadelle du Judaïsme orthodoxe, la grande traduction
alexandrine. Cela correspond bien à la situation suggérée par Justin et
me paraît s'opposer à l'hypothèse d'une diffusion essentiellement chrétienne de la LXX (1). Partout l'Église naissante a dû trouver entre
les mains de la Diaspora juive de langue grecque un texte grec essentiellement identique à celui dont l'autorité traditionnelle s'appuyait
sur le récit merveilleux que nous rapporte la lettre d'Aristée. Je ne
nie évidemment pas que la tradition de ce texte ait pu se nuancer de
façon caractéristique en tel ou tel grand centre juif; mais il semble
bien que dès le Iᵉʳ siècle il avait évincé tous les autres targums grecs
locaux, s'il y en eut jamais de vraiment consistants.

Essayons d'établir maintenant que cette recension est bien, comme
le prétend Justin, l'œuvre de lettrés juifs.

Le fait que le rouleau dont proviennent nos fragments ait été en
possession de réfugiés de la Seconde Révolte est déjà un indice, d'autant
plus que, dans ce nouvel ensemble de grottes, on a trouvé des fragments
hébreux de la Thôrah et des Psaumes ainsi qu'un phylactère parfaitement orthodoxe (avec suppression du Décalogue en signe de raidis-
sement anti-chrétien). Mais ce sont plutôt des arguments de critique
interne qui nous apporteront, je pense, une preuve suffisante.

Précisons tout d'abord que, dans ce qui nous a été conservé de son
œuvre, le recenseur ne peut être accusé d'avoir agi en polémiste gau-
chissant les textes. Il a seulement fait de son mieux pour rendre la
LXX plus fidèle à l'hébreu qu'il avait sous les yeux. Ce n'est donc
pas à des indices doctrinaux que nous reconnaîtrons une main juive.
Mais le fait décisif est que Aquila, le grand champion de l'orthodoxie
rabbinique, a pris pour base notre recension. Pour établir cela, envi-
sageons les vingt-huit cas ou notre recension diffère de la LXX et où,
par ailleurs, la leçon d'Aquila nous a été conservée (2) :

L : *Mic.* I, 4 σαλευθησεται;   II, 7 εισι καλοι;   *ib.* πεπορευνται;
R :   ]σον[;   ]θυναν;   ]ενου;
A :   τακησονται;   αγαθυνουσι;   πορευομενου;

---

(1) Ceci contre ma concession à Kahle en *RB.*, 1952, p. 191.
(2) Sigles : L = LXX; R = Recension récemment découverte; A = Aquila.

L : ιν, 5 την οδον;   ν,   3 αυτων;   ℣. 5 δηγματα   ;
R :   ]ου;   αυτου;   αρχοντας   ;
A : εν ονοματι θεου;   αυτου;   κατεσταμμενους;

L : ℣. 6 τη ταφρω;   ℣. 7 αγρωστιν;   *Jon.* III, 10 μετενοησεν;
R :   παρα[;   χο[;   ]ληθηι;
A : σειρομασταις;   ποαν;   παρεκληθη;

L : *Nah.* III,   8 ετοιμασαι μεριδα;   ℣. 9 της φυγης;   ℣. 14 πλινθον;
R :   μη αγαθυνεις υπ[;   φουδ;   ]λινθε.ου;
A :   μητι αγαθυνης υπερ;   φουδ;   πλινθιου;

L : *Hab.* I,   8 Αραβιας;   ℣. 10 εντρυφησει;   *ib.*   παιγνια;
R :   ]ρας;   ]παιξει;   γ[;
A :   εσπερας;   πομπευσει;   γελασμα;

L : II, 3 εις κενον;   *ib.* υστερηση;   ℣. 4 εαν υποστειληται ουκ ευδοκει;
R :   ]ιαψευσεται;   στραγ[;   σκοτια ουκ ευθεια;
A :   διαψευσεται;   μελληση;   ιδου νωχελευομενου ουκ ευθεια;

L : *ib.*   εκ πιστεως μου;   ℣. 15 σπηλαια;   ℣. 17 ασεβεια;   ℣ 19 εν αυτω;
R :   εν πιστει αυτου;   ]υνην;   αδικια;   εν μεσω αυ-
                                                              [του;
A :   εν πιστει αυτου;   γυμνωσιν;   αδικια;   in medio
                                                              [ejus;

L : III, 9 ποταμων;   ℣. 10   λαοι;   ℣. 14 διανοιξουσι χαλινους   ;
R :   ]μοι;   οργη;   του σκο.... αι ημας το γαυριαμα;
A :   ποταμους;   οργη;   του διασκορπισαι γαυριαμα;

L : *ib.*   πτωχος λαθρα;   *Soph.* I, 4 ιερεων;   ℣. 15   αωριας.
R :   πτωχον κρυφη;   ]ρειμ;   απορίας.
A : πενητα εν αποκρυφω;   τεμενιτων;   συμφορας.

Comme on le voit, Aquila présente des contacts plus ou moins nets avec notre texte en *Mic.* I, 4; II, 7 *a* et *b*; IV, 5; V, 3; *Jon.* III, 10; *Nah.* III, 8, 9, et 14; *Hab.* I, 8 et 10 *b*; II, 3 *a*, 4 *a* et *b*, 17 et 19; III, 10 et 14 *a*, c'est-à-dire 18 fois sur 28. Les témoignages de *Jon.* III, 10; *Nah.* III, 8; *Hab.* II, 3 *a* et III, 14 *a* paraissent particulièrement formels (1). Il semble bien que ce contact ne puisse s'expliquer que par

(1) On notera encore un point de contact entre Aquila et notre recension : l'écriture du tétragramme en lettres « phéniciennes ». A propos d'un petit fragment de Psaumes sur parchemin provenant du Fayyûm et publié par Wessely en 1910 comme faisant partie de la

Une ancienne recension de la LXX des Petits Prophètes.
Hab. i, 14-ii, 5 et ii, 13-15.

une dépendance d'Aquila à l'égard de notre recension. En effet les inconséquences du recenseur anonyme suggèrent qu'il ne s'agit que d'une ébauche dont l'œuvre d'Aquila présente l'aboutissement achevé. Si l'on voulait au contraire voir dans notre texte une recension tardive partiellement inspirée d'Aquila, il faudrait expliquer premièrement comment ce texte peut se trouver déjà très usagé dans une grotte de la Seconde Révolte, deuxièmement comment il a pu acquérir au cours du Second siècle une assez notable diffusion dans les communautés juives de la Diaspora (cf. *infra*) alors qu'il est beaucoup moins fidèle à l'hébreu que la recension d'Aquila supposée existante, et enfin troisièmement pourquoi au siècle suivant Origène ne le connaît plus comme une version en circulation, mais témoigne par contre de la grande vogue d'Aquila.

L'existence de cette première recension juive nous oblige donc à envisager l'œuvre d'Aquila sous un jour un peu différent : il s'agit d'une surrecension et non d'une traduction originale. Aquila eut le mérite d'étendre à toute la Bible sous une forme infiniment plus systématique un effort de recension qui s'était déjà fait jour dans le judaïsme palestinien avant la Seconde Révolte, très vraisemblablement en liaison avec la réforme intégriste et unificatrice qui suivit 70. Mais certaines initiatives que l'on considérait jusqu'ici comme des originalités d'Aquila doivent être restituées au premier recenseur, ainsi par exemple les créations de mots du genre de ποταμωθησονται reconnu par Rahlfs dans la citation que fait Justin de *Mic.* iv, 1.

Symmaque lui aussi manifeste une connaissance directe de notre recension. Il suffit pour s'en persuader d'envisager plusieurs cas où il reproduit, souvent sans changements, certaines de ses leçons caractéristiques alors qu'Aquila avait éprouvé le besoin de les éliminer. Ainsi en *Mic.* v, 7 il a χορτον (cf. χο[ ); en *Hab.* i, 10 a εμπαιξεται (cf.]παιξει); en *Hab.* ii, 3 b στραγγευσηται (cf. στραγ [); en *Hab.* ii, 15 ασχημοσυνην (cf.]υνην); en *Hab.* iii, 14 b πτωχον κρυφαιως (cf. πτωχον κρυφη). A ces cas s'en ajoutent dix autres où la leçon d'Aquila ne nous est pas connue mais où celle de Symmaque trahit une dépendance très probable à l'égard de notre recension :

L :	*Mic.* ii, 8 εξεδειραν;	v, 4 ακρων;	ÿ. 6 τον Ασσουρ;	*Jon.* ii, 5 εξ;
R :	εξεδυσ[;	περατων;	την γην Ασσουρ;	εξ εναντιας;
S :	εξεδυσατε;	περατων;	terram Assur;	απεναντι;

version d'Aquila — attribution contestée par Mercati (*RB.*, 1911, pp. 266-272) — je suggère la possibilité de son appartenance à notre recension dont la diffusion atteignit l'Égypte (cf. *infra*). Le tétragramme y figure aussi en « phénicien ».

L : *ib.* προς τον ναον τον αγιον σου;   IV,   1 συνεχυθη;
R :   προς ναον αγιον σου;   η..μησεν;
S :   προς ναον αγιον σου;   ηθυμησεν;

L : *Nah.* III, 7 καταβησεται;   *Hab.* I, 9 συντελεια;
R :   αποπ[;   παντα εις;
S :   recedet   ;   παντα εις;

L : *ib.* προσωποις αυτων εξ εναντιας;   III, 10 σκορπιζων;
R : του προσωπου αυτων καυσων;   εντιναγμα;
S : του προσωπου αυτων ανεμος καυσων;   εντιναγματα;

En règle générale, Symmaque présente moins d'indépendance qu'Aquila par rapport à notre recension. Lorsqu'il s'en éloigne, c'est pour des motifs littéraires plutôt que littéraux.

Quant à Théodotion, on ne trouve mentionnées que très rarement des leçons caractéristiques de lui pour les passages qui nous intéressent. Cependant, à propos de *Soph.* I, 4 que nous avons mentionné au sujet d'Aquila, il est le seul à avoir conservé la transcription χωμαρειμ de notre recension (Symmaque a βεβηλων). Mais la meilleure façon d'étudier son comportement par rapport à notre texte est de comparer sa recension de Daniel à la longue citation que Justin fait de *Dan.* VII, 9-28 au ch. XXXI du « Dialogue ». Si nous supposons, ce qui est très probable, que Justin témoigne ici encore pour notre recension, nous ne manquerons pas d'être frappés par le fait que Théodotion ne manifeste, ici du moins, aucune connaissance directe de la LXX non-recensée, mais semble avoir pris pour base notre texte. Tout comme Aquila et Symmaque il ne serait donc qu'un surrecenseur et leur base commune serait cette vieille recension palestienne de la fin du Ier siècle. Une telle conclusion suppose, sans doute, que l'on puisse attester par d'autres indices que notre recension a joui, en son temps, d'une diffusion et d'une autorité appréciables.

Si l'on ne veut pas se laisser convaincre par Justin qui se met en scène à Éphèse utilisant notre recension comme un texte reçu par les Juifs du lieu, il nous est loisible de consulter les versions coptes qui nous attesteront qu'elle fut considérée jusqu'en Égypte comme un exact témoin de la « veritas hebraica ». W. Grossouw a prouvé en effet que les très nombreuses assimilations à l'hébreu qui caractérisent le Dodécaprophéton copte (surtout sous sa forme achmimique) ne peuvent s'expliquer adéquatement ni par un recours direct au texte hébraïque, ni par une utilisation constante de l'une ou l'autre des trois grandes versions du Second siècle (1). Si l'on veut établir que c'est de notre recension que les versions coptes tirent tous leurs hébraïsmes, il faut pouvoir prouver qu'aucun de ces hébraïsmes n'est absent de notre recension. J'estime que cette preuve peut être faite. Pour aujourd'hui je me bornerai à relever un certain nombre de coïncidences particulièrement typiques en me servant de l'apparat critique de Grossouw (2). On se rendra compte aisément que notre recension est le seul témoin grec aujourd'hui connu qui groupe toutes ces leçons (3) :

Mic.	iv,	6	ην εκα[κωσα (cf. Grossouw p. 45 n. 3).
	v,	6	εν παρα[ξιφισιν
	v,	7ᵃ	χο[ρτον
Jon.	ii,	6ᶠ	η ελος περιεσχεν την κεφαλην μου
	iv,	1	η[θυ]μησεν
Nah.	iii,	7ᵃ	αποπ[ηδησεται
Hab.	i,	9ᵇ	]του προσωπου αυτων καυσων
	i,	17	εκκεν]ωσει μαχαιραν αυτου
	ii,	3ᵈ	ενφανησετ[...]ιαψευσεται (cf. Gr. p. 68 n. 3)
	ii,	14ᵈ	θαλασσ[
	ii,	15ᵈ	ασχημοσ]υνην
	iii,	13ᵇ	κε]φ[αλ]η εξ οικου ασεβ[
	iii,	13ᵉ	εξε]κενωσας θεμελιους
Soph.	ii,	10	επι λαον κυριου

Mais ce n'est pas seulement en Égypte, patrie de la LXX, que notre recension a pris pied. Nous pouvons peut-être suivre sa trace jusqu'en Grèce (ce qui rendrait toute la vraisemblance désirable à l'attestation par Justin de sa présence à Éphèse). On sait en effet, par le témoignage d'Origène lui-même (4), que ce fut « à Nicopolis près d'Actium » que la Quinta fut découverte. Or les quatre seules variantes connues de la

(1) *The Coptic Versions of the Minor Prophets*. Rome, Pontifical Biblical Institute, 1938, pp. 112 sq.

(2) *Op. cit.*, pp. 18-97. Lorsque Gr. a plusieurs notes critiques sur un même verset, je les distingue par *a*, *b*, *c*...

(3) Notons que l'hypothèse d'une dépendance des versions coptes à l'égard de notre recension est confirmée par la chronologie. On admet en effet généralement que l'origine des versions coptes est à chercher au cours du iiᵉ siècle. Or c'est justement à cette époque que se situe la plus large diffusion de la recension palestinienne. Reste à préciser si le milieu copte où se fit la traduction des Petits Prophètes était déjà purement et simplement chrétien ou s'il ne gardait pas encore quelque attache au judaïsme.

(4) Voir la discussion des textes d'Origène et d'Eusèbe dans *The Cairo Geniza* de P. KAHLE, pp. 161 sqq.

Quinta qui recoupent le contenu de nos fragments leur sont substantiellement identiques :

Q : *Mic.* v, 5 principes hominum;   *ib.* εν παραξιφισιν
R :   αρχοντας ανθρωπων;   εν παρα[

Q : *Hab.* ii, 15 ignominias eorum;   iii, 13 evacuasti fundamentum
R :   ασχημοσ]υνην αυ[τω]ν;   εξε]κενωσας θεμελιους

Q : usque ad collum sela.
R : εως τραχ[ηλου] σελε.

Les très légères variantes qui, dans les deux derniers exemples, distinguent le texte de nos fragments de la Quinta telle qu'elle est citée
par Jérôme n'excèdent pas les divergences que l'on est en droit d'attendre à l'intérieur de la tradition manuscrite d'un même texte. Si l'on
veut encore un argument convergent pour l'identification de notre
recension avec la Quinta d'Origène (1), on remarquera que, selon les
statistiques de Grossouw (2), les hébraïsmes des versions coptes
concordent douze fois de façon indubitable avec des leçons de la Quinta
et ne s'y opposent *jamais* formellement, alors qu'il leur arrive de
contredire quatre fois Théodotion, onze fois Aquila et onze fois Symmaque.

Je ne voudrais pas grossir l'importance de cette recension juive de
la fin du Premier siècle. Il ne s'agit, répétons-le, que d'une première
tentative encore tâtonnante et pleine d'illogismes, certainement limitée
à quelques livres de la Bible. Il n'est pas étonnant que les grandes
recensions du Second siècle l'aient entièrement éclipsée et qu'au début
du siècle suivant Origène ait dû déjà, comme nous aujourd'hui, la
« redécouvrir ». Elle joua cependant en son temps un rôle appréciable :
celui d'amorcer l'œuvre de révision de la LXX qui allait être la grande
tâche des générations qui suivirent. Le travail de l'ancêtre anonyme
d'Aquila et d'Origène mérite donc une publication que nous espérons
pouvoir aborder sans trop tarder. De cette publication nous pouvons
attendre un triple témoignage : premièrement sur l'état du texte de
base de la LXX, deuxièmement sur l'état du texte hébreu utilisé par
le recenseur, troisièmement sur l'exacte originalité de chacun des trois

(1) Je parle ici de la Quinta telle qu'elle est citée par Jérôme et je laisse de côté la question délicate des citations attribuées à la Quinta par le second glossateur marginal du *codex
Barberini*... qui mériterait une étude spéciale.
(2) *Op. cit.*, p. 112.

grands recenseurs du Second siècle. Ce témoignage se trouvera encore élargi si on accepte la quadruple identification que nous proposons aujourd'hui : premièrement avec le texte cité par Justin, deuxièmement avec la base commune d'Aquila, Symmaque et Théodotion, troisièmement avec la source des hébraïsmes des versions coptes, et quatrièmement avec la Quinta d'Origène. Tant que le texte n'est pas édité il ne peut s'agir que de suggestions. Elles appelleront certainement telles ou telles nuances notables, mais j'espère qu'elles pourront servir au moins d'hypothèses de recherche .

Jérusalem, 19 septembre 1952.   D. BARTHÉLEMY, O. P.

Appendice :

Une des parties les mieux conservées de notre recension portant sur les deux premiers chapitres d'Habacuc pour lesquels nous nous trouvons posséder deux textes hébraïques assez différents : celui du *Pésher* de Qumrân (Q pH) et celui de la Bible massorétique (T. M.), voici un très bref apparat critique où j'ai seulement relevé les appuis donnés par la Septante originale (LXX) et sa recension palestinienne (Rec), lorsque leurs témoignages respectifs les départagent nettement, aux deux formes susdites du texte hébraïque. Nombre de cas plus complexes demanderaient toute une discussion. Dans cet aperçu provisoire, je les ai délibérément omis.

	T.M.		QpH	
I, 8	יבאו	: Rec	om.)	: LXX
I, 17	העל כן	: Rec	על כן	: LXX
ibid.	חרמו	: LXX	חרבו	: Rec
II, 2	קורא	: Rec	הקורא	: LXX
II, 6	ויאמר	: Rec	ויומרו	: LXX
ibid.	עליו	: Rec	עלו	: LXX
II, 8	ישלוך	: LXX	וישלוכה	: Rec
II, 19	דומם	: Rec	רומה	: LXX

En six cas sur huit nous trouvons donc la recension palestinienne aux côtés du T. M. tandis que la LXX originale témoignait pour le texte de Qumrân. Cela semble indiquer que la date de 70 ap. J.-C. marque une étape importante dans le processus de recension du texte hébreu, ce que confirme pleinement une comparaison des textes bibliques de la Seconde Révolte avec ceux de Qumrân.

NEW LIGHT ON EARLY RECENSIONS OF THE HEBREW BIBLE

W. F. Albright

The publication of the Dead Sea Scrolls, though still in an early stage, has now reached a point where we can begin to discuss recensional problems in the early Hebrew text of many books of the Bible. In this brief article I wish to point out certain directions along which future research will have to move; it is thus programmatic and lays no claim to being anything but a pioneer attempt. Now that the chronology of the principal types of script used in the Qumran scrolls and fragments is pretty well established, thanks especially to the recent work of Frank M. Cross,

Jr.,[1] refining and extending the results of John C. Trever,[2] the writer,[3] and especially of S. A. Birnbaum,[4] we can attack the recensional problems with more confidence.

Recognition of the existence of early Hebrew recensions is not new. Though there has never hitherto been any clear evidence for different recensions in the extant Hebrew and Samaritan manuscripts, the text of some of the Greek books differs so widely from the Massoretic Hebrew tradition that divergent Hebrew recensions must be assumed.[5] Thus H. M. Orlinsky wrote in his analysis of the present state of Septuagintal studies, published nearly fifteen years ago: " Of course there was at one time more than one text-tradition of the Hebrew Bible. The Hebrew manuscripts used by the several Septuagint translators of the various books in the Old Testament differ at times not in minor details alone, but, as is the case in such books as Jeremiah, Job, Esther, *recensionally* from the masoretic text-tradition. But these text-traditions have long perished . . ." [6]

The greatest textual surprise of the Qumran finds has probably been the fact that most of the scrolls and fragments present a consonantal text which is virtually indistinguishable from the text of corresponding passages in our Massoretic Bible. The new material carries Hebrew examples of the proto-Massoretic text back into the second century B. C., and there are many Qumran manuscripts, long and short, of this type from the last century and a half of the Second Temple, as well as Murabba'ât texts of Massoretic type from the late first and early second centuries A. D.[7] The complete Isaiah Scroll (1QIs[a]), now in Israel, is written in a text which belongs to the proto-Massoretic type, though

[1] See especially his splendid paper in *Jour. Bib. Lit.*, LXXIV (1955), pp. 147-165; I have no suggestions for revision of his chronology.

[2] See BULLETIN, No. 113 (1949), pp. 6-23, and for his important subsequent studies and photographic experiments see *Proc. Amer. Philos. Soc.*, 97 (1953), pp. 184-193, and the revised reprint of the latter in *The Smithsonian Report*, 1953, pp. 425-435.

[3] See most recently BULLETIN, No. 115 (1949), pp. 10-19, in which I referred to most of the material I had been gathering since 1937 for a new study of the palaeography of the Nash Papyrus. It is interesting to note that my original preference for the first half of the period to which I had assigned this papyrus (placed in 1937 somewhere between cir. 150 and 50 B. C., but in no case later than the accession of Herod the Great in 37 B. C.) is now shown by Cross to be better than my 1949 date in the second half of this period.

[4] See especially his monograph, *The Qumran (Dead Sea) Scrolls and Palaeography* (BULLETIN, *Supplementary Studies*, Nos. 13-14, 1952), and his great work, *The Hebrew Scripts* (London, 1955—), now in its second fascicle (for a notice of the first see BULLETIN, No. 139, p. 24).

[5] A beginning along this line was made by the late A. T. Olmstead in his papers in *Am. Jour. Sem. Lang.*, XXX (1913), pp. 1-35, and XXXI (1915), pp. 169-214, with considerable acumen but with very questionable method; against his views see J. A. Montgomery's commentary on *Kings* (ICC, 1951), pp. 251 f., and my comments in *Jour. Bib. Lit.*, LXXI (1952), p. 250. The trouble with Olmstead's treatment is that he assumed a series of late revisions of the *Hebrew*, as well as of the Greek text even *after* the original LXX translation. The Jeroboam story of LXX he considered to go back to a Hebrew original antedating our MT.

[6] *Jour. Amer. Orient. Soc.*, LXI (1941), p. 85b.

[7] This point has been emphasized by the scholars working on the Scrolls; cf. n. 15 below.

it has a much fuller vocalization with the aid of *waw* and *yodh* [8] and does have a few very useful variants, as well as a great many careless readings.[9]

Only a little less surprising than the new evidence for the great age of the consonantal tradition on which the Massoretic text depends, is the discovery of portions of Exodus, Deuteronomy, and especially of Samuel in recensions which are much closer to the LXX than they are to MT, though they usually differ from both and sometimes exhibit a text which is obviously older than either.[10] The earliest so far found fragments of this type seem to go back into the late third century B.C. and are in any case pre-Maccabaean.[11] The new texts of Samuel, especially 4QSam[a] which represents portions of the text of at least two-thirds of the chapters in I and II Samuel, show that Wellhausen and Driver were entirely wrong in considering the LXX translation as so free as often to be a paraphrase of its Hebrew prototype; actually its fidelity to the Hebrew prototype is much greater than has often been assumed. We now know that in the fragments so far described from the Pentateuch and the Former Prophets (Joshua-Judges-Samuel-Kings) the Greek translators were almost slavish in their literalism (though they seldom pushed it to the point of absurdity, as later done by Aquila). When we find sections preserved in the LXX (i.e., in the Egyptian recension of Codex B and its congeners) that are missing in MT, as well as completely different forms of names, we may thus be reasonably certain that they are not inner Greek additions or corruptions, but go back to an older Hebrew recension which differed from MT.

Returning to our proto-Massoretic texts from Qumran, we can now revert to the position shared by tradition and by scholars of the Wellhausen and related schools of criticism, that many of the older books of our Hebrew Bible were edited in approximately their present form in Babylonia and were then brought back to Palestine by the returning exiles during the late sixth and the fifth centuries B.C. This point of view, once taken for granted by most conservatives and liberals alike, has been rejected by many recent students, but is strongly supported by archaeological evidence.[12] We now have most striking confirmatory evidence from the first Qumran Isaiah Scroll, referred to above. In this text we have a number of correct vocalizations of Assyro-Babylonian words and names: *Šar'uṣur* (*ŠR'WṢR*) for MT *Šar'éṣer* and LXX

---

[8] See Dewey M. Beegle, BULLETIN, No. 123 (1951), pp. 26-30; Millar Burrows, BULLETIN, No. 124, pp. 18-20.

[9] See Burrows, *The Dead Sea Scrolls* (New York, 1955), pp. 303-314. However, Burrows's extremely judicious selection by no means exhausts the list of important variants in this scroll, which I have studied repeatedly with my students.

[10] See especially Cross, BULLETIN, No. 132 (1953), pp. 15-26, and *Jour. Bib. Lit.*, LXXIV, pp. 165-172 (cf. *Christian Century*, Aug. 10, 1955, p. 921); Patrick W. Skehan, BULLETIN, No. 136 (1954), pp. 12-15 (cf. n. 27).

[11] See Cross, *Jour. Bib. Lit.*, LXXIV, p. 164.

[12] For the evidence supporting the completeness of the devastation of Judah in the early sixth century and the historicity of the Exile and Restoration see most recently the references in Albright, *The Bible after Twenty Years of Archaeology (1932-1952)*, reprinted by the Biblical Colloquium (Pittsburgh, 1955), *Notes*, p. 3.

Sarasar; turtân (*TWRTN*) for MT *tartān* and LXX *Tanathan*, etc.;
'*Urarat* ('*WRRT*) for MT '*Arārāt* and Greek *Ararath*. There are many
similar correct occurrences of the vowel-letter *W* for *u, o* in 1QIsᵃ, including a considerable number which are not in Beegle's excellent paper,[13]
but these correct vocalizations of Assyro-Babylonian words are particularly striking. In a text handed down in Babylonia such precise tradition
is not at all surprising, since we know from the work of O. Neugebauer
and A. J. Sachs that cuneiform scribes were still active in the latter part
of the first century A. D. In the West it would be very unlikely *a priori*,
and the LXX transcriptions from the second (or even late third) century
B. C. prove that there was no such fixed tradition.

I have maintained for several years that the prototype of the first
Isaiah Scroll came from Babylonia, probably in the second half of the
second century B. C. There is supporting evidence, into which we have
no room to go here.[14] 1QIsᵃ is thus an offshoot of the proto-Massoretic
text-tradition in Babylonia, where it may have developed further for
several centuries after the ancestral Hebrew text was taken by the returning exiles to Palestine; this would help to explain some divergences
from MT, as well as the generally inferior character of the text when
compared with the proto-Massoretic of the second Isaiah Scroll (1QIsᵇ),
etc., which is virtually identical with MT.[15]

Returning now to the Egyptian recension of the LXX, we note that
there is much evidence of pre-Septuagintal Egyptian influence on the text
of several books. I formerly thought that this evidence of Egyptian influence on the LXX pointed to the translators themselves, in the third
century B. C.[16] However, in a period of such strong Greek influence on
the Egyptian Jews, many of whom had been brought to Egypt by the
Lagides as captives or had recently come as traders, it is scarcely likely
that the Jews would have treated the Hebrew consonantal text with such
freedom merely to exhibit their knowledge of native Egyptian. Moreover, we are in a position to demonstrate from the Qumran fragments
so far published that the translators were extremely careful not to depart
from the Hebrew text that lay before them. We are, therefore, compelled

---

[13] BULLETIN, No. 123 (1951), pp. 26-30.

[14] Suffice it to say here that this evidence is partly derived from Essene beliefs
and practices, such as the strong Mazdayasnian and specifically Zervanite dualism
(to which attention has been drawn particularly by K. G. Kuhn, A. Dupont-Sommer,
and Henri Michaud), and the emphasis placed on lustration by water (as still in
Mandaeanism) as well as upon quasi-science (according to Josephus).   There are
also historical arguments pointing to a movement from Babylonia in the second
century B. C. (cf. the Damascus Document, i).

[15] On the other Isaiah scroll and fragments so far published see most recently
Burrows, *The Dead Sea Scrolls*, pp. 314 f.; F. M. Cross in the *Christian Century*,
August 10, 1955, pp. 920. The original publications by the Hebrew University on
behalf of the late E. L. Sukenik, *Ôṣār ham-megillôt hag-genûzôt* (Jerusalem, 1954),
by James Muilenburg, BULLETIN, No. 135, pp. 28-32, and by P. W. Skehan, *Cath.
Bib. Quar.*, XVII (1955), pp. 158-163, provide all the supporting evidence necessary.
There is already a respectable literature on the second Isaiah scroll alone.

[16] Cf. my *Archaeology of Palestine and the Bible* (1932), p. 143, and my observations in *The Biblical Period* (in Louis Finkelstein, *The Jews*, 1949), p. 6.

to reckon with the probability that the translators dealt piously with a text which had been handed down for generations in Egypt itself. We can probably fix the time at which the Egyptian recensions of the Pentateuch and Samuel-Kings were edited about the fifth century B. C. (presumably not before the sixth century or after the fourth in any book).

I shall limit myself to a few examples. The Egyptian name of Joseph appears as *ṢPNTP'NḤ* which, as long ago pointed out by Spiegelberg, stands for an Egyptian *Ḍd-p₃-nṯr-iw.f-'nḫ*, pronounced in the early first millennium approximately *Čepnūtef'anḫ*.[17] This name belongs to a type which was in common use about the tenth century B. C. However, the Greek equivalent in Gen. 41: 45 is *Psonthomphanech* for a Late Egyptian **Psontenpa'anḫ*, " The Creator (or Sustainer) of Life," [18] obviously substituted for a somewhat different consonantal form which had become unintelligible by the Achaemenian period (even assuming that MT had been transmitted correctly to Egypt). The new form of the word made such excellent sense as an appellation of Joseph that we can be quite certain that the editor of the Egyptian recension or a precursor knew Egyptian very well and considered it important to show that he did. There is even more striking evidence in Genesis. We may expect the correct equivalents Heliopolis and Heroönpolis for On and Pithom,[19] respectively, but it is much more remarkable to find Heb. *Góšen*, " Goshen," replaced by "Arabian Gesem" in two passages (Gen. 45: 10 and 46: 34). A year ago Dr. Isaac Rabinowitz pointed out to the Society of Biblical Literature that the peculiar Greek form *Gesem* for *Góšen* evidently goes back to the famous Arabian king Geshem, Nehemiah's foe, mentioned on silver bowls found at or near Tell el-Maskhûṭah, ancient Pithom-Heroönpolis.[20] Since Geshem's rule extended from the eastern Delta of Egypt to the frontier of Judaea on the northeast and at least as far as Dedan (el-'Ulā) in the south,[21] he was a very important chieftain who must have made a name for himself in the half-century immediately preceding the restoration of Egyptian independence under Amyrtaeus (cir. 400 B. C.). Rabinowitz is undoubtedly right in explaining *Gesem Arabías* for Heb. *Góšen* as a reminiscence of the Arabian prince Geshem. This makes it difficult to date the editing of the Egyptian recension of Genesis before about 400 (Geshem presumably reigned between 450 and 420 B. C.) or after the beginning of the Greek period (330 B. C.). A very interesting example of the difference between the Egyptian and Babylonian recensions of Genesis is the fact that the former substitutes "land of the Chaldaeans" for "Ur of the Chaldaeans" in the story of Abram. As suggested by the Book of Jubilees (probably from the first quarter of the second century B. C.) the original Hebrew text included the words rendered "Ur in the land of the Chaldaeans" (*'R B-'RṢ H-KŚDYM*), which the Babylonian Jewish scribes (who knew Ur very well) corrupted by haplography to *'R H-KŚDYM*, "Ur of the Chaldaeans," while the Egyptian Jews (who knew nothing of Ur) corrupted the original text, by the alter-

---

[17] This explanation we owe to Spiegelberg, *Zeits. f. ägypt. Spr.*, XXVII, pp. 41 f.; XXX, pp. 50 ff.; for names of the same formation see the long list in H. Ranke, *Die ägyptischen Personennamen*, pp. 409-412, who attributes them to the outgoing New Kingdom (specifically to the XXth Dynasty), and especially to the XXIst Dynasty and the following period.

[18] For this explanation see *Jour. Bib. Lit.*, XXXVII (1918), p. 132, where I was wrong in regarding the LXX form as original.

[19] In Gen. 46: 28 f., we have a very remarkable substitution in the Egyptian recension of LXX (fortunately B is extant here). Where MT twice offers *Góšᵉnāh*, " to Goshen," the LXX has " by way of Heroönpolis," which the derived Coptic correctly rendered by " Pithom "; where MT has *'arṣāh Góšen*, the LXX substitutes " to the land of Rameses " (just as both versions offer in Gen. 47: 11). The mention of Pithom and Rameses evidently goes back to the Hebrew prototype of LXX.

[20] Cf. provisionally F. M. Cross, *Biblical Archaeologist*, XVIII (1955), pp. 46 f., and my remarks on the chronology in BULLETIN, No. 139, p. 19.

[21] For our previous knowledge of Geshem and the extent of his power see especially my discussion in the Alt *Festschrift* (*Geschichte und Altes Testament*, 1953), pp. 4 ff.

native haplography, to *'RṢ H-KŚDYM*, "land of the Chaldaeans." One might adduce other illustrations, but we have no space.

In Kings we have two very interesting forms of an Egyptian personal name which reflect quite different Egyptian originals. I Kings 11: 19 f. mentions the name of an Egyptian queen of the late XXIst Dynasty, about the second quarter of the tenth century B. C., as *Taḥpenēs* (*THPNYS*); this the Greek reproduces as *Thekemina*, which obviously reflects an entirely different Egyptian name, since there is no indication of inner Greek corruption. While the MT form of the name does look suspiciously like *THPNḤŚ*, Greek Daphne in the northeastern Delta,[22] there is no reason to doubt that the name has been correctly transmitted. If so, it may stand for an Egyptian **T3-ḥn.t-p3* (or *pr*)-*nsw*, "She Whom the King (or Palace) Protects," [23] to be pronounced something like **Taḥnepinse*, or **Taḥepinse* with dissimilation of the first *n*. However, the name may be corrupt, and there are many long names from the XXIst and XXIInd Dynasties which begin and end with the same consonants.[24] *Thekemina*, on the other hand, seems rather transparent; I should identify it provisionally with an Egyptian **T3-k3i-(n.t)-mn*, "The Female Attendant (or the like) of Min," which would be pronounced something like **Tekemin*. In Late Egyptian we have a name with the same meaning and form in *T3-ḥnr.t-(n.t)-mn*, "The Concubine of Min." [25] Min, the god of Koptos, was renowned for his role as an ithyphallic producer of life. The pejorative sense which could be attributed to *k3i* (translated by German scholars as "Dirne") [26] can scarcely have been overlooked by the editors of the Hebrew prototype of the Greek Kings.

It must be emphasized strongly that the Egyptian editions of different biblical books may have quite different recensional backgrounds, and that we know far too little to be dogmatic. I should be inclined to consider the Egyptian Pentateuch as essentially of Babylonian origin, i. e., it generally reflects the text which had probably been established in Babylonia during the sixth century B. C. This text was brought back to Judah and may have become canonical under Ezra's influence in the late fifth century. There are, of course, other possibilities. Some of the sharp deviations which we find, for instance, in Deut. 32, especially in verse 43 where the Greek has eight cola as against four in MT and six in the Qumran fragment recently published by Mgr. Skehan,[27] warn us

---

[22] On this see my observations in the Bertholet *Festschrift* (1950), pp. 13 f., with references to the literature.

[23] For names of this formation see H. Ranke, *op. cit.*, p. 365: 24 f., both from the XXIst Dynasty, and for the substitution of a word for "the king" or "house of the king (*pr-nsw*)" see *ibid.*, p. 355: 23, again from the XXIst Dynasty.

[24] The original Egyptian name may have begun with the feminine article, *t3*, and have ended with (*n.t*)-*ist*, "of Isis," like various names from the same general period cited by Ranke, but this explanation seems less likely.

[25] Ranke, *op. cit.*, p. 367: 2.

[26] There are quite a number of names formed with the word *k3r.t*, *k3i*, *kry*, which is treated by Erman-Grapow, *Wörterbuch der ägyptischen Sprache*, V, p. 101; it may go back to the classical Egyptian word *k3.t*, "vulva" (cf. Heb. *raḥam*) and it is always feminine in personal names, whether it has the feminine ending or not. From the XIXth and XXth Dynasty come names like *T3-k3r.t*, etc. (Ranke, *loc. cit.*, p. 370: 21, 371: 5-6, 8, 11, 14-15) and much later names like *T3-kr-ḥb* or *T3-kr-Dḥw.ty* (*ibid.*, p. 371: 12 f.), "The Concubine of Thoth." Note that the vocalization of the word for "Dirne" seems to have been originally *ku'e*, *kuya* and would have become approximately *ke* in later times. Observe further that the attribution of a name with such definitely pejorative connotation (for the Jews) to the sister-in-law of the Edomite rebel would be on a par with the statement in the Egyptian recension of Kings that Jeroboam's mother was a harlot.

[27] I should propose the following tentative original Hebrew form of the Egyptian

not to underestimate the possibility that the Egyptian Hebrew prototype had been influenced by Palestinian MS readings handed down independently of the Babylonian text-tradition. The complex situation in the earliest fragments of Samuel from Qumran, with which Frank M. Cross is dealing, suggests a basic form of text antedating sixth-century Babylonian copies. Such MSS as 4QSam[a] and 4QSam[b] reflect a text which antedates both the Hebrew prototype of the LXX and the proto-Massoretic text,[28] and may thus preserve textual elements going directly back to the original Deuteronomic Samuel, compiled toward the end of the seventh century B. C. We must patiently await the results of Cross's work before jumping at conclusions.

Other biblical books must eventually be restudied in the light of this program; we may mention particularly the Egyptian Isaiah, which perhaps separated recensionally from the proto-Massoretic text as late as the third century B. C., and Jeremiah, which presumably circulated in Egypt as early as the sixth century—thus perhaps accounting for the drastic divergences in content and order between LXX and MT. All such suggestions must await detailed study of the thousands of unpublished fragments from Qumran IV.[29]

---

recension, on the basis of MT and the new fragment (a word which departs from the Greek translation is marked by an asterisk):

Harnînû šāmáyim 'immô	we-hištahawû lô benê 'Elôhîm
Harnînû gôyîm 'et le'ummô	we-hithazzeqû lô ( ) mal'akê 'El
kî dam *'abādāw yiqqōm	we-nāqām yāšîb le-ṣārāw
u-le-meśanne'āw yešallēm	we-kipper ( ) 'admat 'ammô

The words which are preserved in MT are not italicized but left in Roman type. The new fragment has the first, third, and fourth bicolon substantially as given above, though with two verbal and one morphemic difference. The parallelism in the Egyptian recension is much better than in MT, so there can be little doubt that this text is very ancient. In such cases, where we may have to do with orally transmitted texts, it is dangerous to speak of relative originality of recensions. However, my own impression is that the Egyptian recension, after a few minor corrections on the basis of the other two recensions, presents a satisfactory archaic text.

[28] See above, note 10.

[29] We have not discussed the extremely interesting publication by Mgr. Skehan of a recension of Exodus which conforms closely to the Samaritan text and is actually written in proto-Samaritan script (resembling the latest preëxilic cursive, but not directly derived from it). My long-standing opinion that both the Samaritan and proto-Samaritan scripts are archaizing rather than archaic is shared by S. Yeivin and now by Cross: cf. my remarks in *From the Stone Age to Christianity* (1940), pp. 266, 336, and BULLETIN, No. 115, p. 14; Yeivin, BULLETIN, No. 118, pp. 28-30; Cross, *Jour. Bib. Lit.*, LXXIV, p. 147, n. 1. I doubt whether any of the fragments in proto-Samaritan script antedate the last century B. C. The recension differs only slightly from MT, and it obviously springs from the proto-Massoretic of Qumran.

THE OLDEST MANUSCRIPTS FROM QUMRAN

FRANK M. CROSS, JR.

McCORMICK THEOLOGICAL SEMINARY

DISCOVERY in 1952 of some three hundred fragmentary manuscripts in Cave 4, Qumran, all dating before the First Jewish Revolt, as well as the discovery of documents of the first and second centuries A. D. in the region of Wadi Murabba'at, some with date formulae, have made possible new advances in the study of early Jewish paleography.[1] Were this find of material not sufficient, Qumran has provided a series of ostraca (partly unpublished) in controlled archeological contexts,[2] and Cave 4 itself, like the caves of Murabba'at, has produced associated materials in other scripts, notably Greek, yielding confirmation of the results of Jewish paleography on independent paleographic grounds.

The overwhelming lot of new documents does not materially alter conclusions of previous specialists in Hebrew and Aramaic epigraphy. As early as 1937, the main lines of the development of the script from the

[1] For the sake of clarity, we distinguish here between the "Jewish" script and the older (common) Aramaic script of the 4th–3rd centuries B. C. from which it derives, just as in the case of Nabatean and Palmyrene. It is used, of course, to write Hebrew and Aramaic. Over against it is the resurgent Paleo-Hebrew script of the Maccabean era, descended from Israelite times, but at Qumran archaizing, and roughly contemporary with the Maccabean "Jewish" hand. The present paper does not attempt to deal with the Paleo-Hebrew script; new evidence is in hand, however, which provides a solution in principle.

[2] For example, the practice alphabet from Level I (before 31 B. C.) published by De Vaux, "Fouilles au Khirbet Qumrân," *RB*, LXI (1954), Pl. Xa; cf. p. 229. While the forms are crudely made, it is clear in a number of cases *how* the scribe means to make his letter. *Beth* is corrected; note, however, that in both forms the lower (baseline) horizontal stroke is made from right to left continuous with the vertical; contrary to the cursive, and to the later formal hand, the base does not break through the vertical to the right. The left arm of *gimel* is high and horizontal; *daleth* is fairly narrow and long. *Ṭeth* (note flat bottom), *mem* (broad and short to the point of distortion), *'ayn, pe,* and *shin* (note curved left arms on all specimens) are all characteristically developed forms. *Zayn* has no tendency to bulge to the right at the top; *samekh* is closed, but perhaps too crudely made to be useful; the leg of *qoph* is *moderately* long; the left leg of *'aleph* is lengthened, and inclining towards a vertical rather than a horizontal or crescent stance as in the preceding two stages of the script; the cross-bar of *ḥeth* is lowered. In short, we have a mixture of developed and undeveloped letters characteristic of that stage of the script known as "transition to Herodian," according to typology, here confirmed in an archeological context.

fifth century to the time of the First Revolt had become sufficiently clear to permit W. F. Albright's definitive redating of the Nash Papyrus.[3] It is possible now, however, to clarify a number of obscurities, and to refine the limits within which a given typical script may be dated.

Two crucial tasks of the paleography of our period can be accomplished now with greater precision. The first, and most important, is a detailed description of the parallel courses of evolution of the bookhand (formal script) on the one hand, and the cursive on the other. The organization of a typological series with scores of exemplars of the formal script, both from MSS and inscriptions, is now in progress; this paper deals with the earliest and most problematical section of the series. Similarly, the cursive series can be set up, though with fewer specimens. From Qumran, MSS exhibiting both hands stand side by side from the second century B. C. until the First Revolt. Documents from Murabba'at and associated finds continue the series in the first and second centuries A. D. The cursive hand is rare in biblical scrolls, as might be expected, though frequent in sectarian, and especially Aramaic documents.

A second task is the study of the separation of the related scripts, Jewish, Palmyrene, and Nabatean, from the parent Aramaic script. This effort is aided by new materials in both Palmyrene and Nabatean as well as by the early biblical documents in Jewish script from Qumran, the

---

[3] "A Biblical Fragment from the Maccabaean Age: The Nash Papyrus," *JBL*, LVI (1937), 145–76 (hereafter abbreviated *AN*). Cf. "On the Date of the Scrolls from *'Ain Feshkha* and the Nash Papyrus," *BASOR*, No. 115 (Oct., 1949), pp. 10–19. Albright's original Nash article remains the classical organization of the field of Aramaic and Jewish paleography. Despite the vast increases in epigraphic data, not to mention the finds in the Wilderness of Judah, his date in the Maccabean Period remains undisturbed. Indeed, his original preference for a date in the second half of the second century needs scant revision. All characteristic letters of Nash are earlier in form than 1QIsa[a]. *'Aleph* has a short, curved left arm (aside from early, looped, cursive forms); *beth* is still small and curved; the later form with a rectangular lower right corner has not yet developed; especially significant, *daleth* is long and narrow; *yodh* is a three-stroke form; *mem* is far more narrow, especially at the top, in both medial and final forms; *pe* is rounded at the top and bottom; *resh* is extremely narrow; *qoph* has a very short leg. Birnbaum was the first to relate correctly Nash and 1QIsa[a] ("The Dates of the Cave Scrolls," *BASOR*, No. 115 [Oct., 1949], pp. 20–22). His relative chronology is superb; his absolute chronology appears to be a bit too high. Trever's arguments to date 1QIsa[a] earlier than Nash (J. C. Trever, "A Paleographic Study of the Jerusalem Scrolls," *BASOR*, No. 113 [Feb., 1949], p. 19) are based chiefly on Isaiah's non-use of modified forms of final letters, an idiosyncrasy of the MS, irrelevant to dating. As a matter of fact, we can now show (see below) that the late third century featured a more developed use of final letters than later periods. The cursive forms of Nash: looped *'aleph*, *he*, and looped *taw*, in particular, are mixed with formal types. But these cursive forms must be dated in the cursive series, not in that of the bookhand. In the former they stand quite early. A date in the early Maccabean period, *ca.* 150 B. C., or even slightly earlier, seems best.

latter mostly unpublished as yet. As a matter of fact, exemplars of the early Jewish bookhand and cursive from Qumran span precisely the period of divergence of the Palmyrene and Nabatean hands. This combination of materials enables us to apply more checks from outside in the effort to achieve an absolute chronology for the typological series of Jewish hands in the early period; of course an absolute chronology from the late first century B. C. to the second century A. D. is already closely fixed by datable epigraphs and dated documents of several kinds.

I

THE ARAMAIC SCRIPT OF THE FOURTH CENTURY B. C. AND ITS THIRD CENTURY DERIVATIVES[4]

The Aramaic chancellery script of the Persian Empire was in use from Asia Minor in the northwest, to North Arabia and Egypt to the south, and to Afghanistan eastward. To judge from inscriptional evidence, it remained homogeneous, at least in its essential characteristics, over this broad area until the fall of the Persian power. Studies of the development of Jewish scripts must begin with the cursive hands of the late fifth and fourth century B. C., the immediate (extant) ancestor of the Jewish bookhand, as well as cursive scripts from Egypt from the early third century, the immediate ancestor of the Jewish cursive hand. Our chief exemplars of the fourth-century script, aside from lapidary inscriptions which are not directly useful, are from Egypt, published by

---

[4] The key to Fig. 1 is as follows:

Line 1. An advanced cursive from Elephantine, dating to *ca.* 419 B. C. From Sachau, *Aramäische Papyrus, usw.* (Leipzig, 1911), Pap. 18, Pls. 17–20. The asterisk notes final forms; the siglum ¹ a form from Sachau, Pap. 20. Pl. 23.

Line 2. The Aramaic cursive of the first half of the fourth century B. C. From N. Aimé-Giron, *Textes araméens d'Egypte* (Cairo, 1931), Pl. X, Pap. 87. Cf. also Ostracon 4 *bis*, Pl. I; and Pap. 86 *bis* (393–381 B. C.), 88, 89. The siglum ¹ designates a letter taken from Pap. 88.

Line 3. The cursive of the end of the fourth century. From Sachau, *op. cit., Tafel* 62:2.

Line 4. The Aramaic cursive of the early third century (*ca.* 275 B. C.). From M. Lidzbarski, *Ephemeris für semitische Epigraphik III, Tafel* II. The letter bearing the siglum ² is taken from an ostracon of similar date, *ibid., Tafel* III.

Line 5. The Aramaic cursive of the early third century B. C. From an Edfū papyrus published by A. H. Sayce and A. Cowley, *Proceedings of the Society of Biblical Archaeology*, XXXVII (1915), 217 ff. (cf. G. R. Driver, *The Hebrew Scrolls* [London, 1951], Pl. II); the sigla ³ and ⁴ refer respectively to the papyrus published by Sayce-Cowley, *Proceedings*, XXIX (1907), Pls. I, II (from Edfū), and the ostracon published by Weill, *Revue des études juives*, LXV (1913), 16–23 (from Zâwiyet el-Meitîn).

All forms are traced from enlarged photographs.

Aimé-Giron in 1931,[5] and Papyrus Luparensis.[6] The Aimé-Giron papyri date from the first half of the century, and show only the slightest development from the late cursive script of Elephantine. The Papyrus Luparensis must be dated *ca.* 350 B. C.[7]

Distinctions between broad and narrow strokes within letters are still preserved in the fourth century, though the tendency towards a "monotonous" stroke, to gain sway in the third-century cursive, has already begun.[8] The development of medial letters commences in the late fifth-century cursives. The long downstrokes below the (theoretical) baseline all begin to bend to the left in what may be called "semi-ligatures." So-called "final" letters, actually the older forms preserved where the tendency towards creating "semi-ligatures" is not so strong, are used in late fifth-century and early fourth-century cursives, though not systematically. Medial and final *kaph*, medial and final *pe*, medial (and possibly final) *ṣade*, as well as medial and final *nun* are becoming clearly distinguished. *Mem* in the medial position frequently exhibits a curving left diagonal stroke, as opposed to the older (and "final") straight diagonal. "Medial" *lamedh*, i. e., with a narrow hooked base, is clearly distinguished first in the fourth century.

The extreme difference in the length of various letters below the ceiling line characteristic of the fifth century persists, with *kaph*, *mem*, *nun* (medial as well as final), *pe* (medial and final), *ṣade* (normally), and *taw* extending far beneath a theoretical baseline.

'Aleph in the fourth century is developed beyond fifth-century forms as follows: the left leg is no longer a short, nearly horizontal straight line; it has become a crescent-shaped stroke which usually cuts the diagonal at the base on the lower side, as well as protruding in a high, curved point on the upper left of the diagonal. *Beth* is still gently rounded at the bottom right as it curves to the horizontal. *Daleth* is long and narrow, as in the fifth century, while *resh* is still narrower, but shorter. *He* (see also Fig. 3) is still made in classical fashion, with the horizontal arm drawn from right to left. In the fourth century, there is a notable tendency for the cross-bar of *ḥeth* to bulge upwards following the right vertical downstroke; the cross-bar comes down again for a partial loop to the left vertical downstroke. *Ṭeth* is long, pointed at the base, with a high left arm, little developed from earlier forms. *Yodh* is made with a triple

---

[5] For references to literature, here and below, see n. 4. For convenient reference to fifth-century forms, see F. Rosenthal, *Die aramaistische Forschung* (Leiden, 1939), *Schrifttafel* 3. The new leather documents published by Driver, *Aramaic Documents*, *etc.* (Oxford, 1954), present normally the more formal hand of the period.

[6] See Fig. 2, line 1, and n. 14.

[7] *'Aleph, lamedh, nun, mem, 'ayn*, and especially *ṣade* are here slightly more developed than in the Aimé-Giron texts.

[8] Cf. *AN*, p. 153.

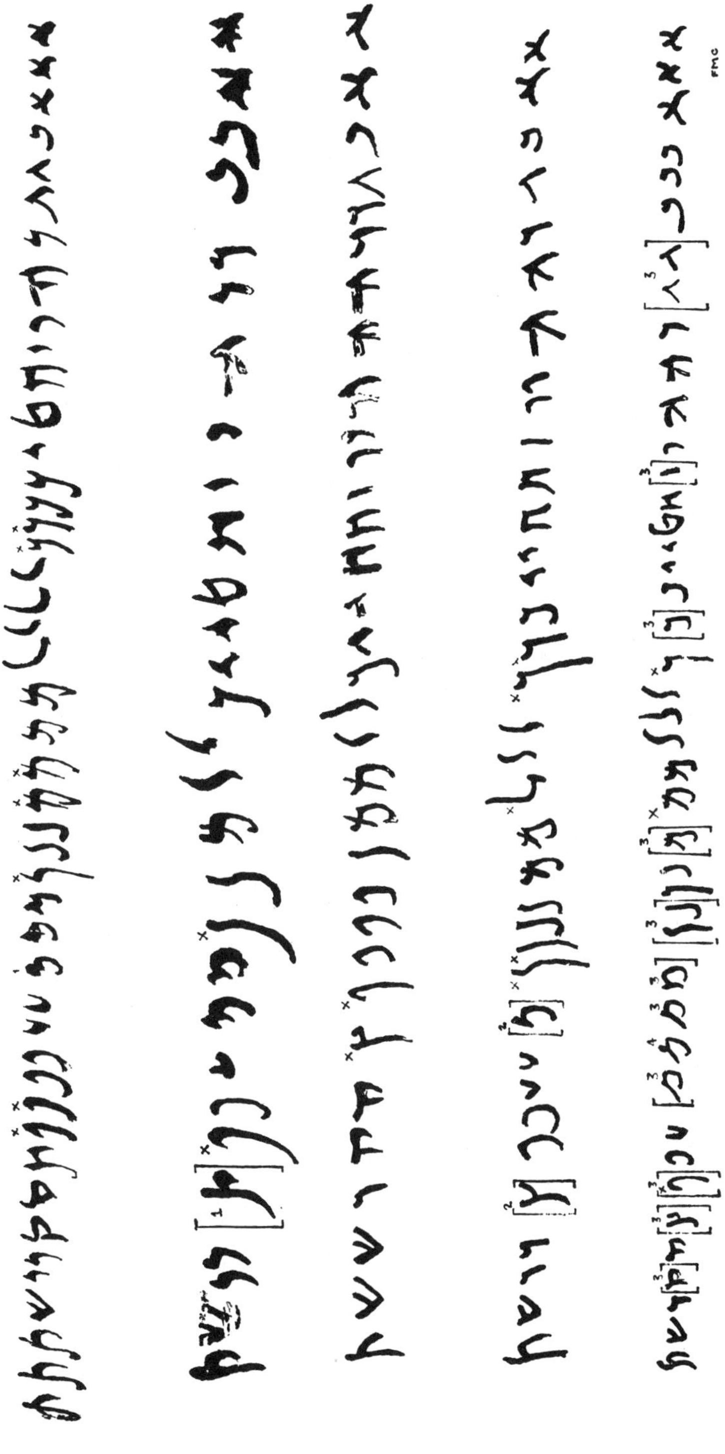

FIGURE 1

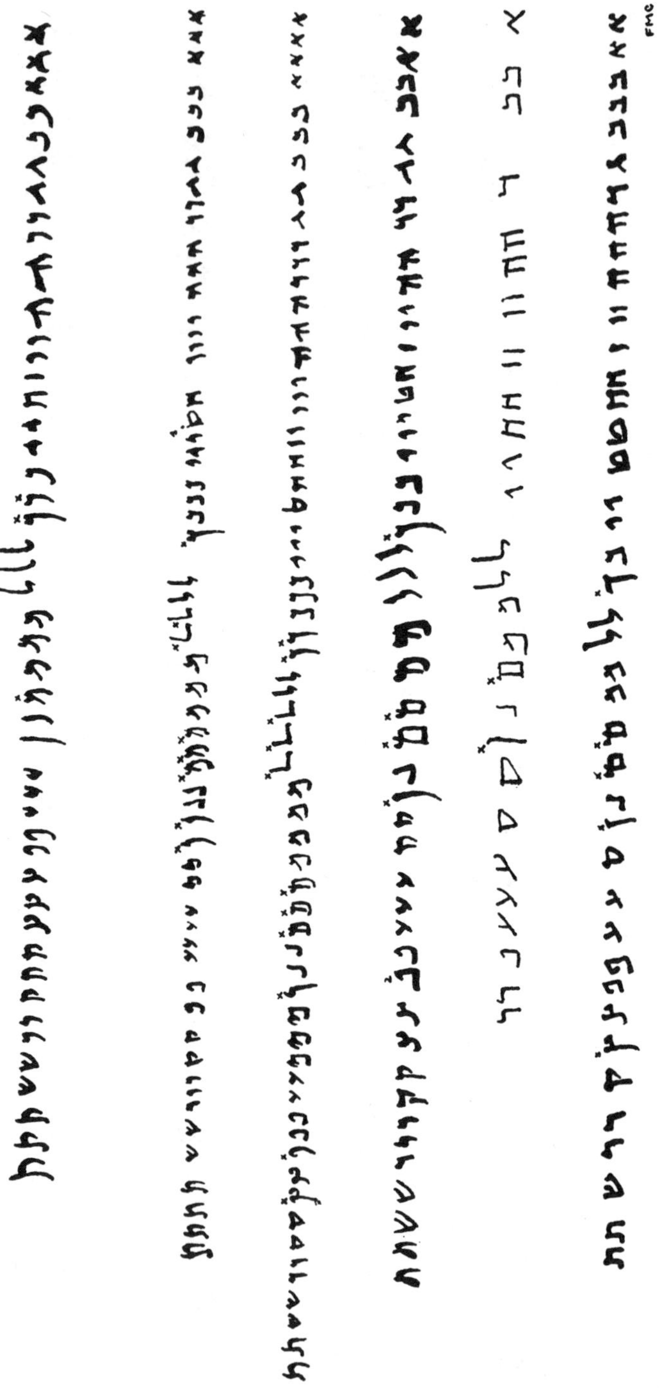

FIGURE 2

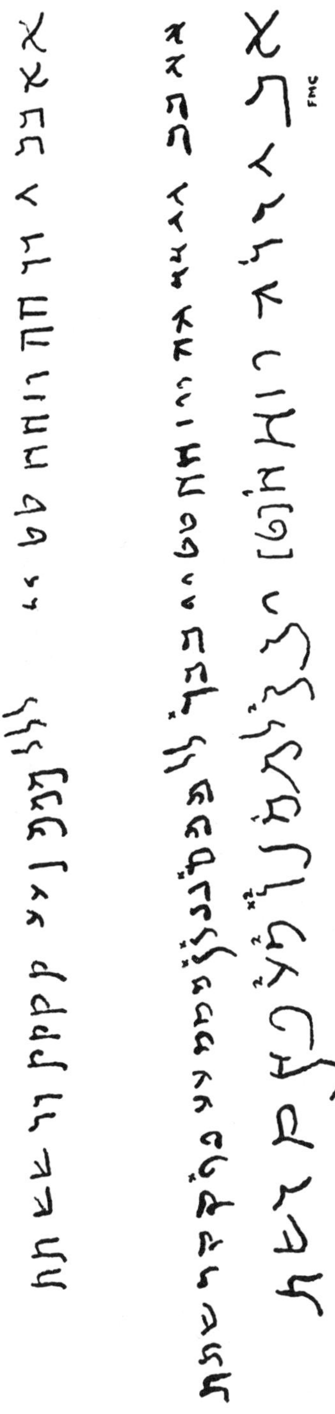

FIGURE 4

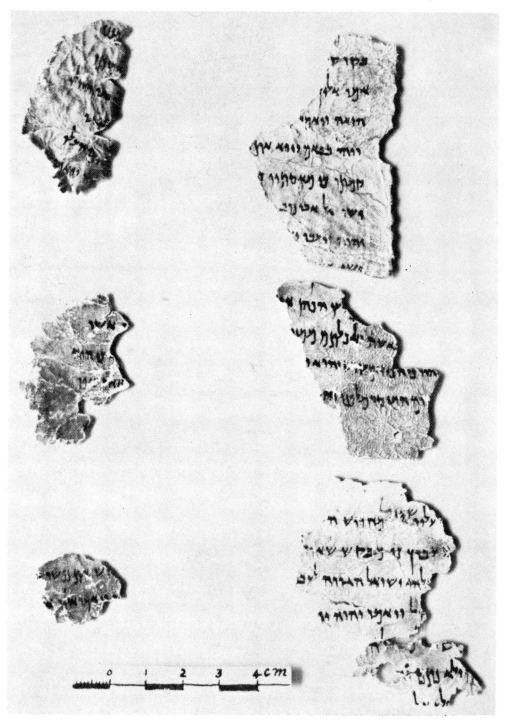

FIGURE 6: 4Q Sam^b

movement; down, then to the left, then curving up and down strongly
again to the right. Medial *nun* is very long still, and preserves often a
curve to the right at the top. *Samekh* in the fourth century loses its
characteristic, complicated head; the letter now resembles a double
hook, the second, rounded and large, emerging from the center of the
first. The lower stroke curls more tightly to the left than in the fifth
century. *'Ayn* remains small and high; a slight tendency for the right
stroke to break through at the base may be noted. *Shin* reveals no curved
strokes as yet, and is small. *Taw* remains very large with a short right
stroke.[9]

The scripts of the third century B. C. from Egypt must all be dated
not later than the first half of the third century, and preferably in the
first decades of that century.[10] The forms are only slightly advanced
over those of the early fourth century, and very slightly beyond those
of the Sachau ostracon (n. 9). Historical circumstances, namely the
rapid decline of Aramaic for business or public purposes in Egypt in
favor of Greek, support such a conclusion, confirming the paleographic
evidence.

The development of medial forms is now approaching its zenith.[11] The
long down-strokes of medial forms of *kaph, samekh, pe, ṣade* are more
tightly bent to the left. So also with *lamedh* whose base is hooked more

---

[9] The late fourth century is represented by a single ostracon, published by Sachau
(*Tafel* 62:2). It has been associated in the past with the ostraca and papyri of the early
third century but is clearly more archaic in script. *Beth* retains its curved lower stroke;
the left leg of *gimel* is very long, with no tendency to "kick up" towards the horizontal;
he is classical, not that of the third-century cursive. *Kaph* is longer than third-century
forms. Medial and final *mem* are little distinguished, and the left diagonal is straight;
neither of these characteristics is necessarily a criterion of antiquity, however, since
they persist in the cursive into the second century. *Lamedh* is archaic, not developed
beyond early fourth-century forms (see below); medial *nun* is especially archaic, being
scarcely bent to the left at the base, and is longer than some cursive fifth-century forms,
much less later third-century types. *Yodh* is intermediate: its two stroke form, normally
like a small, late *gimel*, is the forerunner of the cursive "inverted-V-shaped" *yodh*. The
ṣade has its right arm curled upward and back to the left like mid-fourth-century
types (Fig. 2, line 1). *Shin* is relatively large. In fact, the chief element revealing
development towards third-century cursive scripts is the increased uniformity in size
of letters. *Taw* has a very short right leg, and is less developed than those of Pap. 18.
To this paleographical evidence it may be added that the ostracon has no Greek names
in some sixteen lines of text, unlike the other name-lists of the early third century, where
Greek names fairly swarm.

[10] Cf. *AN*, pp. 154–55.

[11] Actually, this took place in the bookhand, not in the cursive script to which the
third century documents from Egypt belong, as we shall see below. The tendency
towards creation of ligatures or semi-ligatures ceased earlier in the cursive script than
in the formal hand, with an attendant trend towards standardization of forms most
strongly seen in Palmyrene. Here, except in the case of *nun*, all distinctions between
medial and final forms were obliterated.

sharply; its vertical stance, anticipated in the fourth century, is regular; the first evidence of final *lamedh* now appears.[12]

The homogeneity of pen stroke, already noted in the late fourth-century script, is more obvious in the third. *'Aleph* is larger. The right downstroke of *beth* is vertical, and the letter base tends to sweep farther left in cursive (*sensu stricto*) fashion.[13] The left arm of *gimel* is rising with the concurrent tendency to lower its point of departure from the right downstroke. *Daleth* and *resh* are broadening. *He* is regularly made in what is to become the style of the later cursive (see Fig. 3), a major departure from earlier scripts. *Ṭeth* is not yet *squarish* at the bottom, but is opening up, its cross-bar failing usually to cut into the vertical left. *Samekh* is radically changed, the left hook of the fourth-century form giving way to a vertical or, in extreme cursive forms, a long diagonal stroke. The right leg of *taw* is rapidly lengthening.

II

The Earliest Jewish Scripts from Qumran[14]

Two MSS in particular are clear exemplars of the most archaic Jewish hand at Qumran. These are 4QSam[b] (I Samuel), herein published, and an unpublished MS of Jeremiah, 4QJer[a]. Two aspects of the typology of the script are apparent at a glance. The extraordinary differentiation in size of letters in length, characteristic of the Aramaic hand of the fifth and fourth centuries, and largely absent already from the cursive of the third century, is here retained, especially in 4QSam[b]. Secondly, the

[12] See below in the early Jewish bookhand, especially 4QJer[a].

[13] Cf. 4QEccles, and Palmyrene.

[14] A key to Fig. 2 follows. All scripts are traced from photographs with the exception of the Benê Ḥêzîr inscription. Its forms were traced from a photograph of a new squeeze made by the writer, and checked by direct photographs. Sigla: [1], the letter is broken off at the top; [2] final *pe* is not used.

Line 1. An Aramaic script of the mid-fourth century. From the Louvre Papyrus, *CIS* (*Pars Secunda*) I:1, Tab. XVII, Nos. 146 A, B.

Line 2. 4QSam[b] (see Fig. 6).

Line 3. 4QJer[a] (unpublished).

Line 4. A cursive hand from *ca.* 150–125 B. C.: 4QXII[a] (Minor Prophets).

Line 5. The Benê Ḥêzîr inscription from the end of the first century B. C.

Line 6. 4QDeut[j] (unpublished) from *ca.* A. D. 50.

Not included in the chart, but presumed in comparative discussions, are 1QIsa[a] (*ca.* 125–100 B. C.), and the Nash Papyrus (*ca.* 175–150 B. C.). Convenient and accurate typological charts of these scripts may be found in Birnbaum's studies, *BASOR*, No. 115, p. 21, or *The Qumrân (Dead Sea) Scrolls and Palaeography* (*BASOR, Suppl. Studies*, Nos. 13–14 [New Haven, 1952]), pp. 33, 41. The best photographs of Nash are those of Trever, "The Problem of Dating the Dead Sea Scrolls," *The Smithsonian Report* [1953], pp. 425–35, Pl. 17; note also his photographic tables of the script of 1QIsa[a], *ibid.*, Pl. 8.

calligraphic technique, varying wide and narrow strokes of the pen according to fixed canons, is here preserved. Actually, the cursive of the third century has largely lost this finesse and, as we have seen, has become monotonous in stroke. Moreover, as we shall see, a number of letters retain characteristics of the classical script of the late Persian period, already lost in the third-century cursives. On the other hand, a few letters are more developed than early third-century cursives, so that there is no question of dating our MSS in the late fourth century B. C. Rather, it now becomes clear that the formal Jewish bookhand derives from a formal tradition of the early third century, as yet unknown from cursive third-century ostraca and papyri. The existence of this formal script, projected to fill the gap in our extant third-century material, is further confirmed by the typology of the cursive scripts which develop directly from the third-century Aramaic cursive. Two exemplars are given here: line 4 of Fig. 2 (4QXII^a) and line 2 of Fig. 4 (4QEccles, see below). This cursive cannot be treated in detail here, save as it bears directly on problems of dating the bookhand.[15] Obviously, the formal and cursive scripts are always in tension, influencing one another, though the cursive leads. The two traditions, discernible in principle as early as the late fifth century, are clearly distinguished in the third and second

[15] The divergence of the bookhand and the cursive is illustrated in Fig. 3. Here below is a key to the figure.

1. Standard Aramaic cursive (on leather) from the end of the fifth century B. C. From Letter V, G. R. Driver, *Aramaic Documents* (Oxford, 1954).

2. The Aramaic script of the late fourth century B. C. From Sachau, *op. cit.*, *Tafel* 62:2.

3. An Aramaic cursive of the early third century B. C. From Lidzbarski, *op. cit.*, *Tafel* II.

4. 4QEccles., an early Hebrew cursive (*ca.* 175–150 B. C.). Cf. J. Muilenburg, *BASOR*, No. 135 (Oct., 1954), p. 22.

5. From 4QTobit (unpublished). Herodian.

6. An ossuary cursive of the first century A. D. Cf. Bagatti and Milik, "Nuovi Scavi al 'Dominus Flevit,'" *Studii Biblici Franciscani Liber Annuus IV* (1953–54), p. 262, Fig. 11; Savignac, *RB*, XXXIV (1925), Pl. X:2; R. Dussaud, "Comptes d'ouvriers d'une entreprise funéraire juive," *Syria*, IV (1923), 241–49, Fig. 1; etc.

7. A cursive of the second century A. D. From J. T. Milik, "Un contrat juive de l'an 134 après J-C," *RB*, LXI (1954), Pl. IV. Cf. Savignac, *op. cit.*, Pl. x:7; Dussaud, *op. cit.*, *loc. cit.*; De Vaux, "Quelque textes hébreux de Murabba'at," *RB*, LX (1953), Pl. XIII (third signature); etc.

8. From 4QSam^b (end of the third century B. C.).

9. From 4QIsa^d (unpublished; *ca.* 150–125 B. C.).

10. From 4 QEx^e (unpublished; *ca.* 150–125 B. C.).

11. From 4QSam^a. Cf. Cross, *BASOR*, No. 132 (Dec., 1953), p. 17 (*ca.* 50 B. C.).

12. From 4QNumbers^b (unpublished; Herodian).

13. From 4QDeut^j (unpublished; *ca.* A. D. 50).

14. A Murabba'at Fragment of Exodus (early second century A. D.). Cf. De Vaux, *op. cit.*, Pl. XIIa.

centuries. Of course, forms are mixed in certain documents: the Nash
Papyrus, for example, which is none the less dominantly in the tradition
of the bookhand. By the first two centuries A. D., the two are so widely
separated that an intermediate chancellery hand emerges.[16] The development of cursive *he* is shown in Fig. 3. Several other characteristic cursive

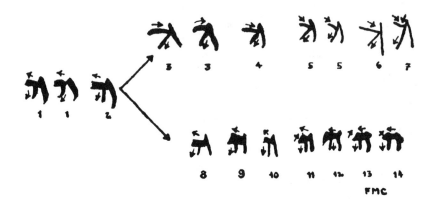

FIGURE 3

forms may be noted. *'Aleph* develops two forms: the looped *'aleph* which
later invades Nabatean, and, in Jewish, the "caret" form, open to the
right, which is derived from forms that omitted the left short leg. *Beth*,
by the second century, reverses the direction in which the lower horizontal
is penned, a development taking place only in the second half of the first
century B. C. in the bookhand. The cursive form develops into the
"figure 2" *beth* of the first century A. D. and later. *Ḥeth* early takes on
the "N-form." *Samekh* develops from third-century forms in the cursive,
being made often without lifting the pen, looping slightly at top left,
and tending to close at the baseline to form a triangular shape. The
form invades both Nabatean and the Jewish bookhand towards the end
of the second century B. C. *'Ayn*, in the cursive, enlarges and rounds
before the right stroke breaks very deeply through; in the bookhand,
on the contrary, the right arm cuts through early, forming an angular
"y-form," which is very small and high. Later *'ayn*, in the cursive, is
made without lifting the pen. Medial and final *mem* are never strongly
distinguished in the cursive; in any case, a single form develops, made
with a continuous motion beginning with the *lower* end of the left diagonal, omitting the broad tick at top left. Finally, it must be said that

---

[16] See Milik, "Une lettre de Siméon bar Kokheba," *RB*, LX (1953), 276, n. 1.

the general characteristics of the cursive are, in the early period, its broadening, shortening, increasingly uniform letters, and later its tendency to simplify to single-letter forms which could be made without lifting the pen. Ligatures become characteristic of the cursive only quite late.

We return to the early Jewish bookhand with special reference to the MSS of Samuel and Jeremiah. *'Aleph* in 4QSam[b] is very small compared with that of 1QIsa[a], or even of third-century cursives. Its left leg is crescent-shaped, breaking through at the bottom, precisely as in fourth-century types, our only clear witness to the form. Of course, from such forms develop the semi-looped leg of Nabatean and Palmyrene *'alephs*, as well as the looped, or half-looped Nash forms. Typologically, the *'aleph* of 4QSam[b] is prior to any known Jewish hand, or any forms extant after the fourth century. This applies to its size, the calligraphic technique (shared with Jer[a]), as well as the treatment of the left leg, the chief typological clue in the case of *'aleph* throughout its late history. *Beth* is small, rounded at bottom right, though the downstroke is moving to the vertical. In Jer[a], it has become vertical or even bulges slightly to the right. In neither case has it approached the larger, square-cornered Isa[a] *beth*. The top is short with sharp ticks, unlike the broader, cursive forms with a rounded right shoulder. The "square-cornered" long baseline has not yet begun to develop. This latter form is the mother to early cursive *beths* (by 125 B. C.) which draw the base from left to right. It may be noted that both Nabatean and Palmyrene exhibit the "square-cornered" *beth*, or "proto-cursive" form. *Gimel*, both in Sam[b] and Jer[a], has developed beyond the fifth-century forms, but is far more archaic

FIGURE 5

than Isa^a, or even earlier second-century forms (4QEccles, 4QXII^a, and unpublished MSS). Third-century forms are closest. The right leg is a straight diagonal, not bowed as later (e. g., Isa^a). The left leg, the more significant paleographically, is normally very long, beginning high on the right leg, if not virtually at the top. It has begun to "kick up" slightly. *Daleth* again finds its nearest parallels in the long, narrow forms of the fourth century, though Nash is comparable, as well as certain third-century forms.[17] The broad, angular cross-bar of Isa^a is far in the future. The long, right downstroke is vertical, and shows no tendency to shift counter-clockwise to a slightly diagonal stance characteristic of the cursive, especially 4QEccles and Palmyrene. *He* is made in classical, formal style. Its top horizontal is thickened heavily; the right vertical is still inclined diagonally and sharply pointed at the top. In Sam^b the tendency to move the left vertical towards the left end of the horizontal top has now begun; however, the leg is still diagonal. Jer^a is more archaic, without the tendency to shift the left leg. They both stand intermediate between the fourth-century scripts and the second-century bookhand. *Waw* is strongly bent at the top; the true "head," or hooked top, is not yet developed (Isa^a and later). *Zayn* is not particularly useful for paleography as long as it remains a simple, vertical stroke. However, it is to be noted that the sharply-pointed top, survival of the technique of the fifth-fourth century, is found in Jer^a (no *zayn* appears in Sam^b). As early as Isa^a, *zayn* tends to bend and thicken slightly at the top. *Ḥeth* in Sam^b sometimes bulges at the center of the cross-bar (see the discussion of fourth-third century forms), a tendency eventuating in "N-shaped" *ḥeth*. 4QEccles and Isa^a are intermediate, with the cross-bar slanting often up to the left downstroke. On the other hand, some forms, especially those of Jer^a are indistinguishable from fifth-century cursives. Note that the left leg often bends left at the bottom, and tapers to a point in archaic style. *Ṭeth* is narrow, tall, with a long left arm, and rounded or pointed bottom. The cross-stroke cuts the left arm. It is undifferentiated from fifth-fourth century forms. In the second century the cross-bar curls, and, especially in the cursive, the left arm shortens. In the first century B. C (earlier in the cursive) the broad flat bottom with rectangular verticals appears. *Yodh* in 4QSam^b is made with three

---

[17] See Fig. 5 which is a drawing of an ostracon from Samaria reading, "(belonging) to Judah," from *ca.* 200 B. C. The long, narrow *daleth* is now certain and characteristic. Formerly it was read ליהוה, "(belonging) to Yahweh." See E. L. Sukenik, "Potsherds from Samaria, Inscribed with the Divine Name," *PEFQS*, 1936, pp. 34–37. Cf. *PEQ*, 1937, pp. 140 f. It may now be said with confidence that no coins, ostraca, or stamps bearing the divine name are extant from the post-exilic period. Sukenik himself corrected most erroneous readings, "Paralipomena Palaestinensia," *JPOS*, XIV (1934), 178–84. See most recently, Vincent, "Les épigraphes judéo-araméennes postexiliques," *RB*, LVI (1949), 275–94, who holds to older views.

motions as in third-century forms and earlier, as well as in Nabatean and Nash. The *yodh* of Jer^a appears sometimes to be an early form of two-movement *yodh*, nearly an inverted, curved "V." It appears only rarely in fourth and third-century materials, but is regular in the early Jewish cursive of the second century. It is also found in the earliest Nabatean inscription (see below), as well as in Palmyrene. By the end of the second century (Isa^a), it is standard. Medial *kaph* is very long and narrow, especially in Jer^a. The downstroke is nearly on the vertical, showing advance from the fifth and early fourth-century forms which slant. The downstroke bends in leftward in the middle, a rudimentary "figure-three" form.[18] The base of medial *kaph* is still a curving, short flourish to the left, reminiscent of its cursive origin in the fifth century, and identical with that of the third century. There is no hint yet of the long, sloping bottom stroke, bent from the vertical downstroke at a virtual right angle (second-century cursives, Isa^a, and later). Final *kaph* is identical with fourth and third-century forms, having a narrow top, and very long vertical downstroke. *Lamedh* in Jer^a always distinguishes an archaic final form with a long horizontal stroke, almost imperceptibly hooked. Sam^b also uses final *lamedh* but not systematically. Medial *lamedh* is characteristically short, its hook downward thin, short, and uncurved. Final *lamedh* appears elsewhere certainly only in the early third century.[19] It traces its origin to the fourth century. The final *mem* of Sam^b is extraordinarily archaic. There is nothing like it after the fifth-fourth centuries. The third-century forms are neither as long nor as narrow, but belong to the cursive tradition preserved in 4QXII^a. The form in Jer^a is less archaic, tending to vertical downstrokes, and with a long base-stroke to the left, anticipating the "closed" forms of Eccles, Nash, Isa^a, and later. Medial *mem* in Sam^b is also more archaic than Jer^a, though both are narrow and very long below the baseline. Contrary to earlier and later cursive *mem*, the left diagonal does not cut the top-stroke. This left diagonal is still very long, but bends leftward. The closest parallels are fourth century (Fig. 2, line 1). *Nun* is very large and long, and sometimes bends right at the top in archaic fashion; however, this latter feature survives in even later scripts. Both final and medial *nun* are identical with fourth and third-century types. In the early second century, *medial nun* is radically shortened, beginning in the cursive.

Samekh is extremely valuable paleographically in this period, since it is in the course of rapid change. The *samekh* of both Sam^b and Jer^a is very archaic. Note the "hooked head" (*not* looped in Sam^b!). The only parallels are in late fifth-century cursives and in the fourth century. The

[18] See *A N*, pp. 166–67.
[19] See above, n. 12.

cursive of the third century develops a new tradition out of which emerges the *samekh* of 4QEccles, Palmyrene, and later scripts. '*Ayn* has been briefly touched on in connection with discussion of the Jewish cursive above. It is small and high, but, unlike the early cursive hands, has "broken through" at the bottom. We must presume that the form developed in the bookhand sometime between the early fourth century and the late third century. At this point third-century cursives are of little aid, since they develop in a different tradition (cf. *samekh*). Medial *pe* is gently rounded at both the top and bottom as in the fourth-third centuries. The later pointed top and rectangular base develop first in the second century cursives, and enter the bookhand as early as 1QIsa[a]. Unfortunately, *ṣade* is missing in Sam[b]. In Jer[a] both the medial forms and the final forms are archaic.[20] The closest parallel to the form of Jer[a] is the *ṣade* of the mid-fourth century. Indeed, nowhere else do we find an example of the tightly curled right arm of *ṣade*.

The chief element of typological interest in the case of *qoph* is its tail. It shortens in the fourth century, and begins to lengthen again in the cursives and formal scripts of the early second century. In Sam[b] and especially in Jer[a] it is at its shortest phase. The "open" head of *qoph* (Sam[b]) is also indicative of relative antiquity (in this period!). *Resh* in Jer[a], and especially Sam[b] has an extremely narrow head. This is the case in fourth century scripts. The cursive of the third century, and the early Jewish cursives (Eccles, XII[a]) already have a broadening form. *Shin* in the archaic period is made with a broad left diagonal, and two straight diagonals to its right. The form persists until a tendency to curve the right-most diagonal develops in the second century (Eccles, Isa[a], as well as unpublished bookhands earlier than Isa[a]). Sam[b] and Jer[a] belong with the archaic scripts both in style of stroke and in form. Still later (first century B. C.), both right diagonals bend back. *Taw* in Sam[b] is extraordinarily large, with a short right leg. Its closest parallels are in Papyrus 18 (419 B. C.!), and Papyrus Luparensis; however, the third-century forms are quite similar, except in calligraphic technique. In Jer[a], the right leg is lengthened (cf. Palmyrene), but *taw* is still very large. Beginning in the third century, the relative size of *taw* is steadily reduced to conform with that of other letters.

The result of our analysis is to show that 4QSam[b], especially, but also Jer[a], belongs to the tradition of the Persian chancellery script of the fourth century B. C. both in its technique of penning letters, and in the size of letters: their length below the ceiling line and their narrowness. Certain letters, '*aleph* (Sam[b]), *daleth*, *he*, *ṭeth*, final *mem* (Sam[b]), *samekh*,

---

[20] It is not impossible that the Nabatean *ṣade* develops from such a form, rather than from the common fifth-century *ṣade*.

ṣade (appears only in Jerᵃ),[21] and *resh* have their closest parallels with fourth-century forms. Another series, *waw, ḥeth, yodh, nun* (medial and final), *qoph, shin,* and *taw* have equally good parallels in the fourth and third centuries. *Beth, gimel, kaph* (medial), *lamedh* (medial and final), *pe* (medial and final) are more developed than fourth-century types, and stand closest to *early* third-century letters. Two letters, *'ayn* (Samᵇ and Jerᵃ) and *medial mem* (Samᵇ), have no precise parallels. Medial *mem* (Samᵇ) is a development of forms like those of Papyrus Luparensis, bypassed in extant third-century documents. The *mem* of Jerᵃ (medial and final) also has no real parallels, but is developed from the types in Samᵇ. *'Ayn* shares early characteristics with fourth century forms but possesses late characteristics not found in the early third century.

It is evident from this data that the archaic Jewish bookhand belongs to a formal tradition which *parallels* the extant cursives of the third century B. C., and that this formal tradition has evolved very slowly after the end of the Persian Empire. This is to be expected, of course, with the disuse of Aramaic for official purposes during the period of Hellenization. The Jewish bookhand, in all probability used chiefly to preserve sacred documents, is, therefore, quite naturally conservative. But before proceeding to an attempt to date these MSS, evidence for checking our conclusions from Nabatean and Palmyrene must be examined.

III

THE SISTER SCRIPTS: PALMYRENE AND NABATEAN[22]

By analysis of the earliest Palmyrene and Nabatean inscriptions, we can project backward, and determine fairly accurately the stage of the Aramaic script at the time each broke off to begin its independent evolu-

---

[21] Both *samekh* and *ṣade* are more formal than their fourth-century counterparts, but show evolution; they are classified here, however, since third-century forms are far more developed.

[22] See Fig. 4. A key to the chart follows:

Line 1. Inscription of Aṣlaḥ (90 B.C.). Gustav Dalman, *Neue Petra-Forschungen, usw.* (Leipzig, 1912), *Abb.* 68, *Inschrift Nu.* 90 (p. 99), cf. J. Cantineau, *Le Nabatéen,* II, No. II. The letters are line-drawn, but freshly traced from Dalman's squeeze.

Line 2. 4QEccles (175–150 B.C.). Traced from natural size photographs. Cf. J. Muilenburg, "A Qoheleth Scroll from Qumran," *BASOR,* No. 135 (Oct., 1954), pp, 20–28.

Line 3. The earliest dated Palmyrene inscription (44 B.C.). Cf. J. Starcky and S. Munajjed, *Palmyra* (Damascus, 1948), p. 26. The siglum ¹ refers to letters taken from a contemporary (or, more likely, slightly earlier) inscription dedicated to *Bêl, Bêlḥammān.* and *Manawāt* (unpublished). The siglum ² refers to the inscription published by Du

tion. This information can be most useful if we can then solve two problems: (1) the points at which the prototypic Nabatean and Palmyrene scripts fit into the typological sequence of the scripts with which we have been working, and (2) the probable "absolute" date when Nabatean and Palmyrene branched off from their parent scripts.[23]

The earliest Nabatean inscription which can be dated certainly is the Aṣlaḥ Inscription of *ca.* 90 B. C.[24] An older inscription found at Khalaṣah belongs to the cursive tradition of the third century, rather than to the tradition out of which the Nabatean lapidary branched, and therefore need not be considered.[25]

The ductus of Nabatean preserves the narrow, long, and irregularly-sized letters of the formal tradition. Indeed, contrary to the trend towards uniformity ("squareness") in script operating in the second and first-century B. C. Jewish scripts, Nabatean develops and exaggerates this element of the old Aramaic hand.[26] The Aṣlaḥ script has only begun this secondary development; the relative size of its letters is close to that of Sam[b]. As a matter of fact, the Aṣlaḥ script shares many characteristics of the earliest Jewish bookhands: *daleth* and *resh* are narrow with small heads; *ḥeth* shares the domed cross-bar with Sam[b] (as well as older scripts and Palmyrene); *ṭeth* has the long left arm; *yodh* is a development of the "three-movement" formal *yodh*; medial *mem* is very narrow and

Mesnil du Buisson (*Inventaire des Inscriptions Palmyréniennes de Doura-Europos* [Paris, 1939]), dated 33 B. C. The line drawings are traced from unpublished photographs of Abbé J. Starcky. The writer is in debt to Abbé Starcky, not only for permission to draw on unpublished material, but also for counsel in matters of Palmyrene epigraphy, a field in which he is unsurpassed. The present group of inscriptions is announced in *Actes du XXI Congrès international des Orientalistes*, Paris, 23–31 juillet, 1948 (*Impr. Nat.*, 1949), p. 111. They will be published by Starcky together with a study of early Palmyrene and Nabatean paleography in the forthcoming volume dedicated to Levi della Vida.

[23] Albright (*AN*, pp. 163–71) deals at length with the early evolution of these two scripts, solving most of the basic problems. Much of the material he treats needs not be rehearsed here.

[24] For literature on this inscription, and those discussed below, see n. 22.

[25] The Khalaṣah Inscription has been assigned by Cowley (*Palestine Exploration Fund Annual* [1914–15], p. 146, Fig. 59) and Albright (*AN*, p. 165) tentatively to Ḥaretat II at the end of the second century B. C. If this script is at all accurately traced, however, it is scarcely developed beyond third-century forms. Note *'aleph, mem,* and especially *'ayn* and *taw* (with a short right leg). All forms are broad, and *daleth, ṭeth, yodh, mem,* and *'ayn* clearly are in the cursive tradition. A date in the reign of Ḥaretat I (contemporary of Antiochus IV) is not excluded paleographically. On the date of the archaic El-'Ulā texts, and of the much disputed Rabbel inscription, see Albright's discussions, *AN*, pp. 164–67, especially n. 57 and p. 167; and "Dedan," *Geschichte und Altes Testament* (*Alt Festschrift*; Tübingen, 1953), p. 7, n. 2.

[26] See now the extraordinary papyrus hand in the text published by Starcky, "Un contrat nabatéen sur papyrus," *RB*, LXI (1954), 161–81.

long (the left diagonal has shortened, however); *nun* is long; *'ayn* is small, high, and tends towards the "y" form; *shin* is archaic; *taw* has a short right leg and is nearly identical with Sam[b]. A number of letters appear, however, never to have evolved through the stage represented by the earliest Jewish hands, but to have diverged from a script of a later period. *'Aleph*, both in Aṣlaḥ and later, derives from an *'aleph* with a semi-looped left leg.[27] *Beth*, with its rectangular right-lower corner, is late, though it may be derived by parallel evolution. *He* is especially advanced; it derives from the formal hand, however. *Ṣade* is problematical; it may well be a survival of the form otherwise unknown later than the fifth and early fourth centuries; it may be a development of the "curled" form represented by Jer[a]. *Samekh*, when it appears in Nabatean (unfortunately it is not found in Aṣlaḥ), is very late; its form has invaded the formal script from the cursive.[28]

Thus we may conclude that Nabatean, like the early Jewish book-hand, testifies to the existence of a formal Aramaic hand, ultimately derived from a chancellery hand of the late Persian Empire, paralleling the vulgar hand of the third century B. C. The point of divergence from this tradition appears to be later in Nabatean than in the earliest Jewish bookhands extant, notably 4QSam[b]. Unfortunately we know little of the early history of the Nabateans from the time of Antigonus' raids against them in 312 B. C., until their dealings with Jason and the Maccabees in the days of Antiochus IV. It is clear, however, that they were exercising considerable autonomy in the days of Ḥaretat I, though their great expansion begins in the days of Ḥaretat II and 'Obodat I at the end of the second century B. C. and the beginning of the first century B. C. In this latter period the script begins a period of rapid evolution towards the classical Nabatean lapidary style. The writer is inclined to believe, however, that the Nabatean script became more or less independent in its development *not later* than the second quarter of the second century, when effective Seleucid and Ptolemaic control of outlying provinces came to an end. It is precisely in the second half of the second century, with the decline of Hellenistic organization in Syria and Egypt, that the Jewish state and Nabatean Arabia are freed to go their own ways. In each case there is nationalistic expansion and resurgent Orientalism. In Judea, the Paleo-Hebrew script is resurrected in Maccabean times, and the Jewish bookhand begins a period of very rapid evolution culminating in the classical Herodian character. Historical circumstances as well as

---

[27] See the *'aleph* of the Rabbel inscription (used medially and in final positions), Cantineau, *op. cit.*, p. 2; the looped form of the Ḥawrān inscriptions from the first century B. C. (published by De Vogüé, *Inscriptions sémitique* [Paris, 1868], Pl. 13:1 equals *CIS* II, 162), and Nash.

[28] E. g., see Rabbel, l. 4.

paleographical evidence suggest that the Nabatean script followed a similar pattern of development.

Palmyrene, by the middle of the first century B. C. when our series of inscriptions begins,[29] has already achieved a strongly individual style. Nevertheless, Palmyrene gives clear-cut evidence of descending from an Aramaic semi-cursive of the first half of the second century, being independent from *ca.* 150 B. C.[30]

The script of 4QEccles, though influenced by formal elements of the Jewish bookhand, is very close to the prototypic script of Palmyra.[31] Both scripts exhibit enlarged, especially broadened forms of letters: *'aleph, beth, daleth, resh, mem,* and *'ayn.* Palmyrene is also characterized by the later (cursive) style in *he, yodh, samekh, 'ayn, ṣade,* and perhaps *qoph.* Note the following typological traits: *'aleph* has the semi-looped left leg; *beth* is large, with an angular base at the right, and long baseline; the stance of *daleth* is tipped forward (cf. 4QEccles); *ḥeth* has the domed cross-bar, and tends to spread its verticals at the base; *samekh* is fairly archaic, but belongs with 4QEccles and the third-century style, not to earlier bookhand styles; *pe* is rounded at the top still, but flattened at the bottom, with a long baseline; *qoph* has a tail; the right leg of *taw* has lengthened. It is possible that a few of these late traits derive from an independent evolution which by coincidence pursues a similar path to that of the Jewish cursives; but not all of them. They are evidence that the prototype of the Palmyrene script must be dated later than the earliest Jewish scripts, not far from the period of the Ecclesiastes hand.

On historical grounds, the divergence of Palmyrene from its parent script is expected in precisely this period. Like Judea and Nabatea, Palmyra became increasingly independent with the breakdown of Seleucid power following the reign of Antiochus IV. It is extremely doubtful if any form of sustained control of Palmyra from Antioch was ever established again after the fall of Seleucia (141 B. C.).

[29] See n. 22 (to Fig. 3, line 3).

[30] Albright in 1937 (*AN*, pp. 168–71), on the basis of Palmyrene texts beginning in 9 B. C. and the third century Egyptian documents, was able to date the divergence of Palmyrene from its cursive prototype between 250 and 100 B. C. The addition of older Palmyrene texts, and especially the discovery of the series of cursive texts from Qumran (4QEccles, 4QXII[a], etc.) permits further narrowing of limits.

[31] As remarked above, the non-use of final forms in Palmyrene is a secondary cursive development, and must be discounted in comparisons with Jewish hands, especially those under formal influence.

IV

The Dating of the Earliest Scripts from Qumran

As we have seen, the relative chronology of Hebrew and Aramaic documents from Qumran in the Jewish script is easily worked out, thanks to the abundance of new data. Absolute dating of the documents poses a more complicated problem, especially in the earlier periods.

At the end of the type-series the paleographer is on sure ground. The dated documents of the first and second centuries A. D. from Murabba'at fix an absolute *terminus ad quem* for the Qumran script types. This is confirmed by archeological data from Qumran, as well as by the long series of Jewish funerary inscriptions from Herodian times.[32]

Similarly, scripts of the first century B. C. can be given absolute dates with some confidence since they stand close in typological sequence to the Herodian materials. Moreover, a *terminus ad quem* at the end of the first century B. C. is fixed from outside by the inscription of the Bᵉnê Ḥezîr,[33] and controls include the Qumran alphabet mentioned above (before 31 B. C.).[34]

As for the earliest materials, the dating of formal Jewish scripts which fall between the documents of the fourth century, the *terminus a quo* for the earliest Jewish bookhand (4QSamᵇ), and the first-century B. C. scripts, is still based primarily on typological sequence. While we can establish their age relative to other members of the series, an absolute dating is made difficult since we cannot presume that the speed of evolution of a script remains constant. The earliest Jewish cursives, which have their *terminus a quo* in the Aramaic vulgar scripts of the early third century, are of some aid. The formal and cursive are in

[32] Most useful are the Helena Inscription (*CIS* II, 156), from ca. A. D. 50–60, the dipinto published by Sukenik, *Tarbîṣ*, VI (1935), 190–96, Pl. III, which closely follows the bookhand of the mid-first century A. D., the Uzziah Plaque (Sukenik, *Tarbîṣ*, II [1929], 288 ff.) from *ca.* A. D. 50. There is no let up in the discoveries of ossuary inscriptions which now constitute an extensive corpus, virtually all of which belong to the Herodian era (30 B. C. to A. D. 70). Since 1953, thirty to forty Hebrew-Aramaic inscriptions from Dominus Flevit have been published. At least one other major find has been made within the last two years (unpublished).

[33] This date, established by De Vogüé, Klein, and Albright, has recently been revised upward by N. Avigad, *Ancient Monuments in the Kidron Valley* (Jerusalem, 1954 [Hebrew]), pp. 62–66, to the first half of the first century B. C. His paleographical arguments are not convincing.

[34] In the past the Gezer Boundary inscriptions have been dated on archeological grounds to the first century B. C. Cf. Macalister, *The Excavation of Gezer* (London, 1912), I, 37–40; III, Pls. X, XI; Lidzbarski, *Handb. d. nords. Epigraphik*, Taf. 43:3; and *AN*, p. 162. The date is not secure, however, and it may be necessary to lower it as observed by Albright (private communication). A date near the time of the First Revolt is not unreasonable. In any case the inscriptions are not suitable for use as controls in absolute dating.

tension, the cursive, especially, influencing the bookhand. Further assistance comes from the related scripts, Nabatean and Palmyrene. It must be admitted that the attempt to date the divergence of the latter scripts from their parent scripts in part leans on the evidence of Jewish paleography. Nevertheless, the juxtaposition of four typological series, each fixed absolutely in the first century B. C. at the lower end of the series, makes possible judgments which cannot be far wrong in terms of absolute dating. Our conclusions in the preceding section have been that Nabatean and Palmyrene stemmed from prototypic scripts which cannot be dated later than the first half of the second century B. C. If this is true, then the first half of the second century is an absolute *terminus ad quem* for the archaic Jewish bookhands which are clearly older than the Nabatean or Palmyrene parent scripts.

In the case of 4QSam^b, we have thus established its extreme range from the late fourth century to the first half of the second century B. C. Actually, we must allow time for evolution on either side of its script. There is, moreover, a probability that the course of change of the script in the Greek period was relatively slow. Finally, by relating the script to the cursive of the third century which precedes it, and to the Jewish cursive which follows it, we can safely narrow this range to the last half of the third century, and possibly as late as the first quarter of the second century B. C. A date for 4QSam^b in the last quarter of the third century B. C. seems suitably conservative. The Jer^a script is in the same horizon, *ca.* 200 B. C., or slightly later.

In conclusion to the paleographic section of this paper, we wish to outline a set of periods in the early Jewish bookhand based on preliminary studies of the biblical scrolls from Qumran. This framework attempts to conform to both the typological and historical evidence. While the organization is tentative, requiring exhaustive analysis, I believe three periods are defined adequately:

1. Archaic, *ca.* 200–150 B. C.
2. Hasmonean, *ca.* 150–30 B. C.
3. Herodian, *ca.* 30 B. C. to A. D. 70.

This analysis is confirmed partly by indirect evidence from Qumran, though it was first drawn up on the basis of paleographic schemata alone. The vast majority of the MSS from Qumran fall into Periods 2[35] and 3, especially the latter half of Period 2, and the latter part of Period 3, precisely the periods when activity at Khirbet Qumran was at its height.[36] Manuscripts from the Archaic Period are exceedingly rare and

---

[35] Significantly, the earliest sectarian MSS fall into Period 2.

[36] The history of occupation of Khirbet Qumran is given preliminary discussion in De Vaux's report, "Fouilles au Khirbet Qumrân," *RB*, LXI (1954), 231–36.

fragmentary; they may be master scrolls brought into the community at its foundation.

V

A Manuscript of Samuel in an Archaic Jewish Bookhand from Qumran: 4QSam^b

To illustrate the earliest Jewish scripts from Qumran, we have chosen to publish 4QSam^b, probably the oldest of the series. The MS is extremely fragmentary and poorly preserved.[37] It consists of seven fragments containing: Fragment 1, I Sam 16 1–11; Fragment 2, I Sam 19 10–17; Fragment 3, I Sam 21 3–7; Fragment 4, I Sam 21 8–10; Fragments 5–7 (continuous), I Sam 23 9–17. The leather is grey where decomposition has not darkened it. Originally, margin and lineation guides had been impressed lightly into the relatively soft leather. The script is delicate; the lines of script are regular, and unusually long. The number of characters per line averages between 71 and 72; variation in length is no more than five characters in either direction (66–77) over all columns preserved, even less in individual columns.

It will be noted that this is the first of the published Qumran MSS whose orthography seems to be systematically more "defective" than the consonantal Masoretic Text (hereafter MT). While the evidence is skimpy, nevertheless it is significant that within our six fragments there are four cases of words using fewer *matres lectionis* than MT.[38] In no single case are more *matres lectionis* used than in MT! Moreover, the text of MT in these sections is relatively defective throughout. We have argued elsewhere that the fullest use of *matres lectionis* was achieved in the Maccabean Era.[39] Whereas we cannot argue too strenuously on the basis of this evidence, it tends to confirm other arguments, and, in turn, to corroborate the pre-Maccabean date of the scroll.

The textual position of the MS stands close to the *Vorlage* of the Old Greek; it is an earlier exemplar of the textual type discovered in 4QSam^a.[40]

---

[37] For reasons of space, a number of technical details, especially measurements, are not given here, but will be recorded in the general publication.

[38] Frg. 1, l. 5 (I Sam 16 6), בבאם for MT בבואם; l. 6 (16 7), קמתו for MT קומתו; Frg. 2, l. 3 (19 12), החלן for MT החלון; Frg. 4, l. 3 (21 10), אפר for MT האפוד. There are, as is expected, a number of Kenn. MSS supporting each of the "defective" 4Q readings in three of the cases. No MS preserves the reading החלן.

[39] Cross and Freedman, *Early Hebrew Orthography* (New Haven, 1952), p. 69, especially n. 24.

[40] Cross, "A New Qumran Biblical Fragment Related to the Original Hebrew Underlying the Septuagint," *BASOR*, No. 132 (1953), pp. 15–26. (Note the following corrections in the reconstruction, p. 26: Col. I, l. 10, for *bymym*, read *ymymh*; Col. II, l. 4, for *bpwr*, read *bprwr*; Col. II, l. 15, following [šw]m[' add]dbry[.) Still a third unpublished MS of Samuel, 4QSam^c, represents a similar textual type.

Fragment 1, I Sam 16 1–11[41]

1	[	[אשלח]ךֿ]	(1–2)
2	[	בקר ק[ח]	(2–3)
3	[	אמר אליך]	(3–4)
4	[	הראה ויאמר]	(4–5)
5	[	ויהי בבאם וירא את אֿלֿיאב	(6–7)
6	[	קמתו כי מאסתיו כֿיֿ	(7–8)
7	[	ישי אל אבינדב[	(8–9)
8	[	יהוה ויעבר ישֿיֿ	(9–10)
9	[	ישי הֿתֿנֿמו	(11)

Commentary to Fragment 1:

L. 1 (vs. 1). Calculation of the line length makes the reconstruction of l. 1 beginning [אשלח]ךֿ fairly certain. No other final *kaph* (or other letter with a long tail) is near enough to fit the count.

L. 2 (vs. 2). Against the MT תקח, 4Q reads ק[ח] with LXX (λάβε). Cf. Syriac (S), *'aḥod*.

L. 4 (vs. 4+). 4Q adds הראה with LXX, ὁ βλέπων. Unfortunately, calculations of space do not help us determine 4Q's reading in this verse below where LXX reads אתי היום (so!) ושמחו (καὶ εὐφράνθητε μετ' ἐμοῦ σήμερον), clearly superior to MT ובאתם אתי בזבח as first demonstrated by Wellhausen, *Der Text der Bücher Samuelis* (Göttingen, 1871), *ad loc*.

L. 5 (vs. 6). 4Q, *mult.* MSS Kenn. read בבאם for MT בבואם (see n. 38).

L. 6 (vs. 7). 4Q *mult.* MSS read קמתו for MT קומתו (see n. 38). 4Q reads מאסתיו for MT מאסתיהו; cf. MT, vs. 1.

4Q must be reconstructed to read האדם (or יביט) כֿ]י לא כאשר יראה etc., [יראה האלהים (LXX, ὅτι οὐκ ὡς ἐμβλέψεται ἄνθρωπος, ὄψεται ὁ θεός). MT כי לא אשר יראה האדם is impossible as it stands, as is generally recognized.[42] However, this is not the point. The fuller text must be read in 4Q to fill out the line. If we follow the LXX, the line is calculated at 72 characters, precisely the mean; if the awkward MT is followed, the line is 61 characters, impossibly short, or in any case, far shorter than the shortest line elsewhere in the fragments. The phrase יראה האלהים appears to have fallen out by haplography due to *homoioarkton*.

L. 8 (vss. 10, 11). As in MT, a paragraph break stood between [באלה] and [ויאמר], to judge from a reconstruction of the line.

---

[41] The *sigla* to the transcription of the text are as follows: ° above a letter equals very uncertain reading; · above a letter, probable reading. The abbreviations in general follow Kittel, ed., *Biblia Hebraica*.

[42] Cf. Driver, *Notes on the Hebrew Text . . . of Samuel* (Oxford, 1913), p. 133.

Fragment 2, I Sam 19 10–17

1	[מפני	]	(10)
2	ל[המיתו	]	(10–11)
3	ד[ו̊ד בעד החלן	]	(11–12)
4	בבגד [° °	]	(12–13)
5	ד[ו̊ד לאמר העלו	]	(14–15)
6	מראש[תיו ויאמר	]	(15–17)

Commentary to Fragment 2:

L. 2 (vs. 10). There is enough room for the introduction of ויהי in the line before הוא<ה>בלילה with the Greek, καὶ ἐγενήθη ἐν τῇ νυκτὶ ἐκείνῃ, clearly the original reading (Wellhausen). However, were it omitted, the line would *not* be excessively short. Hence we cannot argue from space factors in 4Q to the reading.

L. 3 (vs. 12). 4Q reads החלן for MT החלון (cf. n. 38).

L. 4 (vs. 13). Before בבגד, the leather is badly split and distorted by shrinkage. Some traces of letters are preserved on the border twisted down from the split; they hardly conform to read ותכס or any part thereof. But the traces are too indistinct to permit more than speculation as to the actual reading.

L. 5 (vs. 15). The LXX[B] text omits את המלאכים לראות, a transparent haplography by *homoioarkton* (את . . . את), in the *Vorlage* of the Greek. LXX[Luc.], MT, Vulgate (V), S, stand together with the full text. Calculation of the spatial requirements in l. 5 makes certain that 4Q follows the full (and superior) reading.

Fragments 3 and 4, I Sam 21 3–10[43]

1	צויתי̇ך [ואת]		(3)
2	[ו̊נ̊]ע̇ן הכהן את̇	]	(4–5)
3	[מאשה ואכלתם ממנו̊ [ויען]	]	(5–6)
4	וי̊היו כל הנערים קדש והוא ד[רך]	]	(6)
5	פ]נ̊ים המוסר מלפני יהו̊]ה לשום]	]	(6–7)
6	]ם̊ אשר	]	(7–8)
7	ביד]י כי היה	]	(8–9)
8	]א̇חר אפד	]	(9–10)

[43] The lineation can be reconstructed accurately on the basis of Fragment 4 which is continuous, and reveals the end of lines.

Commentary to Fragments 3 and 4:

L. 1 (vs. 3). The reconstruction of the lines requires that the tail of a letter seen on the fragment belong to *kaph*: ‏[צוית]ך‎.

L. 3 (vs. 5+). The reading here is most interesting. Note first the supralinear addition of ‏[א]ך‎ (?) by a corrector. Presumably it is to be placed before ‏מאשה‎ with MT and Greek MSS in the Hexaplaric tradition (LXX^h). LXX^BLuc. and S omit with 4Q*. The addition ‏ואכלתם ממנו‎ in 4Q preserves a reading closely related to the Old Greek reflected in the following variants: LXX^B καὶ φάγεται; LXX^hLuc., *et al.* καὶ φάγονται; Syro-hexaplar (*apud* Barhebraeus), Eus. καὶ φάγετε. Without the phrase, the conditional sentence stands awkwardly without an apodosis; the protasis cannot be construed gracefully with the preceding. 4Q (LXX) is superior in all respects: "If the young men have kept themselves from women, then ye may eat of it." MT arises from haplography and cannot be defended on the principle of *lectio difficilior*.

L. 4 (vs. 6). LXX adds ‏בדרך‎ (εἰς ὁδόν) after ‏בצאתי‎. Without the addition, 4Q is rather too short; but we cannot be certain here.

4Q, LXX (πάντα) read ‏כל‎ against MT ‏כלי‎. Perhaps this is preferable, ‏כלי‎ arising secondarily in anticipation of ‏בכלי‎ below. We then read "Certainly we have been segregated from women, as in the past; whenever I have taken a journey, all the young men have been consecrated even if it was a secular journey; how much more so when today, etc." Thenius, *Die Bücher Samuelis* (2nd ed.; Leipzig, 1864), p. 99; Driver, *op. cit.*, pp. 174–75.

L. 5 (vs. 7). The uncertainty of readings in the first half of l. 5 makes reconstruction difficult. It seems clear, however, that the conflate reading of LXX^B Ἀβειμελεχ ὁ ἱερεὺς τοὺς ἄρτους τῆς προθέσεως, (‏אב/חימלך‎ ‏הכהן את לחם הפנים‎), cannot possibly be fitted into the line. There is evidence in the several recensions of LXX (though scanty in each: CLS[44] doa₂ Eth.) for the omission of ‏הכהן‎ in the Old Greek; however, the Greek tradition is still too long. It seems likely that 4Q here agrees with MT against LXX.

4QSam^b correctly reads ‏המוסר‎ for the ungrammatical reading of MT ‏המוסרים‎ (by attraction to the preceding ‏הפנים‎).

L. 8 (vs. 10 [Fragment 4]). 4Q reads ‏אחר אפד‎ "behind *an* ephod," for MT ‏אחרי האפוד‎.[45] However, here 4Q and MT, S and V stand together with a reading surely more original than the omission of the Old Greek.

---

[44] I. e., MSS so designated in the Cambridge Larger Septuagint (*The Old Testament in Greek*, eds. Brooke, McLean, Thackeray [London, 1927], II:I).

[45] Cf. n. 38 for the orthography: ‏אפד‎.

Fragments 5, 6, and 7, I Sam 23 9-17[46]

1		] (9)
	שאול [ ]° עליו ... מחריש הר[עה]	
2		] (10)
	ש]מ̊ע עבדך כי מבקש שאול [ ]	
3		] (10–11)
	א̊להי ישראל הגידה לעבד[ך]	
4		] (11–13)
	שא]ול ויאמר יהוה יס[ג]ירו	
5		] (13)
	לשא]ו̊ל [כי נ]מ̊לט ד[ו]ד מק̊עׄילה	
6		] (13–14)
	הימי]ם ולא נתנו יה[ו]ה	
7		] (15–16)
	לב]ק̊ש את נפשו וד̊[ו]ד	
	שא]ו̊ל [ו]י̊לך אל [ ]	
8		(16–17)
	ביה[ו]ה ויאמר אליו א̊ל [ ]	

Commentary on Fragments 5, 6, and 7:

L. 1 (vs. 9). The confusion in the order of the phrase corresponding to MT כי עליו שאול מחריש הרעה is considerable in the Greek: LXX[B] ὅτι οὐ παρασιωπᾷ Σαουλ περὶ αὐτοῦ τὴν κακίαν; LXX[Luc.] ὅτι Σαουλ περὶ αὐτὸν γίνεται καὶ οὐ (omit o) παρασιωπᾷ ὁ Σαουλ περὶ αὐτοῦ τὴν κακίαν (clearly conflate, the latter reading equals LXX[B]). There is no way to recover the original 4Q reading. The erasure and insertion of supralinear שאול by a different (though early) hand alters the text into line with the "Masoretic" order. The letters erased are too faint, unfortunately, to be recovered.

L. 2 (vs. 10). The addition of יהוה (i.e., אפ[ו]ד יהוה) and of דוד after ויאמר (1°) is highly likely in 4Q, with LXX. The line is below minimum length without the additions, and slightly *below* average length with *both* additions.

L. 3 (vs. 11). The entire phrase היסגרני בעלי קעילה בידו in MT is certainly absent from 4Q. Some twenty characters are involved. Without

<hr>

[46] The transcription is arranged in longer lines here to give space to include Fragment 6 where readings are in the latter half of the lines. In the preceding transcriptions, we have, of course, telescoped the length of lines. Note well that Frag. 6 is placed too far to the right in the photograph. The clearer top of the two *lamedhs*, traces of which appear at the bottom of Frag. 5, fits with the *lamedh* in נמלט. [The lineation is now fixed by new fragments; the beginning and end of ll. 4 and 5 with their margins are among the fragments.]

the phrase (see below), the line count is 67 characters, only slightly under the general mean for all the fragments (71/72). Moreover, the Old Greek omitted the entire phrase.[47] Finally, since Wellhausen, it has been commonly held that the phrase in MT is a dittograph from vs.12, where it is repeated and obviously belongs. On the other hand, we need with the omission of the phrase to add ועתה with LXX[BLuc.] (καὶ νῦν). Without it, the line count is 63 (below minimum); with it the line is a suitable 67 characters.[48]   In short, the reading of 4Q is supported in part by the LXX[B], and wholly by critical restoration of the passage by textual scholars.

For MT הגד־נא לעבדך, 4Q reads הגידה לעבד[ך]. The reading of the LXX ἀπάγγειλον τῷ δούλῳ σου supports 4Q against MT. Our translator in these books regularly indicates נא by δή (rarely οὖν) in all such passages. In very rare exceptions such as this, we must suppose a different underlying text.

L. 4 (vss. 11–12). In vss. 11b–12a (=MT), LXX has suffered haplography due to *homoioarkton*: καὶ εἶπεν κύριος [καταβήσεται ... καὶ εἶπεν κύριος] ἀποκλεισθήσεται. 4Q here presents the fuller, uncorrupted text. Thus in vs. 11, where MT has suffered dittography and subsequent further corruption, 4Q stands with the Old Greek in preserving the original reading; also, where LXX has suffered haplography, 4Q with MT preserves the original reading!

L. 5 (vs. 13). It is necessary, from clear traces of two *lamedhs* at the bottom of Frag. 5 to reconstruct in the first line of Frag. 6 [now confirmed by new fragments, see n. 46] ויגד לשאול כי נמלט thus following the reading of LXX [Luc.], Eth. against MT, LXX[B]!

L. 6 (vs. 14).[49]   4Q reads יה[וה] with LXX (κύριος) against MT אלהים.

L. 8 (vs. 16). 4Q reads ב[יהו]ה with LXX (ἐν κυρίῳ) against MT באלהים.

For convenience, a reconstruction of Fragments 5–7 follows:[50]

[47] LXX[B] reads εἰ ἀποκλεισθήσεται καὶ νῦν εἰ καταβήσεται etc. However, εἰ αποκλεισθήσεται is clearly displaced here as demonstrated by Wellhausen, *op. cit.*, p. 128. See below on its omission in LXX[B], vs. 12. S omits the whole of vs. 11 in a haplography which, however, presumes the developed Masoretic tradition.

[48] Budde, *The Books of Samuel* (*SBOT*, VIII [Leipzig, 1894]), p. 70 states that ועתה is "unquestionably genuine" on the basis of the LXX alone, and its idiomatic use before questions *in Hebrew*, comparing II Sam 9 11. Our argument from requirements of space certifies this position.

[49] We have not dealt in detail with the readings of place-names in vss. 14, 15 of LXX. There is extensive conflation of transliterated and translated forms of the names leading to some subsequent corruption. Critical restoration of the Old Greek makes clear that LXX and MT do not diverge significantly here, or in any case, not in such fashion as to permit check by calculation of gaps in 4QSam[b].

[50] Obviously, a reconstruction cannot claim accuracy in matters of orthography,

I Sam 23 9–17

שאול]

1   ]עה [מחריש הר . . . וידע דוד כי] עליו
ויאמר [

2   [דוד אל אביתר הכהן הגישה אפד
יהוה ויאמר דוד יהוה אלהי ישראל
שמע ש[מע עבדך כי מבקש שאול
[לבא

3   ]אל קעילה לשחת לעיר בעבורי ועתה
הירד שאול כאשר שמע עבדך
יהוה] אלהי ישראל הגידה לעבד[ך

4   [ויאמר יהוה ירד ויאמר דוד היסגרו
בעלי קעילה אתי ואת אנשי ביד
שא[ול ויאמר יהוה יס[גירו ויקם

5   [דוד ואנשיו כארבע מאות איש ויצאו
מקעילה ויתהלכו באשר יתהלכו
ויגד לשאו[ל [כי נ[מלט ד[וד
מקעילה

6   [ויחדל לצאת וישב דוד במדבר
במצדות וישב בהר במדבר זיף
ויבקשהו שאול כל הימי[ם ולא
נתנו יה]וה בידו

7   [וירא דוד כי יצא שאול לב[קש
את נפשו וד[וד במדבר זיף בחרשה
ויקם יהונתן בן שאו[ל ו[י]לך
אל [דוד חרשה

8   [ויחזק את ידו ביהו[ה ויאמר אליו
אל]תירא

[

(9) . . . . and David knew that Saul was plotting evil against him; then said

David to Abiathar the priest, "Bring here the Ephod of Yahweh." (10) Then David said, "O Yahweh, God of Israel, thy servant has heard definitely that Saul seeks to come

to Keilah, to wreck the city on my account. (11) But now! will Saul come down as thy servant has heard? O Yahweh, God of Israel, tell thy servant."

And Yahweh said, "He will come down." (12) Then

David said, "Will the citizens of Keilah deliver me and my men into the hand of Saul?" And Yahweh said, "They will deliver." (13) So arose

David and his men, about four hundred men, and they departed from Keilah, and they went about wherever they could. When it was told to Saul that David had escaped from Keilah,

he gave up his raid. (14) Then David settled in the wilderness, in its fastnesses; and he remained in the hill-country of the Wilderness of Ziph. And Saul sought him constantly, but Yahweh did not give him into his hand.

(15) Now David saw that Saul had come to seek his life, while he was in the Wilderness of Ziph at Horesh. (16) Then Jonathan, Saul's son, arose and went to David at Horesh;

and he gave him courage through Yahweh. (17) Then he said to him, "Do not fear . . . ."

A brief summary of the textual position of 4QSam[b] may be given as follows:

(1) Readings actually on the leather fragment. In eight cases, one of which is questionable, 4QSam[b] agrees with LXX against MT; in two cases (one of which is not precisely in agreement), 4Q agrees with MT against LXX.

(2) Readings based on spatial requirements in reconstruction. In five cases, two of which are doubtful, 4Q agrees with LXX against MT. In two cases, 4Q agrees with MT against LXX.

or in cases where minor variants existing among MT, LXX and 4Q are not reflected in a derangement of line lengths. In all major cases of divergence, however, we are on fairly sure ground. [For the convenience of readers, a translation of the text has been prepared by the editor. D. N. F.]

(3) Corrections. In two cases, one doubtful, 4Q has been corrected from a reading in line with the LXX to a reading in line with the MT. These are not counted in the totals, either as agreement with LXX or with MT.

Our totals, including three doubtful cases, are as follows: 4Q agrees with LXX against MT thirteen times; 4Q agrees with MT against LXX four times.

Such statistics do not indicate really the full value of this archaic text. Its affinities with the tradition to which the *Vorlage* of the Old Greek belongs is most important, and cannot be neglected in developing new methods and evaluations in future critical studies of the text of Samuel. Nevertheless, the most extraordinary characteristic of the text of 4QSam[b] is the high proportion of original readings which it preserves, whether it be in agreement with the Greek, or in agreement with MT, or against both in its several unique readings.

THE HISTORY OF THE BIBLICAL TEXT IN THE LIGHT OF DISCOVERIES IN THE JUDAEAN DESERT

FRANK MOORE CROSS, JR.

HARVARD UNIVERSITY

THE publication in January, 1953, of fragments of an unknown recension of the Greek Bible gave the first unambiguous warnings of a revolution to come in the textual criticism of the Hebrew Bible.[1] Earlier the publication of the great Isaiah scroll of Qumrân, Cave I (1Q Isa[a]), and later of the second fragmentary roll of Isaiah (1Q Isa[b]), created noise and excitement,[2] but none of the major text-critical schools was forced to shift significant ground. Champions of the *Hebraica veritas* who had increasingly dominated the field, especially in Europe, noted the close affinities of the scrolls with the traditional text. The failure of 1Q Is[a] to produce a significant number of superior readings despite its antiquity embarrassed lingering survivors of the great critical tradition of the nineteenth century, and delighted biblical exegetes and historians who wished to ply their trade without entering the miasmal precincts of text-critical labors. Despite some attention paid to its occasional affinities with the Old Greek,[3] most scholars, whether prompted by traditionalist prejudgment or sheer inertia,

---

[1] D. Barthélemy, "Redécouverte d'un chaînon manquant de l'histoire de la Septante," RB 60 (1953), 18–29. Cf. F. M. Cross, The Ancient Library of Qumrân, rev. ed. (New York, 1961), pp. 28f., n.35 (bibliography), and pp. 174f., n.19 [hereafter abbreviated ALQ[2].] In 1963, Barthélemy published transcriptions of the new recension as well as an analysis of its place in the textual history of the Septuagint: Les devanciers d'Aquila: Première publication intégrale du texte des fragments du Dodécaprophéton (Leiden, 1963) [hereafter, DA]. See also B. Lifshitz, "The Greek Documents from the Cave of Horror," IEJ 12 (1962), 201–07, and Pl. 32B.

[2] Selected items of bibliography can be found in ALQ[2], pp. 177f., n.21. To these should be added M. H. Goshen-Gottstein, Text and Language in Bible and Qumran, pp. vii–xv; pp. 51–85; and Textus III (1963), 130–58; H. M. Orlinsky, "The Textual Criticism of the Old Testament," in The Bible and Ancient Near East, ed. G. E. Wright (New York, 1961), pp. 113–32.

[3] See, for example, the distinguished textual scholar, J. Ziegler, "Die Vorlage der Isaias-Septuaginta (LXX) und die erste Isaias-Rolls von Qumran (1Q Is[a])," JBL 78 (1959), 34–59.

were pleased to label the text vulgar or even sectarian, avoiding thereby a serious reexamination of their text-critical theories.

The recension published by Barthélemy proved to be an extraordinary document. It is a revision of the Old Greek text, revised on the basis of a forerunner of the traditional Hebrew text extant in Palestine toward the middle of the first century of the Christian era. The Recension itself dates probably from the second half of the first century.[4] It should be noted, however, that the *Vorlage* of the Greek text is by no means identical with the surviving *textus receptus*, but may be called Proto-Massoretic, since it differs even more decidedly with the Old Palestinian Hebrew text. In the Minor Prophets, the recension of Barthélemy has been identified with the text used by Origen in the seventh column of the Hexapla, so-called Quinta. That it had wide circulation is suggested by the evidence that it was available to Origen in at least two editions,[5] and survives in the quotations of Justin Martyr's Dialogue and elsewhere.[6] More important, Barthélemy has been able to establish that his recension was the common base of later recensions of the Greek Bible, above all Aquila.[7]

Barthélemy's most significant contribution, perhaps, is the identification of this Greek recension outside the Minor Prophets elsewhere in the Greek Bible. Building on the basis of H. St. John Thackeray's analysis of the Greek style of the Books of Reigns,[8] i.e., Samuel and Kings, he has been able to demonstrate that the sections of Samuel and Kings assigned by Thackeray to "Proto-Theodotion" actually are identical in style with the Recension. The sections in question are 2 Samuel 11:2-1 Kgs. 2:11 (Thackeray's $\beta\gamma$) and 1 Kgs. 22-2 Kgs. 25 ($\gamma\delta$). Thus it

[4] The Greek scripts and Palaeo-Hebrew inserts in "R" (i.e., the Recension of Barthélemy) point to a date about the middle of the first century of our era, or, perhaps better, the second half of the century. See DA, pp. 167f., and C. H. Roberts *apud* P. Kahle, "Problems of the Septuagint," Studia Patristica, ed. Aland and Cross, I (1957), 332.

[5] Cf. P. Katz, "Justin's Old Testament Quotations and the Greek Dodekapropheton Scroll," Studia Patristica, I, 350.

[6] See DA, pp. 228-45 for discussion of other relations of the Recension; Cf. D. Katz, op. cit. (note 5), 345-53.

[7] DA, pp. 246-70.

[8] The Septuagint and Jewish Worship [Schweich Lectures 1920] (London, 1921).

became clear that the Old Greek or Septuagint in these sections has been replaced by the later recension. Other books and sections of the received Greek Bible may belong to this recensional group, appropriately labeled by Barthélemy the *Groupe καίγε*.[9] Ruth and Lamentations are good candidates.[10] Daniel, traditionally assigned to Theodotion, and correctly recognized by a number of scholars as "Proto-Theodotion," seems clearly to belong to the καίγε Recension. Other Theodotionic materials show clear affinities with the Recension and belong at least to the same family.[11]

The καίγε Recension is of decisive bearing on the debate over Septuagint origins. It brings a qualified victory to the Lagarde school, despite Paul Kahle's protestations to the contrary.[12] There is no doubt that this Greek text was an early Jewish attempt to revise the standard Septuagint into conformity with a Proto-Massoretic Hebrew text, just as Aquila represents a sequent attempt to revise this revision in the direction of the official Rabbinic or Massoretic text which had been established by his day. We see, then, a series of attempts to bring the Greek Bible into conformity with a *changing* Hebrew textual tradition.[13] On the

[9] DA, pp. 33–47; pp. 91–143.

[10] The case of Judges is not established by Barthélemy, and insufficient data is presented for Canticles, et al. Much labor is needed to test most of the suggested instances of the καίγε Recension. In the case of the Book of Reigns, Barthélemy's careful study, the data presented below, as well as a dissertation of my student Father D. Shenkel, which goes well beyond Barthélemy in dealing with the recensions in 1 and 2 Kings, put the identification beyond doubt.

[11] E.g., the additions to Old Greek Job, the "Theodotionic" material in Psalms, including "Quinta," etc. Cf. Barthélemy, DA, pp. 41–47. On the "Proto-Theodotionic" text of Daniel, see J. A. Montgomery, The Book of Daniel [ICC] (Edinburgh, 1927), pp. 46–50; J. Ziegler, Susanna, Daniel, Bel et Draco [*Göttingen Septuaginta*] (Göttingen, 1954), p. 28, n. 1 and pp. 61f. Barthélemy's thesis that the καίγε Recension is to be identified with Theodotion must remain *sub judice*. The evidence to equate Theodotion with Jonathan ben Uzziel is highly speculative, and little is actually solved by reassigning the designation "Theodotion." In Samuel-Kings we must still deal, as Barthélemy recognizes, with two "Palestinian recensions" (at least), in the Minor Prophets with both the Sixth Column and Quinta, with Theodotion in the Pentateuch, and so on. Until the character of "late" Theodotion is fully analyzed, perhaps it is better to retain more traditional designations, "Proto-Theodotion" and "Theodotion," rather than shifting with Barthélemy to what may be termed "Theodotion" and "Post-Theodotion."

[12] P. Kahle, "Die im August 1952 entdeckte Lederrolle mit dem griechischen Text der kleinen Propheten . . . ," TLZ 79 (1954), coll. 81–94; Cross, ALQ², p. 171, n.13; Barthélemy, DA, p. 266.

[13] Cf. ALQ², p. 174 and n.19.

one hand these data firmly support evidence, already overwhelmingly clear, that an *Urtext* exists behind the Christian recensions of the Septuagint. On the other hand it also vindicates those who had argued that the special readings of Justin were early, and lends the support of analogy to those who claimed that the "Lucianic" readings of Josephus' biblical quotations were early.[14]

Later in the same year that the first fragments of the Barthélemy text were published, the writer published pieces of a Hebrew manuscript of Samuel from Cave IV, Qumrân (4QSam[a]).[15] Later purchases added a very large number of fragments to the manuscript, and now it is probably the most important as well as the most extensively preserved of some one hundred biblical manuscripts from Cave IV, Qumrân. The text was of a type markedly distinct from the traditional Hebrew text of Samuel, but closely related to the Hebrew *Vorlage* of the Septuagint. There could be no confusion. A text having integrity though widely at variance with the *textus receptus* had come to hand. This text was the herald of a series of non-Massoretic texts, some from Cave IV which have had only preliminary publication, some like the Deuteronomy manuscript from Cave V (5Q1) which have been fully published.[16]

In 1954 Monsignor Skehan published a fragment of the "Song of Moses" which followed the Septuagint text against a defective Massoretic tradition.[17]

In 1955 appeared the writer's study of a third-century B.C. manuscript of Samuel (4QSam[b]). The character of one group of its fragments was summarized as follows:

> 4Q agrees with LXX against MT thirteen times; 4Q agrees with

---

[14] Paul Kahle is thus justified in his fulminations against Rahlf's treatment of the Proto-Lucianic problem. It is ironical, however, that Kahle himself then argued (1947) that the biblical quotations from the historical books in Josephus had later been brought into conformity with the Lucianic text by Christian scribes! (The Cairo Geniza [London, 1947], pp. 150–56).

[15] F. M. Cross, "A New Qumrân Biblical Fragment Related to the Original Hebrew Underlying the Septuagint," BASOR 132 (Dec., 1953), 15–26; cf. corrections of misprints in F. M. Cross, "The Oldest Manuscripts from Qumrân," JBL 74 (1955), 165, n.40.

[16] M. Baillet, J. T. Milik et R. de Vaux, Les "petites grottes" de Qumrân, DJD III (Oxford, 1962).

[17] P. W. Skehan, "A Fragment of the 'Song of Moses' (Deut. 32) from Qumrân," BASOR 136 (Dec., 1954), 12–15; cf. ALQ², pp. 182–84.

MT against LXX four times. Such statistics do not indicate the full value of this archaic text. Its affinities with the tradition to which the *Vorlage* of the Old Greek belongs is most important, and cannot be neglected in developing new methods and evaluations in future critical studies of the text of Samuel. Nevertheless, the most extraordinary characteristic of the text of 4QSam[b] is the high proportion of the original readings which it preserves, whether it be in agreement with the Greek, or in agreement with the MT, or against both in its several unique readings.[18]

In the same year, in fact in the same issue of the Journal of Biblical Literature,[19] Monsignor Skehan published parts of an Exodus manuscript written in a late Palaeo-Hebrew script, probably of the second century B.C. The character of the text is Samaritan, or rather that Palestinian type of text selected by the Samaritan community and surviving alone in it. It may be designated Proto-Samaritan to distinguish it from the specifically Samaritan text-type which underwent further recension.

Thanks to new data from Qumrân and elsewhere, we can correct a false assumption which has long plagued textual study of the Samaritan recension, namely, the view that the text stems from a Samaritan rupture of the fifth or fourth century B.C. As early as 1941, W. F. Albright had recognized that the script of the Samaritan Bible branched off from the Palaeo-Hebrew script not earlier than the first century B.C.[20] The study of the Palaeo-Hebrew script of Qumrân, of the Palaeo-Hebrew script found on an unpublished sealing of a Samaritan governor of the mid-fourth century B.C. as well as on coins and stamps of the fourth to the second century B.C., wholly support this dating. Similarly orthographic evidence, evidence from language, and indeed the character of the text itself confirm it.[21]

In 1958, the writer published his first attempt to deal in a systematic if provisional way with the variety of textual types

[18] F. M. Cross, "The Oldest Manuscripts from Qumrân," JBL 74 (1955), 147–72.

[19] P. W. Skehan, "Exodus in the Samaritan Recension from Qumrân," JBL 74 (1955), 182–87.

[20] From the Stone Age to Christianity (Baltimore, 1941, 1946²), p. 336, n.12.

[21] See the writer's remarks in "The Development of the Jewish Scripts," in The Bible and the Ancient Near East, p. 189, n.4, and in the Harvard dissertation of my student James Purvis dealing with the Samaritan schism (1962).

found among the biblical manuscripts from Cave IV, Qumrân.[22]
It had become clear that at Qumrân we had penetrated to an era
when local texts prevailed, and, so far as the Qumrân community
was concerned, before the promulgation of an authoritative recension. The evidence for textual families for the time being is restricted largely to the Pentateuch, the Former Prophets, and the
Book of Jeremiah. Study has been directed first of all to those
books whose texts are dramatic in their variety, and whose Greek
versions are relatively trustworthy. Isaiah's textual variations
between the Hebrew and Greek are narrow in range, and, unhap-
pily, the Septuagint is notoriously paraphrastic.[23] The Minor
Prophets exhibit slightly more variety, and ample material is
available for their analysis, but full attention has not been
directed upon their exemplars from Cave IV, Qumrân, and the
same is so by and large for the Hagiographa. The Psalter is an
exception, and while its text at Qumrân is close to that of the
textus receptus, the Scroll of Psalms from Cave XI shortly to be
published will be of considerable interest.[24] If the so-called 11Q
Ps[a] is indeed a Psalter, despite its bizarre order and noncanonical
compositions, mostly of the Hellenistic era, then we must argue
that one Psalms collection closed at the end of the Persian period
(the canonical collection), and that another remained open well
into the Greek period (11Q), but was rejected by the Rabbis.
This is not to mention the extensive fragments of Psalms manuscripts from Cave IV, to be published shortly by P. W. Skehan.

In the Pentateuch three types of text are present. Some texts,
especially that of Genesis, are closely allied with the *textus re-*

[22] ALQ[2], pp. 168–94. Other general studies include M. Greenberg, "The Stabilization of the Text of the Hebrew Bible . . . ," JAOS 76 (1956), 161–63; H. M.
Orlinsky, "The Textual Criticism of the Old Testament," in The Bible and the
Ancient Near East, pp. 113–32. The most provocative single study was Albright's
brief "New Light on Early Recensions of the Hebrew Bible," BASOR 140 (1955),
27–33.
[23] Cf. P. W. Skehan, "The Text of Isaias at Qumrân," CBQ 8 (1955), 38–43;
and "Some Textual Problems in Isaias," CBQ 22 (1960), 47–55. References to
Orlinsky's series of detailed studies can be found in the article cited in n.22. See
also E. Y. Kutscher, The Language and Linguistic Background of the Isaiah Scroll
[Hebrew] (Jerusalem, 1959).
[24] See, provisionally, J. A. Sanders, "The Scroll of Psalms (11Q Pss) from
Cave II: A Preliminary Report," BASOR 165 (Feb., 1962), 11–15; "Ps. 151 in
11Q Pss," ZAW 75 (1963), 73–86; "Two Non-Canonical Psalms in 11Q Ps[a],"
ZAW 76 (1964), 57–75.

ceptus; others reflect close relations with the Samaritan, or properly, with the Palestinian text; a third group is closely affiliated with a text of the type which underlies the Septuagint.[25] A text of Numbers (4Q Num[b]) shows unusual characteristics.[26] It regularly follows Samaritan readings, including the long additions from Deuteronomy introduced into the text of Numbers in Proto-Samaritan tradition. On the other hand, when the Massoretic and Samaritan texts agree against the pre-Hexaplaric Greek text (i.e., the Septuagint), this text of Numbers usually agrees with the Old Greek, and it almost never sides with MT against both the Samaritan and Septuagint. It is evidently an early type of Palestinian text which somehow survived.[27]

The Samuel manuscripts from Cave IV are all at wide variance with Massoretic tradition, all with ties to the tradition used in the Septuagint translation. For reasons to be discussed below, we believe them all to belong to the Palestinian textual tradition.

In the case of Jeremiah, one manuscript of three from Cave IV follows the short tradition familiar from the Septuagint. Two represent the type of the traditional text.[28]

I. THE RABBINIC RECENSION OF THE BIBLE.

With the publication of the biblical documents from Murabbaʿât in 1961,[29] Genesis, Exodus, Numbers, and Isaiah, and above all, the great Hebrew Minor Prophets scroll, there can no longer be any reason to doubt that by the beginning of the second century A.D. an authoritative text of the Hebrew Bible had been promul-

---

[25] Some readings from an Exodus scroll (4Q Ex[a]) together with a photograph of a fragment from it are published in ALQ[2], p. 184, n.31; see also the Plate opposite p. 141.

[26] On 4Q Num[a], see already ALQ[2], p. 186 and n.36.

[27] Against the text's having arisen by a simple *crossing* of MSS of Palestinian and Egyptian types stands the evidence of occasional agreement with LXX minuses and occasional omission of LXX plusses, as well as a sprinkling of so-called Proto-Lucianic readings (i.e., 4Q Num–𝔊[L] vs. MT–𝔊[BAO]).

[28] A sample of the text of the shorter recension is published in ALQ[2], p. 187, n.38 (4Q Jer[b]). One of my students, Mr. J. G. Janzen, has shown in a forthcoming Harvard dissertation that a large portion of the plusses of MT in Jeremiah stem from expansionist tendencies of the type familiar for example in the Samaritan Pentateuch. On the contrary, the short text represented at Qumrân and in the Septuagint is exceedingly well preserved.

[29] P. Benoit, J. T. Milik, et R. de Vaux, Les grottes de Murabbaʿât, DJD II (Oxford, 1961), 75–85 (Pls. XIX–XXIV), and 181–205 (Pls. LVI–LXXIII).

gated,[30] the archetype of the Massoretic manuscripts of the Middle Ages. The entire text of the Minor Prophets scroll reveals only five or six real variants, neglecting minor orthographic variation, interchange of 'l and ʿl, and the like. The astonishing fact is that even the minor textual variants which mark the text of Aquila, the Targum, and the Vulgate are largely absent, and it is clear that these versions preserve some genuine survivals of readings which predate the official recension, since in each case older materials were used alongside the newer standard text.[31] Medieval variants are for the most part merely orthographic or secondary, a witness to subsequent development of variant readings which for a number of reasons may coincide with older witnesses.[32] In effect we have found at Murabbaʿât texts which testify to an archetypal recension as the ancestor of all Medieval Hebrew biblical manuscripts. The character of textual variation in Qumrân texts, where manuscripts belong to different textual families, differs *toto caelo* from the variation exhibited in the biblical texts of Murabbaʿât stemming from the circles of Bar Kokhba.

Thanks to the existence at Qumrân of a variety of textual traditions as well as to the evidence of the Greek recensions, we are able to describe somewhat the process by which the official text came into existence. The establishment of the official text followed a pattern unusual in the textual history of ancient documents. Unlike the recensional activity in Alexandria which produced an elegant if artificial and eclectic text of Homer,[33] and quite unlike

---

[30] To this material will be added other fragments from the Naḥal Ḥever (Wâdī Ḥabrā). See provisionally Y. Yadin, Yediot 25 (1961), 49–64, and esp. Pl. 32:2. Cf. Y. Aharoni, "The Caves of the Naḥal Ḥever," ʿAtiqot 3 (1961), 148–75; Y. Yadin, "New Discoveries in the Judaean Desert," BA 24 (1961), 34–50; and J. T. Milik, "Deux documents inédits du Désert de Juda. . . ," Biblica 38 (1957), 255–64. The new discoveries at Maṣada may enable us to push back the existence of the Rabbinic recension, if not its official promulgation, to before A.D. 73. See below.

[31] Compare the writer's remarks in ALQ², p. 170, n.13.

[32] See, for example, Aptowitzer, Das Schriftwort in der rabbinischen Literatur (Sitzungsb. der kais. Akad. der Wiss. in Wien, Phil.-Hist. Klasse Bd. 153:6 [1906]; 160:7 [1908]), and H. L. Strack, Prolegomena critica in Vetus Testamentum hebraicum (Leipzig, 1873). Cf. M. H. Goshen-Gottstein, Text and Language in Bible and Qumrân, pp. x–xii.

[33] Compare S. Lieberman, Hellenism in Jewish Palestine (New York, 1950), pp. 20–27; S. Talmon, "The Three Scrolls of the Law That Were Found in the Temple Court," Textus II (1962), 19–27.

the recensional activity which produced the Hexaplaric recension of the Septuagint or the conflate *textus receptus* of the New Testament, the Rabbinic scholars and scribes proceeded neither by wholesale revision and emendation nor by eclectic or conflating recensional procedures. They selected a single local textual tradition, which may be called the Proto-Massoretic text, a text which had been in existence in rough homogeneity for some time. Evidence for this text-type appears in our sources for the Pentateuch first at Qumrân. In Samuel and Kings it first influences the Septuagint text in the second of the major Jewish recensions, the καίγε or Proto-Theodotionic Recension, made about the middle of the first century A.D. It must be noted, however, that the Proto-Massoretic tradition at Qumrân and underlying the καίγε Recension of Samuel-Kings is not identical with the official text now known from the era between the two Jewish Revolts, and from Aquila. Some recensional activity was involved. A single orthographic tradition, in part archaizing to pre- or non-Maccabaean spelling practices, was systematically imposed. Remarkably, the old Palestinian Palaeo-Hebrew script, as well as the Palestinian text-type preserved in it, was rejected. This rejection cannot be termed anti-Samaritan. The Palaeo-Hebrew script was the national Hebrew script of the Maccabees and was at home among the Essenes of Qumrân. It was the script nostalgically revived in both Jewish revolts against Rome. For a reason we shall expound later, the Rabbis chose a textual tradition of a specific kind never found in pure type in Palaeo-Hebrew, and hence, reluctantly, we suspect, chose the Late Herodian book-hand as the official character. This hand, already an archaizing character in the era of Bar Kokhba, was preserved through many centuries with remarkably slight evolutionary change.

As we have remarked, the Rabbinic text is normally short, not conflate or expansionist in the Pentateuch and Samuel. To be sure, there are secondary expansions in the Pentateuch, but by and large it is a superb, disciplined text. On the contrary, the text of Samuel is remarkably defective, and its shortness is the result of a long history of losses by haplography, the commonest error by far in a text which has not undergone systematic recensional activity, or which has not become mixed by infection from a different textual tradition. Some indisputable evidence can be marshalled of revision and suppression of dramatically corrupt readings in the case of Samuel.[34] At all events, the Rabbinic recension stands in clear contrast to the full texts of the Palestinian and Old Greek traditions. The Proto-Massoretic text of the Pentateuch never passed through the centuries of reworking, revision, and expansion which characterized the development of the Proto-Samaritan tradition; it stood aloof from both this circle of tradition and that of the fuller Egyptian text. In the case of Samuel, it is difficult to understand the selection of the Proto-Massoretic tradition in view of the excellence of the Old Palestinian text-type, available at least at Qumrân.

We shall be speaking later of the local origin of the *textus receptus* and shall argue that its tradition, at least for the Pentateuch and Former Prophets, is the local text of Babylon which emerged in the fourth to second centuries B.C. Anticipating some of the conclusions of the following sections, however, we wish to deal now with the difficult problem of the occasion and date of the promulgation or, if one prefers, the fixing of the official text.

A *terminus ad quem* of c. A.D.100 is well established by the manuscripts taken into the desert by the remnants of Bar Kokhba's forces. A *terminus a quo* is more difficult to fix. Rabbinic reflections of the recensional activity are late, and must be controlled by external data.[34a] There exists at Qumrân no evidence whatever of true recensional activity. Earlier, scholars pointed to the late Isaiah Scroll (1Q Isa[b]) as evidence of a gradual trend toward the Massoretic text. There is no justification whatever for such a view. A text of Deuteronomy from Cave V dating to the early second century B.C. was systematically corrected in the Early Herodian period by a manuscript of Septuagintal type, so that every correction carried the text away from the Proto-Massoretic tradition.[35] In general, the date of a roll from Cave IV, Qumrân, tells us nothing of what we may expect of its textual character. These data would naturally lead one to propose that the main thrust of recensional activity on

---

[34] See for example, ALQ[2], p. 191, n.45.

[34a] Cf. the studies listed in n.33, to which should be added S. Talmon, JJS 2 (1951), 149 f.

[35] 5Q1, DJD III, 169–71; Pl. xxxvi.

the part of the Rabbis must date from between the Jewish Revolts, or in any case no earlier than the era of Hillel, at the beginning of the first century A.D. Unfortunately, we cannot be sure that members of the Essene community, whether living in the desert or in the villages, were not sealed off from contact with Pharisaic Judaism after about 140 B.C.[36] Before this time, when the Essenes and Pharisees merge back into the Ḥasidic movement, there can be no question of their texts being aloof from putative recensional activity. The separation of the non-Massoretic Samaritan text in the same era points in the same direction.

On *a priori* grounds, we should expect the publication of an official text, and thereby the establishment of the distinction between official and *koina* traditions, to have taken place in one of three critical periods. One era would be the late Maccabaean Age, when expulsions from Parthia and a Zionist revival brought floods of Jews from Babylon, Syria, and Egypt back to Jerusalem, and when, owing to the wholesale destruction of biblical texts in the Epiphanian persecution, scribal activity must have been stimulated. Thus, by the beginning of Hasmonaean times, we should suppose (1) that different local texts had immigrated to Judah, no doubt causing such confusion as we find reflected in the library of Qumrân, and (2) that scribal activity was urgent, both because of rival textual traditions and the great loss of Palestinian texts. A second era would be that of the interval between the Jewish Revolts, when both Hebrew and Greek evidence affirms that the official text was regnant. A third period would be that of the great schools of Hillel and Shammai. By Hillel's time, the theological and hermeneutic principles requiring a stable text had come into being.[37] Moreover, Hillel's Babylonian origins could provide a reason for the unexpected Rabbinic rejection of the Palestinian in favor of the Babylonian text as the basis of the recension.

The first era must be rejected, and the likelihood is that,

[36] For the writer's detailed arguments for this date, see ALQ², pp. 109–60, and the literature cited therein. To this should now be added R. de Vaux, L'archéologie et les manuscrits de la Mer Morte (London, 1961), esp. pp. 86–94.

[37] Cf. Kutscher, op. cit., esp. p. 472; Barthélemy, DA, pp. 3–21; and the judicious statements of S. Lieberman, Hellenism in Jewish Palestine, pp. 47–68.

while first recensional activities may have begun as early as Hillel,
effective promulgation of the official text and the demise of rival
texts date to the era between the Revolts, in the days of Aqiba.
This is the easiest way to deal with the evidence from Qumrân.
More impressive, we know that late apocryphal and pseudepigraphical works stemming from Jewish circles in Palestine still
exhibit a variety of biblical texts in works composed as late as
the first century A.D. The New Testament reflects a variety of
Hebrew and Greek biblical traditions. The καίγε Recension, based
on a Proto-Massoretic text, gives evidence on the one hand that
in the mid-first century the Old Palestinian text had been displaced in some Jewish circles. On the other hand, it shows equally
that the official or Massoretic text had not yet come into being,
or at least was not used in the Pharisaic school that produced the
recension. Finally, as we shall be able to show in the next section, the Proto-Lucianic revision of the Septuagint of Samuel,
a recension of the Septuagint revised to conform with a Palestinian text of the second or first century B.C., was still used by
Josephus in his Antiquities, first composed about A.D. 93–94.

2. PROTO-LUCIAN IN SAMUEL AND THE TEXT OF SAMUEL USED
    BY THE CHRONICLER AND JOSEPHUS.

In studying the text of 4Q Samᵃ, I have been forced to note a
series of readings in which the Hebrew of 4Q Samᵃ reflects the
so-called Lucianic recension preserved in the Greek minuscules
boc₂e₂, and the Itala. In other words, 4Q Samᵃ stands with LXXᴸ
against MT and LXXᴮ. These are proper Proto-Lucianic readings in a *Hebrew* text of the first century B.C., four centuries before the Syrian Father to whom the recension is attributed. In
I Sam. 1–2 Sam. 11:1, the text of 4Q Samᵃ (and 4Q Samᵇ) follows closely the readings of the family LXXᴮ, especially when
LXXᴮ and LXXᴸ agree against MT. There are also a sprinkling
of indisputable Proto-Lucianic readings when 4Q Sam stands
with LXXᴸ against MT and LXXᴮ, and even a rare instance
when 4Q Sam and Josephus stand together against all other traditions. A few illustrations follow:

  I. 4Q Samᵃ: I Sam. 5:9

        גתה] ואתו 𝔐 | αυτη B | προς γεθ b′ | προς γεθθαιους boc₂e₂

2. 4Q Sam[a]: 1 Sam. 5:10

ארון האלהים [ארון אלוהי ישראל] 𝔐 | την κιβωτον του θεου

B | την κιβωτον του θεου ιηλ boc₂e₂

3. 4Q Sam[b]: 1 Sam. 23:13

ולשאול הגד כי נמלט [לשאו]ל [כי נ]מלט 𝔐 | και τω σαουλ απη-

γγελη οτι διασεσωσται B | (απηγγελη) τω σαουλ οτι δια-

σεσωσται bioc₂e₂ 𝕲

4. 4Q Sam[a]: 1 Sam. 28:1

במחנה אתה ואנשיך [למ]לחמה יזרעא[ל]ה] 𝔐 | εις πολεμον

συ και οι ανδρες σου 𝕲 | εις τον πολεμον εις ρεγαν (Lat.

RELLA). ΕΙΣΡΕΓΑ/ΡΕΛΑ < ΙΕΣΡΑΕΛΑ. Jos. vi,325.

ΙΕΣΡΑΕΛΑ for יזרעאל appears elsewhere in Josephus.

5. 4Q Sam[a]: 2 Sam. 3:28

מדמי אבנר [ודם [אבנר] 𝔐 | απο των αιματων Αβεννηρ B | αιμα

Αβεννηρ boc₂e₂ Thdt.

6. 4Q Sam[a]: 2 Sam. 5:11 [37a]

וחרשי אבן קיר [וחרשי קיר 𝔐 | και τεκτονας λιθων B | και

τεκτονας τοιχου λιθων (conflate!) b | וחרשי קיר 1 Chr.

14:1 | και τεκτονας τοιχου oc₂e₂ 𝔏.

Moreover, in sections where Chronicles overlaps with Samuel in this section 1 Sam. 1–2 Sam. 11:1,[38] the text of Chronicles normally agrees with 4Q and LXX[BL] against MT.

On the contrary, in 2 Sam. 11:2–2 Sam. 24:25, the relation of 4Q Sam[a] with LXX[B] changes wholly. Now 4Q Sam[a] normally stands with LXX[L], the Lucianic recension,[39] against LXX[B], and LXX[B] normally reflects a Proto-Massoretic tradition. We have seen above that Thackeray and most recently Barthélemy have argued that this section of Samuel is not the Old Greek, but the καίγε or Proto-Theodotionic recension. The evidence of the Samuel manuscripts confirms this conclusion beyond dispute. Further, Josephus and the text of Chronicles also continue to side with 4Q Sam[a] and the Proto-Lucianic text.

[37a] On this text, see the analysis of S. Talmon, Textus I (1960), 167, 152.

[38] That is, in 1 Sam. 31; 2 Sam. 5:1, 6–25; 6:1–23; 7–8; 10; 11:1.

[39] On the Proto-Lucianic character of the sixth column of the Hexapla, see below, n.44.

Some illustrations may be found already published in my
Ancient Library of Qumrân.[40] More follow below:

1. 4Q Samᵃ: 2 Sam. 12:15
   אלוהים [יהוה 𝔐 | κυριος B | ο θ͞ς bgoc₂e₂

2. 4Q Samᵃ: 2 Sam. 12:16
   וישכב בשק] ושכב 𝔐 | και ηυλισθη B | και εκαθευδεν εν σακκω
   boc₂e₂ | . . . επι σακκου Jos. vii,154 | και ηυλισθη εν σακκω
   MN cgjnuvb₂ | etc.

3. 4Q Samᵃ: 2 Sam. 13:3
   הונתן[י]] יונדב[י 𝔐 | ιωναδαμ B | ιωναδαβ 𝕲ᴼ | ιωνναθαν boe₂ |
   ιωναθης Jos. vii, 178. Cf. 2 Sam. 21:21 = 1 Chr. 20:7.

4. 4Q Samᵃ: 2 Sam. 24:17
   הרעה הרעתי] העויתי 𝔐 | והרע הרעותי 1 Chr. 21:17 | ειμι
   ηδικησα B | ο ποιμην εκακοποιησα 𝕲ᴼᴸ. Cf. ο ποιμην Jos.
   vii,328.

5. 4Q Samᵃ: 2 Sam. 24:16 +
   בשקים על פניהם [פנ]יהם מת[כסים בשק]ים > 𝔐 𝕲ᴮᴼᴸ |
   מכסים I Chr.; cf. Jos. vii, 327.

6. 4Q Samᵃ: 2 Sam. 24:18
   ויאמר לו] ויאמר 𝔐 | και ειπεν αυτω B | και ειπεν abovc₂e₂

7. 4Q Samᵃ: 2 Sam. 24:20
   וארנא דש חטים [וארנן דש חטים > 𝔐 𝕲ᴮᴼᴸ | וארנן דש חטים 1 Chr. 21:20 |
   ορουυας δε τον σιτον αλοων Jos. vii, 330.

The agreement between the text of Chronicles and 4Q Samᵃ is
most significant.[41] It makes clear now that the text of the Deuteronomic history used by the Chronicler toward 400 B.C. was
by no means identical with the received text. Yet it is equally
clear that the Chronicler used the Old Palestinian text current
in Jerusalem in his day. That in 1 Sam. 1–2 Sam. 11:1 the Chronicler used a text very closely related to that of 4Q Samᵃ and
LXXᴮᴸ and in 2 Sam. 11:2–24:25 a text closely related to 4Q

----

[40] ALQ², pp. 188–89, n.40a. Samples are chosen arbitrarily from a passage at
the beginning and a passage at the end of the section.

[41] Among other things it means that we can control better the Chronicler's
treatment of his sources. The usual picture painted of the Chronicler violently or
willfully distorting Samuel and Kings to suit his fancy must be radically revised.

Sam^a and LXX^L, but not to LXX^B, yields further evidence for the Old Palestinian substratum in the Lucianic recension.

Perhaps we can now proceed to sketch a general theory of the development of the Hebrew text-types and the Greek recensions of Samuel. There is evidence that the Septuagint of Samuel and Kings was translated from an Egyptian Hebrew text that separated from the Old Palestinian textual tradition no later than the fourth century B.C.[42] This text differed sharply from the *textus receptus*, and while more closely allied to Palestinian texts from Qumrân, nevertheless is distinct from them. This Old Greek text was revised no later than the first century B.C. toward a Hebrew text we can trace in Palestine in the Chronicler and in the three manuscripts from Cave IV, Qumrân. The Greek form is extant in quotations in Josephus, in the substratum of the Lucianic Recension preserved in the Greek minuscules boc$_2$e$_2$, and, surprisingly enough, in the sixth column of Origen's Hexapla to 2 Sam. 11:2–1 Kgs 2:11. Adam Mez first noted that the sixth column in the Hexapla, normally Theodotion, was directly related to the Greek biblical text used by Josephus, and to the Lucianic recension.[43] To Barthélemy must go the credit, however, for fully demonstrating the importance of this material, of freeing the sixth column here of its Theodotionic label, and of dealing systematically with its relations to the family boc$_2$e$_2$. Barthélemy concludes that the column contains the lost Septuagint of this section of Samuel-Kings. Here he errs, not being aware of the new evidence relating to the Proto-Lucianic recension. In fact the column preserves the Proto-Lucianic recension in relatively pure form. The Old Greek is lost in this section as in 2 Kgs (Thackeray's γδ).[44] The first stage, then, in the history of the

[42] See W. F. Albright, "New Light on Early Recension of the Hebrew Bible," pp. 27–33; ALQ², pp. 189f.

[43] A Mez, Die Bibel des Josephus . . . (Basel, 1895). Cf. Barthélemy, DA, pp. 139f.

[44] See Barthélemy, DA, pp. 126–36. The following points should be stressed about θ, i.e., the sixth column in the section βγ of Reigns: (1) the readings follow the Lucian text closely, but occasionally are superior to the witnesses boc$_2$e$_2$; (2) the readings are very often against MT; and (3) the readings often give translations of terms where LXX^B transliterates!

In addition to the new Qumrân evidence, supporting the identification of the Proto-Lucianic recension, we should observe that elsewhere in Samuel there are Greek materials difficult to explain by Barthélemy's hypothesis. For example, in

Greek recensions was the Proto-Lucian recension of the second or first century B.C., revised to conform to a Palestinian Hebrew text.

The second stage is represented by the καίγε recension made about the middle of the first century A.D. The Palestinian tradition underlying the Proto-Lucianic Greek was jettisoned, replaced by the Proto-Massoretic text as the Hebrew base.

The final stage is found in the late Greek recensions of the second century A.D., notably Symmachus, and Aquila, who undertook the further revision of the καίγε text, bringing it into conformity with the official Rabbinic text of Samuel.

Similarly we can schematize the history of the Hebrew textual families. The text of Samuel as it developed from a fifth century archetype split into three branches. (1) The Old Septuagint witnesses to an Egyptian local text. (2) 4Q Sam in its several manuscripts, as well as the Chronicler and Josephus, give witness to a Palestinian tradition at home in Palestine in the fourth century B.C. (Chronicles), the third century B.C. (4Q Sam[b]), the first century B.C. (4Q Sam[a], the Hebrew text underlying the Proto-Lucianic Recension), and the first century A.D. (Josephus' text). (3) The Proto-Massoretic text is known only from the καίγε Greek Recension of the first century A.D. in Samuel. With Egypt and Palestine preempted by local text-types,

---

1 Sam. 17–18, where the Old Greek text has *not* been suppressed, the Old Greek is much shorter than the Massoretic text, and perhaps original in its short form (cf. J. Wellhausen, Der Text der Bücher Samuelis [Göttingen, 1871], pp. 104f.). The Greek minuses in 17:12–31, 55–18:5 are filled in by (1) a recension belonging to the καίγε/Theodotionic group, and (2) the Lucianic recension of boc₂e₂, which, despite its Hexaplaric character, preserves many older readings against the MT, against the Theodotionic recension, and, of course, against the Old Greek (omissions).

Barthélemy's readiness to discard the Lucianic recension, *sensu stricto*, is puzzling. He recognizes that L in boc₂e₂ and in θ of the βγ section go back to a non-Massoretic Hebrew tradition, closely related to the Old Greek. But these data do not require or even support his radical solution.

It may be observed in passing that Barthélemy's selective treatment of Jerome's testimonies to Lucian leaves much to be desired, and that he omits mention of the relatively early and important witness of Pseudo-Athanasius. Compare the judicious recent treatment of these testimonies to Lucian by B. Metzger, Chapters in the History of New Testament Textual Criticism (Leiden, 1963), pp. 3–7. Cf. also S. Jellicoe, "The Hesychian Recension Reconsidered," JBL 82 (1963), 409–18.

In short, I do not perceive any ground for doubting the existence of a "late" Lucianic recension, and, in any case, the evidence for an early or Proto-Lucianic recension, the substratum of the text of Antioch, remains unaffected.

there is no escaping the conclusion, I believe, that the Proto-Massoretic text goes back to a local text preserved in Babylon in the fourth-second centuries B.C., reintroduced into Jerusalem in the Hasmonaean or Herodian period.

4. A THEORY OF LOCAL TEXTS

The evidence marshalled to support a theory of local texts of Samuel can be applied to other recensionally diverse texts from Qumrân, especially to the Pentateuch. In the Pentateuch in the Proto-Samaritan text of Qumrân and in the later Samaritan recension *sensu stricto*, we find, I believe, a text which developed in Palestine in the fifth-second centuries B.C. Its text is marked by "scholarly" reworking; parallel texts were inserted, grammar and orthography brought up to date, explanatory expansions and glosses intruded. As Kahle observed long ago, it is a text which was the work of centuries of growth, not systematic recension.[45] It appears at Qumrân both in Palaeo-Hebrew script, certainly a Palestinian trait, and in the Jewish character. The Samaritan texts have strong relations with the Egyptian *Vorlage* of the Septuagint, and certain texts of Cave IV, notably the 4Q Num[a] manuscript, though of Samaritan type, have *very* strong Egyptian affiliations. It is difficult to avoid the conclusion that this text-type is Palestinian and, like Samuel, closely allied to the Egyptian local text utilized by the translators of the Septuagint in the third century B.C. The oldest witness to the existence of this Palestinian text is to be found in the passages of 1 Chronicles 1–9, which quote from the Pentateuch. Gillis Gerleman has shown that these passages in Chronicles "show greater resemblance to the Samaritan Pentateuch than to the Massoretic."[46]

This leaves the Proto-Massoretic text once again without provenience in Palestine or Egypt, and presumably we must look again to Babylon as the locale for its preservation and emergence as a distinct, if conservative, textual type. It reflects little

[45] P. Kahle, "Untersuchungen zur Geschichte des Pentateuchtextes," Theologische Studien und Kritiken 88 (1915), 399–439 (now republished in Opera Minora [Leiden, 1956], pp. 3–37).
[46] Synoptic Studies in the Old Testament (Lund, 1948), pp. 9–12. As will be evident below, I cannot accept his explanation of the reasons for this phenomenon. Cf. S. Talmon, "The Samaritan Pentateuch," JJS 2 (1951), 146–50.

of the active scribal endeavor which shaped the other recensions, especially the Palestinian. Since it would not have been preserved in Palaeo-Hebrew, perhaps we find here cause for the rejection of the national script for the official text.

It is necessary to take up, finally, some of the objections raised against a theory of local texts. Some scholars, not always those with conservative axes to grind, argue that the manuscripts underlying the official recension must have come ultimately from the Temple library, and hence would be "Palestinian" texts. Further, it is argued that different texts might arise in one locality, and one must therefore distinguish between exact or official texts of the Temple, etc., and vulgar texts.

To the first argument we may readily answer that the manuscripts used in the official recension may well have come from the Temple. The question is when. Obviously various texts had come to Qumrân, to the Temple, into scribes' hands in the era immediately preceding the textual crisis which is the normal precondition for recensional labors. It does not follow at all that the text-type in question derived originally from Palestine because exemplars of the textual tradition finally came to rest in a Palestinian library.

The distinction "official versus vulgar" must be abandoned, however, as anachronistic. Official and vulgar texts do exist, but after official definition, that is, precisely after the promulgation of an official text. To use the term "vulgar" of the Proto-Samaritan recension, because of its reworking and revision, is not wholly unreasonable, though it obviously was not considered a vulgar text in the Samaritan or Qumrân community, nor was it deemed vulgar, I dare say, by the Chronicler. But our evaluation on scientific grounds of the text-critical worth of a text is not identical with the mode of judgment applied by the ancients, and it would be absurd to apply the designation *vulgar* to the old Samuel manuscript, to the manuscript used to revise the Septuagint to produce the Palestinian Greek Recension (Proto-Lucian) — in brief, to manuscripts equal to or superior to the *textus receptus* of Samuel. Or to put it most strongly, I challenge anyone to give a sensible reason for labeling the short, superb text of Jeremiah from Qumrân and underlying the Septuagint a vulgar text.[47] No, the term *vulgar* must be applied to a text denigrated in favor of an official text, whether this be the Rabbinic Bible or Homeric texts, or else it comes to mean merely "non-traditional," or even "unfamiliar."

We must object brusquely also to the notion that textual traditions, each having a known character, of limited number, and each quite distinct from the other, can exist side by side in the same community or locality for centuries. Certainly it runs counter to analogies drawn from other fields of textual criticism. In the classical field, in Septuagint criticism, in the study of the history of the old Latin Bible and the Greek New Testament, scholars have come to recognize that critical or recensional activity regularly follows an era of local textual development.

It must be remembered that recensionally distinct texts are fragile creations; one text, coming in contact with another, immediately dissolves into a mixed text. One set of corrections and centuries of development are destroyed in a twinkling. We may observe that there are few mixed texts at Qumrân, and the Proto-Massoretic text reveals no evidence of mixing in the Torah and Former Prophets. The development of the traditional texts of the Pentateuch and Samuel cannot have taken place in Palestine. Too many centuries were required in their making, and the small community had insufficient space to furnish isolation for two radically distinct texts to mature over a period of centuries in pristine innocence of one another.

[47] For this analysis of the short recension of Jeremiah I am greatly indebted to my student Mr. Gerald Janzen.

THE MASSORETIC TEXT AND THE QUMRAN SCROLLS:
A STUDY IN ORTHOGRAPHY

DAVID NOEL FREEDMAN

I

Some years ago, Frank M. Cross and I made a systematic study of the orthography of representative inscriptions in the different North-West Semitic dialects. These could be dated by epigraphic and other means to the period between the 10th and 6th centuries B.C.E., and thus provided a pattern for comparison with Hebrew inscriptions of the same period. The object of the investigation was to determine the basic principles governing orthographic practice and to trace the course of development and refinement in alphabetic spelling of these dialects and of Hebrew in particular. One result of the study[1] was the establishment of a relative chronology, and with the help of related disciplines, especially that of palaeography, an absolute chronology could also be fixed within limits. Thus it was possible not only to determine the general pattern of orthographic development, and to distinguish its principal phases, but also to date these approximately. Our conclusions may be summarized as follows:

1. The Phoenician phase of consonantal orthography, down to the end of the 10th century B.C.E. This was a purely consonantal spelling, without indication of vowel sounds at all, and is the oldest form of alphabetic writing. It is characteristic of the Proto-Canaanite inscriptions found at Sinai and in Palestine. Ugaritic spelling, with different *aleph* signs to indicate various vowels accompanying the *aleph*, is a special phenomenon arising from the peculiar linguistic situation at Ugarit, and has no echoes in later alphabetic spelling. Phoenician inscriptions, from the earliest to the latest times are written in typically consonantal orthography: in fact they define the nature and details of the system. The earliest Hebrew inscriptions (*e.g.*, the Gezer calendar) exhibit the same characteristics, and clearly belong to this pattern of spelling.

2. The Aramaic phase, from the 9th century, involving the use of *matres lectionis* to represent certain vowel sounds. Two further subdivisions can be distinguished:

---

1. F. M. Cross, Jr., and D. N. Freedman, *Early Hebrew Orthography* (New Haven, 1952).

196

a) The introduction of the vowel letters, *he, waw,* and *yodh* to represent long vowels in the final position: *i.e., he* for *ā, ē, ō, waw* for *ū,* and *yodh* for *ī.* We find this pattern in Aramaic inscriptions from the 9th century on, in the Mesha' Inscription (also 9th century), and in Hebrew inscriptional material from this period (chiefly 8th century on). In short there was a clear shift in Hebrew spelling practice, which may be dated to the 9th century.

b) The gradual introduction of vowel letters, *waw* and *yodh,* in the medial position, to represent *ū* and *ī.* The first examples are found in Aramaic inscriptions from the late 8th century (*e.g., Aš̌šur* spelled with *waw* for *ū*), and now also in Hebrew from approximately the same period, the end of the 8th century (in the so-called Shebna inscription, with the word *'ārūr,* using *waw* foi the *ū* vowel). Such usage, however, remains rare and sporadic in Hebrew until the end of the pre-Exilic period. Thus there are only a few examples in the whole of the Lachish correspondence.

II

While some questions could not be decided because of lack of evidence, and others remain obscure, the general pattern, established by inductive analysis from hundreds of examples, has not been seriously undermined by critics, but has been confirmed by subsequent discoveries. On the assumption that some parts at least of the Old Testament were originally written down in the pre-Exilic period, an effort was made to test the usefulness of our studies in early Hebrew orthography for the investigation of the biblical text. For this purpose a series of studies were made of some of the poems, which on other grounds might be regarded as among the oldest compositions in the O.T. Professor W. F. Albright pioneered with his important paper on the Oracles of Balaam[2], followed by studies on Habakkuk iii[3]; Psalm lxviii[4], and most recently, Deut. xxxii.[5] Cross and I, continuing a long Johns Hopkins concern with this early poetry, as attested by the articles of Albright and before him of Paul Haupt, have published papers on Deuteronomy xxxii[6]; Psalm xviii= 2 Samuel xxii[7], and Exodus xv[8], and have others as yet unpublished. It is our considered judgment that these papers have generally vindicated the applic-

2.   "The Oracles of Balaam", JBL 63 (1944), 207-33.
3.   "The Psalm of Habakkuk", *Studies in Old Testament Prophecy,* ed. H. H. Rowley (Edinburgh, 1950), pp. 1-18.
4.   "A Catalogue of Early Hebrew Lyric Poems (Ps. 68)", HUCA 23/1 (1950-51), 1-40.
5.   "Some Remarks on the Song of Moses in Deuteronomy 32", VT 9 (1959), 339-46.
6.   "The Blessing of Moses", JBL 67 (1948), 191-210.
7.   "A Royal Song of Thanksgiving: 2 Samuel 22 = Psalm xviii", JBL 72 (1953), 15-34.
8.   "The Song of Miriam", JNES 14 (1955), 237-50.

ation of orthographic analysis to selected biblical passages. That they have proved useful in text-criticism and in the clarification of difficult passages can hardly be denied. Used circumspectly they may be helpful in fixing an original date of written composition. Thus, if any of these poems were written down in the age of David and Solomon, we would expect them to have been written in the prevailing orthographic style, *i.e.*, Phoenician consonantal orthography. While the present Hebrew text of the O.T. naturally reflects much later spelling techniques, the presence of examples of archaic spelling ("mistakes" from the point of view of later practice, but quite correct according to earlier usage) would be evidence in support of such an hypothesis. We would not wish to press the case beyond this point, since the evidence is limited, and the conclusions depend to some degree on the presuppositions adopted and the method employed in interpieting the data.

The orthographic approach has proved useful not only in identifying the features of the earliest Hebrew spelling, but also in distinguishing orthographically the dialects of northern and southern Palestine (*i.e.* Israelite and Judahite). A basic difference lies in the pronunciation and spelling of the proto-Semitic diphthongs *aw* and *ay*, which were contracted in the North to *ô* and *ê* respectively while they were preserved uncontracted in the South. Israelite followed Phoenician and Ugaritic in this respect, while Judahite agrees with Aramaic and Arabic. The difference in pronunciation is reflected in the spelling: thus in the North the words for "house" and "death" would be written *bt* and *mt* (pronounced *bêt* and *môt*), while in the South they would be written *byt* and *mwt* (pronounced *bayt* and *mawt*). Comparison of Psalm xviii and 2 Samuel xxii indicated the existence of two recensions of this poem, one written in the standard Judahite spelling characteristic of MT in general, the other in northern orthography.[9] While there has been considerable contamination of the text in the course of transmission, sufficient evidence for the "contracted" orthography survives in the 2 Samuel recension to support substantially the "northern" hypothesis. A further possibility in this direction may be mentioned. The date and provenience of the Book of Job have occasioned much debate among scholars, and it cannot be said that any hypothesis has won general approval as yet. Recently the proposal has been advanced that the book is a product of the northern diaspora, *i.e.* that it comes from the community of Israelites exiled from Palestine after the fall of Samaria in 722 B.C.E.[10] A number of arguments have been adduced in support of this view, but quite apart from these, a provisional examination of the orthography of the Book

9.   "A Royal Song of Thanksgiving", JBL 72 (1953), 15-17.
10.   The suggestion is Albright's. On the North-Israelite diaspora, see "An Ostracon from Calah and the North-Israelite Diaspora", BASOR 149 (1958), 33-36.

of Job shows a surprisingly high incidence of peculiar and even unique spellings which are characteristically northern in character. That is, they reflect contraction of the diphthongs *aw* and *ay* in spelling (and presumably therefore in pronunciation), *e.g.*, the particle *'ôdh* is repeatedly spelled *'d* instead of normal Judahite and biblical *'wd*.[11] The survival in the book of numerous spellings of this sort can hardly be accidental, and may point to a "northern" recension of the Book of Job.

III

In an important sense, however, these studies have been preliminary. The main problem from the beginning has been to determine the place of the MT as a whole (and not simply isolated passages and archaic survivals) in the history of Hebrew orthography, *i.e.*, in what phase of the evolution of Hebrew spelling does the distinctive and characteristic orthography of the MT belong? While the MT is by no means homogeneous, and there is considerable variation not only between the main divisions (*e.g.*, the orthography of the Torah is more conservative than that of the Kethubim, particularly Chronicles) and from book to book, but also on the same page or even in the same verse, there is nevertheless a discernible pattern in the use of *matres lectionis*, though this has not been clearly analysed or described scientifically. One reason for this is the superimposition of Massoretic vocalization on Massoretic spelling in the ordinary printed text of the O.T. For the purpose of clarity in the discussion which follows, let us make the following distinction between spelling and vocalization: by "spelling" we mean the Hebrew letters used to indicate the consonants and certain vowels, *i.e.* the unpointed text. This is sometimes called the consonantal text, but the term is misleading, since some of the letters represent vowels and not consonants. By "Massoretic vocalization" we mean the full system of vowel indication introduced in the latter half of the 1st millennium C.E., which, while combining with the system of vowel letters, nevertheless superseded and distorted the earlier pattern. There is ample evidence to show that the two systems diverge at many points and reflect different periods in the evolution of Hebrew phonology. Thus the vocalization, while preserving older traditions, is nevertheless considerably later than the pronunciation implied in the spelling of the MT.

A cursory examination of MT shows that its spelling does not fit into any phase of pre-Exilic spelling, which even in the latest materials shows only sporadic use of internal *matres lectionis*. On the contrary, MT exhibits consist-

---

11.   Job i, 18, ii, 3, 9, viii, 12, 21.

ent use of internal *matres lectionis* for *ū* and *ī* and the contracted diphthongs *aw* and *ay* (*ô* and *ê* respectively). The representation of *ō* varies considerably (*i.e.*, sometimes the *waw* is used, sometimes not), while *ā* and *ē* are not represented by vowel letters. There is no indication of short vowels.

If Massoretic spelling was clearly post-Exilic—and since the written composition or compilation of any complete book or part of the Old Testament could hardly be attributed to an earlier date, this was only to be expected—it was not at all clear where in the post-Exilic period the orthography of the Massoretic Text properly fits. The *terminus ad quem* was fixed by the adoption of the Massoretic Text with its particular orthography as the official Bible of the Jewish community toward the end of the 1st century C.E. This view has been fully confirmed by the manuscript discoveries in the Murabba'at caves: the biblical MSS, which date from the Second Revolt, *i.e.* before 135 C.E., are Massoretic both in text and spelling. The origins of Massoretic spelling and its emergence as a definable system must be placed much earlier, of course. The discoveries at Qumran in addition to the previously known Nash Papyrus (and to a lesser extent the evidence of Jewish coins of the 2nd and 1st centuries B.C.E.) have enabled us to trace a specifically Massoretic type of spelling back to the latter part of the 2nd century B.C.E., or roughly 100 B.C.E.

For the *terminus a quo* there was in the first place the Exile. In view of critical theories concerning the compilation of the principal parts of the O.T., and in particular of the Torah and Former Prophets, it seemed reasonable to date the emergence of a canonical text to the century after the Exile. When we take into consideration the considerable divergences between the latest pre-Exilic orthography and Massoretic spelling, the 5th century would appear to be the earliest possible occasion for the appearance of Massoretic spelling, while the 4th would be a more reasonable supposition. On general considerations therefore, the emergence of Massoretic spelling could be narrowed to the period between the 5th-4th and the 2nd centuries B.C.E., since by the latter date distinctively Massoretic spelling appears in biblical MSS alongside other more elaborate spelling systems. Greater precision in narrowing the limits could hardly be undertaken because of the deplorable lack of Hebrew inscriptional evidence for the period in question. We are dependent chiefly on seals and stamps, with personal and place names[12], and these add little to our knowledge of the orthographic practice of the period.

12.   Of these, the well-known *yahūd* stamps and the five-letter Jerusalem insignia (*yršlm*) may be mentioned. The *yahūd* stamps are sometimes spelled with the *waw* for *ū*, sometimes without: the former reflects current practice in the 4th (or possibly late 5th) century, while the latter spelling attests the survival of an even older practice. The Jerusalem insignia likewise reflects the persistence of a traditional design and custom of spelling.

IV

While the Qumran scrolls have provided more than ample materials—in fact an overwhelming and embarrassing quantity—for the orthographic practice, or rather confusion of the period from the 2nd century B.C.E. through the 1st century C.E., they could hardly have been expected to supply data for the crucial earlier period in which the origins of Massoretic spelling lie. The Qumran community itself does not antedate the latter half of the 2nd century B.C.E., and the bulk of the manuscript materials necessarily belongs to the period following the settlement there. That some of the MSS, especially of biblical books, might be of an earlier date was a possibility to be considered: thus the great Isaiah scroll could be dated by experts to the latter part of the 2nd century B.C.E., and a fragment of Ecclesiastes to about the middle of the same century. With the refinement of palaeographical analysis in the last few years, and the examination of hundreds and hundreds of documents from this period, a sequence dating of Qumran MSS has proved feasible. Substantial agreement in procedures and results has been achieved by the principal workers in this field, chief of whom is Professor Cross. His provisional study in JBL[13] fixed the order and dates of a wide selection of Qumran MSS within relatively narrow limits. It has now been superseded by his definitive analysis of all presently available Qumran material (in *The Bible and the Ancient Near East*, ed. G. E. Wright, 1961).

With the vast amount of material now available, and with absolute control provided by dated documents interspersed through the latter part of the period, the dating of the Qumran MSS is virtually certain throughout: we may allow a maximum variation of 50 years in the dating of particular MSS. As was to be expected, the large majority of documents from Qumran date from the period of Essene occupation (*i.e.*, from the late 2nd century B.C.E. to the late 1st century C.E.). Nevertheless, Cross has identified several MSS of an earlier date, some from the early and middle 2nd century B.C.E., and a few fragments even older than these. They may have been brought to Qumran by the first settlers, or procured from other sources. In any case, there are now three biblical MSS which belong, according to Cross's analysis, to the period from *ca.* 275–175 B.C.E., and may reasonably be regarded as the oldest surviving fragments of the Bible. These MSS, only one of which has been published in part (4QSam(b))[14] now offer us data concerning Hebrew orthographic practice in the 3rd and early 2nd century B.C.E., thus enabling us to close partially the gap in the history of post-Exilic spelling; the situation in the

13. "The Oldest Manuscripts from Qumran", JBL 74 (1955), 147-72.
14. *Ibid.*, 165-72.

5th–4th centuries remains obscure. In view of the fact that complete publication of these MSS is some years off, and because of their critical importance for the study of Hebrew orthography in the post-Exilic period, and particularly for the origins of Massoretic spelling, Cross has made the necessary transcriptions available to me for a provisional orthographic analysis.[15]

Cross classifies the documents as follows:

1.   The oldest MS is apparently 4QExod(f), containing Exodus xl, 8–27 and dating from *ca.* 275–225 B.C.E. or roughly 250.

2.   4QSam(b) contains 1 Sam. xvi,1–11; xix,10–17; xx,26–xxi,6; xxiii,9–17, and is to be dated *ca.* 250–200 B.C.E., or about 225.

3.   The last is 4QJer(a), containing Jer. xii,17–xiii,6 and xvii,10–25, and is to be dated between 225 and 175 B.C.E., or about 200.

There is no need to press for a precise dating of the MSS in question at this time, and since the science of Hebrew palaeography has not yet achieved the exactitude or the prestige of Greek epigraphy, we can allow considerable leeway without debate. We intend therefore to treat the documents as roughly contemporaneous and as coming from the latter half of the 3rd century or, at the latest, the early part of the 2nd. The fragments comprise a random selection of sufficient length to secure representative orthographic data, though some characteristic forms are lacking for the reconstruction of a complete picture of the manuscripts' orthography. Our concern is especially with the use of vowel letters in the orthography of the documents, and more particularly with the representation of the medial vowels, since the indication of final vowels had long since been regularized, and the pattern of use remained relatively unchanged from the 9th or 8th century on. There is a significant exception to the general rule: in pre-Exilic inscriptions the 3rd masculine singular suffix attached to nouns in the singular is regularly represented by the letter *he*, whereas in these documents, as in MT commonly, *waw* is used. The vowel in question was presumably *ô*, though this is not certain for pre-Massoretic vocalization (*i.e.*, we are dependent upon Massoretic vocalization for this pronunciation: it may have been *uh* in pre-Exilic times and possibly *aw* later, contracted to *ô* in post-Exilic times). Thus the significance of the shift from *he* to *waw* is not altogether clear, though the use of *waw* in this situation is sufficient to demonstrate that our documents belong to a definitely post-Exilic stratum of Hebrew orthography. A second modification of pre-Exilic spelling relates to the 3rd masculine singular suffix with plural nouns (Massoretic *–āw*) which is represented in pre-Exilic inscriptions simply by the letter *waw*, while in the present documents,

15.   I have consulted with Cross, at various stages in the study, and wish to express my appreciation for many helpful suggestions. I must bear responsibility for the conclusions, such as they are.

as in MT generally, by *–yw*. There is some difficulty in explaining the appearance of the pre-Exilic form in the southern dialect, though it seems to derive ultimately from *–ayhu*. The post-Exilic form *–yw* is incompatible with Massoretic vocalization *–aw*, and reflects rather the vocalization *–ayw* from *ayhū* with syncope of the *he* as very often in spoken Hebrew (so Siloam *rēʿēw* for MT *rēʿēhū*, cf. Jer. vi,21 רֵעוֹ, which is wrongly vocalized.[16] Once again we have a characteristically post-Exilic form both in our 3rd century documents and MT.

To sum up: the use of vowel letters in the final position in the documents under consideration is identical with prevailing practice in MT. Thus *he* is used to represent final *ā*, *ē*, and *ô*, e.g., כה (*kô*) in 4QJer(a). *Waw* is used for final *ū* and *ô* (derived from *aw*—the question of the contraction of the diphthong must be considered further), and *yodh* for final *ī* and *ê* (derived from *ay*). So far as the final vowel letters are concerned, it is clear that the general system which goes back to the 9th century B.C.E. underwent specific changes in the post-Exilic period, and that by the 3rd century at the latest they were firmly incorporated into standard orthographic practice. The unanimity of our 3rd century sources, and their identity with Massoretic practice, suggest that the pattern must actually have originated earlier, perhaps in the 4th or even 5th century.

V

It is in connection with the use of medial vowel letters that more fruitful results can be obtained, however. The general pattern is the same in all three documents, and corresponds closely to that of MT, though with certain significant exceptions. We may summarize the evidence as follows:

1. There is no use of vowel letters to represent short vowels, as in MT.

2. The same is true with regard to medial *ā* and *ē*. This is also the common practice of MT.

3. *Waw* is used for *ū* and for *ô* which results from the contraction of *aw*. *Yodh* is used for *ī* and for *ê* which results from the contraction of *ay*. The question as to when these diphthongs contracted is not easily settled. In pre-Exilic orthography the chief evidence for the contraction of the diphthongs is the loss of the original *waw* or *yodh*, while the presence of the *waw* or *yodh* is evidence of its retention. The situation in post-Exilic orthography is complicated by various factors, including the persistence of historical spelling, *i.e.* the preservation of *waw* or *yodh* after contraction, so that the letter becomes

---

16.   *Early Hebrew Orthography*, p. 50, no. 26, and no. 28.

in effect a vowel indicator, and by the evidence of Massoretic vocalization, which indicates that the diphthong was contracted in certain instances, *e.g.* the construct state of nouns like *bêt* and *môt*, and preserved in others, *e.g.* in the artificial forms like *bayit* and *māwet*. If contraction had taken place we would then expect examples of two concomitant phenomena: 1. the occasional loss of originally diphthongal *waw* and *yodh*, since the sounds would fall together with vocalic *ō* and *ē*, which are not always or even regularly represented by the corresponding vowel letters. 2. Extension of the use of *waw* and *yodh* to cases of *ō* and *ē* which did not originate from the corresponding diphthongs *aw* and *ay*. In other words, we would expect similarity in orthographic treatment of sounds which fell together, or at least some overlapping. It is too much to expect that the Hebrew scribes could have maintained a formal, *i.e.* orthographic distinction for any length of time or with consistency when the phonemic support for the distinction had been lost. Even in modern times with our massive scientific knowledge of linguistics, of etymologies, and the principles governing historical spelling, we continually make mistakes in attempting to preserve and reconstruct older forms, and the mistakes fall into the pattern of contamination described above. It can be safely asserted that once different sounds have fallen together, orthographic distinction between them on the basis of historical practice or etymology cannot be long maintained consistently. In MT, the system of vocalization reflects extensive contraction of the diphthongs *aw* and *ay*, and the resulting vowels *ô* and *ê* are assigned the same value as the *ō* and *ē* which derive from the original vowels *ā* (or *u*), and *i* (*i.e. ḥōlem* and *ṣēre*: there are undoubtedly distinctions in quantity, and we should reckon with instances of short *ḥōlem* and *ṣēre*, but the system used does not indicate these, while it does indicate an identity in vowel quality). Massoretic spelling, as distinct from vocalization, is less clear on this point. On the one hand it carefully preserves the distinction between *ê* derived from *ay*, which is consistently represented by *yodh*, and *ē* which is derived from *i*, which is rarely if ever so indicated. This regularity can hardly be explained as a survival of historical spelling, but is rather rooted in a difference in pronunciation. It may be explained in either of two ways, or a combination of them: either the diphthong had actually been preserved and not contracted, or the *ṣēre* is a short vowel as distinct from the contracted diphthong which is long, and is therefore not represented in the orthography. Whether the second explanation can be used to cover all cases of the shift *i* > *ē* is debatable, however. On the other hand, the Massoretic treatment of the *ō* vowel (*ḥōlem*) involves extensive representation of vocalic *ō*, derived from *ā* (rather than *u*, which is not indicated by a vowel letter, thus implying that the vowel is short) as well as diphthongal *ô*, derived from *aw*. This can be taken to mean that the ō sounds have fallen together, and thus that contraction of the diphthong has taken place. On the whole it would appear that Massoretic spelling and vocalization point in the direction of diphthongal contraction: that the contracted diphthongs ô and ê are represented by *waw* and *yodh*, that the vowel ō derived from ā is similarly represented by *waw*, although not consistently, while *e* derived from *i* and *o* derived from *u* are not represented in the orthography because they remained short vowels.

VI

When we turn to the new documents from the 3rd century, we find that two of them, Exod(f) and Jer(a), conform closely to the orthographic pattern of MT, while Sam(b) diverges. The latter makes no use of *waw* to represent the vowel ō (*ḥōlem*), but distinguishes carefully between the diphthong which is always represented by *waw* and the vowel which is not. This implies strongly that the ō vowel was not represented orthographically, and that the contraction of the diphthong had not yet taken place. Since all three MSS come from approximately the same period, it would appear that this was a time of transition, with Sam(b) preserving an older orthographic tradition and the other MSS belonging to the newer pattern. We also seem to have reached the point of origin of Massoretic spelling as such.

The only significant distinctions in spelling practice among the MSS, and between them and MT, concern the use of *waw* as a medial vowel letter for ō (derived from ā). There are other differences, but these are minor and may be mentioned in passing. Thus there are a few instances in which Massoretic vocalization indicates an ī vowel, where the MSS do not have *yodh* to represent the vowel. Sam(b) spells the name "David" *dwd* regularly, as often in MT, even though the second vowel is apparently long, as the spelling (with *yodh*) elsewhere in MT, and in many places in the Qumran scrolls, shows. In Sam(b) (as MT here), we undoubtedly have a case of historical spelling, the survival of the older, pre-Exilic spelling (which we would expect in the case of names particularly) alongside the development of the more "correct" fuller spelling. In Exod(f) at xl, 18, we have ברחיו for MT בריחיו which is more regular. This may also be the survival of an older spelling (*cf.* Jon. ii, 7 בריחה) or more likely a scribal slip reflecting the current slurring of the vowel (which is unaccented) in ordinary pronunciation. There are two similar cases in Jer(a): הושעני for MT הושיעני (xvii, 14) and תבאהו (MT same, xiii, 1), where the expected *yodh* is omitted, probably as a reflection of current pronunciation of the unaccented pretonic syllable (*i.e.*, the vowel was not heard distinctly or regarded as long). Other explanations are possible; in any case such exceptions do not undermine the general pattern, but only prove that scribes are human.

We may now turn to the evidence for the spelling of $\bar{o}$ in our documents:

1. For Sam(b) we have the following— $\bar{o}$ is never indicated in the orthography, with the possible exception of four words:

a) למועד, *lĕ mô 'ēd* (1 Sam xx,35, as in MT). Here the *waw* is etymologic, *i.e.* derived from the diphthong *aw*: **maw'id* > *mô'ēd*.

b) יונתן, *yônātān* (MT יהונתן, but elsewhere יונתן). Here again the *waw* is etymologic, deriving from an original diphthong. MT spelling is archaizing or hypercorrect, since intervocalic *he* was lost early in ordinary pronunciation (MT vocalization is an artificial backformation from *yônātān*). Thus: *yahunatan > * *yawnatan* > *yônātān*.

c) היום, *hayyôm* (xx, 27, 34, as MT). Again the *waw* is to be considered etymologic: *i.e.* *yawm > *yôm*. A second root, *ym*, is reflected in the plural *yāmīm*, as also in the curious (but repeated) form *ym* for "day" in pre-Exilic Judahite materials. We must reckon with a more complex dialectic situation in Judah in which bi-forms of the type *yawm/yam, qawl/qal*, etc., existed side by side.

d) מקום, *māqōm*, (xx,27,37; xxi,3 as MT). This is the most difficult form, since it is usually derived from *maqām (root *qm*). If this derivation is correct then it would be the only case of the use of *waw* for vocalic $\bar{o}$ (from $\bar{a}$) in Sam(b) The consistency of usage with this word (all three cases), and the complete absence of any other examples of such use of *waw* (though there are numerous instances of $\bar{o}$ from $\bar{a}$ in the materials and an impressive number in which MT has *waw* but where Sam(b) omits), indicates that another explanation is implied if not required. On the analogy of Arabic and Syriac formations from the same root[17], we suggest that *māqōm* derives from *maqawm rather than *maqōm, and that the *waw* is etymologic here also. The bi-form *maqām* > *māqōm* may also have existed, since MT preserves a number of cases in which the *waw* is omitted (though only in combining forms with preposition or suffix, where a possible change in pronunciation may be involved). The plural form (*mĕqōmōt*) may likewise be derived from the simple form *maqāmāt rather than one with the diphthong, thus conforming to the pattern suggested in (c) above.

As another illustration of metaplastic formations we may suggest the different spellings of the word Jerusalem. MT spelling of the last syllable is simply *–lm*, implying a pronunciation *–lēm*, while the vocalization (a permanent Qerē) *–ayim* points to an original diphthong *–aym*. We know now that this vocalization is not artificial but derives from a tradition going back at least to the 2nd century B.C.E. as shown by numerous examples in the Qumran scrolls,

17.   *Cf.* Syriac *qawmā, qawmĕthā* and Arabic قوم ,قومة; قامة.

in which the *yodh* appears in the last syllable (*-lym*). This can only signify the diphthongal form *-aym*, as *yodh* is not used to represent either *seghōl* or *ṣēre*.

The principal difference between Sam(b) and MT is in the representation of the *ō* vowel (derived from *ā*), as the following table indicates:

	4Q Sam (b)	Verse	M.T.
1.	בבאם	xvi,6	בְּבוֹאָם
2.	קמתו	xvi,7	קוֹמָתוֹ
3.	החלן	xix,12	הַחַלּוֹן
4.	טהר	xx,26	טָהוֹר
5.	אפד	xxi,10	הָאֵפוֹד

No. 2, the word *qōmātô* is apparently derived from **qāmat* rather than **qawmat*, although we have argued that *māqōm* derives from **maqawm* rather than **maqām*. Our point is that both basic forms existed in the language, that any given substantive may be derived from either root, and that we may expect considerable mixture in the use of forms.

From the evidence presented it is clear that Sam(b) not only uses *waw* as a *mater lectionis* less frequently than MT, but follows a consistent pattern, which is no longer the case with MT: it distinguishes between diphthongal *ô* and vocalic *ō*, thus implying that there was a difference in the pronunciation of these sounds, *i.e.* the diphthong had not yet been contracted. We must in view of these data assign orthographic priority to Sam(b). It reflects a phase of Hebrew spelling earlier than that of MT. Cross drew this conclusion on general grounds along with the important observation that Sam(b) also preserves a text of Samuel which is demonstrably older than that of MT, and apparently even of the *Vorlage* of the LXX.[18] We are dealing therefore with an archaic MS which preserves a tradition, both textually and orthographically, considerably older than the date of the MS itself. As a conservative estimate we suggest the 4th century or even late 5th for the pattern, both textual and orthographic, preserved in Sam(b).

VII

The evidence for the use of *waw* for *ō* in Ex(f), which must now be regarded as the oldest known MS of the Bible, is as follows: the usage is not consistent, though a general pattern emerges—there is extensive use of *waw*, contrary

18.   "The Oldest Manuscripts from Qumran", JBL 74 (1955), 165-72.

to the practice of Sam(b) and closer to what we find in MT. It is to be noted however that the orthography of the MS as a whole is somewhat irregular, unlike Sam(b), which is a model of consistency, and it must therefore be used with caution. The following cases are clear examples of the use of *waw* for $\bar{o}$ (from $\bar{a}$):

	4Q Ex(f)	Verse	M.T.
1.	אותו	xl, 9, 13	אֹתוֹ
	אותם	12, 14, 15, 16	אֹתָם
	but אתו	11	אֹתוֹ
2.	עולם	15	עוֹלָם
3.	לדורותם	15	לְדֹרֹתָם
4.	הארן	20 (3 times), 21	הָאָרֹן
5.	צפן	22	צָפֹנָה

These are apparently all cases of $\bar{o}$ derived from $\bar{a}$; *waw* commonly appears when the $\bar{o}$ occurs under the accent but not always, *cf.* לדורותם. There are notable differences in detail between Ex(f) and MT, though elsewhere MT spells these words as does Ex(f). However the spelling of the *nota accusativi* before suffixes with *waw* is very rare in MT, though common in Ex(f) and in many later Qumran texts. It is clear that by the 3rd century and possibly earlier, *waw* was already being used to represent medial $\bar{o}$. If we are right in supposing that this usage developed as an extension of the use of *waw* for the contracted diphthong $aw > \hat{o}$, then it would mean that the diphthong aw had contracted by the 3rd century at the latest. Since the evidence of Sam(b) points in the other direction, *viz.* that contraction had not yet taken place, and the MSS are roughly contemporary (in fact in Cross's opinion Ex(f) is somewhat older than Sam(b)), we must look for some other explanation of the use of *waw* for $\bar{o}$ (*i.e.*, it may be independent of the use in connection with the diphthong) or suppose that the two MSS reflect a linguistic transition, in which the archaic Sam(b) preserves an older pattern of pronunciation and orthography, while Ex(f) reflects a later, contemporary usage. The orthographic pattern represented by Ex(f) cannot be later than the early 3rd century, and may be as old as the 4th. That of Sam(b) must be correspondingly older, though in view of the date of the MS itself it can hardly ascend beyond the early 4th century, or possibly the late 5th.

There are additional cases in Ex(f) where *waw* is not used although the corresponding word in MT is vocalized with *ḥolem* (and in one case spelled with *waw* in MT):

	4Q Ex(f)	Verse	M.T.
1.	אהרן	xl,12,13	אַהֲרֹן
2.	הכתנת	14	כְּתֹנֶת
3.	משה	16,19,21,23	מֹשֶׁה
4.	הראשן	17	הָרִאשׁוֹן
5.	הכפרת	20	הַכַּפֹּרֶת
6.	פרכת	21,22	פָּרֹכֶת

In some cases the omission of the *waw* may be due to carelessness, in others to the survival of historical spelling, and in still others to a difference in pronunciation or interpretation of the word in question. Thus Nos. 1 and 3 are proper names where we would expect historical spelling, as in MT. No. 2 may have been understood as a singular form, especially as MT also omits the expected *waw* marking the plural. Nos. 5 and 6 may involve a difference in pronunciation especially as MT regularly spells without *waw* (the original vowel behind the *ḥōlem* may have been *u* rather than *ā*, and in these MSS as in MT *ō* from *u* is not represented in the orthography). No. 4 is the only clear case of omission, and this is doubtless a survival of older spelling practice in Ex(f) (the spelling without *waw* occurs elsewhere in MT).

MT and Ex(f) are closer to each other in the matter of the use of *waw* for *ō* than either is to Sam(b). At the same time there are important differences between them; particularly as regards the spelling of *'ōt–*, Ex (f) goes beyond MT generally in the direction of the fuller spelling of the later Qumran MSS.

VIII

The evidence for the use of *waw* for *ō* for the third MS, Jer(a), is as follows: the pattern is very similar to that of Ex(f), and also to that of MT. The following cases illustrate this point:

	4Q Jer(a)	Verse	M.T.
1.	נתוש	xii,17	נָתוֹשׁ
2.	אזור	xiii,1,2,4	אֵזוֹר
3.	יומהו	xvii,11	יָמָיו Q / ימו K
4.	הושעני	14	הוֹשִׁיעֵנִי
5.	אצותי	16	אִצְתִּי
6.	מוצא	16	מוֹצָא
7.	(ב)יום	17,18, *etc.*	(בְּ)יוֹם

	4Q Jer(a)	Verse	M.T.
8.	אבושה	xvii,18	אֵבֹשָׁה
9.	הלוך	19	הָלֹךְ
10.	יבוא	19	יָבֹאוּ
11.	אבותיכם	22	אֲבוֹתֵיכֶם
12.	שמוע	24	שָׁמֹעַ
13.	עשות	24	עֲשׂוֹת

It is clear that there is widespread use of *waw* for *ō*, comparable to what we find in MT, though more extensive in Jer(a) than MT for this passage. *Waw* is used for the contracted diphthong: Nos. 4, 6, 7 and possibly 3 (which is peculiar); *waw* for *ō* from *ā* in the tone position is common: Nos. 1, 2, 9, 12, 13. Nos. 5 and 8 involve difficulties in interpretation of the form, though MT usually omits the *waw*. No. 10 is a case of metathesis in Jer(a) where MT יבאו is the correct reading. No. 11 shows the *waw* used in an unaccented position, though the form may involve a secondary accent: 'ăbōtêkem. There are in addition a number of cases in which *waw* is omitted although MT vocalizes with *ḥōlem*.

	4Q Jer(a)	Verse	M.T.
1.	קרא	xvii,11	קֹרֵא
2.	עזביך	13	עֹזְבֶיךָ
3.	יבשו	13	יֵבֹשׁוּ
4.	אמרים	15	אֹמְרִים
5.	מרעה	16	מֵרֹעֶה
6.	רדפי	18	רֹדְפַי
7.	ישבי	20	יֹשְׁבֵי
8.	רכבים	25	לְכֹבִים

The principal examples involve the Qal active participle, both singular and plural, where in agreement with regular MT practice *waw* is not used. The careful orthographic distinction in a MS not otherwise noted in this fashion suggests that the pronunciation differed, perhaps due to the position of the accent. The *ō* of Massoretic vocalization is confirmed however by later Qumran scrolls (as well as linguistic analysis). The only other instance of omission in Jer(a) is No. 3, where MT also omits the *waw*.

IX

The orthography of these three early scrolls from Cave IV of Qumran is the same in all essentials except for the use of *waw* to represent $ō < ā$; $ô < aw$

is regularly represented by *waw*, while *ō* < *u* is never so represented. Sam (b) apparently does not represent *ō* (from *ā*) at all, while Ex(f) and Jer(a) generally do, though with exceptions (discussed above), which arise either as a result of historical spelling or differences in contemporary pronunciation (as distinguished from Massoretic vocalization); these in turn depend upon the position of the accent and the length of the vowel in question. There is also the possibility of scribal error. None of the MSS is identical with MT in spelling practice in the passages under consideration, and there are general as well as detailed differences. Nevertheless all three exhibit features which can be matched in MT taken as a whole, and MT could be reconstructed from the evidence of the three MSS under consideration.

The earliest or most conservative spelling is that of Sam(b), which probably reflects normative Israelite spelling of the 4th century B.C.E. There are numerous significant differences from 6th century practice to suggest an upper limit for Sam(b)'s orthography in the 5th century. The other two MSS exhibit freer use of *waw* as a *mater lectionis*, but may also be based upon usage going back to the 4th century—not earlier in our judgment since it would then be difficult to explain the survival of the older tradition in a 3rd century MS like Sam(b). In addition, the irregularity in the practice of these MSS suggests that the extended use of *waw* was of recent origin, and that these MSS reflect a period of transition both in spelling and pronunciation.

It may be premature to draw general conclusions about MT on the basis of the material now available, but certain points may be made now. MT shares with all three early MSS the same orthographic practice with regard to final and medial vowel letters, with the single exception of the use of *waw* for *ō* (< *ā*), which varies between Sam(b) and the other documents. This alone argues for a long stable orthographic tradition stemming from scribal schools of the early post-Exilic period. Massoretic practice with regard to the use of *waw* for *ō* might well be described as a compromise between the defective spelling of Sam(b) and the extended orthography of Ex(f), and is in fact very close to that of Jer(a). It may be further argued that Massoretic spelling was delibera ely designed to combine the best features of the different orthographies current in the 4th–3rd centuries, preserving continuity with the older conservative tradition of Sam(b), and at the same time incorporating the helpful features of the newer spelling exhibited in Ex(f) and Jer(a). We may place the origins of Massoretic spelling as a definite orthographic system in the late 3rd or early 2nd century, and describe it as a learned recension based upon the best practice of the preceding period. Apparently with official support, it gained primacy during the next two centuries, and was ultimately successful as the official biblical spelling, sweeping the field of all rivals.

THE QUMRAN MANUSCRIPTS AND TEXTUAL CRITICISM

BY

P. W. SKEHAN
Washington

As indicated in the outline distributed to the members of the Congress, this is in the nature of one more preliminary report, mainly of the Qumran cave 4 materials on which the writer has himself been working. We may begin by recalling the fact, already indicated by F. M. Cross [1]) and confirmed by the further study of J. T. Milik of the various biblical materials from Wadi Murabba'āt, that a definite *terminus ad quem* for the variety of texts that Khirbet Qumran provides occurs between the two Jewish revolts; somewhere before A.D. 135. The standardizing of the text as regards orthography, conformity to a selected prototype which yields in all essentials the consonants of the Masoretic text, and definitive scribal rules for its transmission, was clearly an accomplished fact at the time of the second Jewish revolt: this is verifiable explicitly for several books of the Pentateuch (Gen., Ex., Deut.), for Isaias, and for the Minor Prophets. The Wadi Murabba'āt materials have none of the variability of text, format and orthography that is to be found at Qumran.

It has already been indicated by Prof. Cross that the Qumran manuscripts of Genesis, six in number, provide nothing of special textual interest beyond a few isolated readings. The same is by no means true, however, with respect to the other books of the Pentateuch, in which we are clearly dealing in many cases with recensional variations. For the paleo-hebrew scroll of Exodus of which a preliminary announcement was published by the writer, [2]) there is still no definitive indication as to whether or not one can class it as Samaritan in any sectarian sense. In view of the known attitude of the community towards the "men of Ephraim and Manasses", however, the probabilities are all against it. We may now add the fact that

---

[1]) *Biblical Archaeologist* 17, 1954, 11 and 19.
[2]) *Journal of Biblical Literature* 74, 1955, 182-187.

Cross is preparing a manuscript of Numbers (4 Q Num^b) in square-letter script that contains expanded readings hitherto known only from the Samaritan recension—a manuscript with text that is in other respects of a mixed character, going sometimes with LXX against Sam. and MT, and sometimes with MT against LXX and Sam. When one adds to this a manuscript of Exodus (4 Q Ex^a) of distinctly Septuagintal type, [1]) and the ending of the Song of Moses from Deuteronomy published by the writer, [2]) which has also pronouncedly Septuagintal affiliations, it becomes clear that, with the exception of Genesis, the books of the Pentateuch still circulated in Palestine down to the First Revolt in copies with varying recensional backgrounds.

This may perhaps be the point for a reflection of a more general character. There are, it will be recalled, some 100 biblical manuscripts from cave 4 at Qumran. At the end of two years' acquaintance, in varying degrees, with these materials, the writer is still not aware of internal evidence which would urge either that any one of these manuscripts was copied from another identifiable manuscript among the finds, or that any two had a common immediate prototype. Put in another way, this is to say that the biblical manuscripts of the fourth cave at Qumran have a spread in time of some three hundred years; that their origins are to some extent necessarily diverse, and that nothing in the materials to my knowledge shows that there was a specific type of text for any book to which the community felt itself especially committed, and which it endeavored to propagate from the scriptorium of the settlement.

Coming back to the Pentateuch in particular, one fact that should perhaps be stressed is that Qumran is not giving us, in these books, a multiplicity of unknown readings. Nor does it absolve us of applying to the readings it does provide, whether or not these are in accord with a known Greek or Samaritan text, the same critical judgment with which we approach the Masoretic text itself. Partisans of a supposed superiority of the Septuagint in particular still tend today, as in earlier times, to regard the evidence of the Greek as though from place to place, and from book to book, it were all on one plane. Nothing could, of course, be further from the truth; and even in such an instance as the end of Deut. xxxii, where materials from the LXX and material from Qumran combine to suggest that

---

[1]) Cf. Prof. CROSS' report in *Revue biblique* 63, 1956, 56.
[2]) In *BASOR* 136, 1954, 12-15.

the Masoretic text is in certain respects defective, it is still the fact that these alternative recensions themselves are on specific points demonstrably corrupt and inferior. [1])

The books of Judges, Kings, Esdras-Nehemias and Chronicles in Qumran cave 4 have not yielded enough material for serious textual discussion. Prof. Cross has already indicated that in Josue and Samuel there is a strong Septuagintal cast to the Hebrew manuscripts from Qumran 4. This is the less surprising in that for Samuel in particular the Masoretic text has long been recognized as partly in disorder and as containing lacunae which the Septuagint and the Old Latin help to fill. From the twofold viewpoint of the amount of text preserved, and the direct value of that text as a source of fruitful criticism of the Masoretic tradition, the Books of Samuel are in fact unique at Qumran.

For the remaining books it may be briefly said that the only areas in which notable and extensive differences from the consonantal text of the Masora are still possible would be the Minor Prophets and Jeremias. The writer has been working on one manuscript of the Minor Prophets, from about Herodian times, and finds that it presents the early books in the order given in the Masora, and that nearly all its verifiable text is quite ordinary, except for a rather full orthography of the known Qumran type. The texts of Ezechiel, and of the *Ketubim* as a whole, offer no differences of recensional character, and a quite limited number of interesting variants.

For Isaias, the complete scroll from cave 1 remains textually the most interesting document, and there is nothing among the 15 manuscripts of cave 4 which is recensionally different from the received consonantal text, or yields improved readings in any signi-

---

[1]) I refer in particular to the reading ʾmr *Yhwh* in Dt. xxxii 37; though in my judgment the secondary and conflate character of verse 43 in these witnesses is equally patent. Incidentally, it is now possible, another piece of the "Song of Moses" manuscript (4Q Dt ⁹) having been acquired this year, to clarify the very troublesome arrangement of the stichoi in Dt. xxxii 37ᵇ-41ᶜ, the next to last column of that text. When it was published in *BASOR* I felt obliged to assume, methodologically, that the text must have been written uniformly, either one or two hemistichs to the line. Neither arrangement could lead to a satisfactory result; I therefore assumed a number of lacunae. Though the new fragment is a small one, it is sufficient to show that the column had some lines with two hemistichs, and others with only one: of an 11-line column, lines 1-4, 9 and 10 had each one hemistich; while lines 5-8 and 11 had two. There is nothing else quite like this at Qumran, and it can only be attributed to the individual scribe's desire to end his text, as he in fact did, exactly with the bottom of his final column.

ficant degree. Only a few detailed considerations suggest themselves.
Probably our oldest manuscript (4Q Is^h) contains Is. xlii 4-11; in
xlii 4 it already has the well-known variant *b^erīt 'ōlam* for *b^erīt 'am*.
Since the reading is quite impossible, we have no reason to be
grateful. Published mention has already been made ¹) of the late
manuscript (4Q Is^c) which contains such names as *Yhwh, Yhwh
ṣb'wt, 'lwhynw*, and the like, in paleohebrew script. This is almost
unique among square-letter biblical manuscripts in Qumran cave 4; ²)
but it occurs again in biblical materials from two other caves. In
general, also in non-biblical manuscripts, this is a late phenomenon
at Qumran; and our oldest witness to a differentiation in script for
the tetragrammaton is still probably the Fuad papyrus of Deuteronomy
in Greek, ³) in which the name appears in the square-letter Hebrew
script.

The point perhaps still deserves to be stressed, that among other
things which the large scroll from cave 1 illustrates for us is an
exegetical process at work within the transmission of the text itself,
in Hebrew. In J. ZIEGLER's excellent *Untersuchungen zur Septuaginta
des Buches Isaias*, ⁴) he provides two extensive chapters (pp. 103-134;
134-175) on the relationship of the LXX of Isaias to the other Old
Testament books, and on the reciprocal influences, within the book,
of one passage on another where some association of thought or
phraseology has led to harmonizing. In the former of these chapters
he allows (p. 105) for the possibility that borrowings from the other
O.T. books into the text of Isaias may already have been present
in the translator's *Vorlage*; in the other chapter he leaves open (p. 134)
the like possibility that the harmonizing of similar or related passages
within the book of Isaias may also have been done, in many cases,
in a Hebrew text leading up to the copy which stood before the
translator. Now, IQ Is^a and the LXX of Isaias are not recensionally
connected, though they have an occasional reading in common;
but they are mutually illustrative, because the cave 1 manuscript
gives us, for the first time in Hebrew, the kind of glossed and reworked
manuscript that the LXX prototype must have been. I subjoin to

---

¹) By the writer, in *Catholic Biblical Quarterly* 17, 1955, 42-43.

²) One occurrence of *'lwhym* which seems to belong to a badly deteriorated
MS. of Leviticus remains to be verified.

³) W. G. WADDELL, "The Tetragrammaton in the LXX", in *JTS* 45 (1944)
158-161: P. Fouad Inv. 266, lxx Deut. xxxi 28-xxxii 7.

⁴) *A. T. Abhandlungen xii*, 3; Münster i. W., 1934.

this paper a list of some twenty-seven passages in the large scroll containing unique readings, each of which is dependent on another passage in Isaias or on a specific reading from some other prophetical book. [1]) The phenomenon is too frequent and well-defined, especially in the second half of the scroll, to be indeliberate. It is in fact a part of the technique which, when applied more consistently and on a broader scale, produced the Samaritan recension of the Pentateuch. The process is, as already stated, an exegetical one, excluded for the future by the definitive standards of text transmission that accompanied the stabilization of the consonantal text between the two revolts. Since Isaias was quite evidently the most studied book outside the Pentateuch, it understandably reflects the result of this study in pronounced degree, on the one hand in 1Q Is^a and on the other in the LXX rendering. Of the cave 4 manuscripts of Isaias none seems to be of this type. In 4Q Is^c, the latest of them, the text of Is. xi 9 has been accommodated to that of the very similar verse Hab. ii 14—but that is about all.

It has been in conjunction with the text of Isaias that the writer has examined to some extent the likely effects of the extrabiblical documents at Qumran in providing us with text-critical materials for the O.T. itself. This examination has been tentative, and has been centered on a book for which we have now fragments of quite a number of manuscripts showing, as already indicated, rather little significant variability in the text. It is therefore hardly surprising that the conclusion thus far is largely negative: allusions and *lemmata* in the extrabiblical documents may yield some points of detail, but will not alter our understanding of the textual history of the book. This is by no means to exclude the eventual importance of

---

[1]) Is.

i 7 cf. Lev. xxvi 32; Is. lii 14.	Is. xlvi 5 cf. xl 25; xiv 14.
i 15 cf. lix 3.	xlvii 12 cf. Jer. iii 25.
ii 20 cf. xvii 8.	li 3 cf. li 11; xxxv 10.
xxxii 11 cf. xxxii 12 and Jer. xlix 3.	li 6 cf. xl 26.
xxxiv 4 cf. Mich. i 4.	lii 8 cf. liv 7; Zach. i 16.
xxxvi 4 cf. xxxvii 10.	lii 12 cf. liv 5.
xxxvi 11 cf. xxxvi 12.	lvii 11 cf. xlvii 7.
xxxvii 4 cf. Jer. xxi 7; xxxviii 4.	lvii 12 cf. lvii 13.
xxxvii 31 cf. xxxvii 4.	lix 7 cf. Hab. i 3.
xxxvii 32 cf. ii 3.	lx 13 cf. xxxv 2.
xxxviii 6 cf. xxxvii 35; 2 Kgs. xx 6.	lx 21 cf. lxi 3
xl 18 cf. xl 25.	lxii 9 cf. Ps. cxlviii 5, 13; Is.
xliv 15-16 cf. xliv 19; xlvii 14.	lxvi 9.
xlv 1 cf. xlv 2.	
xlv 9 cf. xlv 10.	

careful study along these lines, as more and more material continues to be published; here tribute has of course to be paid to the thoughtful exploratory article of C. RABIN in the *JTS* of last year. [1]) Two considerations would, in fact, suggest that the scope for such study may be somewhat larger and more challenging even than Dr. RABIN has indicated. One, already mentioned, is that there is not now any good evidence, so far as I know, that the sect committed itself to consistently transmitting a standardized form of text for any biblical book. The other is that the principle of "limited variability", as Dr. RABIN has described it, with analogies especially from Coran transmission, is still visible at work within the Jewish tradition, preserving and expounding consonantal variants from the known Masoretic standard, as late as the Targum to the *Ketubim*. Since we already know that the *peshers* of Qumran can contain a *lemma* and an explanation which are in fact at odds with one another as to the text, we can be quite sure that both they and the other extrabiblical documents will bear repeated scrutiny before the last variant has been identified and evaluated. On the other hand, the writer has already had occasion to indicate [2]) that genuine variants which do occur, for example in the large Isaias scroll from cave 1, are at times matched in the extrabiblical materials from Qumran by the standard Masoretic reading for the same place.

For the Psalms, the outline you have received suggests a good deal of preoccupation with the external arrangement. For this there are two reasons. One is the fact that the Qumran cave 4 manuscripts reflect a practice of transmitting the Psalm text in a form in keeping with the verse structure, parallel with the more mechanical mode of transmission contained in the later codices and printed bibles. The other is the omissions and rearrangements of entire Psalms, which do occur, and which raise the question how far they may be significant.

With respect to arrangement in verse form, the most interesting document is 4Q Ps[b], carefully prepared on whitish leather, in a hand of the Herodian period, 18 lines to the column, at least eight columns to the skin; each line contains a single hemistich. The Psalms now represented are xci-xciv, xcix-c, cii-ciii, cxii-cxvi, cxviii. Psalm cxvii (the short one) was certainly included. Psalms civ-cxi were demonstrably omitted, though several fragmentary manuscripts from 4Q

---

[1]) "The Dead Sea Scrolls and the History of the Old Testament Text", *JTS* n.s. VI, 1955, 174-182.

[2]) In *CBQ*, 17, 1955, 41.

contain one or more Psalms from this part of the book (Pss. civ-cv, cvii, cix). Considering the short, narrow columns with ample spacing between, it is most unlikely that 4Q Ps^b ever contained the entire Psalter. Its text is quite close to the Masora, even in orthography. In Ps cii 20 it gives *mimᵉ῾ôn qodšô* for the Masoretic *mimᵉrôm qodšô*; but the verb *hišqîp* and the parallel hemistich both favor the Masoretic reading.

4Q Ps^a is apparently of the Hasmonean period. As indicated in the outline, this Ms arranges the Psalms and their titles as they still appear in the Masora: there is no special separation between title and text, the *selah* appears as though part of the continuous text, and stichometric arrangement is not observed. What remains of it are portions of Pss. v-vi, xxxi, xxxiii, xxxv-xxxvi, xxxviii and lxxi, liii-liv, lxvi-lxvii and lxix. Psalm xxxii was omitted (as is the case also in another, unpublished, ancient portion of a Psalter, not from cave 4 at Qumran). Psalm lxxi, which has no title, is given in continuous text with Psalm xxxviii, as though it were part of the same Psalm. The best explanation the writer can offer for this is that the 6th and final verse of Psalm lxx is quite similar in thought and diction to the last verse of Psalm xxxviii, and that on this basis some scribe or reciter of the Psalms grouped Psalms xxxviii and lxxi, having in mind the sequence lxx-lxxi. In view of the presence among our fragments of Psalms lxvi-lxvii and lxix, an explanation based on the identity of Psalm xl 13-18 with all of Psalm lxx would encounter difficulties.

4Q Ps^a presents both some good readings and some quite bad ones. In Ps. xxxviii 20 for (*wᵉ᾽ōyᵉbay*) *ḥayyîm* (*῾āṣēmû*) of MT, this Ms. reads *ḥinnām* as is required by the parallelism. In Ps. lxix 11, for MT's *wā᾽ebke(h)* (*baṣṣôm napšî*) the Ms. has *wā᾽ak*. In Ps. lxxi 6 for the well-known *crux* (*mimmᵉ῾ê ᾽immî ᾽attāh*) *gôzî*, the Ms. reads *῾ozzî*. But in Ps. lxix 4, where MT has *kālû ῾ēnay mᵉyaḥḥel* (*lē᾽lôhāy*), this Ms. has *kālᵉyû šinnay*, or, if you prefer, *šānay*.[1]) And in Ps. xxxviii 21 for MT's *yiśṭᵉnûnî taḥat rodᵉpî ṭôb*, the Ms. has *yᵉśossûnî taḥat dābār ṭôb*.

Two other Mss. of the Psalter deserve brief mention. Of one (4Q Ps^d) there are extant fragments of only Psalms civ and cxlvii— including the fragment on which Psalm cxlvii ends and Psalm civ *begins*. The other (4Q Ps^c) is a late and very regular hand, with tittled

---

[1]) *Šinnay* suggested itself first, because of the opposite corruption in Cant. v 12, where for *῾ēnā(y)w* A. VACCARI rightly restores *šinnā(y)w*.

alephs, with the standard order of the Psalms (Pss. xlviii-lii are best preserved), but with the Qumran type of full orthography. Like 4Q Is^c, it would seem to come from the closing years of the sectarian settlement. Occasionally, as in Psalms xviii, xxvii and xxxvii, it shows an arrangement with two hemistichs to the line. In Ps. xviii 33-36 this arrangement is, however, a mechanical one which no longer fits the parallelism. Consistent examples of this type of arrangement are found only in the two Mss. (4Q Ps. ^g, ^h) of the long alphabetic Psalm cxix.

We come now to the Septuagint materials with which Qumran cave 4 provides us. Of a leather ms. of Numbers, written about 30 letters to the line in a hand of the first century B.C., there are extant portions of iii 30-iv 14. Some of the fragments were recovered from the cave itself in the controlled excavation by the archaeologists. With this paper will be published the transcription of iii 40-42 and iv 6-9: two fairly continuous passages which represent more than half of the material.

4Q LXX Numbers

iii 40-42   α]ΡΙΘΜΗϹΟ[ν παν πρωτοτοκον αρσεν
των υι]ΩΝΙϹΡΑΗΛΑΠ[ο μηνιαιου και επανω
και λαβ]ΕΤΟΝΑΡΙΘΜΟΝ[εξ ονοματος 41 και
λημ]ΨΕΙΤΟΥϹΛΕΥΙΤΑ[ς εμοι εγω Κυριος
αντι παντων] ΤΩΝ ΠΡ[ωτοτοκων των υιων
Ισραηλ και τα κτη]ΝΗΤ[ων λευιτων αντι
παντων των πρ]ΩΤΟΤΟΚΩΝ[εν τοις κτηνεσιν
των υιων Ισραη]Λ ⁴²ΚΑΙΕΠ[εσκεψατο Μωυσης
ον τροπον ενετ]ΕΙΛΑΤ[ο

    40. αριθμησον: all other witnesses επισκεψαι. Cf. Numb. iii
        15, αριθμησον M^mg b g s^mg v^mg w Sahidic.
        Ισραηλ: note absence of abbreviation.
        λαβε: supposed, with AFGM, etc., λαβετε BF.
        αριθμον: so BG, etc.; αριθμον αυτων AFMN, etc.
    41. λημψει: *lege* λημψη, codd.

iv 6-9.   διω]ϹΤΗΡΑϹ[⁷και
επι την τραπεζαν την προ]ΚΕΙΜΕΝΗΝ Ε
πιβαλουσιν επ αυτην ιμ]ΑΤΙΟΝΥ[α]ΚΙΝΘ·
νον και δωσουσιν επ αυ]ΤΗϹΤΑΤ[ρυ]ΒΛΙ
α και τας θυισκας και τ]ΟΥϹΚΥΑΘΟΥϹΚΑΙ

τα σπονδεια εν οις σπε]Ṅ∆ΕΙΕΝΑΥΤΟΙϹ
και οι αρτοι οι δια παντ]ΟϹΕΠΑΥΤΗΙΕϹΟ
νται⁸ και επιβαλουσιν επ αυτ]ΗΝΙΜ[ατιον
κοκκινον και καλυψουσι]ṄΑΥΤΗΝΚΑ[λυ
μματι δερματινω υακιν]ΘΙΝ̇[ωι και δι
εμβαλουσιν δι αυτης τους δι]ΩϹΤΗΡΑϹ
⁹και λημψονται ιματιον υακιν]ΘΙΝΟΝΚΑΙ
καλυψουσιν την λυχνιαν τη]Ϲ̄ΦΑΥϹΕΩϹ
. . . . κ]ΑΙ

6. διωστηρας: all witnesses αναφορεις; cf. LXX Exod.
7. υακινθινον: all witnesses ολοπορφυρον.
   δωσουσιν επ αυτης: G c k x only; other mss. *omit.*
   εν αυτοις: d g n p t only; other mss. *omit.*
   επ αυτη: codd. επ αυτης.
8. διωστηρας: as verse 6.
9. της φαυσεως: την φωτιζουσαν mss.; του φωτος b w;
   Armen. *ut vid.* του φωτος (? της φαυσεως); cf. LXX
   Gen. i 15.
   και: the line may have read και τους λυχνους και τας
   λαβιδας και (*omit* αυτης *bis*).

In general, the text is that which we know; for example in iv 7
the expression την τραπεζαν την προκειμενην is a unique occurrence
in the LXX to represent *šulḥan happānîm*, and the reading occurs
identically in our fragments. There are, however, notable variations
in diction which indicate a deliberate recensional treatment of the
book at a very early period. The reading αριθμησον in iii 40 is to
be found in no other manuscript in this place; but various forms
of the verb αριθμειν are a characteristic feature of codex A nine
times in Numbers ii, and again in iii 16, as against the επισκεπτειν
of the codex B. This latter verb is of course the standard LXX
equivalent for פקד in the book of Numbers and elsewhere; and it
occurs (at least its first two letters occur) in the Qumran manuscript
in iii 42. In Numbers iv 6 and 8, the term for the carrying-poles or
baddîm in our manuscript alone is διωστηρας, all other Greek witnesses
having αναφορεις; but the term διωστηραι is used for *baddîm*
regularly in the LXX of Exodus. On the other hand, in Numb. iv
11 of the Qumran MS. the same Hebrew term is represented by
αρτ[ηρας], a word otherwise known to us in LXX only from Neh.

iv 11, where the Hebrew is quite different. In Numb. iv 9, the equivalent for *m^enôrat hammā'ôr* is not την λυχνιαν την φωτιζουσαν as in practically all manuscripts, but uniquely [την λυχνιαν τη]ς φαυσεως, using for *mā'ôr* a rendering that occurs otherwise in LXX only in Gen. i 14-15 and Ps. lxxiii (lxxiv) 16, with four scattered occurrences (Exod. xxv 5-6; *Sym.*, Exod. xxxv 8; *Al.*, Lev. xxiv 1) in the known hexaplaric materials. The impression which the writer derives from this is that a somewhat awkward Greek rendering of Numbers has been reworked anciently to yield the recension contained in our later codices.

The papyrus manuscript of Leviticus (4Q LXX Lev^b), of which again some fragments were obtained from the controlled excavations, is in a hand closely akin to that of the Fuad papyrus of Deut., and is datable accordingly to the first century B.C. Averaging about 27 letters to the line, it presents us with numerous fragments of chapters 2 to 5 of the book, from which ten separate segments of text can be pieced together (ii 3-5; ii 7; iii 4; iii 9-13; iv 6-8; iv 10-11; iv 18-20; iv 26-29; v 8-10; v 18-24). Its only special feature is that in the midst of the Greek text familiar from the LXX codices, the divine name here appears not as Κυριος, but as ΙΑω — a form previously known to us in manuscript only from the margin of the codex Q of the Prophets. The reading των εντολων Ιαω in iv 27 is ineluctable; and in iii 12 the last two letters of the same name can be verified— Κυριος does not occur in the document. This new evidence strongly suggests that the usage in question goes back for some books at least to the beginnings of the Septuagint rendering, and antedates such devices as that in the Fuad papyrus or the special scripts in the more recent Hebrew manuscripts of Qumran and in later Greek witnesses.

We come finally to the scroll of Leviticus on leather (4Q LXX Lev. ^a), of which we have Lev. xxvi 2-16 in lines of about 47 letters. This is the full length of one column of 28 lines, with stitching broken away at the left, where the margin is intact for the last 12 lines. The upper left of the column and the ends of all the lines are missing; the hand is apparently of the first century A.D. A new section at xxvi 14 is marked by a spacing of about three letters' width within the line and by a horizontal paragraph mark in the margin. Unfortunately, the divine name in any form does not occur in the preserved text.

That text is in the main the rendering of Leviticus with which we are familiar; nevertheless, in the limited material we have (of which a full publication will be subjoined to this paper) there are ten separate readings which are unique. Of these, nine are farther from a mechanical rendering of the Masoretic text than what is contained in the codices; one is closer, though this one (l. 15) depends on an inference as regards the quantity of text to fill a gap. None of these unique readings has anything to offer for the criticism of the Hebrew consonantal text itself. There are also five readings for which the Qumran MS. provides direct evidence, on which the later Greek codices are notably divided; with regard to these the scroll shows no systematic affiliation. Two of the unique readings, in the writer's judgment, can only be extremely early. In xxvi 11, for και ου βδελυξεται η ψυχη μου υμας, the Qumran reading is και ου βδε-λυξομαι υμας; and in xxvi 12, for (και υμεις εσεσθε μοι) λαος the Qumran text has εθν[ος]. Of these Qumran readings, the former introduces an anthropomorphic turn which is not in the original text; and the latter, in rendering ʿam by εθνος, violates the pattern by which LXX regularly applies εθνος to the gentiles, and λαος to the people of Israel. The general impression with which the writer is left is that we have here one more book of the O.T. in which a single early Greek rendering seems to have undergone a good deal of what we would today call critical revision, in the period even before Origen.[*]

PATRICK W. SKEHAN

[*] For the Septuagintal materials, see also P. Kahle, "The Greek Bible and the Gospels: Fragments from the Judaean Desert," Studia Evangelica [I.] ed. Kurt Aland et al., (Texte und Untersuchungen ... 73), Berlin, Akademie-Verlag, 1959, pp. 613-621 (especially 615-618).

ΦΟΒΗΘΗΣΕΣΘΕ Ο...
ΡΕΤΗΣΘΕ ΚΑΙ ΤΗΣΗ...
ΗΤ ΗΥ...ΩΕΝΙΚΑ ΡΠΟΙ...
...ΤΟΝ ΕΙΣ ΥΜΩΝ ΚΑ...
...ΜΗΤΟΣ...ΕΣΩ...
...ΤΕΡΟΝ Κ...

...ΤΗΝΥ...
...ΤΗΝ ΚΝ ΕΝ ΤΙ...
...Κ ΟΘΕΝ ΥΜΑΣ...ΤΗΕ...
...Α ΠΟΛΕΜΟΝ...ΓΟ...
...Ε ΤΟΥΣ ΕΧΘ ΥΜΩΝ Α...
...ΚΥ ΝΟΣ ΕΙΣ ΥΜΩΝ Ο...
...ΥΜΑΣ Κ ΠΑΛ ΕΘ ΥΜ...
...ΚΑ...ΕΑΛΚΟ ΕΙ ΥΜ...
...ΗΑΙΑ ΔΗ ΚΗ ΝΟ...
...ΕΙ ΟΤ ΩΝ ΗΣΩ...

...ΜΟΥ...ΕΑΤΕΟΜΩΥΜΑΣ ΚΑ...
ΚΑΙ ΤΜΕΚΟ ΚΟΘΟ ΦΟΒΩΛΟΙ ΕΘ...
ΖΕΑΤΠΩΝ ΥΜΑΣ ΕΠΗ ΘΟΑΠΤ...
ΣΥΝΕ ΤΕΤΑ ΕΝ ΖΥΝΟΝ Τ...
ΜΕΤΑ ΠΑΡΡΗΣΙΑΣ ΕΑ...
ΤΡΟΣΤΑΓΜΑΤΑ ΜΟΥ Κ...
ΓΜΑΣ ΙΜΟΥ ΙΕΡΟΣΟΧΟ...
ΤΑΣ ΕΝΤΟΛΑΣ ΜΟΥ...
ΚΑΙ ΕΓΩ ΠΟΙΗΣΩ...
ΨΩΡΑΝ ΚΑΙΤΟ...
ΚΑΙ ΤΗΝ ΥΥ...
ΥΜΩΝ...

4 Q LXX Lev.ᵃ Lev. xxvi 2-16.

μο]ΫΦΟΒΗΘΗϹΕϹΘΕΕΓ[ω

πο]ΡΕΥΗϹΘΕΚΑΙΤΑϹΕΝΤ[ολας

τη]ΙΓΗΙΥΜΩΝΕΝΚΑΙΡΩΙΑΫ[του

κ]ΑΙΤΟΝΞΥΛΟΝΕΝΚΑ[

5   ]ΑΜΗΤΟϹ[τον]ΤΡΥΡΓ[ητον

σ]ΠΟΡΟΝΚ[αιφα]ΓΕϹΘ[ε

κ]ΑΤΟΙΚΗϹ[ετε

ε]ΙΡΗΝΗΝΕΝΤ[ηι γηι υμων] ΚΑΙ[

]ΕΚΦΟΒΩΝΥΜΑϹ[καια]ΠΟΛΩ[

10   κ]ΑΙΠΟΛΕΜΟϹΟΥΔΙ[ελε]ΥϹΕΤ[αι

διωξεσθ]ΕΤΟΥϹΕΧΘΡΟΥϹΥΜΩΝ[κ]ΑΙ[

διωξ]ΟΝΤΑΙΠΕΝΤΕΥΜΩΝΕ[κατον

μ]ΥΡΙΑΔΑϹΚΑΙΠΕϹΟΥΝΤΑ[ι

μαχαιρα]ΙΚΑΙΕΠΙΒΛΕΨΩΕΦΥΜΑϹ[

15   μο]ΥΗΔΙΑΘΗΚΗΕ[σ]ΤΑΙ[

παλαι]ΑΜΕΤΑΤΩΝΝΕΩ[ν

ΚΑΙΟΥΒΔΕΛΥΞΟΜΑΙΥΜΑϹΚΑΙ[

ΚΑΙΥΜΕΙϹΕϹΕϹΘΕΜΟΙΕΘΝ[ος

ΞΑΓΑΓΩΝΥΜΑϹΕΓΓΗϹΑΙΓΥ[πτου

20   ϹΥΝΕΤΡΙΨΑΤΟΝΖΥΓΟΝΤ[ου

ΜΕΤΑΠΑΡΡΗϹΙΑϹ   ΕΑΝ[

ΠΡΟϹΤΑΓΜΑΤΑΜΟΥΑΛ[λα

ΓΜΑϹΙΜΟΥΠΡΟϹΟΧΘΙϹ[ηι

ΤΑϹΕΝΤΟΛΑϹΜΟΥΑΛ[λα

25   ΚΑΙΕΓΩΠΟΙΗϹΩ[

ΨΩΡΑΝΚΑΙΤΟ[ν

ΚΑΙΤΗΝΨΥ[χην

ΥΜΩΝ[

l. 2.   An omission of about the length of και ποιησητε αυτας must be supposed.

l. 3.   τηι γηι υμων: codd. υμιν cf. MT.

l. 4.   τον ξυλον εν κα[   ]: MSS. τα ξυλα των πεδιων αποδωσει τον καρπον αυτων = MT. τον ξυλον *sic*; εν κα[ιρω αυτου...?]

l. 5.   αμητος: as B*Ay Ethiopic; αλοητος Bᵃᵇ FGMN etc. Lev. xxvi 5 is the source of Amos ix 13 LXX, where the same confusion exists; in Lev. αμητος is thus a very early corrupttion (MT *dayiš* = αλοητος) and Amos LXX could primitively have adopted either term.

        τρυγ[ητον]: corrected from σπορον by the same hand; the σπο is cancelled and the ρ dotted, in the MS.

l. 9.   [ο] εκφοβων υμας: as F bmn Armen. Cyr.; υμας ο εκφοβων B etc.

l. 10. και πολεμος ου διελευσεται [δια της γης υμων]: in its primitive place, as in MT; so G, etc.; BᵃᵇAFM etc. have it twice, here and before verse 6; B* before verse 6 only; gnpt Ethiopic omit it entirely.

l. 12. πεντε υμων: εξ υμων πεντε codd.

l. 15. [μο]υ η διαθηκη ε[σ]ται [μεθ υμων?]; codd. και στησω την διαθηκην μου μεθ υμων as MT.

        For παλαια και παλαια παλαιων of codd. this MS. can have had no more than παλαια παλαιων cf. MT.

l. 16. μετα των νεω[ν]: codd. εκ προσωπου νεων.

l. 17. ου βδελυξομαι υμας: all witnesses ου βδελυξεται η ψυχη μου υμας.

l. 18. μοι as FGMN etc.; μου BAkx.

        εθνος : all witnesses, and 2 Cor. vi 16, λαος (b w Armen. ᵉᵈ· εις λαον).

l. 19. εγγης for εκ γης.

l. 20. τον ζυγον τ[ου δεσμου]: so dnt Lat. Origen ˡᵃᵗ; most witnesses τον δεσμον του ζυγου.

l. 22. μου: omit ταυτα as Boh. Ethiop. Lat.

l. 23. [προστα]γμασι μου; all witnesses, κριμασιν μου.

l. 24. αλ[λα ωστε?]: codd. ωστε; d n Armen. και; Ethiop. και ωστε.

ASPECTS OF THE TEXTUAL TRANSMISSION OF THE BIBLE IN THE LIGHT OF QUMRAN MANUSCRIPTS

SHEMARYAHU TALMON

I

The discovery of the Scrolls from the Judaean Desert has added a new dimension to Biblical text criticism. It goes without saying that these MSS which precede the oldest extant MSS of the MT by more than a millennium, in view of their antiquity, are of unsurpassed importance for an investigation into the early history of the text of the OT. Much already has been learned from research carried out so far. More is to be expected from the edition of yet unpublished MSS, and from an ensuing evaluation of their contribution to a better understanding of the processes by which the Bible text was transmitted.[1]

The new material often helps in elucidating the genesis, and the history of individual variants in which one or more of the ancient VSS differ from the MT. They also open up new possibilities for the recovery or the reconstruction of the factors which underlie textual variation. The sifting of these cases, their classification, and a statistical assessment of the frequency of their appearance may make possible the systematic presentation of the processes which can be proved empirically to have been conducive to the emergence of *variae lectiones*. The pertinent information gained from these first-hand sources, because of their scope and their primacy, should enable scholars to improve on previous attempts along these lines, such as F. Delitzsch's *Lese- und Schreibfehler im Alten Testament* (Berlin–Leipzig 1920).

Prior to the discovery of the Qumran Scrolls, observations on the skill and the peculiarities of the ancient copyists of the Biblical text could be inferred only from the analysis of variants which are extant in mediaeval Heb. MSS,

---

1   A valuable summary of these aspects of the Scrolls may be found in Frank M. Cross, Jr., *The Ancient Library of Qumran*, revised edition (1961) 161–194, where pertinent earlier literature is quoted. See further: H.M. Orlinsky, "The Textual Criticism of the Old Testament", *The Bible and the Ancient Near East, Essays in Honor of W.F. Albright*, ed. G.E. Wright (New York 1961) 113–132; D. Barthélemy, *Les Devanciers D'Aquila* (Leiden 1963); W.H. Brownlee, *The Meaning of the Qumrân Scrolls for the Bible* (Oxford 1964).

226

or had to be abstracted from deviating translations in the ancient VSS. With the pre-Christian Hebrew Scrolls from Qumran at our disposal, we now are in a position to verify principles established by inference, and to put them to a practical test. The Scrolls afford us a completely new insight into ancient scribal craft and give us an unexampled visual impression of the physical appearance of the manuscripts in which arose the Biblical *variae lectiones*. We now can observe at close range, so to say *in situ*, scribal techniques of the Second Commonwealth period which left their impression on the Bible text in subsequent stages of its history. We can perceive the manuscriptal realities which were the breeding ground of the variants that crop up in the extant witnesses to the text of the Bible.

That the Qumran Scrolls indeed exhibit scribal conventions and techniques which were generally prevalent in Jewry of the Second Commonwealth is easily proved from the fact that the sectarian scribes in many details followed rules which tally with those laid down by the Rabbis for Torah-scribes of the "normative" community.[2] There is obviously nothing specifically sectarian in the external appearance of the Qumran Scrolls, nor in the scribal customs to which their copyists adhered.[3] The same holds true for the majority of the deviating readings found in them. The impression of dissention that goes with the Biblical Scrolls from Qumran derives from the secession of their scribes from normative Judaism, and has no roots in the MSS as such. That is to say, it must be attributed to socio-historical processes which engulfed these scrolls, but in no way to their textual or manuscriptal character. Genetically the Biblical texts from Qumran are "Jewish". They became "sectarian" in their subsequent history.

What makes the evidence of the Scrolls especially valuable is the fact that they present not just one horizontal cross-section view of a stabilized version, such as is the Massoretic *textus receptus*. Because of their textual diversity, the kaleidoscope of the textual traditions exhibited in them: their concurrence here with one, here with another of the known Versions, or again in other cases their textual exclusive individuality, the Biblical MSS found at Qumran, in their totality present, in a nutshell as it were, the intricate and variegated problems of the OT Hebrew text and Versions. The concentration of processes

---

2   This was pointed out by the late E.L. Sukenik already in 1947 in his first report on the Scrolls: א.ל. סוקניק, מגילות גנוזות... סקירה ראשונה (ירושלים תש״ח) א–יא

3   A notable exception are the enigmatic scribal marks or symbols found in the margins of Is-a for which, as yet, no adequate explanation was offered. See: *The Dead Sea Scrolls of St. Mark's Monastery* 1, ed. M. Burrows (New-Haven 1950) p. XVI. It appears that these signs are peculiar to Is-a. Only some of the simpler ones turn up also in other Qumran MSS.

which obtain in the history of the Bible text, in a comparatively small corpus of MSS, small in comparison with the bulk of Hebrew — Massoretic and Samaritan —, Greek, Aramaic, Syriac, Latin *etc.* MSS which have to be sifted, collated and compared in the course of the critical work on the Bible text, a corpus which moreover is relatively homogeneous with respect to time and place of provenance, make the Qumran Scrolls an ideal subject for a pilot-study on these processes. Although the results gained from an analysis of the Qumran material cannot be applied without qualification to the wider field of comparative research into the MT and the VSS, we may derive from them certain working hypotheses which then have to be verified by application to the wider problem.

Thus the situation at Qumran reflects on a basic issue in OT textual research, namely the moot problem of the establishment of a Hebrew *textus receptus*. The coexistence of diverse text-types in the numerically, geographically and temporally restricted Covenanters-community; the fact that (some or most of) the conflicting MSS, very probably, had been copied in the Qumran *Scriptorium*; and that no obvious attempts at the suppression of divergent MSS or of individual variants can be discovered in that voluminous literature, proves beyond doubt that the very notion of a Biblical *textus receptus* had not yet taken root at Qumran. The superscribed corrections in 1QIs[a] (henceforth Is-a) which in the majority of cases, though by no means in all, bring the deviant basic text in line with MT,[4] or with a proto-Massoretic textual tradition (1QIs[b] = Is-b) cannot be adduced in evidence for a supposed tendency to revise Is-a towards an established Qumran recension. This evidence is set off, in fact is neutralized by a Deuteronomy MS from Cave 5, roughly contemporary with Is-a.[5] Here the corrections in practically every instance run counter to the proto-Massoretic tradition, and align themselves with a Septuagintal text-type.

We have no reason to doubt that this "liberal" attitude towards divergent textual traditions of the Bible was prevalent also in "normative" Jewish circles of that period, *i.e.* in the second and first centuries B.C.E. It actually can be shown that according to Rabbinic testimony, even the model codices that were kept in the Temple precincts not only exhibited divergent readings, but represented conflicting text-types.[6] Phenomenologically speaking the situation that prevailed in the *'azarah* may be compared, though with quali-

4   Cp. J. Hempel, "Beobachtungen an der 'syrischen' Jesajarolle vom Toten Meer (DSIa)", ZDMG 101 (1951) 149.
5   See: M. Baillet – J.T. Milik – R. de Vaux, *Les petites grottes de Qumrân*, DJD 3 (Oxford 1962) 169–171, pl. XXVI.
6   Cp. S. Talmon, "The Three Scrolls of the Law That Were Found in the Temple

fications, with the one that obtained in the *Scriptorium* at Qumran. The difference consists in the fact that in the end the Temple codices were collated, probably in the first century C.E., and what is more important, that Rabbinic Judaism ultimately established a model text and strove to banish deviant MSS from circulation. However at this stage the comparability of "normative" with Qumran practice breaks down. The active life span of the Covenanters-community ends sometime in the first century B.C.E., although sporadic attempts at restoration vibrate into the first or possibly into the second century C.E. However also the latest manuscripts from Qumran which give evidence to the local history of the Bible text in the crucial period, the last decades before the destruction of the Temple, do not present the slightest indication that even an incipient *textus receptus* did emerge there, or that the very notion of a model recension ever was conceived by the Covenanters.[7]

The presentation of the sum total of the Biblical documents from Qumran as a small-scale replica of the "MT and VSS" issue, derives further support from one more characteristic of that material. The Qumran finds exhibit, as stated, a basic homogeneity with regard to the time and the place of their provenance. There are no grounds to doubt that these MSS were written in Palestine, and that a great majority of them, if not all, were copied at Qumran. It also may be considered as established that, some odd items excepted, the bulk of the MSS in the Qumran library was copied within a span of not more than three hundred years, approximately from the middle of the third century B.C.E. to the middle of the first century C.E.[8] In view of these circumstances the marked diversity of textual traditions which can be observed in these MSS presumably derives from the temporal and/or geographical[9] heterogeneity of the *Vorlagen* from which the Qumran MSS, or some of them, were copied. Thus, in addition to the horizontal cross-section view of the Bible text at Qumran during the last phases of the Second Commonwealth period, the Qumran material also affords a vertical cross-section view of the transmission

---

Court", *Textus* 2 (1962) 14–27 (henceforth TSL). Also the deviant readings in the Apocrypha and the NT point in the same direction.

7 Cp. P.W. Skehan, "The Qumran Manuscripts and Textual Criticism." *Suppl. to VT*, 4 (Leiden 1957) 149.

8 Cp. Frank M. Cross, Jr., "The Development of the Jewish Scripts", in : *The Bible and the Ancient Near East*, 133.

9 The case for an existence of local recensions of the Bible text in view of the Qumran evidence, recently was argued by W.F. Albright, "New Light on Early Recensions of the Hebrew Bible", BASOR 140 (1955) 27–33; F.M. Cross, Jr., *The Ancient Library of Qumran*, 188–194; see also the latter's forthcoming paper in HThR in which unpublished material from Qumran Cave 4 was utilized. The present author is indebted to Prof. Cross for permission to read this paper in typescript.

of the Bible text, in which are reflected various chronological layers, and geographical or social-strata traditions.[10] These circumstances further enhance the similarity of the problems relating to the Bible text at Qumran with those adhering to the wider issue of the relations of the MT and the VSS.

The situation which obtains at Qumran holds out one more possibility of comparison with another phase in the history of the Bible text. In conformity with a basic characteristic of Second Commonwealth Judaism — normative and dissenting alike — the Covenanters' religious concepts were Bible-centred. Their original literary creations, such as the *War-Scroll*, the *Hodayot*, the *Sectarian Manual*, and the *Zadokite Documents* swarm with *verbatim* Bible quotations, paraphrases and allusions.[11] Their most fundamental beliefs and practices reflect the attempt to recapture, and to typologically re-live Biblical Judaism.[12] It is this Scripture-piety which produced the *pesher* technique, so indicative of the Covenanters' system of Bible hermeneutics, by the aid of which Biblical history was actualized, and made existentially meaningful. In this unceasing process of quotation, interpretation and adaptation, the Bible text at Qumran was exposed to a fate which is comparable to that which the *hebraica veritas* experienced on a wider scale in Rabbinic Judaism, and in the orbit of Jewish and Christian communities that had recourse to translations of the Hebrew original. The deliberate insertion of textual alterations into Scripture for various reasons of dogma, style *etc.*, the uncontrolled infiltration of haphazard changes due to linguistic peculiarities of copyists, or to their characteristic concepts and ideas, which may be observed in the transmission of the Bible text at large, have their counterparts in the "Qumran Bible". The study of these phenomena at Qumran again is facilitated by the comparative compactness of the material, and by the decidedly more pronounced manner in which they become manifest. We thus encounter in the Qumran writings developments of Biblical text-transmission which may be considered proto-types of phenomena that emerge concurrently and subsequently in the text-history of the Bible in Jewish and Christian tradition, albeit in less concentrated form, and at different grades of variation.

10 For a discussion of these issues cp. E.Y. Kutscher, הלשון והרקע הלשוני של מגילת ישעיהו השלמה ממגילות ים המלח (ירושלים תשי״ט), esp. pp. 45–70.

11 Basic information on the utilization of the Bible in these works is provided in the scholarly editions of the texts. A detailed discussion of the Biblical quotations and allusions in the *Hodayot* pl. I–III is offered by P. Wernberg-Moller in his article in the present volume.

12 This aspect of Qumran Sectarianism often is referred to in the voluminous literature on the Covenanters. See also my forthcoming discussion of "The 'Desert Ideal' in the Bible and at Qumran", in: *Studies and Texts* 3, ed. A. Altmann (Philip W. Lown Institute of Advanced Judaic Studies, Brandeis University).

II

The foregoing general remarks will be illustrated in this paper by an analysis of the manuscriptal conditions which, in the first stage, fathered the development of "double-readings",[13] and ultimately were conducive to the Massoretic techniques of variant-preservation in the *Kethîb–Qerê* system, and in the Midrashic *'al tiqrê* technique.

Two main types of conflation must be clearly distinguished. On the one hand, a double reading may result from the routine insertion into the main text of marginal or intralinear corrective notes and annotations together with the readings which they were meant to supersede. On the other hand, conflation will result from the premeditated intentional effort on part of a scribe to preserve variant readings which he considered equal in value and worthy of preservation.[14] This type of conflation is a well-attested trick-in-hand of the transmitters of the Bible text. It was widely practiced by scribes and copyists, Jews and Christians, throughout centuries, in the Heb. original and in translations.

Lacking a universally recognized device of variants-notation, not to be confused with correction, the parallel readings either were recorded in the margins and between lines, or else were incorporated *prima manu* (*p.m.*) into the textbase, whenever this could be done without serious disruption of syntax or distortion of sense. But also when the variant initially had been noted *p.m.* outside the normal text-base, it easily could be transferred into the text by a subsequent copyist who used the annotated MS as his *Vorlage*. Although the practical results of variants-conflation will coincide with those of the routine conflation of a mistake with its correction, the two phenomena must be kept apart. Routine conflation always is due to a copyist's default and runs counter to the original corrector's intentions. Variants-conflation *secunda manu* indeed also results from scribal lapse, but it always puts into effect the purport of the first-hand collator, namely the intentional preservation of variant readings.

Methodologically, therefore, the two types of conflation outlined above are different. But in practice we have no safe means to decide in each case whether the marginal or intralinear notation from the outset was intended to replace a reading in the main text, whether it was meant to be added to the text base,

---

13 See the present writer's "Double Readings in the Massoretic Text", *Textus* 1 (1960) 144–184 (henceforth DRMT); and the notes on Ex. 15:2 and 1 Sam. 15:32a in VT 4 (1954) 206–207, respectively VT 11 (1961) 456–457.

14 On these, see the present author's "Synonymous Readings in the Textual Traditions of the Old Testament", *Scripta Hierosolymitana* 8 (1961) 335–383 (henceforth SROT).

or whether it was considered a mere note, to be kept apart from the text proper also at subsequent copyings. The external similarity of emendation, restitution and annotation, all of which were entered in the margins or between lines, could be conducive to conflation by mistaken interpretation of the collators' notations.

It is one of the great advantages of the Biblical MSS from Qumran that in them we yet can perceive conflation in the different stages of its execution. The Qumran Scrolls furnish us with the means to trace step by step the intentional preservation of alternative readings on the one hand, and the perpetuation by default of scribal mistakes together with their corrections on the other hand.

III

Let us first consider the category of routine conflations which resulted from the mistaken insertion of superscribed or adscribed corrections into the text base.

Superscription or marginal adscription as a means of correction was as familiar to the sectarian scribes as it is to the modern writer or copyist. It is unfortunate that in most cases, especially in Is-a, it cannot be decided whether the first hand is at work correcting a recognized and admitted mistake, or whether a second hand thought fit to emend a text with which the initial scribe had found no fault. On the whole the corrections are towards the MT. Accordingly they are ascribed to a second hand who used a proto-Massoretic MS as his *Vorlage*. However there are significant exceptions to this rule.

These two different types of correction make themselves manifest in the very first line of Is-a in which we find three cases of superscribed single letters: בִּימֵי, וִירוּשָׁלַ͏ם, יְשַׁעְיָהוּ. The first two seemingly are instances of corrected lapses which, at the same time, bring the text of Is-a in line with the (proto-) Massoretic readings. In the third the opposite is the case: a normal MT-type reading (בימי) is (mis)corrected towards the Aramaic determined morphology of the sectarian copyist. The first two may be ascribed to the initial scribe with much probability, the third with absolute certainty.

On pl. iv, 3 (Is. 3:25b) the insertion amounts to two letters. A typical variant reading — וגבוריך (2nd pers. plur. fem. of גבור), supported by all VSS,[15] which is a better parallel to מתיך of the first stichos than is the Massoretic וגבורתך (2nd pers. sing. fem. of גבורה) was corrected towards the reading exhibited in the MT by the superscription of ות : וגבוריך (2. pers. plur. fem. of

---

15 T: ועבדי נצחנך ; G: οἱ ἰσχύοντες ὑμῶν; Aq.: οἱ δυνατοί σου; V: fortes tui. See also: A. Rubinstein, VT 4 (1954) 320.

גבורה). However no full identity with the MT reading was achieved. Here we seem to be dealing not with a corrected mistake *p.m.*, but rather with a (subjective) emendation *s.m.* based on a MT-type *Vorlage*.

Similarly, complete words were added to the basic text of Is-a by superscription. Again we can differentiate between omissions by default which were filled in *p.m.* or possibly *s.m.*, and between emendations of what a second hand interpreted as a textual mistake perpetrated by the initial copyist. Thus the superlinear סוחריה in Is. 23:8 certainly is a correction *p.m.* of an obvious omission in the basic text. That by this correction Is-a is brought in line with the MT is an accidental corollary, and is immaterial for the issue on hand.

In Is. 8:17 the acc. part. את was inserted by superscription before פניו, in accordance with the prevalent usage of Is-a. Here the superlinear correction goes against the MT, and most certainly stems from the original copyist.

Much less clear is the situation with regard to the word צבאות which is added over מה יעץ ה׳ על מצרים in Is. 19:12. The basic text of Is-a, as it stands, causes no difficulties. Th correction makes it identical with the MT (=T,G) which reads ה׳ צבאות in this verse, in vv. 16, 18, 25, and especially in v. 17 where imagery is employed which is virtually identical with the imagery of v. 12. But, on the other hand, also the single tetragrammaton is well represented in this chapter (vv. 19, 20, 21, 22). Accordingly it seems preferable to ascribe the insertion of צבאות in v. 12 to the emendatory activities of the MT-oriented corrector, and not to the first hand. The same goes for the superlinear addition of אבני in Is. 14:19 to the basic reading of Is-a יורדי אל בור which indeed may, but need not be a simplified reading[16] of the somewhat obscure Massoretic: יורדי אל אבני בור (=G, V). Whatever the case may be, the restitution of אבני adjusts Is-a to the MT.

The random examples adduced so far clearly show that superscription was a technique recognized by the scribe and the corrector of Is-a as a means for restituting letters or words which had been omitted by default from the text base. These interlinear and marginal notations contained a tacit, but nevertheless explicit directive for future copyists to restore the superscribed or adscribed textual items into the text base of their own copies for which the annotated MS served as *Vorlage*. This restoration would be a mere mechanical re-transfer from the margin or from between the lines into the line proper,

---

16 In the main tradition of T אבני is not rendered: נחתי לגוב בית אבדנא. MSS. f, c insert אבני before לגוב whereas in the First and Second Bomberg Bible (b, g) the word follows upon לגוב. Qimḥi's commentary (ed. L. Finkelstein), as quoted in A. Sperber's edition of the Targum, has the interesting variant: לסייפי (גוב בית) אבדנא. Could לסייפי be a miswritten לסיפי which thus would tally with אדני that seems to underlie V: *ad fundamenta laci*. Cp. Kedar's discussion of this reading on p. 187 of this volume.

and would not require any re-adjustment in the text-base of the *Vorlage*.
Since such corrections *p.m.*, or *s.m.* of omissions and mistakes perpetrated *p.m.*
most probably constituted the majority of marginal notations, they created
a psychological readiness in copyists to restore superscriptions or adscriptions
which they found in their *Vorlage* into the main text of their own copy. Herein
may be found the roots of routine conflation.

It is here that the Qumran Scrolls lend the support of manuscriptal facts
to theoretical considerations. Let us first discuss some cases of hypothetical
doublets which could have arisen, but in fact did not arise from such an Is-a
reading. An intriguing instance of correction by superlinear insertion is found
in Is. 43:3. Here the basic text of Is-a has no equivalent for מושיעך of the MT.
Its shorter reading אני ה׳ אלהיך קדוש ישראל is syntactically without fault,
although metrically it lacks somewhat in length in comparison with the second
half-verse. A second hand whose *ductus* is clearly distinguishable from that
of the first, and who uses defective as against the latter's *plene* spelling (אלוהיכה),
added גואלך between the lines. This is a good synonymous reading of the
Massoretic מושיעך.[17] Thus the difference between Is-a and the MT which in
the first stage consisted of the lack of one word, in the second stage developed
into a *varia lectio*. A subsequent collator, not a mere copyist, of Is-a and the
(proto-) MT easily could have combined the two readings into a non-extant
doublet: אני ה׳ אלהיך קדוש ישראל מושיעך (ו)גואלך for which cp. *e.g.* Is. 49:26
(MT=Is-a): כי אני ה׳ מושיעך וגואלך אביר יעקב (=G, T).

The probability of routine-conflation increases when we consider not re-
storative but corrective superscriptions which are meant to "replace" a component of the text-base. As a rule the tendency towards conflation will be
checked by appropriate marks which prescribe the excision from the text[18]
of the component that is to be replaced by the marginal notation. There are
two instances of this kind, which hypothetically could have resulted in *conflatio*.

1. Is. 21:1   Is-a: ממדבר בא מארץ רחוקה נוראה
                MT: ממדבר בא מארץ נוראה

The basic reading of Is-a which is reflected in S: מן ארעא רחיקתא, perhaps
inadvertently substituted מארץ רחוקה, which is found nine times in the OT[19]
including one mention in Is. 39:3, for the *hap. leg.* מארץ נוראה[20] of MT which
underlies G: φοβερὸν, and T (?): חסינן. The superscription of נוראה with the

17 Cp. SROT, 379–380.
18 Cp. Sifre (ed. Horowitz, 80): נקוד עליו מלמעלה ולמטה מפני שלא היה זה זה מקומו.
19 Seven times connected with the verb בוא: Deut. 29:21; Josh. 9:6, 9; 1 Ki. 8:41 =
    2 Chr. 6:32; 2 Ki. 20:14, and esp. Is. 39:3. Cp. Kutscher, *op. cit.*, 478.
20 However twice נורא ...מדבר is found: Deut. 1:19; 8:15.

concomitant deletion of רחוקה may confidently be attributed to a second hand by reason of the different *ductus*. Thus we deal here with the subjective emendation *s.m.* of a possibly *bona fide* reading *p.m.*

2. Is. 12:6   Is-a: צוהלי ורוני ־בּתּ ציון

   MT: צהלי ורוני יושבת ציון

The basic reading of Is-a: בת ציון presents a to all means and purposes synonymous variant of MT's יושבת ציון. Whereas S: עמורתא דציון clearly sides with the MT[21], T's כנשתא דציון[22] appears to go with Is-a *p.m.*, although the evidence is not altogether decisive. Again it would appear that a *bona fide* variant reading of the first hand, was subsequently (*s.m.*?) corrected towards the MT by the superscription of יושבת. However it seems that the concomitant deletion here affects only the second letter of the word בת[23], thus creating the basis for a reading יושבת בציון which indeed comes nearer to MT than Is-a *p.m.*, but is not identical with it. This reading is mirrored in G: οἱ κατοικοῦντες ἐν Σιων.

It does not require much imagination to reconstruct the reasoning of a copyist of Is-a who, in spite of the deletion mark in Is. 21:1, and because of the only partial deletion in 12:6 would have interpreted the superscriptions not as substitutions for components found in the text-base, but rather as faultily omitted intrinsic parts of it, which he therefore restored to their proper place without altering the text-base. In both cases this could easily be done. In Is. 21:1 it would have resulted in the doublet מארץ רחוקה (ו)נוראה for which cp. Deut. 1:19 — המדבר הגדול והנורא. In 12:6 the outcome would have been יושבת בת ציון for which cp. *e.g.* בתולת בת ציון (Is. 37:22 = 2 Ki. 19:21).

Such a hypothetical development is even more imminent in the following instance of hypercorrection:

1QIs^a 41:20

In Is. 41:20 a series of four synonymous verbs is used to describe the future

21 Cp. Is. 10:24 MT: ישב ציון, T: יתיב ציון, S: דעמר בצהיון; Jer. 51:35 MT: ישבת ציון T: לכנשתא דציון, S: אשתביו דציון (probably resulting from an intentional or unintentional confusion of √ישב with √שבה).

22 Cp. Is. 1:8; 16:1; 52:2; 62:11 MT: בת ציון, T: כנשתא דציון, S: ברת צהיון.

23 Kutscher (*op. cit.*, 474) maintains that בת was struck out altogether.

recognition by the poor and the destitute of God's mighty deeds: למען יראו וידעו וישימו וישכילו יחדו כי יד ה׳ עשתה זאת. The MT here is supported by the *verbatim* rendition of the first two and the fourth verb in T (...דיחזון וידעון ויסתכלון), and by the latter's interpretative rendering of the crucial third: וישוון דחלתי על ליבהון. However Is-a reads here ויבינו, and has וישימו as a superscription, most probably introduced *s.m.* The basic ויבינו clearly is a variant reading. Whether it is due to a mere interpretation of the apocopated וישימו (לבם) or whether it is a true *varia lectio*, may be left undecided at present. The G translation ἐννοηθῶσιν, which may reflect ויבינו, possibly strengthens the latter proposition. But, since this specific verb is a *hap. leg.* in the Greek translation of Isaiah the evidence is not conclusive. Also the fact that the combination שים (לב) — ידע recurs in v. 22 in inverted order, both in the MT and in Is-a: הגידו ונשימה לבנו ונדעה, makes us believe that ויבינו of Is-a, instead of וישימו in the MT, results from faithful adherence to a *Vorlage* which is yet mirrored in S: ונתבינון, and not from slovenly word substitution.

Of more importance for the issue on hand is the fact that the superscribed emendation וישימו subsequently was disqualified by its enclosure within deletion-dots. Thus the basic non-MT ויבינו was restored to its original validity.[24] This two-stage correction might have led an imaginary copyist to consider the interlinear וישימו as a restituted omission and not as an emendation. As a result he would have conjoined this verb with ויבינו, thus creating the hypothetical doublet: למען יראו וידעו וישימו ויבינו וישכילו יחדו....

It is obvious that the chances of an actual conflation will considerably ncrease in cases in which a variant reading is superscribed or adscribed without iny accompanying critical symbols.

1QIsᵃ 36:11

Is. 36:11   Is-a: דברנא עם עבדיך עמנו ארמית
            MT: דבר נא אל עבדיך   >   ארמית

The redundant עמנו of Is-a, which has no equivalent in the VSS, was entered in the right hand margin exactly in line with the following word ארמית. עמנו is a parallel reading of עם עבדיך with which the preceding line ends.[25] Thus we

---

24 Cp. *e.g.* Is. 49:14 where the non-Massoretic superscribed emendation ואלוהי is deleted by "pointing" in favour of the basic ואדוני (= MT).

25 Kutscher (*op. cit.*, 430) assumes that עמנו in the first part of Is. 36:11 echoes עמנו in the

have here a true variant-notation, a *Qerê*-type entry which was registered alongside the *Kethîb*-type reading עם עבדיך, and was never meant to be integrated into the text proper. However the probability of its integration is much furthered by the favorable manuscriptal conditions which could easily induce a copyist of Is-a to take עמנו as an integral part of the original text-base.

We can now proceed from hypothetical to actual routine conflation. While in the preceding instances Is-a was presented as a possible basis for an ensuing doublet in an imaginary MS for which it might have served as the *Vorlage*, in the examples to follow the faulty doublet actually occurs in Is-a.

We presume that a reading *cum* superscribed emendation lies at the basis of the following doublet in Is-a 51:11 which, however, was emended *post facto*, by the erasure of one of its components.

The extant text of Is-a reads here ופזורי ה׳ ישובו, as against ופדויי ה׳ ישובון of MT which is supported by the VSS.[26] In the parallel, Is. 35:10, both MT and Is-a read ופדויי ה׳. Moreover, whereas the root פדה is represented twice more in the Book of Isaiah (1:27; 29:22), פזר is not found in it at all. Even if one assumes that the sectarian scribe substituted ופזורי for ופדויי under the influence of scriptures which use √פזר in reference to Israel's dispersion (Jer. 50:17; Joel 4:2; Esth. 3:8),[27] his reading still must be considered the *lectio difficilior*, with a fair claim at originality. Accordingly, ופזורי may be deemed a synonymous reading of ופדויי, and its textual equivalent. This equivalence is further indicated by the fact that ופדויי actually had been written also in the text-base of Is-a where it preceded ופזורי, but was subsequently erased, possibly by a second hand. If indeed this was the case, the scroll initially contained the doublet ופדויי ופזורי ה׳ which, as we assume, resulted from a conflation of the main reading with a supralinear or marginal variant which the scribe of Is-a had found in his *Vorlage*.[28]

---

second part of the parallel verse 2 Ki. 18:26 — ואל תדבר עמנו יהודית. This supposition is highly improbable in view of the fact that in Is. 36:11b Is-a altogether deviates from MT, and from the parallel reading in 2 Kings.

26 G: καὶ λελυτρωμένοις; T: ופריקא דיוי; S: פריקוהי דמריא.

27 Cp. Kutscher, *op. cit.*, 207.

28 Cp. Kutscher, *op. cit.*, 433. A similar situation may underlie the present text form of Is-a in Is. 2:4: ושפט בין הגואים והוכיח-בין עמים רבים. The crossing out of בין and the superscribed *lamed* bring Is-a into conformity with MT, whereas in the preceding instance the erasure fortified the deviance of Is-a from MT. The reading of Is-a indeed may be explained as a conscious, or unconscious harmonization with the first stichos of the verse (Kutscher, *op. cit.*, 489), but in itself it is the *lectio difficilior*. הוכיח with the dat. pron. *lamed* is found in the parallel passage Mic. 4:3, and prevails in the OT (Job 32:12; Prov. 9:7, 8; 15:12; 19:25, and esp. Is. 11:4), whereas הוכיח בין is found only twice (Gen. 31:37; Job 9:33).

IV

Now we can turn to the premeditated retention of parallel readings by conscious conflation, as reflected in Qumran Biblical MSS.

We find in the Scrolls, just as in the MT and the VSS, fully-fledged doublets which have been already incorporated in the basic text. These may be arranged under the following two headings:

1. Doublets which are reflected also in extra-Qumran Bible texts, and therefore obviously are rooted in an all-Jewish (not specific-sectarian) textual tradition.

2. Doublets which are found only in Qumran MSS. These cases, which may be assumed with much probability to have arisen at Qumran, illustrate the collation activities of the sectarian scribes. At the same time Qumran MSS, and especially Is-a, present instances of interlinear or marginal critical notations which in MT or in one of the VSS have become part and parcel of the main text. Here the Qumran material fulfills two functions:

3. (A) It illustrates the manuscriptal conditions which are the basis of double-readings, and enlightens us on the technical aspects of conflation. (B) It assists in the discovery of presumed doublets in other extant text-traditions of the Bible.

Not in all cases are we in a position to determine the sources from which the constituent variants of a doublet were culled, due to the paucity of non-standardised textual traditions which survived the normalising attention of scribes and revisers. Yet often one of the components of a doublet (*e.g.* in Is-a) turns up as a single reading in the MT or in one of the extant VSS. This can cause no surprise in view of the disparity of the textual traditions of the Biblical books which may be observed at Qumran. In the same fashion as the harmonization of variant readings by conflation was practised by Greek or Aramaic translators and copyists, and by scribes of the MT, it was employed by the Covenanters. Also in this respect the atmosphere of scribal activities at sectarian Qumran resembles that which prevailed in normative circles.

At the present, our interest lies with the particular Qumran text-traditions, and not with the text of a given Biblical book as such. Accordingly all the illustrations to be adduced quite naturally will be cases of textual deviations of a Qumran MS from the MT and/or from one or more of the ancient VSS.

1. Double-readings in Qumran MSS which presumably derived from a *Vorlage.*

a) In Is. 37:9 the reading of Is-a: וישמע וישוב וישלח מלאכים
undoubtedly combines the MT wording in Is.   וישמע   >   וישלח מלאכים
with that of the MT parallel in 2 Ki. 19:9   >   [29]וישב וישלח מלאכים

---

29 Cp. DRMT, 133. The sectarian scribe's awareness of the MT readings in 2 Ki. chs.

Since the doublet is reflected also in G: καὶ ἀκούσας ἀπέστρεψεν[30] καὶ ἀπ-
έστειλεν ἀγγέλους, it may be considered as being derived from a text-type
which was utilized both by the sectarian scribe and the Greek translator.

b) Is. 51:23 Is-a: ושמתיהו ביד מוגיך ומעניך אשר אמרו לנפשכי שוחי ונעבורה
MT: ושמתיה ביד מוגיך > אשר אמרו לנפשך שחי ונעברה
G: καὶ ἐμβαλῶ αὐτὸ εἰς τὰς χεῖρας τῶν ἀδικησάντων σε
καὶ τῶν ταπεινωσάντων σε
T: ואמסרינה ביד דהוו מונן ליך
S: ביד ממככניכי

Here, as in many other cases, it cannot be decided by any objective means
whether the MT, probably supported by T (cp. Is. 49:26), and S (?), has a
defective text, or whether Is-a indeed presents a conflation. If, by rule of
thumb, the shorter MT reading is taken to be original, the redundant ומעניך
of Is-a may be explained as an interpretative gloss of the *hap. leg.* מוגיך or
else simply as a parallel reading. The two roots √יגה and √ענה are employed
in *parallelismus membrorum* in Lam. 3:33. Whatever the case, the doublet
is proved to antecede the text of Is-a by its appearance in the translation of
G.[31] It is possible that the common *Vorlage* was influenced by the similarity
of ideas and expressions in Is. 60:14: ו(א)הלכו אליך שחוח (כול) בני-מְנַאֲצַיִךְ מעניך
והשתחוו על כפות רגליך (כול) מנאציך.

c) 1 Sam. 2:24 4Q Samᵃ: [אל בני לוא טובה הש]מועה אשר אנוכי שו[מע
אל תעשון כן כי לו]א טוב]ות השמועות] אשר אני שומע
MT: אל בני כי לוא טובה השמעה אשר אנכי שומע
G: μὴ τέκνα ὅτι οὐκ ἀγαθὴ ἡ ἀκοὴ ἣν ἐγὼ ἀκούω
μὴ ποιεῖτε οὕτως ὅτι οὐκ ἀγαθαὶ αἱ ἀκοαὶ ἃς
ἔγω ακούω[32]

The Qumran text is very fragmentary. However, the restoration, as proposed
by its editor F.M. Cross, Jr.,[33] may be considered almost certain, in view

18–20 which differ from those found in the parallel account of Is. chs. 36–39, and his
utilization of both text-traditions, significantly illuminate the early textual history of
the Book of Isaiah. This issue will be discussed in a separate publication.
30 In the Origenic tradition the word is shown to be an addition to the Hebrew text by
means of an obelus.
31 This fact has fathered the suggestion (BH) to insert וביד מונן (cp. Is. 49:26) after
ביד מוגיך. G renders מוניך — θλίψαντες. Accordingly we may assume that the, with
regard to MT, redundant καὶ τῶν ταπεινωσάντων σε in Is. 51:23 indeed stands
for Is-a ומעניך. The Greek words in question are absent from Aq., Sym., and Orig.
32 The second line is omitted in the Luc. tradition, and in some late witnesses.
33 F.M. Cross, Jr., "A New Qumran Biblical Fragment Related to the Original Hebrew
Underlying the Septuagint," BASOR 132 (1953) 15–26.

of its virtual identity with the Greek rendition. Again it can be stipulated that
the doublet was found in a textual precursor of 4Q Sam[a] which both the Qumran
copyist and the Greek translator used as their *Vorlage*.

2.   Doublets which arose in the basic textual tradition of Is-a.

   In the examples to follow only one of the components of a presumed doublet
in Is-a is yet extant singly in other textual traditions. Accordingly we assume
that here conflation arose in the Qumran Scroll. In some cases this assumption can be supported, though not proved, by circumstantial evidence. The
decision to classify these double-readings as intra-Is-a conflations can be
maintained only as long as the doublets are not found also in extra-Is-a text-
traditions.

   a)   A clear case of an extended variants-combination may be found in Is.
38:19–20. The two verses actually are mere reiterations with only slight variations in spelling, and one possible sense-variant. At the same time it is obvious
that Is-a adhered to a sentence division which differs from that of the MT,
and probably underlies also G.[34]

19 (a): חי חי הוא יודכה כמוני היום אב לבנים יודיע אל אמתכה ה' להושיעני

20 (b): חי חי < יודך כמוני היום אב לבנים והודיע אלוה אמתך ה' להושיעני

   None of the extant witnesses to the Book of Isaiah exhibits this doublet
which thus is shown to be of particular Qumran vintage. It is obvious that
the doubling could not have resulted from a scribal mistake, as is suggested
by Kutscher,[35] and this for two reasons:

   Accidental dittography of complete syntactical units may be assumed
only when evident manuscriptal reasons can be adduced to back up this
assumption, mainly *homoioteleuton* or *homoioarkton*. Neither of these can
account for the present doublet in spite of the phrase אל אמתך which in MT
recurs at the end of both v.18 and v.19. According to the proposed
syntactical analysis, in Is-a the phrase does not close v.19, but is followed
by ה' להושיעני with which the verse ends.

   Against the assumption of accidental doubling militates the even weightier
fact that the textual peculiarities of the (b) reading which exhibits a defective
spelling (אמתך, יודך), as against the *plene* spelling of the (a) text (אמתכה, יודכה)
were faithfully preserved.

   On ground of the spelling alone we can confidently state that the (b) variant
stems from a text-type which differed from that of the Is-a text-base, where,

---

34   Some further concurrences of sentence-division between Is-a and G against MT, were
   discussed by the present author in "DSIa as a Witness to Ancient Exegesis of the Book
   of Isaiah", *Annual of the Swedish Theological Institute* (= ASTI) 1 (1962) 62–72.

35   *Op. cit.*, 432.

plene spelling prevails. On the other hand, the interlinear and marginal corrections in Is-a often are distinguished from the basic text by their defective
spelling. Compare *e.g.* the superscribed גּוֹאֵלָךְ in 43:3 with the lower-case
אֱלֹהַיְכָה. Thus we may surmise that variant (b) in 38:20 and some of the marginal
or interlinear corrections were derived from the same extra-Is-a text, or text-
types.

Can this *Vorlage* of the (b) reading be further defined? The variant of (b)
והודיע, as against יודיע of (a), is of no help. But the remaining *varia lectio*
אלוה might point the way. It is evident that (b) here reads the divine epithet
'eloah (אלוה) instead of the proposition אֶל in MT.[36] The (b) reading is not
supported by any other witness, whereas the MT variant is possibly, although
only poorly, attested in S's rendition of אל אמתך by the direct object ונחוה
הימנותך, reflected also in the redundant paraphrase יחוון גבורתך of T.[37] Sym.'s
περὶ τῆς ἀληθείας σου seems to mirror אֶל / עַל אמתך. The other VSS have
preserved a medial stage between אֶל of MT and אלוה of (b). T's main reading:
דכל אלין קשוט, and possibly also G's: ἃ ἀναγγελοῦσιν τὴν δικαιοσύνην σου
which is clarified by the marginal καὶ τοῦτο ἀναγγεῖλαι in MS. Q and Syr.
Hex., reflect the consonantal base of MT and (a) vocalised אֶל, which is the
apocopated form of the demonstr. pron. אלה. For the Targum this was already
recognized by Qimḥi *ad loc.* who comments: "It appears that Jonathan translated this אל as if (it were pointed) with *ṣere*, like הארצות האל (Gen. 26:3, 4)."
He then goes on and quotes with disapproval Ibn Ezra who, following T,
interpreted אל אמתך to mean אלה האמונות — "these are the creeds/tenets". It
seems, in fact, that Qimḥi suspected Ibn Ezra of implying that he had based
his comment on an actual variant vocalization אֶל, since he emphatically
professes: "In no book have I seen אל pointed otherwise than with *segol*, and
in the construct-state with אמתך."[38]

The vocalization of אל as the plur. demonstr. pron., as it transpires from
the Aramaic and Greek renditions, and from Ibn Ezra's commentary, is now
supported by the consonantal variant אלה found in the incomplete Isaiah
Scroll (Is-b). However, we cannot be certain whether the scribe of Is-b, like
T and G, took אלה to represent the plur. demonstr. pron., or whether he

36 Here we differ from Kutscher (*op. cit.*, 432) who maintains that אל simply was omitted
     in the (a) reading, as is the case in MS. Ken. 96.
37 I.L. Seeligmann, *The Septuagint Version of Isaiah* (Leiden 1948) 69, considers אל (את)אמתך
     of MT the probable original reading.
38 ונראה כי יונתן תרגם אל זה כמו בציר~י כמו הארצות האל שתרגם אבהן לבן יחוון גבורת ויודון
     למימר דכל אילן קשוט. וכן פירש החכם ראב~ע, וזהו לשון פירושו: אב לבנים יודיע אלה
     האמתות, ואני תמה בזה כי לא ראיתי בשום ספר אלא אל נקוד סגולה וסמוך במקום עם אמתך.
     והמסרת אל אמתך שנים והם אלה השנים אשר הן בפסוק כי לא שאול תודך ובפסוק חי חי.
     Cp. S. Loewinger, VT 4 (1954) 157, n. 3.

considered it a defective spelling of אלוה, siding with (b). But it may be considered as certain that the copyist of Is-a thus interpreted the consonantal group אלה in his (a)-type *Vorlage*, and transferred it to his own MS with the *waw* filled in, as a variant reading.

If the textual development indeed followed the above reconstructed pattern, the doublet in Is-a 38:19–20 would give witness that the scribe of Is-a collated a proto-Massoretic with a (proto-) Is-b text with the resulting conflation of the present (a) and (b) variants.

From here follow some further considerations which will be discussed at a later stage.

b) Is. 14:2   Is-a: ולקחום עמים רבים והביאום אל אדמתם ואל מקומם

                   MT: מקומם < < ולקחום עמים רבים והביאום אל

                   T(P): לאתרהון ויובלונונון

                   T(R): ויובלונונון לארעהון

                   G: εἰς τὸν τόπον αὐτῶν

The conflation of אל מקומם with אל אדמתם smoothed over by the insertion of the conjunct. *waw*, is found in Is-a only. In this case both the conflated readings are preserved singly in extant textual witnesses: אל מקומם is the reading of MT, G, S, and is reflected in one branch of the T tradition (Cod. Reuchlinianus, ed. de Lagarde), whereas another MS of T (Bibl. Nationale MS. 1325) mirrors the parallel reading אל אדמתם.[39] This circumstance decisively weakens Kutscher's implied suggestion that Is-a merely harmonized אל מקומם of v. 2a with על אדמת(ם) of vv. 1 and 2b.[40]

c) Is. 35:9   Is-a: ופריץ חיות בל לוא יעלנה

                   MT: יעלנה < ופריץ חיות בל

The double negation בל לוא, which has no equivalent in MT or the VSS, suggests that the scribe of Is-a conflated two readings.[41] In view of the fact that Is-a faithfully retains the twenty odd occurrences of בל in the Book of Isaiah,[42] and by virtue of the *plene* spelling of לוא[43] which is characteristic for the Is-a base, this latter variant should be deemed primary in the present

39 Not mentioned by Kutscher *op. cit.*, 429.

40 If one accepts Gottstein's supposition, for which no manuscriptal evidence can be adduced, that T originally had the compound reading לארעהון ולאתרהון (*Biblica* 35 [1954] 35), the doublet in Is-a would have to be classified as derivative from a *Vorlage*.

41 See also Kutscher, *op. cit.*, 430. In Is. 33:21 the two words are employed synonymously in *parallelismus membrorum*.

42 Among these are found three cases of triple בל in one verse (33:20; 40:24; 44:9), and three of double בל (26:10, 14; 33:23).

43 One MS Ken. — לא.

setting. Thus בל must be considered a synonymous reading which was collated into the MS from a (proto-) Massoretic-type text, such as *e.g.* Is-b.

d) Is. 62:7   Is-a: עד יכין ועד יכונן ועד ישים את ירושלים תהלה בארץ
             Is-b: ע[   ]ו   ]ם את[
             MT: עד יכונן ועד ישים את ירושלים תהלה בארץ
             T: עד דיתכין ועד דישוי
             S: עדמא דנתקנכי ועדמא דנעבדכי
             G: ἐὰν διορθώσῃ καὶ ποιήσῃ

The synopsis of all the extant witnesses to this verse reveals a typical case of textual expansion if the Is-b reading is considered original, or of contraction in Is-b if MT or one of the VSS is chosen as departure point for the textual comparison. Either way, Is-a exhibits a conflated reading.

The shortest reading, with only one verb in the sentence, is found in Is-b. Its preserved text is very fragmentary indeed, but may be reconstructed as follows: [45] [ואל תת[נו דמי לכם[44] ע[ד יש]ים את [ירושלים ת]הלה בארץ. The reading לכם, against לו in MT and Is-a (=T: מן קדמוהי) which is supported by G's ὑμῖν, proves that Is-b presents here a deviant text tradition, to which also the absence of תמיד in the preceding verse (found in all other VSS) gives evidence. Viewed against this background, the omission in Is-b of MT's and Is-a's יכונן[46] (= G: διορθώσῃ, T: דיתכין) cannot be considered a *lapsus calami* resulting from *homoioarkton*.

MT and all the VSS have two verbs, the first of which is obviously doubled in Is-a: עד יכין ועד יכונן. Since this duplication has no parallel in any other witness, it may be ascribed, with much probability, to the scribe of Is-a. What it boils down to is a combination of two forms of the causative of the *hif'il* formation יכין and the *polel* formation יכונן. Both formations are found in the Book of Is., in MT as well as in Is-a: the *hif'il* in 9:6; 14:21; 40:20 (MT: להכין; Is-a: להוכין); the *polel* in 45:18; 51:13; 54:14 (MT: תכונני; Is-a: תתכונני). Stylistically one cannot be preferred over the other, and they must be considered

---

44 The reading of Is-b in 62:6–7: אל דמי לכם [ואל תת[נו דמי לכם, lets one suspect that in MT and Is-a this obvious doublet was camouflaged by variation to read: אל דמי לו ואל תתנו דמי לכם. G has preserved only the first component of the suspected doublet: οὐκ ἔστι γὰρ ὑμῖν ὅμοις. The main tradition of T exhibits the first variant in an apocopated form (K: להון; b, g,: לא פסיק לכון).

45 Cp. Zeph. 3:19: ושמתים לתהלה ולשם בכל הארץ. Nowhere in the Bible does √כון carry a double object. May we assume two possible basic readings for Is. 62:7, namely עד ישים את ירושלים תהלה בארץ and עד יכונן את ירושלים?

46 In the *lacuna* between the preserved ע of עד and the final ם of the following word, there is room for four to five letters at most.

synonymous. One is inclined to postulate that the scribe of Is-a culled them from two MSS that were at his disposal, and conflated them in his copy.[47]

e) Is. 40:19 Is-a: הפסל ויעשה מסך חרש

MT: נסך חרש < הפסל

T: הא צלמא נגרא עביד

G: μὴ εἰκόνα ἐποίησεν τέκτων

Aq.: μὴ γλύπτον ἐχώνευσεν

The redundant ויעשה of Is-a which is reflected in T's עביד, S's דעבד, and G's ἐποίησεν probably is a variant of MT: נסך (miswritten in Is-a as מסך[48]), which was correctly rendered ἐχώνευσεν by Aq. More confident than Kutscher, and in spite of the garbled syntax of Is-a, we tend to propose that its scribe conflated a MT-type and an extra-Massoretic reading in his copy.

f) Is. 30:6   Is-a: משא בהמות נגב בארץ צרה וציה וצוקה

MT: וצוקה < משא בהמות נגב בארץ צרה

All the VSS concur here with MT in recording only two appositions to בארץ as against three in Is-a. The word-pair צרה וצוקה is found again, though divided, in Is. 8:22, and once more, with a slight variation, in Zeph. 1:15: יום צרה ומצוקה. In other formations the roots $\sqrt{צרר}$ and $\sqrt{צוק}$ appear as pairs also in Deut. 28:53, 55, 57; Jer. 19:9; Ps. 119:143. Never is the redundant ציה of Is-a combined with either. This makes the Is-a reading a *lectio difficilior* which can hardly be explained by Kutscher's contention that ציה — "parched land" spuriously arose in the text under the influence of אין מים (MT: מהם) in the continuation of the verse.[49] Accordingly we are led to assume that ציה is a variant reading for either צרה or צו(ו)קה (possibly due to graphic confusion) which was incorporated by the scribe into his text.

g) Is. 40:18 Is-a: ואל מיא תדמיוני אל ומה דמות תערוכו לי

MT: ואל מי   תדמיון אל ומה דמות תערכו לו

MT here has the support of all the VSS. The variant reading of Is-a, which in fact constitutes a doublet, accordingly must be considered an inner-Is-a

---

47 A somewhat similar situation obtains in MT to Is. 35:5. Cp. DRMT, 177.

48 For an interesting example of the also otherwise abundantly documented interchange of נ–מ see B. Kedar–Kopfstein's note on Is. 14:31 in *Textus* 2 (1962) 143–145. Kutscher's supposition (*op. cit.*, 195) that Is-a in 40:19 possibly substituted the Rabbinic מסך for Biblical נסך is ingenious but hardly warranted in view of the retention of נסך in 44:10. There T renders it: אתיך, S: נסיכא, Theod.: χωνευσεν, whereas G omits the word.

49 Kutscher (*op. cit.*, 429) compares Ps. 63:2. As a contrasting image also Is. 41:18 = Ps. 107:35 can be adduced.

development. It appears that the scribe combined two wordings of an idea which is found twice in ch. 40, in v. 18 and again in v. 25, and which are kept distinct in MT and the VSS. The basic difference between them is in that one refers to God, the direct object, by the noun אל and the 3rd. pers. pron. לו; while in the other He, being the speaker, refers to himself by the 1st pers. pron. לי and the pronominal suffix נִי:[50]

v. 18: לו   תדמיון אל

אל מי(א)   ומה דמות תער(ו)כו

v. 25: לי   תדמיוני

h) A fairly obvious case of conflation of two interrogative particles may be found in

Is. 36:19 Is-a: וכיא ההצילו

MT: וכי   הצילו

The VSS support MT in that only one interrogative word is mirrored in them, but it is not possible to decide which of the two: כי or הַ was in their respective *Vorlage*.

The non-MT variant (ה(הצילו constitutes the retention of a form which had been already employed in the preceding verse (36:18, MT = Is-a), whereas כי is a variational form of interrogation.

A class by themselves are the doublets which result from a combination of parallel readings that present the same word-stock, but differ in the word order.[51].

i) Is. 22:14 Is-a: אם יכפר לכם העוון הזה לכמה

MT: אם יכפר > העון הזה לכם

T: אם ישתביק   חובא הדין לכון

S: לא תסבון לכון חטיתא

G: ὅτι οὐκ ἀφεθήσεται ὑμῖν αὕτη ἡ ἁμαρτία

One of the readings conflated in Is-a had the pers. pron. לכם precede the subject העון. This order — אם יכפר לכם העון הזה — which also is reflected in G and S, is well represented in a Yemenite textual tradition, as evidenced by the quotation of the verse in one Yem. MS of the Bab. Tal. Taʿanit 11a, and in some MSS of the (Yem.) Midrash ha-Gadol to Gen. 37:29 (MSS. ש,ד; ed. M. Margulies 637, 18), and to Ex. 32:6 (MSS. ה,כ,ס,; ed. M. Margulies

50 Kutscher (*op. cit.*, 56, 250, 447) assumes a mere contamination of v. 18 by v. 25, but this seems unlikely.

51 Examples of inverted word-order in Is-a in comparison with MT, were assembled by Kutscher, *op. cit.*, 450–451.

681, 9). In the other reading the pers. pron. followed upon the noun. This is the arrangement of MT, supported by T, and one MS of G.[52]

The difference in spelling לכם against לכמה may point to the derivation of the two readings from different text-types.[53]

j) Is. 57:18   Is-a: ואשלם לוא תנחומים לוא ולאבליו
MT: ואשלם < נחמים לו ולאבליו
T: ואשלים < תנחומין להון
S: ופרעה < בויאא לה
G: καὶ ἔδωκα αὐτῷ παράκλησιν ἀληθινήν

The reading of MT (=T, S), in which the dat. pron. לו follows upon the direct object, was conflated in Is-a with the reading presented by G in which it precedes it. The force of the G evidence is somewhat weakened by the omission in its translation of the second dat. object ולאבליו. This may have caused the transfer of the dat. pron αὐτῷ. However the same word-order is maintained also in MSS of G, in Aq., Sym., Theod. and Orig., where the missing clause is restored.

k) Is. 64:1   Is-a: תבעה אש לצריכה להודיע שמכה לצריכה
MT: תבעה אש < להודיע שמך לצריך
G: καὶ κατακαύσει πῦρ τοὺς ὑπεναντίους καὶ φανερὸν ἔσται τὸ ὄνομα κυρίου ἐν τοῖς ὑπεναντίοις
T: להודעא שמך לסנאי עמך

In view of the exegetical difficulties inherent in this verse it cannot be decided for definite whether the first לצריכ(ה) simply was omitted in MT (followed by T, Sym., Theod.,) or whether it accrued in Is-a (followed by G). In the first case, לצריכ(ה) would be the dat. object of both the verbs תבעה and להודיע. In the second a conflation of the following two readings must be assumed:

לצריכה להודיע שמכה
להודיע שמכה לצריכה

Also the most closely amalgamated type of conflation found in MT, the crossing of two variants in one word which results in hybrid readings, is not absent from Is-a.

l) Is. 1:31   Is-a: והיה החסנכם לנעורת ופעלכם לניצוץ
MT: והיה החסן   לנערת ופעלו לניצוץ

Here the Is-a reading results from the combination of a noun defined by

52   Cp. J. Ziegler (ed.), *Isaias* (Göttingen 1939) *ad loc.*
53   Cp. Is. 38:20, above, p. 108–109.

the def. art. החסן (MT) with its parallel definition by the 2nd pers. plur. poss. suffix חסנכם[54] which is reflected in the 3rd pers. plur. poss. suffix found in the main VSS — G: ἡ ἰσχὺς αὐτῶν

> T: תקפהון
>
> S: עושינהון

m) The enigmatic אייאמים of Is-a as against איים of MT in Is. 34:14 can possibly be explained as a hybrid reading.[55] We propose tentatively that the scribe combined the otherwise attested איים, some sort of desert – being (Is. 13:22, Is-a: אים; Jer. 50:39), with the *hap. leg.* ימים (Gen. 36:24) which carries a similar connotation. The VSS are of no help here, since the Heb. synonyms would be similarly translated.

n) An uncompleted case of hybrid reading of the same type may be found in Is. 30:23 where the present text of Is-a אשר תזרע את האדמה[ה] has been super-imposed upon the variant (אדמת)ך. The *hē* at the end of the word אדמה clearly is a correction of an underlying *taw*. The initially intended definition by the 2nd pers. sing. poss. suffix אדמתך (= G: τῆς γῆς σου) was superseded by the definition with the aid of the def. art. האדמה (= MT; T: ית ארעא).

Conflation possibly may explain the following reading of Is-a.

o) Is. 61:6   Is-a: חיל גואים תואכלו ובכבודם תתיאמרו[56]

MT: חיל גוים תאכלו ובכבודם תתימרו

The phrase ובכבודם תתימרו is a *crux interpretum*. No satisfactory deriva-tion for תתי(א)מרו has been proposed.[57] T: תתפנקון, S: תשתבחון and G: θαυασ-θήσεσθε[58] are of no help. But the Is-a reading in conjunction with Aq.'s rendition may point the way.

We assume for Is-a a combination of the MT spelling תתימרו (possibly

---

54   Cp. האהלי (Josh. 7:21), החציו (*ib.* 8:33), ההרותיה (2 Ki. 15:16), and see DRMT, 178–179. After considering the possibility of conflation, Kutscher seems to prefer the doubtful explanation that the scribe of Is-a (inadvertently?) transferred from one determination to the other in the process of writing (*op. cit.*, 445).

55   The possibility was suggested by Kutscher, *op. cit.*, 238 (צורת כלאים) who tentatively explains the form as a combination of איי+אמ+ים (*ib.*, 165). Mr. A. Hurvitz has drawn my attention to a comparable case of proper nouns conflation in the Genesis Apocryphon XXI, 29, ed. N. Avigad and Y. Yadin [Jerusalem 1956]). Here a seeming combination of זוזים (Gen. 14:5) with זמזומים (Deut. 2:20) resulted in ולזוזמיא.

56   At first sight this could be explained as a *plene* spelling of תתימרו with the *alef* serving as *mater lect.* for *patah*. Cp. Is. 30:31 MT: יכה, Is-a: יאכה.

57   Cp. E. Nötscher, VT 1 (1951) 300: מור – אמר – ימר

58   J. Ziegler (*op. cit.*, 168) following Fischer and Wutz, supposes that influence of Aram. דמר, and of the in content similar passage Is. 60:5 may explain the use of θαυμάζειν in the instance under review.

reflected in Sym.'s στρηνιάσατε) with a spelling תתאמרו which is mirrored in the renderings of Theod. and Aq.

Theod.'s ὑψωθήσεσθε clearly is derived from אמר in the meaning "high", for which cp. Is. 17:6,9 אמיר (בראש) = "branch", "tree-top" (?).[59] In a different connotation אמר appears to be reflected in Aq.'s rendition: πορφυρωθήσεσθε, (faultily quoted by Hier., in his commentary as: πόρφυρα ἐνδύσεσθε). We propose that the translator here had in mind the Rabbinic "hem of a garment", which sometimes was made of purple, cp. Mishnah Nega'im 11, 10: חלוק שנראה בו נגע מציל את האמריות שבו, אפילו הן ארגמן. In translating καὶ ἐν δόξῃ αὐτῶν πορφυρωθήσεσθε, Aq. probably took ובכבודם תתאמרו to mean: "Ye will put on their splendour (like) purple", thus exhibiting his familiarity with Rabbinic language. We may assume that this same concept underlies the conflated reading תתיאמרו of Is-a.[60]

p) Is. 57:17 Is-a: ואהסתר ואקצופה
    MT: הסתר ואקצף

    G: καὶ ἀπέστρεψα τὸ προσωπόν μου ἀπ' αὐτοῦ καὶ ἐλυπήθη

T: מליקית שכינתי מנהון and S: ואתפנית ורגזת do not bear on the issue.

Kutscher explains the redundant hē of Is-a אהסתר as due to Aram. influence.[61] Thus both verbs would be (inverted?) imperfects.[62] However, a case can be made for the supposition that Is-a contains a fully developed doublet which may be observed *in statu nascendi* in MT. The underlying alternative variants then would be ואסתר ואקצו(ו)פ(ה) — הסתר וקצו(ו)ף.[63]

The assumption that in one variant וקצף was read as an absolute inf. is borne out by the vocalization of the *waw* with *shewā* in MT, and by G's rendering it as a 3rd. pers. sing. which points to a consonantal stock קצף without the prefixed *aleph* of the 1st pers. sing. imperf.

q) Is. 11:9 Is-a: כי תמלאה הארץ דעה
    MT: כי מלאה הארץ דעה

Here, as in similar cases in the MT,[64] we postulate that in Is-a the 3rd pers. sing. fem. perf. מלאה (= MT) was conflated with the parallel imperf. form תמלא which possibly is reflected in T's: ארי תתמלי, and S's: דתתמלא.

---

59 Theod.'s translation is not preserved here. G. is of no help.
60 Cp. Is. 3:22 MT: המחלצות והמעטפות, G: τὰ χεριπόρφυρα κὰι τὰ μεσοπόφυρα.
61 *Op. cit.*, 149. G.R. Driver construes the interpolated hē as an attempt on part of the scribe to correct אסתר to הסתר (JTS N.S. 2 [1951] 18).
62 Kutscher, *op. cit.*, 266.
63 Cp. A. Rubinstein, VT 4 (1954) 200–201.
64 Cp. Is. 63:3 MT: אגאלתי, Is-a: גאלתי, below p. 124.

3. (A) Is-a readings and corrections which constitute the basis of double-readings found in MT.

a) On pl. iii, 20–25 (Is. 3:15–18) Is-a three times records the tetragrammaton accompanied by what in the MT is considered its *Qerê perpetuum* — אדוני. In v. 18 the Tetragrammaton is written in the line, with אדוני inserted on top of it. In v. 17 the situation is reversed. In both cases the superscribed reading is presented as a correction by the "pointing" of the lower-case reading. Here the corrector quite clearly indicated the superiority of, or his preference for the superlinear variant. Obviously this is a matter of choice which is not rooted in the intrinsic primacy of one or the other reading since the correction alternately goes both ways, but rather derives from the idiograph of the *Vorlage* used by the corrector, which was not identical with the MT. MT reads in both verses אדני. In both these instances the substitution character of the superscription is made manifest by the pointing of the variant to be deleted. This is sufficient safeguard against the mistaken combination of the two by a later copyist. We encounter a different situation in the remaining instance, the first in the row of three, which has a direct bearing on the issue on hand, the emergence of double-readings. In v. 15 the superlinear אדוני is added without the deletion of the lower-case Tetragrammaton (cp. also 28:16; 30:15; 65:13). It is impossible to decide whether the omission of the deletion-points is due just to a *lapsus calami* on part of the corrector, *p.m.* or *s.m.*, or whether the express purpose of the correction was the restoration of what the corrector considered to be an accidentally missing אדוני. Thus the superscribed word would constitute not a variant of the one in the line, but rather an addition to it. The latter assumption derives support, though not proof, from the MT which in fact reads the double-name אדוני יהוה. The doublet, and such it appears to be, accordingly did not arise in Is-a, but rather stems from a proto-Massoretic text-type which possibly preceded Is-a, but certainly is external to its textual tradition. Thus Is-a *p.m.* represents the earliest text-form of this specific case, Is-a *s.m.* the transitional stage, and MT the ultimate doublet-phase, also present in Aq.: κυριος κυριος (πιπι πιπι).

b) Is. 24:4 MT: אמללו מרום עם הארץ
           Is-a: אמלל מרום עם הארץ

As Kutscher correctly observed, the reading of the verb in the sing. (אמלל) proves that the lack of עם in the text-base of Is-a is not just a case of faulty omission, subsequently corrected. The shorter text of Is-a underlies also the renditions of G (οἱ ὑψηλοί τῆς γῆς) and S (רומה דארעא) which have no equivalent for עם. This is moreover missing also in one MS Ken. T follows MT: תקוף עמא דארעא. Accordingly the reading עם (הארץ) may be conceived of as a parallel of מרום(הארץ) which in Is-a was collated between the lines from a not anymore extant text-type. At a subsequent copying for which a MS of the Is-a type served as *Vorlage*, the superscribed variant was misconstrued as a corrected omission, and was reinstated in the text proper. This resulted in a doublet, as exhibited by the present MT.

In passing we may observe that a similar conflation of עם (הארץ) with דלת (הארץ), the very opposite of מרום (הארץ), occurred in the MT of 2 Ki. 24:14: לא נשאר זולת דלת עם הארץ. Here again the word עם is not translated in G: οἱ πτωχοὶ τῆς γῆς. It appears that in this case the two basic readings may still be found singly in parallel passages:

2 Ki. 25:12: ומדלות הארץ   ; ומדלת הארץ :cp. Jer. 52:16
Jer. 39:10: ומן העם הדלים   ; ומדלת העם :cp. Jer. 52:15 [65]

c) Is. 21:17 MT: ושאר מספר קשת גבורי בני־קדר ימעטו
Is-a: גבורי בני קדר

The shorter basic reading of Is-a, without the (redundant?) בני, underlies the main Targumic tradition: גיברי ערבאי, and Theod.: ...τῶν ἰσχυρῶν κηδάρ. It also is found in one MS Ken.[66] The parallel reading בני קדר, which was interpolated between the lines in Is-a, is found singly in G: ...υἱῶν κηδάρ. MT, followed by G: τῶν ἰσχυρῶν υἱῶν κηδάρ, S: גברא דבני קדר and some witnesses of T (L[RN]): גברי דבני ערבא, presents the double reading which resulted from the integration of the superscribed variant into the text proper.

d) Is. 56:12 MT: והיה כזה יום מחר יתר גדול מאד
Is-a: ויהי כזה היום ומחר יתר גדול מואד

The shorter basic reading here has the support of T: ותהי שירותנא דמחר טבא מדיומא דין סגיאה לחדא, and possibly of S: ונותר לן סוגאא דטב. One MS and some printed editions of T (bogf) though mirror MT: רבא סגיאה לחדא. G does not render the verse at all. Aq., Theod. and Sym. restored the missing passage in complete agreement with MT. The same pertains to Orig.[67]

In view of T's (and S's) concurrence with the base of Is-a, we are inclined to assume that the superscribed גדול constitutes a variant notation which at a subsequent stage of copying was embodied in the main text, thus creating the doublet found in MT.

---

65   These passages will be discussed separately.
66   Cp. Kutscher, *op. cit.*, 439 who, though, fails to mention the evidence of T and Theod. which supports the basic Is-a text.
67   Cp. Kutscher, *op. cit.*, 442 at a future occasion.

e)   Is. 61:1 MT: יען משח ה׳ אתי לבשר ענוים שלחני לחבש לנשברי־לב לקרא
לשבוים דרור ולאסורים פקח־קוח

Is-a: יען משח ה׳ אותי לבשר ענים ^{שלחני} ולחבוש לנשברי לב לקרוא
לשבויים דרור ולאסורים פקח קוח

MT is supported by all VSS. The shorter Is-a text may well have resulted
from the omission of שלחני which subsequently was restored as a superscription. However the *waw* prefixed before לחבוש makes it quite clear that שלחני
cannot have been an integral component of the basic Is-a reading, unless it
is conjoined with לבשר ענוים (שלחני), against the Massoretic sentence division.
It therefore may be surmised that the superscribed שלחני represents a variant
reading שלחני לנשברי לב, not otherwise attested, which the writer or corrector
of Is-a collated into his copy. If that is the case, MT would exhibit a faulty
conflation of the two variants. While לחבוש לנשברי לב appears to be the
smoother expression (cp. Ez. 34:4, 16), the reading שלחני לנשברי לב can be
maintained, by its comparison with 2 Sam. 10:3 – כי שלח לך מנחמים; Ps.
111:9 – פדות שלח לעמו. In the first reading the whole series of infinitive
constructs לבשר, לקרא, לחבש, etc. would be dependent on the finite verb
משח אתי. In the second, only לבשר would be dependent on משח, while the finite
שלחני would open a new series of infinitive constructs.

3. (B)   One more category of double-readings in the MT, on which the
Qumran Scrolls throw light, remains to be mentioned. These are readings in
which a Qumran MS will exhibit only one component in its text-base, without
any superlinear or marginal variant-notation, as against a fully fledged doublet
in the MT. Some such instances have been discussed by the present author
in a previous publication in which the MT served as the point of departure.[68]
Further suggestions are made in what follows.

It goes without saying that in many cases of a supposed doublet in the MT,
the single reading in the Is-a which serves as the controlling standard can be
interpreted as a defective reading resulting from faulty omission. The situation is comparable to the choice between a dittography in one text or a haplography in another, where either decision would result in a satisfactory reading.
A good example of such a situation may be seen in

Is. 3:22 MT: המחלצות והמעטפות והמטפחות והחריטים
Is-a: והמחלצות והמעטפות   >   והחריטים

Here the Greek and the Targumic evidence appears to support MT, and a
haplography in Is-a is as good an assumption as a variant conflation in MT.

---

68   DRMT, 162 (Is. 14:12), 163 (12:2), 168 (35:8), 169 (37:18), 177 (25:5).

It is possible, though, to present the in Rabbinic Hebrew widely used מטפחת (found only once in the OT, Ruth 3:15), as an interpretative reading of the *hap. leg.* (ת)מעטפה which is extremely rare also in Rabbinic language (Tos. Kelim B. B. 5, 4; ed. Zuckermandel, 595).

The scales can be tipped in favour of the doublet assumption whenever it is supported by one of the following:

Concurring evidence of an independent ancient Version.

Where no such support is forthcoming:

One component of the double-reading can be shown to be redundant on grounds of metrical, syntactical or sense considerations, or else can be explained as a harmonizing intrusion from a parallel passage.

We shall open this series with the analysis of a MT reading which already at some previous occasion was presented as arising from conflation by its comparison with a parallel MT reading, and with its rendition in G, and whose doublet-nature now can further be substantiated with the aid of Qumran evidence.

a) 2 Sam. 5:11 MT: וחרשי עץ וחרשי אבן קיר[69]

      4Q Samᵃ: וחרשי > קיר

We postulate that the redundant אבן in MT represents the reading וחרשי אבן which is yet extant in Gᴮ: καὶ τέκτονας λίθων, and for which cp. also 1 Chr. 22:15 – וחרשי אבן ועץ (G: οἰκοδόμοι λίθων καὶ τέκτονες ξύλων).

The synonymous Qumran variant וחרשי קיר turns up in MT and G of the parallel passage, 1 Chr. 14:1,[70] and in the Lucianic tradition (oc₂e₂): καὶ τέκτονας τοίχου. The MT doublet underlies two Greek minuscules: καὶ τέκτονας τοίχου λίθων. T paraphrases: וארדיכלין דאומנין בבנין כותליא.[71] It is feasible that בבנין arose out of the Heb. אבן, which in MS. y possibly turns up as ואבנין after the rendition of וחרשי עץ: ונגרי דאומנין למקץ אעין ואבנין.

b) Is. 26:6   MT: תרמסנה רגל רגלי עני   פעמי דלים

      Is-a: תרמסנה > רגלי ענײם פעמי דלים

The redundant רגל (sing.) of MT, which is the reading of S: רגלא, has no equivalent in the Greek tradition, and is also absent from one MS Ken. It is, probably, a variant of רגלי (plur.) which was inserted into the text base (= T).

---

69 This passage will be published by F.M. Cross, Jr., in his forthcoming paper in HThR.

70 In inverted order: וחרשי קיר וחרשי עצים.

71 Cp. S: ואומנא דראפא דאסתא.

c) A probable case of conflation, possibly involving a misreading,[72] is the following:

Is 59:13 MT: דבר עשק וסרה הרו והגו מלב דברי־שקר

Is-a: ודברו עושק וסרה והגוא מלב דברי שקר <

The VSS support the consonantal base of MT as it stands and follow also the Massoretic sentence division, which has a break after וסרה, taking הרו together with הגו as the regnant verbs of דברי שקר. All the Greek sources, and S (בטנן) derive הרו from √הרה "to conceive, to become pregnant". G and Sym. render it by κύειν, Theod. and Aq. by (ἐν γάστρι) λαμβάνειν. Thus understood הרו makes a poor parallel for the remaining verbs דבר and הגה, and at the same time clearly shows the translators' dependence on an earlier verse in the same chapter, 59:4. There הרה parallels ילד, and is again rendered by κύειν in G,[73] these being the only two instances in which G employ this verb in the OT.[74] It is feasible that הרו intruded into MT 59:13 from v. 4, possibly due to the correspondence of ideas expressed in those two verses, and the further similarity of the phrases employed in them – v. 4: דבר שוא; v. 13: דבר עשק. If that is the case, the combination הרו והגו would not constitute a true doublet.

However, with some grammatical license, הרו can be, and probably should be derived from √ירה – "to teach, to instruct", as was done, and correctly so, by some mediaeval commentators, e.g. Qimḥi (in his father's name), and Rashi (as a second proposition to its derivation from √ירה "to shoot, to throw", for which he quotes Ex. 15:4). הרו...דברי שקר[75] thus would make an excellent alternative reading of הגו...דברי שקר,[76] and could well be taken as a variant notation which was conflated with the basic reading. The restored two variants, individually make for a better metric structure than the present doublet:

דבר ע(ו)שק וסרה (ו)הרו מלב דברי שקר (ו)הגו

d) Is. 57:18 MT: נחומים לו ולאבליו < ואנחהו ואשלם

Is-a: ואשלם לוא תנחומים לוא ולאבליו <

The renditions of G: καὶ παρεκάλεσα[77] αὐτὸν, T: וארחים עליהון and S: וביאתה[77] convincingly show that MT ואנחהו[78] probably should be emended

---

72 If הרו is seen simply as a miswritten dittography of הגו; cp. BH.
73 Sym.: ἐν γάστρι ἐλαβον.
74 The noun κύησις is used in Ruth 4:13.
75 Cp. Is. 9:14; Hab. 2:18 – מורה שקר(ו).
76 Cp. Is. 33:18 – לבך יהגה אימה; Prov. 24:2, et al.
77 The ensuing noun נחומים is translated by the same root, and so is לנחם in 61:2.
78 Retained, though, by Aq.: και καθοδηγησα.

to read ואנחמהו (cp. BH). In that case, ואנחמהו could well be a parallel variant of ואשלם נחמים לו[79] which in this combination is not found again in the OT,[80] whereas the *pi'el* of נחם is recurrently employed in the Book of Isaiah and elsewhere to describe God's reconciliatory intentions for Israel (49:13; 51:3, 12; 52:9; 61:2; 66:13; further 40:1; 54:1; 12:1). Thus the redundant ואנחמ(ה)הו would have to be considered a variant-gloss which intruded into the text-base of MT (but is missing from two MSS Ken.), and resulted in a cumbersome lengthening of the second half-verse.

e) Is. 24:22 MT: ואספו אספה אסיר על בור וסגרו על מסגר

Is-a: אספו אספה > על בור וסגרו על מסגר

On ground of the lopsided parallelism and the unwieldy structure of the MT, and in view of the fact that G renders only ואספו... על בור of the first half-verse,[81] Seeligmann raised doubts as to the original authenticity of the words אספה אסיר.[82] He then hesitatingly, although to my mind correctly, suggested to take אסיר as a corrupted variant gloss of ואספו, namely ואסרו. This assumption derives further support from the Origenic and Lucianic traditions which do render אספה but again omit אסיר: καὶ συνάξουσι συναγώγην αὐτῆς[83] εἰς δεσμωτήριον καὶ ἀποκλείσουσιν εἰς ὀχύρωμα. The Hebrew original of this reading which is also reflected in T: ויכנשונונון מכנש לבית אסירי ויגונונון לבית עגנא (where לבית אסירי appears to equal בור), has now been recovered in Is-a, whose text, at the same time, witnesses to the originality of אספה.

We therefore can endorse, with only a slight adjustment, Seeligmann's conclusion that the variant notation (אסרו) < אסיר,[84] "must have crept into the Hebrew text during the centuries that elapsed between the composition of the Septuagint and that of the later (Greek) versions", since Sym.'s rendition, as quoted by Eus., already reflects the word in question: καὶ ἀθροισθήσονται ἀθροισμὸν δεσμίου εἰς λάκκον καὶ συγκλεισθήσονται εἰς συγκλεισμόν.

---

79 G translate ואשלם – ἔδωκα and לשים in 61:3 – δοθῆναι. Did they read the same verb in both verses? An interchange between שלם and שים can be observed also in 1 Sam. 2:20 MT: ישם ה' לך , 4 Q Samᵃ: ישלם (= G: ἀποτίσαι). See: F.M. Cross, Jr., BASOR 132 (1953) 22.

80 The noun נחומים is found twice more in the OT, Hos. 11:8 and Zech. 1:13. In Is. 66:11 תנחמים is employed, for which cp. Jer. 16:7, and Job 15:11; 21:2 (תנחמות). None of those is construed with שלם.

81 καὶ συνάξουσι καὶ ἀποκλείσουσιν εἰς ὀχύρωμα κὰι εἰς δεσμωτήριον, with על בור transferred to the end of the verse. The crucial phrase εἰς δεσμωτήριον is absent from the Orig. and Luc. tradition.

82 *Op. cit.*, 63.

83 The additional phrase obviously stems from Theod., as maintained by Seeligmann, *ib*.

84 Possibly representing אספו אספה אסרו אסור(ה) or some reading like it.

In the following two instances the doublets assumedly found in the MT, occur in the form of hybrid readings:

f) Is. 63:3   MT: וכל מלבושי אגאלתי
Is-a: וכול מלבושי גאלתי

The phrase is missing in G, and is rendered paraphrastically in T: וכל חכימיהון אסלעים. Sym. and the Luc. revision restore: καὶ πάντα τὰ ἐνδύματά μου ἐμόλυνα. The queer form אגאלתי has been explained as a possible Aramaism, or simply as a miswritten גאלתי (BH),[85] which latter we find now in Is-a.

We suggest to explain אגאלתי as a combination of the not extant אגאל with the alternative variant גאלתי (= Is-a, and S: פלפלת). The former would take up the 1st pers. imperf. which is mirrored in ואדרכם ....וארמסם of MT (cp. also ...ויז). These words are omitted from Is-a whose text here is much shorter. The latter (גאלתי) would follow the 1st pers. perf., as found in דרכתי at the opening of the verse.

An identical conflation of a perf. with an imperf. form, is found in the Scroll reading to Is. 11:9: תמלאה, MT: מלאה.[86]

g) Is. 23:11   MT: ה׳ צוה אל כנען לשמד   מעזניה
Is-a: ה׳ צוה אל כנען להשמיד מעוזיה
G: ἀπολέσαι αὐτῆς τὴν ἰσχύν
T: לשיצאה תוקפהא

Kutscher offers the learned but unconvincing explanation of the unusual MT reading as possibly being an attempt on behalf of the prophet to employ a characteristically Phoenician plur. ending נם instead of the usual ם ending. He admits though that the נם ending never is found in inscriptions with an appended 3rd pers. plur. fem. poss. pron.[87]

We suggest that מעזניה in MT arose from a conflation of מעוזיה[88] of Is-a, for which cp. in this context (Is. 17:9; 23:4, 13), with a parallel reading מעוניה,[89] which is not extant for the passage under review. The synonymity of מעוז and מעון as an epithet of God can be proved

1. from their serving alternately in combination with a third synonym — מחסה,
Joel 4:16: וה׳ מחסה לעמו ומעוז לבני ישראל
Ps. 91:9: כי אתה ה׳ מחסי עליון שמת מעונך

85 Cp. Kutscher, op. cit., 264.
86 Cp. above, p. 117.
87 Op. cit., 493.
88 The plur. of מעוז is found only in Dan. 11:19, 38, 39.
89 The plur. מעונים from מעון is not extant in the Bible. מעונות occurs in Jer. 21:13; Na. 2:13; Job 37:8; 38:40; Cant. 4:8.

2. from their being employed alternately in one and the same context,

   Jer. 16:19: ‏ה׳ עזי ומעזי ומנוסי‏[90]

   Ps. 90:1: ‏אדני מעון אתה היית לנו‏[91]

3. from their being used alternately in a recurring passage,

   Ps. 31:3: ‏היה לי לצור מעוז‏

   71:3: ‏היה לי לצור מעון‏

   In both passages a noun derived from $\sqrt{\text{עזז}}$ is found in the continuation, ‏ואתה מחסי עז‏ — 71:7, ‏כי אתה מעוזי‏ – 31:5.

V

The coexistence at Qumran of varying text-formations of the Bible, and the
absence of any noticeable attempt at establishing one universally recognized
recension of binding force, must have confronted the Qumran scribes with
the problem of what attitude to take towards these conflicting not yet assessed
and rated textual traditions. The individual scribe could solve this problem
by adhering faithfully to the MS which he had chosen, or had been assigned,
as the *Vorlage* for his own copy. In a reasonable number of instances, such
as were discussed above, he could perpetuate parallel readings which he found
in other MSS that were at his disposal, by noting them in the margins or
between the lines of his own copy or, sometimes, by integrating them in his
text-base. Now, these devices, which were a common stock-in-trade of the
ancient Bible scribes regardless of their socio-religious affiliations, are mere
practical expediences that may work fairly well, up to a certain point, for the
individual copyist, but cannot satisfactorily solve the problem of the community's disposition towards divergent, but equally well documented, readings.
In Bible MSS which are intended for public use, critical annotations must be
kept to a practical minimum. In fact even these relatively few marginal entries
will tend to disappear at subsequent copyings by sheer routine omission, unless
they are absorbed into the text proper. Even where authoritative guidance is
absent we may find a spontaneous tendency towards the simplification and
the stabilisation of the textual traditions of the Holy Writ and other hallowed
books. This process cannot be expected to culminate in complete unification,[92]
but it will effectively circumscribe the scope, and reduce the number of textual

---

90 Cp. further Is. 25:4; Na. 1:7; Ps. 27:1; 28:8; 37:39, *et al.*

91 Some MSS of MT read here ‏מעוז‏. Also a graphical confusion of ‏נ-ו‏ may have caused
    the interchange. Cp. Josh. 15:29 where the MT reads ‏ובזיותיה‏ for the patently correct
    ‏ובנותיה‏ (=G *ad loc.* and MT Neh. 11:27).

92 Cp. DRMT, 146–150.

types which are allowed a continued existence, until, if ever, conscious official redactional activities set in.

The impending gradual disappearance of variant readings which, on object-ive grounds, could not be declared to be intrinsically inferior to those which happened to have taken root in the predominant textual traditions, may well have been viewed with misgivings by those concerned with the preservation of Scripture. The practical advantage of traditing a fairly standardized text-type for communal-cultic purposes was set off by an understandable appre-hension for the unrecoverable loss of, to all appearances, valid and venerated textual traditions of the Biblical books, which per force would result from the above outlined process. Contradictory as it may sound, such *pro* and *ante* deliberations seem to have produced diverse techniques of non-manuscriptal variant preservation which helped balancing the tipped scale of the favoured text-tradition(s) that became increasingly predominant, to the exclusion, and the, to all intent and purposes, complete suppression of less favoured *variae lectiones*.

Here again, a comparison with attitudes and techniques that were current in the normative community is in order.

The prevalence in Rabbinic circles of trends of thought, such as were out-lined above, may have been responsible for the perceptible latitude in the em-ployment of the Bible text in scholarly discussion which conspicuously con-trasts the unceasing efforts to establish an exclusive *textus receptus* for public worship and for official text-transmission. Whereas deviant readings were banned from books which were earmarked for these latter categories, they were readily accepted and used as bases for Midrashic exposition.[93] In fact, at times it appears that such an officially discarded variant was not employed merely as just a convenient peg upon which to hang a Midrash that was on hand, but rather that the Midrash in question was constructed on a variant that had been barred from the *textus receptus* in order to give it a non-manu-scriptal lease on life. This supposition especially applies to the specific type of the *'al tiqrê* Midrash,[94] in which an established text is suspended, as it were, and another reading becomes the point of departure for an ensuing Midrashic comment, by means of the introductory formula: "do not read..., but rather read...". A famous case in point is the *'al-tiqrê* Midrash (Bab. Tal. Berakot 64a) which hinges on reading in Is. 54:13 – בוניך – "thy builders", instead of MT : בניך – "thy sons" (cp. G: τέκνα; T : בנך), a variant which now has turned up in Is-a as an emended reading: ב'ניכי.[95] Similarly, the Midrash:

93 Cp. TSL, 14–15; 386–374 (1932).
94 נ"ה טורשינר, אל תקרי, אשכול, אנציקלופדיה ישראלית ב'
95 Cp. Kutscher, *op. cit.*, 171 who points out that the Midrash appears to echo the reading

אל תקרי זרועו (בשר) זרועו אלא (בשר) זַרְעוֹ" (Bab. Tal. Shab. 33a)[96] can be anchored
in the different textual traditions of Is. 9:19. Here the MT (= Is-a) reading:
איש בשר זר(ו)עו י(ו)אכלו — "they shall eat every man the flesh of his own
arm" (G: τοῦ βραχίονος αὐτοῦ) is abandoned, as it were, for a variant זרעו –
"his offspring", which underlies T's paraphrastic rendering: גבר נכסי קריביה
ייבזון, and Sym.'s rendition: τοῦ πλησίου αὐτοῦ. Both readings seemingly were
conflated in the main stream of G^AB: τοῦ βραχίονος τοῦ ἀδελφοῦ αὐτοῦ.

We do not propose that every extant al-t. Midrash can be shown to have
arisen from a yet identifiable textual variant. This certainly is not the case.
Variae lectiones which supposedly triggered off the emergence of many a
Midrash of this type have been lost for us, together with the (suppressed)
MSS which exhibited them. Here is a possible example. Is. 2:22 (missing in
G) warns before reliance on man "for wherein is he to be accounted of" –
כי במה נחשב הוא. The MT reading בַּמֶּה is reflected in T: וכלמא חשיב הוא,
S: מטל דאיך מנא חשיב, and Aq.: ἐν τίνι ἐλογίσθη αὐτός. Now this phrase,
among others, is employed in an al-t. Midrashic comment on Prov. 16:5
(Bab. Tal. Sotah 4b) as p r o o f that "everyone that is proud in heart is an
abomination to the Lord": "'Ula said (he is considered) as if he had built a
bamah", and then goes on to quote Is. 2:22, winding up with: "אל תקרי במֶה אלא
בָמָה". At first glance it appears that here a mere different vocalization of the
same consonantal group is involved. But the fact that the point of departure
for the exposition in question is a Biblical proverb which castigates "the proud
in heart", suggests another possibility: an interchange between ב and ר, with the
resulting reading רמה in Is. 2:22. This word can be construed as a (synonymous)
parallel of במה (Ez. 16:24, 25, 31, 39), and in fact sometimes is textually confused
with it (Jud. 4:5 MT: רמה, G^B: βαμα; 1 Sam. 22:6 MT: רמה, G^BL: במה; cp.
DRMT, 157–158). Or else רמה can be derived from √רום — "to be exalted".
In an association with גבה לב (Prov. 16:5) this would bring to mind the expression
רום (לב) – *hybris* which recurrently is referred to in Is. 2:11, 12, 17, adjacent
to במה in 2:22. Interestingly, this latter concept emerges in the V rendition of
Is. 2:22: e x c e l s u s reputatus est ipse, which accordingly also may be
based on a reading רמה.[97]

Moreover this specific type of Midrash progressively degenerated, and ultima-

of Is-a, and stresses the fact that the first בניך in MT of Is. 54:13 was retained in
Is-a. Also in 49:17 Is-a reads בוניכי instead of MT: בניך. But there the copyist may have
been influenced by the context. See. H.M. Orlinsky, *Tarbiz* 24 (1954) 4 ff. Cp. further the
Midrashic comments in Bab. Tal. Sotah 12b on 1 Chr. 2:18, and in Cant. Rab. 137
on Cant. 1:5 where בוניה respectively בונות is implied instead of MT: בניה, respectively
בנות.

96 Cp. Yalqut on Isaiah *ad loc.* (ed. J. Spira, 75), *et al.*
97 Cp. Kedar's remarks in the present volume, p. 183.

tely the *'al tiqrê* formula often was employed, even when the Midrash in question could not be related to an actually extant reading, by definition originally a *sine qua non* requirement, and had become a mere exegetical *Spielelement*.[98] *Vice versa* the introductory formula of a genuine *'al tiqrê* Midrash often was dropped, so that now the same exposition sometimes is preserved in parallel versions, both with and without that formula.[99]

These short remarks which are intended but to sketch cursorily the genesis and some phases of development of the *'al tiqrê* Midrash lead one to presuppose the existence of a transition stage from manuscriptal notation to extra-manuscriptal Midrashic preservation of Biblical variant readings. It appears that also these aspects of text-transmission can yet be traced in Qumran writings.

A few comments on the textual character of the variants which assumedly underlie the *'al tiqrê* Midrash, and many a Midrash not so designated, are called for, before we enter into a discussion of the pertinent Qumran material.

In a majority of cases the textual variations involved are of the simplest and most common types: interchange of graphically similar letters or of auriculary close consonants; haplography or dittography; continuous writing of separate words or division of one word into two; *plene* or defective spelling; metathesis, differences of vocalization, sometimes entailing a change of verb conjugation. Some cases of more complicated textual phenomena do not affect the overall impression.

With respect to the issue on hand, we note that only under exceptionally favourable circumstances can we hope to find the very same reading recorded both as a variant-notation in a yet extant Hebrew manuscript or as a double-translation in one of the VSS, and at the same time also in its non-manuscriptal form as the basis of an *'al tiqrê* Midrash. Such a propitious concurrence of independent evidence characterizes the following instance, although in the Midrashic factor the *'al tiqrê* formula is not present.

98 This and related techniques of variation on Biblical themes in Midrash-exegesis, were discussed and illustrated by I.L. Seeligmann in his valuable study "Voraussetzungen der Midraschexegese", *Suppl. to VT* 1 (1953) 150–181, esp. 159–160.

99 The Sam. variant in Num. 11:32 – (ה)שחוטו להם וישחטון (ed. Blayney) as against MT וישטחו להם שטוח is reflected in an *al-t.* Midrash in Sifre Num. § 98 (ed. Friedmann 26b) which is adduced *in extenso* without the introductory formula in Bab. Tal. Yoma 75b; Jer. Tal. Nazir 53c IV, 6, and in Yalqut Shim'oni I, 635 on Num. 11:32. Another Sam. variant in Ex. 12:17 – המצוה את ושמרתם (= G: καὶ πυλάξεσθε τὴν ἐντολὴν ταύτην) as against MT – המצות את appears to underlie the *al-t.* Midrash (cp. Rashi *ad loc.*) in Mekilta d'Rabbi Ishmael, Tractate Pisḥa, ch. 9 (ed. Horowitz-Rabin, 32; ed. Lauterbach, 74) which again is quoted without the formula in Mekilta d'Rabbi Shim'on b. Yoḥai (ed. Epstein-Melamed, 22:3); cp. further Rashi to Bab. Tal. Yoma 33a; Meg. 6b.

In this case a double translation of the two letters אל in G (and possibly also in T) to Ps. 29:1 is involved. The crucial passage in MT: הבו לה׳ בני אלים is rendered by the Greek translator: ἐνέγκατε τῷ κυρίῳ υἱοὶ θεοῦ

ἐνέγκατε τῷ κυρίῳ υἱοὺς κριῶν,

and by T: הבון קדם י״י תושבחתא כתי מלאכיא בני אלים.

Here the first line in G, and the first phrase in T, conceive of the underlying Hebrew text as of an invitation to divine beings, υἱοὶ θεοῦ — כתי מלאכיא, to praise God (תושבחתא), taking אלים (בני) in the vocative as a plur. of the common noun אל = god (cp. Ex. 15:11; Ps. 89:7; Dan. 11:36, et al.). In its general meaning the passage thus may be compared e.g. with Ps. 97:7 and Job 38:7, to which latter also Ibn Ezra ad loc. alludes. This most natural explanation is further reflected in the Rabbinic tradition which identifies בני אלים as "angels" — מלאכי שרת.[100] However the second rendition of G – υἱοὺς κριῶν – clearly derives from the plene spelling בני אילים = "(young) rams" (for which cp. בן ראמים in v. 6), construed as the syntactical object, and paralleling כבוד ועז in the second half-verse. The same possibly also applies to the redundant בני אלים in T, and certainly to Jerome's translation: adferte filios arietum.

The above evidence indicates that the variant spelling אילים at some time or other was extant in manuscripts, and was retained in the extra-Massoretic Greek tradition in the form of a variant notation (cp. also T). In the Massoretic manuscriptal tradition this variant-reading אילים was discarded to the exception of some odd copies. But it did enjoy a Midrashic after-life. Shoḥer Tov ad loc. (ed. Buber, 116) relates בני אלים to Israel, who are likened to helpless sheep over whom God will appoint David as shepherd; or again, and this time more in line with the Greek-Latin conception, presents Israel as "the sons of men slaughtered like sheep. Abraham said: I slaughter, Isaac said I am slaughtered".

As already stated, this example is a rare case in which are yet preserved both ends of the transition process: the textual variant-notation in the form of a doublet in one (set of) extra-MT witness(es), side by side with the Rabbinic tradition in which the variant that was ejected from the MT was made the basis of a Midrash. However, ordinarily we shall have to content ourselves with illustrating the transition from one phase to the other by drawing on examples which individually reflect only one of them, but which, if viewed in conjunction, typologically represent the transition-process in toto.

We now can revert to the double-reading in Is-a 38:19 which was discussed on page 109, and in which we seem to discern the typical characteristics of a potentia 'al tiqrê Midrash. Again the pregnant consonant combination אל is involved.

---

100 Cp. Seder Eliahu Rab. ch. 2 (ed. Friedmann, 12).

As noted, Is-a here records in its text-base the variant והודיע אלוה אמתך along-side יודיע אל אמתכה which is the reading found in MT. The transition from MT אֶל to Is-a אלוה, or *vice versa*, may be considered as textually exceedingly simple, especially since a potential intermediate stage – אלה – is yet extant in Is-b. We thus may take as certain the manuscriptal coexistence, towards the end of the Second Temple period, of the above three readings which most prob-ably derived from one another, either in the order אלוה → אלה → אל or אלוה → → אל → אלה or אלוה ← אלה → אל. The problem of the actual historical devel-opment is of no relevance to the present issue. The scribe of Is-a obviously did not feel competent to decide on the respective merits of אל and אל(ו)ה, or else deemed both worthy of preservation, and therefore, rather than choosing between them, integrated the two readings in the text of his copy.

At this juncture we are well within the phase of manuscriptal variants notation which, however, took place in one witness only, *viz.* Is-a, whereas in our other Hebrew sources and in the ancient VSS a decision was reached as to the retention of one reading and the rejection of the other(s). Now, it does not require much imagination to visualize the discarded variant אלוה cropping up in Midrashic literature in the formulation: אל תקרי אל אלא אלוה. True, such a Midrash is not extant, to my knowledge, but it would have been in the very best tradition of the type to embark on an exposition which utilizes the simple graphic or linguistic variation אלוה — אלה — אל which was found in Biblical MSS for the fashioning of an exegetical comment with theological or ideological undertones.

This pattern of development indeed can be observed in Qumran writings of the *pesher*-type which shares many features with the Rabbinic Midrash without being identical with it. In this setting we can perceive the simultaneous utiliza-tion of variant readings for expository purposes when only one of the given possibilities is quoted as actual Scripture. Here are three illustrations of the phenomenon in question.

a) Hab. 1:11 MT: אז חלף רוח ויעבר ואשֵׁם זו כחו לאלהו is quoted as: וישם זה כוחו לאלוהו in 1QHp IV, 9–10. The MT reading, which derives אשם from √אשם — "to be guilty", is supported by G: ἐξιλάσεται and T: וחב. In the ensuing comment, which is based on the first part of the above Scripture, 1QHp clearly shows acquaintance, both with its own Biblical reading and also with that of MT (G, T), and with the Massoretic sentence-division: (a) פשרו על מושלי הכתיאים אשר בעצת בית אשמ[תם] יעבירו איש מלפני רעהו (b)[מושלי]הם ז[ה אחר זה יבואו לשחית את ה[ארץ?]... The second *pesher* (b), in which the salient word is לשחית — "to despoil, to lay waste", in all prob-ability mirrors וישם of the *Vorlage* from which 1QHp quoted, the verb being understood as derived from שמם. The first exposition (a), in which בית אשמ[תם]

"[their] house of guilt" is the pivotal expression, obviously is based on אָשֵׁם as found in the MT which reading, though, is not explicitly quoted. However, it is possible that this very reading actually was adduced furtheron in 1QHp (IV, 14–15)[101] where another *pesher* is introduced, but was lost for us in a *lacuna*: ...זה כוחו לאלוהו פשרו   ז[ה אחר זה יבואו לשחית את ה]ארץ?   ז[ה. If this indeed can be maintained, we would have here what amounts to a variant-notation, in quotation, together with two Midrash–like expositions which are based alternatively on the one and the other of the parallel variants.

b) Hab. 2:16 MT: שתה גם אתה והערל – "drink thou, and *uncover* your-self"[102] is quoted in 1QHp XI, 9 as: שתה גם אתה והרעל — "drink thou, and become *intoxicated*", a change of concept which may have resulted from a simple metathesis. Here MT is supported by T, and 1QHp by G,[103] Aq. and S.

The interesting feature of this example is that, notwithstanding his own reading והרעל, the author of 1QHp sets his *pesher* to the tune of the MT variant והערל in its obvious, but in Hab. 2:16 unsuitable derivation from the root ערל – "uncircumcised": כי לוא מל את ערלת לבו – "he did not circumcise (the foreskin of) his heart". Without employing the very formula, the *pesher* here exhibits the technical intricacies which characterize the Rabbinic 'al tiqrê Midrash. We observe a similar suspension of an explicit Qumran reading in favour of an extra-Qumran variant which becomes the departure point for a Midrashic exposition.

The same factors seem to have been at work in the following instance, in which, though, the actual Biblical quotation was lost in a *lacuna*, and has to be restored by inference.

c) The first word on col. ii, 1 of 1QHp – יטופר preceded by a *lacuna* at the lower margin of col. i, is the end of a quotation of Hab. 1:5, a verse which in the MT opens: ראו בגוים והביטו – "Behold ye among the *nations*, and regard...". The *pesher* which is only partially preserved never mentions the word בגוים – "nations", but instead refers three times in a row to "the traitors" – הבוגדים. It certainly can be postulated, as is done by I.L. Seelig-

---

101 Unless we assume that in this instance the sectarian author quoted only the second part of the verse starting, against the Massoretic sentence-division, with [וישם], and now deriving the word from √שֹים.

102 This appears to be the required translation of the phrase, rather than RV: "and be as one uncircumcised". ערל here should be taken in the meaning of ערם. The metaphor is rooted in a situation like the one described in the tale of Noah's drunkenness (Gen. 9:2) which well may have been in the back of the prophet's mind. In addition to the above similarity, cp. Hab. 2:17 – יכסך with Gen. 9:23 – ויכסו; 2:15 – למען הביט על with ib. – ראו לא אביהם ערות. Cp. further Lam. 4:21.

103 Which presents a double-translation: διασαλεύθητι καὶ σείσθητι. Cp. M. Stenzel, VT 3 (1953) 97–99.

mann,[104] that the Biblical *Vorlage* with which the author of 1QHp was familiar, in fact contained the *varia lectio* הבוגדים. But one also could postulate that 1QHp here presents a case of a typical variant-Midrash. Bypassing the reading בגוים which he actually may have quoted, the author anchored his actualizing paraphrase in a parallel variant בבוגדים which he found in a manuscript of the text-type that seems to underlie G's οἱ καταφρονηταί[105]. Thus the emerging situation would be comparable to that which we encountered in the previous example.

The foregoing analysis leads us to conclude that the category of the variant-Midrash which in Rabbinic literature is best, though not exclusively, represented by the '*al tiqrê* type, in the Qumran writings is exemplified by the variant-*pesher*. The Qumran material thus offers proof for the high antiquity of this Midrashic category. At the same time the combined evidence of Qumran and Rabbinic techniques proves the contention that variant readings in the Biblical textual traditions were viewed with relative equanimity by both groups, and even were perpetuated by diverse manuscriptal and non-manuscriptal devices.

This conclusion opens up a new avenue of approach to the problem of the genesis and the early history of the *Kethîb-Qerê* variants, an issue which we hope to discuss in a separate publication.

104 In his review of K. Elliger, *Studien zum Habakkuk Commentar vom Toten Meer* (Tübingen 1953) in *Kirjath Sepher* 30 (1954) 40.
105 It is of interest to remark that a similar pair of variants may be observed in Prov. 10:3 where the Ben Chajim edition and some MSS read בונדים instead of רשעים which is found in other MSS and printed editions, and also underlies the VSS.

The Biblical Scrolls from Qumran and the Text of the Old Testament

Patrick W. Skehan

Catholic University

So many partial lists of Old Testament manuscripts from Qumran exist in the scholarly literature that it seems necessary to begin this account with a full inventory. The numbers to be given are minimal. They are given in four separate groups, for cave 1, for caves 2, 3, 5-10, for cave 4, and for cave 11; thus for the published material those especially interested can verify how these totals have been arrived at. A manuscript which contains any Psalm and no extant non-biblical material is counted as a Psalms manuscript. Three isolated bits from cave 4 are not counted, however; and 11Q Ps^a and 4Q Ps^f, both of which are definitely Psalms manuscripts incorporating non-biblical compositions, are included. A manuscript which contains any of the Minor Prophets is counted as a manuscript of the Twelve, as the evidence seems to require. The four manuscripts which indicate inclusion of two biblical books in a single scroll (two of Gen.-Ex., two of Lev.-Numb.) are counted one to each of the biblical books concerned. Since one of these manuscripts (4Q paleoEx^l) contains of Genesis only the bottoms of two letters from its last line of text, one could add one each to the totals for Exodus, Leviticus, Numbers, but hardly to that for Genesis. Tentative identifications have been passed over when too little text is extant for certainty as to the nature of the manuscript.

There are, then, the following manuscripts. From cave 1: Genesis 1, Exodus 1, Leviticus 1 (with Numbers), Deuteronomy 2, Judges 1, Samuel 1, Isaiah 2, Ezekiel 1, Psalms 3, and Daniel 2. From the "minor caves" 2, 3, 5-10: Genesis 3, Exodus 3, Leviticus 2, Numbers 3, Deuteronomy 5, Kings 2, Isaiah 1, Jeremiah 1, Ezekiel 1, Minor Prophets 1, Psalms 4, Job 1, Ruth 2, Song of Songs 1, Lamentations 3, and Daniel 1. From cave 4: Genesis 11 (one includes Exodus), Exodus 11, Leviticus 4, Numbers 2 (one includes Leviticus), Deuteronomy 18, Joshua 2, Judges 2, Samuel 3, Kings 1, Isaiah 15, Jeremiah 3, Ezekiel 3, Minor Prophets 7, Psalms 17, Job 3, Proverbs 2, Ruth 2, Song of Songs 3, Ecclesiastes 2, Lamentations 1, Daniel 5, Ezra 1, Chronicles 1. From cave 11: Leviticus 1, Ezekiel 1, Psalms 3.

Included in this inventory are the ten manuscripts in the paleo-Hebrew script, which are four copies of Leviticus (one each from caves 1, 2, 6, and 11), two each of Genesis, Exodus, and Deuteronomy, one of Numbers and one of Job. Translation materials are not included. Of Septuagint Greek texts, Qumran furnishes portions of Exodus (7Q1), Leviticus (4Q LXX Lev^a, ^{b}), and Numbers (4Q LXX Numb); and there are Aramaic targums of Leviticus (from cave 4) and of Job (from both 4 and 11).

These lists do not include materials of varying date from sites in the Judean desert other than the Qumran area such as the Wadi Murabba'āt, Masada, Engeddi, Khirbet Mird, and Wadi Khabra, though some of these texts will need to be mentioned in what follows. Neither do the lists take into account the extensive paraphrases of Torah texts from cave 4 being studied by J. Strugnell, nor the substantial number of phylacteries and mezuzas, with their excerpts (not always the traditional ones) of key Torah passages. No such lists can be absolutely definitive,[1] but the gleanings from further study of caves 4 and 11 cannot be expected to alter these totals by more than a few slight bits.

Qumran and the Canon

It will be noticed from the above that Esther alone, of the Hebrew canon of the Old Testament, has still not been found at Qumran. It is easy to discount an argument from silence, but when one considers the late origin of the Purim festival with which Esther is connected, its partial identification with the victories of Judas the Maccabee (whose Hasmonean kindred were abhorred at Qumran), and the rigidity in matters of the liturgical calendar that characterized the Qumran group, it seems more likely that the book was avoided than that it was simply not known. After the colophon to the Septuagint text of Esther, though of doubtful value for dating the translation, is usually taken to indicate that even in Greek the book of Esther was circulating by about 75 B.C. at the latest.

The recognized authority of the Torah and the Latter (Writing) Prophets at Qumran is beyond dispute on the basis of formal citations and commentary in addition to the copies of the text. The composite book of the Minor Prophets was known at Qumran in the Hebrew order of the books, and in its integrity; the inference that lies ready to hand from Ben Sira 49:10 is thus confirmed from the manuscripts. The "Former Prophets" (Josh., Judg., Sam., and Kings) are adequately represented, and show, like a part of the Torah evidence, a text type with Septuagintal affiliations. Among the "Writings," the Psalms occupy a privileged place. While in at least two manuscripts the canonical Psalms are combined with other hymnic or wisdom compositions, there can be no doubt at all of the existence of the Psalm collection we know, and of its attribution in a general way to David. Job, Proverbs, and four of the five *Megilloth* are quite adequately represented; the only really scanty evidence is that for Ezra-Nehemiah and Chronicles. Daniel was much used at Qumran in it part-Hebrew, part-Aramaic text, without the expansions known from the Greek, as 1Q 72 already shows.

Most of the "Apocrypha" retained as canonical in the Vulgate are not represented at Qumran; so for I-II Maccabees, Judith, Baruch, and the Wisdom of Solomon. One can hardly suppose that the Qumran group would have shown special favor to the books which were composed in Greek (II Macc. and Wis.), or to the Greek text which survives to us from elsewhere of the others. Yet a bit of the Letter of Jeremiah (Baruch 6 in the Vulgate)

---

1. The Psalms total above includes a cave 4 fragment of Psalm 89 being studied by Fr. J. T. Milik, which is in addition to the otherwise exhaustive Psalms inventory published by J. A. Sanders, *Catholic Biblical Quarterly*, XXVII (1965), 114-23.

did turn up in Greek, in 7Q2. The case of Tobit, of which cave 4 contains four Aramaic manuscripts and one Hebrew one, is somewhat different; it is the long text of the Greek Sinaiiticus manuscript and of the Old Latin version that is supported at Qumran. Also well enough known at Qumran was the book of Ben Sira (Ecclesiasticus); besides the stichometric fragments of 2Q 18, there are now to be included the first half and the last two words of the acrostic poem in 51:13-30. This occurs in 11Q Ps^a, columns 21-22, recently published by J. A. Sanders in *Discoveries in the Judaean Desert, IV*. It is not too much to infer that the scribe of 11Q Ps^a or some predecessor of his wished to count this piece among the 4050 compositions he attributes to David, along with a scattering of other Hebrew texts that are currently in nobody's canonical list.[2]

These data for the history of the Canon should be weighed in the light of various other considerations. Not liking Hasmoneans, the Qumran group would not have been partial to I Maccabees even in Hebrew, were it available to them in that form. On the other hand, they had ten copies of the various sections of Enoch in Aramaic (still without the *Parables,* chaps. 37-71), and eleven copies of the *Book of Jubilees* in Hebrew. Since they studied and applied the *Jubilees* calendar of 364 days, they no doubt took this book which enshrined it quite seriously. Of their own sectarian compositions, we know of fourteen copies of the community rule (*Serek,* or "Manual of Discipline"), ten of the Zadokite "Damascus Document," seven of the Thanksgiving Hymns (*Hodayot*), seven of the War Scroll, and six of the sapiential work represented in 1Q 26. Then there are three manuscripts of the *Testament of Levi* in Aramaic and one of the Hebrew *Testament of Nephthali.* All in all, the Qumran library gives the impression of a certain selectivity, but hardly of any fine distinction between a closed canon and all other texts.

Qumran and Septuagint Studies

The fragment of 4Q LXX Numb shown in Figure 12 will serve to illustrate one contribution of the Qumran texts to our knowledge of Septuagint origins.[3] The years after the second World War witnessed a lively controversy, centered in England, between two distinguished scholars now dead, Paul Kahle and Peter Katz. Kahle insisted strenuously that in view of the confusion of evidence and the variations of reading inherent in the use of the Greek Old Testament in our earliest literary sources (Philo, the New

2. Study of Ben Sira in this period will be further stimulated by the portions of thirteen fragmentary columns of it, from 39:37 to 44:20, announced by Y. Yadin, *Yediot,* XXIX (1965), 120-2 (Hebrew), as having been recovered at Masada in a hand of the early first century B.C. The connections of the Cairo geniza fragments of Ben Sira with a presumptive Qumran prototype have been stressed again by A. A. DiLella in *Catholic Biblical Quarterly,* XXIV (1962), 245-67, and in his *The Hebrew Text of Sirach: A Text-critical and Historical Study,* The Hague, 1965.

3. The manuscript has been partially published, including this piece, by the present writer in *Supplements to Vetus Testamentum,* IX (1957), 155-7.

Testament, Josephus, and early Church writers), any attempt to recover a single pre-Christian rendering in its primitive form from the extant manuscripts must be an illusory quest. He proposed instead that the Greek Old Testament grew after the fashion of the Palestinian Aramaic targums, in a welter of divergent and unrelated oral traditions that afforded no fixed form of text for general acceptance before the 4th century A.D. This position, which in the United States was strongly opposed by H. M. Orlinsky, always

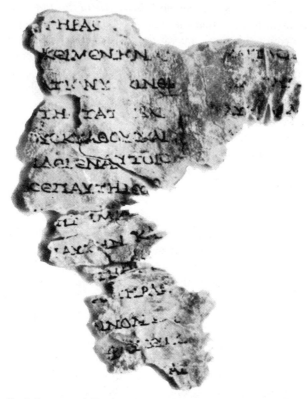

Fig. 12. The Greek fragment of Numbers from cave 4 at Qumran designated 4Q LXX Numb. Photo courtesy The Palestine Archaeological Museum.

had against it the evidence of the ancient secondary versions from the Greek namely the Old Latin, the Coptic, and the Ethiopic. It was further belied by the two pre-Christian bits of Deuteronomy in Greek which had been recovered from Egypt before the Qumran discoveries (papyrus Rylands gr. 458 and papyrus Fuad inv. 266). To these the Qumran caves have added the four LXX manuscripts of Exodus, Leviticus, and Numbers enumerated above, plus the Letter of Jeremiah fragment. All fit quite clearly into the textual tradition that we know from the great 4th century manuscripts and thus counter the sweeping theory of Kahle with tangible facts. For example, the second line of text in the fragment here illustrated contains the Greek word *[pro]keimenēn.* To place this in Numbers 4:7 with their aid of a Septuagint concordance, it was necessary only to fit the verb form with the proper prepositional prefix ("pro-"), broken away with the missing beginning of the line. Yet in the whole Greek Old Testament this is the only place where this particular turn of phrase, "(the table) lying before (the Divine Presence)" is to be found (RSV: "table of the bread of the Presence"); the rendering is hardly an obvious or necessary one. Hence we are dealing with basically only one translation, in our fragment and in the later manuscripts.

The same fragment poses problems of its own, however. The last complete word it contains is the word *phauseōs,* a part of the phrase "(the lampstand) of the lighting" in Numbers 4:9, where the later Greek tradition regularly reads "the light-giving lampstand" (RSV: "the lampstand for the light"). Now it happens that the Greek word in our fragment also occurs in Genesis 1:14-15 in connection with the same Hebrew word as in the Numbers passage. One way or another, it seems clear that the Septuagint text has at this point undergone a deliberate retouching of some sort.

Rather than from the Qumran texts, however, the key to a large part of the confusion in Septuagint textual evidence and the history of its transmission has come from a Greek Minor Prophets manuscript almost certainly from the Wadi Khabra, published by D. Barthélemy, O.P.[4] In this manuscript, which he dates from the second half of the first century A.D., Barthélemy has identified a reworked form of the LXX translation of the Minor Prophets done in Palestine in accord with developing rabbinic hermeneutical principles, with the purpose of bringing the Greek text more closely into line with the Hebrew manuscripts in use there in the early first century A.D. These Hebrew manuscripts were still not completely standardized, as in the consonants of the now received Masoretic text, but they stood closer to the Masoretic text than did the Hebrew prototype of the original Alexandrian Septuagint for these books.

This early reworking of the Greek Old Testament text does not stand alone. In the Minor Prophets tradition, Barthélemy has been able to equate it with the seventh column, or *quinta editio* (V^a), of Origen's Hexapla; with a series of approximations to the Hebrew in the Sahidic Coptic secondary version from the Greek, and in the Freer codex in Greek; and with the citations in Justin Martyr in the mid-2nd century A.D. The recension has certain fixed characteristics which make it possible to go further; most obvious, though only one of a whole complex of similar features, is the recurrent rendering

---

4. In *Les dévanciers d'Aquila, Supplements* to *Vetus Testamentum,* X (1963).

of the Hebrew particle *gām* by *kaige* in Greek. Here Barthélemy was able to build on earlier studies of H. St. J. Thackeray in the Greek books of King-doms (Samuel-Kings), and also to trace the same recension through a number of other Old Testament books. To summarize the results of this, the recension in question includes in its scope the later supplements to the short LXX texts of Job and Jeremiah, the "Theodotion" text of Daniel, the "Septuagint" renderings of Lamentations and (probably) Ruth, the text of II Samuel to I Kings 2:11 and of I Kings 22 and all of II Kings in the "Septuagint" column of Origen's Hexapla and in our printed Bibles. This recension, whose exact limits remain to be marked out, Barthélemy then equates with the work of "Theodotion," whom he situates in A.D. 30-50 and identifies with the Jonathan ben Uzziel of Jewish targumic and talmudic tradition.

Prescinding from the identification of "Theodotion" with Jonathan, the relationships described and the insights they afford do much to relieve Septuagint studies of certain continual embarrassments. It appears to be the "Theodotion" form of Daniel that is cited in the New Testament and by Clement of Rome; if so, something of what has been ascribed to the 2nd century personage Theodotion was already extant in the preceding century. Barthélemy's demonstration of the existence of an extensive work of revision of the Greek text in first century Palestine removes this anomaly. In addition, the relationship between "Theodotion" and Aquila (*ca.* 135 A.D.) is set straight, because Barthélemy can show that Aquila's work depends on this "Theodotionic" revision, which it supplements, refines, and in the end, smothers with labored and rigidly applied devices.

Once the concept of widespread recensional activity in the Greek Old Testament text in Palestine by the first century A.D. is accepted, ramifications of it are not difficult to find. The secondary recension of the Greek Sirach, best known from codex 248 and the Old Latin, and now available for intensive study in J. Ziegler's critical edition of the book,[5] is quoted in the *Teaching of the Twelve Apostles* (Sir. 12:1 at *Did.* i:6, see *Biblica* LXIV (1963), 533-536); hence this is basically a first century recension. The variant Greek text of Proverbs 2:21 is quoted by Clement of Rome (I Clem. xiv:4); thus the reworked form of the first nine chapters of the Greek Proverbs is a product of the same early period. And in Ezekiel, J. Ziegler has shown that papyrus 967 (the Beatty-Scheide manuscript) displays a pre-Origen, first century A.D. recensional treatment of the text. In fine, instead of being at the beginnings of a "critical" reworking of the Greek text on the basis of the Hebrew, Origen comes near the end of the process, which was otherwise an entirely Jewish undertaking, in which Aquila built on "Theodotion," which itself built on earlier materials.

5. *Septuaginta* XII,2: *Sapientia Jesu filii Sirach*, edited by J. Ziegler, Göttingen, 1965.

The nature of those earlier materials will take us back to the evidence afforded by the Hebrew manuscripts of Qumran. One last reflection on the Greek Numbers fragment seems necessary, however. It has been seen by good Greek paleographers, and dated tentatively at about the turn of the era, too early, seemingly, for Barthélemy's Jonathan ben Uzziel personage, whom he puts between 30 and 50 A.D. Yet the retouchings in the Greek text of Numbers in this fragment are already such as to suggest the Greek "Theodotionic" reviser. There are other reasons, we shall see, for placing the origins of revision work on the Greek text in Palestine prior to the Christian era; and it seems possible that Barthélemy puts his "Theodotionic" reviser slightly too late.

Greek Bible Revision in Palestine before the Christian Era

The key to the next step, forward in research, but backward in time, lies in the text of Samuel. We have noticed that there was a revision of its Greek text, part of the undertaking ascribed to Theodotion, which dates in fact from about the turn of the era. Was this revision founded, as we might offhand expect, on a translation made in Egypt in about the 3rd century B.C.? Besides the "Theodotionic" materials isolated by Thackeray and dated for us by Barthélemy's researches, there exists still another body of evidence for the Greek text of Samuel which has preoccupied scholars for a long time, and which has seemed inconsistent with any such Egyptian explanation. This is the text which, in biblical manuscripts is associated with Syrian sources and the memory of Lucian of Antioch (died A.D. 312). It cannot be of 4th century A.D. date because, as A. Mez pointed out in 1895, it is substantially the text of Samuel used by Josephus Flavius before A.D. 94. Barthélemy has been able to show that for those parts of Samuel and Kings (see above) in which the "Theodotionic" recension has invaded the general stream of Septuagint transmission through its use by Origen in the 5th column of his Hexapla, the adjoining material in the 6th column, an older text that formed the basis for the "Theodotionic" one, is in fact the same text that appears in the Lucianic manuscripts and in Josephus.

It is at this point that the Hebrew manuscripts from Qumran cave 4 begin to assume their full importance. Prof. F. M. Cross, Jr., has followed upon Barthélemy's publication with a study[6] which has as only the first of its merits the fact that it specifies the exact nature of this "Lucianic" text of Samuel in Greek. From an examination of the various Greek texts in the light of his Hebrew evidence, Cross is able to show that the "Lucianic" text also is a reworking of a still older Greek text, with the purpose of bringing it

---

6. *Harvard Theological Review*, LVII (1964), 281-99. Cross' earlier studies on his Samuel texts can be traced through this article and the Anchor Book edition of his *Ancient Library of Qumran* (1962).

into line with the state of the Hebrew text of Samuel in Palestine itself, perhaps toward the end of the 2nd, and certainly in the first century B.C. Thus besides a proto-Theodotion, we now have a proto-Lucian.

There are, then, three important stages of transmission of the text of Samuel (and Kings) in Greek, all three of them prior to the fixing of the Hebrew tradition with the received consonantal text near the end of the first cent. A.D. These are:

1. The earliest Alexandrian rendering, largely preserved for us in codex B, but only for the sections I Samuel 1:1—II Samuel 11:1 and I Kings 2:12 —II Kings 21:43.[7] This may be supposed, with H. St. J. Thackeray,[8] to be the full extent of this first translation; it is certainly all that is extant.

2. The "proto-Lucianic" revision from the Hebrew, of the 2nd-first centuries B.C., done in Palestine, and including all of Samuel-Kings. This is found especially in the minuscule manuscripts b, o, c_2, e_2, in Josephus, and partly in the 6th column materials from Origen's Hexapla.

3. The "proto-Theodotionic" recension of the first century A.D., which regularly builds on "proto-Lucian" and brings it much closer to what we now know as the Masoretic type of Hebrew text, though the two forms are by no means identical.

In the reconstructed "Septuagint" text of his Hexapla, Origen employed the first version of Samuel-Kings where it existed, and where it did not, he chose the third. Thus the nature and date of the second, or proto-Lucianic recension became obscured, and it took on for the future the character of a missing link, whose restoration to its proper place in the sequence makes a true historical perspective on the development of the Greek text possible for the first time. Since the same proto-Lucianic revision has survived to us also in our evidence for Exodus through Deuteronomy in Greek, where once again its date and significance have never been clear, it can be but small wonder that a scholar of Kahle's calibre should have despaired of any unraveling of the resultant web. Cross, in his critique of Barthélemy, holds to a real function for the Theodotion of *ca.* A.D. 180, and for Lucian at the beginning of the 4th century. One proximate task in Septuagint studies, however, would seem to be the endeavor to ascertain how much of the function normally attributed to these worthies was already performed for them in the centuries before they were born, and with the priorities between them reversed.

Qumran and the Transmission of the Hebrew Text

In this matter, once again, the books of Samuel play a crucial role; and it is through the same article of Cross that new perspectives on their

---

7. There is a transposition here; II Kings 20 and 21 are given in the Greek in the reverse order, hence the 43 verses for what is actually Masoretic text II Kings 20.
8. *The Septuagint and Jewish Worship*, 2nd ed. 1923, pp. 16-28 and 114-5.

Hebrew text become available. The Qumran cave 4 evidence for Samuel is copious (in 4Q Sam[a]; see fig. 13), is in part early (4Q Sam[b], end of the 3rd century B.C.), and there exist both in Hebrew and in Greek substantial bodies of related material against which to test it. To present only the results, Cross finds in the books of Samuel a chain of evidence for a distinctive Palestinian text type, the archetype to which he would place in the 5th

Fig. 13. Leather fragments of I Samuel 1-2 from 4Q Sam[a]. Photo courtesy The Palestine Archaeological Museum.

century B.C. This line of transmission is witnessed to by the Chronicler (4th century B.C.), by 4Q Sam[b] (3rd century B.C.), by 4Q Sam[a] jointly with the proto-Lucianic Septuagint (first century B.C.), and finally by Josephus (at the end of the first century A.D.). It is the type of text to which, in its Lucianic manuscript witnesses, J. Wellhausen appealed in

1871 as a means of healing, if possible, the defects in the Masoretic tradition. For with all due respect to the scholars who would have it otherwise, it has long been held by serious students of Samuel that in their case the Masoretic text presents us with a truncated text with notable omissions, both deliberate and accidental; it is a text that is much below the standard of excellence observable in the received text of other Old Testament books.

Over against this early Palestinian text with its five centuries of traceable history, Cross sets a text that would have branched off as a local text in Egypt, not later than the 4th century B.C.; from this is derived the Old Greek rendering preserved to us in codex B as far as II Samuel 11:1 inclusive, where it stops. More sharply divergent from the Palestinian form of earlier times is the first century A.D. text reflected in the proto-Theodotionic materials; in general the Hebrew they suppose may be labeled proto-Masoretic. Close to, but not identical with this is our extant Masoretic text.

Faced with the problem of where the two latter texts, seemingly intrusive in Palestine, may have had their origin, Cross recalls that the rather frequent loss by homoioteleuton (similarity of ending) which the Masoretic text of Samuel manifests is suggestive of transmission in comparative isolation; and given the date of the appearance, first of proto-Theodotion and then of the Masoretic text form, he refers them "back to a local text preserved in Babylon in the fourth-second centuries B.C., reintroduced into Jerusalem in the Hasmonean or Herodian period" (p. 297). Some such solution does appear to be demanded by the data at hand.

Moving on from the books of Samuel, one can admit, with Cross, that the study of the Hagiographa and the Minor Prophets in the Qumran cave 4 materials is not at the point where clear inferences can be drawn regarding early textual families in these books. To quote him again, "The evidence for textual families for the time being is restricted largely to the Pentateuch, the Former Prophets, and the book of Jeremiah. Study has been directed first of all to those books whose texts are dramatic in their variety, and whose Greek versions are relatively trustworthy" (p. 286). The reflection is perhaps not out of place, that the texts which are dramatic in their variety (i.e., part Septuagintal, part Palestino-Samaritan, part proto-Masoretic) are in most cases those of the very books whose authority is longest and most firmly fixed. Genesis is an exception; its Qumran text is, says Cross, already allied with the *textus receptus*.

The present writer has had occasion to work on half a dozen Torah manuscripts from Qumran cave 4, five of them in the old paleo-Hebrew script and the sixth a separate copy of Deuteronomy 32. This last, with the Qumran evidence for Septuagintal readings in Hebrew in all parts of the Song of Moses, has been discussed by both Cross and myself before now. Two of

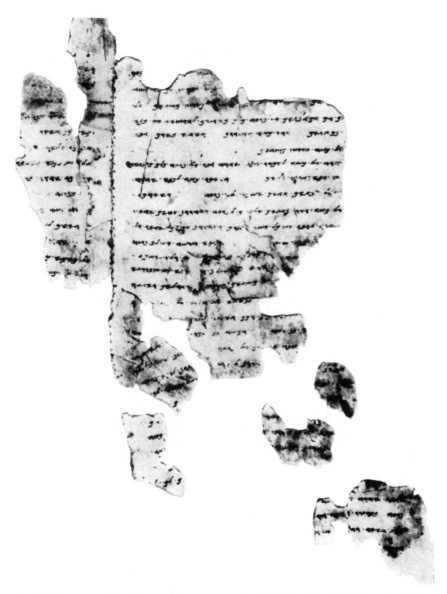

Fig. 14. Fragments of the "Samaritan" type manuscript of Exodus, 4Q paleoEx^m, in paleo-Hebrew script. Photo courtesy The Palestine Archaeological Museum.

the others are too limited in scope for a good text sampling; and a not very careful Deuteronomy had best be considered with the large number of manuscripts of the book being studied by Cross. That leaves two copies of Exodus; the "Samaritan" type manuscript (4Q paleoEx^m; see fig. 14) already a number of times described, and 4Q paleoEx¹, a manuscript in a tiny hand of perhaps the beginning of the first century B.C. This last is quite near to the received text, with only slight concessions to the tendency towards expanded readings for the sake of clarity and smoothness.

For the books from Exodus through Deuteronomy, what emerges thus far when the 4Q manuscripts are placed in the context of the Samaritan recension, the Old Greek, the proto-Lucianic Greek, which makes itself felt also in these books, and finally of the Masoretic text, is that in some degree all these witnesses (the Old Greek least, the Samaritan text type most) *except* the Masoretic text give evidence of a continuous expansionist tendency in text transmission in pre-Christian Palestine. This expansionist feature involves syntatical smoothing, harmonization of related passages, borrowings from one section or one book to another of supplementary materials, and sometimes an expanded orthography. A comparison of the short form of Jeremiah, known now from its appearance in 4Q Jer^b as well as from the Septuagint, with the fuller Masoretic form of the book suggests that the editing of the latter consisted largely of the application, presumably in Palestine, of similar expansionist techniques to the shorter text.

The fullest instance of the expansionist technique is, of course, the "Samaritan" recension of the Torah. This was complete in all its essentials by the beginning of the 2nd century B.C. at the latest, as 4Q paleoEx^m (early in that century) shows. As Cross, following W. F. Albright, has repeatedly emphasized, the actual branching off of the Samaritan sectarian textual tradition, as such, from this developing Palestinian type does not antedate the period of John Hyrcanus I toward the end of that same century. In the standard Hebrew text of Exodus 36-39 we have what may be one of the earliest manifestations of this expansionist mentality, and one which, apart from the Greek tradition, has won universal acceptance. Whatever God tells Moses to have done, it must be said explicitly that the Israelites actually did at Moses' bidding, normally in the same order and in the same detail; this is the rationale for the chapters in question.

Of the tendency for a sacred text transmitted in Palestine in the period between the Exile and the first century A.D. to grow by accretion and reworking on the basis of its own integral logic, so that the form becomes expanded but the substance remains the same, we may see other instances in the editorial process that has given us the book of Ezekiel, in the complete Qumran Hebrew scroll of Isaiah (1Q Is^a) and, independently, in the Septuagint form of that prophet. The underlying attitude is one of explicit reverence for a text regarded as sacred, an attitude of explaining (as we would put it) the Bible by the Bible in the very transmission of the text itself; but it is not the attitude of stern adherence to an unalterable Hebrew consonantal text that we meet with regularly after A.D. 70.

If this be a fair estimate of the evidence, what of the sound, tightly organized, unexpanded text of the Torah that stands in our Bibles? How has it not (except perhaps for the chapters of Exodus noted above) undergone the kind of development present in varying degrees in our other witnesses? Cross, in the article referred to, would root the Masoretic text of the Torah in a conservative Babylonian tradition, as he does for the books of Samuel. In any case, the received Hebrew text of the Torah appears again as an exceptional text, but this time, as an exceptionally good text.

With the recent publication of the Psalms scroll 11Q Ps^a and the non-Biblical materials which it contains, there will undoubtedly be a period of renewed speculation as to how far we can see the Psalter as a closed collection in the days of the Qumran community. Fr. J. Starcky is about to publish in the *Revue biblique* a collection of three non-biblical hymns, one of which is the "Apostrophe to Zion" of the cave 11 Psalter. Since these have been established as being part of a manuscript (4Q Ps^f) already known for the canonical Psalms 22, 107, and 109, the question will arise again there. With no special desire to press for an overly conservative answer to the question, the present writer will close this interim report by mentioning three small facts that seem to him to indicate dependence of the cave 11 Psalter on the complete collection of Psalms as we know it. One is that Psalm 133, which is detached from the group of "Songs of Ascents" in 11Q Ps^a, still retains the same title as the other Psalms of this group. A second is that Psalms 151A and B, compositions written for David on the basis of the text of Samuel, appear *after* the prose narrative about all David's compositions in the cave 11 collection (along with Pss. 140, 134, which in a reshuffling of the order may simply have been skipped at some earlier place). The third is that Psalm 146 stands in columns [i] -ii in 11Q Ps^a, and Psalm 145 in cols. xvi-xvii; yet after the 11Q text of Psalm 146:9 there stands an extra line based on Psalm 145:9 and 12.

The Contribution of
the Qumrân Discoveries to the Study of
the Biblical Text*

F. M. CROSS, Jr.

Harvard University

I.

THE most striking feature of the biblical manuscripts found in the vicinity of Qumrân is the diversity of their textual traditions. We refer, not to the multiplicity of individual variant readings within manuscripts nor to the variety of orthographic traditions in which copies of biblical works are inscribed, but to the plurality of distinct text types preserved.[1]

This plurality of textual families was not immediately manifest owing to the happenstance of discovery which directed attention first to the text of Isaiah at Qumrân. The two great scrolls from Cave I, together with the dozen or so fragmentary scrolls of Isaiah from Cave IV, proved on careful analysis to belong precisely to the Proto-Massoretic tradition, that is to the textual family from

---

* Address delivered on the occasion of the dedication of The Shrine of the Book, April 21, 1965.
[1] See most recently, F. M. Cross: The History of the Biblical Text in the Light of the Discoveries in the Judean Desert, *Harvard Theological Review* 57 (1964), pp. 281-299; S. Talmon: Aspects of the Textual Transmission of the Bible in the Light of the Qumrân Manuscripts, *Textus* 4 (1964), pp. 95-132; P. Wernberg-Moller: The Contribution of the *Hodayot* to Biblical Textual Criticism, *Textus* 4 (1964), pp. 133-175; P. W. Skehan: The Biblical Scrolls from Qumrân and the Text of the Old Testament, *BA* 28 (1965), pp. 87-100.

which our received text derived.[2] The text of Isaiah at Qumrân gave an important and unambiguous witness to the antiquity of the Proto-Massoretic tradition, and the several manuscripts illustrated vividly the range of variation and development within a textual family at home in Palestine in the last two centuries of the Second Commonwealth.[3]

Non-traditional text types were first recognized when study was directed to the biblical manuscripts of Cave IV. An excellent example is the text of Jeremiah. A Hasmonaean manuscript, 4QJer[b], contains the so-called short recension of Jeremiah,[4] a text type identical with that which underlies the Old Greek (Septuagint) translation. The latter is about one-eighth shorter than the received text. The Proto-Massoretic family is also represented at Qumrân, especially well in 4QJer[a], a manuscript from ca. 200 B.C.[5] Study of the two textual traditions in the light of the new data makes clear that the Proto-Massoretic text was expansionist, and settles an old controversy. Those who have defended the originality of the traditional text by arguing that the Greek translator abbreviated the Hebrew text before him are proved wrong. The Septuagint faithfully reflects a conservative Hebrew textual family. On the contrary, the Proto-Massoretic and Massoretic family is marked by editorial reworking and conflation, the secondary filling out of names and epithets, expansion from parallel passages, and even glosses from biblical passages outside Jeremiah.[6]

---

[2] The literature on the Isaiah scrolls is immense and growing; for recent discussions and bibliography, one may note the following: P. W. Skehan: The Qumrân Scrolls and Textual Criticism, *VT* Supplement IV (1957), pp. 148-160; H. M. Orlinsky: The Textual Criticism of the Old Testament, *The Bible and the Ancient Near East*, New York, 1961, pp. 113-132; F. M. Cross: *The Ancient Library of Qumrân*, New York, 2nd ed., 1961, pp. 177 ff. (hereafter *ALQ²*); J. Ziegler: Die Vorlage der Isaias—Septuaginta (LXX) und die erste Isaias-Rolle von Qumrân (IQIs[a]); *JBL* 78 (1959), pp. 34-59; S. Talmon: DSIs[a] as a Witness to Ancient Exegesis of the Book of Isaiah, *Annual of the Swedish Theological Institute* 1 (1962), pp. 62-72; E. Y. Kutscher: *The Language and Linguistic Background of the Isaiah Scroll* (Hebrew), Jerusalem, 1959; M. H. Goshen-Gottstein: Theory and Practice of Textual Criticism, *Textus* 3 (1963), pp. 130-158; and *The Book of Isaiah: Sample Edition with Introduction*, Jerusalem, 1965.

[3] On the Palestinian origin of the Proto-Massoretic text of Isaiah, Jeremiah, and certain other books, see below.

[4] A fragment of the poorly preserved manuscript is cited in Cross: *ALQ²*, p. 187, n. 38.

[5] On the script and date of this manuscript, see Cross: The Development of the Jewish Scripts, *The Bible and the Ancient Near East*, Fig. 1, line 5, and pp. 136-160. On the orthography of this manuscript, see D. N. Freedman: The Massoretic Text and the Qumrân Scrolls, A Study in Orthography, *Textus* 2 (1962), pp. 87-102.

[6] For detailed documentation, see the forthcoming Harvard dissertation on the two recensions of Jeremiah by Mr. J. G. Janzen. As instances of glosses from outside Jeremiah, he cites Jer. 28:16, 29:32, and 48:45-6 (all omitted in the Old Greek). In analyzing several categories of conflation in the

The text of Samuel found in three manuscripts from Cave IV is non-Massoretic. 4QSam[a], an extensively-preserved manuscript of ca. 50-25 B.C.,[7] contains a text-type closely related to the *Vorlage* of the Septuagint.[8] Its precise textual relationships can be defined even more narrowly. It is allied with the text of Samuel used by the Chronicler about 400 B. C. It is even more closely allied to the Greek text of Samuel used by Josephus, and surviving in a substratum of the Lucianic recension of the Septuagint. In short, its textual family is Palestinian, and corresponds to the Greek recension usually called Proto-Lucianic.[9] 4QSam[c], written by the same scribe who copied the *Sérek Hay-yáḥad* (1QS), preserves the same Palestinian text-type. The archaic manuscript of Samuel from Cave IV (4QSam[b]), dating from the third century B. C.,[10] belongs to an early stage of this Palestinian tradition.

Divergent textual families are represented also in the Pentateuch. A palaeo-Hebrew manuscript of Exodus (4QpalaeoEx[m]),[11] and a Herodian scroll of Numbers (4QNum[b])[12] present a textual tradition closely allied to the Samaritan, a Palestinian text-form characterized by wide-spread glosses, expansions from parallel passages, and like editorial activity.[13] We note that these textual traits of the Proto-Samaritan family are remarkably similar to those of the Proto-Massoretic (and Massoretic) text of such books as Jeremiah described above, and Isaiah, to be discussed below. In contrast to these expansionistic texts, however, the Massoretic text of the Pentateuch was remarkably short and conservative. One other manuscript may be cited to illustrate these deviant textual families found at Qumrân: 4QEx[a].[14] This Herodian exemplar stands

---

Massoretic tradition, Janzen concludes that 'in the number of expansions from parallel passages [in Jeremiah], M[assoretic] exceeds G[reek] by a ratio of 6:1'.

[7] On the dating, see Cross: The Development of the Jewish Scripts, Fig. 2, line 3, and pp. 166-181.

[8] See provisionally, F. M. Cross: A New Qumrân Biblical Fragment Related to the Original Hebrew Underlying the Septuagint, *BASOR*, 132 (1953), pp. 15-26; and the corrections in *JBL* 74 (1955), p. 165, n. 40.

[9] On the 'Proto-Lucianic' and Palestinian character of the text of Samuel at Qumrân, see the writer's detailed discussion: *Harvard Theological Review*, 57 (1964), pp. 292-299 (hereafter *HTR*).

[10] Cf. Cross: The Oldest Manuscript from Qumrân, *JBL* 74 (1955), pp. 147-172; and The Development of the Jewish Scripts, pp. 145-158, and Fig. 1, line 4.

[11] Parts of this manuscript, formerly labeled 4QEx[α], were published by P. W. Skehan: Exodus in the Samaritan Recension from Qumran, *JBL* 74 (1955), pp. 182-187.

[12] See provisionally, Cross: *HTR* 57 (1964), p. 287 and n. 27.   [13] Cf. the older studies of P. Kahle: Untersuchungen zur Geschichte des Pentateuchtextes, *Opera Minora* (1956), pp. 5-26; S. Talmon: The Samaritan Pentateuch, *Journal of Jewish Studies* 2 (1951), pp. 144-150; and the forthcoming Harvard dissertation by Bruce Waltke on the textual character of the Samaritan Pentateuch.   [14] See provisionally the fragment published in *ALQ*[2], Pl. opposite p. 141, and p. 184, n. 31.

very close to the Hebrew text used in Egypt by the Greek translator of the Septuagint.[15]

II.

The plurality of textual types from the Judean Desert fall into distinct families limited in number. Their diversity is not fluid or chaotic but conforms to a clear and simple pattern.[16] In the Pentateuch and Former Prophets, all textual traditions known from Qumrân and from the southern Judean Desert belong to three families. In the Latter Prophets only two families are extant. Moreover, none of these text-types is unknown. They have left their witnesses in textual traditions available before the discovery of the caves of Qumrân, in the received text, in the Septuagint and its recensions, in apocryphal Jewish works, in the New Testament, in the Samaritan Pentateuch, and in Josephus.

The Hebrew textual families have left clearest traces in the Greek Bible. We are able to trace a series of as many as three stages in the recensional history of the Septuagint before the emergence of the Massoretic text. The Old Greek preserves a non-traditional text-type which is represented at Qumrân, for example, by 4QEx[a] and especially 4QJer[b]. In the second or first century B. C., the Septuagint was revised in Palestine to conform to a Hebrew text then current, represented at Qumrân by the manuscripts of Samuel from Cave IV; this is the Proto-Lucianic recension of the Greek Bible best known, perhaps, from Josephus, and the special readings of a small group of Greek witnesses.[17] No

---

[15] 4QEx[a] also exhibits readings which are clearly 'Palestinian,' however, and we may observe that the Old Palestinian text of Exodus (i.e., the text of the fourth-third centuries B. C.) stood far closer to the *Vorlage* of the Septuagint than to the Samaritan text (*sensu stricto*). This is to be expected, however, if we are correct in describing the Egyptian text as a branch of the Old Palestinian, and if the recent analysis of Waltke is sound, showing that the Samaritan recension was influenced secondarily by the developed Massoretic tradition.

[16] Within a textual family, there is, if course, a considerable range of minor variation, especially in texts of an expansionist character. An example of 'minor variations' are those found in certain Palestinian texts owing to the introduction of new, so-called *plene* orthographic style in the Maccabaean and Hasmonaean periods, an innovation that affected only a part of the texts in this tradition (see below).

[17] The clearest witness to the Proto-Lucianic text actually is to be found in the sixth column of the Hexapla to 2 Sam.11:2-1; Kgs.2:11 (normally Theodothionic elsewhere). It is found as the substratum of the Lucianic Recension (hence 'Proto-Lucian') of Samuel-Kings, in the cursives boc₂e₂, in Joshua-Judges in the groups K gn dpt, and more faintly in the Pentateuch in the families gn dpt and (in Deuteronomy) θ. In the Former Prophets, especially, the Old Latin also is often a witness to the Proto-Lucianic recension. See the discussion with references to the literature in the writer's paper in *HTR* 57 (1964), pp. 292-297.

later than the beginning of the first century A. D., portions of the Greek Bible were revised a second time, this time to the Proto-Massoretic text. This Greek recension, called Proto-Theodotian or καίγε, is extensively preserved in a manuscript of the Minor Prophets from the Naḥal Ḥever.[18] In Jeremiah its text-type is preserved in Hebrew in 4QJerᵃ, in Greek in the supplementary additions to the Old Greek. In Samuel-Kings it has replaced the Old Greek in most witnesses in the section II Samuel 11:2-I Kings 2:11 and in II Kings.[19] These three stages in the history of the Greek Bible, the Old Greek, the Proto-Lucianic recension, and the καίγε recension reflect in turn the three families of the Hebrew text isolated in the finds at Qumrân.[20] If one distinguished the fully developed Massoretic text from the Proto-Massoretic, a fourth stage may be discerned, represented by the Hebrew text-type found, for example, at Murabba'ât and Maṣada, reflected in Greek in the revision of the καίγε recension prepared by Aquila in ca. 130 A. D.

III.

Any reconstruction of the history of the biblical text before the establishment of the traditional text in the first century A. D., must comprehend this evidence: the plurality of text-types, the limited number of distinct textual families, and the homogeneity of each of these textual families over several centuries of time. We are required by these data, it seems to me, to recognize the existence of local texts which developed in the main centers of Jewish life in the Persian and Hellenistic age.[21]

---

[18] This manuscript has now been published by D. Barthélemy: *Les devanciers d'Aquila,* Leiden, 1963.

[19] Cf. Barthélemy, *op. cit.* (above, n. 18); Cross: *HTR* 57 (1964), pp. 281-299; and S. Jellicoe: *JAOS* 84 (1964), pp. 178-182.

[20] It need scarcely be said that these stages are not found for every book in the Hebrew Bible, either in Hebrew or Greek, and in the case of many books, especially those which became canonical late, never existed.

[21] A theory of local texts was adumbrated by W. F. Albright in his study, New Light on Early Recensions of the Hebrew Bible, *BASOR* 140 (1955), pp. 27-33. Against Albright, we should argue, however, that the local textual families in questions are not properly called 'recensions'. They are the product of natural growth or development in the process of scribal transmission, not of conscious or controlled textual recension. The steady accumulation of evidence from the Desert of Judah has enabled us to elaborate a 'general theory' and to document it in considerable detail. See the chapter on The Old Testament at Qumrân in *ALQ²*, and The History of the Biblical Text in *HTR* 57 (1964), pp. 281-299. A similar approach is presented in the forthcoming article of P.W. Skehan on Bible. Texts and Versions in the *New Catholic Encyclopedia,* and in the Harvard dissertation of J. D. Shenkel: *Chronology and Recensional Development in the Greek Text of Kings,* 1964.

We may sketch the history of the local texts as follows. Three textual families appear to have developed slowly between the fifth and first centuries B. C., in Palestine, in Egypt, and in a third locality, presumably Babylon. The Palestinian family is characterized by conflation, glosses, synoptic additions and other evidences of intense scribal activity, and can be defined as 'expansionistic'. The Egyptian text-type is often but not always a full text. In the Pentateuch, for example, it has not suffered the extensive synoptic additions which mark the late Palestinian text, but is not so short or pristine as the third or Babylonian family. The Egyptian and Palestinian families are closely related. Early exemplars of the Palestinian text in the Former Prophets, and Pentateuchal texts which reflect an early stage of the Palestinian tradition, so nearly merge with the Egyptian, that we are warranted in describing the Egyptian text-type as a branch of the Old Palestinian family. The Babylonian text-type when extant is a short text. Thus far it is known only in the Pentateuch and Former Prophets. In the Pentateuch it is a conservative, often pristine text, which shows relatively little expansion, and a few traces of revision and modernizing. In the books of Samuel, on the contrary, it is a poor text, marked by extensive haplography and corruption. While it is not expansionistic, it is normally inferior to the Old Palestinian tradition preserved in 4QSam[b], and often to the Egyptian despite the more conflate traits of the latter.[22] It is not without significance that the oldest manuscripts from Qumrân are uniformly of the Palestinian family, or rarely, of Egyptian provenience. The first appearance of what we term the Babylonian text-type appears in the Former Prophets in the Proto-Theodotionic (καίγε) recension of the Greek Bible, and at Qumrân not at all. The evidence is more complex in the Pentateuch, but I am now inclined to believe that genuine exemplars of the Babylonian text-form at Qumrân are exceedingly rare, and late in date.

The grounds for the localization of these textual families are both theoretical and specific. In the textual criticism of ancient works, it is an axiom that texts which develop over a long span of time in geographical isolation tend to

---

[22] Cf. the conclusions reached by the writer in his paper. The Oldest Manuscripts from Qumrân, pp. 165-172. A study of an additional column of this text will be published shortly.

[23] Several old manuscripts of Pentateuchal books have escaped the severe reworking that produced the late Palestinian or Proto-Samaritan text, e. g., the early Hasmonaean text of Genesis-Exodus (4Q Gen[a] = 4Q Ex[b]). However, in key readings these manuscripts sometimes display Palestinian or Egyptian readings. Perhaps their assigment to a textual family should be left *sub judice*. Earlier the writer had assigned them to the Proto-Massortic tradition.

develop special characteristics, corrupt or secondary readings, haplographies and expansions, recalculated numbers and chronologies, etc., as well as preserving a pattern of primitive readings. These traits and peculiarities are transmitted producing series of filiated readings which distinguish the family. In turn, when textual families are detected, each with a particular series of special readings or traits, it must be postulated that such textual families arose in separate localities, or in any case, in complete isolation. Distinct textual families take centuries to develop but are fragile creations. When manuscripts stemming from different textual traditions come into contact, the result is their dissolution into a mixed text, or the precipitation of textual crisis which results in recensional activity, and often in the fixing of a uniform or standard text.

Our new evidence for Hebrew textual families yields, on examination, specific grounds for assigning each tradition to a certain locality, to Egypt, to Palestine, and to Babylon. The Hebrew text-type which was used by the Alexandrian translators of the Septuagint may be attributed to Egypt. Supporting such an attribution is not merely the provenience of the Old Greek text. W. F. Albright has collected evidence of pre-Septuagintal Egyptian influence on the text of the Pentateuch and Former Prophets.[24] We have noted above that frequently the Egyptian text-type is closely allied with the Palestinian family, precisely the relationship which might have been posited of an Egyptian local text on *a priori* grounds. It should be said, however, that the range of agreement between the Egyptian and Palestinian text fluctuates rather widely in different biblical books. In the Pentateuch it is only in the earlier stages of the Palestinian text that there is a real convergence of the two traditions, suggesting that the Egyptian text separated relatively early, no later than the fourth century B. C., from the main Palestinian stream. In Samuel, the two families are much more closely related, suggesting that the archetype of the Egyptian text split off no earlier than the fourth century. In Jeremiah, on the other hand, the Egyptian text is to the farthest degree unrelated, requiring a special explanation, namely that the text of Jeremiah at home in Egypt derived from a time near or before the beginning of the special development of the Palestinian family, thus in the fifth or even the sixth century B. C. In Isaiah, or in certain of the later books, where the Egyptian tradition is virtually identical with the Palestinian, we are led to conclude that the Hebrew text underlying the Old

---

[24] See his discussion in *BASOR* 140 (1955), pp. 30-33.

Greek separated from the Palestinian quite late, or indeed that a Palestinian Hebrew manuscript was used for the Greek translation.

By far the majority of the Hebrew witnesses from Qumrân belong to the Palestinian family. The evidence for the identification of the Palestinian family is most easily delineated in Samuel. The three manuscripts of Samuel from Cave IV, while not directly filiated, contain a single textual tradition, known at Qumrân as early as the third century (4QSam[b]), the early first century B.C., (4QSam[c]), and in the late first century B. C., (4QSam[a]). The earliest distinctive witness to a text of the type of these manuscripts is found in the Chronicler. As has been shown elsewhere, the Chronicler, shortly after 400 B. C., cited a text of Samuel which stands in close agreement with the manuscripts of Qumrân, but, as is well known, sharply diverges from the received text.[25] In the second or early first century B. C., the same Palestinian text-form was used to revise the Septuagint: the Proto-Lucianic recension. Finally Josephus at the end of the first century A. D., made use of this Palestinian Greek recension in writing his *Antiquities.* The Proto-Massoretic tradition appears in no witness to the text of Samuel before the early first century A. D., and then in the second Palestinian recension of the Septuagint, 'Proto-Theodotion.' In the Pentateuch, the evidence is closely parallel. It has been observed that in the Chronicler's citations from the Pentateuch, his text stands closer to the Samaritan recension than to the Massoretic.[26] There can be little doubt, I believe, that he utilized the prevailing Palestinian text. At Qumrân two stages of the Palestinian text are represented, an early form and the Proto-Samaritan form, the former standing closer to the *Vorlage* of the Septuagint, the latter more expansive including long synoptic interpolations found also in the Samaritan Pentateuch. The Samaritan Pentateuch, as we have shown elsewhere, derives from the Palestinian family, separating from the common Palestinian not earlier than the Hasmonaean era.[27] Other witnesses to this non-traditional, Palestinian textual family are scattered through Jewish apocryphal works and the New Testament. An especially useful example is the book of Jubilees. In its scriptural cita-

---

[25] See Cross: *ALQ²,* pp. 188 f. and n. 40a; *HTR* 57 (1964), pp. 292-297; and the forthcoming paper of Werner Lemke: The Synoptic Problem in the Chronicler's History, *HTR* 58 (1965), pp. 349-363.

[26] Cf. G. Gerleman: *Synoptic Studies in the Old Testament,* Lund, 1948, pp. 9-12, and especially S. Talmon: *op. cit.* (above, n. 13), pp. 146-150.

[27] See Cross: The Development of the Jewish Scripts, p. 189, n. 4; and the Harvard dissertation of J. D. Purvis: *The Samaritan Pentateuch and the Origin of the Samaritan Sect,* 1964, shortly to be published in monograph form; and Cross: *HTR* 59 (1966), pp. 201-211.

tions,[28] it regularly sides with the Septuagint and the Samaritan (most often with the former), and in its readings in common with the Massoretic text, it is regularly joined by the Samaritan. This is, of course, precisely the pattern of the earlier forms of the Palestinian text. Charles in his analysis of the biblical text used by the author of Jubilees notes also its frequent alignment with the Syriac Bible.[29] This datum is also significant since in the Former Prophets and in the Pentateuch, the Syriac is often a witness to Palestinian readings.

A word may be said about the orthography and script used in manuscripts of the Palestinian textual family.

Hasmonaean and Herodian exemplars of the Palestinian family often exhibit a *plene* style of orthography, far fuller than that we are accustomed to in the Massoretic text. The introduction of this new style[30] began sporadically in the third century, but was developed systematically in the Maccabaean era, and reached its most extreme form in the Hasmonaean age. The extreme, or baroque phase of the style is often associated with archaizing or, most often, pseudo-archaic grammatical forms. The best known text in this style is, of course, the great Isaiah scroll (1QIs^a). The extreme form of the style is, however, relatively rare. In its milder, dominant form, it appears regularly in texts inscribed in the Palaeo-Hebrew script, and in modified form is the style surviving in the Samaritan Pentateuch. The emergence of the style is most likely to be attributed to the literary activity which attended the nationalistic revival of the Maccabaean Age.

All manuscripts, so far as I am aware, inscribed in the new Palestinian orthography contain a text-type which on other grounds must be called Palestinian.[31] The same is true of manuscripts written in the Palaeo-Hebrew character. Script and orthography thus may be useful clues in assigning texts to the Palestinian family. Of course, the great majority of our witnesses to the Palestinian text-form are not written in Palaeo-Hebrew script, and many in every period are inscribed, not in the new, or Maccabaean style but, in a more archaic, or archaizing orthography. We may cite again the Palestinian texts of the three

---

[28] See provisionally, R. H. Charles: *The Book of Jubilees*, Oxford, 1902, pp. xxxiii-xxxix, for analysis of the textual affinities of Ethiopic Jubilees.   [29] *Ibid.*
[30] Its primary trait is the use of *waw* to mark *ō* derived from etymological *ā*. Earlier orthographies restricted the use of *waw* to signify *ū*, and later *ō* derived from the diphthong *-aw*. See Cross and Freedman: *Early Hebrew Orthography*, New Haven, 1952, pp. 69 f.; and D. N. Freedman: *Textus* 2 (1962), pp. 87-102.   [31] We cannot agree with the view of W. F. Albright: *BASOR* 140 (1955), pp. 29 f., that the text of 1QIs^a is Babylonian.

Samuel manuscripts from Cave IV. 4QSam^b, the archaic Samuel, is written in an orthography which is not only defective, but which has no parallel after the fourth century B. C. Long-$\bar{o}$ is marked by *waw* only when it derives ethmologically from the diphthong *-aw*.[32] Massoretic orthography is typologically much more developed and hence later. 4QSam^c is inscribed in the baroque new style, replete with such forms as *hw'h* and *mw'dh*. 4QSam^a, from the early Herodian period is written in the standard form of the new orthography.

The third or Babylonian textual family cannot be localized on the basis of direct evidence. We have described its traits which are very different from those of the Palestinian and Egyptian textual families, and have noted that it has appeared so far only in the Pentateuch and in the Former Prophets, and then only in relatively late witnesses. Texts of this family are never found inscribed either in Palaeo-Hebrew script or in the new orthography developed in Palestine in the Maccabaean Era. Its orthographic tradition is not especially early, however, deriving in the main from orthographic usage which was first established in the third century B. C., and which continued to be widely used until the end of the Second Commonwealth.

The assignment of the family to Babylon rests on several lines of argument. It is a distinctive text-type, distant from both the Egyptian and Palestinian families. It must have arisen in isolation. On the one hand it cannot have arisen in a late eclectic recension to judge from the pattern of its superior readings (especially in the Pentateuch). This would be too much to ask of the text-critical skills of the Rabbis. On the other hand, it is not a text drawn from a single or several old manuscripts, so archaic as to escape or predate the development of the Palestinian and Egyptian families. It is a text-type with a long independent history to judge from its special set of secondary readings (especially in Samuel-Kings).[33] Since we know well the textual families of Palestine and Egypt, we must look elsewhere for its locale, most naturally to Babylon. Further, examination of the Palestinian witnesses to the text at Qumrân and in citations in Palestinian Jewish literature in no way prepares us for the sudden

---

[32] Occasionally very archaic orthographic practices appear in 4QSam^b. An example is the 'pre-Exilic' use of *he* for the 3.m.s. suffix *-ô* (<-uh <uhu), found in the following reading in 1 Sam. 20:38: *ᶜlmh*, LXX τοῦ παιδαρίου αὐτοῦ, revised in MT to *hnᶜr*.

[33] James D. Shenkel has shown (see above, n. 21) that in one section of the chronology of the Kingdom, the Egyptian and Palestinian tradition is based on one set of calculations, the Massoretic and Proto-Massoretic on another, the latter demonstrably secondary. The secondary system first appears in Kings in the καίγε recension, in our extant witnesses.

emergence of this text-type as a signifiant, much less dominant or standard text. Its choice in the time of Hillel as the textual base of a new revision of the Septuagint is the first hint of its coming importance. By the end of the first century A. D., it has become dominant, or in any case standard, to judge from its exclusive use in the texts from Maṣada, Murabbaᶜât, and the Naḥal Ḥever. The simplest explanation of these data, it seems to me, is found in placing the development of this text-type in Babylon during the interval between the fifth century and the second century B. C., and to fix the time of its reintroduction into Palestine no earlier than the Maccabaean period, no later than the era of Hillel.

IV.

Before sketching the history of the biblical text from the time of its separation into textual families until the establishment of the Massoretic recension, it will be useful to analyze briefly an alternate theory of the development of the biblical text. This is the view which attempts to explain the complex data we have presented in terms of a distinction between a standard text and vulgar texts. In application, the Massoretic text is deemed 'standard', all non-traditional text-types 'vulgar'.

I have often argued that the terms *standard* and *vulgar* are anachronistic. Both imply that a standard exists, either that authorities have designated one text-type as standard, or to say the same thing, that an official recension has been promulgated. But this is precisely not the case in the period under discussion. There is no tendency toward the stabilization of the text at Qumrân, no drift toward the traditional text. Indeed neither in the Palestinian Greek witnesses nor in the citations of Jewish works composed in this era is there any evidence earlier than the time of Hillel that the recensional activities had begun which would ultimately establish an authoritative text.

Let us suppose, however, that our analysis is wrong, and that a standard text did exist in Palestine alongside vulgar text types over these early centuries. What kind of picture emerges? As for the Pentateuch and the Former Prophets, we must say that no one used the standard text. The Chronicler used a vulgar text in the composition of his history. The author of Jubilees ignored the standard text. Palestinian revisers of the Greek translation chose, not the standard Hebrew text but the vulgar for their important labours. The Zadokite priests[34]

---

[34] Cf. Cross: *BA* 26 (1963), p. 121.

of Samaria chose the vulgar text for their official recension. . . *mirabile dictu*. From a text-critical point of view, it is even more extraordinary that the standard text exercised no influence on the vulgar text. That there was no mixing, no contact, could be explained only, I believe, if the 'standard' text were the property of a tiny cabal, secretly preserved, copied, and nourished. Moreover, even if all this were true, we should have to ask, why do the vulgar texts fall into two distinct, homogeneous families?—that is, if one wishes to dispose entirely of resort to an explanation in terms of local texts. Such a picture of the textual situation can only be described as bizarre, and we are left wondering why the little circle who hid the standard text away for these centuries suddenly decided to publish it.

Perhaps there are other grounds upon which we may legitimately label Massoretic or Proto-Massoretic texts 'standard', non-traditional text-forms 'vulgar'. Our criterion might be one particular characteristic of the text itself. Since the Pentateuch and Former Prophets in the received text are clearly short texts, perhaps we may discover here a valid criterion to distinguish the standard from the vulgar text-forms. As is well-known, the Alexandrian grammarians based their recension of Homer on the principle of the superiority of the short reading. While haplography also produces short readings, and the text of Samuel is demonstrably defective by reason of extensive haplography, there can be no denying that the received text of the Pentateuch is a marvelously compact and well-preserved text, from the point of view of the modern textual critic. The difficulty arises when we look at the received text outside the Pentateuch and the Former Prophets. The traditional texts of Isaiah, Jeremiah and Ezekiel, for example, are notoriously expansionistic, marked by conflations, readings added from parallel passages, and harmonizing. The Egyptian text of Jeremiah and 4QJer[b] contains a text tradition which is drastically shorter as well as far superior to the Massoretic text. Indeed the texts of these books possess all the expansionistic traits charateristic of the 'vulgar' (Palestinian) textual family. This is true of the Proto-Massoretic texts of Isaiah, Jeremiah, and Ezekiel at Qumrân; it is also true of the developed Massoretic texts of these books.[35] In short, the criterion cannot be sustained.

---

[35] It may be observed that the Proto-Massoretic text of 1QIs[a], and the Egyptian Hebrew text underlying the Septuagint, often go beyond the other Proto-Massoretic texts of Qumrân, as well as the Massoretic text in the extent of their expansionistic character (cf. P. W. Skehan: *VT* Supplement IV [1957], p. 152). However, the expansions, happily, are not always the same as those in MT, and we are given some control of the additions, double readings, etc., in the Massoretic text.

The criteria of orthographic or linguistic development have occasionally been used to ferret out 'vulgar' text forms. It is true that the Rabbis chose an orthographic and linguistic tradition which by-passed the innovations of Maccabaean orthography, and the archaizing and modernizing features preserved in this orthography. But as we have seen, Proto-Massoretic manuscripts may appear in late orthography, non-traditional manuscripts in the most archaic. The same must be said for late or early, archaic or modernizing grammatical forms. It was probably the choice of the Pentateuch text which established orthographic principles for the remainder of the Bible, not the selection of an orthographic tradition which determined the choice of text.

These criteria will not justify the use of the distinction *standard/vulgar* in describing the text-forms later to be selected and established as the Massoretic recension. This is because no one textual family was selected by the Rabbis or scribes when the era of textual crisis and recension arrived. In the Pentateuch, a Babylonian, or in any case, non-Palestinian textual tradition was chosen, in the Latter Prophets a Palestinian.

v.

If we put together all the evidence now at hand, woven together, to be sure, with occasional skeins of speculation, I believe that the history of the biblical text can be outlined as follows. Sometime in the Persian period, probably in the fifth century B.C., local texts began to diverge and develop in Palestine and Babylon. Certainly the Priestly edition of the Tetrateuch and the Deuteronomic edition of the Former Prophets cannot antedate the late sixth century B.C. Presumably the local texts stem from copies of the Law and Former Prophets whose literary complexes had come into final form in Babylon in the sixth century, and which were then brought back to Palestine. The traditions concerning the text of Ezra may reflect these circumstances.[36] In any case we must project the 'archetype' of all surviving local texts of these books roughly to the time of the Restoration.

In the early fourth century, the Chronicler used an early form of the developing Palestinian text, and sometime about this time the Egyptian text of the

---

[36] See D. N. Freedman: The Law and Prophets, *VT* Supplement IX (1962), pp. 250-265. With possible exception of the short text of Jeremiah, we know no evidence of the survival of Exilic editions of a biblical work surviving independently in Palestine.

Pentateuch broke off from the Old Palestinian text, to begin its independent development. The separation of an Egyptian text of Jeremiah was probably earlier, that of the text of the Former Prophets rather later. Meanwhile in Babylon the third of the incipient textual families was developing, continuing in isolation until its reintroduction into Palestine, perhaps in the Maccabaean era when longings for Zion and Parthian expulsions coincided to bring large numbers of the Jews to Palestine, or perhaps later in the second or first century B. C. At all events, the Babylonian textual family was not selected for the early (Proto-Lucianic) revision made in the second or early first century B. C. It was taken up in the Proto-Theodotionic reworking of the Old Greek translation prepared in Palestine at the beginning of the first century A. D.

Probably the Proto-Theodotionic recension of the Old Greek coincided with earliest recensional endeavours on the Hebrew text of the Pentateuch and Prophets. In any case between the era of Hillel and the first Jewish Revolt the Massoretic text came into being. The principles which guided the scholars who prepared the recension were unusual. The recension was not characterized by wholesale revision and emendation, nor by eclectic or conflating procedures. Nor was a single, local textual family chosen. In the Pentateuch the current Palestinian text-type was rejected, and along with it the Palaeo-Hebrew script and orthographic innovations that marked certain of its exemplars. Rather the conservative, superb text of Babylonian origin, recently introduced into Palestine, was selected for the standard text. In the Former Prophets, the same pattern was followed, a Babylonian text was chosen, despite the existence of the superior Old Palestinian textual family. Presumably the pattern was set by the selection of the Pentateuch. In the Latter Prophets, the scholars shifted textual families. In these books a Palestinian text was chosen, perhaps because Babylonian texts were not available. However that may be, the orthographic type chosen was not the new *plene* style common in many Palestinian manuscripts beginning in Maccabaean times.

The process of recension was basically one of selecting traditions deriving from two old textual families available in Palestine in the first century A. D.

There was some leveling through, not always successful, of the conservative orthographic style chosen, and some revision, within narrow limits, was undertaken.[37] The process was not evolutionary or adventitious, but one of careful

---

[37] Cf. *ALQ²*, p. 191 and n. 45.

selection between sharply differing traditions. It was in short a systematic if not radical process of recension.

The promulgation of the new, standard recension evidently took place sometime near the mid-first century A. D. The text used to prepare the καίγε recension at the beginning of the century is Proto-Massoretic, not Massoretic. Readings which differ both from the older Greek, and from the developed Massoretic text are not few or insignificant, especially in Samuel and Kings. While the Proto-Massoretic text is well-known in many books at Qumrân, there is no exemplar of the Massoretic text, and no evidence of its influence. On the other hand, the Rabbinic recension appears to have been the accepted text in other circles by 70 A. D., and in the interval between the Jewish Revolts against Rome, became the reigning text in all surviving Jewish communities. Its victory was complete and rival textual traditions shortly died out, except as they were preserved frozen in ancient translations or survived in the text of an isolated sect such as the Samaritans.

LUCIAN AND PROTO-LUCIAN

TOWARD A NEW SOLUTION OF THE PROBLEM *

EMANUEL TOV

Much new material on the Septuagint revisions has been revealed recently through both archaeological finds and philological investigations. The present paper deals with one of these recently discovered revisions — the so-called proto-Lucianic revision. Since any analysis of this revision is by its very nature closely related to Lucian's revision, we shall first outline the three major opinions profferred on the nature of his revision and the essence of the MSS boc_2e_2.

From Ruth 4: 11 onwards, Lucian's revision is contained in boc_2e_2, as has been suggested by de Lagarde and corrected by Rahlfs. Our remarks, however, will be limited to the four books of Reigns since they have been the subject of the majority of investigations concerning Lucian's revision.

Alfred Rahlfs' thorough study *Lucian's Rezension der Königsbücher*, published in 1911 [1], formed the basis of the *communis opinio* on Lucian until the last two decades. Rahlfs described how, on the one hand, Lucian brought the Old Greek into conformity with the Hebrew, while, on the other hand, he removed the Old Greek from MT by freely revising its language and style. Rahlfs further realized that Lucian's fourth century revision reflects many ancient variants, which Rahlfs named proto-Lucianic since they are also to be found in various sources preceding Lucian by several centuries. We shall later return to these proto-Lucianic elements.

It was Rahlfs' great achievement to have described the three layers composing Lucian's text. As a rule, however, he underestimated the importance of proto-Lucianic elements [2], and his views doubtlessly need revision also in view of recent findings and studies.

* A paper read in the *IOSCS* section of the VIIth Congress of the *IOSOT* (Uppsala, August 7, 1971) and previously at the Biblical Symposium in Jerusalem (February 28, 1971). The writer wishes to express his thanks to Prof. I. L. Seeligmann for helpful comments and encouragement. I am also much indebted to Prof. F. M. Cross who has stimulated my interest in the problems discussed in this paper.

[1] *Septuaginta Studien* 3 (Göttingen 1911).
[2] Cf. P. L. HEDLEY, *HThR* 26 (1953) 69 : « Rahlfs has always admitted that Lucian may

A completely novel view of the nature of boc₂e₂ was suggested in
1963 by Père Barthélemy in his *Devanciers d'Aquila* ³. After describing the characteristics of the newly discovered *kaige* revision,
Barthélemy turned to a precise analysis of the second part of 2 Sam.
Barthélemy showed that in this section the main LXX MSS contain
the *kaige* revision, while the Old Greek, surprisingly enough, is found
in boc_2e_2. In order to prove this, Barthélemy showed that boc_2e_2
and the other MSS have a common basis, and he further demonstrated that the *kaige* revision revised the tradition embodied in
boc_2e_2 in conformity to the Hebrew. The details of Barthélemy's
views are too well-known to bear repeating.

It must be granted to Barthélemy that, as a rule, *kaige* is more
literal than boc_2e_2; but this situation does not necessarily imply
that *kaige* revised boc_2e_2. The relationship between *kaige* and boc_2e_2
could be viewed differently.

The following remarks should be made with regard to Barthélemy's
views:

1. His examples are selective and exclude those showing that
boc_2e_2 are more literal than *kaige*.

2. There is much internal evidence in boc_2e_2 indicating that they
contain a revision, even in the second part of 2 Sam ⁴.

3. Barthélemy's conclusions refer to the whole of the LXX, while
his investigation is limited to one section of Reigns.

4. Finally, Barthélemy dismisses the historical evidence concerning
Lucian's revisional activities with too much ease ⁵.

A third view of boc_2e_2 was proposed in 1964 by F. M. Cross, Jr. ⁶.
While working on the 4QSamᵃ manuscript, Cross realized that this
Hebrew source contains many proto-Lucianic readings ⁷. In light
of this new evidence, Cross suggested that boc_2e_2 are composed of
two different layers: a substratum containing a proto-Lucianic revision of the Old Greek towards a Hebrew text like 4QSamᵃ, and a
second layer containing the historical Lucian's corrections. Cross'

have used a Syrian text that differed from those current in other districts, but he has consistently depreciated the value of the recension ».
  ³ *SVT* 10 (1963).
  ⁴ Cf. especially S. P. BROCK, « Lucian *redivivus*, Some Reflections on BARTHÉLEMY'S
Les Devanciers d'Aquila », in F. L. CROSS (ed.), *Studia Evangelica* V (= *TU* 103) 176-181.
Cf. also Brock's unpublished dissertation quoted in n. 40.
  ⁵ Cf. F. M. CROSS, Jr., « The History of the Biblical Text in the Light of Discoveries in
the Judaean Desert », *HThR* 57 (1964) 295, n. 44.
  ⁶ *Ibid.*, 281-299.
  ⁷ Cross has published only a few examples of proto-Lucianic readings of 4QSamᵃ; the
complete text has yet to be published.

thesis has been elaborated by several of his students, mainly by Shenkel in his study on the books of Reigns [8].

While I agree with the position that boc_2e_2 are composed of two layers [9], I would question whether the substratum is indeed a proto-Lucianic *revision*. Has it really been established that this substratum was a revision rather than simply another Greek text? Why need one assume such a revision? If such an assumption is necessary to explain those elements in boc_2e_2 which approximate the LXX to MT, it must be pointed out that Lucian derived such elements mainly from the « Three » and the fifth column of the Hexapla, as Rahlfs has shown.

As a result of the above reflections and on the basis of my own study of Lucian and other ancient sources, I would like to propose a new working hypothesis on the nature of boc_2e_2. My suggestion is programmatic and tentative, based on pilot studies rather than on systematic investigations of all the sources involved. This work still remains to be done, and, in fact, many studies are needed to verify this working hypothesis.

Like Cross, I propose that boc_2e_2 in the books of Reigns are composed of two layers. The second layer is the historical Lucian, and I suggest that its substratum contained either *the* Old Greek translation or any Old Greek translation. We shall later return to this problem. Although one may continue to use the term proto-Lucianic (or pre-Lucianic) when referring to the elements of the Old Greek substratum, one should not assume a proto-Lucianic *revision* as such, since the existence of such an intermediary stage has not yet been proved. One could thus suggest that our proposal forms a compromise between the views of Barthélemy and Cross.

I should like to support the working hypothesis with the following five arguments:

1. — It has always amazed me that the text of boc_2e_2 is evidenced in so wide a range of sources, both before and after Lucian's supposed *floruit* (300). Of these sources, the proto-Lucianic are, of course, the most interesting. These include:

the Hebrew 4QSam[a] [10],

two so-called « proto-Lucianic » papyri, namely the Manchester

---

[8] J. D. SHENKEL, *Chronology and Recensional Development in the Greek Text of Kings* (Cambridge, Mass., 1968).

[9] The fact that diametrically opposed tendencies are visible in boc_2e_2 makes such an assumption very plausible.

[10] See F. M. CROSS, Jr., *op. cit.*

Pap. Ryl. Greek 458 of Deut. [11] and Pap. 2054 of Psalms,
the various fragments of the Vetus Latina [12],
the substratum of the Armenian translation [13],
the text quoted by Josephus [14],
the text quoted by Pseudo-Philo in his *Biblical Antiquities* [15],
the text quoted by various Church Fathers: Clemens of Alexandria [16], Theophilus of Antioch [17], Tertullian [18], Hippolytus [19], Cyprian [20] and Origen [21].

To these sources one should probably add the Coptic translation of the Greek [22] and possibly certain elements in the Peshitta [23].

Contrary to the beliefs of some scholars [24], I disagree with the opinion that the enumerated sources have been retouched by so-called « Lucianic revisers ». In some instances such an assumption is either impossible or close to impossible.

The list of sources which reflect the text of boc$_2$e$_2$ after the historical Lucian is equally large. It contains both the text quoted by

---

[11] Cf. the literature quoted by P. KAHLE, *The Cairo Geniza* [2] (Oxford 1959) 220-223 and in addition : J. HEMPEL, *ZAW* NF 14 (1937) 115-127; A. ALLGEIER, *Biblica* 19 (1938) 1-18; J. HOFBAUER, *ZKT* 62 (1938) 385-389.

[12] B. M. METZGER, *Chapters in the History of NT Criticism* (Leiden 1963) 31-32 mentions several studies on the relationship between Lucian and the Vetus Latina. See further : J. WELLHAUSEN, *Der Text der Bücher Samuelis* (Göttingen 1871) 221-224; H. VOOGD, *A Critical and Comparative Study of the Old Latin Texts of the First Book of Samuel, unpubl. diss.* Princeton 1947 (not accessible to me); R. THORNHILL, *JThSt* 10 (1959) 233-246; J. CANTERA, *Sefarad* 23 (1963) 252-264; id., « Puntos de contacto de la « Vetus Latina » con la recension de Luciano y con otras recensiones griegas », *Sefarad* 25 (1965) 69-72; cf. also Brock's dissertation mentioned in n. 40.

[13] Cf. B. JOHNSON, *Die armenische Bibelübersetzung als hexaplarischer Zeuge im 1. Samuelbuch* (Lund 1968) 158. In a paper read in the *IOSCS* section of the VIIth Congress of the *IOSOT* (Uppsala, August 8, 1971), Johnson further emphasized this feature of the Armenian translation.

[14] Cf. A. MEZ, *Die Bibel von Josephus* (Basel 1895); A. Rahlfs, *op. cit.*, 80 ff.; H. St. J. THACKERAY, *Josephus, The Man and the Historian* (1929; reprinted N. Y. 1967) 87 ff.

[15] Cf D. J. HARRINGTON, S. J., « The Biblical Text of Pseudo-Philo's *Liber Antiquitatum Biblicarum* », *CBQ* 33 (1971) 1-17.

[16] Cf. D. BARTHÉLEMY, *op. cit.*, 136 (*pace* A. Rahlfs, *op. cit.*, 118 ff.).

[17] Cf. A. RAHLFS, *op. cit.*, 114 ff.

[18] Cf. P. CAPELLE, *Le Texte du Psautier latin en Afrique* = *Collectanea biblica latina* IV (Rome 1913) 200 (*pace* A. Rahlfs, *op. cit.*, 138 ff.).

[19] A. RAHLFS, *op. cit.*, 123 ff.

[20] Cf. especially B. FISCHER, « Lukian-Lesarten in der Vetus Latina der vier Königsbücher », *Miscellanea biblica et orientalia R. P. Athanasio Miller oblata* = *Studia Anselmiana* XXVII-XXVIII (Rome 1951) 169-177; R. CAPELLE, *op. cit.*, 203-204.

[21] A. RAHLFS, *op. cit.*, 139 ff.; D. BARTHÉLEMY, *op. cit.*, 136 ff.

[22] Cf. J. B. PAYNE, « The Sahidic Coptic Text of I Samuel », *JBL* 72 (1953) 51-62; however, it is not certain whether the Old Coptic text is as early as Payne surmises (250 A. D.).

[23] Cf. the data collected by Th. STOCKMAYER, *ZAW* 12 (1892) 218-223; however, Stockmayer's conclusion, which is phrased in the title of his article (« Hat Lucian zur seiner Septuagintarevision die Peschito benützt? » : yes!), cannot be vindicated.

[24] See especially L. DIEU, « Retouches Luciniques sur quelques textes de la vieille version latine (I et II Samuel) », *RB* NS 16 (1919) 372-403.

various Church Fathers [25] and the text reflected in the Gothic, Sla-
vonic and so-called Syro-Lucianic translations of the LXX. Some
of these sources are undoubtedly based on Lucian, but in other cases
it has yet to be determined whether the post-Lucianic sources are
based on the ancient substratum of boc_2e_2 only or whether they
reflect the Lucianic text as a whole. This is especially true since some
of these sources are very close to Lucian's *floruit* and /or are not derived
from the area of Antioch.

It cannot be coincidental that so many diverse sources reflect a
proto-Lucianic text in the books of Reigns. The only logical solution
appears to be that all the above-mentioned sources reflect elements
of either *the* Old Greek translation or a single Old Greek translation
underlying Lucian's revision. The non-Lucianic MSS contain a different, and, sometimes later, text tradition. We shall later dwell on the
differences between boc_2e_2 and the non-Lucianic MSS.

2. — The studies dealing with the character of the assumed proto-
Lucianic revision stress that this revision generally left the Old Greek
unrevised [26]. This view is based upon a comparison of translation
options in boc_2e_2 and the Old Greek which shows that both have a
common vocabulary [27], on Shenkel's investigation of the identical
chronological systems of the two as opposed to the chronological
systems of MT and the *kaige* revision [28], and on the fact that both
traditions start the third book of Reigns at 1 Ki. 2: 11 [29]. But if the
assumed proto-Lucianic revision is so close to the Old Greek and
frequently left it unrevised, would it not be more fair to characterize
the substratum of boc_2e_2 as Old Greek rather than a proto-Lucianic
revision?

3. — It has been recognized by scholars [30] that the contents of the
Hexapla's sixth column in the second part of 2 Sam. are very close
to boc_2e_2. For Barthélemy the sixth column thus contains the Old
Greek, while the other MSS in that section contain the *kaige* revision.
For Cross it contains the proto-Lucianic revision « in relatively pure
form » [31]. Since in this section Origen placed the *kaige* revision in the
fifth column, it would be more understandable in our opinion for

---

[25] Asterius Sophista, Diodore of Tarse, Eustathius, Lucifer, Ambrose, Augustine, Theo-
dore of Mopsuestia, John Chrysostom, Theodoret, Jacob of Edessa.

[26] See especially J. D. SHENKEL, *op. cit.*

[27] *Ibid.*, 11 ff., 113 ff.

[28] *Ibid.*, *passim.*

[29] Cf. J. D. SHENKEL, *op. cit.*, 10 ff. and further section 2 of the appendix to this paper.

[30] Cf. e. g., D. BARTHÉLEMY, *op. cit.*, 128 ff.

[31] F. M. CROSS, Jr., *op. cit.*, 295.

the Hexapla's sixth column to contain the Old Greek than an unknown revision about which we possess no ancient records. Furthermore, a probable parallel is found in 2 Kings, where Burkitt suggested long ago that the *Quinta* contains the Old Greek [32]. One notes that, as in the second part of 2 Sam., the main MSS of 2 Ki. contain the *kaige* revision, and here, also, boc$_2$e$_2$ resemble one of the columns of the Hexapla, in this case the *Quinta*. However, the resemblance between boc$_2$e$_2$ on the one hand, and the sixth column on the other, has yet to be investigated in detail.

4. — In a recent article in *HThR* [33], Klein has rightly shown that the additions in the Greek Chronicles harmonizing the text with 2 Ki. reflect the textual tradition of boc$_2$e$_2$ rather than *kaige* [34]. This situation would seem to indicate that the translator of Chronicles, naturally enough, took the Old Greek text as his basis [35].

5. — In another recent article in *HThR* [36], Shenkel demonstrated that in the synoptic sections of Samuel and Chronicles the Greek Chronicles is based on the Old Greek of Samuel. He found that in the *kaige* sections there is a much greater agreement with boc$_2$e$_2$ of Samuel than in the non-*kaige* sections [37]. An analysis of Shenkel's data proves that in all sections the Greek Chronicles is based upon the Old Greek, which in the *kaige* sections is reflected in boc$_2$e$_2$.

We have adduced five arguments in favor of our working hypothesis that the substratum of boc$_2$e$_2$ contains *the* Old Greek or Old Greek elements. We therefore suggest that the study of boc$_2$e$_2$ should

---

[32] F. C. BURKITT, « The so-called Quinta of 4 Kings », *Proceedings of the Society of Biblical Archaeology* 24 (1902) 216-219.

[33] R. W. KLEIN, « New Evidence for an Old Recension of Reigns », *HThR* 60 (1967) 93-105.

[34] The alternative explanation that the historical Lucian harmonized the two Greek texts has been discussed by KLEIN and ALLEN in *HThR* 61 (1968) 483-495.

[35] This possibility, which seems to us the best explanation of the evidence, is rejected by Klein after some consideration : « This pre-*kaige* text, which served as the source for the Par supplements, could be either the Old Greek hitherto unknown, or, as seems more likely, the proto-Lucianic recension » (*ibid.*, 104).

[36] J. D. SHENKEL, « A Comparative Study of the Synoptic Parallels in I Paraleipomena and I-II Reigns », *HThR* 62 (1969) 63-85.

[37] According to Shenkel's statistics, 74 % of the words of 1 Par 17-18 agree with the OG of 2 Sam 7-8 (non-*kaige*) and 3 % disagree with the OG in favor of boc$_2$e$_2$ in that section. On the other hand, 56 % of the words in 1 Par 19 agree with the *kaige* MSS of 2 Sam 10 and 13 % disagree with the same MSS in favor of boc$_2$e$_2$. The amount of agreement between 1 Par 19 and the boc$_2$e$_2$ MSS in 2 Sam 10 is actually much greater than the numbers indicate: 1. the 56 % agreement between 1 Par 19 and the *kaige* MSS of 2 Sam 10 include many instances when *kaige* is identical with boc$_2$e$_2$; it would actually be more correct to state that in such cases 1 Par agrees with boc$_2$e$_2$ of 2 Sam 10 while the *kaige* revision has left the text unrevised. 2. The number of assumed agreements between 1 Par 19 and the Old Greek of 2 Sam 10 would have been larger than 13 % if the historical Lucian had not inserted his own revisions in boc$_2$e$_2$.

be founded on a new basis, different from that of previous research. The contents of boc_2e_2 should be studied anew, especially in the light of the proto-Lucianic sources. While the above-mentioned five arguments partially relied on studies which have already been published, few studies have seen light on which a renewed investigation of boc_2e_2 may rely. Therefore, I carried out some pilot studies, and it seems to me that an internal investigation of boc_2e_2 supports the working hypothesis which I have suggested.

When starting to elucidate the details of the working hypothesis in the light of the above-mentioned arguments, one will immediately discover that it is no easy task to define criteria for unraveling the three layers of which boc_2e_2 are composed, viz. the Old Greek substratum, Lucian's borrowings from the « Three » and the fifth column of the Hexapla, and Lucian's own corrections. Criteria have to be defined as to which elements belonged or could have belonged to any one of the three layers. In this respect one of the main problems is that certain characteristics of boc_2e_2 which scholars have always assigned to the historical Lucian were actually extant in Lucian's *Vorlage*. In a short and very instructive article, Father Bonifatius Fischer showed in 1951 (cf. n. 20) not only that the so-called Lucianic tendencies were already extant in the Vetus Latina, but also that the Vetus Latina — no doubt an early translation of the Old Greek — reflected some of these tendencies against boc_2e_2 and the other MSS of the LXX. In other words, additions of subjects, objects and names, changes between nouns and pronouns, short contextual additions, harmonistic additions, certain translation equivalents, several doublets, some linguistic changes and translations instead of transliterations [38] are not late Lucianic phenomena, but belonged to the very first stratum of the LXX. To these examples one may add several in which boc_2e_2 reflect the original Greek text which has been corrupted in all other MSS. And, last but not least, the most striking examples of proto-Lucianic elements are provided by those readings which reflect early variants. These variants, which can rather easily be pinpointed and which are of immense importance for Biblical scholarship, form the largest group of proto-Lucianic readings [39].

---

[38] Even though it appears illogical that original renderings would have been changed by a later hand to transliterations (mainly of unknown words), the present writer hopes to have established this process for some of the LXX revisers; see « Transliterations of Hebrew Words in the Greek Versions of the O. T. — A Further Characteristic of the *kaige*-Th. Revision? », *Textus* 8 (1971).

[39] Some categories of proto-Lucianic *readings* are exemplified in the appendix to this paper.

Since it can be proved that certain readings of boc₂e₂ were extant
in pre-Lucianic sources, one must consider the possibility that many
typologically similar readings were pre-Lucianic as well. This point
should not be overstressed, however, since it is not impossible that
in some cases the historical Lucian acted according to the same principles which guided the original translators.

In concluding this point, I should like to emphasize once again the
importance of the Vetus Latina and other pre-Lucianic sources in
pinpointing the ancient elements of boc₂e₂. It seems to me that an
investigation into the first stratum of boc₂e₂ is of primary importance
in solving the « riddle of boc₂e₂ ».

A second line of investigation will attempt to pinpoint readings
which the historical Lucian derived from the « Three » and from the
Hexapla's fifth column. This investigation is limited by its very nature
since Lucian's sources have been preserved only partially. From the
outset it is probable that the majority of the quantitative revisions
towards MT are derived from the « Three » of the fifth column, but
again on this point one should be cautious. The second category of
proto-Lucianic readings in the appendix shows that some of Lucian's
quantitative revisions may already have been found in his Greek
Vorlage.

Much research has to be done on the changes which Lucian himself
introduced. One immediately thinks of several Atticistic changes
such as the replacement of Hellenistic forms as εἶπαν and ἐλάβοσαν
with εἶπον and ἔλαβον, λήμψει with λήψει and of the change of the
passive aorist ἐγενήθη to the middle aorist ἐγένετο. [40].

Lucian probably also introduced certain stylistic corrections, such
as the insertion of synonymous words. However, much investigation
remains to be done in this field as well; a comparative study of trans-
ation equivalents in the different sections and MSS of the LXX
should determine which boc₂e₂ synonyms were introduced by Lucian
and which belonged to the old substratum. In this respect also, the
Vetus Latina and other pre-Lucianic sources are of help [41].

I must end my paper with an open question. I have suggested
that the substratum of boc₂e₂ contains either *the* Old Greek transla-

[40] After I finished writing this paper, I had the opportunity to read S. P. Brock's unpublished dissertation, *The Recensions of the Septuagint Version of I Samuel* (Oxford 1966).
In this pioneering and thorough study, Brock discusses several Atticizing and stylistic
changes by the historical Lucian.

[41] For example, of the few stylistic changes which Brock assigned to Lucian in his article
mentioned in n. 4, two are already evidenced in the Vetus Latina (cf. the translations of
שלום in 2 Sam. 11: 7 and of חי in 2 Sam. 11: 11).

tion or any single Old Greek translation. The non-Lucianic MSS contain the *kaige* revision in two sections in the books of Reigns, and in three sections they reflect a text which is usually described as the Old Greek. My suggestion poses few problems in the *kaige* sections: here *the* Old Greek is contained in the substratum of boc_2e_2, while *kaige* and the second stratum of boc_2e_2 reflect later corrections of this old substratum [42]. However, how should one explain the relationship between boc_2e_2 and the other MSS in the non-*kaige* sections? It appears to me that in these sections we should continue to characterize all non-Lucianic MSS as the Old Greek. But in the instances in which boc_2e_2 deviate from the other MSS I suggest a modification of the general opinion on the latter MSS for which I consider two alternatives:

1. — In his publication of 4QLXX Lev[a] [43], Monsignor Skehan has shown that in many details the Qumran fragment reflects the Old Greek, while all extant MSS have been retouched. This situation shows how little one should trust the MSS of the LXX, especially when they reflect MT literally. In the historical books there obtains a situation which parallels the problem raised by 4QLXX Lev[a]: whenever the boc_2e_2 reading is at variance with MT or renders it freely, the reading found in the remainder of the MSS, as a rule, agrees with MT, and could thus represent a later revision. In other words, in the non-*kaige* sections the substratum of boc_2e_2 *always* represents the Old Greek, while the other MSS *as a rule* reflect the Old Greek, but *at times* their text has been retouched.

2. — As an alternative possibility it may be suggested that both the boc_2e_2 reading and the one found in the other MSS represent two parallel Old Greek traditions.

Since the relationship between the readings of boc_2e_2 and that of the other MSS may, as a rule, be described as that between an original and its revision, one may prefer the first possibility. However, at the present state of knowledge of the proto-Septuagint question it is hard to solve this problem. I have therefore characterized the substratum of boc_2e_2 as containing either *the* Old Greek or any Old Greek translation. The latter possibility allows for the existence of other Old Greek translations.

---

[42] Since there is no doubt that boc_2e_2 and the other MSS of the LXX are genetically interrelated in all sections of the books of Reigns, it is likely that the *kaige* revision was based upon the Old Greek substratum of boc_2e_2. However, it has yet to be determined whether this substratum of boc_2e_2 was identical with the assumed *Vorlage* of *kaige* or whether one should posit two closely-related Old Greek traditions (OG[1] and OG[2]).

[43] P. W. Skehan, *SVT* 4 (1957) 148-160.

In conclusion, I propose that the existence of a proto-Lucianic revision of the LXX has not been established. I further suggest that the substratum of boc₂e₂ contains either *the* Old Greek or any single Old Greek translation. It should perhaps be noted that the correctness of the first suggestion does not hold any implication for the validity of the second.

APPENDIX

Some categories of proto-Lucianic readings reflected in boc₂e₂ in the books of Reigns.

1. <u>Proto-Lucianic variants</u> ($\neq$ MT) — the majority of the proto-Lucianic readings belong to this section.

2 Sam. 13:3	MT	יונדב
	4QSamᵃ	[י]הונתן
	boe₂ Syrᴶ (txt)	Ἰωναθαν
	B*a₂	Ἰωναδαμ
	Bᵃ⁽ᵛⁱᵈ⁾ᵇ AMN rell Arm Co Eth Thdt	Ἰωναδαβ
	Jos. *Ant.* VII, 178	Ἰωναθης
	(cf. F. M. Cross, *HThR* 57 (1964) 294)	

2 Sam. 18:2	MT	וישלח דוד
	boz(mg)c₂e₂	καὶ ἐτρίσσευσε Δαυειδ (וישלש דוד)
	LXX (rell)	καὶ ἀπέστειλεν Δαυειδ
	Laᵛ·²	et tripartitum fecit

2. boc₂e₂ = La = MT $\neq$ LXX — the historical Lucian could have derived these readings from the « Three » or the Hexapla's fifth column, but since they are reflected in La, they may have been original.

I Sam. 1:6	MT	בעבור הרעמה
	boghe₂ Chr(vid)	διὰ τὸ ἐξουθενεῖν αὐτήν
	LXX (rell)	om.
	Laᵛ	quia ad nihilum reputabat eam

2 Ki. 17:21	MT	קרע
	borc₂e₂	ἐρράγη
	LXX (rell)	om.
	La Cypr	dissipatus est

3. Ancient doublets

1 Sam. 16:14	MT	ובעתתו
	boc$_2$e$_2$ Syr^J	συνεῖχεν ... καὶ ἔπνιγεν αὐτόν
	LXX (rell)	ἔπνιγεν αὐτόν
	La^v	comprehendit ... et soffoca-bat eum

Cf. further B. Fischer, « Lukian-Lesarten... », 177.

4. boc$_2$e$_2$ reflect the OG from which the corrupt text form of the other MSS has developed

1 Sam 9:24	MT	לאמר העם
	Nabe-osvwyz(mg)b$_2$c$_2$e$_2$(txt) Syh^J (mg) Thdt	παρὰ τοῦ λαοῦ (מאת העם)
	B	παρὰ τοὺς ἄλλους
	A	παρὰ τοῦ α͞ου
	La^b = boc$_2$e$_2$	(acc. to Brooke-McLean; Belsheim's edition was not available to me)

1 Sam. 10:2	MT	בגבול
	bioc$_2$e$_2$	ἐν (τοῖς) ὁρίοις
	gv	τῷ ὁρίῳ
	LXX (rell)	ἐν τῷ ὄρει
	La^{bv}	in finibus

1 Ki 18:32	MT	תעלה
	oc*$_2$e	θααλα
	bz(mg)c$_2^a$?	θαλαα
	dip	θαλααν
	LXX (rell)	θάλασσαν

5. boc$_2$e$_2$ contain a translation while the other MSS contain a transliteration

2 Sam. 17:29	MT	שפות בקר
	a(mg)bgoz(mg)c$_2$e$_2$ Arm	γαλαθηνὰ μοσχάρια
	LXX (rell)	σαφωθ βοῶν (or sim.)
	La^b	vitulos saginatos

La^v lactantes vitulos

Clem. Alex. I, 98   μοσχάρια γαλαθηνά

Cf. further B. Fischer, « Lukian-Lesarten... », 176.

6. boc$_2$e$_2$ add subjects or objects (these additions could reflect variants)

1 Sam. 10:23	MT	om.
	bhoxb$_2$c$_2$e$_2$ Co	Σαμουηλ
	LXX (rell)	om.
	La^{bv}	Samuel
1 Ki. 21:20	MT	om.
(20:20)	bioc$_2$e$_2$	'Ηλιας
	LXX (rell)	om.
	La^{Luc}	Helias

Cf. further B. Fischer, « Lukian-Lesarten... », 176.

7. Contextual additions (these additions could reflect variants)

1 Sam. 30:15	MT	om.
	Mbgioy^{b}za$_2$c$_2$e$_2$ Arm	καὶ ὤμοσεν αὐτῷ
	LXX (rell)	om.
	La^v	et iuravit ei David
1 Sam. 9:3	MT	om.
	bdghiopc$_2$e$_2$	καὶ ἀνέστη Σαουλ καὶ παρέλαβεν ἕν τῶν παιδαρίων τοῦ πατρὸς αὐτοῦ μετ' αὐτοῦ καὶ ἐπορεύθη ζητεῖν τὰς ὄνους Κις τοῦ πατρὸς αὐτοῦ
	LXX (rell)	om.
	Peshitta	וקם שאול ואזל ודבר עמה לחד מן טליא למבעא אענא דאבוהי

8. The internal division of the books of Reigns

In the following sources III Reigns starts at 1 Ki. 2:12:
boc$_2$e$_2$ Vat. Syr. 162 (cf. A. Rahlfs, *Septuaginta-Studien* III,

16, n. 1), Jos. *Ant. Jud.* (book VII includes 1 Ki. 1:1 — 2:11), Diod, Thdt, Syr^J. Cf. further A. RAHLFS, *ib.*, 186 ff.

9. Translation technique

1 Sam. 9:27	MT	(ב)קצה
	b'b(txt)oz(mg)c₂e₂ Arm	ἄκρον
	LXX (rell)	μέρος
	La^b	in loco summo

2 Sam. 11:7	MT	(וישאל דוד) לשלום יואב ולשלום העם ולשלום המלחמה
	boc₂e₂	εἰ ὑγιαίνει 'Ιωαβ καὶ εἰ ὑγιαίνει ὁ λαὸς καὶ εἰ ὑγιαίνει ὁ πόλεμος
	LXX (rell)	εἰς εἰρήνην 'Ιωαβ καὶ εἰς εἰρήνην τοῦ λαοῦ καὶ εἰς εἰρήνην τοῦ πολέμου
	La^b	recte est Joab et recte est populus et recte est exercitus belli

1 Sam. 4:4	MT	ישב הכרבים
	boza^?c₂e₂	οὗ ἐπεκάθητο τὰ Χερουβιμ
	LXX (rell)	καθημένου Χερουβειμ
	La^bv	ubi sedebat in cherubin

10. Grammatical changes

1 Sam. 1:19	MT	וישתחוו ... ויבאו
	boc₂e₂	προσεκύνησαν ... καὶ ἐπορεύθησαν
	LXX (rell)	καὶ προσκυνοῦσι ... καὶ πορεύονται
	La^v	adoraverunt ... abierunt

1 Sam. 2:25	MT	ואם
	bozc₂e₂ Syr^J Or Chr	ἐὰν δε
	LXX(rell)	καὶ ἐάν
	La^v Cypr	si autem

The Hebrew University, Jerusalem.   Emanuel Tov.

The Evolution of a Theory of Local Texts

Frank Moore Cross
Harvard University

The primary focus of interest in the present essay is upon questions of Greek recensions in the books of Reigns. I wish, however, to
introduce my discussion by reviewing the data on divergent Hebrew text
types garnered largely from the discoveries in the Wilderness of Judah.
One cannot overstress the importance of this new knowledge of Hebrew textual traditions, each with its own integrity and special characteristics,
for the discussion of Greek recensions. Nor can one forget the long-time
impasse between what we may call translation theories and recension theories devised to explain the origins and development of the Greek Bible.
So long as the history of the Hebrew text remained obscure, no consensus
was gained in the study of text forms of the Greek Bible. In the books
of Samuel, the effective use of the Greek Bible in the reconstruction of
the Hebrew text declined from the publication of Wellhausen's dissertation (1871)[1] until it reached a nadir in the textual studies of P. A. H.
de Boer.[2] Even the discovery of the Dodekapropheton from the *Naḥal Ḥéber*
and its publication and brilliant analysis by Father Barthélemy did not
convince all Septuagint specialists that the major strata in the manuscripts of the Greek Bible consisted primarily of an Old Greek translation and a series of recensions of that translation. No small part of
the intransigence of such scholars stemmed from the anachronistic assumption that a single Hebrew textual tradition prevailed throughout the interval of the development of the Greek Bible. In fact we must deal with a
complex history of Hebrew textual traditions before the emergence of the
recension which lies at the base of the Massoretic text in the course of
the first century of the Christian era. The history of the Hebrew text
parallels precisely the history of the Old Greek translation, and its recensions. Each sequence or development in one has its reflex in the other
and furnishes data to date the parallel sequence. Any theory of the development of the history of the Greek text must comprehend the data supplied
by both the history of the Hebrew text and the history of the Greek text

if it is to be adequate. To deal exclusively with one or the other or
primarily with one or the other is to court or create too simple or asym-
metrical solutions and hypotheses.

 1. The publication of the great Isaiah Scroll of Cave 1, Qumrân ɪ
in 1950 gave us our first glimpse at a Palestinian text of Isaiah of the
mid-second century B.C.[3] Cave 4, Qumrân has provided an additional fifteen fragmentary manuscripts to the two exemplars from Cave 1. These
spread in date from the early second century B.C. (earlier than 1QIs[a]) to
the late Herodian period, some two centuries and a half. All the Qumrân
manuscripts of Isaiah belong to a single textual tradition, and may be
described as congeners of the archetype of M, i.e., proto-Massoretic in
our terminology. All these manuscripts of Isaiah share the expansionistic character of the traditional texts of Isaiah, Jeremiah, and Ezekiel,
that is, they are marked by conflate readings, explicating pluses, double
readings, and like harmonization. While the Old Greek text of Isaiah, or
rather its *Vorlage*, belongs to a different textual tradition, it is one
which is closely allied and shares the expansionistic or "full" attributes
of the proto-Massoretic tradition. It may be observed, indeed, that the
text of 1QIs[a] and the Hebrew text underlying the Septuagint often go
beyond the other proto-Massoretic texts of Qumrân, as well as the Massoretic text in the extent of their expansionistic tendency. However, the
expansions, fortunately, are not always the same as those in M, and we
are given some control of the additions, double readings, etc., in the
Massoretic tradition.[4]

 There is every reason to believe that the text of Isaiah at Qumrân,
over the interval of two and a half centuries represented by manuscripts,
reflects a text at home in Palestine. It follows that the Massoretic text
is a recension of the Palestinian text of Isaiah. As we shall see, the
Palestinian text was characterized by intensive scribal reworking and expansion, especially in the Maccabaean era late in its history. Again, the
close relationship between the proto-Massoretic text and the Septuagint
tradition is expected to judge from other instances where we have reason
to believe the *textus receptus* stems from the Palestinian biblical text.
The baroque orthographic tradition found in the 1QIs[a] scroll (among many
others) is a mark of a Palestinian text. It is refracted in orthographic

practice of the Maccabaean age in inscriptions from Palestine, and frequently is found in the Palaeo-Hebrew manuscripts of the Pentateuch as
well as in the Samaritan scribal tradition which branched off from the
common Palestinian practice in the first century B.C.[5]

Most of the one hundred eighteen biblical manuscripts from Cave 4,
Qumrân must be identified similarly as "proto-Massoretic" and "Palestinian" in type. This is true of manuscripts of Ezekiel, the Minor Prophets, and the Writings, most of which appear to have expansionistic
texts both in the *textus receptus* and at Qumrân. Expecially obvious
cases include the "full" texts of Ezekiel, Proverbs, Psalms, and Job.
Job also appears in Palaeo-Hebrew at Qumrân. The point is noteworthy
since all the Palaeo-Hebrew texts from Qumrân contain a Palestinian textual tradition.[6]

2. Deviation from this pattern of "proto-Massoretic" = "Palestinian" does occur at Qumrân in three groups of manuscripts, the most significant manuscripts we possess for the reconstruction of the history of the
biblical text before its stabilization in the Pharisaic recension (M).
All came under my eye first in the examination of the manuscript fragments from Cave 4. Virtually all of these Hebrew witnesses from Qumrân
do bear the marks described above of the Palestinian text (as might be expected);[7] but they are not proto-Massoretic.

Three manuscripts of Jeremiah were recovered from the excavations in
Cave 4, Qumrân. Two, 4QJer[a] dating from the end of the third century B.
C.[8] and 4QJer[c] from no earlier than the end of the first century B.C.,
present the long text of Jeremiah with virtually no significant deviations
from the traditional text (M). Certainly they are to be labeled proto-
Massoretic and Palestinian. The third manuscript, dating from the Hasmonaean period, it should be noted, is radically different in its textual
tradition preserving the short textual tradition of the book of Jeremiah
known hitherto only from the Old Greek translation.[9] As has often been
observed, these two textual traditions may differ recensionally in origin.
So great is their difference in length and order that the long text cannot
be supposed to have developed between the second half of the third century
B.C., the date of the Old Greek translation, and the fixing of the Palestinian textual tradition in the Massoretic recension of Jeremiah. As a

matter of fact, there is no room at all if we suppose the Septuagint of
Jeremiah was translated from a Palestinian text type of the third century
B.C. The full-blown, expansionistic text of Jeremiah is already present
at Qumrân in the third century B.C.! Moreover, the Hebrew textual tradition underlying the Greek and 4QJer[b] is a short, pristine form of the
text of Jeremiah, comparable only to the short, conservative Massoretic
text of the Pentateuch. Like the latter, it shows few expansionistic
glosses or conflations, few traces of revision and modernizing. I cannot
believe that these radically variant textual types were transmitted side
by side in Palestine over many centuries. As I have argued elsewhere,[10]
distinct textual families take centuries to develop but are exceedingly
fragile creations. When manuscripts stemming from different textual traditions come into contact, the result is their dissolution into a mixed
text, or the precipitation of a textual crisis which results in recensional activity, and often in the fixing of a uniform or standard text.
The short text of Jeremiah must have developed in isolation, in a community in which it was not exposed to the intense scribal activity which produced the long Palestinian recension, indeed in a community in which its
text was rarely copied and restricted in use and circulation. I should
argue further that the short text of Jeremiah branched off very early from
the Palestinian textual tradition, perhaps as early as the fifth, or even
the sixth century B.C. (within a generation or two of Jeremiah's death in
Egypt). The evidence drawn from an analysis of these variant textual traditions of Jeremiah appears to be most satisfactorily and parsimoniously
comprehended by a theory of local texts, distinguishing the short text of
Jeremiah as Egyptian in origin and attributing 4QJer[b] or its archetype to
the Jewish community in Egypt which persisted through the Persian and Hellenistic ages.[11]

The manuscripts of the Pentateuch from Cave 4, most clearly manuscripts of Exodus, Numbers, and Deuteronomy, also exhibit traits which
identify them as Palestinian. They tend to be fuller than M, characterized by explicating pluses, synoptic or parallel readings intruded in the
text, well known from the Samaritan recension of the Pentateuch, harmonizing: in short, by expansions. Many MSS appear in the full Maccabaean
orthography best known from 1QIs[a]; many appear in the moderately full

orthography reflected in the Samaritan Pentateuch, both markers of a Palestinian style ultimately rejected by M. Such manuscripts as 4QPalaeoEx^{m12}
and 4QNum^{b13} clearly reflect a common Palestinian tradition of which the
Samaritan recension is a late collateral witness. There can be no question of these being Samaritan manuscripts. This text type is found in
both the palaeo-Hebrew and Jewish character, early and late at Qumrân.
It is a textual tradition found in the Chronicler,[14] in Jubilees, in the
New Testament, and in other Hellenistic Jewish works.

These Palestinian manuscripts stand much closer to both G^{BL} and the
Samaritan tradition than to M. Yet even the earliest Qumrân exemplars
are clearly distinct from the Hebrew textual tradition underlying the
Septuagint. We have to do with three distinct textual traditions, a Palestinian text type, the *Vorlage* of the Old Greek, both fairly full texts,
and the short, relatively pristine text preserved in the Massoretic text.
When forced to label these three textual traditions, *all well known before
the discoveries at Qumrân in fact*, we are faced with two plausible alter-
nates, I believe. We can search for isolated socio-religious communities
(to use Shemaryahu Talmon's terminology) in Palestine which might have
guarded these textual traditions and preserved them intact. Or we can
look to major Jewish communities, inside and outside of Palestine, which
may have nurtured and preserved these variant text types over centuries in
isolation. The first alternative in the case of the Pentateuch is difficult to maintain in view of the evidence that priests in Samaria (of Zadokite extraction), priests at Qumrân of Essene affiliation, as well as
various Jewish authors, all used the same Palestinian text. We cannot
attribute the three textual families to the Jewish parties in Palestine.
The rise of the three major parties must be dated to the second century
B.C.,[15] too late to give the textual types a sectarian *Sitz im Leben*. The
Ḥasidic communities out of which both the Essenes and Pharisees sprung
evidently knew only the Palestinian textual tradition found in the third
and second century B.C. manuscriptions found at Qumrân. Once again, it is
simplest to look to the Jewish community in Egypt as the conservators of
the text type used in the Greek translation made in Alexandria.[16] The
textual family out of which the archetype of the Pharisaic recension was
made differs radically from both the Egyptian and Palestinian textual

tradition. It shows no influence of the local traits which marked the
development of the Palestinian text and stands even further aloof from
the Egyptian than does the Palestinian text. We have been inclined to
seek its origin in the third major Jewish community in the Persian and
Hellenistic ages, in Babylon.

We turn finally to the Former Prophets, especially to Samuel, the
most fully preserved of the biblical manuscripts from Cave 4, Qumrân.
Joshua seems to fit to the pattern found in Qumrân Samuel texts. Judges
and Kings unfortunately are extant at Qumrân only in a few small fragments.

The three Samuel manuscripts from Qumrân are all fuller than M.
4QSam^a and 4QSam^c exhibit most of the traits of the Palestinian tradition
in the Pentateuch and in the Major Prophets and Writings. They are much
fuller texts than the *textus receptus*. Many of their pluses are expansionistic, and they reveal contamination by the popular Palestinian
orthography of the Maccabaean period. 4QSam^b, the archaic Samuel scroll
of the mid-third century B.C., on the other hand, was inscribed in a
uniquely primitive orthographic tradition, far more defective than the
later Samuel MSS, and for that matter, than any of the other scrolls from
Qumrân. Its affinities with the *Vorlage* of the Old Greek (G^{BL} in 1
Samuel) are close, but the most extraordinary characteristic of 4QSam^b is
its high proportion of original readings, whether they be in agreement
with the Greek, or in agreeeent with M, or against both in its relatively
frequent unique readings.[17]

The Massoretic tradition in Samuel is wholly absent from Qumrân. Our
earliest evidence of its existence is the *kaige* Recension which replaces
the Old Greek in the βγ section of Reigns. In view of the date of the
Dodekapropheton of Barthélemy, we must date its appearance in Palestine no
later than the beginning (sic!) of the first century of the Christian
era.[18] On the other hand, the Palestinian tradition found in the Cave 4
manuscripts of Samuel is reflected in the text of Josephus,[19] the closest
ally to the Qumrân textual tradition, in Pseudo-Philo,[20] and, remarkably
enough, in the text of the Chronicler in synoptic passages,[21] certifying
its Palestinian origin.

The received text of Samuel (M) resembles in its outward traits the
Pentateuchal tradition we have called Babylonian.[22] It is remarkably
short especially over against the Palestinian tradition of 4QSam[a], 4QSam[c],
and Josephus. Its orthographic style is close to that of the Massoretic
text of the Pentateuch though often even more defective (primitive). In
fact, it is a text in a poor state of preservation. While it is uncon-
taminated by the scribal reworking which expanded the other two textual
families, especially the late Palestinian text of Samuel, it is a text
riddled with haplographies, some of paragraph length.[23] It appears to
stem from a locale in which Samuel was not intensively used[24] and in
which scribal traditions were extremely conservative, presumably from the
same milieu as the received (Babylonian) text of the Pentateuch. In view
of the fact that the Old Greek of Samuel, while allied fairly closely with
the Qumrân texts of Samuel, is nevertheless distinct,[25] we must again
recognize three parallel streams of textual tradition, three distinct
local texts, as in the Pentateuch.

     3. In our reconstruction of the history of the Old Greek and its
recensions we find the history of the Hebrew text recapitulated. The Old
Greek translation of the Pentateuch and Samuel transmits a Hebrew textual
tradition at home in Egypt, and ultimately a branch of the Old Palestinian
text of the fifth or at latest fourth century. Its text form is full in
these books,[26] inferior in the Pentateuch to proto-Massoretic (Babylonian)
text, and inferior in Samuel to the Old Palestinian exemplar 4QSam[b]. On
the other hand it is, over all, clearly superior to the proto-Massoretic
(Babylonian) text of Samuel.

     The second stratum is the so-called proto-Lucianic recension, a sub-
ject to which we shall return. It consists apparently of a light sprinkling of readings derived from the Palestinian textual family of the type
found in the three Samuel manuscripts from Qumrân, to which the Old Greek
was sporadically corrected. To this proto-Lucianic recension we should
assign the text of Samuel in Josephus, and in my view an early stratum of
the Lucianic recension (boc_2e_2 in Reigns), and the sixth column of the
Hexapla in Reigns section βγ (2 Sam. 10:1-1 Kgs. 2:11).[27] Whether the Itala
was translated from the proto-Lucianic recension or translated from the
Old Greek is not certain and must be determined in future studies. I am

inclined to assign its base provisionally to the proto-Lucianic tradition. The "proto-Lucianic" recension can be discerned only in the Pentateuch and Former Prophets. Much confusion has entered the discussion at this point. Proto-Lucianic readings are discerned in Samuel according to the formula $G^L \neq MG^B$.[28] Readings where G^L agrees with M against G^B are inadmissible since they may be Hexaplaric readings or corrections arising in a late stratum of the Lucianic text. However, in Isaiah, Jeremiah, and and Ezekiel, in the Minor Prophets and in most if not all of the Hagiographa, the textual base of M is the Palestinian text. Thus proto-Lucianic readings cannot be discerned owing to the restrictions of our method of isolating them. "Proto-Lucianic" readings in such cases are corrections to the Palestinian, i.e., the proto-Massoretic, text and cannot ordinarily be distinguished from *kaige* revisions to the proto-Massoretic text or later Hexaplaric corrections to the standard Massoretic text. In the past, the primary data for isolating the proto-Lucianic recension derived from the $\beta\gamma$ and $\gamma\delta$ sections of Reigns. With the demonstration by Barthélemy that in these sections the *kaige* Recension has replaced the Old Greek, most of this evidence disappeared. Many readings formerly labeled proto-Lucianic are merely Old Greek, the substratum of the Lucianic tradition preserved in boc_2e_2.

The third recension we may call *kaige* or proto-Theodotionic, now best known from the *Dodekapropheton* of Barthélemy and sections $\beta\gamma$ and $\gamma\delta$ of Reigns (2 Sam. 10:1-1 Kgs. 2:11; 1 Kgs. 22:1-2 Kgs. 25:30). Confirmation that 2 Sam. 10:1-1 Kgs. 2:11 ($\beta\gamma$) is recensional is overwhelmingly given by 4QSam[a] which has scores if not hundreds of readings in this section which follow the formula 4QSam[a] $G^L \neq G^B M$.[29] The date of the *kaige* Recension is early first century of the Christian era (at latest) to judge from the date of the script of the *Dodekapropheton*. Its base is proto-Massoretic, the earliest evidence for the presence of the Babylonian text of Samuel in Palestine. Symmetry would suggest that the *kaige* Recension was made from the proto-Lucian recension rather than directly from the Old Greek, but we have no basis upon which to establish its precise textual base, again owing to methodological restrictions.[30] Typologically, the *kaige* Recension should be later in origin than the proto-Lucianic since it is the first evidence of the presence of the proto-Massoretic text in

Palestine, dominated from the time of the Chronicler by the Palestinian
text of the Pentateuch and Samuel. It is, moreover, the first of a continuing series of recensions toward a text of Babylonian type which includes later revisions of the Theodotionic school and Aquila. Thus we
should date the proto-Lucianic Greek no later than the first century B.C.,
and as Barthélemy has suggested, proto-Lucianic activity may have begun
on the Old Greek from the moment of its introduction into Palestine, in
the late third or second century B.C.

The recensions of Aquila and the Hexapla bring us to the era after
the Massoretic Hebrew recension of the Babylonian textual tradition had
become authoritative. The Hebrew recension evidently dates from the era
of Hillel[31] since it is the exclusive textual form found at Maṣada (before
A.D. 73) and in the hands of the soldiers of Bar Kosiba (spanning the
interval between the Jewish Revolts, A.D. 70-135). The new, standard
recension is wholly absent from Qumrân. It is curious that neither the
full orthography of the Maccabaean era and later nor the palaeo-Hebrew
script was adopted in the text now promulgated by the Pharisaic school.
These are evidently additional signs of its non-Palestinian background.

4. The discussion of the problems of the proto-Lucianic and Lucian
have been greatly advanced by the papers of Barthélemy and Tov.[32]

Tov suggests that there are two strata in the Lucianic recension,
"the second layer is the historical Lucian, and...[the first layer] its
substratum contained either *the* Old Greek translation or any Old Greek
translation."[33] We need not, I believe, spend time in discussing the
latest stratum of the Lucianic text. Barthélemy is willing to go so far
as to speak of *"une recension grécisante"* though he persists in his doubts
that the martyr Lucian took any role in its creation. We can agree also
with Tov to the degree that he reckons with the Old Greek as the substratum of Lucianic text. There are in my view, however, three strata,
not two, in the Lucianic text of Reigns. Tov's two-strata analysis describes the Lucianic recension elsewhere in the Greek Bible where the
textus receptus is the *Palestinian* text. The third or middle stratum in
my view are corrections of the Old Greek to a Palestinian Hebrew text type
in Reigns where *three* textual traditions exist, and where the *textus receptus* is *non-Palestinian*. The strata of the Lucianic recension are thus

symmetrical with the three text types: Old Greek (Egyptian), proto-Lucian (Palestinian), Lucianic proper (Babylonian). Proto-Lucian readings belong to three formulae: G^L(4QSam) $\neq$ G^B/M (in which M and G^B are not in agreement),[34] 4QSam Josephus M $\neq$ G^B, and 4QSam Josephus $\neq$ G^{BL}M.[35] The second formula in the past has been explained away with the assertion that Josephus on these occasions corrected his Greek Bible by his Hebrew text. The addition of 4QSam complicates the equation making this explanation problematic. I do not believe Josephus corrected to Palestinian readings; if he did, he is a "proto-Lucianic" reviser himself! The third equation in my judgment regularly identifies proto-Lucianic readings in Josephus hitherto beyond our control. An excellent example of such a reading is the lost paragraph found in 4QSam[a] and Josephus[36] before 1 Sam 11:1 describing an earlier otherwise unknown campaign of Nahash, king of Ammon. The temporal reference *wyhy kmw hdš*, "after a month" found in 4QSam[a] (G^{BL} και εγενηθη ως μετα μηνα), and hopelessly corrupted in M (10:27b *wyhy kmhryš*) is a reference back to this lost episode, certifying its originality in the text of Samuel. Here we have an instance in my view of a "proto-Lucianic" reading or rather a Palestinian reading in Josephus' Greek text which was suppressed in the later history of the Lucianic recension.

The proto-Lucianic text in Samuel in my view was essentially G with intruded Palestinian readings, many (as in 4QSam[a] and Josephus) in agreement with M. One may question whether it was a recension carried out at one time and place, or a text form arising in a tendency or drift toward the Palestinian text effected by various, unsystematic correctors. I do not believe we are yet in a position to answer this question although it may be that continuing research in Palestinian witnesses, especially in the Samuel scrolls from Qumrân, and in the biblical text quoted by Josephus, will finally provide an answer.

Notes

1. Julius Wellhausen, *Der Text der Bücher Samuelis* (Göttingen: Vandenhoeck, 1871).

2. Cf. F. M. Cross, *BASOR* 132 (1953), 25 and references.

3. W. F. Albright's early contention that the prototype of 1QIs[a] derived directly from Babylon has proved wrong. His identification of its text-type, however, as "proto-Massoretic" has been reinforced steadily by newer data. See his paper "New Light on Early Recensions of the Hebrew Bible," *BASOR* 140 (1955), 27–33.

4. Cf. P. W. Skehan, "The Qumran Manuscripts and Textual Criticism," *VT Supplement* IV (1957), 152.

5. See the writer's discussion in "Aspects of Samaritan and Jewish History in Late Persian and Hellenistic Times," *HTR* 59 (1966), 208–211 and references, especially the monograph of James D. Purvis, *The Samaritan Pentateuch and the Origin of the Samaritan Sect*, Harvard Semitic Monographs 2 (Cambridge: Harvard University Press, 1968).

6. See below on the Pentateuchal texts in Palaeo-Hebrew allied to a Palestinian tradition common to both Qumrân and Samaria. The Palaeo-Hebrew script, firmly rejected in the Pharisaic recension of the first century of the common era, may also have found its way to Egypt. Professor Orlinsky has astutely discerned that the Greek text of Job was translated from a Palaeo-Hebrew manuscript; see provisionally his *Studies in the Septuagint of the Book of Job V* (*HUCA* 36 [1965], pp. 40, 43–46) and esp. § C (forthcoming).

7. Note that this statement alters the position I took in my earliest papers. I now believe that the 4Q MSS of Samuel are Palestinian and that the archaic Pentateuch MSS I first took to be proto-Massoretic are in fact Old Palestinian as opposed to the usual late Palestinian Pentateuchal texts. In short, the situation in the Pentateuch precisely parallels that in Samuel (see below, n. 11).

8. The discovery of the dated manuscripts from the Wâdî Dâliyeh of the late fourth century B.C. and the El-Qôm ostraca inscribed in Aramaic and Greek with date formula of the mid-third century B.C. now provide firm pegs for dating derivatives of the Aramaic character used in Palestine. The chronology of the earliest Qumrân biblical scrolls proposed in the writer's paper, "The Development of the Jewish Scripts," *BANE*, pp. 133–202, must be labeled "minimal," and may be low by a generation. 4QEx[f] and 4QSam[b] certainly are mid-third century B.C. at latest, and 4QJer[a] belongs to ca. 200 B.C.

9. Preliminary publication of one fragment of 4QJer[b] was given in *AJQ*[2], p. 187, n. 38; see now J. G. Janzen, *Studies in the Text of Jeremiah*, Harvard Semitic Monographs 6 (Cambridge: Harvard University Press, 1973). Cf. F. M. Cross, *IEJ* 16 (1966), 82, n. 6.

10. *IEJ* 16 (1966), 87.

11. Father Barthélemy (*Proceedings of IOCS, 1972*, p. 60), noting my unwillingness to adopt Albright's argument that the Hebrew text used by

the Greek translators had undergone recensional work in Egypt, then
writes "I honestly think that F. M. Cross should give up his 'Egyptian
Hebrew text' of Samuel-Kings, for its distinctive quality has only been
shown (?) a propos of an Egyptian queen's name. It would be better to
begin the textual history of Samuel with the old Palestinian form which
the fragments from Cave IV, Qumrân have brought to light, and which more
or less constitute the *Vorlage* of the old Septuagint, concerning which a
process of recensional activity of a proto-Lucian type must have been
begun almost as soon as the translator had finished his work." Let me
say first of all that I should accept immediately Barthélemy's critique
of Albright's interpretation of the Egyptian queen's name. I have also
argued against Albright that the local textual families discerned in the
variant textual traditions of which we have witness in Samuel and in much
of the Pentateuch are not properly called "recensions." They are the
product of natural growth or development in the process of scribal transmission, not of conscious or controlled textual recension (*IEJ* 16 [1966],
85, n. 21). In the case of Jeremiah, recensional activity *may* have been
involved in the origin of the two surviving local texts. [See now E.
Tov, "L'Incidence de la critique textuelle sur la critique littéraire
dans le livre de Jérémie," *RB* 79 (1972), 189-199.] In any case, my arguments for identifying an Egyptian textual tradition have never rested on
Albright's evidence for Samuel-Kings. In my publication of the first
fragments of 4QSam^a (recovered in Father Roland de Vaux's excavations in
Cave 4), I assumed that the text of 4QSam^a was a congener of the *Vorlage*
of the Old Greek (G^{BL}). With the study of other fragments of 4QSam^a and
4QSam^c (from ca. 100 B.C.), and especially 4QSam^b from the mid-third century B.C., I became increasingly dissatisfied with this explanation as
over simple. The text of 4QSam^b was much superior to the contemporary
Hebrew text used by the Alexandrian translators, and not infrequently in
agreement with M when the latter preserved a superior reading. While
4QSam^a often was in agreement with G^{BL} (G^L in section βγ) in readings
where M was haplographic, they agreed much less often in readings arising
in expansions or other secondary readings. In short, I believe that both
in the Pentateuch and in Samuel-Kings we have three distinct textual
families. While what I have called the Egyptian and Palestinian are more
closely affiliated, and evidently go back to an Old Palestinian archetype,
I believe this archetype to be no later than the fourth century in the
case of Samuel. In the case of the two texts of Jeremiah, I think the
reasons for positing an Egyptian as well as a Palestinian text are com-
pelling; in the case of the three textual families of the Pentateuch, I
think the arguments are strong for identifying an Egyptian textual tradition, and in the case of Samuel-Kings, the arguments are not weak, and my
tripartite division of tradition is bolstered by the analogy with the
Pentateuch.

12. Fragments of this large scroll were published by P. W. Skehan,
"Exodus in the Samaritan Recension," *JBL* 74 (1955), 182-187.

13. For sample readings, see *ALQ*^{2}, p. 186, nn. 35-36.

14. Cf. G. Gerleman, *Synoptic Studies in the Old Testament* (Lund,
1948), pp. 9-12, and especially S. Talmon, "The Samaritan Pentateuch," *JSS*
2 (1951), 146-150.

15. Cf. the writer's essay, "The Early History of the Qumrân Community," *New Directions in Biblical Archaeology*, eds. D. N. Freedman and J. C. Greenfield (New York: Doubleday, 1969), pp. 63-79.

16. We make this assertion in the face of the claims of the Letter of (Pseudo-)Aristeas (§ 176) that the Jewish highpriest sent to Ptolemy both translators and scrolls engraved in gold. The letter is, of course, propaganda intended to establish the Septuagint as authoritative.

17. Cf. F. M. Cross, "The Oldest Manuscripts from Qumrân," *JBL* 74 (1955), 165-172.

18. Barthélemy's dating of the Dodekapropheton is minimal, and we cannot suppose that the copy of the Greek text found in the Nahal Ḥéber is the autograph.

19. See the forthcoming dissertation of Eugene Ulrich which compares the text of Josephus with the Qumrân manuscripts of Samuel. It shows clearly, I believe, that there is no reason to suppose that Josephus made use of a Hebrew text. Rather, he simply used a Greek text of Samuel of proto-Lucianic type.

20. See D. J. Harrington, "The Biblical Text of Pseudo-Philo's *Liber Antiquitatem Biblicarum*," *CBQ* 33 (1971), 1-17.

21. See *ALQ*^{2}, pp. 188f. and n. 40a; *HTR* 57 (1964), 292-297; and Werner Lemke, "The Synoptic Problem in the Chronicler's History," *HTR* 58 (1965), 349-363.

22. S. Talmon in the *Cambridge History of the Bible* (Cambridge, 1970), p. 197, insufficiently recognizes the resemblance of the textual traditions surviving in M in the Pentateuch and Samuel. He correctly describes the short text of the Pentateuch as compact and pristine, the short text of Samuel as haplographic and corrupt. However, these are the descriptions of the modern textual critic. From the point of view of the ancient scribe, both texts were short and primitive in orthography. Had the rabbis sought the best text of Samuel, best from a scientific, text-critical perspective, obviously they would have chosen a manuscript like 4QSam^b which no doubt would have been available to them. In fact they rejected the common Palestinian tradition.

23. See below on the paragraph missing in 2 Sam. 11 from M and G^{BL} but preserved in 4QSam^a and Josephus, and certainly original.

24. Haplography is by far the most common scribal error as typists and linotype operators will ruefully testify. The textual critic's preference for the *lectio brevior* derives from his experience with textual traditions which have suffered conflation and secondary expansion which is the rule in the majority of textual traditions with long histories. He must be on his guard, however, against the occasional textual tradition in which haplography and secondary omissions are frequent as well as the occasional haplography in a prevailingly full text.

25. See above note 11.

26. Jeremiah presents a rare exception to this characterization.

27. As my student Dr. Walter Bodine has shown, the sixth column in

Judges is a "Palestinian recension," corrected to Hebrew text, which is unrelated to the *kaige*-Theodotionic recension (in Judges found in G^B). In Judges, however, this Palestinian recension is not found in the Lucianic witnesses (gn pt and congeners). This suggests that the term "proto-Lucianic," appropriate in Reigns, is too limited a designation for the recension in question.

28. The formula is useful, of course, only where it can be shown that G^B and G^L reflect genuine Hebrew readings which differ from each other and from M.

29. The examples in ALQ^2, pp. 188-189, n. 40a, and in *HTR* 57 (1964), 294, are arbitrarily chosen from the beginning and the end of the section as noted. See also now the extensive textual notes to Samuel in the *New American Bible* where many new readings from 4QSam[a] are cited.

30. George Howard in his paper "Frank Cross and Textual Criticism," *VT* 21 (1971) has attacked my views on the proto-Lucianic recension. I should have been happier had he shown some knowledge of my more recent discussions, notably the lecture published in *IEJ* 16 (1966), 81-95. In any case, he asserts (pp. 442f.) that "perhaps the most salient problem connected with Cross' theory is his assumption that the καίγε recension is a revision of the Proto-Lucianic text as represented by minuscules boc₂e₂. There is absolutely no uncertainty in Cross' mind that this is true. 'There is no doubt,' he says, 'that this Greek text was an early attempt to revise the standard Septuagint into conformity with a Proto-Massoretic text.'" I must confess to some bewilderment. Does Professor Howard suppose that my term "standard Septuagint" means the "proto-Lucianic recension"? I have never used it so. Had he looked elsewhere he would have discovered that I have written of "the Proto-Theodotionic reworking of the Old Greek translation." As a matter of fact, I have never written that the *kaige* Recension was made from the proto-Lucianic recension, and can assure Professor Howard that his remark that "there is absolutely no uncertainty in Cross' mind" is inaccurate. There is nothing but uncertainty in my mind on this issue. Howard also asks how I can identify "an Egyptian Hebrew text of Samuel-Kings with a Greek text that no longer exists." Of course the Old Greek is not lost in sections other than βγ and γδ so that we can calculate its characteristics over against M and the Samuel MSS of Qumrân. The Itala also may be a witness to the Old Greek in βγ and γδ rather than to the proto-Lucianic recension. In any case, an Old Greek stratum in boc₂e₂, in Josephus, and in the Itala persists, in the latter two cases overwhelmingly dominates. Here I stand with Barthélemy in effect. At most the proto-Lucianic text is a light revision of the Old Greek, consisting of occasional corrections to the closely allied Palestinian text. The Old Greek thus is not unknown to us; it is not lost in such a radical sense. I wonder what Professor Howard thinks. Does he suppose that the *Vorlage* of the Old Greek, after sharing many traits and readings with G^L, Josephus, 4QSam[a], and 4QSam[c] suddenly shifted at the beginning of 2 Samuel 10 into a proto-Massoretic text type while Josephus, G^L and the Qumrân Samuel MSS persisted unchanging in their non-Massoretic character?

31. Cf. F. M. Cross, *IEJ* 16 (1966), 90f.; see now also, Barthélemy,

"Les problèmes textuel de 2 Sam 11, 2-1 Rois 2, 11," pp. 24f., who adds to my arguments for a Hillelite date.

32. E. Tov, "Lucian and Proto-Lucian," *RB* 79 (1972), 101–113; and D. Barthélemy, "Les problèmes textuel de 2 Sam 11, 2-1 Rois 2, 11, reconsiderés à la lumière de certaines critiques de *Devanciers d'Aquila*," *Septuagint and Cognate Studies* 2 (1972), 16-89.

33. "Lucian and Proto-Lucian," p. 103.

34. Tov would argue, I am sure, that in the formula G^L 4QSam $\neq$ MG^B, where M and G^B are in agreement, the text of G^B was corrected secondarily toward M. Thus G^B would take on a very different character from that we have generally attributed to it, having suffered very extensive Hebraizing and/or Hexaplaric contamination. Indeed, G^B would have the strange look - having exceedingly frequent corrections to M which involve the omission of Greek readings, very rare corrections to M where M has a plus over the common Greek witnesses (asterisked passages in the Hexapla). I prefer to regard most of the shorter readings of G^B as primitive, stemming from its *Vorlage*.

Even so, there remain a sprinkling of proto-Lucianic readings which cannot be identified as Old Greek. To introduce "another Old Greek" rather than *the* Old Greek is, in the present state of our knowledge, a less "parsimonious" solution than positing a proto-Lucianic stratum.

See also Ralph W. Klein, "New Evidence for an Old Recension of Reigns," *HTR* 60 (1967), 93-105.

35. *Antiq.* 6.68-71.

36. *HTR* 57 (1964), 295f., n. 44.

The Textual Study of the Bible - A New Outlook

Shemaryahu Talmon
Hebrew University

I The History of the Bible Text - The Present Stage of Research

The discovery of the biblical manuscripts from Qumran triggered a widespread renewed interest in the comparative textual research of the Bible, and foremost in the history of the Bible text.[1] Of special importance in this respect was the late W. F. Albright's attempt in 1955 to throw "New Light on Early Recensions of the Bible."[2] In retrospect, it may be said that this short article in fact became the launching pad of a whole new school in biblical textual studies, in the formation of which Frank M. Cross, Jr. has played a dominant role. It appears, though, at present that the impetus effected by Albright's initial paper, and accelerated by later papers and monographs in which followers of the "three recensions" school developed the new lines, recently has perceptibly slowed down, possibly or even probably because scholars quite legitimately now are busy consolidating the new positions won during the last twenty years or so. This situation prompts me to present here some thoughts about new directions which should be and could be profitably explored in the field of textual research in direct conjunction with the wider realm of biblical studies. These new tasks are not incumbent exclusively on scholars whose preoccupation is the Bible text proper and the history of its transmission in the original Hebrew and in the Versions,[3] but rather do they call for the cooperation of students in areas of biblical research which traditionally are considered separate domains of investigation.

Before mapping out some such new avenues, it seems advisable to offer in a nutshell a summary of the main stages that have led to the situation which one encounters now in biblical textual studies.[4]

Before the discovery of the biblical scrolls from Qumran, i.e., until the middle of this century, an impasse had occurred with respect to theories about the early history of the Bible text, its genesis, and the ways and vicissitudes of its subsequent development. Rival conceptions had hardened into two polarized theories: de Lagarde's "Urtext" hypothesis

321

and P. Kahle's "Vulgaertexte" theory, with some scholars working out variations on the basic ideas within the framework of one or the other. One
had turned away, to a large degree, from theorizing about those ultimately unattainable "first stages," i.e., the earliest form or forms of the
Bible text. Instead scholars became preoccupied with the sifting of extant variants, and tried to establish "textual families," especially
within the field of the Greek translations, and the relations of these
families to each other. Textual errors, assumed or real, were collected,
collated and categorized, and attempts were made to devise by a synopsis
of all Versions a typology or typologies of inter-versional emendations.[5]

One wonders why, in view of these variegated endeavours, no attempt
was made to publish an eclectic text of the Hebrew Bible, parallel to what
von Gall, e.g., did for the Samaritan Pentateuch.[6] True, scholars occasionally tried their hand at re-establishing the presumed original text of
this or that piece of biblical literature.[7] But one refrained, and in my
judgment justifiedly so, from going all the way by putting before the
reader a reconstructed, supposedly original text of Hebrew Scriptures.
The situation has not changed to this very day. At best, scholars will
speculate on the "proto-text" of one or another version, but will not
attempt to recover the Hebrew Urtext of a biblical book, let alone of the
entire Bible.

The discovery of the Qumran biblical material opened up new horizons.
After some initial doubts and varying appreciations of its antiquity, the
preponderant majority of scholars subscribed to the opinion that the bulk
of the scrolls and fragments discovered at Qumran stem from the last two
centuries B.C.E. and the first century C.E., with some dating certain
fragments earlier into the third, and even fourth century B.C.E.[8] One now
had access to biblical manuscripts from a very early period which previously had been altogether beyond the scope of textual research proper, i.e.,
research based on actual manuscript evidence.

The sifting and evaluating of individual variants continued, and with
renewed vigor. The field was enriched by the crop of novel readings that
turned up in Hebrew manuscripts from Qumran, and by the emergence of what
sometimes can be taken to be the "Hebrew originals" of previously known
versional variants. At the same time, new possibilities opened up for

manuscript-based investigations into the early history of the Bible text. These possibilities were made especially attractive by the circumstance that, *mutatis mutandis*, the Qumran biblical material *in toto*, and the problems that it presents to the student, approximate the Massoretic Text and Versions issue. Concomitant with the horizontal cross-section of the Bible text at Qumran during the last phases of the Second Temple period, the material affords us a vertical cross-section, i.e., a diachronic view which reflects at least three centuries of the history of the Bible text, within a closely circumscribed geographical setting. It thus can cause no wonder that the Qumran manuscripts soon became the point of departure for a novel theory with respect to the early history of the biblical text.

As said, it was W. F. Albright who laid the foundations of the new hypothesis. An analysis of the Qumran biblical materials available in 1955 led him to the suggestion that most manuscripts and fragments essentially can be aligned with the known ancient Versions of the Bible, including the MT, which *in toto* can be traced back to three local revisions that solidified in Babylon, Palestine and Egypt during the second half millennium B.C.E. Albright's mere sketch of this theory was fully worked out by Frank M. Cross who thus defined its bases: "Any reconstruction of the biblical text before the establishment of the traditional text in the first century A.D. must comprehend this evidence: the plurality of text-types, the limited number of textual families, and the homogeneity of these textual families over several centuries of time. We are required by these data...to recognize the existence of *local texts* which developed in the main centers of Jewish life in the Persian and Hellenistic age."[9] Cross commendably introduced a significant change in Albright's terminology: "Against Albright, we should argue, however, that the local textual families in question are not properly called 'recensions.' They are the product of natural growth or development in the process of scribal transmission, not of conscious or controlled scribal recension."[10]

This theory, which is yet in the process of being revised and further refined by Cross and his students, appears to have attracted surprisingly little comment either from European scholars, with few exceptions, or for that matter, Israeli students of the Bible text. It has remained largely confined to a rather restricted setting on the American scene. One does

not gain the impression that the "three local texts" hypothesis has
aroused, as it surely deserves, a new debate on the basic issues in question. Actually one seems to observe again a concentration on partial
problems which indeed are constituents of the overall theory,[11] and a
concomitant shying away, as it were, from the very heart of the matter.
Much attention is given to the internal developments of the Greek Version
or Versions, evoked especially by Barthélemy's critical appraisal of the
fragments of a Greek Dodekapropheton from Qumran[12] which sparked a spate
of publications on the *kaige* revision of the Old Greek translation.[13]
The question of the relationship of this revision to Theodotion and
proto-Theodotion,[14] to Lucian and proto-Lucian,[15] to Josephus' Greek
text,[16] and to the MT is in the forefront of ongoing textual research.
This reflects on the major problem of the internal composition of Reigns,[17]
and the unity or compositeness of the Greek translation of other biblical
books.[18] Of exceeding importance is the renewed debate on whether the
diverse Greek sources, or at least some, e.g., Aquila and Symmachus,
should be judged independent translations made directly from the Hebrew
original, or whether they are rather in the nature of revisions of one
basic first translation. This discussion has some repercussions on the
"two-translators" theory which had been proposed by Thackeray,[19] Baab,[20]
Herrman-Baumgaertel[21] and others,[22] by which one attempted to explain the
inner linguistic and sometimes terminological diversity or duality of the
Greek renditions of several biblical books, e.g., Jeremiah and Ezekiel.
Now, a trend makes itself felt to substitute for "two translators" "one
translator and a reviser."[23]

    In reference to the *Urtext* versus *Vulgaertext* debate, recent develop-
ments, on the whole, appear to weigh the scales in favour of a more consolidated concept of the early text of the Bible, although it would seem
that the new school has not aligned itself outright with the de Lagardi-
ans.[24] While highly appreciative of the systematic effort to bring some
method and order into the baffling diversity of text-types and textual
variants which can be observed at Qumran, and certainly within the wider
compass of the Hebrew Text and Versions, I yet entertain some reservations
with regard to certain major aspects of the "three local families" theory.
The theory implies that the three local texts derived directly from one

Hebrew proto-type, and that this archetype is to be dated at the latest
in the fifth century B.C.E., that is to say more than half a millennium
earlier than de Lagarde's *Urtext* or Rosenmueller's *Ur-rezension*. I would
yet maintain, as I did several years ago, that notwithstanding the additional information and further analyses along these lines which have been
forthcoming lately, the "three local texts" hypothesis cannot satisfactorily explain the restricted plurality of text-types at the end of the
pre-Christian era.[25] It appears that the extant text-types must be
viewed as the remains of a yet more variegated transmission of the Bible
text in the preceding centuries, rather than as witnesses to solely three
archetypes. The more ancient manuscripts are being discovered and published, the more textual divergencies appear. The relatively limited number of distinct textual families which are extant at the end of the pre-
Christian era may be explained to have resulted from two factors, among
others: historical vicissitudes which caused other textual families to
disappear; and the lack of a major prerequisite for the preservation of a
text tradition, namely its acceptance by a sociologically definable integrated body.

This last factor raises an issue which is not sufficiently considered by students of the Bible text: the social and societal aspects of
the preservation of literature, first and foremost of sacred literature.
A hallowed text-form adopted by a specific group has a decidedly integrating effect. A *Gruppentext* is as much a socializing agent as is a *Gruppen-
sprache*. This certainly applies to the Massoretic Text which became the
standard version of the Synagogue; the Samaritan Hebrew Pentateuch which
gained authoritative status in the Samaritan community; the Greek Version,
and later the Latin, that were hallowed by the Church. One does not encounter the same degree of textual solidification at Qumran. The diversity of textual traditions preserved in the Covenanters' library may in
part have resulted from the variegated sources of provenance of at least
some of the manuscripts. These probably were brought to Qumran by members
of the Community who hailed from diverse localities in Palestine, and from
various social strata. From the very outset, one therefore should expect
to find in that library, as indeed one does, a conflux of text-traditions
which had developed over a considerable span of time in different areas of

Palestine, and also outside Palestine, as in Babylonia, and in different
social circles. These diverse *Vorlagen* were continuously copied by the
Covenanters' scribes at Qumran, even in the restricted compass of their
scriptorium. The relatively short period of uninterrupted existence of
the Covenanters' community possibly was not conducive to the emergence of
one stabilized text form, if they were at all concerned about establishing
a *textus receptus*.[26] It stands to reason that also other constituted
deviant Jewish communities may have embraced one specific text-type in
their time. But with the disappearance of these groups also their respective literary heritages disappeared or were suppressed, and with them
their particular biblical textual traditions.

The scope of variation within all these textual traditions is relatively restricted. Major divergencies which intrinsically affect the
sense are extremely rare. A collation of variants extant, based on the
synoptic study of the material available, either by a comparison of parallel passages within one Version, or of the major Versions with each other,
results in the conclusion that the ancient authors, compilers, tradents
and scribes enjoyed what may be termed a controlled freedom of textual
variation. The exact limits of this "variation-scope," though, cannot be
accurately established intuitively, nor can they be gauged from mere
sample collations. An investigation into this matter, based on a thorough
and comprehensive synopsis of all types of variants, glosses, intentional
modifications, etc., which can be ascertained in our sources is an urgent
desideratum.

The limited flux of the textual transmission of the Bible appears to
be a legitimate and accepted phenomenon of ancient scribal tradition and
not a matter which resulted from sheer incompetence or professional laxity.
This fact, and our ignorance of literary standards and norms practised in
the crucial period of the second half-millennium B.C.E., seems forever to
proscribe any endeavour to restitute an assumed original of the biblical
books. Beyond that, there arises an operational problem which harasses
the editor of a critical edition of the Bible, and with which e.g. we are
at present faced, working on the Book of Jeremiah for the Hebrew University Bible Project. The one-time existence of a short text of the Book,
deduced from the Greek Version which exhibits a text which is considerably

shorter than the MT,[27] gains further probability from the Hebrew fragments of Jeremiah found at Qumran. The preliminary reports published by
their prospective editor, Frank Cross, and now also by J. G. Janzen, suggest that Qumran has preserved for us fragments of what amounts to a
Hebrew *Vorlage* of the short Greek Text of Jeremiah.[28] The considerable
difference in sheer bulk makes labelling these traditions "pristine" and
"expansionist" sound rather inadequate.[29] The very comparability of so
widely divergent traditions seems to be questionable. From here follows
the further question, whether the collation of the short Greek and/or
Hebrew text in the apparatus of the considerably fuller Massoretic Version
can at all be justified on methodological grounds. Similar considerations
pertain to the Book of Esther.[30] The variance of the Greek traditions
among themselves, and *vis-à-vis* the Hebrew, appears to preclude a systematic collation of these widely divergent texts.

In view of these facts, I would propose that a major problem to be
investigated with regard to the history of the Bible text is not so much
the existence of a limited plurality of text-types, but rather the loss of
other presumably more numerous textual traditions. Thus phrased, the
issue of whether a single *Urtext* broke up into "three distinct local families" in which subsequently and separately manuscript variants emerged,
or whether conversely, primal traditions which varied among themselves to
a limited degree progressively lost their lease on life and ultimately
crystallized in a restricted number of *Gruppentexte* should be studied from
a new angle.

II "Higher" and "Lower" Criticism - New Perspectives
The Albright-Cross hypothesis has considerably extended the historical reach of the enquiry into the history of the Bible text. Kahle already
had attempted to push the study of the history of the text in all its ramifications beyond the *terminus non ante quem* which his predecessors had
tacitly or explicitly considered as the starting point of their investigation, namely the end of the Second Commonwealth or the early period after
the destruction of the Temple in 70 C.E.[31] The "three textual families"
theory penetrates deeper into history, since it assumes that these textual
families "developed slowly between the fifth and first centuries B.C., in

Palestine, in Egypt, and in a third locality, presumably Babylon."[32]
Thus, the investigation of textual phenomena, and of the developmental
history of the Bible text is carried down into a period in which some
biblical literature was yet being authored, and other parts were being redacted or edited. To put it differently, in that period diverse literary
processes which affected biblical writings in their totality, then were
carried out concurrently. The recognition of this circumstance should
have alerted scholars to some new issues and endeavours in the wider field
of biblical studies: the investigation of the possible comparability and
likely interdependence of literary phenomena which, on the surface, obtain
on different levels of the literary process. If the history of the Bible
text is no longer considered to become the object of systematic study only
after the creative impulse, i.e., after the authoring of biblical literature had come to an end, but rather as partly overlapping with it, then it
obviously becomes legitimate to probe into the possibility that the textual enquiry, designated "lower criticism," may illuminate issues that are
usually debated in the orbit of "higher criticism." The "shorter" versus
the "expansionist" text of Jeremiah on the surface is a textual problem
and thus comes under the heading of "lower criticism." But if the roots
of the question go as deep as the fifth century B.C.E., the issue, in
fact, connects and concurs with problems of "higher criticism," namely the
presumed intrusion of non-Jeremianic material into the book ascribed to
the prophet.

Another illustration of the same issue is the pericope in Isaiah ch.
38 which reports on Hezekiah's illness and the prophet's intervention as a
healer could be similarly viewed. The absence of Hezekiah's מכתב,[33] the
King's prayer-psalm[34] recorded in the Book of Isaiah (ib. vv. 9-20), both
from the parallel in 2 Kings 20 and 2 Chr. 32 (where also other parts of
the narrative in which the prayer is set are missing),[35] prima facie is a
structural problem which belongs in the realm of "higher criticism." As
against this, the somewhat different textual order of the components of
the pericope in the First Isaiah Scroll (1QIs[a]) will correctly be dealt
with as an issue of "text," and thus comes under the heading of "lower
criticism."[36] Would it not be in order to investigate whether one set of
problems could not have some bearing on the other, foremost the "textual"
on the "structural"?

In the present context, a full analysis of the rather complex problem
would be cumbersome, and therefore will be discussed in a separate paper.
Here it must suffice to outline the main points involved, highlighting
their bearing on the issue under review. In doing so, we shall concen-
trate on the Hebrew text, with only occasional references to Versional
variants.

Of the four extant Hebrew parallels, 2 Chr. 32 presents by far the
shortest and Is. 38 the most expansive text. The latter also is reflected
in 1QIs[a] with one significant deviation, shortly to be analysed. 2 Kings
20 occupies a medial position with respect to the extent of text presented.
There can be little doubt that the Chronicler's text, which clearly is
based on the 2 Kings version, has been severely abbreviated. The account
comprises 22 verses in Is. 38, and 11 in 2 Ki. 20. It was compressed into
one single verse in 2 Chr. 32:24. The process of editing appears to have
been carried out rather mechanically by telescoping the beginning of the
narrative - למות (עד) חזקיהו(י) חלה ההם הימים בימים (cp. 2 Ki. 20:1 and Is. 38:1
MT and 1QIs[a]) - with the catchphrase - ומופת נתן לו - which alludes to the
"sign" - אות (2 Ki. 20:8-11; Is. 38:7-8, 22) - given by the prophet to the
king to assure him that he will recover from his illness. The two components were awkwardly combined by the apocopated phrase ויאמר לו, presumably referring to Isaiah, with the contents of the message missing. LXX
has here the more fitting but probably "improved" rendition καὶ ἐπήκουσεν
(וישמע or BH: ויעתר) [κυριος] αὐτῷ which does not require a direct object.
Neither the summary in 2 Chr. 32:4 nor the full narrative in 2 Ki. 20:1-11,
reflected also in both the MT and 1QIs[a] of Is. 38, exhibit any hint that
would make the reader expect the additional psalm - מכתב - which follows
in Is. 38:9-20 upon the conclusion of the narrative. This obvious addition which elaborates on Hezekiah's short prayer (ib. vv. 2-3) bears witness to a paraphrastic tendency that affected the prophetic narrative,[37]
most probably after it had been incorporated into the Book of Isaiah.
Upon weighing the evidence, the expanded Isaiah parallel is found to be
secondary to the shorter, or more "pristine" Kings account. In essence,
the issue is of a structural nature and pertains to the field of "higher
criticism." It resembles the contrast between the short Greek (and Qumran
Hebrew) and the expanded Massoretic text of Jeremiah, which standard

procedure considers a textual problem, and which is discussed under the
heading of "lower criticism."

A "textual" dimension attaches to the relationship between the two
witnesses to the Isaiah text, the MT and 1QIs^a. The Qumran text lacks
verses 38:21-22 which in the present MT conclude the composite narrative
(vv. 1-8) *cum* prayer-psalm (vv. 9-20) pericope: "Then Isaiah said, 'Let
them take a cake of figs, and apply it to the boil, that he may recover.'
And Hezekiah said, 'What is the sign that I shall go up to the house of
the Lord?'" It is generally agreed that these two verses are misplaced
in the MT, probably as a result of *homoioteleuton*, since both the מכתב and
the concluding appendix end on the words בית יהוה, preceded in one instance by על (Is. 38:20) and in the other by the graphically similar אעלה
(*ib.* v. 22). Therefore they are generally transposed after v. 6, to a
position parallel to the one they occupy in the 2 Kings arrangement. The
verses clearly were before a reviser of 1QIs^a. He supplied the missing
passage *s.m.* by squeezing most of v. 21 into the remainder of the last
line of ch. 38 - omitting, though, the word ישאו - and then wrote the
word ויחי and all of v. 22 vertically in the left-hand margin. However,
the fact that the first scribe neatly ended his copying of ch. 38 by using
up only about one-fourth of the last line, leaving the remainder blank,
seems to suggest that his *Vorlage* contained a shorter text than the MT.
This supposition gains in probability when one bears in mind that 1) the
unemended 1QIs^a text and the MT without the appendix read smoothly, indeed
read better than the fuller 2 Kings text; 2) Hezekiah's question מה (ה)אות
כי אעלה בית יהוה, with the telling reference to the fig-cure in 2 Ki.
20:8 - כי ירפא יהוה לי - conveniently left out in the Is. reading, is a
pedantic and superfluous enlargement; 3) the reference to a fig-pad דבלת
תאנים which the prophet prescribed as a cure for the King's affliction
makes Isaiah the type of wonder-healer that is known from prophetic narra-
tives in the historiographies, but is altogether out of tune with the
traditions told about him in his book. The reference to the "cure" (v.
21) in the appendix to Is. 38 thus is recognized as a secondary intrusion
from the 2 Kings parallel.[38] 4) The definition of the King's malady as
שחין - "boil" (NEB) - on the surface looks like an "informed" interpretation of the very general remark that Hezekiah had been taken critically ill

בימים ההם חלה חזקיה למות (2 Ki. 20:1; cp. *ib.* v. 13; Is. 38:1; cp. 39:1).
In actual fact it is a tendentious elaboration which probably was intended
to present the king's illness in the typical manner of a divinely decreed
affliction. Whereas חלה usually refers to any illness which affects man
in the course of nature (cp. e.g. Gen. 48:1; 1 Sam. 19:14; 30:13; 1 Ki.
14:15; 15:23, 17:17; 2 Ki. 8:7, 29; Neh. 2:2 *et al.*), שחין like דבר -
plague[39] and equally צרעת - leprosy[40] in the narrative parts of biblical
literature, is conceived of as a *topos*, a sign of divine wrath (Ex. 9:9-
11; Deut. 28:27, 35), especially in the Job story (Job 2:7).[41] Since the
fig-pad element is not alluded to in the compressed 2 Chr. account nor in
the base text of 1QIs[a], it is conceivable that it should be viewed as an
alternate tradition of the sun-dial sign which also indicates God's acceptance of Hezekiah's prayer. This latter is present in all four versions of
the narrative, including the catch-phrase reference ומופת נתן לו in 2 Chr.
32:24.

   We are led to the suggestion that the retrospective reference to the
healing of Hezekiah's illness, defined as שחין, and the recapturing of the
sun-dial sign in MT Is. by the question put into the king's mouth, constitute an appendix. Together with the main narrative in vv. 1-8, it is intended to form an inclusio-like frame for the inserted prayer-psalm מכתב:
while v. 21 (the fig-pad) is a topical doublet of vv. 7-8 (the sun-dial
sign), v. 22 links the renewed reference to the King's illness in Is. 39:1
(= 2 Ki. 20:12) with the initial narrative, thus arching, as it were, over
the intrusive element of the prayer-psalm.[42] The present 1QIs[a] text indeed contains the psalm. But the omission of the closing verses, i.e.,
the fig-pad parallel and the *inclusio*, seem to reflect a shorter version
in which the psalm and the "fig-pad" episode had not yet been incorporated
into the Isaiah version of the 2 Kings tradition. 1QIs[a], with the prayer-
psalm, thus represents, on the one hand, a medial stage of structural development between MT Is. and MT Kings, and lacking the fig-pad reference,
on the other hand, appears to have a more pristine tradition than MT Kings
in which the sun-dial sign and the fig-pad already are conflated.

   The above analysis rooted in structural criteria that divide MT Is.
from MT Kings (and Chr.), on the one hand, and in textual criteria which
constitute a deviation of 1QIs[a] and MT Chr. from MT Is. and Kings, on the

other, clearly illustrates the interdependence of the two phenomena and
of the respective disciplines of structural-"higher" and textual-"lower"
criticism. It reveals the parallelism of the "fig-pad" and the "sun-dial"
signs which presumably had been alternately employed in parallel versions
of the Hezekiah story. The transposition of MT Is. 38:21-22 after v. 6
in order to align the text with MT Kings, subscribed to by virtually all
commentators and translators, must be considered improper procedure, both
from the viewpoint of structural and of textual analysis.

             III Biblical Stylistics and the Textual Study of the Bible
     It would appear that another field of comparative research is even
closer at hand than the "lower" and "higher" criticism issue. It concerns
the study of biblical stylistics on the one hand and the textual study of
the Bible on the other. In this area of prospective interdisciplinary
research, new ground can be broken.[43]
     Let me explain what I have in mind.
     It may be considered an established practice in biblical studies to
separate the discussion of stylistics from the study of the forms and the
history of the Bible text. The subject-matter examined in the one field
is adjudged to be intrinsically different from that which comes under
scrutiny in the other. Biblical stylistics are taken to deal exclusively
with the ways and techniques of literary creativity, while in the study of
the text one is concerned with processes which were operative in the preservation and transmission of the finished product. Consequently, distinctive methods seem to be required for an analytical investigation into
these disparate fields of research. These distinctive methods again call
for a specialization and a degree of expertise which result in a rigid de-
partmentalization of the study of biblical literature. The scholar who
has made the problems of biblical stylistics his main pursuit will be drawn
away from questions which pertain primarily to the history of the Bible
text. On the other hand, the student who has chosen as his domain the
comparative study of the witnesses to the Bible text seldom will occupy
himself with the genesis of literary forms or with the evolution of biblical stylistic devices. The few notable exceptions that there are only
prove the rule. The resulting division of labor further widens the gulf

between these two areas of biblical studies which become oriented towards different frameworks of references and which are subjected to analysis by different sets of tools. In practice we arrive at the crystallization of two self-contained disciplines covering two areas which barely touch upon each other.

In this division also a time element is involved. The study of biblical stylistics is rooted in the phase of biblical literary creativity which is taken to have come to an end in the initial stages of the codification of biblical literature, when style stopped developing. Roughly at that stage divergent textual traditions emerged which make possible the study of the textual history of the Bible. The dividing line between these two phases may be set approximately at the end of the third century B.C.E.[44]

As a technical corollary of the division between biblical stylistics and the study of the Bible text in matters of method, these issues often are examined independently of each other in specialized works whose scope is consciously limited to the one or the other. On the one hand, there are histories and descriptions of the "biblical literature" which take no notice of textual problems whatsoever, such as, e.g., K. Budde, *Geschichte der althebraeischen Literatur* (Leipzig 1909), J. Hempel, *Die althebraeische Literatur und ihr hellenistisches-juedisches Nachleben* (Potsdam 1930), and A. Lods, *L'histoire de la littérature hébraïque et juive* (Paris 1950). On the other hand, concerns of stylistics and literature, together with other problems, are altogether excluded, e.g., from F. Buhl, *Canon and Text of the Old Testament* (Edinburgh 1892), B. J. Roberts, *The Old Testament Text and Versions* (Cardiff 1951) and E. Wuerthwein, *Der Text des Alten Testaments*[4] (Stuttgart 1973) which deal solely with aspects of the textual history of the Bible. Even more revealing is the arrangement of the discussion of these subject matters in comprehensive Introductions to the (Literature of the) Old Testament. The part or parts which deal with style and literary forms usually precede the analysis of the biblical books in their traditional order, while the formation of the canon and the history of the Bible text are dealt with in what amounts to an appendix.[45] This arrangement forcefully underlines the distinctiveness of the field of biblical stylistics from that of the study of the Bible text. With this division of spheres goes the notion that a transfer of analytical tools from one to the other can hardly be justified, since one cannot assume *prima facie* any inherent similarity in the processes under observation in the one and in the other.

One certainly has to acknowledge the methodological necessity and the practical advantages which are provided by this division of the spheres of study. However, since we are dealing with one closely-knit complex of literature - notwithstanding the variety and diversity of phenomena involved - we should ask ourselves whether or not there are common basic features which can be discerned in these different emanations of biblical literary creativity. We do not refer to the widely practised employment of stylistic criteria, such as *parallelismus membrorum*, for the emendation of a supposedly faulty text. What we have in mind are fundamental formative elements which assumedly were operative on the author level as stylistic patterns and in the transmission-stage as their editorial and textual modification.

The mere quest for such common fundamental elements in biblical literature *ab initio* implies that we do not rule out the possible transfer of principles and formative techniques from the sphere of literary composition to that of textual transmission. In fact we expect such transfers to occur to a high degree of probability in a literature which experienced the transition from a state of relatively flexible and modifiable oral tradition to a more stabilized written transmission and ultimately to textual uniformity. The transition from one stage to the other was not disruptive, but rather was it a smooth and gradual process which moreover affected biblical literature in a staggered sequence: different biblical books were subjected to the progressive stages of transition at different periods. This even-flowing development allowed for a continuum of values and for a transfer of standards from one stage to another, by means of variation and adaptation. Thus, stylistic conventions which had been of decisive importance in the formation of oral tradition did not cease from being operative in the stage of written transmission.[46] They also left their imprint on the work of editors and revisers, and are reflected in scribal techniques which were conducive to textual stabilization. Therefore, in analyzing the processes and methods that are mirrored in the

transmitted text-forms of the biblical books which represent the final
written crystallization of initially oral traditions, we should not lose
sight of the continuous impact of basic stylistic maxims on processes of
textual transmission.

Let me illustrate the continuity posited here by an example of a
scribal technique which most probably was employed already in the biblical
setting on different levels of the creative literary process, and persisted in the same duality of employments in post-biblical writings. In
the scribal category of *finis* notations, biblical literature twice employs
the technical term עד הנה. Both instances are found in the Book of Jeremiah. It seems likely that in one, Jer. 48:47b, the notation עד הנה משפט
מואב which concludes the Oracle against Moab (48:1-47) was part of that
unit before it became integrated into the Book of Jeremiah. We may surmise that it is the concluding remark of an author, although the definition of the term in this context would be rather difficult. In the second
instance, Jer. 51:64b, the notation עד הנה דברי ירמיהו decidedly should be
ascribed to an arranger or editor of the book who appended it here after a
preceding expansion of the collection of oracles credited to Jeremiah.
The *finis* notation at the end of ch. 51 quite definitely proves ch. 52 to
be in the nature of an appendix.[47]

The very same term עד הנה again serves as a *finis* notation in the
post-biblical collection of proverbs that are known under the name of
Ben-Sira. There it introduces a colophon-like summary, appended to the
end of ch. 51, which is closed by a doxology of the type found at the end-
ings of each of the five collections which constitute the Book of Psalms:
עד הנה דברי שמעון בן ישוע שנקרא בן סירא: חכמת שמעון בן ישוע בן אלעזר בן
סירא. יהי שם יי מבורך מעתה ועד עולם.   There can be little doubt that this
notation stems from the pen of a copyist or an editor of Ben-Sira's proverbs, and not from the pen of the author, who in fact had closed his book
by a preceding colophone that comes at the end of ch. 50:29 (42): מוסר[48]
שכל ומשל אופנים לשמעון בן ישוע בן אלעזר בן סירא... Now, while the
author's colophon is extant in all versions of the book, the line עד הנה
דבר שמעון בן ישוע... in 51:30b (56b) which we take, with others,[49] to be a
scribe's or an editor's notation, is found only in the Hebrew text and is
missing from the Greek, the Syriac and the Latin.

The proposed analysis of the employment of the *finis* notation thus
illustrates the persistence of a biblical literary technique which has
its equivalent in pre-biblical Mesopotamian scribal tradition and in post-
biblical literature. At the same time it exemplifies the diversified
employment of one and the same technique on different stages of the literary process - by an author, an editor or arranger, and possibly a copyist - and thus proves the literary process to constitute a continuum which
facilitates the transfer and the adaptability of underlying basic norms
and concepts.

IV

The assumed continuity of literary maxims and techniques, employed by
literati who were active in the creation, preservation and transmission
of the literary product, viz. the books of the Bible, becomes practically
a certainty when, as is done by the "three recensions" school, the process
of text recension and preservation is taken to have begun as early as the
fifth century B.C.E. It stands to reason that at that stage of the development of biblical literature, and also before it, authors and copyists
were not clearly separable classes of literary practitioners. One rather
may presume that a *unio personalis* was the rule: an author often served,
when the need or the occasion arose, also as the editor, transmitter,
scribe or copyist of his own works or of the work of others.[50] A comprehensive integrated concept of the diverse facets of this literary process
would help us better to understand the biblical prophet's variegated
literary pursuits which crystallize in the complexity of a prophet "book."[51]
In the early post-exilic period, Ezra the Scribe represents this type of
literate. Later in the Mishnaic period, the eminent Tanna R. Meir (second
century C.E.), Akiba's most prominent disciple, was active both as a creative teacher and as a prodigious scribe.[52] Now, if the post-exilic fifth
century and the Tannaitic סופר alike indeed was a man of many parts, a
comprehensive literate who could be author, editor, transmitter, scribe or
copyist when performing different aspects of his profession, it surely
must be agreed that his literary techniques would not automatically change
whenever he turned from one task to another. Quite to the contrary, it
may be taken for granted that some basic canon of literary conventions

would be followed by him in all the variegated performances of his craft,
obviously with some variation and adaptation of the basic rules and modes
to the specific requirements. It is possible, or even probable, that such
scribes were busy at Qumran with copying sanctified literature while creativity of a biblical or a quasi-biblical stance continued,[53] as can be
deduced e.g. from the supernumerary compositions in the Psalms Scroll from
Qumran Cave 11,[54] the *Hodayoth*, and possibly the Temple Scroll, etc.[55]

We can go one step further. The contemporaneity of the diverse literary processes of authoring, editing and copying, with regard to different components of the biblical canon, makes it likely that similar literary
traditions were followed, at least to some degree, also by men who specialized in one specific aspect of the literary process, if such speciali-
sation had already begun to emerge. That is to say, the professional
copyist in his work would follow, mechanically and instinctively or deliberately, literary prototypes and techniques by which the historiographer abided and which the historiographer emulated, let us say, from the
narrative or the oratory biblical style. The phenomenon could be defined
as "variations on common basic literary standards." This continuity of
literary modes over the centuries, and across the diverse aspects of the
literary process, appears to be reflected in the gamut of connotations
that attach to such a basic term as כתב in biblical and in post-biblical
rabbinic literature. The famous *Baraitha* in Baba Bathra 14b-15a defines
by the term כתב Moses' authoring of the Torah (the Balaam Pericope and the
Book of Job) - משה כתב ספרו ופרשת בלעם ואיוב; the compilation of the Book
of Psalms by David with the help of (or transmitted by) ten sages of old -
דוד כתב ספר תהלים עיי עשרה זקנים; as well as the transmission or the
canonisation of Isaiah, Proverbs, Song of Songs and Ecclesiastes by (King)
Hezekiah and his college - חזקיה וסיעתו כתבו ישעיה, משלי, שיר השירים וקהלת.
Our modern differentiation between the diverse aspects of the literary
process, for which we also would coin and employ different terms, simply
did not concern the ancients, who entertained, so it seems, an all-
inclusive comprehensive view of literature.

The same comprehensiveness seems to be reflected in the diverse manifestations of what I would define as "basic literary modes." The issue
requires a full-fledged study. Here space permits only the presentation
of some examples.

Returning for a moment to *parallelismus membrorum* which we mentioned
in passing, it certainly is true that this basic device of biblical and
other ancient Near Eastern writers is not to be taken as merely an orna-
mental figure,[56] but rather as "the main building principle"[57] of biblical poetry and to some extent also of biblical prose. One concurs with L.
Alonso-Schoekel's statement that *parallelismus membrorum* "ist kein rein
auesserliches Stilmittel, sondern eine Haltung und eine Denkweise."[58] If
this is indeed the case, it would be shortsighted to assume that this
fundamental principle was employed exclusively by "productive" writers and
had no impact whatsoever on the "reproductive" arranger, scribe and copyist. *Parallelismus membrorum* and the underlying tendency to reiterate
matters stated once in a somewhat different phrasing, together with some
other cardinal literary modes, must be considered emanations of fundamental Semitic and Hebrew thought processes and literary concepts which
permeate the entire range of biblical literary activity.

IV Stylistic and Textual Interchangeability of Words

Let me begin by discussing the phenomenon of "interchangeability"
rooted in pragmatic synonymity[59] which often results from the break-up of
word-pairs[60] that sometimes are in the nature of a *hendyadys*.

Ia. On the creative-literary level, interchangeability expresses itself
in the employment of a word-pair in *parallelismus membrorum*, in a fixed
(A-B) or an indiscriminate order (A-B or B-A)[61] where one component in
practice can substitute for the other.

1. A pair in case is אדם - איש.[62] In Is. 2:9 we encounter the pair in the
A-B sequence: וישח אדם || וישפל איש. In Is. 31:8 the sequence is B-A:
ונפל אשור בחרב לא-איש || בחרב לא-אדם תאכלנו (cp. further: Job 9:12; 38:26;
Prov. 30:2 etc.). Because of their synonymity, אדם and איש can serve
alternately in one and the same idiom. Is. 21:9 has רכב איש whereas in
22:6 we encounter the parallel expression רכב אדם. Cp. further Is. 2:20 -
ימאסרן איש [= 1QIs[a]; G] with Is. 31:7 - ביום ההוא ישליך האדם את אלילי כספו
אלילי כספו [= 1QIs[a]; G].

2. How do we now assess the character of the very same interchange when
it occurs between two MT parallels such as

Ps. 105:14   לא הניח אדם לעשקם   compared with

1 Chr. 16:21   ‎לא הניח לאיש לעשקם.

Is this instance to be considered a *textual variant* or a *stylistic variation*?

b.   The issue becomes further complicated when one comes to consider this
very same interchange of אדם and איש when it occurs between the MT and a
translation and between a biblical Hebrew text and its citation in extrabiblical literature.

In the rendition of

3.   Lev. 27:28-29   אך כל חרם אשר יחרם איש ליהוה מכל אשר לו

מאדם ובהמה ומשדה אחזתו ... כל חרם אשר יחרם

מן האדם לא יפדה

the Aramaic Targums clearly follow the MT in differentiating consistently
between גבר and אנש. In contradistinction, the LXX uniformly render both
Hebrew words by ἄνθρωπος. This is in keeping with the apparent inconsist-
ency of the LXX in rendering the two Hebrew terms[63] which are kept well
apart by Aquila - איש = ἀνήρ, אדם = ἄνθρωπος with a limited number of exceptions.[64]   In view of the foregoing examples, it can be surmised that
this Greek custom does not reflect consistency but rather may indicate the
continuity of the biblical synonymous employment of the pair of words as a
literary device[65] which as a result could be used interchangeably.

c.   This suggestion can be buttressed by the following observation. The
biblical verses quoted above turn up as a telescoped quotation in the
Damascus Fragments which read (*editio* C. Rabin):

4.   CD ix, 1:   ‎... כל אדם אשר יחרים אדם מאדם

Although there are some queries with regard to the exact interpretation of
the passage,[66] it should not have gone unnoticed that the Qumran text in
its threefold reiteration of the noun אדם[67] reflects the Greek threefold
mention of ἄνθρωπος. It thus presents additional proof for the one-time
existence of a text-tradition of Leviticus which differed from the MT in
precisely the same interchange of אדם and איש which constitutes the core
of the variation between two identical verses in parallel accounts (Ps.
105:14 and 1 Chr. 16:21) and in recurring imagery within one and the same
biblical book in the Massoretic Version (Is. 21:9 and 22:6; 2:20 and 31:7).

IIa. Another example of the same kind is the following:

5. ‏וראה שאול כל - ‏איש גבור‎ serves as a *hendyadys*, e.g. in 1 Sam. 14:52 -

‏ולנעמי מודע לאישה איש גבור חיל‎ and in Ruth 2:1 - ‏איש גבור וכל בן חיל‏,

which can be broken up into its two components which then serve separately

in a parallelistic structure, as in Jer. 14:9 - ‏כאיש נדהם || כגבור לא יוכל‎

‏להושיע‏.[68]

b. So far we certainly are in the realm of biblical stylistics. Is this

yet so when the two terms in question are employed alternately in two

parallel expressions but in two different books of the Bible:

6. Ps. 24:8 ‏יהוה עזוז וגבור יהוה גבור מלחמה‎ as against

    Ex. 15:3 ‏יהוה איש מלחמה‏, or should this be counted as a "textual vari-

ant"?

c. By established rules, we certainly must consider the same interchange

as a textual variant when it occurs between two Versions:

7. In distinction from the above MT reading in Ex. 15:3: ‏יהוה איש מלחמה‏,

the Samaritan reads there ‏יהוה גבור מלחמה‏.[69] It seems that this decidedly

textual variation, irrespective of whether it is unpremeditated or inten-

tional, illustrates the persistence of modes of style in the practices of

text transmission. The tradent or the copyist of the Samaritan Version

made use of the same controlled freedom in the transmission of the text

vis-à-vis the MT as did the writer of Psalm 24 in respect to Ex. 15, or

vice versa. Should these two instances, indeed can they, be dealt with in

complete separation from each other, one under the discipline of stylis-

tics and the other under textual criticism?

III. ‏שים‎ and ‏נתן‎ are a pair of synonymous verbs which are employed inter-

changeably

a. on the creative-stylistic level in parallel members of one and the

same sentence, in either the A-B or the B-A order, as e.g. in the follow-

ing instances to which many more could be added:

8. Gen. 27:37 ‏ואת כל אחיו נתתי לו לעבדים‎ II   ‏הן גביר שמתיו לך‎

    Josh. 7:19   ‏ותן לו תודה‎ II ‏שים נא כבוד ליהוה אלהי ישראל‎

    Ez. 4:2   ‏ושים עליה כרים סביב‎ II   ‏ונתת עליה מחנות‎

Hos. 11:8   אשימך כצבאים II   איך אתנך כאדמה

b. The two verbs can be alternately employed in the same context, as e.g.
in the matter of appointing a king. The basic passage:

9. Deut. 17:14-15   אשימה עלי מלך ... שום תשים עליך מלך ... מקרב אחיך
                       תשים עליך מלך לא תוכל לתת עליך איש נכרי

is reflected in the wording of 1 Sam. 8:5-6 which deals with the negotia-
tions between Samuel and the people that preceded the election of Saul.
There, as well as in 1 Sam. 9:23-24 שים and נתן are consistently employed
as alternatives (cp. further Hos. 13:10-11).[70]

c. Again, שים and נתן can serve alternately in a given idiom.

10. Whereas in Lev. 26:6; Num. 25:12; Hag. 2:9 and 1 Chr. 22:9 the
notion of "peace" is expressed by נתן שלום, Num. 6:26 has the phrase:
וישם לך שלום..

11. The opposite notion of "destruction and waste" can be indicated
either by אשימך שממה (Jer. 6:8) or alternately by ואתנך לחרבה ולחרפה (Ez.
5:14). A similar interchange obtains between Mal. 1:3: ואת עשו שנאתי
ואשים את הריו שממה and Ez. 35:1-9 where the combination נתן שממה[71] is recurrently used to describe the future fate of Edom (vv. 3, 7, 9), but
where also שים turns up in a similar phrase עריך חרבה אשים (v. 4).[72]

d. While all the above instances come under the heading of stylistic
interchanges, the very same verb-couple constitutes the variant element in
two *variae lectionis* between the MT and the Samaritan Version.

12. Ex. 40:22 MT reads: ויתן את השלחן, the Samaritan: וישם את השלחן.

13. In Lev. 8:9 an inverted situation obtains: MT has twice וישם את
המצנפת whereas Sam. in both instances reads ויתן.

We surely must ask ourselves whether the Sam. deviation from the MT is
intrinsically different from the interchange of the two verbs in question
in synonymous expressions in the MT, such as discussed above, or in parallel members of a biblical verse. Unless definite criteria can be established for a methodological differentiation between the above identical
phenomena, the Sam. variants *vis-à-vis* the MT must be viewed as emanations
of the same literary-stylistic modes and processes which underlie the

internal interchangeability of the two verbs. In editing the biblical
text of Leviticus, one would record the Sam. readings for practical purposes as variants in the apparatus. But this appositioning of the one
reading in the main text and the other in the apparatus in no way can reflect on their relative merits, nor does it establish the variation to be
of a "textual" (in distinction from being of a "stylistic") nature.

e. The complexity of the issue increases when translational Versions are
brought into the picture.

14. The Greek verb-pair τιθῆναι and διδόναι exhibits the same, or at
least a similar, interchangeability as the Hebrew pair נתן and שים.[73] Both
Greek verbs, in complete parallelism with the two Hebrew equivalents, express e.g. the notion of appointing someone to office. It therefore cannot cause any surprise that in the LXX either one of the Hebrew pair can
be rendered by either one of the Greek pair. The usual rendition of נתן
would be διδόναι[74] whereas שים is preponderantly rendered by τιθῆναι.[75]
However, in Jer. 1:5 MT: נביא לגוים נתתיך is translated in LXX: τέθεικά
δε (cp. v. 10).[76] The same situation obtains in v. 18, MT: נתתיך, LXX:
τέθεικά δε and in v. 15, MT ונתנו, LXX: καὶ θήσουσιν. In Jer. 9:10(11)
the LXX renders the double employment of נתן in MT (ונתתי ... אתן) once
by δώσω and once by θήσομαι, possibly to avoid repetition. Josephus,
however, preserved also in the first instance a form of τιθῆναι: καὶ θήσω,
and thus may reflect a tradition which rendered the Hebrew root נתן twice
by τιθῆναι, unless he avoided repetition by rendering like Aq. the second
mention - δώσω.

f. A conflux of the literary and the textual interchangeability of שים
and נתן can be observed in the Book of Ezekiel with respect to the idiom
נתן פנים ב or שים .. , in the meaning of 'turn accusingly or threateningly
towards someone or something.'

15. In 6:2; 13:17; 21:2 (G 20:46); 21:7 (G 21:2); 25:2; 28:21; 29:2;
38:2 the LXX render the expression by στηρίξω which translates שים/שום
in Jer. 17:5; 21:10; 24:6; Am. 9:4.

16. The same stem is employed twice to render נתן, in
Ez 14:8 MT: ונתתי פני באיש ההוא
          LXX: στηριῶ

15:7 MT: משרפי את פני בהם ... ונתתי את פני בהם

LXX   'εν τῷ στηρίξαι   στηριῶ[77]

g. while these cases can be categorized as "textual interchanges," the pragmatic synonymity of the word-pair נתן/שים quite legitimately became a fructifying element in biblical and subsequently in post-biblical midrashic expostulation. In the description of Israel's iniquities in ch. 14, the two verbs alternate in a recurring phrase. Once the reading is

17. Ez. 14:3 MT: ומכשול עונם נתנו נכח פניהם

        LXX: ἔϑηκαν   ,   while in

    14:4,7 MT: ומכשול עונו ישים נכח פניו

        LXX: τάξη   the variation with שים is

introduced. At the culmination of the passage, when Judah is threatened with retribution, measure for measure, the two verbs are skilfully combined in midrash-fashion imagery:

18. 14:8 MT: ונתתי פני באיש ההוא II והשמתיהו לאות ולמשלים

        LXX: ϑήσομαι   στηριῶ

It is probable that the unusual hiph. of שים here was chosen on purpose. It suggests a possible derivation of the form והשמתיהו from the root שמם[78] in evoking an association with

    15:8 MT: ונתתי את הארץ שממה

        LXX: καὶ δώσω τὴν γῆν εἰς ἀφανισμόν

and obviously was thus understood by the Greek translator of 14:8: ϑήσομαι αὐτὸν εἰς ἔρημον καὶ εἰς ἀφανισμόν.[79]

It is of interest to note that the midrashic utilization of the pragmatic synonymity of שים-נתן was carried over into post-biblical literature. The Qumran Pesher of Habakkuk (1QHab[p] v. 1 ff.) quotes verbatim:

19. Hab 1:12MT: יהוה למשפט שמתו, but then goes on to interpret the phrase: וביד בחירו יתן אל את משפט כול הגוים. Although the choice of יתן in this instance may be a mere free variation, in view of the foregoing discussion, it is better taken to constitute a post-biblical reflex of a biblical stylistic-textual tradition.

V   Stylistic and Textual Conflation

Another phenomenon which can be observed on diverse levels of the
biblical literary tradition is that of "doubling" or "conflation." Again,
I intend to indicate here only the main lines of approach which I think
should be followed in a full-fledged investigation of the issue. I shall
do so by choosing an inverted order of presentation, beginning with
"doubling" on the textual level, and tracing from there the impact of the
same phenomenon on the "stylistic" levels.

IVa. The issue of "double readings" resulting from textual conflation is
well known and so widespread that it requires little if any illustration.
Conflation can be observed in a wide variety of configurations in the
Hebrew Versions of the Bible - MT, Samaritan Pentateuch, Qumran biblical
manuscripts - as well as in the ancient translations. In a previous discussion of this phenomenon, I proposed to explain the motivation of the
scribe or the translator to record more than one reading in a given context as revealing his reverence for transmitted readings between which he
could not choose, with the aid of the criteria at his disposal.[80] Textual
conflation thus is not merely a technical corollary of multiple text transmission, but at the same time also points to an important aspect of the
ancient literati's attitude towards the biblical text.[81] The awe for the
hallowed material and a basic conservatism balanced the concomitant tendency to modulate and diversify, and thus helped in bringing about a progressive stabilization of the Bible text. The inclination to preserve
diverging traditions, which should not be identified with a predisposition
towards "expansion," becomes especially strong in later strata of the textual evidence, such as e.g. the Lucianic revision of the LXX. However, it
is by no means restricted to them. "Doublets" turn up also in the main LXX
tradition on which the Lucianic revision is based. Often such doublets
result from the conflation of diverging Hebrew readings which were preserved alternately in two parallel accounts in the MT. Thus the

20. LXX of 2 Sam. 7:13 αὐτὸς οἰκοδομήσει μοι οἶκον τῷ ὀνόματί μου combines the MT הוא יבנה בית לשמי with the variant in the parallel 1 Chr.
17:12 - הוא יבנה לי בית. There the Greek follows the Hebrew verbally.[82]

b. An analogous situation obtains in the following instance, except that here the Greek doublet appears in the Chronicles reading.

21.   1 Chr. 19:3   οὐχ ὅπως ἐξεραυνήσωσιν τὴν <u>πόλιν</u> τοὺς κατασκοπῆσαι
                    τὴν <u>γῆν</u>

      2 Sam. 10:3   ἀλλ οὐχι ὅπως ἐρευνήσωσιν τὴν <u>πόλιν</u> καὶ κατασκοπήσωσιν
                    αὐτὴν καὶ τοῦ κατασκεψασθου αὐτήν

The LXX of Chr. exhibits a combination of the parallel readings in the MT
which deviate from each other in the alternate employment of עִיר and אֶרֶץ
which in the context were considered to be of pragmatic equivalence:

1 Chr. 19:3   בעבור לחקר ולהפך ולרגל הארץ באו
2 Sam. 10:3   [85]בעבור לחקר את [84]העיר ולרגלה ולהפכה באו

It is of interest to note that within the 2 Sam. tradition the said interchange of עִיר and אֶרֶץ was preserved in T[J].[86] The main manuscript evidence
renders הָעִיר somewhat surprisingly ית אַרְעָא, i.e. exhibits, as it were, the
Chronicles variant. However, some manuscripts (y w)[87] and printed editions which represent the Tiberian tradition (T), adjusted the translation
to the MT by reading: ית קרתא.

    The above MT variants, and their "conflation" in the LXX of Chroni-
cles, indicate, as said, that עִיר and אֶרֶץ were considered by the Hebrew
biblical writers to be a pair of pragmatically synonymous nouns which
therefore could be substituted for each other under controlled circumstances. Again, as already stated, we have no reason to assume that this
"freedom of variation," in this as in other such cases, was restricted to
the Hebrew authors of Samuel and Chronicles. To the contrary, we may expect that identical or similar interchanges affected the text tradition of
the above vocables also in different settings. This indeed is the case.
It is found, at least three times in the Book of Jeremiah:

22α. Jer. 4:29 MT: מקול פרש ורמה קשת ברחת כל העיר
                 LXX: χώρα

Here, V, S and Sperber's main text of T[J] follow the MT, with T[J] ms. g reading אַרְעָא. Jerome adduces in his commentary[88] both readings: (civitas
sive) regio. Again,

β.   Jer. 29:7 MT: ודרשו את שלום העיר
                LXX: τῆς γῆς

All other ancient Versions reflect the MT in the above and in also the following instance:

γ. Jer. 40:5 MT: בערי יהודה

    LXX: ἐν γῇ Ιουδα[89]

Commentators tend to prefer in these passages the Greek reading over the
Hebrew (at least with regard to the first two cases), and justify their
decision by considerations of contents and meaning.[90] One tends to explain the "inferior" MT reading in 4:29 as a possible *lapsus calami* engendered by העיר in the second half of the verse.[91] Volz (*op.cit.*, p. 31)
even posits that an assumed abbreviation (ץ)אר was misunderstood as = עיר
ער. This reconstruction and the professed preference for the Greek readings are unwarranted in the light of the recognition of עיר and ארץ as a
pair of interchangeable synonyms, which also are employed parallelisti-
cally, as e.g. in Is. 1:7$^{a\alpha}$ || 7$^{a\beta}$; Lev. 26:33$^{b\alpha}$ || 33$^{b\beta}$; 31 || 32 *et al.*

c. In other instances, the doubling gives evidence to Vokabel-Varianten[92]
in the Greek tradition which a copyist saw fit to combine, as e.g. in:

23. Am. 6:9-10 MT: והיה אם יותרו עשרה אנשים בבית אחד ומתו ונשאו דודו
                        ומסרפו

     LXX: καὶ ἔσται ἐὰν ὑπολεφθῶσιν δέκα ἄνδρες ἐν οἰκία
             μιᾷ ... καὶ ὑπολειφθήσουνται οἱ καταλοιπος καὶ
             λήμψονται οἱ οἰκεῖοι αὐτῶν...

In some cases, the double translation has preserved for us two different
interpretations of the Hebrew text which may go back to divergent Hebrew
Vorlagen, or else originated in the translation setting. They sometimes
reveal a "midrashic" impact. The crucial term ואמיץ in Am. 2:16 MT: ואמיץ
לבו בגבורים is derived in the tradition either from אמץ or, by way of inversion, from מצא. Both derivations were conflated in some Greek witnesses, among them a third century papyrus fragment, to read: ὁ κραταιὸς
οὐ μὴ εὑρήσαι. The interchange of אמץ and מצא which generated this Greek
doublet in no way is restricted to the Greek version or to the translations alone. It emerged also in the synoptic study of other witnesses to
the Bible text, e.g., Deut. 32:10 MT: באַרץ מדבר[93] ימצאהו Sam: יאמצהו.

d. A comparable case of a Hebrew *Vokabel-Variante* appears to underlie the
LXX doublet in:

24. 2 Sam. 20:19: εἰ ἐξέλιπον ἃ ἔθεντο οἱ πιστοὶ τοῦ Ισραηλ ... ἐγώ
εἰμι εἰρηνικὰ τῶν στηριγμάτων Ισραηλ where the MT reads: אנכי שלמי אמני
ישראל. Whereas εἰρηνικά renders שלמי of the MT (=T^J: שלמין), ἃ ἔθεντο[94]
clearly reflects a no longer extant Hebrew reading שמו. Barthélemy considers ἔθεντο to be "la forme ancienne," while "la second phrase (i.e.,
εἰρηνικά) parte la signature du recenseur palestinen" of the *kaige* group.[95]

The Greek doublet appears to point to the interchangeability of the
two Hebrew roots שלם and שים. This supposition is buttressed by the fact
that they also constitute the measure of variation between 1 Sam. 2:20

25. MT: ישם יהוה לך זרע מן האשה הזאת   and
     LXX: ἀποτίσαι σοι κύριος   which now has turned up
in 4QSam^a:
There can be little doubt that the Greek version here reflects the Qumran
reading. ἀποτίνειν renders some thirty times forms of שלם, whereas the
case under review is the only instance where it would reflect שים.[97]

Again, it would seem that the "textual variability" of שלם and שים
which generated the "double reading" in the LXX to 2 Sam. 20:19 emanated
from their "stylistic variability." This may be seen from the following
example.

26. There are four occurrences in biblical literature of the phrase: שלם
רעה תחת טובה (Gen. 44:4; Jer. 18:20; Ps. 38:21; Prov. 35:12) and three
additional partial mentions of it (1 Sam. 24:20; 2 Sam. 3:39; Prov. 13:21).
As against these we find once the reading Ps. 109:5 - רעה תחת) וישימו עלי
טובה) which is correctly rendered by LXX: καὶ ἔθεντο κατ᾽ ἐμοῦ and by T:
ושרון עלי. In view of the above parallel examples, there is no need to
emend the MT to read simply וישלמו.[98] Neither is there scope for M.
Dahood's proposition to retain וישימו, but to link with it the closing
words of the preceding verse: ואני תפלתי, and to translate "My prayer they
set down to my debit."[99] The interchangeability of שים and שלם on the "textual" level has led us to the recognition of the same interchangeability
on the "stylistic-formative" level which is reflected in the singular
wording שים רעה in Ps. 109:5 instead of the usual phrase שלם רעה, and makes
any emendation unwarranted.

27. The recognition of the stylistic interchangeability which inheres in
the verb-pair שׁים - שׁלם on the one hand, and in the pair שׁים - נתן on the
other hand, leads to the conclusion that an interchange of שׁלם - נתן/שׁים
underlies also the variation between the MT and the LXX in the following
instance:

Is. 57:18 MT: ואשׁלם נחמים לו ולאבליו   (= 1QIs[a], T[J], S)

          LXX: καὶ ἔδωκα αὐτῷ   (= נתן אתן or שׁים) (אשׁים).[100]

     The contention that what on the surface appear to be inner-Greek
cases of "textual conflation" sometimes are the reflex of a Hebrew stylistic phenomenon is further borne out by the following example:

28. 1 Sam. 25:12 MT: ויגידו לו ככל הדברים האלה   is rendered verbally

           in LXX: κατὰ τὰ ῥήματα ταῦτα

However, in v.9 which constitutes the narrative basis of this reference,

the MT: וידברו אל נבל ככל הדברים האלה   is represented twice in the

LXX: καὶ λαλοῦσιν τοὺς λόγους τούτους ... κατὰ πάντα τὰ ῥήματα ταῦτα
It may be assumed that the LXX mirrors two alternative renditions of ככל
הדברים האלה or, what is more likely, two original parallel Hebrew wordings:
את הדברים האלה and ככל הדברים האלה.

e. The interchangeability of these expressions, despite the slight difference in their connotations, can be easily proved from an inner-Hebrew comparative analysis of parallel passages:

29. Deut. 32:46   לשׁמר לעשׂות את כל דברי התורה הזאת
     Josh. 1:7   לשׁמר לעשׂות ככל התורה אשׁר צוך משׁה

30. Jer. 27:12   ואל צדקיהו דברתי ככל הדברים האלה
        34:6   וידבר .. אל צדקיהו .. את כל הדברים האלה

31. The two expresions interchange generally in the Book of Jeremiah.
Next to את כל דברים האלה (16:10; 19:2 et al.), also ככל הדבר(ים) האלה is
used (27:12; 42:5 et al.).[101]

     A similar interchange obtains between the parallel or synonymous pair
(acc. pronoun +) את כל (ככל) אשׁר צוה and other equivalents, such as עשׂה,
אמר etc.

32. Jer. 1:7 MT: (ו)את כל אשׁר אצוך, LXX: καὶ κατὰ πάντα 35(42):10;

36(43):8; 50(27):21 - (acc. pronoun +) MT: ‫ככל אשר צוה‬,
LXX: κατὰ πάντα.[102]

f. Of the same type is the linguistically legitimate employment of partitive (‫)מ(ן‬, in the sense of *e numero*,[103] for the all-inclusive direct accus.
prefaced by ‫את‬. Let us illustrate this feature by again adducing at first
what appears to be a "double reading," this time in the MT.

33. Num. 13:33 MT: ‫ושם ראינו את הנפלים בני ענק מן הנפלים‬ (= Sam.; Trgs.)

     LXX: [om.] καὶ ἐκεῖ ἑωράκαμεν τοὺς γίγαντας

Whether or not one accepts the likely definition of the second Hebrew
clause as a gloss,[104] it stands to reason that prior to the identification
of the ‫בני ענק‬, who are mentioned exclusively in Conquest traditions (cp.
Num. 13:22, 28; Deut. 1:28; 2:10, 11; 9:2; Josh. 11:22; 14:12; 15:13, 14;
21:11; Judg. 1:20), with the ‫נפלים‬ who turn up only in the antediluvian
tradition of Gen. 6:4, the verse Num. 13:33 had been extant in two slightly
divergent readings. One employed the direct object clause ‫את הנפלים בני‬
‫ענק‬ in identifying the ‫נפלים‬ as *benē ʿanaq*, whereas the partitive clause
‫בני ענק מן הנפלים‬ presented the *benē ʿanaq* as being part of the ‫נפלים‬.
What interests us here, though, is not the exegetical issue but rather the
textual conflation of two parallel readings in the MT.

g. The very same "textual-stylistic" difference constitutes three or four
times the core of variation between the MT and the Sam., with the Greek
and other verstions aligning themselves here with the one, there with the
other:

34: Ex. 18:12 MT: ‫ויבא אהרן וכל זקני ישראל‬   (= LXX: Targs.)
     Sam: ‫ויבא אהרן ומזקני ישראל‬

35. Ex. 20:24(21)
  MT: ‫וזבחת עליו את עלתיך ואת שלמיך את צאנך ואת בקרך‬ (= LXX, TFr.)[105]
  Sam: ‫וזבחת עליו את עלתיך ואת שלמיך מצאנך ומבקרך‬ (= T^Sam,T^O,T^J)[106]
and possibly

36. Num. 23:10 MT: ‫ומספר את רבע ישראל‬ (= LXX, T^Sam)
     Sam: ‫ומי ספר מרבעת ישראל‬[107] (= T^O, T^J ?)

One last example -

37. Lev. 11:28 MT: והנשא את נבלתם   (cp. v.40; 15:10)

     Sam: והנשא מנבלתם   (= LXX, MT 11:25).

The interchange of והנשא את נבלתם (Lev. 11:28) with מנבלתם (ib. v.25) in
the MT proves that we are concerned with a phenomenon of stylistic synonymity which reverberates in variant readings in diverse witnesses to the
biblical text.

h.   38. In Prov. 15:14 MT: לב נבון יבקש דעת ופני כסילים ירעה אולת, the
gerē reading ופי instead of the kethīb ופני could be explained to have
arisen from a simple scribal error, or from contamination by the adjacent
mention of פנים in v.13a, or else from the approximation of לב II פני/פי
to the parallel couple לב II שפתים in 15:7. Because of these considerations, and because of the fact that the LXX - στόμα, S and T - ופומהון
give substance to the gerē reading, most commentators prefer it over the
kethīb.[108] This preference indeed may be justified. However, in view of
the recurrence of the very same interchange in biblical[109] and post-
biblical writings, the explanation of the variance between the kethīb on
the one hand and the gerē and the Versions on the other as resulting from
mere scribal processes, graphic error or contamination does not seem to be
satisfactory. There are two instances of the same variation between פי
and פני in the textual tradition of Ben-Sira:[110]

39. B-S 1:29 (26): אל תתלהלה בפני אדם ובשמתיך השמר   (= S, Syh, L)
     G: ἐν στόμασιν[111]

40.   8:11 (15): אל תזוח מפני ליץ להושיבת כאורב לפניך (= S: לפני)
     G: τῷ στόματί σου[112]   (= L: oritu)[113]

A similar relationship obtains between the MT and the main Greek tradition
in

41. Neh. 2:13 MT: ואל פני עין תנין
     LXX: καὶ πρὸς στόμα πηγῆς τῶν συκῶν

It is further possible that the Greek renditions of the two alternative
readings were combined in

42. Jer. 4:1 MT: ואם תסיר שקוציך מפני ולא תנוד
     LXX: ἔαν περίελῃ τὰ βδελύγματα αὐτοῦ ἐκ στόματος αὐτοῦ καὶ
           ἀπὸ προσώπον μόυ εὐλαβηθῇ

Because of the similar terminology, the translator presumably associated
the Jeremiah passage with

Zech. 9:7 MT: והסירתי דמיו מפניו ושקוציו מבין שנים

LXX: καὶ ἐξαρῶ τὸ αἷμα αὐτῶν ἐκ <u>στόματος</u> αὐτῶν καὶ τὰ βδελύγ-
ματα αὐτῶν ἐκ μέσου ὀφθύτων αὐτῶν.[114]

i. What is of importance in the present context is that the interchangeability of פנים/פני and פה/פי has left some traces also within the Hebrew
textual tradition, and possibly is rooted in a stylistic convention. A
phrase based on פה in

43. Num. 12:8 MT   פה אל פה אדבר בו ... לא כן עבדי משה   (= Vss)
turns up with a פנים variation in

Ex. 33:11 MT: ודבר ה' אל משה פנים אל פנים   (= Vss)
and is reflected also in

Deut. 34:10 MT: ולא קם נביא עוד בישראל כמשה אשר ידעו ה' פנים אל פנים (= Vss)
which at the same time appears to constitute a reminiscence of

Num. 12:6 MT: אם יהיה נביאכם יהוה במראה אליו אתודע בחלום אדבר בו (= Vss).
Similarly, the reading of

44. Ps. 80:17 MT: מגערת פניך יאבדו (= Vss) is to be retained[115] as a variation of the more usual image which appears to connect the concept of God's
fury with an auditive impression emanating from His mouth. Cp. e.g. Ps.
104:7: "At your roar - געדתך - they fled, at the sound of your thundering
they took flight"; Ps. 18:16 (= 2 Sam. 22:16): "At your roar - גערתך -
Yahweh, at the blast from your nostrils" etc. (cp. further Is. 51:20). In
Prov. 13:1, 8 and Eccl. 7:5 גער is connected with שמע (cp. also Gen. 37:10;
Jer. 29:27; Zech. 3:2).[116]

45. Viewed in the light of the foregoing discussion, also the reading Num.
33:8 MT: החירת[117] ויסעו מפני should be judged as a variation on פי החירת
that occurs in the preceding verse (Num. 33:7,[118] cp. Ex. 14:9), and which
probably is the more correct transliteration of an Egyptian place name.[119]
If this argument can be maintained, one suspects that the MT contained a
textual or stylistic doublet in

46. Ex. 14:2 - ויחנו לפני פי החירת. It is probable that the reading פני
החירת instead of פי החירת resulted from a substitution, considered quite

legitimate, of one member of this word-pair for the other, and that this interchange was facilitated by the Hebrew place name פני(ר)אל[120] which like פי החירת is constructed of the name of a deity and the prefixed noun פני which here replaces the Egyptian פי whose Hebrew translation would be בית.[121]

j. Upon analysis it thus becomes apparent that the proclivity to conflate does not emerge late, as it were, in the frame of text transmission, but rather has deep roots in earlier stages of biblical literature. It would be considered another basic literary mode. This mode expresses itself on the "creative" level, e.g. in the intentional retention of synonymous alternate idioms in a given unit, irrespective of its compass. Here are some illustrations of this feature:

47. 1 Sam. 18:12 tells us that Saul feared David because God was with him: וירא שאול מלפני דוד כי היה יהוה עמו. Verse 15 in the same chapter repeats the statement, but gives as the reason for Saul's fear the fact that David succeeded in whatever he did: וירא שאול אשר הוא משכיל מאד.

48. A similar case is Deut. 31:24: ויהי ככלות משה לכתב את דברי התורה הזאת על ספר עד תמם. The verse poignantly picks up the *finis* formula עד תמם of v.30, and the word ויכל of v.1 preserved in the Qumran text tradition and mirrored in the Greek καὶ συνέτελεσεν, but probably mistakenly read וילך in MT: וילך משה וידבר את הדברים האלה אל כל ישראל.

49. In some instances this type of stylistic conflation comes at the end of a more comprehensive unit. In the Sinai traditions, Israel's readiness to accept God's commandments is expressed in Ex. 19:8 by their saying: Whatever God said we will *do* - כל אשר דבר יהוה נעשה. The same idea underlies the request that Moses mediate between them and God, with the undertaking that they will "listen," i.e., "obey" and "do" what God commands, 20:19: ויאמרו אל משה דבר אתה עמנו ונשמעה. The two decisive expressions נעשה and נשמעה were combined in the culminating statement in 24:7: ויאמרו כל אשר דבר יהוה נעשה ונשמע.[122] This combination on its part is reflected in an inverted order of its components in Deut. 4:24:[123] ואתה תדבר אלינו את כל אשר ידבר יהוה אלהינו אליך ושמענו ועשינו.

k. At this stage, we enter the realm of "higher criticism," if we follow

established practice and terminology, since the above examples seem to
derive from different sources. But is this really the case? Does this
variation in Deuteronomy compared with the three Exodus passages indeed
reflect a different source? Could not simply be concerned with another
instance of stylistic conflation with added inversion?

How do we judge the following case against the background of the
foregoing discussion?

50. MT of Jer. 44:3 exhibits what at first glance may be taken as a
double reading:[124] מפני רעתם אשר עשו להכעסני ללכת לקטר לעבד לאלהים אחרים.
Upon further investigation one finds that one of the two expressions -
לקטר לאלהים אחרים - is employed in the latter part of the book, in that
very chapter, not less than nine times (vv.5,8,15,17,18,19,21,23,25), and
turns up only twice in the earlier part (1:16; 19:4). Against this, the
other - לעבד אלהים אחרים - is used exclusively in the first part of the
book, up to chapter 35 (8:2; 11:10; 13:10; 16:11, 13; 22:9; 25:6; 35:15),
and never occurs after 44:3. The conflation in 44:3 thus is recognized
as another "transition doublet," most probably of the stylistic variety,
and therefore should be retained. A problem, though, arises with the
collation of the Greek evidence. The overwhelming Old Greek tradition has
θυμιᾶν, i.e. לקטר only. Exceptions are the Hexapla (with asterisk) and
one minuscule (538) which exhibits Lucianic influence which add καὶ λατ-
ρεύειν. Can the shorter LXX reading here be judged "pristine" and superior
to the MT reading which on the surface appears to contain a textual conflation? Or should we not rather accept the stylistic vindication of the
apparent "textual doublet," and explain the shorter Greek reading to have
resulted from a wrongly applied reductionist tendency?[125]

1. Another clear case of retention of two alternate expressions and the
concomitant emergence of a stylistic transition doublet can be observed in
the Book of Jeremiah.

51. In the first chapter (1:8, 19) we encounter twice the expression אתך
אני להצילך which the LXX render ἐξαιρεῖσθαί σε. The same expression turns
up with a variation in Jer. 30:11[126] אתך אני להושיעך. The main Greek
tradition here has no rendition at all of the Hebrew text. But the Hexapla

and Theodotion have retained a translation in which להושיע is rendered
by σῴζειν. The same holds true for the preceding verse. The third mention of the same phrase comes exactly in the middle between the above instances, and here the MT exhibits a transition doublet: Jer. 15:20 אתך
אני להושיעך ולהצילך, accurately rendered in Tᴶ למפרקך ולשיזבותך, whereas
the Greek has only one verb: τοῦ σῴζειν. In the next verse ... והצלתיך
ופדיתיך is consistently translated in Tᴶ ואשיזבינך ... ואפרקנך, but the
LXX again have only one verb - ἐξαιρεῖσθαί δε - which patently is meant to
render והצלתיך.

One could surmise that the MT represents here a conflate expanded
text, and could define the Greek as "pristine." However, taking into
account other cases of "transition doublets," we are inclined to give
preference to the fuller MT which exhibits a good biblical stylistic practice, and to regard the shorter Greek version as resulting from a pedantic
mistaken predilection for brevity.

52. A similar situation obtains in the Book of Ezekiel. Here a singular
reference in the first part of the book, Ez. 10:19 MT: שער בית יהוה
הקדמוני, rendered in the main Greek tradition ἀπέναντι, is set off by the
recurring reference in the latter part, 44:1 MT: שער ממקדש החיצון הפונה
קדים (cp. 46:1, 12; 47:1, 3) which the Greek translates consistently κατ'
ἀνατολάς.[127] In one intervening instance, again a "transition doublet"
occurs: 11:1 MT: שער בית יהוה הקדמוני הפונה קדימה which the Greek faithfully renders: τὴν κατέναντι τὴν βλέπουσαν κατ' ἀνατολάς.[128]

53. A less distinct case of a structural transition doublet may be found
in Jer. 15:11 MT: אם לוא הפגעתי בך בעת רעה ובעת צרה. Interestingly
enough, here the Versions reflect the apparent conflate Hebrew text,[129]
with Tᴶ exhibiting a paraphrastic rendition.[130] The first of the two crucial idioms - עת רעה - is employed four more times in the book, 2:27,[131]
28; 11:12, 14, all of which precede the mention in the above transition
doublet. The second - עת צרה - turns up twice more. Once, as could have
been expected in view of the previous examples, subsequent to the doublet,
in 30:4. However, the other occurs in 14:8, i.e., before the doublet,
thus marring the expected symmetry of distribution. It nevertheless remains evident that the author of 15:11 (and one does not seem to doubt the

ascription of the verse to Jeremiah) purposefully retained here a combination of expressions which he uses elsewhere alternately.[132] The same
alternation may be observed, e.g., in Psalm 37. In describing the righteous'
hope for delivery in times of stress, the poet once defines these as עֵת
רָעָה (v.19), and once as עֵת צָרָה (v.39).

m. In the following instance of idioms-conflation in the book of Jeremiah,
the "textual" and the "stylistic" aspects are most manifestly intertwined
and constitute two interrelated emanations of one basic literary phenomenon.

Throughout the book, the two alternate expressions בָּעֵת הַהִיא (3:17;
4:11; 8:6; 31:1) and בַּיָּמִים הָהֵם(ה) (3:16, 18; 5:18; 31:19; 33:16) are
employed without any discernible pattern of distribution. In all cases,
T[J] faithfully renders the Hebrew in accord with the MT: בְעִדָּנָא הַהוּא - בָּעֵת
הַהִיא and בַּיָּמִים הָהֵם - בְּיוֹמַיָּא הָאִנּוּן. LXX render the first expression consistently ἐν τῷ καιρῷ ἐκείνῳ,[133] and the second ἐν ταῖς ἡμέραις ἐκείναις.

In these instances, the MT exhibits a conflation of the two expressions which is mirrored in T[J] and in the LXX:

54. Jer. 50:4 MT: בַּיָּמִים הָהֵם וּבָעֵת הַהִיא[134]

         T[J]:   בְּיוֹמַיָּא הָאִנּוּן וּבְעִדָּנָא הַהוּא

(27:4, 20) LXX: ἐν ταῖς ἡμέραις ἐκείναις καὶ ἐν καιρῷ ἐκείνῳ
In the third - 33:15[135] - no LXX rendition is extant,[136] but the Hexapla
(with asterisk), Theod. and Luc, as could be expected, have preserved the
above faithful Greek translation of the Hebrew.

Interestingly enough, these doublets occur as the last mentions of the
expressions under review in the book (33:15; 50:4, 20) with the one exception of בַּיָּמִים הָהֵם in 33:16. We cannot be far off in assuming that they
were meant to tie together the alternate idioms in what amounts to a
"summary-doublet."

In addition to these, the LXX alone exhibit one further such doublet,
exactly at the opposite end, i.e., at the beginning of the book preceded in
3:16 by one single mention of ἐν ταῖς ἡμέραις ἐκείναις

55. 3:17 MT: בָּעֵת הַהִיא

        T[J]:   בְּעִדָּנָא הַהוּא

        LXX: ἐν ταῖς ἡμέραις ἐκείναις καὶ ἐν καιρῷ ἐκείνῳ[137]

In view of this situation, the unavoidable conclusion presents itself that
the stylistic combinatory process exhibited in the MT and Versions in Jer.
33:15 (with the exception of LXX); 50:4, 20 transcended to the Greek translational level in 3:17. The *obelos* in the Hexapla relative to the second
clause makes it unlikely that the Old Greek is based on a Hebrew *Vorlage*
different from the MT which already contained the doublet. Any discussion
of the textual problem involved certainly must be informed by its stylistic background.

n. In some other instances, "conflation" turns up in a "summary doublet":

56. Jos. 9:27: ויתנם יהושע ביום ההוא חטבי עצים ושאבי מים לעדה ולמזבח יהוה
welds together significant alternate terms of the two parallel narrative
strands in the chapter. לעדה echoes v.21 and the "tribal leaders" variant
of the event reported: ויאמרו אליהם הנשיאים יהיו ויהיו חטבי עצים ושאבי
מים לכל העדה. As against this, למזבח יהוה reflects the "Joshua" variant
and the crucial verses 22-23 in which Joshua appoints the Gibeonites to
become: חטבי עצים ושאבי מים לבית יהוה.

We surely must ask ourselves to what degree the conflation of the expression עדה with בית יהוה or מזבח is, methodologically speaking, different
from the conflation of salient expressions which characterize different
versions of one and the same motif in biblical literature, as, e.g.,

57. Deut. 32:10 tells of God's finding Israel in the desert: ימצאהו בארץ
מדבר.[138] Ps. 80:9, in distinction, considers the Exodus to have been the
initial encounter of God and His people. The redemptive event is likened
to the transplantation of the vine Israel from Egypt to the fertile grounds
of Canaan,[139] גפן ממצרים תסיע. Is it too farfetched to assume that Hosea
combined these two separate motifs by saying that God *found* Israel like
grapes in the desert: כענבים במדבר מצאתי ישראל (Hos. 9:10)?

c. While in the previous instances some vestige of the possibility that
the doublets under review resulted from "textual" conflation yet remains,
the following example patently belongs to the realm of biblical stylistics
pure and proper. It is an instance of combination of literary images which
culminates in a duplex or mixed metaphor. Both constitutive elements express figuratively protection from danger. One likens it to sheltering in
the shade of a tree.

58. Jud. 9:15   ויאמר האטד אל העצים ... באו חסו בצלי

and, transferred to the human scene:

Is. 30:2-3 ;לעוז במעוז פרעה ולחסות (החסות) בצל מצרים (לכלימה)

the other to seeking safety under the wings of a bird:

Ps. 91:4   באברתו יסך לך II ותחת כנפיו תחסה

again transferred to a different scene:

Ruth 2:12   .מעם יהוה אלהי ישראל אשר באת לחסות תחת כנפיו

In this second image, the notion of shadow obviously is immaterial. Nevertheless, we twice find the two expressions stylistically combined in:

59. Ps. 36:8   ובני אדם בצל כנפיך יחסיון

      57:2   ,ובצל כנפיך אחסה

with a further variation in:

60.   17:8   בצל כנפיך תסתירני[140]

There can be no doubt whatsoever that here we are concerned with a literary-
creative phenomenon which must be ascribed to the authors of the above
psalms and not to an editor or a copyist.

      The last examples analyzed lead us back to the ones with which we
began our discussion in this section. Again, a basic maxim of biblical
literature, the interchangeability of pragmatically synonymous words and
expressions from which sometimes resulted a combining of the alternate
elements was found to be operative in diverse developmental strata of biblical writings. On the "textual" level it fathered "double readings" in
practically all witnesses to the Bible text. On the "stylistic" level it
engendered "literary conflation," "transition doublets,"[141] "summary doublets" and "mixed" or "amalgamated metaphors." Once the inherent similarity
which underlies all these emanations of one fundamental phenomenon is
recognized, extreme caution is required when one comes to judge in specific
instances whether one is confronted with a late copyist's "textual conflation" or with an author's primary "stylistic-structural amalgam." The decisions whether in a given case a "fuller" reading points to an underlying
"expansionist" tendency, and whether the "shorter" variant represents a
"pristine" tradition, must be informed by a concomitant literary analysis
of the "stylistic" motivations that may underlie the "textual" facts.

VI Stylistic Metathesis and Textual Inversion

One other basic mode of biblical writing in the widest sense of the word appears to be the principle of "inversion." Its impact is of special weight and importance within the setting of "repetition" for which biblical writers and editors exhibit a distinct propensity.[142] This concerns not only repetition of single words,[143] often erroneously deleted by the ancient translators, and for that matter also by modern scholars,[144] but also the reiteration of whole phrases, either in a direct sequence or as "distant parallels."[145] "Reiteration" is an important feature of Hebrew and also of ancient Canaanite, foremost of Ugaritic composition. It makes for fixity of form and pattern. "Inversion" introduces movement into this fixity and variation into stereotype patterns. Repetition and variation by inversion thus should be viewed as primary complementary principles of biblical literature. Being such, we have no reason to believe that they were embraced solely by the creative writer. Rather, we should expect them to have been followed also by arrangers, revisers and editors whose endeavours affected biblical writings in subsequent stages of "inlibration." In fact, we may assume from the very outset that the effect of these standards can be traced also in the latest stages of the history of the biblical literature, i.e., in the diverse forms of its written textual transmission.

a. The most widely represented and best known manifestation of "inversion" in biblical literature is the chiastic arrangement of reiterative components in parallelistic sentence structure. The phenomenon had been already recognized by medieval Jewish commentators,[146] but became common knowledge in the wake of Bishop Lowth's treatise on biblical *parallelismus membrorum*,[147] probably the most essential feature of biblical writing which had its counterparts and antecedents in ancient Near Eastern literature.[148] The increasing preoccupation with comparative research and the recognition of modifications within the principle of *parallelismus membrorum* which make themselves manifest in Ugaritic literature produced new insights into the diversified employments of *parallelismus membrorum* and chiasm in biblical literature.[149] The intensity and multi-facetedness of research in this field highlights the centrality of the issue under review.

There is no need to illustrate here in detail the abundantly employed
technique of parallelistic chiasm in adjacent cola. It prevails in poetic
passages, but is found also in prose compositions which often exhibit this
distinct literary feature. The following two examples will suffice:

61. Is. 28:7[150]   ומשכר תעו[151] ‖ רגם אלה ביין שגו
            כהן ונביא שגו בשכר ‖ נבלעו מן היין[152]
                    שגו בראה[153] ‖   תעו מן השכר

The interdependence of stylistic and textual considerations become apparent already in this first case. In distinction from the chiastic A-B ‖
B-A arrangement in the MT of the first two lines, the LXX twice exhibit
the A-B sequence and retain only parts of the third line: οὗτοι γὰρ οἴνῳ
πεπλανημένοι εἰσίν ‖ ἐπλανήθησαν διὰ τὸ σικερα; ἱερεὺς καὶ προφήτης
ἐξέστησαν διὰ τὸν οἶνον[154] ‖ ἐσείσθησαν ἀπὸ τῆς μέθης τοῦ σικερα.[155]
It cannot be decided on objective grounds whether the translator had a
different *Vorlage* at his disposal, or whether he preferred the simple
parallelistic structure to chiasm, legitimately availing himself of the
literary licence to introduce slight changes into the text before him.

62. Prov. 1:26   אלעג בבא פחדכם ‖ גם אני באידכם אשחק
        1:27   ואידכם כסופה יאתה ‖   בבא כשאוה פחדכם
We shall turn now to cases of "distant chiastic parallelism" which transcend the confines of one verse or adjacent verses, arching over at least
one intervening verse:

63. Jer. 16:4   ולא יקברו ‖ לא יספדו
        16:6   ולא יספדו[156] ‖ לא יקברו

64. Jer. 3:7   יהודה [157]בגודה אחותה
         3:8   בוגדה יהודה אחותה
         3:10   בגודה אחותה יהודה

b. In the following examples, distant chiastic parallelism is a formative
element in passages which belong to different literary units in one and
the same book:

65. Ez. 24:16   ולא תבכה ולוא תבוא דמעתך ‖ ולא תספד
        24:23   ... ולא תבכו ‖ לא תספדו
        27:31   ובכו אליך במר נפש מספד מר

This example elicits the attractive suggestion, which yet has to be further investigated, that literary inversion may be connected with reversal
of contents. That is to say, when in a positive statement a word-pair is
used in the A-B pattern, the B-A pattern will be chosen by the author, or
by another writer who refers to this statement, in a recurrent employment
when the statement takes on a negative sense, or vice versa.[159]

66. Jer. 2:27   אמרים לעץ אבי אתה II ולאבן את ילדחני[160]
        3:9   ותנאף את האבן ואת העץ[161]

67. Is. 5:11   הוי משכימי בבוקר שכר ירדפו II מאחרי בנשף יין ידליקם
        5:22   [162]הוי גבורים לשתות יין II ואנשי חיל למסך שכר

68. Ez. 16:3   אביך האמרי II ואמך חתית
        16:45   אמכן חתית II ואביכן אמרי

69. Ez. 17:17   ולא בחיל גדול ובקהל רב יעשה ... במלחמה
        38:15   רכבי סוסים כלם קהל גדול וחיל רב[163]

70. Is. 40:21   הלא תדעו II הלא תשמעו
        48:8   גם לא שמעת II גם לא ידעת

c. In the next cases, the chiastic parallelism is rooted in a word-couple
which in (a) actually resembles a hendyadys, and involves the further feature of the break-up pattern, and in (b) introduces a third component for
the sake of variation. The construct ארץ מולדת (Gen. 11:28; 24:7; Jer.
22:10; 46:16; Ez. 23:15) and the syndetic parataxis ארץ ומולדה[164] (Gen.
12:1; 24:4; 32:10; Num. 10:30, cp. also Gen. 31:3), in the break-up pattern are the basis of chiastic parallelism in:

71. Esth. 2:10   לא הגידה אסתר את עמה ואת מולדתה
        2:20   אין אסתר מגדת מולדתה ועמה
        8:6   כי איככה אוכל וראיתי ברעה אשר ימצא את עמי II
                  ואיככה אוכל וראיתי באבדן מולדתי

72. Esth. 5:10   וישלח ויבא את אהביו ואת זרש אשתו
        5:14   ותאמר לו זרש אשתו וכל אהביו
        6:13   ויספר המן לזרש אשתו ולכל אהביו ...
                  ויאמרו לו חכמיו וזרש אשתו

d.   Inverted parallelism can be applied to more comprehensive speech units.
Thus, e.g., the formula והייתי לכם לאלהים ואתם תהיו לי לעם is employed in
the Book of Jeremiah in alternating A-B and B-A arrangements. The A-B
pattern is used in the first and in the two last mentions of the formula
(Jer. 7:23 and 31:1, 33), forming an *inclusio*-like frame for the B-A examples (11:4; 24:7; 30:22).

   Inversion sometimes is present in what may be described as inner-
biblical quotations. In some such cases a passage is recurrently used in
one book, either by the author or an editor.

73. Deut. 7:5	ומצבתם תשברו	‖	מזבחתיהם תתצו
	ופסיליהם תשרפון באש	‖	ואשרהם תגדעון
12:3	ושברתם את מצבתם	‖	ונתצתם את מזבחתם
	ופסילי אלהיהם תגדעון[165]	‖	ואשריהם תשרפון באש

In two parallel passages which deal with transgressions which are to be
punished by stoning, the procedure once is described in the A-B and once
in the B-A pattern:

74. Deut. 13:10-11	ידך תהיה בו בראשונה ויד כל העם באחרונה	α
	וסקלתו באבנים ומת	β
17:5-7	וסקלתם באבנים ומתו ...	β
	יד העדים תהיה בו בראשונה ויד כל העם באחרונה	α

e.   Independent employment of a common phrase or formula by two authors or
quoting of the one by the other[166] constitutes the matter of the following
instances of distant chiastic parallelism:

75. Jer. 18:18	כי לא תאבד תורה מכהן ועצה מחכם ודבר מנביא
Ex. 7:26	ובקשו חזון מנביא ותורה תאבד מכהן ועצה מזקנים

76. Ps. 95:6-7	ואנחנו עם מרעיתו	‖	נברכה לפני יהוה עשנו כי הוא אלהינו
			רצאן ידו
100:3	ולו אנחנו עמו וצאן	‖	דעו כי יהוה הוא אלהים הוא עשנו
	מרעיתו		

77. Jer. 51:58	ולאמים בדי אש ויעפו	‖	ויגעו עמים בדי ריק
Hab. 2:13	ולאמים בדי ריק יעפו	‖	וייגעו עמים בדי אש

A somewhat more involved situation obtains in a formula which appears

to have originated in the Book of Deuteronomy, and turns up recurrently as
an inverted quotation in Jeremiah and Ezekiel.

78.   Deut. 32:35-36   כי קרוב יום אידם‏^167 II   לי נקם ושלם לעת תמוט רגלם
      Jer. 46:21   עת פקדתם‏^168 II   יום אידם בא עליהם

     In the following instances, one member of the synonymous pair is em-
ployed in an apocopated form, *pars pro toto*, either by retaining יום:

79.   Jer. 50:27   כי בא יומם עת פקדתם‏^169
      50:31   כי בא יומך עת פקדתיך
      Ez. 21:30, 34   אשר בא יומו(ם) בעת עון קץ‏^170,

or by mentioning only איד‏^171:

80.   Jer. 49:8   כי איד עשו הבאתי עליו עת פקדתיו, and somewhat differently
      Ez. 35:5   בעת אידם בעת עון קץ

f.   In some of the above examples, inversion could be discerned not only
as a stylistic phenomenon, *sensu stricto*, but also as a structural principle which, to a degree, ties together "distant parallels." In some instances, we suggest that the two thus connected references may be viewed
as complementary units of a literary frame of the *inclusio* or *Ringkomposition*‏^172 type, which together delineate the extent of a given unit. It
must be stressed that we are concerned with a phenomenon that can be established only empirically. Our approach perforce must remain descriptive.
No prescriptive dimension can be attached to the results of the enquiry.
In other words, principles which are elicited from selected passages by
careful analysis cannot be employed subsequently to revise by them other
units which do not follow plainly the same or similar lines of structure.‏^173

     These restrictions apply to a degree to most aspects of literary
analysis, and more so with respect to biblical writings whose canon of
literary concepts and techniques was not handed down to us by the ancient
writers themselves, but must be distilled by the student from the material.
They are especially stringent in the issue under review, distant parallelistic inversion which serves as an *inclusio*, since in it the diverse phenomena of style, structure and text tradition are intricately interwoven. The
analysis involves aspects of literary criticism which, as stated previously,
usually are considered under separate headings. Moreover, since we have no

definitely objective means by which to control the results of our analysis,
the discernment of actual illustrations of this technique, and their
appraisal, depend to some extent on the sensibility of the individual
scholar, and of his readers, to such literary intricacies and on his
susceptibility to accrediting biblical writers with the technical accom-
plishments that are prerequisite for their application in literary practice.

With this caveat in mind, we can now turn to the presentation of the
said technique, again demonstrating it by only a few examples.

81. An interesting illustration of intricate structuring can be seen in 1
Sam. ch.18. Although differing over details, commentators are unanimous
in the identification of vv.17-28 as a unit which is set apart from the
context, internally by subject matter, and externally by the features of a
Ringkomposition, or by the *Wiederaufnahme*[174] of vv.15-16 in vv.29-30.
There can be no doubt that the diverse components of the passage were not
simply juxtaposed but rather were they skilfully interwoven with each
other, though without disguising the underlying compositeness. The overall issue requires a more detailed treatment than can be given in the present context. Therefore, we shall limit our analysis to the pericope 18:20-
28 which, as is well known, in itself is composite. The passage combines
two vignettes that depict Saul's attempts to ensnare David in what he hopes
would become a fatal fight with the Philistines, by offering him in marriage either both his daughters - בשתים תתחתן בי היום - (v.21b),[175] or else
first the elder Merab and then the younger Michal. The narrative reflects
salient motifs of the Jacob - Laban and his two daughters episode (Gen.
29:15-30), and possibly is modelled upon this prototype.

The Merab passage (vv.17-19) which ends in her being given in marriage
to one Adriel of Meholah (cp. 2 Sam. 21:8 where Merab instead of Michal
must be read with the Pesh. and LXX[L]), possibly is an intrusive element,
and is missing in the LXX version. In any case, it can be clearly separated from the Michal pericope which is encased between

18:20   ותאהב מיכל בת שאול את דוד

and the complementary "distant inverted parallel":

18:28   ומיכל בת שאול אהבתהו

The stylistic relationship of these two distant parallels may be likened
to that which often obtains between two adjacent cola in which identical
verbs are recurrently employed: in the first, the predicate, a verb in
the imperfect *(yqtl)* with waw consecutive, will precede the substantive;
in the second, the predicate in the perfect *(qtl)* will follow upon the
substantive. This schema is widely employed in biblical [176] as well as in
Ugaritic literature. [177]

     The discernment of an ancient stylistic-structural technique in the
instance under review gives support to the results of compositional analysis arrived at by the literary-historical method.

g. A textual problem connects with the issue in the following instance.

82. In the introduction to the Book of Esther, Ahasuerus' courtiers are
referred to by the term חֵיל פָּרַס וּמָדַי (1:3). This sequence "Persia and
Media" is retained in the three other mentions in ch.1 (vv.14, 18, 19).
These are all that there are until we come to the finale. There, in 10:2,
the last reference לְמַלְכֵי מָדַי וּפָרַס is best understood as a "distant inverted parallel" of 1:19 (בִּדְתֵי)פָּרַס וּמָדַי [178] which together encase the
Esther-Mordechai-Ahasuerus story proper which begins in 2:1 [179] and which
the redactor of the book wishes to conclude with the "chronistic appendix"
10:1-3. [180]

     It is of interest to note that the LXX follow the MT as far as the
three first mentions of the term are concerned (1:3, 14, 18) [181] but reverse the order with respect to the remaining two cases which are crucial
for our argument. [182]   In distinction from the preponderant sequence in
ch.1, the rendition of v.19 is Μήδων καὶ Περσῶν [183] (against the MT), and
in 10:2 Περσῶν καὶ Μήδων (also against the MT). Thus the LXX preserve the
chiastic relationship of these two references, but reverse the internal
order. The effect of the inverted distant parellelism thus is retained
also in the Greek.

83. Passing from narrative to poetry, *inclusio* by "distant inverted parallelism" can be illustrated by two recurring cola in David's Lament over
Saul and Jonathan. Our sole concern is structural, and therefore real or
imagined cruxes of interpretation will not engage our attention here.

(α-β) הצבי ישראל על במותיך חלל II איך נפלו גבורים   2 Sam. 1:19

(β-α) איך נפלו גברים (בתוך המלחמה) II יהונתן על במותיך חלל   1:25

In this instance, the LXX and T[J] reflect the MT in all details, including
the traditional reversed order of the components under review, as correctly observed by S. Gevirtz in the most recent detailed study of the
poem.[184] But neither Gevirtz nor previous commentators[185] appear to have
given heed to the *inclusio* pattern which arises from this repetition.
Just as vv.17-18 are in the nature of a superscription to the "Lament" and
are shown to be such by their exclusion from the *inclusio*, so v.26, though
intimately related to the "Lament" is proved by it to be in the nature of
an "afterthought" which refers solely to Jonathan and makes no mention of
Saul. It is cemented to the "poem" by the repetition of a reflex of בתוך
המלחמה (v.25[a]) and v.21[b] in the closing line (v.27[b]), and by the repetition of the phrase איך נפלו גבורים (vv.19[a] and 25[a]) in v.27[a]. The above
two lines constitute the frame of a congruent structure which embraces the
whole poem. Its second half constitutes an inverted reflection of the
first: v.25 parallels v.19; v.24 II v.20; v.23 II vv.21[b]-22. V.21[a] is an
expansion which calls for a separate analysis.

84. A good example of *Ringkomposition* in prophetic literature, defined by
Zimmerli as *Rahmung*,[186] is found in Ez. 43:7-9.

v.9:   עתה ירחקו את זנותם ופגרי מלכיהם ממני ושכנתי בתוכם לעולם,

takes up in an inverted telescoped sequence two salient phrases of

v.7   ויאמר אלי ... את מקום כסאי ... אשר אשכן שם בתוך בני
ישראל לעולם ולא יטמאו עוד ... בזנותם ובפגרי מלכיהם ...

The two verses encase v.8 which is a distinct reflex of the prophet's
Temple-oracle in ch. 8:7-12.[187] It shares with that passage the references to a wall inside the Temple building - קיר (8:7-8, 10) and תעבות -
"abominations" (8:9, cp. 6 and 13) which equals גלולים (8:10) in the combination with עשה (8:9, 12, cp. v.6). By means of the inclusion in inverted parallels, the short text-segment Ez. 43:7-9, introduced by v.6 is
recognized as a self-contained sub-unit.

In an analogical fashion, *Ringkomposition* seems to be involved in the pair
of inverted parallels in

85. Is. 13:9 .. הנה יום יהוה בא אכזרי ועברה וחרון אף‖לשום הארץ לשמה (α-β)

(β-α) על כן שמים ארגיז ותרעש הארץ ממקומה ‖בעברת יהוה צבאות 13:13
וביום חרון אפו

The tenor of the included passage, 13:10-12, which is of a cosmic-general
character and remindful of the "doxologies" in Amos (4:12-13; 5:8-9; 9:5-
6), decidedly sets it apart from the "oracle against Babylon" in which it
is enveloped (13:1-8 and 14ff.). To put it differently: Is. 13:9-13,
encompassed by inverted parallels, quite legitimately could be taken as a
sub-unit which may have had a literary history of its own and which was
inserted into the oracle against Babylon, either by the prophet himself
or by a reviser. Viewed thus, what was defined as an *inclusio* assumes the
function of a *Wiederaufnahme* which served to delineate the extent of the
secondarily integrated material. This double entendre is basic to "inverted distant parallelism." It is often difficult to decide whether in a
particular instance such parallelism should be taken as a structural-
literary principle of the *inclusio* type and should be ascribed to the
author, or whether it should rather be viewed as a "repetitive resumption,"
i.e., as a structural device of an "arranger" or an "editor." This inherent duality is highlighted in the following example: By content, imagery
and compositional circumstance, the above unit presents some similarities
with Jer. 30:22-31:1. This passage again is structured on the principle
of "inverted distant parallelism":

86. 30:22   והייתם לי לעם II ואנכי אהיה לכם לאלהים
31:1   והמה II ישראל [189] בעת ההיא נאם יהוה אהיה לאלהים לכל משפחות
יהיו לי לעם[188]

We should mention from the outset that the separation of the second member
from the preceding text, as indicated by the chapter division, is open to
debate. This division follows one Hebrew manuscript tradition and the
Greek (38:1), and begins an altogether new pericope with 31:1. Our printed
editions are arranged accordingly, including BH. However, a number of old
Hebrew manuscripts,[190] among them the noted Leningrad codex which underlies the BH, have an empty space *after* 31:1, and none before it. This
proves that their *sedarim* division connected 31:1 with the preceding
verses[191] and regarded it as a subscription rather than a superscription,[192]

as the chapter system implies. This massoretic division, though, has a
new *parashah* begin with 30:22, and thus does not put in full relief the
inclusio pattern posited here.

The above two parallels develop a short oracle of doom against "the
wicked" which basically is of a general nature. By means of the parallels,
and the context, it becomes a vision of hope for Israel:

30:23   הנה סערת יהוה חמה יצאה סער מתגורר על ראש רשעים יחול

30:24   לא ישוב חרון אף יהוה עד עשתו ועד הקימו מזמות לבו באחרית הימים

                                                                תתבוננו בה.

J. Bright correctly says of these verses: "They sit loosely in context
here and may have been inserted to place further stress upon the judgment
of Israel's foes hinted at in vss. 11, 16, 20c."[193] But, like other commentators mentioned further on, he altogether disregards the *inclusio* by
which the short passage is framed. Bright also refers to the assumed
source of this intrusion, namely the repetition of these verses in Jer.
23:19-20, with minor variations and without the *inclusio*. There, in his
judgment, "they fit splendidly after v.18 etc."[194] In this appreciation
he sides with, e.g., P. Volz: "30:23-24 aus 23:19-20 wiederholt,"[195] and
"es ist nicht ein versprengter jeremianischer Spruch, sondern ein spaeterer
Beitrag."[196] Also W. Rudolph, S. Mowinckel, H. Schmidt[197] and others
stress the originality of the version in ch.23. As against this, Streane
does not express a definite opinion with respect to the genuineness of
vv.23-24 in ch.30,[198] but states emphatically that they were introduced
into 23:19-20 from ch.30.[199] H. Cornill is less definite. He rejects the
said "Achtzeiler" in ch.23 and admits that in ch.30 "wuerde er passen,"
but then concludes that also here we have a secondary intrusion: "die
beiden Verse (sind) hier aus spaeteren Stimmungen und Verhaeltnissen heraus
interpoliert."[200]

It should have become apparent that in the case under review the
stylistic-structural phenomenon connects with a literary-historical problem, namely the genuineness of the said passage in either Jer. 23:19-20 or
in 30:23-24 or in both. The failure to observe the two-sidedness of the
issue, to analyze the implications that arise therefrom, and to bring them
to bear on the overall question underlines the lack of coordination in
modern biblical studies of "stylistics" with "literary-historical" research.

We have yet to consider the "textual" dimension of this case. The
investigation of the minor variations between the two Hebrew versions has
not contributed to solving the question of the genuineness of the one or
the other or both. Nor are the differences between the two Greek renditions of import in this matter.[201] But the collation of the Hebrew with
the Greek shows that the LXX has no rendition for the first of the two members of the assumed "chiastic parallelism," i.e. for Jer. 30:22. Cornill
tends to discard the MT here for a variety of reasons, including two that
concern us here directly: "v.22 ist ein isolierter schlecht gebauter
Zweizeiler, welcher LXX fehlt, 31,1 uebel vorwegnimmt und schon durch die
in dem ganzen Complex (chs.) 30 31 unerhoerte Anrede in der 2. Pers. Plur.
hinlaenglich verdaechtig waere."[202] P. Volz, echoed by W. Rudolph (ad
loc.) defines it as "ein formelhafter Ausdruck" and an addition which
"fehlt in G mit Recht."[203] The possibility that a "reductionist tendency"
of the LXX here may have ruined a perfect Hebrew stylistic-structural
device[204] simply never was considered. This is hardly an admissible procedure. In view of the forgoing discussion, the shorter LXX reading at
the best can represent a different redaction of the Jeremiah text, but certainly should not be given preference over the MT, mistakenly designated
"expansionist."

f. The variegated employment of "inversion" as a stylistic and structural
tool in a diversity of forms forcefully underlines the deep-seated effect
this technique had on biblical literature in the "creative" and the "recen-
sionist" stages. Consequently, we may expect this literary phenomenon to
have affected biblical writings also in the transmission stage: within the
text tradition of one Version, foremost the MT; in inter-Version variants;
and in extra-biblical quotations from Scriptures.

The conflux of the stylistic principle of "inversion" with the predilection for the preservation of stylistic variables by conflation sometimes results in "textual doublets" in which two inverted parallel expressions are conjoined. I have discussed some cases of this phenomenon in
detail in earlier publications.[205] Therefore I shall illustrate it here
by only a few examples in which the literary analysis helps in solving an
exegetical crux:

87. 2 Kings 5:18   (α)   לדבר הזה יסלח יהוה לעבדך

(γ)   בבוא אדני בית רמון להשתחות שמה והוא נשען על ידי

(β)   והשתחויתי בית רמון

(β')   בהשתחויתי בית רמון

(α')   יסלח נא[206] יהוה לעבדך בדבר הזה

Although many emendations of this apparently clumsy bit of diction have been
suggested, Montgomery correctly concludes that the MT which is reflected
also in the ancient Versions [207] is best retained.[208] It appears that in
the present Hebrew text two variants were conjoined which differ in the
inverted arrangement of the two lines α–α' and β–β', of which α–α' in addition present an internal chiasm:[209]

1.   לדבר הזה יסלח נא יהוה, עבדך ... והשתחויתי בית רמון

2.   בהשתחויתי בית רמון ... יסלח נא יהוה לעבדך בדבר הזה

     The ensuing two examples are somewhat more speculative

88. Num. 14:27   עד מתי לעדה הרעה הזאת אשר המה מלינים עלי

את תלנות בני ישראל אשר המה מלינים עלי[210] שמעתי

The MT is mirrored in the ancient Versions,[211] but nevertheless seems to
contain a doublet of inverted parallel readings. We suggest the following
reconstruction of the underlying variants:

(α)   עד מתי לעדה הרעה הזאת[212]

(β–α)   אשר המה מלינים עלי את תלנות ישראל }

(α–β)   את תלנות ישראל אשר המה מלינים עלי } or

(α)   שמעתי

89. Lev. 11:21   כל איש אשר בו מום[213]... מום בו[214]... את לחם אלהיו לא יגש
להקריב

The immediately following opening phrase of v.22 .. לחם אלהיו should in
fact be connected with v.21 and should be understood as a variant of את לחם
אלהיו. One of these variants is missing in the Sam. Pent. which combines
elements of both to read: כל איש ... לא יגש להקריב את לחם אלהיו. מקדשי
הקדשים ... We propose to reconstruct the following inverted parallels:

את לחם אלהיו לא יגש להקריב

כל איש ... אשר מום בו

לא יגש להקריב לחם אלהיו[215]

and to read v.22 with the Samaritans: מקדשי הקדשים ומן הקדשים יאכל[216].

90. Lev. 17:14   כי נפש כל בשר דמו בנפשו הוא (α)

                      ואמר לבני ישראל דם כל בשר לא תאכלו (β)

                      כי נפש כל בשר דמו הוא[217] כל אכליו יכרת (α′)

The Versions, with the exception of the Targums, do not render the contextually difficult בנפשו which most probably is an intrusive element from
Gen. 9:4. Thus, the *stichoi* α and α′ are fully identical, are in better
accord with the similar phrases in v.11, and suggest the above reconstruction of the inverted parallel readings that were combined in the verse.

91. 1 Sam. 28:19   ויתן יהוה גם את ישראל עמך ביד פלשתים (α)

                      ומחר אתה ובניך עמי (β)

                      גם את מחנה ישראל יתן יהוה ביד פלשתים (α′)

The Versions render the crucial *stichoi* α and α′ almost verbally. (The
most probably paraphastic changes in the Greek translation are of no concern in the present context.) In spite of the unanimity of our sources,
commentators generally recognize α and α′ as parallels and tend to delete
one of them although without analyzing the genesis of the doublet.[218] The
suggestion to view it as another instance of conflation of inverted synonymous readings appears to be a satisfactory explanation.[219]

g. Stylistic inversion constitutes an intra-Version variation between two
parallel wordings of the same subject matter, e.g., in the following instances:

92. 2 Sam. 22:45   בני נכר יתכחשו לי II לשמוע אזן ישמעו לי (α-β)
     Ps. 18:45   לשמע אזן ישמעו לי II בני נכר יכחשו לי[220] (β-α)

93. 2 Sam. 5:11 (אבן) וחרשי עץ II חרשי עץ with אבן[221] missing in 4QSama[222]
     1 Chron. 14:1   וחרשי קיר II וחרשי עצים

94. Ex. 23:18   לא תזבח על חמץ דם זבחי II ולא ילין חלב חגי עד בקר (= Sam)
     34:25   לא תשחט על חמץ דם זבחי II ולא ילין לבקר זבח חג הפסח (= Sam)
Notwithstanding some differences in wording, there is no mistaking the
basic identity of these verses which are embedded in two versions of a
short cultic catalogue of the pilgrim festivals.[223]

h. Viewed against this background, the widely encountered textual phenomenon of inter-Version variation in the form of syntactical inversion cannot
be judged to be merely an indication of ordinary scribal laxity. Many such

instances of textual inter-Version variation, even though not all, rather
should be considered evidence for the existence of equally valid text-
traditions which cannot be reduced to one common archetype, and/or scribal
manifestations of stylistic conventions which were continuously and legitimately operative in the transmission stage of biblical literature.

These factors are more readily recognized in a synopsis of Hebrew
Versions than in a collation of Hebrew readings with translational variants. To be sure, attention must be paid to the expected impact from
changing conventions of syntax in a collation of Hebrew inversion-variants
in sources which may have been affected by diachronic linguistic developments, such as MT versus Sam. or Qumran material.[224] This aspect, though,
more particularly requires consideration when inversion-variants in the
Hebrew original and in translations are compared, especially in a non-
Semitic target language. Here, the greater probability that peculiarities
of the meta-language may have induced a translator or a copyist to trans-
pose syntatical elements must be carefully evaluated. A cautious analysis
will reduce the number of instances in the translations that should right-
fully be dealt with under the heading of "original inversion variants"
stemming from a Hebrew *Vorlage*. However, the remaining cases suffice to
demonstrate the impact of legitimate stylistic inversion on translational
Versions which makes itself manifest in textual transposition.

α. A sampling of inversion-variants in non-massoretic witnesses to the
text of the Bible will sufficiently illustrate the validity of the above
argument. We shall first adduce examples from the Samaritan Hebrew Pentateuch Version and then present comparable evidence from the Qumran Scrolls.
The discussion of these will be kept to a bare minimum:

95.	Ex. 5:3 MT:	נלכה נא דרך שלשת ימים במדבר
	Sam:	נלכה נא המדברה דרך שלשת ימים
96.	Lev. 20:13 MT:	תועבה עשו שניהם מות יומתו
	Sam:	תועבה עשו מות יומתו שניהם
97.	20:22 MT:	ולא תקיא אתכם הארץ
	Sam:	ולא תקיא הארץ אתכם

In the above instances, the inversion amounted to a reversal of the

order of some syntatical components (such as can be found in intra-MT
parallels, e.g., 2 Sam. 7:20-1 Chr. 17:18; 2 Sam. 6:17-1 Chr. 16:1; 2 Sam.
10:11-1 Chr. 19:12) which often also constitutes the element of variation
between the MT and parallel Qumran material.

β. In the following cases, the relation between the MT and Q material reflects the A-B versus the B-A arrangement of the two components of a pair
of synonyms:

98. Is. 49:6 MT:[225]   ונצורי ישראל להשיב   להקים את שבטי יעקב
               Isa: ונצירי יעקוב להשיב   להקים את שבטי ישראל

99.   49:25 MT: מלקוח עריץ ימלט[226]   גם שבי גבור יקח
               Isa: ושבי עריץ ימלט[227]   גם מלקוח גבור ילקח

100.   52:13 MT: הנה ישכיל עבדי ירום ונשא וגבה מאד
               Isb:[228]   ירום וגבה ונשא מאד[229]

In other instances, inversion effected a syntatical rearrangement in Qumran parallels vis-à-vis the MT which is of the same type as the one observed between MT and Samaritan variants (examples 95-97) as well as between intra-MT parallels:

101. Is. 36:12 MT: האל אדניך ואליך שלחני אדני (= 2 Kings 18:27)
               Isa: האליכמה ועל[230] אדוניכמה שלחני אדוני

102.   1:30 MT: וכגנה אשר מים אין לה
               Isa: וכגנה אשר אין מים לה

103.   37:7 MT: הנני נותן בו רוח
               Isa: הנני נותן רוח בוא[231]

104.   38:19 MT: חי חי הוא יודך כמוני היום[232]
               Isb: היום כמוני

105.   62:8 MT: אם אתן את דגנך עוד מאכל לאיביך
               Isb: עוד את דגנך

106. 2 Sam. 24:16 MT: om.
               4QSama: (פנ)יהם מת(כסים בשק)ים[233]
     1 Chr. 21:16 MT: מכסים בשקים על פניהם

A collation of the MT with Qumran parallels also reveals instances of

inversion of complete sentence parts, which was found to constitute the
element of variation between intra-MT parallels (examples 92-93) and which
sometimes resulted in 'double-readings' (examples 87-91). A case in point
is

107. Is. 37:33 MT: ולא יורה שם חץ ולא יקדמנה מגן ולא ישפך   (= 2 Ki.19:32)
עליה סללה

Isᵃ: ולוא ישפוך עליהא סוללה ולוא ירא שם חץ ולוא יקדמנה מגן

γ. There is ample documentation for changes of word-order in the LXX tradition or part of it *vis-à-vis* the MT as well as between the major witnesses to the Greek text. Discussing this issue with reference to the
text of Jeremiah, Ziegler quotes Origen who in his letter to Africanus
poignantly remarks on the numerous (syntactical) inversions:[234] πολλὰ δὲ
τοιαῦτα καὶ ἐν τῷ Ιερεμίᾳ κατενοήσαμεν, ἐν ᾧ καὶ πολλὴν μετάθεσιν καὶ
εναλλαγην τῆς λέξεως τῶν προφητευομένων εὕρομεν (Migne PG 11,50 B). It
remains, though, an open issue whether, as Ziegler does, it is correct to
define[235] the numerous examples of word-order variants in the A text *vis-à-
vis* the MT as *Umstellungen*, implying that the Greek tradition in these
cases changed the Hebrew text: "Es koennen 40 Stellen genannt werden, wo
A allein oder von einigen abhaengigen Zeugen begleitet, eine Umstellung
vornimmt," presumably for Greek stylistic reasons.[236] A similar explanation is offered for *Umstellungen* in the B text tradition in comparison with
the MT where this is followed by the A text, although the suggestion is
weighed that B preserved in such instances an original different word
sequence.[237] However, what was not pondered at all is the possibility that
at least some cases of inverted word-order in the Greek translation may reflect the same margin of stylistic licence which can be observed in a collation of parallel Hebrew traditions of the Bible text.

This suggestion gains in probability in instances in which the LXX
concur with the MT arrangement of the verse, whereas the hexaplaric or the
Lucianic revision, which preponderantly correct towards the MT, exhibit a
surprising inverted arrangement. In analyzing some such cases in the Greek
tradition of Isaiah, Ziegler rather carefully raises the question whether
such transpositions indeed can be ascribed to Origen or whether they were
not already contained in his *Vorlage*: "Bei den Umstellungen erhebt sich

wiederum die Frage, ob sie alle auf Origenes zurueckgehen. Es ist moeglich,
das bereits in dessen Vorlage solche Umstellungen standen."[238] Bearing
in mind the preceding discussion, we are inclined to answer this question
more decidedly in the affirmative, especially when the inversion involves
the transposition of components of a pair of synonyms in one of the revisions, and a *fortiori* in the basic LXX tradition:

108. Jer. 2:19 MT: תיסרך רעתך ‖ ומשבותיך תוכחך

            LXX: παιδεύσει σε ἡ ἀπόστασια σου ‖ καὶ ἡ κακία ἐλέγξει σε
The second Greek noun κακία renders 89 times the Hebrew רעה which is the
first noun in the MT. In view of this fact, it is only natural to assume
that ἀποστασία renders here משובה,[239] being derived from ἀφίσταναι which
translates שוב and שבב, e.g., in Jer. 3:14. It therefore is not surprising that the hexaplaric tradition adjusted the Greek to the MT by invert-
ing the two translational nouns. Similarly, we discern an identical case
of inversion of a pair of parallels in:

109. Jer. 8:20 MT: עבר קציר ‖ כלה קיץ
         LXX: διῆλθε θέρος ‖ παρῆλθευ ἄμητος   and

110. Prov. 26:1 MT: כשלג בקיץ ‖ וכמטר בקציר
         LXX: ὥσπερ δρόσος ἐν ἄμητῳ ‖ καὶ ὥσπερ ὑετὸς ἐν θήρει
In five other passages θέρος renders the Hebrew noun קיץ (Gen. 8:22; Zach.
14:8; Ps. 74[73]:17; Prov. 6:8; 30:25 [24:60]), whereas ἄμητος translates
14 times קציר (and once קצר). Only once more, in addition to the above
instances, it is used to translate קיץ (Micah 7:1).

     The proposed identification of ἄμητος with קציר is buttressed by a
comparison of Prov. 26:1 with

111. Is. 18:4 MT: כחם צח עלי אור ‖ כעב טל בחם קציר
         LXX:ὡς φῶς [240]καύματος ‖ καὶ ὡς νεφέλη δρόσου ἡμέρας ἀμήτου
                      μεσημβρίας
νεφέλη δρόσου recalls δρόσος in Prov. 26:1, both terms being connected in
the two instances with ἄμητος = קציר. In parenthesis we may add that the
rearranged word-order of the LXX in the first *stichoi* of Is. 18:4 possibly
reflects an original reading. It is suggested that the difficult עלי אור
should be read[241] טל עלי אור (ט) or טל אור (ט), an expression which is employed
in Is. 26:19 - כי טל אורת טלך.

Accordingly we would emend Is. 18:4 to read: בֹּחֹם צַח (כֹּטֹל) עֲלֵי אוֹר || כְּעָב
קל בֹּחֹם קָצִיר; or in accord with the Greek positioning of φῶς at the beginning of the verse: (כֹּטֹל) עֲלֵי אוֹר בֹּחֹם צַח[242] || כְּעָב מֹל בֹּחֹם קָצִיר. Outside the LXX, ἄμητος always equals 'crop-harvest.' It never carries the connotation of 'summer' which attaches to קַיְץ that also can mean 'summer-fruit' (cp., e.g., Am. 8:1-2), exactly as does θέρος in extra-LXX usage. It is, therefore, reasonable to posit that the Greek translation of Jer. 8:20 and Prov. 26:1 inverted the MT sequence of the nouns קַיְץ and קָצִיר.

In the last example to be discussed, the reversal of the massoretic word sequence in the LXX certainly can be explained to have arisen from translational stylistic reasons or from 'literary logic':

112. Jer. 4:28 MT: עַל כִּי דִבַּרְתִּי זַמֹּתִי || וְלֹא נִחַמְתִּי וְלֹא אָשׁוּב מִמֶּנָּה

      LXX: διότι ἐλάλησα καὶ οὐ μετανοήσω ὥρμησα καὶ οὐκ
            ἀποστρέφω ἀπ᾽ αὐτῆς

The MT here presents two word-pairs of opposite meanings, arranged in an a-a' b-b' order, whereas the Greek displays the more elegant a-b a'-b' pattern. Although it must be admitted that we may be concerned here with an inner-Greek inversion effected by a translator, we feel inclined to accord as much probability to the suggestion that the present Greek text reflects a Hebrew inversion variant displayed in its *Vorlage*.

δ. Having retraced the impact of stylistic inversion on the textual transmission of the Bible text in various Hebrew and translational witnesses, we shall now turn to the investigation of the effect which this literary phenomenon had on quotations from biblical literature in post-biblical writings. The transposition of syntactical elements of a biblical verse in its secondary employment as a quotation in Qumran and rabbinic writings, or in the Apocrypha, often is interpreted to have resulted from scribal laxity or from lapses of memory, assuming that the post-biblical author quoted by heart and did not rely on a written source.[243]

It is agreed from the outset that in a large percentage of cases of quotational inversions the above explanations indeed are valid. It may further be assumed that in other instances, inverted quotations reflect Hebrew or possibly translational variants which the quoting author found in his *Vorlage* of the biblical text in question. However, in view of the

foregoing discussion, it is suggested that also in this sphere of biblical
text transmission the possibility should be considered that the principle
of 'controlled variation' which was the legitimate right of biblical
authors, editors, and likewise of transmitters and copyists retained a
lease on life also in the post-biblical period and was utilized by writers
who employed biblical quotations as building stones in their own compositions. We have no reason to doubt that if already in the early post-
biblical period the later emerging insistence on literal exactness with
regard to the Bible text would have been the established norm, rabbinic
and Qumran authors would have meticulously abided by this norm. Even
after discounting the inversion variants which can be readily explained to
have resulted from transmissional phenomena such as mentioned above, some
of the remaining instances require a different interpretation.

Rabbinic literature presents us with many instances of a fruitful
employment of transposition and inversion in Scripture quotations for
midrashic-exegetical and homiletic purposes, to the extent that it coined
a special technical term for this technique - סרוס,[244] and established the
exegetical rule - סרס המקרא ודרשהו - 'invert (or rearrange) a verse and
(then) expound it.'[245] It would appear that in essence this method was
considered a means by which to re-establish the supposedly original syntactical order of a verse which in the MT seemingly presented a case of hys-
teron proteron.[246] Like other literary-textual terms, such as אל תקרא -
... אלא ... 'do not read ... , but rather ...,'[247] סרוס in the course of
time lost its original exact technical connotation,[248] and inversion became a midrashic Spielelement in Scripture quotations. However, the progressive dissipation of exactness in the employment of the term and the
technique should not prevent us from recognizing the initially literary-
technical character of the rabbinic concept of סרוס.

Qumran writings have not preserved for us any specific terminology by
which to identify literary phenomena and techniques that were operative in
the Covenanters' setting. However, there is no lack of proof that
quotation-inversion was fully accepted by Qumran authors, whether deliberately and consciously or as a matter of tradition and routine. In some
instances, as, e.g., in the comparison of

113.   CD I,2:   כי ריב לו עם כל בשר || ומשפט יעשה בכל מנאציו with

    Jer. 25:31:   כי ריב ליהוה בגוים || נשפט הוא לכל בשר (= Vss),

we are concerned with a simple reversion and paraphrase of the biblical text.

The midrashic-paraphrastic character of transposition becomes even more apparent in the following examples:

114.   Zech. 11:11:   וידעו כן עניי הצאן השמרים אתי (= Vss)

    CD VII,20:   והשומרים אותו הם עניי הצאן

115.   Is. 59:5:   ביצי צפעוני בקעו || וקורי עכביש יארגו

    CD V,13-14:   קורי עכביש קוריהם || ובצי צפעונים ביציהם

In other instances it would appear that the possible employment of literary chiasm to express by it contrasting moods or meanings to which attention already was drawn[249] may be reflected in inverted quotations in Qumran literature, e.g.:

116.   Ps. 119:22:   גל מעלי חרפה ובוז

    1QH II,33-34:   וישימוני לבוז ולחרפה

Since the combination חרפה ובוז, probably a hendyadys, is unique in biblical Hebrew, little doubt is left that we are dealing here with a direct quotation by the author of 1QH from Psalm 119.

117.   Ez. 22:26:   בין קדש לחל לא הבדילו || ובין הטמא לטהור לא הודיעו

    CD VI,17:   ולהבדיל בין הטמא לטהור || ולהודיע בין הקודש לחול

The unique combination of elements and the ensuing reference to the Sabbath in both instances again make it abundantly clear that CD VI,17 presents a paraphrased inverted quotation of Ez. 22:26. Similarly,

118.   Deut 32:22   כי אש קדחה באפי ותיקד עד שאול תחתית ותאכל ארץ ויבלה ותלהט מוסדי הרים is paraphrased with inversion of the main syntactical elements in 1QH XVII,13   (אוכל)ה משאול תחתיה   ואש[250] מוסדי הרים (ביקוד).   The proposal to read [ביקוד] or possibly [בלהוט] at the beginning of the line, rather than [בחשרף] with Licht, derives from the recognition of the dependence of the Hodayoth passage on the text of Deut. 32:22, which Licht failed to recognize,[251] and illustrates the potentials of stylistic analysis for textual research.

Similar instances of quotation inversion may be observed in a comparison of, e.g.

119. 1QW I,1-2 with Is. 11:14,

120. 1QW XI,7 with Num. 24:18,

121. 1QH VIII,23-24 with Jer. 17:6-8, and many more examples that follow the same pattern.

VII 'Biblical' and 'Post-biblical' - The Issue of Literary Continuity

The rich crop of quotation variants from biblical writings in Qumran compositions suggests that 'inversion' was considered by their authors a legitimate quotation technique. In this, as in many other matters, Qumran writers obviously followed basic trends and tenets of biblical literature. Since some of the earlier Qumran works are contemporaneous with the latest parts of the biblical canon, such as, e.g., the second half of the Book of Daniel, the comparability of the two sets of literature becomes almost self-evident. The specific issue discussed here, viz. the interrelation of biblical stylistics and the history of the Bible text and its relation to biblical qutations in Qumran writings, must be viewed in the wider setting of the Qumran Covenanters' ideology and their historical conceptions. The Covenanters conceived of themselves as the 'biblical Israel.' In their self-understanding, they identified their community with the 'remnant' of biblical prophetic visions (Is. 6:13; 7:3; 10:20-22; 46:3; Jer. 23:3; Micah 2:2 etc.). The 'New Covenanters' were, in their own view, the 'holy seed' (Is. 6:13; 7:3; Ezra 9:2 etc.), the direct descendants of pre-exilic Israel, who had returned to the Land. As a reward for their faithfulness to Israel's God and their steadfast adherence to His commandments they, and only they, had been saved from the utter dissolution of Israel and the destruction of the Temple (CD I,4-8; II,8; etc.). In their community, pre-exilic Israel was embodied and reconstituted.[252]

In actual fact, the emergence of the Qumran community occurred in a historical setting which from the point of view of nascent rabbinic Judaism must be defined as post-biblical, whatever definition is accorded to this term. However, conceptually speaking, the Covenanters perceived themselves as standing within the framework of the biblical period, not less so than, e.g., the author of the Book of Daniel. In this fundamental aspect, the

'commune of the Bene Zadok' differs radically from other biblicizing ramifications of post-exilic Judaism that considered the biblical period a
closed chapter in the history of Israel, a period which served them as a
major source of inspiration. These contemporaneous Jewish communities,
and foremost rabbinic Judaism, consciously had terminated the writing of
'biblical' literature. They innovated new styles and types of literary
composition: the Apocrypha on the one hand and on the other the Mishnah
and the various forms of Midrash. The emerging 'oral Torah' was deliberately segregated from the biblical 'written Torah.'[253]

The rationalist teaching of the Rabbis found its expression in literary forms which most probably by intention differed fundamentally from
the biblical literary genres in which was concretized the inspired teaching
of former generations. In contradistinction, the Qumran Covenanters did
not subscribe to the idea that the biblical era had been terminated, nor
did they accept the concomitant notion that 'biblical' literature and literary standards had been superseded or replaced by new conceptions. It
appears that the very concept of a 'canon of biblical writings'[254] never
took root in their world of ideas, whatever way the term 'canon' is defined. Ergo, the very notion of a closing of the canon was not relevant.
This applies to the completion of the canon of Scriptures as a whole, and
also to the closure of its major components. It would seem that not only
did the complex of the Hagiographa remain an open issue, but also the collection of prophetic books was not considered sealed. Prophetic or quasi-
prophetic 'inspiration' continued to inform the leaders of the Qumran community, who did not subscribe to the rabbinic dictum that with 'the demise
of the last (i.e., the post-exilic) prophets Haggai, Zechariah and
Malachi (prophetic) inspiration had departed from Israel' (Tos. Sotah 13,2
ed. Zuckermandel 318,21-23; Bab. Tal. Sotah 48b; Sanh. 11b, etc.; and Seder
Olam 30).[255] Qumran literati condidered biblical literature a living matter, and participated in the ongoing process of its creation. Their attitude to the biblical books and to the text of Scriptures may be better compared to that of the author of the Book of Chronicles toward earlier biblical writings, rather than to that of rabbinic authors toward the books of
the canon. Like the Chronicler, or for that matter the author of Daniel,
they related to the biblical literature from within, and not from without

its orbit, as did the authors of the Apocrypha and the Rabbis. Like the
Chronicler, the copyist and possibly also the author of the Psalms Scroll
from Cave 11 (11Q Ps[a]),[256] as well as the authors of the Hodayoth, the
Damascus Documents and similar works, introduced into the copies based
upon their *Vorlagen*, and into their biblical quotations, paraphrases, word-
substitutions and glosses and skipped phrases and passages which they considered unsuitable. In all these aspects they maintained a biblical
stance, worked in a biblical vein, and used biblical stylistic techniques.

   I am fully aware of the fact that a great number, probably an overwhelming majority, of Qumran variants in biblical scrolls and in Bible
quotations resulted from insufficiently controlled copying and/or sometimes
represent diverging *Vorlagen*. But I would also maintain that an undeter-
mined percentage of these *variae lectiones* derive from the impact of ongoing literary processes of an intra-biblical nature, as illustrated by the
examples adduced above. This proposition, no doubt, calls for further detailed investigation. However, already at this preliminary stage its
potential importance for biblical studies becomes apparent when it is discussed within the frame of reference established by the 'three recensions'
or 'three text-types' school. As was stressed at the very outset of this
presentation, this new hypothesis has widened the scope of biblical textual
research. It purports to evince the history of the text, as far back as
the third century B.C.E., basing its arguments on manuscript evidence, and
has deduced from this evidence preceding stages of the text in as early as
the fifth or even sixth century B.C.E. In other words, in the Qumran
material coalesce the phase of creative authoring of biblical literature
with the ancillary phase of text transmission. The synchronous execution
of these intrinsically different processes within the orbit of one set of
literature, viz. the biblical writings, lends additional force to the suggestion that the diverse practitioners, the authors and the copyists, *mutatis mutandis*, employed the same or similar literary tenets and techniques.
In view of the inherent ideologically biblical stance, Qumran literature,
which chronologically speaking is set in the Hellenistic and Roman periods,
closes to a large degree the developmental gap between biblical and rabbinic literature. The literary and stylistic analysis of Qumran works thus
could provide new insights into the interdependence of these diverse sets

of ancient Hebrew writings and could help in recapturing some aspects of
the continuance of biblical literary norms into what customarily is designated as the post-biblical period.

It is hoped that the foregoing discussion sufficiently illustrated
the hypothesis that in ancient Hebrew literature no hard and fast lines
can be drawn between authors' conventions of style and tradents' and copyists' rules of reproduction and transmission. It may be said that in
ancient Israel, and probably also in other ancient Near Eastern cultures,
especially in Mesopotamia, the professional scribe seldom if ever was
merely a slavish copyist of the material which he handled. He rather
should be considered a minor partner in the creative literary process. To
a degree, he applied on the reproductive level norms and techniques which
had informed his predecessors, the ancient authors, and which had become
his literary legacy. The right to introduce variations into the biblical
text, within limits, had come to the Bible-oriented copyists and quoting
authors of post-biblical works, together with the transmitted writings.
Mechanical faithfulness to the letter of the sanctified traditional literature is to become the rule only after the undirected and intuitive process
of canonisation had completed its course, i.e., not earlier than the first
century B.C.E. and not later than the second century C.E. The recognition
of the ongoing impact of stylistic techniques and norms on the textual
transmission of the biblical literature which results from the above analysis must be given due attention in the scholarly discussion of issues pertaining to the 'Text and Versions' of the Bible.[257]

Notes

1. The publications in this field are far too numerous to be recorded here. The pertinent material is listed in the standard bibliographies of Qumran studies, viz. W. S. LaSor, "Bibliography of the Dead Sea Scrolls 1948-1957," *Fuller Library Bulletin* 31 (1958). Fuller Theological Seminary Bibliographical Series 2 (Pasadena, Calif. 1958); Chr. Burchard, *Bibliographie zu den Handschriften vom Toten Meer*, vol. I, *BZAW* 76 (Berlin 1957); vol. II, *BZAW* 89 (Berlin 1967); J. A. Fitzmyer, "A Bibliographical Aid to the Study of the Qumran Cave IV Texts," *CBQ* 31 (1969) 59-71; B. Jongeling, *A Classified Bibliography of the Finds in the Desert of Judah 1958-1969* (Leiden 1971), *et al.*

2. *BASOR* 140 (1955) 27-33.

3. The term "Version" is used here in reference to all witnesses of the Bible text, including the MT which, *sensu stricto*, is but a version of the now unattainable original Hebrew text.

4. A more detailed account may be found in S. Talmon, "The Old Testament Text," in: *Cambridge History of the Bible* vol. I etc., reprinted in the present volume.

5. A complete listing of pertinent bibliographical material would transcend the scope of this essay. Some notable works are, e.g.: F. Delitzsch, *Die Lese- und Schreibfehler im Alten Testament* (Berlin und Leipzig 1920); J. Kennedy, *An Aid to the Textual Amendment of the Old Testament* (Edinburgh 1928); F. Perles, *Analekten zur Textkritik des Alten Testaments* (Muenchen 1895); *Neue Folge* (Leipzig 1922), *et al.*

6. A. von Gall, *Der hebraeische Pentateuch der Samaritaner* (Giessen 1918). Like von Gall's main text, such an eclectic edition of the MT would present a hypothetical text which never had had a manuscript existence. See my remarks on this issue in "Aspects of the Text of the Hebrew Bible," in: *Biblical and Armenian Studies* ed. M. Stone, Suppl. to *Sion* vol. I (forthcoming).

7. Cp., e.g., F. M. Cross - D. N. Freedman, *Studies in Ancient Yahwistic Poetry* (Baltimore 1950); Cross, "A Royal Song of Thanksgiving: II Sam. 22 = Psalm 18," *JBL* 72 (1953) 15-34; *idem*, "The Song of Miriam," *JNES* 14 (1955) 237-250; I. L. Seeligmann, "A Psalm from Pre-Regal Times," *VT* 14 (1964) 75-92; *et al.* A. Bruno, *Rhytmische Untersuchungen von Genesis etc.* (1953-1959) has not convinced scholars that rhythmic considerations are a sufficient basis for full-scale text reconstructions.

8. A convenient summary of the history of the Qumran discoveries and a survey of theories about their dating and the identity of the Covenanters may be found in the standard works on these finds. See, most recently: J. A. Sanders, "The Dead Sea Scrolls - A Quarter Century of Study," *BA* 36,4 (1973) 110-148.

9. F. M. Cross, Jr., "The Contribution of the Qumran Discoveries to the Study of the Biblical Text," *IEJ* 16 (1966) 85.

10. *Ib.* n. 21.

11. For surveys consult: H. M. Orlinsky, "The Textual Criticism of

the Old Testament," in: *The Bible and the Ancient Near East, Essays in Honour of W. F. Albright*, ed. G. E. Wright (New York 1961) 113-132; S. Jellicoe, *The Septuagint and Modern Study* (Oxford 1968); F. M. Cross, Jr., "The Evolution of a Theory of Local Texts," *SCS* 2 (1972) 108-126 (reprinted in this volume); J. A. Sanders, *op. cit.*

12. D. Barthélemy O.P., *"Les Devanciers d'Aquila* etc.,*" SVT* X (Leiden 1963).

13. Cp. D. Barthélemy, "A Reexamination of the Textual Problems in 2 Sam. 11:2 - 1 Kings 2:11 in the Light of Certain Criticisms of *Les Devanciers d'Aquila*," *SCS* 2 (1972) 16-89; E. Tov, "The State of the Question: Problems and Proposed Solutions," *ib.*, 3-15.

14. K. G. O'Connell, *The Theodotionic Revision of the Book of Exodus*, Harvard Semitic Monographs 3 (Cambridge, Mass. 1972) and current publications surveyed there.

15. Cp. the survey presented by E. Tov, *op. cit.*; *idem* "Lucian and Proto-Lucian - Toward a New Solution of the Problems," *RB* 79 (1972) 101-103.

16. For a discussion of the pertinent issues and for current bibliography consult: G. Howard, "*Kaige* Readings in Josephus," *Textus* VIII (1973) 45-54.

17. Cp. items listed in note 13, and especially D. W. Gooding's studies: "Ahab According to the Septuagint," *ZAW* N.F. 35 (1964) 269-280; "Pedantic Timetabling in 3rd Book of Reigns," *VT* 15 (1965) 153-166; "The Septuagint Version of Solomon's Misconduct," *ib.* 325-335; "Temple Specifications: a Dispute in Logical Arrangement Between the MT and the LXX," *VT* 17 (1967) 143-172; "Text-Sequence and Translation-Revision in 3 Reigns ix 10-x 33," *VT* 19 (1969) 448-463; J. D. Shenkel, *Chronology and Recensional Development in the Greek Text of Kings*, Harvard Semitic Monographs 1 (Cambridge, Mass. 1968).

18. E.g., the Book of Daniel. Cp. P. Grelot, "Les versions grecques de Daniel," *Biblica* 47 (1966) 381-402; A. Schmitt, "Stammt der sogenannte θ'-Text bei Daniel wirklich von Theodotion?" *MSU* 9 (Goettingen 1966).

19. H. St.J. Thackeray, "The Bisection of Books in Primitive Septuagint MSS," *JThSt* 9 (1907/80 88-98; "The Greek Translators of Jeremiah," *JThSt* 4 (1902/3) 245-266; "The Greek Translators of Ezekiel," *ib.*, 398-411; "The Greek Translators of the Prophetical Books," *ib.*, 578-585; "The Greek Translators of the Four Books of Kings," *JThSt* 8 (1906/7) 88-98.

20. O. J. Baab, "A Theory of Two Translators for the Greek Genesis," *JBL* 52 (1933) 239-243.

21. J. Herrmann - F. Baumgartel, *Beitraege zur Enstehungsgeschichte der Septuaginta, BWAT* ii,5 (Stuttgart 1923).

22. E.g., G. C. Workman, *The Text of Jeremiah* (Edinburgh 1889); P. F. Frankl, "Studien ueber die Septuaginta und Peschitto zu Jeremia," *MGWJ* 21 (1872) 444-456; 497-509; A. W. Streane, *The Double Text of Jeremiah* (Cambridge 1896); G. B. Gray, "The Greek Version of Isaiah: Is it the Work of a Single Translator?," *JThSt* 12 (1911) 186-293; N. Turner, "The Greek

Translators of Ezekiel," *JThSt* 7 (1956) 12-24; T. Muraoka, "Is the Septuagint Amos viii 12 - ix 10 a Separate Unit?," *VT* 20 (1970) 496-500 contra
G. Howard, "Some Notes on the Septuagint of Amos," *VT* 20 (1970) 108-112,
and recent publications mentioned in these articles.

23. This theory was applied to the LXX of Jeremiah by E. Tov in an
unpublished thesis: "The Septuagint Translation of Jeremiah and Baruch"
(Hebrew University, Jerusalem 1973) where also recent literature is
adduced. See further n. 13.

24. P. Kahle has restated his views in: *Die hebraeischen Handschriften aus der Hoehle* (Stuttgart 1951); *The Cairo Geniza*[2] (Oxford 1959); "Der
gegenwaertige Stand der Erforschung der in Palaestina neu gefundenen
hebraeischen Handschriften," *ThLZ* 79 (1954) 81-94, etc. Proponents of the
de Lagarde school like H. M. Orlinsky and P. Katz have not expressed themselves unequivocally on the 'three recensions' theory.

25. See my remarks in *CHB*, 193ff. (reprinted in this volume).

26. S. Talmon, "Aspects of the Textual Transmission of the Bible in
Light of the Qumran Manuscripts," *Textus* IV (1964) 95ff.

27. K. H. Graf, *Der Prophet Jeremia erklaert* (1862) xl ff., calculated that 2700 Hebrew words of the MT, or about one-eighth of the overall
text, are not represented in the LXX. Cp. also F. Giesebrecht, *Das Buch
Jeremia*[2], *HAT* (Goettingen 1907) xxv ff.; A. W. Streane, *op. cit.*; E. Tov,
"L'incidence de la critique textuelle sur la critique littéraire dans le
livre de Jérémie," *RB* 79 (1972) 189-199.

28. F. M. Cross, Jr., *The Ancient Library of Qumran*, rev. ed. (New
York 1961) 186-187; *idem*, "The Contribution of the Qumran Discoveries to
the Study of the Biblical Text," *IEJ* 16 (1966) 82; J. G. Janzen, *Studies in
the Text of Jeremiah*, Harvard Semitic Monographs 6 (Cambridge, Mass. 1973).

29. Cp. E. Tov, *RB* 79 (1972) 189ff.

30. A concise survey of the problem may be found in C. A. Moore,
Esther, *AB* (New York 1971) lxi ff.; *idem*, "A Greek Witness to a Different
Hebrew Text of Esther," *ZAW* 79 (1967) 153-158; *idem*, "On the Origins of
the LXX Additions to the Book of Esther," *JBL* 92 (1973) 382-393.

31. Cp. Kahle's writings mentioned in n. 24.

32. F. M. Cross, Jr., *IEJ* 16 (1966) 86.

33. It is immaterial for our present purpose whether the MT=Is[a] reading מכתב is retained or whether מכתם is preferred.

34. I. Engnell defines the composition 'Royal Psalm of Lament.' See:
"Figurative Language of the O.T." in: *Critical Essays on the O.T.*, trans.
J. T. Willis (London 1970) 265.

35. A detailed textual analysis was given by H. M. Orlinsky, "The
Kings-Isaiah Recensions of the Hezekiah Story," *JQR* 30 (1939/40) 33-49.
Cp. further: J. Begrich, *Der Psalm des Hiskia*, *FRLANT* N.R. 25 (Goettingen
1926).

36. An ancillary attempt to probe into the possible overlapping of
issues of 'higher' and 'lower' criticism is made by E. Tov, *RB* 79 (1972)
189-199.

37. For this type of homiletic expansion which initially may have been of an extra-scriptural character see S. Talmon, "Pisqah Be'emsa‘ Pasuq and 11QPs[a]," *Textus* V (1966) 12-21.

38. *Vide* Y. Zakowitz, "2 Kings 20:7 - Isaiah 38:21-22," *Beth Mikra* 17 (1972) 302-305 (Hebrew).

39. Cp., e.g., Ex. 5:3; 9:3, 15; Lev. 26:25; Num. 14:12, 2 Sam. 24:13-15; Ez. 5:17; 7:15, *et al.*

40. Cp., e.g., Num. 12:10; 2 Ki. 5:27; 15:5; 2 Chr. 26:20-23, *et al.*

41. It may be assumed that the elaboration which introduces שׁחין into the Hezekiah narrative constitutes a typological approximation to the tradition about King Uzziah's affliction by צרעת (2 Ki. 15:5 = 2 Chr. 26:19-21).

42. This technique of 'recapitulation' is widely employed in the biblical writings and can also be found in other literatures of the ancient Near East. The phenomenon which is to be discussed elsewhere in greater detail can be found, e.g., in Essarhaddon's vassal treaties. See for the present: R. Frankena, "The Vassal Treaties of Essarhaddon and the Dating of Deuteronomy," *Oudtestamentische Studien* 14 (1965) 128, 132. I am indebted to Dr. J. H. Tigery for bringing this reference to my attention.

43. In some Introductions to biblical literature, stylistics are not discussed at all, and likewise literary forms and textual history. Issues of 'canon' are dealt with in a rather cursory fashion. See, e.g., S. R. Driver, *An Introduction to the Literature of the O.T.*, rev. ed. (New York 1950).

44. The schematic division which appears to obtain in biblical studies can be illustrated by the following table:

Discipline	Literary Process	Techniques	Practitioner	Period
Biblical Stylistics	Creative Writing	Composition (predominantly oral)	Poet, Narrator, Historiographer, etc.	1200 -
Literary Criticism	Compilation, Redaction	Oral and Written Tradition	Compiler, Redactor	900 -
Study of Text	Reproduction	Written Transmission	Copyist	300 -

45. This system is exemplified in the 'Introductions' by O. Eissfeldt[3] (Tuebingen 1964); E. Sellin - G. Fohrer (Heidelberg 1965); M. Z. Segal (Jerusalem 1946, Hebrew). In spite of some departures from this model also F. Bleek - J. Wellhausen[5] (Berlin 1866), C. H. Cornill (Tuebingen 1905), R. H. Pfeiffer (New York/London 1941), *et al.*, follow the same lines.

46. The assumed profound difference between the forms of oral tradition and written transmission should be toned down considerably. An investigation into transitional stages and into the possible transfer of techniques from one to the other is an urgent desideratum. These issues were not touched upon in such systematic works as E. Nielsen's *Oral Tradition*, STB 11 (London 1954) and A. B. Lord's *The Singer of Tales* (New York 1970),

especially pp. 124-138. For a suggestive new approach to the problem with reference to the rabbinic 'oral law' see J. Neusner, "Types and Forms in Ancient Jewish Literature: Some Comparisons," *History of Religions* vol. 11,4 (1972) 354-390; *idem*, "The Rabbinic Traditions About the Pharisees Before A.D. 70, The Problem of Oral Transmission," *JJS* xxii (1971) 1-18.

47. The growth in stages of the latter part of the Book of Jeremiah (chs. 45-52) will be discussed in a separate publication.

48. R. Smend, *Die Weisheit des Jesus Sirach* (Berlin 1906). Verse numbers in brackets refer to M. Z. Segal's edition of the book (Jerusalem 1953, Hebrew).

49. Cp. Segal, *op. cit.* 350,13; 363 *ad loc.* G. H. Box - W. O. E. Oesterley in: R. H. Charles, *The Apocrypha and Pseudepigrapha* vol. I (Oxford 1913) 511-512 and 517, define both notations as 'subscriptions' without further clarifications.

50. An illustration of the interdependence of these diverse literary processes may be found in S. Talmon - M. Fishbane, "Aspects of the Literary Structure of the Book of Ezekiel," *Tarbiz* xlii (1972/73) 27-41 (Hebrew).

51. The required integrative approach in exegesis of biblical literature is most fruitfully applied by W. Zimmerli, *Ezechiel*, BKAT (Neukirchen-Vluyn 1969).

52. A detailed portrait of R. Meier may be found in W. Bacher, *Die Aggada der Tannaiten*, vol. ii (Strassburg 1890) 1-69. Tradition has it that R. Meier dedicated one-third of his income from his scribal activities to the maintenance of needy scholars (Midrash Koh. Rabba *ad* Eccl. 2:18ff.).

53. See below, examples 113-121.

54. J. A. Sanders, *The Psalm Scroll of Qumran Cave 11 (11QPs^a)*, DJD IV (Oxford 1965); *idem, The Dead Sea Psalms Scroll* (Cornell 1967).

55. To be edited by Y. Yadin. For the present see the editor's preliminary observations: "The Temple Scroll," in *Jerusalem Through the Ages* (Jerusalem 1968) 72-84 (Hebrew).

56. S. Mowinckel, "Zum Problem der hebraeischen Metrik," *Festschrift A. Bertholet* (Tuebingen 1950) 391.

57. S. Segert, "Problems of Hebrew Prosody," *SVT* 7 (1960) 285.

58. L. Alonso-Schoekel, "Die stylistische Analyse bei den Propheten," *ib.*, 164.

59. Most synonymities are in fact of the pragmatic type and are not necessarily rooted in etymology. They reflect the 'conditioned meanings' which result from the actual employment of two words in parallelistic structures in a given literary context. Cp. M. Dahood, in: ed. L. R. Fisher, *Ras Shamra Parallels Analecta Orientalia* 19 (Roma 1972) 83; M. Z. Kaddari, "On Semantic Parallelism in Biblical Hebrew Poetry," *Lešonénu* XXXII (1967/68) 37-45.

60. Cp. E. Z. Melamed, "Break-up of Stereotype Phrases as an Artistic Device in Biblical Poetry," *Scripta Hierosolymitana* VIII, ed. C. Rabin (Jerusalem 1961) 115-144; S. Talmon, "Synonymous Readings in the Textual

Tradition of the O.T.," *ib.*, 335ff.; M. Dahood, *Psalms*, AB vol. I, xxiv; II, xxiii; III, xxxix-xli and indexes *s.v.* 'Break-up of Stereotyped Phrase.'

61. An up-to-date survey of the rapidly growing literature on this stylistic phenomenon which is shared by biblical with Ugaritic literature is given by M. Dahood in *Ras Shamra Parallels*, 73ff. To the list presented there, add Y. Avishur, "Pairs of Synonymous Words in the Construct (and in Appositional Hendyadys) in Biblical Hebrew," *Semitics* 2 (1971/72) 17-81.

62. Cp. S. Talmon, *op. cit.*, 359.

63. אִישׁ is translated ἀνήρ 764x and ἄνθρωπος 400x. אָדָם is rendered ἄνθρωπος 460x and ἀνήρ 27x. Cp. E. C. Dos Santos, *An Expanded Hebrew Index for the Hatch-Redpath Concordance to the Septuagint* (Jerusalem n.d.) *x.v. cit.*

64. Cp. J. Reider, *An Index to Aquila etc.*, completed and revised by N. Turner, *SVT* 12 (Leiden 1960) *s.v. cit.*, with further additional corrections by E. Tov, *Textus* VIII (1973) 164-174.

65. Cp. T. Muraoka, "Literary Device in the Septuagint," *ib.* 25.

66. The *hif'il* יחרים suggests that the phrase is a contracted quotation from Lev. 27:28 MT אֲשֶׁר יַחֲרִם אִישׁ ... מֵאָדָם with an interchange of אָדָם and אִישׁ, and not from v.29, *pace* C. Rabin, *The Zadokite Documents* (Oxford 1954) 45 and others, who adjust the CD reading to the *hof'al* that occurs in MT Lev. 27:29 אֲשֶׁר יָחֳרַם מִן הָאָדָם. The assumed dependence on v.29 causes the further suggestion that the second mention of אָדָם in CD ix,1 which has no counterpart in the MT is a free addition of the Qumran author (Rabin, *ib.* n.3). A comparison of the CD reading with the parallel MT passage leads one to propose that in any case the first אָדָם should be emended to חֶרֶם:

Lev. 27:29   אַךְ כָּל חֵרֶם אֲשֶׁר יַחֲרִם אִישׁ ... מֵאָדָם

CD ix,1   > כָּל אָדָם אֲשֶׁר יַחֲרִים אָדָם > מֵאָדָם

67. Most translators of the passage throughout read אָדָם - 'man.' Cp. Rabin, *loc. cit.*; M. Burrows, *The Dead Sea Scrolls* (New York 1955) 358; A. Dupont-Sommer, *The Essene Writings from Qumran*, tr. G. Vermes (Cleveland and New York 1961) 148, *et al.* Th. Gaster, *The Dead Sea Scriptures* (New York 1964) 85 distinguishes between 'man' and 'fellow being.'

68. Cp. S. Talmon, *op. cit.*, 370-371.

69. Cp. S. Talmon, *ib.*, 373.

70. שִׂים interchanges with שִׁית, as e.g. in

Jer. 2:15   וַיָּשִׁיתוּ אַרְצוֹ לְשַׁמָּה עָרָיו נִצְּתָה מִבְּלִי יֹשֵׁב

4:7   לָשׂוּם אַרְצֵךְ לְשַׁמָּה עָרַיִךְ תִּצֶּינָה מֵאֵין יוֹשֵׁב

Therefore it also can form a parallel pair with נתן, as e.g. in

Jer. 3:19   אֵיךְ אֲשִׁיתֵךְ בַּבָּנִים וְאֶתֶּן לָךְ אֶרֶץ חֶמְדָּה

71. For reasons of assonance and paronomasy one would have expected here the combination שִׂים שַׁמָּה instead of נתן שַׁמָּה.

72. Comparable variations in the composition of idioms and epithets can be observed in the Versions. For the LXX see T. Muraoka, *op. cit.*, especially p. 25ff.

73. See W. Bauer, *Griechisches Woerterbuch zum N.T.*[2], tr. W. F. Arndt and F. W. Gingrich (Chicago 1965) *s.v. cit.*

74. Some 1450x, and almost 300x more with a preposition. As against this τιθηναι renders נתן only some 150x, and another 180x with prepositions.

75. Altogether close to 400x. διδοναι is employed as a rendition of שים 27x. Cp. Dos Santos, *op. cit., s.v. cit.*

76. All references are to the text and apparatus of the LXX Goettingen edition where available. In other instances the Cambridge (A. E. Brooke - N. McLean) or A. Rahlfs's *Septuaginta* (Stuttgart 1950) are used.

77. Ms. B here reads δώσω, possibly in approximation to the MT.

78. A. B. Ehrlich prefers this derivation in his מקרא כפשוטו, vol. iii (1901) 310. But in his *Randglossen zur hebraeischen Bibel*, vol. v (Leipzig 1912) 48, he adopts the widely accepted emendation of the unusual *hif'il* to the *qal* form ושמחיהו.

79. See Ehrlich, *ib.*

80. Cp. S. Talmon, "Double Readings in the MT," *Textus* I (1960) 144-184.

81. Cp. S. Talmon, "Aspects, etc.," *Textus* IV (1964) 95-132.

82. A similar case may be observed in 2 Sam. 5:14-16 where the MT parallel reading of 1 Chr. 14:4-8 (+ ואלפלט ונגה) turns up in what amounts to an appendix in the LXX (2 Sam. 5:16[a]).

83. For the phenomenon of such inner-Greek variants see J. Ziegler, "Die Vokabel-Varianten der O-Rezension im griechischen Sirach," *Festschrift G. R. Driver* (Oxford 1963) 172-190 = *Sylloge* (Goettingen 1971) 615-633.

84. Chr. Ginsburg lists one printed edition and BH[4] four Mss which read here הארץ.

85. The MT of Sam. is distinguished from the Chr. parallel by a more balanced structure.

86. Not too much weight, though, can be accorded to the Targumic evidence which derives from late manuscripts or even early printed editions.

87. The Targums are quoted according to S. Sperber's edition, *The Bible in Aramaic* (Leiden 1959-1968).

88. Cp. his *Commentarius* ed. Vallarsi, *ad loc.* On Jerome's *sive* readings see J. Ziegler, "Die Septuaginta Hieronymi im Buch des Propheten Jeremias" in: *Colligere Fragmenta, Festschrift A. Dold* (Beuron 1952) 13-24 = *Sylloge*, 345-356.

89. With the exception of the cases listed here, the LXX never render עיר by χωρα or γη which translate ארץ, אדמה, שדה, מדינה. Hatch-Redpath do not list עיר under χωρα (1418a) or γη (240c), nor χωρααor γη under עיר (254).

90. *Vide* e.g., P. Volz, *Studien zum Text des Jeremia* (Leipzig 1920) 31,217; W. Rudolph, *Jeremia*, HAT (Tuebingen 1947) 30,154; J. Bright, *Jeremiah*, AB (New York 1965) 208. Volz admits, though, that in Jer. 40:5 "beides ist

moeglich" (*op. cit.*, 278).

91. Thus Volz and Rudolph, *loc. cit.*

92. See n.83.

93. LXX: αὐταρκήσεν and TO: צרכיהון סמיק possibly reflect a *hif‘il* reading ימציאהו.

94. Recorded by F. Field, *Origenis Hexaplorum Quae Supersunt*, vol. I (Oxford 1875) 578 as an *állos* reading.

95. Cp. D. Barthélemy, *Les Devanciers, etc.*, 72, 132-33.

96. The editor of this fragment, F. M. Cross, Jr., considers the Qumran reading superior to the MT (*BASOR* 132 [1952] 22). In view of the above discussion this preference cannot be sustained on objective grounds.

97. *Vide* Hatch-Redpath *s.v.*

98. Thus F. Buhl in *BH*.

99. See his *Psalms*, AB, vol. III, 101.

100. The rendition of שלם by δίδωμι possibly resulted from an inner-Greek process facilitated by the fact that שלם predominantly is rendered by a compositum of δίδωμι viz. ἀποδίδωμι.

101. Cp. the doublet in 1 Sam. 2:23, and my analysis in *Textus* I, 180.

102. Jer. 35(42):18 - καθότι.

103. Cp. W. Genesius - E. Kautzsch, *Hebrew Grammar*, 2nd Engl, ed. A. E. Cowley (Oxford 1910) 382. 119 v.w.

104. G. B. Gray, *Numbers*, ICC (Edinburgh 1903) 151.

105. Targ. מן חורך ומן ענך.

106. Targ. ית ענכון וית תורכון.

107. It follows that the Sam. text is not intrinsically different from the MT and that the clause there is understood as a partitive rather than as an all-inclusive direct object. In this Sam. goes with the Targumic tradition - T[O]: חדא מן ארבעתי משריתא T[J]: חדא מארבע משריתא דישראל דישראל. Both the MT masc. form רבע and the Sam. fem. form רבעת are pragmatically synonymous with עפר. W. F. Albright's suggestion that MT את רבע actually is a misread תרבע = Acc. *turbu'tu* (*JBL* LXXIII [1944] 213) which also is found in the forms *turbu'u, turubû, turubu, tarbu'um* (W. v. Soden, *Orientalia* XXII [1954] 343) makes the synonymity of this noun with עפר certain. Cp. the detailed analysis presented by S. E. Loewenstamm, "Notes on the Origin of Some Biblical Figures of Speech," in: *Studies in the Bible, Presented to M. H. Segal* (Jerusalem 1964) 183-187 (Hebrew).

108. See, e.g., C. H. Toy, *The Book of Proverbs*, ICC (Edinburgh 1904); B. Gemser, *Spruecher Salomos*, HAT (Tuebingen 1963); W. McKane, *Proverbs*, OTL (Philadelphia 1970); H. Ringgren, *Sprueche/Prediger*, ATD (1962) *ad loc.*

109. Cp. 2 Sam. 17:9 MT: על פני הבאר; Mss. and Seb. read על פי possibly adjusting the text to the prevailing idiom (Gen. 28:2, 3, 8, 10). — It further is reasonable that Prov. 10:6 ברכות לראש צדיק ופי רשעים יכסה חמס

should be understood or should be actually read וּפְנֵי, with G. Beer, *BH*; Gemser, *op. cit.*; Toy, *op. cit. ad loc.*; I. L. Seeligmann, *SVT* I (1953) 164 who correctly compares Jer. 51:51; Ps. 44:16; 69:8, Job 9:24; against McKane, *op. cit.* and R. B. Y. Scott, *Proverbs/Ecclesiastes*, AB (New York 1965) *ad loc.* who translate the phrase 'speech' or 'mouth of the wicked.' Scott further renders יכסה - 'uncovers' instead of the correct rendition 'conceals' (McKane). The assumed interchange of פְנֵי/פִי would help in understanding the difficult לפי קרת in Prov. 8:3 MT: ליד שערים לפי קרת to mean לפני קרת - 'outside the city.' For לפני קרת cp. פני העיר (Gen. 33:18); על פני יריחו (Deut. 32:49; 34:1) and similar idioms. A good Ug. parallel would be present in 2 Aqht V:6-7 (*CTA* 17 V:6-7): *ytb.bap. t̪ġr. tḥt adrm. dbgrn* (cp. also 1 Kings 22:10 and R-S Parallels I,46).

110.   Cp. J. Ziegler, *Sylloge*, 182.

111.   Box - Oesterley *apud* R. H. Charles, *Apocrypha, etc.*, 321.

112.   H. P. Rueger, *Text und Textform im hebraeischen Sirach*, BZAW 112 (Berlin 1970) 99.

113.   An assumed interchange of פִי / פְנֵי may be of some help in re- covering the 'original' reading of CD III,4 (ed. Rabin, 11): ויעגשר לפני משגותם which I. Lévi correctly read לפי. This reading may be compared with 1QS IX,14: להבדיל ולשקול בני צדוק לפי רוחו. It is further possible that in CD IX,9-10 (ed. Rabin, 45-46) איש אשר ישביע על פני השדה אשר לא לפנים השפטים או מאמרם לפנים should be understood as לפי II מאמרם, both meaning 'according to the judges' instruction.'

114.   Cp. further Hos. 2:17(19). - The assumed association by the translator of Jer. 4:1 with Zech. 9:7 does not militate against the assump- tion that the LXX to Jer. 4:1 contains a doublet, as implied by J. Ziegler, *ib.* The instance must be judged against the background of other inter- changes between פִי - פְנֵי such as are discussed in examples 38-41, 43-45, and especially the MT doublet in Ex. 14:2 (ex. 46). *Beitraege zur Ieremias Septuaginta* (Goettingen 1958) 90.

115.   Thus, e.g., H. Graetz, *Kritischer Kommentar zu den Psalmen II* (Breslau 1883) 470-472; A. B. Ehrlich, *Die Psalmen* (Berlin 1905) 196; M. Buttenwieser, *The Psalms* (Chicago 1938) 609 *ad* Ps. 79:12; C. A. Briggs, *The Book of Psalms*, II (Edinburgh 1925) 209; W. O. E. Oesterley, *The Psalms*, II (London 1939) 368; against F. Buhl, *BH*[4]: *prps* פיך. The MT also is fol- lowed by M. Dahood, *Psalms*, II, AB, 260 who, though, interprets פנים - 'fury' (*op. cit.*, I, 133, 207; *Biblica* 44 [1963] 548).

116.   M. Dahood, *ib.*, failed to take these facts into account in his comment on the passage.

117.   Sam., some MT Mss., printed editions, and *seb.* read מפי which reading also is reflected in the Latin and Syriac renditions.

118.   LXX render here ἐπὶ στόμα Εὔρωθ, in Num. 33:8 ἀπέναντι Εὔρωθ and in Ex. 14:2, 9 ἀπέναντι τῆς ἐπαύλεως, misreading חירת as חצרת = 'court- yards.' For the graphic interchange of ancient Hebrew *yod* and *ṣade* cp. S. Talmon, "The Town Lists of Simeon," *IEJ* 15 (1966) 233-241, and literature adduced there.

119.   The component *pi* = 'house' occurs once more in Ez. 30:17 in the

Egyptian *nom. loc.* פיבסת LXX: Βον Βαστον.

120. In Gen. 32:31, 32 the LXX do not transcribe but rather trans-
late Εὖδος (τοῦ) θεοῦ. This is an adequate rendition of the Hebrew פניאל.
The critical note in *BH* 'ראיאל ?' is gratuitous. In Jud. 8:8, 9, 17; 1
Kings 12:25 the LXX transliterate φανουηλ.

121. Thus understood, פניאל would equal בית אל. The biblical traditions about Peni(u)el indeed exhibit striking similarities with those pertaining to Bethel (Gen. 28:11-19). There are two traditions constitute an
inclusio-like frame for the Jacob - Esau confrontations, one preceding
Jacob's flight before his brother, the other signaling his return to
Canaan, and the re-encounter with Esau. At both locations the patriarch
experienced a theophany which in each case culminated in a covenant between him and the deity, and in the change of his name to 'Israel' - Gen.
32:28-29 and 35:9-10, unless the latter passage is understood as a Peni'el
insert into a Bethel tradition. If P(n)i'el is taken to be another 'bethel,' Jeroboam's I choice of this city as his capital after abandoning
Shechem is more readily explained (1 Kings 12:25).

122. Cp. Jer. 35:10   ונשב באהלים ונשמע ונעש ככל אשר צונו יונדב אבינו
       with *ib.* v.18   יען אשר שמעתם על מצות יונדב אביכם ותשמרו את כל
                           מצותיו ותעשו את כל אשר צוה אתכם

123. The complementary techniques of 'stylistic conflation' and
'break-up pattern' are discussed in the publications listed in note 60.

124. Cp. *Textus* I (1960) 163-164.

125. Such a reductionist tendency possibly may be observed also in
the LXX rendition of Jer. 1:17. See my analysis of this case: "An Apparent Redundant MT Reading - Jer. 1:17," *Textus* VIII (1973) 160-163. - The
shorter Greek text obviously will be accorded preference by scholars who
tend to identify 'short' with 'pristine,' and 'long' or 'fuller' with 'expansionist.' See, e.g., E. Tov, *RB* LXXIX (1972) 195, and H. W. Juengling,
"Ich mache dich zu einer ehernen Mauer," *Biblica* 54 (1973) 1-24 which came
to my attention only after the completion of this paper. The tendency to
delete as secondary what appears to be redundant phrases or words is a
highly dubious procedure which violates the character of biblical writing.
(Cp. J. Muilenburg, "A Study in Hebrew Rhetoric: Repetition and Style," *SVT*
I (1953) 99.

126. In addition to the instances discussed here, נצל is found six
times in the Book of Jeremiah (7:10; 15:21; 20:13; 21:12; 22:3; 39:17)
whereas הושיע is employed sixteen further times (2:28; 3:23; 4:14; 8:20;
11:12 twice; 14:8, 9; 17:14; 23:6; 30:7, 10; 31:7; 33:16; 42:11; 46:27).
No pattern of distribution within the book can be recognised.

127. Th. renders both Heb. terms uniformly κατ' ἀνατολάς. Sym. and
Syh. translate in 10:19 ἀνατολικη. In the two other mentions of קדמוני
with reference to 'gate' (47:8, 18; cp. further 48:1, 2, 6, 7, 8, 18) the
LXX too render ἀνατολάς.

128. T^J renders the two terms uniformly מדנחאה.

129. This case, and examples 5 and 8, were not listed by E. Tov, *op.*

cit., who presented a classification of 'amplifications' without aiming at an exhaustive listing of all instances.

130. Most commentators do not discuss the doublet. See, e.g., C. H. Cornill, *Das Buch Jeremia* (Leipzig 1905); F. Giesebrecht, *Das Buch Jeremia*, GHAT (Gottingen 1907); P. Volz, *Studien zum Text des Jeremia* (Leipzig 1920); *idem*, *Der Prophet Jeremia*, KAT (Leipzig 1928); W. Rudolph, *Jeremia*, HAT (Tuebingen 1954); J. Bright, *Jeremia*, AB ad loc.

131. S. Mandelkern, *Veteris Testamenti Concordantiae*, wrongly records here: ‏ובעת צרתם‎.

132. Another parallel pair which is based on the same synonyms is ‏יום צרה‎ (Jer. 16:19) and ‏יום רעה‎ (*ib.* 17:17, 18; 51:2).

133. In 31:1 Ziegler relegates to the apparatus the prevalent reading ἐν τῷ χαιρῷ and records in the main text the B-S-A-106'-46 rendition ἐν τῷ χρόνῳ.

134. The same double phrase turns up in the MT, LXX and T^J of Joel 4:1.

135. Cornill, *op. cit.*, 497 deletes ‏ובעת ההיא‎ together with ‏נאם יהוה‎ in 50:4, 20 "aus metrischen Gruenden," but retains the MT in 33:15, hardly sound methodological procedure. Volz, KAT, 423-425 takes 50:4, 20 to be parts of more comprehensive 'glosses,' and does not apply himself to the above textual problem. Rudolph, *op. cit.*, follows the MT in all three instances.

136. Jer. 33:14-26 is the most extensive consecutive MT unit which is omitted in the LXX.

137. None of the commentators cited remarks on this case.

138. It is immaterial for the present discussion whether the *hif‘il* ‏ימצאהו‎ or the *qal* ‏ימצאהו‎ is read here.

139. Cp. Ex. 15:17.

140. Cp. further Ps. 61:5 ‏אחסה בסתר כנפיך‎, and the parallel idiom Gen. 19:8 ‏באו בצל קרתי‎ for which Ug. *ʿrb.bzl.ḥmt* (Krt: 159 = CTA 14 III:159) may be compared.

141. Also other cases of presumed textual doublets, in fact, may be stylistic transition doublets, as, e.g., 2 Kings 11:13^a – ‏הרצין העם‎ compared with vv.4, 6, 11 ‏הרצים‎ and vv.13^b, 17 ‏העם‎; *ib.* 11:19 ‏הרצים וכל עם הארץ‎ cp. with vv.4, 6, 11 ‏הרצים‎ and with vv.14, 18, 20 ‏עם הארץ‎. Further: *ib.* 10:6^a ‏ראשי אנשי בני אדניכם‎ compared with vv.1, 2, 3, 6^b ‏בנים, בני אדניכם‎, v.8 ‏ראשי בני המלך‎ and v.7 ‏שבעים איש ... בני המלך‎. See S. Talmon, *Textus I*, 167.

142. Cp. Muilenburg, SVT I, 97ff.

143. The same feature may be observed in Ug. literature. See M. Dahood's remarks in *R-S Parallels*, 79-80.

144. Cp. Muilenburg, *op. cit.*, 99 and Dahood, *ib.*

145. We use the term somewhat differently from M. Dahood, *ib.*, 80-81.

146. Especially by Rashi, Ibn Ezra and David Kimhi. See G. B. Gray, *The Forms of Hebrew Poetry* (London 1915) 17-18.

147. R. Lowth, *De Sacra Poesi Hebraeorum Praelectiones Academicae* (1753), tr. G. Gregory, *The Forms of Hebrew Poetry* (London 1847). A very useful "Annotated Bibliography on Hebrew Poetry from 1915 to the Present" may be found in D. N. Freedman's Prolegomenon to the reissue of G. B. Gray's book (New York 1972) xli-liii.

148. See M. Dahood's discussion of this phenomenon in *R-S Parallels*, I ch.2, 71ff.

149. See the selection of publications in this field given by D. N. Freedman, *ib*.

150. Cp. Gevirtz, *Patterns*, 39, and example 67 *infra*.

151. For the pair *yyn* // *škr* cp. Is. 5:22; 24:9; 29:9; 56:12; Prov. 20:1; 31:4; Ug. 601:3-4, 16. Cp. further M. Dahood, *R-S Parallels* II, 248 (p. 209) where additional biblical examples are listed.

152. For the inverted couple *škr* // *yyn* cp. Is. 5:11; Prov. 31:6 and in Ug. 2 Aqht I:31-32; II:5-6; 19-20 (CTA 17 I:31-32; II:5-6, 19-20). For additional biblical examples consult M. Dahood, *ib.* II, 543 (p. 351).

153. The Greek translators derived בראה from *r'h* = 'see': LXX: φάσμα - φαντάσμα Sym.: ἐν ὁράσει. As against this, the T^J rendition - אתפניאו בזר מיכל בסים - implies that the translator associated בראה with 'food,' possibly connecting the term with 2 Sam. 12:17 MT: ולא ברה אתם לחם; T^J: ולא אכל עמהון לחמא. בסים = 'pleasant, tasty,' most probably is a free addition. In a review of A. L. Oppenheim, *Assyrian Dictionary* vol. XVI (1962), S. R. Driver posited the existence of a root *r'h* II = *rwh*. The interchange of *r'h/rwh* also can be observed in Is. 34:5 MT: רותה בשמים חרבי = LXX: ἐμεθύσθη, as against 1QIs^a: כיא תראה בשמים = T^J: ארי אתגלי; Ps. 60:5 MT: קשה הראית עמך ייך נשחה בעת וראי שמחת לב (47) :השקיתנו יין תרעלה B-S 31:28 [] for which cp. ושושן רעדוי. The same phenomenon appears to underlie the employment of *r'h* in synonymous parallelism with *śb'*, as in Ps. 16:11; 91:16; Job 10:15 and Is. 53:11. For a discussion of this latter verse see: I.L. Seeligmann, "ΔΕΙ ≡ ΑΙ ΑΥΤΩΙ ΦΩΣ," *Gershom G. Scholem Jubilee Volume* (Jerusalem 1958) pp. 1ff. (Hebrew). Additional examples of the same interchange may be found in Ps. 69:33 ראו ענוים ישמחו = 'the humble drank and rejoiced' (since wine proverbially makes the heart glad - Ps. 104:15), when compared with Ps. 22:7 יאסלו ענוים וישבעו. See also Prov. 23:31; Job 20:17 where אל ירא parallels יינק in the preceding verse; Eccl. 2:1 - אנסכה בשמחה וראה בטוב; and possibly also Job 33:21 MT: יכל בשרו מראי ושפי עצמותיו לא ראו = 'his flesh withered because of lack of moisture *(mem privativum)* and the marrow (?) of his bones was not moistened' (i.e., they dried up), bearing in mind the reference to food in the preceding verse. - D. Winton Tomas, *VT* XII (1962) 599-600, proposed to read *rww* for *'w* in Prov. 31:4^b in parallelism with *šth* in the first colon. - the assumed interchange of *r'h/rwh* caused a mistranslation in the Greek to 1 Macc. 6:34 - καὶ τοῖς ἐλέφανσιν ἔδειξαν (= הראו) αἷμα σταφυλῆς καὶ μόρων in order to induce them to go into battle, which surely goes back to a Hebrew *Vorlage* ואת הפילים הרוו דם ענבים = 'they made them *drunk* with the blood of grapes,' i.e. with wine (cp. 3 Macc. 5:1-2). Thus correctly A. Kahane, *The Book of 1 Maccabees*, in: *The Apocrypha, etc.*

vol. II, p. 88 *ad loc.* Grimm, *Kurzgefasstes Exegetisches Handbuch* (1853) refers to Aelian, *De Animal* XXIII,8 for proof that spiritous liquors were *given* (my italics) to elephants in order to excite them. In the case under review (1 Macc. 6:34), though, the liquor only "was *shown* to them, for had they drunk of it they would have got out of control."

154. O' L'- 233-456 403' 770 Syh. Syl Tht. Hi. read + διὰ τὸ σικερα κατεπόθησαν adjusting the Greek text to the Hebrew. Ms. 538 has simply τὸ σικερα for τὸ οἶνου.

155. A clear case of conflation of the transliteration - σικερα with the translation - μέθη.

156. The pair *qbr* // *spd* in this order parallels *bkh* // *qbr* in Job 27:15 and in Ug. 62:16-27 (CTA 6 I:16-17); 1 Aqht:111, 126, 140, 146 (CTA 19 III:111, 126, 140, 146), since *bkh* and *spd* are employed in parallelism and as interchangeable synonyms, either in the A-B or the B-A pattern, in biblical (Gen. 23:2; 2 Sam. 1:12; 3:31-32; Is. 22:12; Ez. 24:16; 27:31; Joel 2:12; Eccles. 3:4; Esth. 4:3) and in Ug. literature (1 Aqht:171-172, 183 = CTA 19 IV:171-172, 183). See S. Gevirtz, *Patterns, etc.*, 71-75; Dahood, *R-S Parallels*, 143, no. II,106).

157. The LXX do not render the word in either of the three occurrences. J. Bright, *op. cit.,* records the omission only for vv.8 and 10. ἡ ἀδελφή αὐτῆς is added in all three instances in a number of Lucianic manuscripts which, though, have also in v.7 the sequence of MT v.8 אחותה יהודה. O, λ and Syh. exhibit the MT order. In vv.8 and 10, O-233 and Q adjust the Greek to the MT by adding ἡ ἀδελφή αὐτῆς in the appropriate positions, but do not supply the phrase in v. 7. For α', ϑ' the addition can be established only in v.10.

158. The recurring a-b-c sequences in vv.7 and 10 form an *inclusio* frame for the a-c-b sequence of v.8. Vv.7-10 are thereby set apart as a small unit within the wider setting of vv.6-12[a] (cp. Bright, *op. cit.*, 26).

159. To the best of my knowledge this possibility was not been considered in the study of chiasm and inversion. Cp. also examples 69-70 and further Joel 1:7, 12 גפן || תאנה (negative) - 2:22 תאנה || גפן (positive); Hag. 1:10 טל + שמים || יבול + ארץ (negative) - Zech. 8:12 ארץ || טל + שמים + יבול + (positive).

160. For *'ṣ* // *'bn* cp. 2 Sam. 5:11, and my remarks on the assumed doublet in *Textus* IV (1964) 121; Is. 60:17; Hab. 2:19. The same simple sequence of the nouns is present in Ex. 7:19; 1 Ki. 5:32; 2 Ki. 19:18; 22:6; Is. 37:19; Ez. 20:32; Zech. 5:4; 1 Chr. 22:14; for Ug. parallels see *'nt* III:19-20; IV:58-59 (CTA 3 III:19-20; IV:58-69); 1001 rev:13, and M. Dahood, *R-S Parallels*, 302; II, 44.

161. Cp. further Ez. 26:12; Eccl. 10:9; 1 Chr. 22:15; 2 Chr. 34:10 and my remarks on this last example in *Textus* I (1960) 182-184. The instance is not listed by M. Dahood in *R-S Parallels*, 100; II, 9. For a Ug. parallel cp. 52:66 (CTA 22:66).

162. For the sequence *yyn* // *škr* cp. example no. 61.

163. The retention of the adjectives *gdl* // *rb* in the order in which they are employed in Ez. 17:17 accompanied by an inversion of order of the

nouns *qhl* // *ḥyl*. Thus a distant chiastic relation between Ez. 17:17 and 38:15 is achieved.

164. Cp. Avishur, *op. cit.*, 44.

165. Ignoring the obvious distant chiasm and following the LXX, J. Hempel *(BH)* gratuitously adjusts the order of the components in this verse to Deut. 7:5 by transposing תגדעון and תשרפון.

166. On intentional inversion in quotations see M. Seidel, "Parallels in the Book of Isaiah and the Book of Psalms," *Sinai* 38 (1958) 149-172; 229-240; 272-280; 333-355 (Hebrew).

167. The term יום איד by itself is widely employed in biblical litera-ture, e.g., 2 Sam. 22:19 = Ps. 18:19; Jer. 18:17; Ob. 12-13; Job 21:30.

168. פקדתם echoes ושלם of Deut. 32:35. Cp. further:

Jer. 25:12	והיה ... אפקד על מלך בבל
25:14	ושלמתי להם כפעלם
51:52	ופקדתי על פסיליה
51:54	כי אל גמלות יהוה שלם ישלם

Jer. 32:18 ומשלם עון אבות אל חיק בניהם is derived from Ex. 20:5; 34:7 פקד עון אבות על בנים (cp. Num. 14:17; Deut. 5:9).

1 Sam. 2:20 4QSam[a] = LXX ישלם יהוה לך זרע מן האשה הזאת

2:21 כי פקד יהוה את חנה

169. Cp. Jer. 6:15; 8:12.

170. The sequence יום (אידם) עת of Deut. 32:35-36 is maintained in Ez. 7:7, 12 בא העת קרוב (הגיע) היום.

171. For single '*yd* cp. Jer. 48:16; 49:32; Job 18:12; 21:17; 30:12; 31:3, 23; Prov. 1:26, 27; 6:16; 17:5; 14:22.

172. The phenomenon of *inclusio* was discerned frequently in the Book of Psalms by M. Dahood in his commentary (*AB*, vol. I-III, index *s.v. inclu-sio*). The concept and the term *Ringkomposition* generated in the study of classical literature, especially the Greek epic. See W. A. A. van Otterlo, "De Ringkompositie als Opbouwprincipe in de epische Gedichten van Homerus," *Verhandl. der Koninklijke Nederlandsche Akademie van Wetenschappen Afd. Letterkunde, Nieuwe Reeks, Deel* 51, no. 1 (Amsterdam 1948) 1-95 (I am in-debted to Dr. E. Tov for bringing this work to my attention); *idem*, "Unter-suchung ueber Begriff, Anwendung und Enstehung der griechischen Ringkomposi-tion," *Mededeelingen der Nederlandsche Akademie van Wetenschappen, Afd. Letterkunde, Nieuwe Reeks, Deel* 6, nos. 1-4 (Amsterdam 1943) 131-176 (with a bibliographical survey of the study of the *Ringkomposition*.

173. See S. Talmon - M. Fishbane, *op. cit.*, 27ff.

174. The term was introduced into the study of biblical literature by C. Kuhl, "Die Wiederaufnahme - ein literarkritisches Prinzip?," *ZAW* 64 (1952) 1-11, who thus rendered in German H. Wiener's English term 'resump-tive repetition' (*The Composition of Judges II 11 to 1 Kings II 46* [London 1929] 2). The German term had been previously used in classical studies. Cp. e.g., van Otterlo, "Untersuchungen." - The literary phenomenon thus defined already had been discerned in some specific cases by medieval Jewish commen-tators as will be shown in a separate publication.

175. בשתים was thus understood by medieval Jewish commentators, e.g., Rashi, Kimḥi, Levi ben Gershom, Isaiah of Trani. Similarly T^J. The passage containing the phrase is lacking in LXX, but was restored in O + L where ἐν ταῖς δύσιν appears to reflect the same interpretation. This is rejected by H. P. Smith, *Samuel*, ICC (Edinburgh 1912) 174, who renders the phrase 'on two conditions.' Cp. also S. R. Driver, *Notes on the Hebrew Text etc. of Samuel* (Oxford 1913) 152-153; M. H. Segal, *Samuel* (Jerusalem 1956) 153 (Hebrew), *et al.* R. Kittel's emendation בשׁ(נ)חים *(BH)* is altogether unwarranted, nor can A. B. Ehrlich's proposed reading ב(פל)שׁחים *(Randglossen* II, 233), or N. H. Tur-Sinai's reconstruction, suggested with some hesitation, בֹּשֵׁתָ מֵהתחתך בי - 'you are ashamed...' (מקרא) פשׁוטו של vol. II, 166) be recommended.

176. Cp., e.g., Gen. 4:2^b //2^b ; 3^b //4^a; 4^b//5^a. The inverted sequence obtains, e.g., in Ps. 29:10^a//^{b}; 1 Sam. 14:25//26. An interesting example of a textual doublet which reflects this principle may be found in 2 Sam. 8:14 וישם נצבים באדום נצבים בכל אדום שם נצבים for which see S. Talmon, *Textus* I, 177.

177. See M. Held, "The *yqtl - qtl* Sequence of Identical Verbs in Biblical Hebrew and Ugaritic," *Studies and Essays in Honor of A. A. Neuman* (Leiden 1962) 281-290.

178. The term occurs again in the Book of Daniel 8:20 where the sequence 'Media and Persia' prevails (5:28; contrast 6:9, 13, 16: מדי כדת ופרס with Esth. 1:19). This fact, though, can hardly be construed to establish a special affinity of the appendix Esth. ch.10 with the Book of Daniel.

179. See the present author's "Wisdom in the Book of Esther," *VT* XIII (1963) 416-453.

180. For the problems concerning this appendix, see D. Daube, "The Last Chapter of Esther," *JQR* 31 (1946-47) 139-147, and the summary of the state of the question in H. Bardtke, "Neuere Arbeiten am Estherbuche, Eine Kritische Wuerdigung," *Ex Oriente Lux* 19 (1965-66) 519-549.

181. The Targums concur with the MT throughout.

182. Neither of the chiasms involved has attracted the attention of commentators.

183. The hexaplaric recension exhibits the inverted sequence.

184. S. Gevirtz, *Patterns*, 77-78, 95.

185. This arrangement which is based on the recognition of the underlying *inclusio* pattern differs considerably from the one proposed *int. alii.* by S. E. Loewenstamm, "On the Chiastic Structure in the Bible," in: *E. Auerbach Volume*, Publication of the Israel Bible Society, vol. I (1955) 27-30 (Hebrew).

186. See W. Zimmerli, *Ezekiel*, BKAT II (Neukirchen-Vluyn 1969) 1083.

187. The interdependence of Ezekiel's vision of the future temple, especially of 40:1 - 43:12, often has been noted. See most recently S. Talmon - M. Fishbane, *op. cit.*

188. For an analysis of the overall use of this formula in the Book of Jeremiah, *vide supra*, p. 68.

189. This addition usually is explained as a widening of the promise to include in it also the northern tribes.

190. See the list given in C. D. Ginsburg's edition (London 1926) *ad loc.*

191. This conclusion is buttressed by the fact that the *haftarah* for the second day of the New Year festival begins with Jer. 31:2.

192. *Pace* J. Bright, *Jeremiah AB*, 280.

193. *Ib.*

194. *Op. cit.*, 152.

195. P. Volz, *Jeremia*, 279.

196. P. Volz, *Der Text, etc.*, 194.

197. See W. Rudolph, *Jeremia*, 131.

198. A. W. Streane, *Jeremiah*, 186.

199. *Op. cit.*, 143.

200. H. Cornill, *Jeremia*, 329. He is followed by Giesebrecht, Duhm, Peake and others. See P. Volz, *Jeremia*, 238.

201. See commentaries *ad loc.*

202. H. Cornill, *Jeremia*, *loc.cit.*

203. P. Volz, *Der Text, etc.*, 227.

204. For some further examples of *inclusio* with inverted parallelism see Jer. 8:4-11; Ez. 12:25-28; 40:1ff.-43:12, and the discussion of this case in S. Talmon - M. Fishbane, *op. cit.*

205. See *Textus* I, 175, 177; IV, 115; *Scripta Hierosolymitana* VII, 175.

206. According to the Massoretic tradition, the word "is to be written but not read." It is not rendered in T[J] and in the Luc. revision.

207. The LXX have no equivalent for MT: לדבר הזה. Ms B[+] and the Hexapl. revision add (with asterisk) τῷ ῥήματι τούτω. L: + καὶ περὶ τοῦ λόγου τούτου.

208. Cp., e.g., J. A. Montgomery, *The Books of Kings*, ICC (Edinburgh 1951) 375, 379.

209. It may be conjectured that in this instance the present second hemistich was accidentally transferred from its previous position after the present third. A restitution of the assumed original sequence would restore an *inclusio* pattern based on inverted parallels.

210. By translating περὶ ὑμῶν = עליכם, the LXX make Aaron and Moses the object of the statement, referring it back to v.2. Thus v.27[b] is not any more a mere repetition of v.27[a] in which God is the object.

211. Sam.: הם for MT: המה is of no consequence.

212. For a similar ellipsis of an expectable verb after the question cp. Is. 6:11; Ps. 6:4 and 90:13.

213. Cp. vv.17, 18.

214. Observe the chiastic structure and cp. v.23.

215. Cp. v.17, MT: לא יקרב להקריב לחם אלהיו, Sam.: לא יגש.

216. Against the Massoretic system which has a major divider after מקדשי קדשיכם.

217. On the vocalization הוא (α´) instead of היא (α) see S. Talmon, "The Three Scrolls of the Law that were found in the Temple Court," *Textus* II (1962) 14-17. This variation cannot serve as a criterion for deciding on the relative antiquity of the two parallels.

218. *Vide*, e.g., J. Wellhausen, *Der Text der Buecher Samuelis* (Goettingen 1872) 141; Smith, *Samuel*, *ICC*, 242-243; Driver, *Samuel*, 218; Segal, *Samuel*, 218.

219. Further instances of partially preserved doublets may be found, e.g., in Ex. 23:2; 1 Kings 10:28; Ps. 10:9; 2 Chr. 1:17.

220. See Cross - Freedman, "2 Sam. 22 - Ps. 18," *ad loc*.

221. The word '*bn* is either a gloss or a variant reading for *qyr*. See S. Talmon, *Textus* IV, 121.

222. See F. M. Cross, Jr., *HThR*, 1964.

223. See M. Noth, *Das zweite Buch Moses*, ATD (Goettingen 1959) 154-155, 216ff.; U. Cassuto, *Exodus* (Jerusalem 1967) 304-305, 446.

224. These considerations apply to some degree also to inner-massoretic inversion variants in parallel traditions that stem from chronologically different linguistic strata. In a discussion of inversion variants in Kings - Chronicles or Historiographies - Psalms, etc., the factor of changing syntactical norms must be taken into account. Cp., e.g., A. Kropat, *Die Syntax des Autors der Chronik*, BZAW 16 (Berlin,1901); A. Hurwitz, *The Transition Period in Biblical Hebrew (Jerusalem 1972, Hebrew)*, and the bibliography listed there; idem, "Diachronic Chiasm in Biblical Hebrew," in: *The Bible and the History of Israel* (Jerusalem, 1972) 248-255 (Hebrew).

225. Cp., e.g., Is. 37:32 MT: מירושלים מהר ציון; Is[a]: ⌣, possibly influenced by 2:3.

226. MT stands here in a chiastic relation to the preceding verse whereas Is[a] presents the same sequence in both instances.

227. Cp. further Is. 52:7 MT: רגלי מבשר משמיע שלום מבשר טוב משמיע ישועה
                 Is[a]:   "   "   משמיע   "   משׁ( )   "   מבשׂר   "   "

228. It should be stressed that in contrast to Is[a] which altogether diverges from the MT in many instances, Is[b] may be considered a proto-massoretic manuscript which rarely differs from the MT, as is well known.

229. Cp. further Is. 63:9 MT: וינטלם וינשאם; Is[a]: ⌣.

230. Cp. 2 Kings 18:27 MT: העל אדניך ...

231. Cp. further Is[a] 61:7; 63:17, *et al.*

232. Is[a] presents two readings of this phrase which are distinguished from each other only by some minor spelling variants.

233. Cp. Cross, *HThR* 1964.

234. J. Ziegler, ed., *Ieremias*, 44, n.1.

235. *Op. cit.*, 55-56; cp. further *idem*, *Isaias*, 24.

236. *Ieremias*, 44.

237. Ziegler, ed., *Isaias*, 72.

238. *Op. cit.*, 72-73, 89.

239. Unless one assumes the unlikely position that κακία renders here, and only here, משובה which in all other instances is translated ἁμαρτία, ἀποστροφή, etc.

240. φῶς is an erroneous translation of 'wr II which refers here to some kind of herbage, as in 2 Kings 4:39. The Greek translator also had difficulties with ṣh which he somehow identified with shrym - midday. Modern translations follow the LXX slavishly: RSV: 'sunshine'; NEB: 'summer sun'; ZB: 'Sonnenlichte'; SB: 'lumière.'

241. The expression may be compared with Prov. 19:12 וכטל על עשב and Deut. 32:1 כשעירים עלי דשא וכרביבים עלי עשב - 'like fine rain upon the grass and like showers on young plants' (NEB). There these idioms follow upon references to mṭr and ṭl. טל אור(ות) should be understood as an elliptic expression signifying 'dew upon herbage' that falls at the end of the rain season or in the summer. Thus correctly RSV: 'dew of herbs.' Translations such as NEB: 'sparkling light'; ZB: 'Tau der Lichter'; SB: 'rosée lumineuse' are far off the mark.

242. An inscription in ancient Hebrew characters from Tell Arad - בשלשת(1) ירח צח(2) - published by Y. Aharoni - R. Amiran, *BIES* N.S. XXVII (1963) 229-230, makes it plausible that in Is. 18:4 reference is made to the name of the summer-harvest month. Cp. further Jer. 4:11 where the term ṣh is connected with the threshing season. - Tos. Ta'anit 1:7 (ed. Zuckermandel, 215 ll. 16-17; ed. Lieberman, 325, ll. 35-38) refers to the summer season by the term ḥm which follows there upon qṣyr and qyṣ.

243. Numerous variants in the biblical scrolls from Qumran were explained to have arisen in this manner, just as variants in Bible quotations in rabbinic literature often were taken to have resulted from citation by heart. See, e.g., H. L. Strack, *Prolegomena Critica in V.T.* (Leipzig 1873) 60, and the discussion of the matter in V. Aptowitzer, *Das Schriftwort in der Rabbinischen Literatur* (photographic reprint New York 1970) 21ff.

244. See W. Bacher, *Die exegetische Terminologie der Juedischen Traditionaliteratur* I (Leipzig 1899) 136-137; II (Leipzig 1905) 144.

245. *Sifrē Bamidbar* 9:6 (ed. Friedmann, 17b, 1. 13); 15:33 (*ib.*, 33b, 1. 28); 17:9 (*ib.*, 49b, 1. 7); also Bab. Tal. B.B. 119b; Jer. Tal. R.H. 58b *ad* Ps. 144:14; *Gen. Rabba* 33(1) *ad* Ps. 36:7, *et al.*

246. Num. 17:2 where El'azar is mentioned before Moses is considered

by R. Joshijah an inverted verse - הרי זה מקרא מסורס - (Sifrē Bamidbar, 49b 1. 7). For further examples consult Bacher, ib.

247. See S. Talmon, Textus IV, 125ff.

248. Bacher renders srs by 'castriren = castrate' (op. cit. I, 136). The Hebrew term is better translated 'invertieren' or 'transponieren' (op. cit. II, 144). Cp. M. Jastrow, Dictionary of Talmud Babli, etc., II (New York 1943); E. Ben Jehuda, Thesaurus, etc., VIII (Jerusalem 1940); A. Kohut, Aruch Completum VI (New York 1955) s.v. srs. - The verb srs and the noun srys are not extant in biblical Hebrew. The biblical noun srys is an Akk. loanword - ša rēši - which designates predominantly officials at foreign courts. In this connotation the term is employed in an Aramaic inscription (Donner-Roellig no. 224 1.5), and should be rendered there: 'einer von meinen Beamten' rather than 'Eunuchen.'

249. See supra, examples 65, 69, 70 and note 159.

250. See J. Licht, The Thanksgiving Scroll (Jerusalem 1957) 207 (Hebrew). Licht draws attention to the similar imagery in 1QH III, 30-33.

251. The phrase [ד]ברתה ביד מושה כאשר (1QH XVII, 12) refers not only to Ex. 34:7 MT: נשא עון ופשע וחטאה, paraphrased in 1QH: עון [פשע לשאת] וחטאה (ib.), but also to the mention of Deut. 32:22 in the next line.

252. This interpretation of Qumran socio-historical ideology will be further developed elsewhere. For the present, see S. Talmon, "Qumran und das Alte Testament," Frankfurter Universitaetsreden Heft 12 (Frankfurt am Main 1972) 84-100.

253. These terms, and especially 'oral Torah,' merit renewed attention in the light of J. Neusner's recent investigations. See his "The Rabbinic Traditions about the Pharisees before A.D. 70, The Problems of Oral Transmission," JJS XXII (1971) 1-18.

254. The very term 'canon' in reference to the collection of the O.T. books requires further clarification which would do full justice to rabbinic pronouncements on this issue. A provocative, rather untraditional approach to the problem may be found in J. A. Sanders, Torah and Canon (Philadelphia 1972); idem, "Cave 11 Surprises and the Question of Canon," McCormick Quarterly XXI (1968) 1-15 where recent discussions of the matter are listed.

255. The issue was dealt with by E. E. Urbach, "When did Prophecy Cease?," Tarbiz XVII (1946) 1-11 (Hebrew).

256. The question whether 11QPs[a] should be considered a copy of the biblical Book of Psalms, as is maintained by most scholars and foremost by its editor J. A. Sanders, or whether it rather should be viewed as a liturgical collection of psalms, as reasoned by M. H. Goshen-Gottstein, Textus V (1966), and S. Talmon, ib., 11 ff., requires further analysis.

257. My thanks are due to Dr. E. Tov for some valuable comments and suggestions.

Palestinian Manuscripts
1947-1972

J. A. Sanders

The spring of 1972 marked the twenty-fifth anniversary of the discovery of the Qumran manuscripts. 1947 was the beginning of a period of more than fifteen years during which ancient manuscript materials have been recovered along the west littoral of the Jordan Fault as far north as the Wadi ed-Daliyeh and as far south as Masada. Publication of the manuscripts continues apace in widely scattered periodicals and titles.

The response to my "Palestinian Manuscripts 1947-1967" (*JBL* 86 [1967] 431-44) was very gratifying and indicates the continued need, there expressed, for a readily available listing of the *loci* of the *editiones principes*, and in some instances the *editiones principales*, of the materials so far published. The bibliography by B. Jongeling (*A Classified Bibliography of the Finds in the Desert of Judah 1958-1969* [1971]) brings the earlier work of William LaSor up to date and is very useful. Indeed, when it first appeared I thought I should not have to update my much leaner listing. But students working with me on the scrolls have made clear the continuing need of a simple list of where the photographs and responsible transcriptions have been published, or those available since the beginning.

The format here is basically that of the earlier list; the only change is that of reversing the order of Caves 4 and 11, so that now they appear in numerical order.

In the near future a good bit of material will have been published. J. T. Milik's 4Q Aramaic Enoch materials, *The Books of Enoch* (see below under I.A.c.2.), are in page proof at Oxford (though not in the *DJD* series). Milik has submitted articles on 4QMelch to *JJS* and on 4QMelch[ar] to *RB*, both of which are scheduled to appear in forthcoming issues of those journals. Milik's definitive edition of all the Cave 4 materials assigned to him is also at the publisher's in Oxford and will probably constitute the next two volumes of the *DJD* series: these will include all of the Qumran Cave 4 materials we would call apocrypha or pseudepigrapha, that is, non-biblical

401

Jewish literature known before Qumran, and all the Qumran sectarian literature not already published in *DJD* 5 (or, possibly, to be published in Jean
Starcky's lot) along with miscellaneous materials including the "Son of
God" fragment. John Strugnell's work is progressing well and will cover
two volumes in the *DJD* series: these are essentially the hymnic materials,
including 4QHodayot and similar literature, plus some miscellaneous fragments including a paraphrase document with long quotations from the Pentateuch. Materials assigned to J. Starcky are all Aramaic, non-biblical
and/or non-recognizable literature, and will constitute one *DJD* volume. F.
M. Cross, Jr., and Msgr. P. W. Skehan are charged with all the 4Q biblical
literature: there will be some three volume of these. Cross has about 70
mss of Pentateuchal and prophetic (except Isaiah and one ms of the Twelve)
books and plans to publish the Joshua, Judges and Samuels fragments first
(see below I.A.c.1.). Skehan has the paleo-Hebrew and LXX fragments of the
Pentateuch, all of the Isaiah materials, as well as Proverbs, Psalms and
others of the Writings; Skehan also has one ms of the Twelve Prophets.

I wish to express gratitude to Msgr. Skehan, as well as to Fr. J. A.
Fitzmyer, S.J., and Frank Moore Cross, for reading this manuscript in draft
and for several valuable suggestions for improvement in it.

Contents

Abbreviations of Publications

ALQ	F. M. Cross, *Ancient Library of Qumran*[2] (Anchor 1961)
ALUOS	*Annual of Leeds University Oriental Society*
BA	*Biblical Archaeologist*
BASOR	*Bulletin of the American Schools of Oriental Research*
DJD	*Discoveries in the Judaean Desert of Jordan*
DSPS	J. A. Sanders, *The Dead Sea Psalms Scroll* (Cornell 1967)
HTR	*Harvard Theological Review*
IEJ	*Israel Exploration Journal*
JBL	*Journal of Biblical Literature*
JSJ	*Journal for the Study of Judaism*
JSS	*Journal of Semitic Studies*
JTC	*Journal for Theology and Church*
JTS	*Journal of Theological Studies*
NAB	*New American Bible* (St. Anthony Guild edition)
NDBA	*New Directions in Biblical Archaeology,* ed. D. N. Freedman and J. C. Greenfield (1969)
NTS	*New Testament Studies*
OS	*Oudtestamentische Studien*
PEQ	*Palestine Exploration Quarterly*
RB	*Revue Biblique*
RQ	*Revue de Qumran*
SBF	*Studii Biblici Franciscani*
SWDS	*Scrolls from the Wilderness of the Dead Sea* (Smithsonian Exhibit Catalogue, American Schools of Oriental Research 1965)
ThLZ	*Theologische Literaturzeitung*
VT	*Vetus Testamentum*
ZAW	*Zeitschrift für die alttestamentlich Wissenschaft*
ZDPV	*Zeitschrift des Deutschen Palästina-Vereins*

Other Abbreviations

AIAR	Albright Institute of Archaeological Research	CD	Damascus Document (from Cairo Genizah)
ap	Apocryphon	DibHam	Words of the Luminaries
ar	Aramaic	gr	Greek
Ber	Berachot	H	Hodayot (Thanksgiving Hymns)

Hen	Enoch	PsAp	Apocryphal Psalms
Hev	Nahal Hever Caves	PsDan	Daniel pseudepigraphon
JerNouv	New Jerusalem	1Q etc.	Qumran Cave 1 etc.
Jub	Jubilees	S	Manual of Discipline
M	War Scroll	Sa	Rule of the Congregation
Melch	Melchizedeq	Sb	Collection of Blessings
Mess	Messiah	SirSabb	Shir ha-Shabbat
Ord	Ordinances	Sl 39-40	Angelic Liturgy
P	Pesher	Temple	The Temple Scroll
paleo	paleo-Hebrew script	tg	Targum
pBless	Patriarchal Blessings	TLevi	Testament of Levi
Phyl	Phylactery	Tob	Tobit
PrNab	Prayer of Nabonidus	Wiles	Wiles of a Harlot
PrLit	Liturgical Prayers	XII	Dodecapropheton

I. Manuscripts

    A. Wadi Qumran

        a. Cave 1

1QIs^a 1QS 1QpHab	M. Burrows, *et al.*, *The Dead Sea Scrolls of St. Mark's Monastery*, 1 (1950), 2:2 (1951); *Scrolls from Qumran Cave 1* (AIAR and Shrine of the Book, 1972) - Trever's original color prints.
1QS	J. Licht, *Megillat has-serakim* (1965) and A. R. C. Leaney, *The Rule of Qumran* (1966). Cf. J. T. Milik, *RB* 67 (1960) 412-16 for 4Q variants: see also 5Q11 and 5Q13 in *DJD* 3.
1QpHab	W. H. Brownlee, *The Text of Habakkuk in the Ancient Commentary from Qumran* (1959) K. Elliger, *Studien zum Habakkuk Kommentar* (1953).
1QIs^b 1QM 1QH	E. L. Sukenik, *Oṣar ham-megillot hag-genuzot* (1948, 1955).
1QM	Y. Yadin, *The Scroll of the War ...* (1962).
1QH	J. Licht, *Megillat ha-hodayot* (1957). S. Holm-Nielsen, *Hodayot Psalms from Qumran* (1960).

	M. Delcor, *Les Hymnes de Qumran* (1962).
1QSa Sb DM etc.	D. Barthélemy and J. T. Milik, *DJD* 1 (1955): of large 1Q scrolls and of other biblical, apocryphal and sectarian materials. Cf. J. C. Trever, *RQ* No. 19 (1965) 335-44 for plates of fragments transcribed in *DJD* 150-55; A. Y. Samuel, *Treasure of Qumran* (1966) 205-08; *SWDS* 29-30.
1QapGen	N. Avigad and Y. Yadin, *A Genesis Apocryphon* (1956).
	J. A. Fitzmyer, *The Genesis Apocryphon of Qumran Cave 1*[2] (1971); cf. 1Q20 in *DJD* 1.
CD	S. Schechter, *Documents of Jewish Sectaries*, 1 (1910). S. Zeitlin, *The Zadokite Fragments* (1952) for photographs. C. Rabin, *The Zadokite Documents*[2] (1958) for transcription. (Fragments also from 4Q)
1QDan[a,b]1QNoah frag 2 1QPrayers frags 2-3	J. Trever, *RQ* No. 19 (1965) 323-36, Pls. i-vi.
b. Caves 2-3, 5-10	M. Baillet and J. T. Milik, *DJD* 3 (1962): fragments of biblical, apocryphal and sectarian materials: 2Q1-33, 3Q1-15, 5Q1-25, 6Q1-31, 7Q1-19, 8Q1-5, 9Q (pap), 10Q (ostr). Includes 3Q15, the copper scroll ed. by J. T. Milik; cf. J. M. Allegro, *Treasure of the Copper Scroll* (1960).

c. Cave 4

1. Biblical

4QEx[a]	F. M. Cross, *ALQ* 184-85: transliteration only.
4QEx[c]	F. M. Cross, *JTC* 5 (1968) 13-16.
4QpaleoEx[m]	P. W. Skehan, *JBL* 74 (1955) 182-187. Cf. *SWDS* 16, 26.
4QEx[f]	F. M. Cross in *SWDS* 14, 23.
4QLXXLev[a]	P. W. Skehan, *VT* suppl 4 (1957) 159-60. Cf. *SWDS* 15, 25.

4QLXXNu	P. W. Skehan, *VT* suppl 4 (1957) 155-56; photo in *BA* 28 (1965) 91.
4QDt^n	F. M. Cross in *SWDS* 20, 31-32; H. Stegemann, *RQ* No. 22 (1967) 217-27,
4QDt^q (Deut 32)	P. W. Skehan, *BASOR* No. 136 (Dec. 1954) 12-15. N.B.: *VT* suppl 4 (1957) 150, n.1.
4QSam^a	F. M. Cross, *BASOR* No. 132 (Dec. 1953) 15-26. Cf. *SWDS* 14, 24-25.
4QSam^b	F. M. Cross, *JBL* 74 (1955) 147-72.
4QSam^{a,b,c}	F. M. Cross, *NAB* (1970) text notes.
4QIs^a	J. Muilenburg, *BASOR* No. 135 (Oct. 1954) 28-32.
4QJer^b	F. M. Cross, *ALQ* 187 (transliteration).
4QXII^c	M. Testuz, *Semitica* 5 (1955) 147-72.
4QPs^{a-q}	All pre-Masoretic Psalter materials, published and unpublished, are catalogued and indexed in *DSPS* 143-55.
4QPs^b	P. W. Skehan, *CBQ* 26 (1964) 313-22. Cf. *SWDS* 20, 30-31.
4QPs^f cols vii-x	J. Starcky, *RB* 73 (1966) 352-71: three "apocryphal" psalms in a Psalter ms.
4QPs^q	J. T. Milik, *Biblica* 38 (1957) 245-55.
4QPs89	J. T. Milik, *RB* 73 (1966) 94-106.
4QQoh^a	J. Muilenburg, *BASOR* No. 135 (Oct. 1954) 20-28.

   2. Apocryphal

4QHen ar	J. T. Milik, *RB* 65 (1958) 70-77: Another Aramaic fragment, possibly from Enoch, may be found in M. Testuz, *Semitica* 5 (1955) 37-38. Cf. J. T. Milik, *HTR* 64 (1971) 333-78. See next entry.
4QHenGéants^{a,b}	J. T. Milik in *Tradition und Glaube* (K. G. Kuhn Fest., ed. G. Jeremias, *et al.*, 1971) 117-127, Pl. 1 (frag of 4QGéants^a only). According to Milik in the *HTR* 64 article *(op. cit.)* there will be 12 Enoch mss, including this one, in Milik, *The Books of Enoch, Aramaic Fragments of Qumran Cave 4* (Oxford, 1972). Cf. 6Q8, 1Q23 (plus frags).

4QJub^f (etc.)	J. T. Milik, *RB* 73 (1966) 94-104.
4QTLevi ar^b	J. T. Milik, *RB* 62 (1955) 398-406. Cf. *SWDS* 16, 25-26.
4QPrNab ar 4QpsDan ar^{a-c}	J. T. Milik, *RB* 63 (1956) 4-7-415.
(4QTob ar^{a-d} hebr^a	J. T. Milik, *RB* 73 (1966) 522. A list, only, of extant materials.)

3. Pesharim

4Q158-186	J. M. Allegro with A. A. Anderson, *DJD* 5 (1968). All of the following 4Q materials published by Allegro are included in *DJD* 5 with the exception of 4QPBless; on the other hand, *DJD* 5 includes 15 mss not published before. Extreme caution is advised in use of *DJD* 5. Two publications are necessary companions to it: J. Strugnell, *RQ* No. 26 (1970) 163-276, and J. A. Fitzmyer, *CBQ* 31 (1969) 59-71 (a bibliographic aid).
4QpIs^a (4Q161)	J. M. Allegro, *JBL* 75 (1956) 174-87: Document III; *DJD* 5, 11-15, Pls. IV-V.
4QpIs^{b-d} (4Q162-64)	J. M. Allegro, *JBL* 77 (1958) 215-21; *DJD* 5, 15-28, Pls. VI-IX.
4QpIs^e (4Q165)	*DJD* 5, 28-30, Pl. IX.
4QpHos^b (4Q166)	J. M. Allegro, *JBL* 75 (1956) 89-95; *DJD* 5, 32-36, Pl. X, formerly 4QHos^a.
4QpHos^a (4Q167)	J. M. Allegro, *JBL* 78 (1959) 142-47; *DJD* 5, 31-32, Pl. X, formerly 4QHos^b.
4QpMic? (4Q168)	*DJD* 5, 36, Pl. XII.
4QpNah (4Q169)	J. M. Allegro, *JBL* 75 (1956) 89-95; J. M. Allegro, *JSS* 7 (1962) 304-08; *DJD* 5, 37-42, Pls. XII-XIV. Cf. *SWDS*, 17, 26-27; A. Dupont-Sommer, *Semitica*, 13 (1963) 55-88; Y. Yadin, *IEJ* 21 (1971) 1-12.
4QpZeph (4Q170)	*DJD* 5, 42, Pl. XIV.
4QPss^a (4Q171)	J. M. Allegro, *PEQ* 86 (1954) 69-75, Pl. XVIII.
(formerly 4QpPs37)	J. M. Allegro, *JBL* 75 (1956) 89-95, Pls. 3-4.

J. M. Allegro, *The People of the Dead Sea Scrolls*
Pls. 48 and 50 (86-87); *DJD* 5, 42-49.

H. Stegemann, *RQ* No. 14 (1963) 235-70 (Stegemann's
article sorts it all out.)

H. Stegemann, *RQ* No. 22 (1967) 193-210 for col. 1
lines 20-27.

4QpPs60 (4Q171)   *DJD* 5, 49-50, Pl. XVII.

4QpPss^b (4Q173)   *DJD* 5, 51-53, Pl. XVIII (pPss 127, 129 and 118?).

(4Q172)   *DJD* 5, 50-51, Pl. XVIII (apparently pesharim on
unidentified biblical? texts).

4. Sectarian

4QFlorilegium   J. M. Allegro, *JBL* 75 (1956) 174-87: Document II;
(4Q174)   Allegro, *JBL* 77 (1958) 350-54; *DJD* 5, 53-57, Pls
XIX-XX. Cf. Y. Yadin, *IEJ* 9 (1959) 95-98.

4QPBless (?   J. M. Allegro, *JBL* 75 (1956) 174-87: Document I.
pGen49)   Cf. H. Stegemann, *RQ* No. 22 (1967) 211-17.

4QTestimonia   J. M. Allegro, *JBL* 75 (1956) 174-87: Document IV:
(4Q175)   *DJD* 5, 57-60, Pl. XXI.

4QM^a (b-e)   C. H. Hunzinger, *ZAW* 69 (1957) 131-51. Cf. *SWDS*,
18, 29.

pap4QM^e,f   M. Baillet, *RB* 71 (1964) 356-59, 365-71.

4QS1 39-40   J. Strugnell, "The Angelic Liturgy at Qumran," *VT*
(4QSirSabb)   suppl 7 (1960) 318-45.

4QDibHam   M. Baillet, "Les Paroles des luminaires," *RB* 68
(1961) 195-250. Cf. *SWDS* 18, 28-29.

4QOrd (4Q159)   J. M. Allegro, *JSS* 6 (1961) 71-73; *DJD* 5, 6-9, Pl.
II.

4QWiles (Harlot) J. M. Allegro, *PEQ* 96 (1964) 53-55; *DJD* 5, 82-85,
(4Q184)   Pl. XXVIII.

4QMess ar   J. Starcky, "Un Texte messianique araméen de la
grotte 4 de Qumrân," *Mémorial du Cinquantenaire
de l'Ecole des langues orientales anciennes de
l'Institut Catholique de Paris* (1964) 51-56. Cf.
SWDS 16, 27-28; and J. A. Fitzmyer, *CBQ* 27 (1965)
348-72.

4QCryptic (4Q186)   J. M. Allegro, "An Astrological Cryptic Document
from Qumran," *JSS* 9 (1964) 291-94; *DJD* 5, 88- 1,
Pl. XXXI. (According to J. T. Milik in *HTR* 64
[1971] 366 this is a portion of the Henoch literature.)

pap4QPrLit   M. Baillet, *RB* 71 (1964) 354-55, 360-65: liturgical prayers close to Allegro's 4Q Prayers.

4QPssJosh   P. A. Spijkerman, *SBF* 12 (1961-62) 325 (photograph
only).

4QTanhumim (4Q175) *DJD* 5, 60-67, Pls. XXII-XXIII.

4QCatena[a,b]   *DJD* 5, 67-75, 80-81, Pls. XXIV-XXV and XXVII.
(4Q177, 182)

4QLamentations   *DJD* 5, 75-77, Pl. XXVI.
(4Q179)

4Q--- (4Q178,   *DJD* 5, 74-75, 81-82, 85-87, Pls. XXV, XXVI, XXIX-
183, 185)   XXX.

4Q Prayers or   J. M. Allegro, *ALUOS* 4 (1962-63) 3-5; *DJD* 5, 77-80,
Ages of Crea-   Pls. XXVII-XXVIII. Cf. J. A. Sanders, *JBL* 88
tion (4Q180-181)   (1969) 286-287.

4QPhyl[a-d]   K. G. Kuhn, *Phylakterien aus Höhle 4 von Qumran,*
1957.

4QD[a] 4QPhyl I   J. T. Milik, *RB* 73 (1966) 94-106.
(4QS variants)   J. T. Milik, *RB* 67 (1960) 412-416.

4Q Halakah[a]   J. T. Milik in *DJD* 3 (1962) 300.

4Q ʻAmran[a-d]   J. T. Milik, *RB* 79 (1972) 77-97, Pl. 1.

d. Cave 11

   1. Biblical

11QLev   A. S. Van der Woude in *Bibel und Qumran* (H. Bartke
Fest. 1968) 153-55 (Lev 9:23-10:2 in Heb with
LXX readings).
Cf. J. Strugnell in *RB* 77 (1970) 268.

11QEz   W. H. Brownlee, *RQ* No. 13 (1963) 11-28.

11QtgJob   J. Van der Ploeg and A. S. van der Woude, *Le Targum
de Job de la grotte XI de Qumran* (1971).

11QPs[a]	J. A. Sanders, *DJD* 4 (1965); J. A. Sanders, *The Dead Sea Psalms Scroll* (1967). For fragment E of 11QPs[a] cf. Y. Yadin, *Textus* 5 (1966) 1-10 and *DSPS* 155-65. Cf. also J. A. Sanders, *NDBA* 101-16.
11QPs[b]	J. van der Ploeg, *RB* 74 (1967) 408-12.
11QPsAp[a]	J. van der Ploeg, *RB* 72 (1965) 210-17: a scroll containing both biblical and apocryphal psalms; v.d. Ploeg in *Tradition und Glaube* (K. G. Kuhn Fest., 1971) 128-39 and Pls. II-VII; cf. *DSPS*, p. 145.
XQPhyl 1-4	Y. Yadin, *Tefillin from Qumran* (1969), from *Eretz Israel* IX.

2. Apocryphal

11QJub	A. S. van der Woude in *Tradition und Glaube* (Kuhn Fest., 1971) 140-46 and Pl. VIII. Also see above under 11QPsAp[a] - except that in the case of the Qumran Psalter PsAp means only psalms not in the MT-150 Psalter, nothing more.

3. Sectarian

11QMelch	A. S. van der Woude, *OS* 14 (1965) 354-73. Cf. M. de Jonge and A. S. van der Woude, *NTS* 12 (1966) 301-26; J. A. Fitzmyer, *JBL* 86 (1967) 25-41; M. P. Miller, *JBL* 88 (1969) 467-69; and D. F. Miner, *JSJ* 2 (1971) 144-48.
11QTemple	Y. Yadin, *BA* 30 (1967) 135-39; *NDBA* 139-48; *IEF* 21 (1971) 6-8 and Plate 1 (photograph, transcription and apparatus for col. 64, lines 6-13); *RB* 79 (1972) 98-99 transcription of col. 57, lines 17-19).
11QBer	A. von der Woude in *Bibel und Qumran* (Bartke Fest. 1968) 253-58. Cf. J. Strugnell in *RB* 77 (1970) 268.
11QJerNouv[ar]	B. Jongeling, *JSJ* 1 (1970) 58-64.

B. Wadi Murabba'at   P. Benoit and J. T. Milik, *DJD* 2 (1971): Frag-
                       ments of biblical, religious, commercial, con-
                       tractual, military and other documents in
                       Hebrew, Aramaic, Greek, Latin and Arabic, on
                       leather, papyrus and ostracon.

C. Wadi ed-Daliyeh   F. M. Cross, "The Discovery of the Samaria Papyri,"
                       BA 26 (1963) 110-21; F. M. Cross, *HTR* 59 (1966)
                       202-11: preliminary report and evaluation only;
                       cf. F. M. Cross, *NDBA* 41-62.

D. Khirbet Mird
    papMird A   Milik, *RB* 70 (1963) 526-39; *Biblica* 42 (1961) 21-27.
    Mird Acts cpa   C. Perrot, *RB* 70 (1963) 506-55.
    papMir 1-100^{arab} A. Grohmann, *Arabic Papyri from Khirbet el-Mird*
                       (1963).

E. Nahal Ḥever, Ṣe'elim and Mishmar
    ḤeverXII^{gr} D. Barthélemy, *Les Devanciers d'Aquila*, *VT* suppl
                       10 (1963) 163-78.
    5-6Ḥever Ps 15-16 Y. Yadin, *IEJ* 11 (1961) 40.
    pap5-6Ḥever 1-15   *Ibid.*, 40-52 (Bar Kokhba letters in Hebrew, Ara-
                       maic and Greek; papyrus except 1, which is on
                       wood).

    pap?5-6Ḥever A-C   J. Starcky, *RB* 61 (1954) 161-81 (Nabataean contract).
    pap?Ḥever^{aram} J. T. Milik, *Biblica* 38 (1957) 255-68; cf. Starcky,
                       61 (1954) 182-90 (two Jewish property contracts).
    34Ṣe'elim 1A-B,2   Y. Aharoni, *IEJ* 11 (1961) 21-24; *Yediot* 25 (1961)
                       19-33 (1A and 1B are phylacteries, Ex. 13:2-16;
                       2 letters in Hebrew).

    pap34Ṣe'elim   B. Lifshitz, *IEJ* 11 (1961) 53-58, 205; *Yediot* 25
      1-8^{gr} (1961) 65-73 (onomastica).

    pap1Mishmar^{gr} B. Lifshitz, *IEJ* 11 (1961) 59-61; *Aegyptus* 42
                       (1963) 240-56, 2 plates (the adelphoi fragments).

    pap1Mishmar   P. Bar-Adon, *IEJ* 11 (1961) 27; *Yediot* 25 (1961) 34-
                       38.

F. Masada   Y. Yadin, *IEJ* 15 (1965) 1-120 (also published
                       separately under title Masada): preliminary

report. Yadin, *Masada: Herod's Fortress and
the Zealots' Last Stand* (1966), a popular report; cf. p. 179 (Jubilees, Lev 8-12) and p.
187 (Ezek 37, Deut 32-34) for unpublished mss.
Cf. *DSPS* 143-54 for description of Psalter
materials.

Mas Ben Sira   Y. Yadin, *The Ben Sira Scroll from Masada* (1965).
Cf. J. T. Milik, "Un fragment mal placé dans
l'édition du Siracide de Masaca," *Biblica* 47
(1966) 425-26, and P. W. Skehan, *JBL* 85 (1966)
260-62.

II. Study Aids

M. Baillet, *et al.*, "Le Travail d'edition des fragments manuscrits de
Qumran," *RB* 63 (1956), remains the basic reference to the contents of
the Cave 4 literature. F. M. Cross, "A Catalogue of the Library of
Qumran," *ALQ* 30-47, gives a reliable overview of the full eleven-cave
complement. *ALQ*[3] will appear sometime in 1975. J. Hempel, *Die Texte
von Qumran in der heutigen Forschung* (1962), is a fund of information
on the state of scholarship to 1960 on nearly all questions related
to the scrolls. P. W. Skehan's "The Biblical Scrolls from Qumran and
the Text of the Old Testament," *BA* 28 (1965) 87-100, offers a full
account of the Qumran biblical materials, updated in *NDBA* 89-100; and
Appendices II and III in *DSPS* 143-49 specify in detail the scope and
content of all preMasoretic Psalter texts. For OT textual criticism,
Cross, "The Contribution of the Qumran Discoveries to the Study of
the Biblical Text," *IEJ* 16 (1966) 81-95 should be added to the titles
listed in *DSPS* 153.

K. G. Kuhn, *Konkordanz zu den Qumrantexten* (1960) is supplemented by his
"Nachtrage zur Konkordanz zu den Qumran texten," *RQ* No. 14 (1963) 196-
234. Kuhn, *Rückläugfiges Hebraisches Wörterbuch* (1958) can be helpful where final letters of words are preserved.

A. M. Habermann, *Megillot midbar Yehudah* (1959), and E. Lohse, *Die Texte
aus Qumran* 2 (1971), provide vocalized texts of the major documents
from Caves 1 and 4; and Habermann has a limited concordance.

Ch. Burchard, *Bibliographie zu den Handschriften vom Toten Meer*, I
  (1957) and II (1965) have been supplemented by H. Stegemann in *ZDPV*
  83 (1967) 95-101.

W. S. LaSor, *Bibliography of the Dead Sea Scrolls 1948-1957* (1958).

B. Jongeling, *A Classified Bibliography of the Finds in the Desert of
  Judah 1958-1969* (1971).

F. M. Cross, "The Development of the Jewish Scripts," *The Bible and the
  Ancient Near East*, ed. G. E. Wright (Anchorbook 1965) 170-264, is the
  standard work on Hebrew and Aramaic palaeography from earliest times
  through the Second Jewish Revolt.

H. Braun, *Qumran und das Neue Testament* 1 (1962), 2 (1966) is very helpful to NT students as well as *NT Abstracts* from Weston College.

(Extreme caution must be used in consulting the apparati to the Isaiah
  and Psalms Fascicles [Nos. 7 and 11] of the Biblia Hebraica Stutt-
  gartensia.)

Contributors

William Foxwell Albright
The Johns Hopkins University

Dominique Barthelemy
Université de Fribourg

Frank Moore Cross
Harvard University

David Noel Freedman
University of Michigan

Moshe H. Goshen-Gottstein
The Hebrew University of Jerusalem

James A. Sanders
Union Theological Seminary (New York)

Patrick W. Skehan
Catholic University of America

Shemaryahu Talmon
The Hebrew University of Jerusalem

Emanuel Tov
The Hebrew University of Jerusalem

Joseph Ziegler
Universität Würzburg

415